PIGEON COVE, CAPE ANN.

NOOKS AND CORNERS
OF THE
NEW ENGLAND COAST

Samuel Adams Drake

AUTHOR OF
"OLD LANDMARKS OF BOSTON," "HISTORIC FIELDS AND MANSIONS OF MIDDLESEX," &C.

WITH NUMEROUS ILLUSTRATIONS

HERITAGE BOOKS
2008

HERITAGE BOOKS
AN IMPRINT OF HERITAGE BOOKS, INC.

Books, CDs, and more—Worldwide

For our listing of thousands of titles see our website
at
www.HeritageBooks.com

A Facsimile Reprint
Published 2008 by
HERITAGE BOOKS, INC.
Publishing Division
100 Railroad Ave. #104
Westminster, Maryland 21157

Entered according to Act of Congress, in the year 1875, by
Harper & Brothers
In the Office of the Librarian of Congress, at Washington.

— Publisher's Notice —
In reprints such as this, it is often not possible to remove blemishes from the original. We feel the contents of this book warrant its reissue despite these blemishes and hope you will agree and read it with pleasure.

International Standard Book Numbers
Paperbound: 978-1-55613-399-2
Clothbound: 978-0-7884-7342-5

Inscribed by Permission,

AND WITH SENTIMENTS OF HIGH RESPECT,

TO

HENRY WADSWORTH LONGFELLOW.

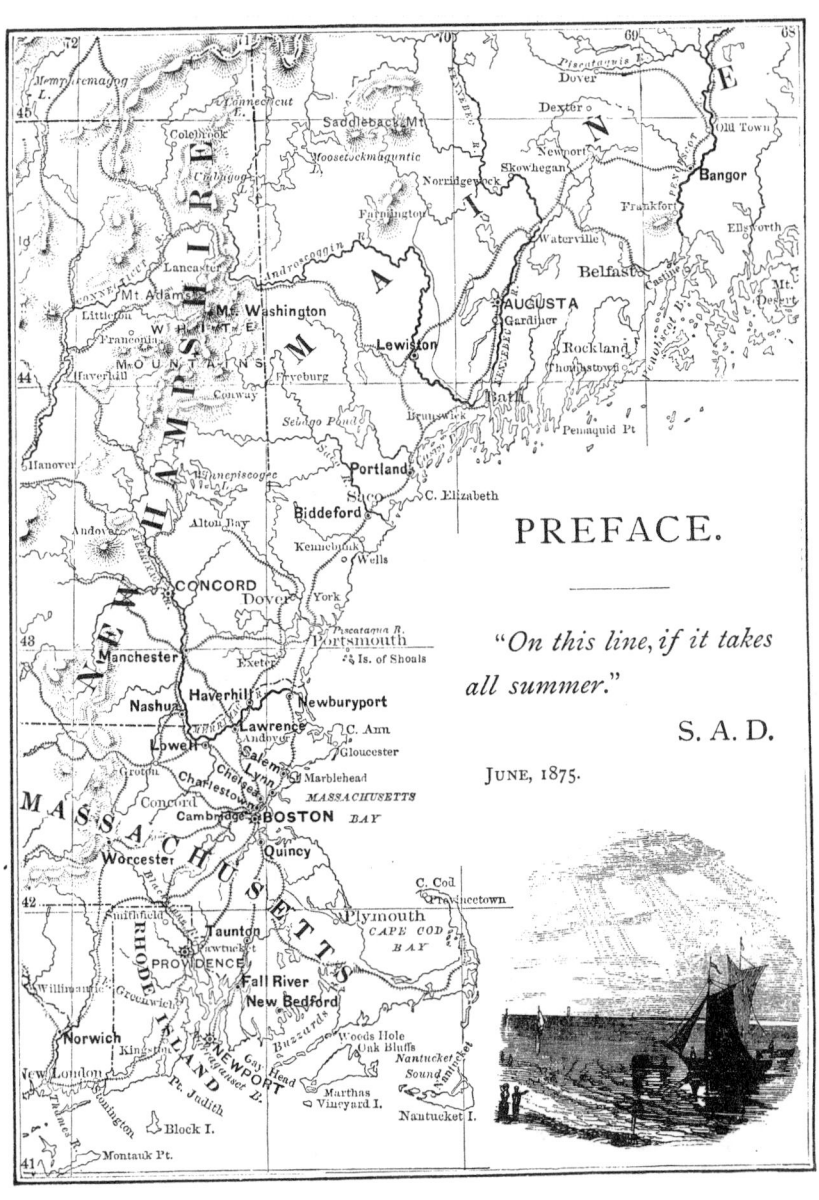

PREFACE.

"*On this line, if it takes all summer.*"

S. A. D.

June, 1875.

CONTENTS.

CHAPTER I.
NEW ENGLAND OF THE ANCIENTS.

Norumbega River and City.—Early Discoverers, and Maps of New England.—Mode of taking Possession of new Countries.—Cruel Usage of Intruders by the English.—Penobscot Bay.—Character of first Emigrants to New England.—Is Friday unlucky?......................Page 17

CHAPTER II.
MOUNT DESERT ISLAND.

About Islands.—Champlain's Discovery.—Mount Desert Range.—Somesville, and the Neighborhood.—Colony of Madame De Guercheville.—Descent of Sir S. Argall.—Treasure-trove.—Shell-heaps.—South-west Harbor.—The natural Sea-wall.—Islands off Somes's Sound...... 27

CHAPTER III.
CHRISTMAS ON MOUNT DESERT.

Excursion to Bar Harbor.—Green Mountain.—Eagle Lake.—Island Nomenclature.—Porcupine Islands.—Short Jaunts by the Shore.—Schooner Head.—Spouting Caves.—Sea Aquaria.—Audubon and Agassiz.—David Wasgatt Clark.—F. E. Church and the Artists.—Great Head.—Baye Françoise.—Mount Desert Rock.—Value of natural Sea-marks.—Newport Mountain, and the Way to Otter Creek.—The Islesmen.—North-east Harbor.—The Ovens.—The Gregoires.—Henrietta d'Orleans.—Yankee Curiosity.. 40

CHAPTER IV.
CASTINE.

Pentagoët.—A Fog in Penobscot Bay.—Rockland.—The Muscongus Grant.—Colonial Society.—Generals Knox and Lincoln.—Camden Hills.—Belfast and the River Penobscot.—Brigadier's Island.—Disappearance of the Salmon.—Approach to Castine.—Fort George.—Penobscot Expedition.—Sir John Moore.—Capture of General Wadsworth.—His remarkable Escape.—Rochambeau's Proposal.—La Peyrouse 58

CHAPTER V.
CASTINE—*continued*.

Old Fort Pentagoët.—Stephen Grindle's Windfall.—Cob-money.—The Pilgrims at Penobscot.—Isaac de Razilly.—D'Aulnay Charnisay.—La Tour.—Descent of Sedgwick and Leverett.—Capture of Pentagoët, and Imprisonment of Chambly.—Colbert.—Baron Castin.—The younger

Castin kidnaped.—Capuchins and Jesuits.—Intrigues of De Maintenon and Père Lachaise.—Burial-ground of Castine.—About the Lobster.—Where is Down East?...................Page 73

CHAPTER VI.
PEMAQUID POINT.

New Harbor.—Wayside Manners.—British Repulse at New Harbor.—Porgee Factory.—Process of converting the Fish into Oil.—Habits of the Mackerel.—Weymouth's Visit to Pemaquid.—Champlain again.—Popham Colony.—Cotton Mather on new Settlements.—English *vs.* French Endurance.—L'Ordre de Bon Temps.—Samoset.—Fort Frederick.—Résumé of the English Settlement and Forts.—John Nelson.—Capture of Fort William Henry.—D'Iberville, the knowing One.—Colonel Dunbar at Pemaquid.—Shell-heaps of Damariscotta.—Disappearance of the native Oyster in New England.. 87

CHAPTER VII.
MONHEGAN ISLAND.

Scenes on a Penobscot Steamer.—The Islanders.—Weymouth's Anchorage.—Monhegan described.—Combat between the *Enterprise* and *Boxer*.—Lieutenant Burrows................. 102

CHAPTER VIII.
FROM WELLS TO OLD YORK.

Wells.—John Wheelwright.—George Burroughs.—On the Beach.—Shiftings of the Sands.—What they produce.—Ingenuity of the Crow.—The Beach as a High-road.—Popular Superstitions.—Ogunquit.—Bald Head Cliff.—Wreck of the *Isidore*.—Kennebunkport.—Cape Neddock.—The Nubble.—Captains Gosnold and Pring.—Moon-light on the Beach.............. 109

CHAPTER IX.
AGAMENTICUS, THE ANCIENT CITY.

Mount Agamenticus.—Basque Fishermen.—Sassafras.—The Long Sands.—Sea-weed and Shellfish.—Foot-prints.—Old York Annals.—Sir Ferdinando Gorges.—York Meeting-house.—Handkerchief Moody.—Parson Moody.—David Sewall.—Old Jail.—Garrison Houses, Scotland Parish... 123

CHAPTER X.
AT KITTERY POINT, MAINE.

York Bridge.—Poor Sally Cutts.—Fort M'Clary.—Sir William Pepperell.—Louisburg and Fontenoy.—Gerrish's Island.—Francis Champernowne.—Islands belonging to Kittery.—John Langdon.—Jacob Sheaffe.—Washington at Kittery... 141

CHAPTER XI.
THE ISLES OF SHOALS.

De Monts sees them.—Smith's and Levett's Account.—Cod-fishery in the sixteenth Century.—Sail down the Piscataqua.—The Isles.—Derivation of the Name.—Jeffrey's Ledge.—Star Island.—Little Meeting-house.—Character of the Islesmen.—Island Grave-yards.—Betty

Moody's Hole.—Natural Gorges.—Under the Cliffs.—Death of Miss Underhill.—Story of her Life.—Boon Island.—Wreck of the *Nottingham*.—Fish and Fishermen.................Page 153

CHAPTER XII.
THE ISLES OF SHOALS—*continued.*

Excursion to Smutty Nose.—Piracy in New England Waters.—Blackbeard.—Thomas Morton's Banishment.—Religious Liberty *vs.* License.—Custom of the May-pole.—Samuel Haley.—Spanish Wreck on Smutty Nose.—Graves of the Unknown.—Terrible Tragedy on the Island.—Appledore.—Its ancient Settlement.—Smith's Cairn.—Duck Island.—Londoner's.—Thomas B. Laighton.—Mrs. Thaxter.—Light-houses in 1793.—White Island.—Story of a Wreck. 175

CHAPTER XIII.
NEWCASTLE AND NEIGHBORHOOD.

The Way to the Island.—The Pool.—Ancient Ships.—Old House.—Town Charter and Records.—Influence of the Navy-yard.—Fort Constitution.—Little Harbor.—Captain John Mason.—The Wentworth House.—The Portraits.—The Governors Wentworth and their Wives.—Baron Steuben.. 196

CHAPTER XIV.
SALEM VILLAGE, AND '92.

The Witch-ground.—Antiquity of Witchcraft.—First Case in New England.—Curiosities of Witchcraft.—Rebecca Nurse.—Beginning of Terrorism at Salem Village.—Humors of the Apparitions.—General Putnam's Birthplace.—What may be seen in Danvers........................ 208

CHAPTER XV.
A WALK TO WITCH HILL.

Salem in 1692.—Birthplace of Hawthorne.—Old Witch House.—William Stoughton, Governor.—Witch Hill.—A Leaf from History.. 220

CHAPTER XVI.
MARBLEHEAD.

The Rock of Marblehead.—The Harbor and Neck.—Chat with the Light-keeper.—Decline of the Fisheries.—Fishery in the olden Time.—Early Annals of Marblehead.—Walks about the Town.—Crooked Lanes and antique Houses.—The Water-side.—The Fishermen.—How the Town looked in the Past.—Plain-spoken Clergymen and lawless Parishioners.—Anecdotes.—Jeremiah Lee and his Mansion.—The Town-house.—Chief-justice Story.—St. Michael's Church.—Elbridge Gerry.—The old Ironsides of the Sea.—General John Glover.—Flood Ireson's, Oakum Bay.—Fort Sewall.—Escape of the *Constitution* Frigate.—Duel of the *Chesapeake* and *Shannon.*—Old Burial-ground.—The Grave-digger.—Perils of the Fishery...... 228

CHAPTER XVII.
PLYMOUTH.

At the American Mecca.—Court Street.—Pilgrim Hall and Pilgrim Memorials.—Sargent's Picture of the "Landing."—Relics of the *Mayflower.*—First Duel in New England.—Old Colony

Seal.—The "Compact."—First Execution in Plymouth.—Old "Body of Laws."—Pilgrim Chronicles.—View from Burial Hill.—The Harbor.—Names of Plymouth.—Plymouth, England.—Lord Nelson's Generosity.—Plymouth the temporary Choice of the Pilgrims.—The Indian Plague.—Indian Superstition.—Who was first at Plymouth?—De Monts and Champlain.—Champlain's Voyages in New England.—French Pilgrims make the first Landing.—Why the Natives were hostile to the Pilgrims of 1620.—Confusion among old Writers about Plymouth.—Among the Tombstones of Burial Hill.—The Pilgrims' Church-fortress.—What a Dutchman saw here in 1627.—Military Procession to Meeting.—Ancient Church Customs.—Puritans, Separatists, and Brownists.—Flight and Political Ostracism of the Pilgrims.—Their form of Worship.—First Church of Salem.—Plymouth founded on a Principle........Page 261

CHAPTER XVIII.

PLYMOUTH, CLARK'S ISLAND, AND DUXBURY.

Let us walk in Leyden Street.—The way Plymouth was built.—Governor Bradford's Corner.—Fragments of Family History.—How Marriage became a civil Act.—The Common-house.—John Oldham's Punishment.—The Allyne House.—James Otis and his Sister Mercy.—James Warren.—Cole's Hill, and its obliterated Graves.—Plymouth Rock.—True Date of the "Landing."—Christmas in Plymouth, and Bradford's Joke.—Pilgrim Toleration.—Samoset surprises Plymouth.—The Entry of Massasoit.—First American Congress.—To Clark's Island.—Watson's House.—Election Rock.—The Party of Discovery.—Duxbury.—Captains Hill and Miles Standish.—John Alden.—"Why don't you speak for yourself?"—Historical Iconoclasts.—Celebrities of Duxbury.—Winslow and Acadia.—Colonel Church.—The Dartmouth Indians............ 283

CHAPTER XIX.

PROVINCETOWN.

Cape Cod a *Terra incognita*.—Appearance of its Surface.—Historical Fragments.—The Pilgrims' first Landing.—New England Washing-day.—De Poutrincourt's Fight with Natives.—Provincetown described.—Cape Names.—Portuguese Colony.—Cod and Mackerel Fishery.—Cod-fish Aristocracy.—Matt Prior and Lent.—Beginning of Whaling.—Mad Montague.—The Desert.—Cranberry Culture.—The moving Sand-hills.—Disappearance of ancient Forests.—The Beach.—Race Point.—Huts of Refuge.—Ice Blockade of 1874-'75.—Wreck of the *Giovanni*.—Physical Aspects of the Cape Shores.—Old Wreck at Orleans............ 304

CHAPTER XX.

NANTUCKET.

The old Voyagers again.—Derivation of the Name of Nantucket.—Sail from Wood's Hole to the Island.—Vineyard Sound.—Walks in Nantucket Streets.—Whales, Ships, and Whaling.—Nantucket in the Revolution.—Cruising for Whales.—The Camels.—Nantucket Sailors.—Loss of Ship *Essex*.—Town-crier.—Island History.—Quaker Sailors.—Thomas Mayhew.—Spermaceti.—Macy, Folger, Admiral Sir Isaac Coffin............ 324

CHAPTER XXI.

NANTUCKET—*continued*.

Taking Blackfish.—Blue-fishing at the Opening.—Walk to Coatue.—The Scallop-shell.—Structure of the Island.—Indian Legends.—Shepherd Life.—Absolutism of Indian Sagamores.—

CONTENTS. 13

Wasting of the Shores of the Island.—Siasconset.—Nantucket Carts.—Fishing-stages.—The Great South Shoal.—Sankoty Light.—Surfside...Page 343

CHAPTER XXII.
NEWPORT OF AQUIDNECK.

General View of Newport.—Sail up the Harbor.—Commercial Decadence.—Street Rambles.—William Coddington.—Anne Hutchinson.—The Wantons.—Newport Artillery.—State-house Notes.—Tristram Burgess.—Jewish Cemetery and Synagogue.—Judah Touro.—Redwood Library.—The Old Stone Mill.. 356

CHAPTER XXIII.
PICTURESQUE NEWPORT.

The Cliff Walk.—Newport Cottages and Cottage Life.—Charlotte Cushman.—Fort Day and Fort Adams. — Bernard, the Engineer. — Dumplings Fort. — Canonicut. — Hessians. — Newport Drives.—The Beaches.—Purgatory.—Dean Berkeley.. 373

CHAPTER XXIV.
THE FRENCH AT NEWPORT.

Behavior of the Troops.—Monarchy aiding Democracy.—D'Estaing.—Jourdan.—French Camps.—Rochambeau, De Ternay, De Noailles.—Efforts of England to break the Alliance.—Frederick's Remark.—Malmesbury and Potemkin.—Lord North and Yorktown.—George III.—Biron, Duc de Lauzun.—Chastellux, De Castries, Vioménil, Lameth, Dumas, La Peyrouse, Berthier, and Deux-Ponts.—The Regiment Auvergne.—Latour D'Auvergne.—French Diplomacy.. 386

CHAPTER XXV.
NEWPORT CEMETERIES.

Rhode Island Cemetery.—Curious Inscriptions. — William Ellery.—Oliver Hazard Perry.—The Quakers.—George Fox.—Quaker Persecution.—Other Grave-yards.—Lee and the Rhode Island Tories.—Coddington and Gorton.—John Coggeshall.—Trinity Church-yard.—Dr. Samuel Hopkins.—Gilbert Stuart... 398

CHAPTER XXVI.
TO MOUNT HOPE, AND BEYOND.

Walk up the Island.—"Tonomy" Hill.—The Malbones.—Capture of General Prescott.—Talbot's Exploit.—Ancient Stages.—Windmills.—About Fish.—Lawton's Valley.—Battle of 1778.—Island History.—Mount Hope.—Philip's Death.—Dighton Rock.—Indian Antiquities.... 407

CHAPTER XXVII.
NEW LONDON AND NORWICH.

Entrance to the Thames.—Fisher's Island.—Block Island.—New London.—Light-ships and Light-houses.—Hempstead House.—Bishop Seabury.—Old Burial-ground.—New London Harbor.—The little Ship-destroyer.—Groton and Monument.—Arnold.—British Attack on Groton.—Fort Griswold.—The Pequots.—John Mason.—Silas Deane.—Beaumarchais.—John Ledyard.—Decatur and Hardy.—Norwich City.—The Yantic picturesque.—Uncas, the Mohegan Chieftain.—Norwich Town.—Fine old Trees.—The Huntingtons.........................Page 420

CHAPTER XXVIII.
SAYBROOK.

Old Saybrook.—Disappearance of the Yankee.—Old Girls.—Isaac Hull.—The Harts.—Connecticut River.—Old Fortress.—Dutch Courage.—The Pilgrims' Experiences.—Cromwell, Hampden, and Pym.—Lady Fenwick.—George Fenwick.—Lion Gardiner.—Old Burial-ground.—Yale College.—The Shore, and the End... 441

INDEX 451

LIST OF ILLUSTRATIONS.

	PAGE
Pigeon Cove, Cape Ann. *Fr'tispiece.*	
Map.................... *In Preface.*	
Head-piece.....................	18
Jacques Cartier...............	20
Captain John Smith...........	21
Pierre du Guast, Sieur de Monts	23
Sir Humphrey Gilbert.........	24
Fac-simile of first Map engraved in New England.....	25
Tail-piece....................	26
Mount Desert, from Blue Hill Bay.......................	27
Map of Mount Desert Island..	28
Samuel Champlain............	29
Head of Somes's Sound........	32
Echo Lake....................	33
Cliffs, Dog Mountain, Somes's Sound.....................	37
The Stone Wall...............	38
Entrance to Somes's Sound ...	39
Professor Agassiz.............	40
View of Eagle Lake and the Sea from Green Mountain...	43
Cliffs on Bald Porcupine......	44
Southerly End of Newport Mountain, near the Sand Beach.....................	45
Cave of the Sea, Schooner Head	46
Cliffs at Schooner Head.......	47
Devil's Den and Schooner Head	48
Great Head...................	51
The Ovens, Saulsbury's Cove..	55
Tail-piece....................	57
Castine, approaching from Islesboro....................	58
General Henry Knox..........	61
General Benjamin Lincoln	62
Fort Point....................	63
View from Fort George	66
Sir John Moore...............	67
Fort Griffith..................	68
Fort George...................	69
Tail-piece....................	72
Ruins of Fort Pentagoët.......	73
Pine-tree Shilling.............	75
Colbert.......................	79
Lobster Pot...................	85
Tail-piece....................	86
Old Fort Frederick, Pemaquid Point.....................	87
"The Land-breeze of Evening"	88
Cotton Mather................	94
Ancient Pemaquid	95

	PAGE
Charlevoix....................	96
French Frigate, Seventeenth Century....................	98
Hutchinson...................	99
Monhegan Island	102
Thatcher's Island Light, and Fog-signals, Cape Ann......	103
Graves of Burrows and Blythe, Portland...................	107
Tail-piece (Burrows's Medal)..	108
Gorge, Bald Head Cliff........	109
Old Wrecks on the Beach.....	112
The Morning Round	119
What the Sea can do.........	123
York Meeting-house..........	134
Jail at Old York...............	136
Pillory.......................	137
Stocks........................	137
Old Garrison House..........	139
Tail-piece....................	140
Portsmouth, New Hampshire, from Kittery Bridge.........	141
Navy Yard, Kittery, Maine....	142
Block-house and Fort, Kittery Point.....................	144
Sir William Pepperell's House, Kittery Point	145
Sir William Pepperell.........	146
Kittery Point, Maine..........	148
Governor Langdon's Mansion, Portsmouth.................	150
Tail-piece....................	152
Whale's-back Light...........	153
Portsmouth and the Isles of Shoals (Map)................	154
Shag and Mingo Rocks, Duck Island......................	158
Meeting-house, Star Island....	163
The Graves, with Captain John Smith's Monument, Star Island	165
Gorge, Star Island............	169
Tail-piece....................	174
Cliffs, White Island...........	175
Blackbeard, the Pirate	178
Smutty Nose	182
Haley Dock and Homestead...	183
Ledge of Rocks, Smutty Nose.	186
South-east End of Appledore, looking South.............	187
Duck Island, from Appledore..	188
Laighton's Grave.............	190
Londoner's, from Star Island..	191

	PAGE
Covered Way and Light-house, White Island...............	193
White Island Light...........	194
Tail-piece	195
Wentworth House, Little Harbor.....................	196
Point of Graves...............	197
Old House, Great Island......	198
Old Tower, Newcastle.........	199
Gate-way, old Fort Constitution.......................	200
Sir Thomas Wentworth, Wentworth House, Little Harbor.	201
Marquis of Rockingham.......	202
In the Wentworth House, Little Harbor...................	203
Lady Hancock's Portrait in the Wentworth House..........	204
Governor Benning Wentworth.	206
Baron Steuben................	207
Witch Hill, Salem	208
Custom-house, Salem, Massachusetts....................	211
Rebecca Nurse's House........	213
Procter House.................	214
Birthplace of Putnam.........	217
Putnam in British Uniform...	218
Endicott Pear-tree............	218
Tail-piece (Putnam's Tavern Sign)......................	219
Washington Street, Salem.....	220
Birthplace of Hawthorne......	221
Shattuck House...............	221
Room in which Hawthorne was born......................	222
The old Witch House..........	223
Fragment of Examination of Rebecca Nurse..............	224
Thomas Beadle's Tavern, 1692.	225
Interior of First Church, Salem	227
Ireson's House, Oakum Bay, Marblehead.................	228
Great Head...................	229
"The Churn".................	230
Drying Fish, Little Harbor....	232
Unloading Fish	235
A Group of Antiques..........	237
Lee Street.....................	239
Tucker's Wharf—the Steps ...	241
Gregory Street	242
Lee House....................	245
Town-house and Square.......	247
St. Michael's, Marblehead......	248

LIST OF ILLUSTRATIONS.

	PAGE
Elbridge Gerry	249
The Gerrymander	250
"Old North" Congregational Church	251
Samuel Tucker	252
General Glover	253
Fort Sewall	255
Powder-house, 1755	256
James Lawrence	257
Glimpse of the Seamen's Monument and old Burial-ground	258
Lone Graves	260
"Sitting, stitching in a mournful Muse"	260
The Hoe, English Plymouth	261
Map of Plymouth	262
Pilgrim Hall	263
Brewster's Chest, and Standish's Pot	263
Landing of the Pilgrims	264
Carver's and Brewster's Chairs	265
Mincing Knife	265
Peregrine White's Cabinet	265
Standish's Sword	266
The Old Colony Seal	267
Map of Plymouth Bay	269
Champlain's Map. — Port Cape St. Louis	274
Tail-piece	282
The Pilgrims' first Encounter. Building on the Site of Bradford's Mansion	283
Site of the Common House	286
The Allyne House	287
The Joanna Davis House, Cole's Hill	288
Plymouth Rock in 1850	289
The Gurnet	296
Watson's House, Clark's Island	297
Election Rock, Clark's Island	298
Church's Sword	302
Tail-piece	303
Provincetown, from the Hills	304
Cohasset Narrows	305
Highland Light, Cape Cod	306
Washing Fish	309
Mackerel.—A Family Group	313
Pond Village, Cape Cod	315
Picking and sorting Cranberries—Cape Cod	317
Sand-hills, Provincetown	318
Life-boat Station.—Trial of the Bomb and Line	321
Tail-piece (A "Sunfish")	323
Nantucket, from the Sea	324
Map of Cape Cod, Nantucket, and Martha's Vineyard	325
Approach to Martha's Vineyard	326
A Bit of Nantucket—the Housetops	328
Last of the Whale-ships	332
Whaling in the olden Time	333
Whale of the Ancients	334
E. Johnson's Studio, Nantucket	341
Tail-piece	342
Nantucket. — Old Windmill, looking oceanward	343
Captured Porpoise and Blackfish	345
The Blue-fish	346
Blue-fishing	347
Homes of the Fishermen, Siasconset	352
The Sea-bluff, Siasconset	353
Hauling a Dory over the Hills, Nantucket	354
Light-house, Sankoty Head, Nantucket	355
Tail-piece	355
Newport, from Fort Adams	356
Old Fort, Dumpling Rocks	358
Old-time Houses	360
Residence of Governor Coddington, Newport, 1641	361
Newport State-house	363
Commodore Perry's House	364
Jewish Cemetery	365
Jews' Synagogue, Newport	366
Judah Touro	367
The Redwood Library	368
Abraham Redwood	369
The Old Stone Mill	370
The Perry Monument	371
Tail-piece	372
Boat Landing	373
The Beach	374
Cliff Walk	375
The Cliffs	376
A Newport Cottage	377
Charlotte Cushman's Residence	377
Spouting Rock	378
The Dumplings	380
Hessian Grenadier	381
Coast Scene, Newport	382
The Drive	383
Purgatory Bluff	383
Whitehall	384
Washington Park, Newport	385
D'Estaing	386
Earl Howe	388
Rochambeau	388
Rochambeau's Head-quarters	389
Louis XVI	389
Military Map of Rhode Island, 1778	390
Lafayette	391
Baron Vioménil	391
Trinity Church, Newport	392
Chastellux	392
Lauzun	393
Mathieu Dumas	394
Deux-Ponts	395
De Barras	395
Latour D'Auvergne	396
Tail-piece	397
Graves on the Bluff, Fort Road	398
Tombstones, Newport Cemetery	399
Perry's Monument	401
Oliver Hazard Perry	401
Friends' Meeting-house	402
George Fox	403
Charles Lee	404
Mount Hope	407
The Glen	408
A Rhode Island Windmill	409
William Barton	410
Silas Talbot	410
Prescott's Head-quarters	411
Agricultural Prosperity	412
From Butts's Hill, looking North	413
Quaker Hill, from Butts's Hill, looking North	414
Battle-ground of August 29, 1778	414
King Philip, from an old Print	415
Inscription on Dighton Rock	416
Old Leonard House, Raynham	419
New London in 1813	420
New London Harbor, north View	421
New London Light	421
New London in 1781 (Map)	422
Old Block-house, Fort Trumbull	423
A Light-ship on her Station	424
Court-house, New London	425
Bishop Seabury's Monument	426
Groton Monument	427
Benedict Arnold	429
Storming of the Indian Fortress	430
Silas Deane	431
Stephen Decatur	433
Rustic Bridge, Norwich	434
Old Mill, Norwich	435
Signatures of Uncas and his Sons	436
Uncas's Monument	437
Arnold's Birthplace	437
Elm-trees by the Wayside	438
General Huntington's House	438
Mansion of Governor Huntington	439
Congregational Church	440
Tail-piece	440
Peter Stuyvesant	441
Isaac Hull	444
A Moss-grown Memorial	446
Tail-piece	449

THE NEW ENGLAND COAST.

CHAPTER I.

NEW ENGLAND OF THE ANCIENTS.

"This is the forest primeval. The murmuring pines and the hemlocks,
  Bearded with moss, and with garments green, indistinct in the twilight,
  Stand like Druids of Old, with voices sad and prophetic,
  Stand like harpers hoar, with beards that rest on their bosoms.
  Loud from its rocky caverns the deep-voiced neighboring ocean
  Speaks, and in accents disconsolate answers the wail of the forest."
                                              LONGFELLOW.

IN many respects the sea-coast of Maine is the most remarkable of New England. It is serrated with craggy projections, studded with harbors, seamed with inlets. Broad bays conduct to rivers of great volume that annually bear her forests down to the sea. Her shores are barricaded with islands, and her waters teem with the abundance of the seas. Seen on the map, it is a splintered, jagged, forbidding sea-board; beheld with the eye in a kindly season, its tawny headlands, green archipelagos, and inviting harbors, infolding sites recalling the earlier efforts at European colonization, combine in a wondrous degree to win the admiration of the man of science, of letters, or of leisure.

Maine embraces within her limits the semi-fabulous Norumbega and Mavoshen of ancient writers. Some portion of her territory has been known at various times by the names of Acadia, New France, and New England. The arms of France and of England have alternately been erected on her soil, and the flags of at least four powerful states have claimed her subjection. The most numerous and warlike of the primitive New England nations were seated here. Traces of French occupation are remaining in the names of St. Croix, Mount Desert, Isle au Haut, and Castine, names which neither treaties nor national prejudice have been quite able to eradicate.

The name of Norumbega, or Norembegue, the earliest applied to New England, is attributed to the Portuguese and Spaniards. Jean Alfonse, the pilot of Roberval, the same person who is accredited with having been first to navigate the waters of Massachusetts Bay, gives them the credit of its discovery. It is true that Marc Lescarbot, the Parisian advocate whose relations are the foundations of so many others, was at the colony of Port Royal in the year 1606, with Pontgravé, Champlain, and De Poutrincourt. This writer discredits all of Alfonse's statement in relation to the great river and coast of Norumbega, except that part of it in which he says the river had at its entrance many islands, banks, and rocks. In this fragment from the "*Voyages Aventureux*" of Alfonse, the embouchure of the river of Norumbega is placed in thirty degrees ("trente degrez") and the pilot states that from thence the coast turns to the west and west-north-west for more than two hundred and fifty leagues.[1] The most casual reader will know how to value such a relation without reference to the sarcasm of Lescarbot, when he says, "And well may he call his voyages adventurous, not for himself, who was never in the hundredth part of the places which he describes (at least it is easy to conjecture so), but for those who might wish to follow the routes which he directs the mariner to follow." After this, his claims to be considered the first European navigator in Massachusetts Bay must be received with many grains of allowance.

Champlain, who remained in the country through the winter of 1605, on purpose to complete his map, has this to say of the river and city of Norumbega; he is writing of the Penobscot:

"I believe this river is that which several historians call Norumbegue, and which the greater part have written, is large and spacious, with many islands; and its entrance in forty-three and forty-three and a half; and others in forty-four, more or less, of latitude. As for the declination, I have neither

---

[1] "Et que passé cette riviere la côte tourne à l'Ouest et Ouest-Norouest plus de deux cens cinquante lieues," etc.

read nor heard any one speak of it. They describe also a great and very populous city of natives, dexterous and skillful, having cotton cloth. I am satisfied that the major part of those who make mention of it have never seen it, and speak from the hearsay evidence of those who know no more than themselves. I can well believe that there are some who have seen the embouchure, for the reason that there are, in fact, many islands there, and that it lies in the latitude of forty-four degrees at its entrance, as they say; but that any have entered it is not credible; for they must have described it in quite another manner to have removed this doubt from many people." With this protest Champlain admits the country of Norumbega to a place on his map of 1612.

In the "*Histoire Universelle des Indes Occidentales*," printed at Douay in 1607, the author, after describing Virginia, speaks of Norumbega, its great river and beautiful city. The mouth of the river is fixed in the forty-fourth and the pretended city in the forty-fifth degree, which approximates closely enough to the actual latitude of the Penobscot. This authority adds, that it is not known whence the name originated, for the Indians called it Agguncia.[1] It also refers to the island well situated for fishery at the mouth of the great river. On the map of Ortelius (1603) the two countries of Norumbega and Nova Francia occupy what is now Nova Scotia and New England respectively. The only features laid down in Nova Francia by name are "R. Grande Orsinora," "C. de Iaguas islas," and "Montagnes St. Jean." These localities answer reasonably well to as many conjectures as there are mountains, streams, and capes in New England; there is no projection of the coast corresponding with Cape Cod. Champlain names the River Penobscot, Pemetegoit. By this appellation, with some trivial change in orthography, it continued known to the French until its final repossession by the English.[2]

Turning to the "painful collections of Master Hakluyt," the old prebendary of Bristol, we find Mavoshen described as "a country lying to the north and by east of Virginia, between the degrees of 43 and 45, fortie leagues broad and fifty in length, lying in breadth east and west, and in length north and south. It is bordered on the east with a countrey, the people whereof they call Tarrantines, on the west with Epistoman, on the north with a very great wood, called Senaglecounc, and on the south with the mayne ocean sea and many islands." In all these relations there is something of fact, but much more that is too unsubstantial for the historian's acceptance. The voyages of the Norsemen, of De Rut, and Thevet are still a

---

[1] The monk André Thevet, who professes to have visited Norumbega River in 1556, says it was called by the natives "Agoncy."

[2] According to the Abbé Maurault, Pentagoët, in the Indian vocabulary, signifies "a place in a river where there are rapids." On the authority of the "History of the Abenaquis," Penobscot is, "where the land is stony, or covered with rocks."

disputed and a barren field. I do not propose here to indulge in speculations respecting them.

Francis I. demanded, it is said, to be shown that clause in the will of Adam which disinherited him in the New World for the benefit of the Spaniards. Under his favor, the Florentine Verazzani put to sea from Dieppe, in *Le Dauphine*, in the year 1524.[1] By virtue of his discoveries the French nation claimed all the territory now included in New England. The astute Francis followed up the clew by dispatching, in 1534, Jacques Cartier in *La Grande Hermine*. Despite the busy times in Europe, near the close of his reign, Henry IV. continued to favor projects confirming the footing obtained by his predecessors. Until 1614, when the name of New England first appeared on Smith's map, the French had the honor of adding about all that was known to the geography of its sea-board.

JACQUES CARTIER.

There can now be no harm in saying that Captain John Smith was not the first to give a Christian name to New England. The Florentine Verazzani called it, in 1524, New France, when he traversed the coasts from the thirty-fourth parallel to Newfoundland, or *Prima Vista*. Sebastian Cabot may have seen it before him; but this is only conjecture, though our great-grandfathers were willing to spill their blood rather than have it called New France. According to the "Modern Universal History," Cabot confessedly took formal possession of Newfoundland and Norumbega, whence he carried off three natives. In the "*Theatre Universel d'Ortelius*" there is a map of America, engraved in 1572, and very minute, in which all the countries north

---

[1] It is curious that three Italians—Columbus, Cabot, and Verazzani—should lead all others in the discoveries of the American continent.

and south are entitled New France. "The English," says a French authority, "had as yet nothing in that country, and there is nothing set down on this map for them."

In Mercator's atlas of 1623 is a general map of America, which calls all the territory north and south of Canada New France. New England does not find a place on this map. Canada is down as a particular province. Virginia is also there.

Captain John Smith's map of New England of 1614 contains many singular features. In his "Description of New England," printed in 1616, the Indian names are given of all their coast settlements. Prince Charles, however, altered these to English names after the book was printed. The retention of some of them by the actual settlers might be accidental, but they appear much as if scattered at random over the paper.

CAPTAIN JOHN SMITH.

"Plimouth" is where it was located six years after the date of the map. York is called Boston, and Agamenticus "Snadoun Hill." Penobscot is called "Pembrock's Bay."

The name of Cape Breton is said to occur on very early maps, antecedent even to Cartier's voyage. A map of Henry II. is the oldest mentioned. "Nurembega" is on a map in "*Le Receuil de Ramusius*,"[1] tome iii., where there is an account of a Frenchman of Dieppe, and a map made before the discovery of "Jean Guartier." It is asserted that the Basque and Breton fishermen were on the coast of America before the Portuguese and Spaniards. Baron La Hontan says, "The seamen of French Biscay are known to be the most able and dexterous mariners that are in the world." It is pretty certain that Cape Breton had this name before the voyages of Cartier or Champlain. The Frenchman of Dieppe is supposed to be Thomas Aubert, whose discovery is assigned to the year 1508.

The atlas of Guillaume and John Blauw has a map of America in tome i. There is a second, entitled *Nova Belgica* and *Nova Anglica*. New England extends no farther than the Kennebec, where begins the territory of *Nova Franciæ Pars*, in which Norumbega is located. The rivers Pentagouet and Chouacouet (Saco) appear properly placed. The map bears certain marks in

---

[1] Giambetta Ramusio, the Venetian.

its nomenclature, and the configuration of the coast, of being compiled from those of Champlain and Smith.[1]

Researches made in England, France, and Holland, at the instance of Massachusetts and New York,[2] have resulted in the recovery of many manuscript fragments more or less interesting, bearing upon the question of priority of discovery. Of these the following is not the least curious. If credence may be placed in the author of the "*Memoires pour servir à l'Histoire de Dieppe*," "*Recherches sur les Voyages et decouvertes des Navigateurs Normands*," and "*Navigateurs Français*," the continent of America was discovered by Captain Cousin in the year 1488. Sailing from Dieppe, he was carried westward by a gale, and drawn by currents to an unknown coast, where he saw the mouth of a large river.

Cousin's first officer was "un étranger nommé Pinçon ou Pinzon," who instigated the men to mutiny, and was so turbulent that, on the return of the caravel, Cousin charged him before the magistrates of Dieppe with mutiny, insubordination, and violence. He was banished from the city, and embarked four years afterward, say the Dieppois, with Christopher Columbus, to whom he had given information of the New World.[3]

In the "*Bibliothèque Royale*" of Paris there is, or rather was, existing a manuscript (dated in 1545) entitled "*Cosmographie de Jean Alfonce le Xaintongeois.*" It is undoubtedly from this manuscript that Jean de Marnef and De St. Gelais compiled the "*Voyages Aventureux d'Alfonce Xaintongeois*," printed in 1559, which includes an expedition along the coast from Newfoundland southwardly to "une baye jusques par les 42 degrés, entre la Norembegue et la Fleuride," in 1543.

Of Jean Alfonse it is known that he was one of Roberval's pilots, in his voyage of 1542 to Canada, and that he returned home with Cartier. Roberval expected to find a north-west passage, and Jean Alfonse, who searched the coast for it, believed the land he saw to the southward to be part of the continent of Asia. His cruise within the latitude of Massachusetts Bay is also mentioned by Hakluyt. The claim of Alfonse to be the discoverer of Massachusetts Bay has been set forth with due prominence.[4] Alfonse and Champlain were both from the same old province in the west of France.

It goes without dispute that the older French historians knew little or

---

[1] Champlain's map of 1612 is entitled "CARTE GEOGRAPHIQVE DE LA NOVVELLE FRANCE FAICTTE PAR LE SIEVR DE CHAMPLAIN SAINT TONGOIS, CAPPITAINE ORDINAIRE POVR LE ROY EN LA MARINE. *Faict len* 1612." All the territory from Labrador to Cape Cod is embraced in this very curious map. Some of its details will be introduced in successive chapters as occasion may demand. There is another map of Champlain of 1632, *fort detaillé*, but of less rarity than the first.

[2] By Ben Perley Poore and John Romeyn Brodhead.

[3] "Massachusetts Archives, French Documents," vol. i., p. 269.

[4] Rev. B. F. De Costa's "Northmen in Maine."

nothing of Hakluyt and Purchas. So little did the affairs of the New World engage their attention, that in the "History of France," by Father Daniel, printed at Amsterdam in 1720, by the Company of Jesuits, in six ponderous tomes, the discoveries and settlements in New France (Canada) occupy no more than a dozen lines. Cartier, Roberval, De Monts, and Champlain are mentioned, and that is all.

When a vessel of the old navigators was approaching the coast, the precaution was taken of sending sailors to the mast-head. These lookouts were relieved every two hours until night-fall, at which time, if the land was not yet in sight, they furled their sails so as to make little or no way during the night. It was a matter of emulation among the ship's company who should first discover the land, as the passengers usually presented the lucky one with some pistoles. One writer mentions that on board French vessels, after sighting Cape Race, the ceremony known among us as "crossing the line" was performed by the old salts on the green hands, without regard to season.

PIERRE DU GUAST, SIEUR DE MONTS.

The method of taking possession of a new country is thus described in the old chronicles: Jacques Cartier erected a cross thirty feet high, on which was suspended a shield with the arms of France and the words " *Vive le Roy.*" Sir Humphrey Gilbert, in 1583, raised a pillar at Newfoundland, with a plate of lead, having the queen's arms "graven thereon." A turf and a twig were presented to him, which he received with a hazel wand. The expression "by turf and twig," a symbol of actual possession of the soil and its products, is still to be met with in older New England records.

Douglass, the American historian, speaking of Henry IV., says, "He planted a colony in Canada which subsists to this day. May it not long subsist; it is a nuisance to our North American settlements: *Delenda est Carthago.*"

The insignificant attempt of Gosnold, in 1603, and the disastrous one of Popham, in 1607, contributed little to the knowledge of New England. But the absence of any actual possession of the soil did not prevent the exercise of unworthy violence toward intruders on the territory claimed by the English crown. In 1613 Sir Samuel Argall broke up the French settlement begun at Mount Desert in that year, opening fire on the unsuspecting colonists before he gave himself the trouble of a formal summons. Those of other nations fared little better, as the following recital will show:

SIR HUMPHREY GILBERT.

Purchas relates that "Sir Bernard Drake, a Devonshire knight, came to Newfoundland with a commission; and having divers good ships under his command, he took many Portugal ships, and brought them into England as prizes.

"Sir Bernard, as was said, having taken a Portugal ship, and brought her into one of our western ports, the seamen that were therein were sent to the prison adjoining the Castle of Exeter. At the next assizes held at the castle there, about the 27th of Queen Elizabeth, when the prisoners of the county were brought to be arraigned before Sergeant Flowerby, one of the judges appointed for this western circuit at that time, suddenly there arose such a noisome smell from the bar that a great number of people there present were therewith infected; whereof in a very short time after died the said judge, Sir John Chichester, Sir Arthur Bassett, and Sir Bernard Drake, knights, and justices of the peace there sitting on the bench; and eleven of the jury impaneled, the twelfth only escaping; with divers other persons."

Captain John Smith says: "The most northern part I was at was the Bay of Penobscot, which is east and west, north and south, more than ten leagues; but such were my occasions I was constrained to be satisfied of them I found in the bay, that the river ran far up into the land, and was well inhabited with many people; but they were from their habitations, either fishing among the isles, or hunting the lakes and woods for deer and beavers.

"The bay is full of great islands of one, two, six, eight, or ten miles in length, which divide it into many faire and excellent good harbours. On the east of it are the Tarrantines, their mortal enemies, where inhabit the

French, as they report, that live with these people as one nation or family."

If the English had no special reason for self-gratulation in the quality of the emigrants first introduced into New England, the French have as little ground to value themselves. In order to people Acadia, De Monts begged permission of Henri Quatre to take the vagabonds that might be collected in the cities, or wandering at large through the country. The king acceded to the request.[1]

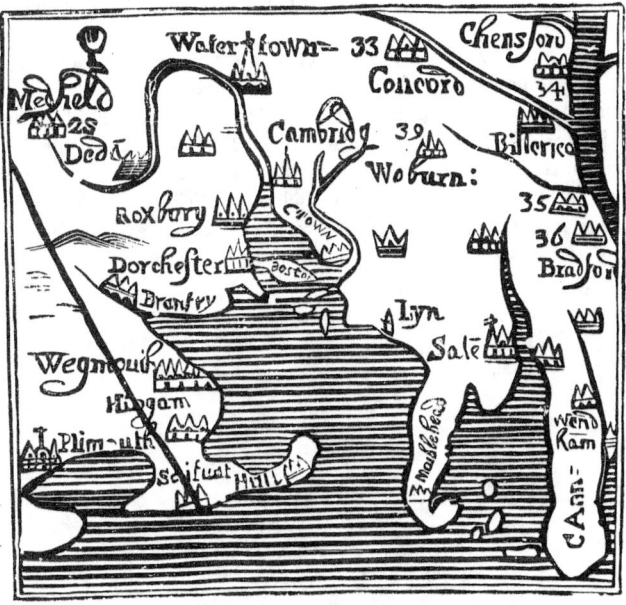

FAC-SIMILE OF FIRST MAP ENGRAVED IN NEW ENGLAND.

Again, in a memoir on the state of the French plantations, the following passage occurs: "The post of Pentagouet, being at the head of all Acadia on the side of Boston, appears to have been principally strengthened by the sending over of men and courtesans that his majesty would have emigrate there for the purpose of marrying, so that this portion of the colony may receive the accessions necessary to sustain it against its neighbors."[2]

These statements are supported by the testimony of the Baron La Hontan, who relates that, after the reorganization of the troops in Canada, "several ships were sent hither from France with a cargo of women of ordinary reputation, under the direction of some old stale nuns, who ranged them in

---

[1] "Mass. Archives, French Documents."   [2] Ibid.

three classes. The vestal virgins were heaped up (if I may so speak), one above another, in three different apartments, where the bridegrooms singled out their brides just as a butcher does ewes from among a flock of sheep. The sparks that wanted to be married made their addresses to the above-mentioned governesses, to whom they were obliged to give an account of their goods and estates before they were allowed to make their choice in the seraglio." After the selection was made, the marriage was concluded on the spot, in presence of a priest and a notary, the governor-general usually presenting the happy couple with some domestic animals with which to begin life anew.

When the number of historical precedents is taken into account, the superstition long current among mariners with regard to setting sail on Friday seems unaccountable. Columbus sailed from Spain on Friday, discovered land on Friday, and returned to Palos on Friday. Cabot discovered the American continent on Friday. Gosnold sailed from England on Friday, made land on Friday, and came to anchor on Friday at Exmouth. These coincidences might, it would seem, dispel, with American mariners at least, something of the dread with which a voyage begun on that day has long been regarded.

MOUNT DESERT, FROM BLUE HILL BAY.

CHAPTER II.

MOUNT DESERT ISLAND.

"There, gloomily against the sky,
The Dark Isles rear their summits high;
And Desert Rock, abrupt and bare,
Lifts its gray turrets in the air."
                            WHITTIER.

ISLANDS possess, of themselves, a magnetism not vouchsafed to any spot of the main-land. In cutting loose from the continent a feeling of freedom is at once experienced that comes spontaneously, and abides no longer than you remain an islander. You are conscious, in again setting foot on the main shore, of a change, which no analysis, however subtle, will settle altogether to your liking. Upon islands the majesty and power of the ocean come home to you, as in multiplying itself it pervades every fibre of your consciousness, gaining in vastness as you grow in knowledge of it. On islands it is always present—always roaring at your feet, or moaning at your back.

Islands have had no little share in the world's doings. Corsica, Elba, and St. Helena are linked together by an unbroken historical chain. Homer and the isles of Greece, Capri and Tiberius loom in the twilight of antiquity. Thinking on Garibaldi or Victor Hugo, the mind instinctively lodges on Caprera or Jersey. An island was the death of Philip II., and the ruin of Napoleon. In the New World, Santo Domingo, Cuba, and Newfoundland were first visited by Europeans.

The islands of the New England coast have become beacons of her history. Mount Desert, Monhegan, and the Isles of Shoals, Clark's Island, Nantucket, The Vineyard, and Rhode Island have havens where the historian or antiquary must put in before landing on broader ground. I might name a score of others of lesser note; these are planets in our watery system. On this line many peaceful summer campaigns have been brought to a happy conclusion. Not a few have described the more genial aspects of Mount Desert. It has in fact given employment to many busy pens and famous pencils. I am not aware that its wintry guise has been portrayed on paper or on canvas. The very name is instinctively associated with an idea of desolateness:

> "The gray and thunder-smitten pile
> Which marks afar the Desert Isle."

Champlain was no doubt impressed by the sight of its craggy summits, stripped of trees, basking their scarred and splintered steeps in a September sun. "I have called it," he says, "the Isle of Monts Déserts."

In a little "*pattache*" of only seventeen or eighteen tons burden, he had set out on the 2d of September, 1604, from St. Croix, to explore the coast of Norumbega. Two natives accompanied him as guides. The same day, as they passed close to an island four or five leagues long, their bark struck a hardly submerged rock, which tore a hole near the

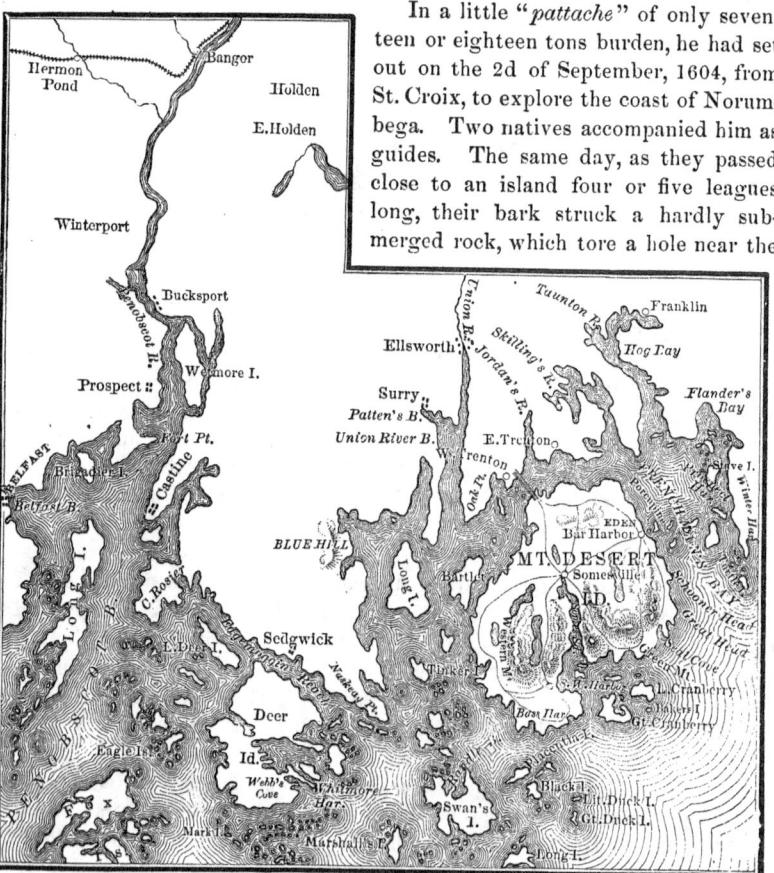

MAP OF MOUNT DESERT ISLAND.

keel. They either sailed around the island, or explored it by land, as the strait between it and the main-land is described as being not more than a hundred paces in breadth. "The land," continues the French voyager, "is very high, intersected by passes, appearing from the sea like seven or eight mountains ranged near each other. The summits of the greater part of these are bare of trees, because they are nothing but rocks." It was during this voyage, and with equal pertinence, Champlain named Isle au Haut.[1] According to Père Biard, the savages called the island of Mount Desert "*Pemetiq*,"

SAMUEL CHAMPLAIN.

"meaning," says M. l'Abbé Maurault, "that which is at the head." A crowned head it appears, seen on land or sea.

It is curious to observe how the embouchure of the Penobscot is on either shore guarded by two such solitary ranges of mountains as the Camden and Mount Desert groups. They embrace about the same number of individual peaks, and approximate nearly enough in altitude. From Camden we may skirt the shores for a hundred and fifty miles to the west and south before meeting with another eminence; and then it is an isolated hill standing almost upon the line of division between Maine and New Hampshire that is encountered. On the shore of the main-land, west of Mount Desert, is Blue Hill, another lone mountain. Katahdin is still another astray, of grander proportions, it is true, but belonging to this family of lost mountains. Although they appear a continuous chain when massed by distance, the Mount

---

[1] "Champlain's Voyages," edit. 1613. Mount Desert was also made out by the Boston colonists of 1630. The reader is referred for materials of Mount Desert's history to Champlain, Charlevoix, Lescarbot, Biard, and Purchas, vol. iv.

Desert range is, in reality, broken into little family groups, as exhibited on the map.

Another peculiarity of the Mount Desert chain is that the eastern summits are the highest, terminating generally in precipitous and inaccessible cliffs. I asked a village ancient his idea of the origin of these mountains, and received it in two words, "Hove up." The cluster numbers thirteen eminences, to which the title "Old Thirteen" may be more fitly applied than to any political community of modern history. This assemblage of hills with lakes in their laps at once recalled the Adirondack region, with some needful deductions for the height and nakedness of the former when compared with the greater altitudes and grand old forests of the wilderness of northern New York.

Should any adventurous spirit, after reading these pages, wish to see the Desert Isle in all its rugged grandeur, he may do so at the cost of some trifling inconveniences that do not fall to the lot of the summer tourist. In this case, Bangor or Bucksport will be the point of departure for a journey of from thirty to forty miles by stage. I came to the island by steamboat from Boston, which landed me at Bucksport; whence I made my way *via* Ellsworth to Somesville.

After glancing at the map of the island, I chose Somesville as a central point for my excursions, because it lies at the head of the sound, that divides the island almost in two, is the point toward which all roads converge, and is about equally distant from the harbors or places of particular resort. In summer I should have adopted the same plan until I had fully explored the shores of the Sound, the mountains that are contiguous, and the western half of the island. In twenty-four hours the visitor may know by heart the names of the mountains, lakes, coves, and settlements, with the roads leading to them; he may thereafter establish himself as convenience or fancy shall dictate. At Somesville there is a comfortable hostel, but the larger summer hotels are at Bar Harbor and at South-west Harbor.

The accentuation should not fall on the last, but on the first syllable of Desert, although the name is almost universally mispronounced in Maine, and notably so on the island itself. Usually it is Mount D*esart*, toned into D*esert* by the casual population, who thus give it a curious significance.

Mount Desert is one of the wardens of Penobscot Bay, interposing its bulk between the waters of Frenchman's Bay on the east and Blue Hill.Bay on the west. A bridge unites it with the main-land in the town of Trenton, where the opposite shores approach within rifle-shot of each other. This point is locally known as the Narrows. When I crossed, the tide was pressing against the wooden piers, in a way to quicken the pace, masses of newly-formed ice that had floated out of Frenchman's Bay with the morning's ebb.

You get a glimpse of Mount Desert in sailing up Penobscot Bay, where its mountains appear foreshortened into two cloudy shapes that you would fail to know again. But the highest hills between Bucksport and Ellsworth display the whole range; and from the latter place until the island is reached their snow-laced sides loomed grandly in the gray mists of a December day. In this condition of the atmosphere their outlines seemed more sharply cut than when thrown against a background of clear blue sky. I counted eight peaks, and then, on coming nearer, others, that at first had blended with those higher and more distant ones, detached themselves. Green Mountain will be remembered as the highest of the chain, Beech and Dog mountains from their peculiarity of outline. A wider break between two hills indicates where the sea has driven the wedge called Somes's Sound into the side of the isle. Western Mountain terminates the range on the right; Newport Mountain, with Bar Harbor at its foot, is at the other extremity of the group. In approaching from sea this order would appear reversed.

The Somesville road is a nearly direct line drawn from the head of the Sound to the Narrows. Soon after passing the bridge, that to Bar Harbor diverged to the left. Crossing a strip of level land, we began the ascent of Town Hill through a dark growth of cedar, fir, and other evergreen trees. A little hamlet, where there is a post-office, crowns the summit of Town Hill. Not long after, the Sound opened into view one of those rare vistas that leave a picture for after remembrance. At first it seemed a lake shut in by the feet of two interlocking mountains, but the vessels that lay fast-moored in the ice were plainly sea-going craft. Somesville lay beneath us, its little steeple pricking the frosty air. Cold, gray, and cheerless as their outward dress appeared, the mountains had more of impressiveness, now that they were covered from base to summit with snow. They seemed really mountains and not hills, receiving an Alpine tone with their wintry vesture.

After all, a winter landscape in New England is less gloomy than in the same zone of the Mississippi Valley, where, in the total absence of evergreen-trees, nothing but long reaches of naked forest rewards the eye, which roves in vain for some vantage-ground of relief. Jutting points, well wooded with dark firs, or clumps of those trees standing by the roadside, were agreeable features in this connection.

A brisk trot over the frozen road brought us to the end of the half-dozen miles that stretch between Somesville and the Narrows. The snow craunched beneath the horses' feet as we glided through the village street; in a moment more the driver drew up with a flourish beside the door of an inn which bears for its ensign a name advantageously known in these latitudes. A rousing fire of birchen logs blazed on the open hearth. Above the mantel were cheap prints of the presidents, from Washington to Buchanan. I was made welcome, and thought of Shenstone when he says,

> "Whoe'er has travel'd life's dull round,
> Whate'er his fortunes may have been,
> Must sigh to think how oft he's found
> Life's warmest welcome at an inn."

THE NEW ENGLAND COAST.

HEAD OF SOMES'S SOUND.

An island fourteen miles long and a dozen broad, embracing a hundred square miles, and traversed from end to end by mountains, is to be approached with respect. It excludes the idea of superficial observation. As the mountains bar the way to the southern shores, you must often make a long *détour* to reach a given point, or else commit yourself to the guidance of a deer-path, or the dry bed of some mountain torrent. In summer or in autumn, with a little knowledge of woodcraft, a well-adjusted pocket-compass, and a stout staff, it is practicable to enter the hills, and make your way as the red huntsmen were of old accustomed to do; but in winter a guide would be indispensable, and you should have well-trained muscles to undertake it.

The mountains have been traversed again and again by fire, destroying not the wood alone, but also the thin turf, the accumulations of years. The woods are full of the evidences of these fires in the charred remains of large trees that, after the passage of the flames, have been felled by tempests. At a distance of five miles the present growth resembles stubble; on a nearer approach it takes the appearance of underbrush; and upon reaching the hills you find a young forest repairing the ravages made by fire, wind, and the woodman's axe. "Fifty years ago," said Mr. Somes, "those mountains were covered with a dark growth." Cedars, firs, hemlocks, and other evergreens, with a thick sprinkling of white-birch, and now and then a clump of beeches, make the principal base for the forest of the future on Mount Desert — provided always it is permitted to arrive at maturity. Hitherto the poverty or greed of the inhabitants has sacrificed every tree that was worth the labor of felling. In the neighborhood of Saulsbury's Cove there are still to be seen, in inaccessible places, trees destined never to feel the axe's keen edge.

Mine host of the village tavern, Daniel Somes, or "Old Uncle Daniel," as he is known far and near, is the grandson of the first settler of the name who emigrated from Gloucester, Massachusetts, and "squatted" here — "a vile phrase"—about 1760. Abraham Somes built on the little point of land in front of the tavern-door, from which a clump of shrubs may be seen growing near the spot. Other settlers came from Cape Cod, and were located at Hull's and other coves about the island. I asked my landlord if there were any family traditions relative to the short-lived settlement of the French, or traces of an occupation that might well have set his ancestors talking. He shook his gray head in emphatic negative. Had I asked him for "Tam O'Shanter" or the "Brigs of Ayr," he would have given it to me stanza for stanza.

There are few excursions to be made within a certain radius of Somesville that offer so much of variety and interest as that on the western side of the Sound, pursuing, with such wanderings as fancy may suggest, the well-beaten road to South-west Harbor. It is seven miles of hill and dale, lake and stream, with a succession of charming views constantly unfolding themselves before you. And here I may remark that the roads on the island are generally good, and easily followed.

The map may have so far introduced the island to the reader that he will

ECHO LAKE.

be able to trace the route along the side of Robinson's Mountain, which is between the road and the Sound, with two summits of nearly equal height, rising six hundred and forty and six hundred and eighty feet above it.. At the right, in descending this road, is Echo Lake, a superb piece of water, having Beech Mountain at its foot. You stumble on it, as it were, unawares, and enjoy the surprise all the more for it. Broad-shouldered and deep-chested mountains wall in the reservoirs that have been filled by the snows melting from their sides. There are speckled trout to be taken in Echo Lake, as well as in the pond lying in Somesville. Of course the echo is to be tried, even if the mount gives back a saucy answer.

Next below us is Dog Mountain. It has been shut out from view until you have uncovered it in passing by the lake. Dog Mountain's eastern and highest crest is six hundred and eighty feet in the air. How much of resemblance it bears to a crouching mastiff depends in a great measure upon the imagination of the beholder:

> *Ham.* "Do you see yonder cloud that's almost in shape of a camel?
> *Pol.* "By the mass, and 'tis like a camel indeed.
> *Ham.* "Methinks it is like a weasel.
> *Pol.* "It is backed like a weasel.
> *Ham.* "Or like a whale?
> *Pol.* "Very like a whale."

Between Dog and Brown's Mountain on its eastern shore the Sound has forced its way for six or seven miles up into the centre of the island. At the southern foot of Dog Mountain is Fernald's Cove and Point, the supposed scene of the attempted settlement by the colony of Madame the Marchioness De Guercheville. Mr. De Costa has christened Brown's Mountain with the name of Mansell, from Sir Robert Mansell, vice-admiral in the times of James I. and Charles I. The whole island was once called after the knight, but there is a touch of retributive justice in recollecting that the English, in expelling the French, have in turn been expelled from its nomenclature.

Turning now to what Prescott calls "historicals" for enlightenment on the subject of the colonization of Mount Desert, it appears that upon the return of De Monts to France he gave his town of Port Royal to Jean de Poutrincourt, whose voyage in 1606 along the coast of New England will be noticed in future chapters. The projects of De Monts having been overthrown by intrigue, and through jealousy of the exclusive rights conferred by his patent, Madame De Guercheville, a "very charitable and pious lady" of the court,[1] entered into negotiation with Poutrincourt for the founding of Jesuit missions among the savages. Finding that Poutrincourt claimed more than he could conveniently establish a right to, Madame treated directly with Du Guast, who

---

[1] She was one of the queen's ladies of honor, and wife of the Duke of Rochefoucauld Liancourt.

ceded to her all the privileges derived by him from Henry IV. The king, in 1607, confirmed all except the grant of Port Royal, which was reserved to Poutrincourt. The memorable year of 1610 ended the career of Henry, in the Rue de la Ferronerie. In 1611 the fathers, Père Biard and Enemond Masse, of the College d'Eu, came over to Port Royal with Biencourt, the younger Poutrincourt. During the next year an expedition under the auspices of Madame De Guercheville was prepared to follow, and, after taking on board the two Jesuits already at Port Royal, was to proceed to make a definitive settlement somewhere in the Penobscot.

The colonists numbered in all about thirty persons, including two other Jesuit fathers, named Jacques Quentin and Gilbert Du Thet.[1] The expedition was under the command of La Saussaye. In numbers it was about equal to the colony of Gosnold.

La Saussaye arrived at Port Royal, and after taking on board the fathers, Biard and Masse, continued his route. Arriving off Menan, the vessel was enveloped by an impenetrable fog, which beset them for two days and nights. Their situation was one of imminent danger, from which, if the relation of the Père Biard is to be believed, they were delivered by prayer. On the morning of the third day the fog lifted, disclosing the island of Mount Desert to their joyful eyes. The pilot landed them in a harbor on the east side of the island, where they gave thanks to God and celebrated the mass. They named the place and harbor St. Sauveur.

Singularly enough, it now fell out, as seven years later it happened to the Leyden Pilgrims, that the pilot refused to carry them to their actual destination at Kadesquit,[2] in Pentagöet River. He alleged that the voyage was completed. After much wrangling the affair was adjusted by the appearance of friendly Indians, who conducted the fathers to their own place of habitation. Upon viewing the spot, the colonists determined they could not do better than to settle upon it. They accordingly set about making a lodgment.[3]

The place where the colony was established is obscured as much by the relation of Biard as by time itself. The language of the narration is calculated to mislead, as the place is spoken of as "being shut in by the large island of Mount Desert." The Jesuit had undoubtedly full opportunity of becoming familiar with the locality, and his account was written after the dissolution of the plantation by Argall. There is little doubt they were inhabiting some part of the isle, as Champlain in general terms asserts. Meanwhile the grassy slope of Fernald's Point gains many pilgrims. The brave ecclesiastic, Du Thet, could not have a nobler monument than the stately cliffs graven by

---

[1] Champlain: Mr. Shea says he was only a lay brother.

[2] This has a resemblance to Kenduskeag, and was probably the present Bangor.

[3] Charlevoix says the landing was on the north side of the island.

lightning and the storm with the handwriting of the Omnipotent. The puny reverberations of Argall's broadsides were as nothing compared with the artillery that has played upon these heights out of cloud battlements.

During the summer of 1613, Samuel Argall, learning of the presence of the French, came upon them unawares, and in true buccaneer style. A very brief and unequal conflict ensued. Du Thet stood manfully by his gun, and fell, mortally wounded. Captain Flory and three others also received wounds. Two were drowned. The French then surrendered.

Argall's ship was called the *Treasurer*. Henri de Montmorency, Admiral of France, demanded justice of King James for the outrage, but I doubt that he ever received it. He alleged that, besides killing several of the colonists and transporting others as prisoners to Virginia, Argall had put the remainder in a little skiff and abandoned them to the mercy of the waves. Thus ended the fourth attempt to colonize New England.

Argall, it is asserted, had the baseness to purloin the commission of La Saussaye, as it favored his project of plundering the French more at his ease, the two crowns of England and France being then at peace. He was afterward knighted by King James, and became a member of the Council of Plymouth, and Deputy-governor of Virginia. During a second expedition to Acadia, he destroyed all traces of the colony of Madame De Guercheville. It is pretty evident he was a bold, bad man, as the more his character is scanned the less there appears in it to admire.

Brother Du Thet, standing with smoking match beside his gun, was worthy the same pencil that has illustrated the defense of Saragossa. I marvel much the event has not been celebrated in verse.

An enjoyable way of becoming acquainted with Somes's Sound is to take a wherry at Somesville and drift slowly down with the ebb, returning with the next flood. In some respects it is better than to be under sail, as a landing is always easily made, and defiance may be bidden to head winds.

One of the precipices of Dog Mountain, known as Eagle Cliff, has always attracted the attention of the artists, as well as of all lovers of the beautiful and sublime. There has been much search for treasure in the glens hereabouts, directed by spiritualistic conclaves. One too credulous islander, in his fruitless delving after the pirate Kidd's buried hoard, has squandered the gold of his own life, and is worn to a shadow.

When some one asked Moll Pitcher, the celebrated fortune-teller of Lynn, to disclose the place where this same Kidd had secreted his wealth, promising to give her half of what was recovered, the old witch exclaimed, "Fool! if I knew, could I not have all myself?" Kidd's wealth must have been beyond computation. There is scarcely a headland or an island from Montauk to Grand Menan which according to local tradition does not contain some portion of his spoil.

Much interest is attached to the shell heaps found on Fernald's Point and at Sand Point opposite. There are also such banks at Hull's Cove and elsewhere. Indian implements are occasionally met with in these deposits. It is reasonably certain that some of them are of remote antiquity. Williamson states that a heavy growth of trees was found by the first settlers upon some of the shell banks in this vicinity.[1] Associated with these relics of aboriginal occupation is the print in the rock near Cromwell's Cove, called the "Indian's Foot." It is in appearance the impression of a tolerably shaped foot, fourteen inches long and two deep. The common people are not yet freed from the superstitions of two centuries ago, which ascribed all such accidental marks to the Evil One.

CLIFFS, DOG MOUNTAIN, SOMES'S SOUND.

In my progress by the road to South-west Harbor, I was intercepted near Dog Mountain by a sea-turn that soon became a steady drizzle. This afforded me an opportunity of seeing some fine dissolving views: the sea-mists advancing, and enveloping the mountain-tops, cheated the imagination with the idea that the mountains were themselves receding. A storm-cloud, black and threatening, drifted over Sargent's Mountain, settling bodily down upon it, deploying and extending itself until the entire bulk disappeared behind an impenetrable curtain. It was like the stealthy approach and quick cast of a mantle over the head of an unsuspecting victim.

Very few were abroad in the storm, but I saw a nut-cracker and chickadee making the best of it. I remarked that under branching spruces or fir-trees the grass was still green, and the leaves of the checker-berry bright and glossy as in September. On this road admirable points of observation constantly occur from which to view the shifting contours of Beech and Western mountains, with the broad and level plateau extending along their northern base-

---

[1] "History of Maine," vol. i., p. 80.

line far to the westward. Retracing with the eye this line, you see a little hamlet snugly ensconced on the hither slope of Beech Mountain, while the plateau is rounded off into the bluffs rising above Eagle Lake.

South-west Harbor is usually the stranger's first introduction to Mount Desert. The approach to it is consequently invested with peculiar interest to all who know how to value first impressions. Its neighborhood is less wild and picturesque than the eastern shores of the island, but Long Lake and the western range of mountains are conveniently accessible from it; while, by crossing or ascending the Sound, avenues are opened in every direction to the surpassing charms of this favored corner of New England.

At South-west Harbor the visitor is usually desirous of inspecting the sea-wall, or *cheval-de-frise* of shattered rock, that skirts the shore less than three miles distant from the steamboat landing. And he may here witness

THE STONE WALL.

an impressive example of what the ocean can do. An irregular ridge of a mile in length is piled with shapeless rocks, against which the sea beats with tireless impetuosity.

Fog is the bane of Mount Desert. Its frequency during the months of July and August is an important factor in the sum of outdoor enjoyment. Happily, it is seldom of long continuance, as genial sunshine or light breezes soon disperse it.

There is, however, a weird sort of fascination in standing on the shore in a fog. You are completely deceived as to the nearness either of objects or of sounds, though the roll of the surf is more depended upon by experienced ears than the fog-bell. In sailing near the land every one has noticed the recoil of sounds from the shore, as voices, or the beat of a steamer's paddles. Coming through the Mussel Ridge Channel one unusually thick morning, the fog suddenly "scaled up," discovering White Head in uncomfortable proximity. The light-house keeper stood in his door, tolling the heavy fog-bell that

ENTRANCE TO SOMES'S SOUND.

we had believed half a mile away. Our pilot gave him thanks with three blasts of the steam-whistle.

Off the entrance to the Sound are several islands—Great Cranberry, of five hundred acres; Little Cranberry, of two hundred acres; and, farther inshore, Lancaster's Island, of one hundred acres. The eastern channel into the Sound is between the two last named. Duck Island, of about fifty acres, is east of Great Cranberry; and Baker's, on which is the light-house, is the outermost of the cluster.

The cranberry is indigenous to the whole extent of the Maine sea-board. It grows to perfection on the borders of wet meadows, but I have known it to thrive on the upland. The culture has been found very remunerative in localities less favored by nature, as at Cape Cod and on the New Jersey coast. Some attempts at cranberry culture have recently been made with good success at Lemoine, on the main-land, opposite Mount Desert. Blueberries are abundant on Mount Desert. I saw one young girl who had picked enough in a week to bring her seven dollars. Formerly they were sent off the island, but they are now in good demand at the hotels and boarding-houses. In poorer families the head of it picks up a little money by shore-fishing. He plants a little patch with potatoes, dressing the land with sea-weed, which costs him only the labor of gathering it. His fire-wood is as cheaply procured from the neighboring forest or shore, and in the autumn his wife and children gather berries, which are exchanged for necessaries at the stores.

At the extreme southerly end of Mount Desert is Bass Harbor, with three islands outlying. It is landlocked, and a well-known haven of refuge.

PROFESSOR AGASSIZ.

CHAPTER III.

CHRISTMAS ON MOUNT DESERT.

"You should have seen that long hill-range,
  With gaps of brightness riven—
How through each pass and hollow streamed
  The purpling light of heaven—"
                                        WHITTIER.

HAVING broken the ice a little with the reader, I shall suppose him present on the most glorious Christmas morning a New England sun ever shone upon. "A green Christmas makes a fat church-yard," says an Old-country proverb; this was a white *Noël*, cloudless and bright. I saw that the peruke of my neighbor across the Sound, Sargent's Mountain, had been freshly powdered during the night; that the rigging of the ice-bound craft harbored between us was incased in solid ice, reflecting the sunbeams like burnished steel. The inscription on mine host's sign-board was blotted out by the driving sleet; the brown and leafless trees stood transfigured into objects of wondrous beauty. I heard the jingle of bells in the stable-yard and the stamping of feet below stairs, and then

> "I heard nae mair, for Chanticleer
> Shook off the pouthery snaw,
> And hail'd the morning with a cheer,
> A cottage-rousing craw."

The roads from Bar Harbor and from North-east Harbor unite within a short distance of Somesville, and enter the village together. Within these highways is embraced a large proportion of those picturesque features for which the island is famed. In this area are the highest mountains, the boldest headlands, the deepest indentations of the shores. It is not for nothing, therefore, that Bar Harbor has become a favorite rendezvous of the throngs

> "That seek the crowd they seem to fly."

On Christmas-day the road to Bar Harbor was an avenue of a winter palace more sumptuous than that by the Neva. Every spray of the dark evergreen trees was heavily laden with a light snow that plentifully besprinkled us in passing beneath the often overreaching branches. The stillness was unbroken. Blasted trees — gaunt, withered, and hung with moss like rags on the shrunken limbs of a mendicant — were now incrusted with ice-crystals, that glittered like lustres on gigantic candelabra. On the top of some rounded hill there sometimes was standing the bare stem of a blasted pine, where it shone like the spike on a grenadier's helmet. It was a scene of enchantment.

I saw frequent tracks where the deer had come down the mountain and crossed the road, sometimes singly, sometimes in pairs, and in search, no doubt, of water. The foot-prints of foxes, rabbits, and grouse were also common. During the day I met an islander who told me he had shot a fat buck only a day or two before, and that many deer were still haunting the mountains. Formerly, but so long ago that only tradition preserves the fact, there were black bear and moose; and traces of beaver are yet to be seen in their dams and houses. Red foxes and mink, and occasionally the black fox, greatly valued for its fur, are taken by the hunters. In order to make the roads interesting to nocturnal travelers, rumor was talking of a panther and a wolf that had been seen within a short time.

In the day when these coasts were stocked with beaver, its skin was the common currency of the country, as well of the Indians as of the whites. It was greatly prized in Europe, and constituted the wealth of the savages of northern New England, who were wholly unacquainted with wampum until it was introduced among them by the Plymouth trading-posts on the Penobscot and Kennebec.

The wigwam of a rich chief would be lined with beaver-skins, and, if he were very rich, his guests were seated on packs of it. Then, as now, a suitor was not the less acceptable if he came to his mistress with plenty of beaver. It was the Indians' practice to kill only two-thirds of the beaver each season, leaving a third for increase. The English hunters killed all they found, rapidly exterminating an animal which the Indian believed to be possessed of preternatural sagacity.

Our road, after crossing a northern spur of Sargent's Mountain, which lifts itself more than a thousand feet above the sea, led on over a succession of hills. Beyond Sargent's, Green Mountain stood unveiled, with what seemed the tiniest of cottages perched on its summit. Ere long Eagle Lake lay outstretched at the right, but it was in the trance of winter. The painter, Church, whose favorite ground lay about due south, christened the lake, doubtless with a palmful of water from its own baptismal font. The roadway is thrown across its outlet where the timbers of an old mill, that some time ago had gorged itself with the native forest, lay rotting and overthrown.

Green Mountain overpeers all the others. On its summit you are fifteen hundred and thirty-five feet higher than the sea. On this account it was selected as a landmark for the survey of the neighboring coasts. It is not difficult of ascent, as the mountain road built by the surveyors is considered practicable for carriages nearly or quite to the top. I had anticipated ascending it, but the new-fallen snow rendered walking difficult, and I was forced to content myself with viewing it from all sides of approach.

An acquaintance with the sierras of either half of the continent exercises a restraining influence in presence of an upheaval comparatively slight, yet it is only in a few favored instances that one may stand on the summits of very high mountains and look down upon the sea. New England, indeed, boasts greater elevations at some distance from her sea-coast, among which the Mount Desert peaks would appear dwarfed into respectable hills. On a clear day, and under conditions peculiarly favorable, a distant glimpse of Katahdin and of Mount Washington may be had from the crest of Green Mountain. In summer the little house is open for the refreshment of weary but adventurous pilgrims.

Here I would observe that the island nomenclature is painfully at variance with whatever is suggestive of felicitous *rapport* with its natural characteristics. The name of Mount Desert, it is true, is singularly appropriate; but then it was given by a Frenchman with an eye for truth in picturesqueness. In the year 1796, when the north half of the island was formed into a township, it was called, with sublimated irony, Eden. Green Mountain is not more green than its neighbors. At the Ovens I saw plenty of yeast, but not enough to leaven the name. Schooner Head is not more apposite.

CHRISTMAS ON MOUNT DESERT.

VIEW OF EAGLE LAKE AND THE SEA FROM GREEN MOUNTAIN.

Just before coming into Bar Harbor there is an excellent opportunity of observing the cluster of islands to which it owes existence. These are the Porcupine group, and beyond, across a broad bay, the Gouldsborough hills appeared in a Christmas garb of silvery whiteness. The Porcupine Islands, four in number, lie within easy reach of the shore, Bar Island, the nearest, being connected with the main-land at low ebb. On Bald Porcupine General Fremont has pitched his head-quarters. It was the sea that was fretful when I looked at the islands, though they bristled with erected pines and cedars.

The village at Bar Harbor is the sudden outgrowth of the necessities of a population that comes with the roses, and vanishes with the first frosts of autumn. It has neither form nor comeliness, though it is admirably situated for excursions to points on the eastern and southern shores of the island as far as Great Head and Otter Creek. A new hotel was building, notwithstanding the last season had not proved as remunerative as usual. I saw that pure water was brought to the harbor by a wooden aqueduct that crossed the valley on trestles, after the manner practiced in the California mining regions, and there called a flume. There is a beach, with good bathing on both sides of the landing, though the low temperature of the water in summer is hardly calculated for invalids.

From Bar Harbor, a road conducts by the shore, southerly, as far as Great Head, some five miles distant. After following this route for a long mile,

CLIFFS ON BALD PORCUPINE.

as it seemed, it divides, the road to the right leading on five miles to Otter Creek, and thence to North-east Harbor, seven miles beyond. Excursions to Great Head, and to Newport Mountain and Otter Creek, should occupy separate days, as the shores are extremely interesting, and the scenery unsurpassed in the whole range of the island.

In pursuing his explorations at or near low-water mark, it will be best for the tourist to begin a ramble an hour before the tide has fully ebbed. The tides on this coast ordinarily rise and fall about twelve feet, and in winter, as I saw, frequently eighteen feet. Hence the advance and retreat of the waves is not only rapid, but leaves a broader margin uncovered than in Massachusetts Bay, where there is commonly not more than eight feet of rise and fall. In many places along the arc of the shore stretching between Bar Harbor and Great Head, the ascent to higher ground is, to say the least, difficult, and, in some instances, progress is forbidden by a beetling cliff or impassable chasm. As time is seldom carefully noted when one is fairly engaged in such investigations, it is always prudent first to know your ground, and next to keep a wary eye upon the stealthy approach of the sea.

SOUTHERLY END OF NEWPORT MOUNTAIN, NEAR THE SAND BEACH.

There is a pleasant ramble by the shore to Cromwell's Cove; but here onward movement is arrested by a cliff that turns you homeward by a cross-path through the fields to the road, after having whetted the appetite for what is yet in reserve.

Schooner Head is reached by this road in about four miles from Bar Harbor, and three from the junction of the Otter Creek road. I walked it easily in an hour. The way is walled in on the landward side by the abrupt precipices of Newport Mountain, in the sheer face of which stunted firs are niched here and there. Very much they soften the hard, unyielding lines and cold gray of the crags; the eye lingers kindly on their green chaplets cast about the frowning brows of wintry mountains. This morning all were Christmas-trees, and the ancients of the isle hung out their banners to greet the day.

Emerging from the woods at a farm-house at the head of a cove, a foot-path leads to the promontory at its hither side. It is thrust a little out from the land, sheltering the cove while itself receiving the full onset of the sea. An intrusion of white rock in the seaward face is supposed by those of an imaginative turn to bear some resemblance to a schooner; and, in order to complete the similitude, two flag-staffs had been erected on the top of the cliff. At best, I fancy it will be found a phantom ship to lure the mariner to destruction.

I did not find Schooner Head so remarkable for its height as in the evidences everywhere of the crushing blows it has received while battling with storms. "Hard pounding this, gentlemen; but we shall see who can pound longest," said the Iron Duke at Waterloo. Here are the rents and ruins of ceaseless assault and repulse. The ocean is slowly but steadily advancing on both sides of the continent; perchance it is, after all, susceptible of calculation how long the land shall endure.

I clambered among the huge blocks of granite that nothing less than steam could now have stirred, although they had once been displaced by a few drops of water acting together. A terrible rent in the east side of the cliff is locally known as the Spouting Horn. Down at its base the sea has worn through the rock, leaving a low arch. At the flood, with sufficient sea on, and an off-shore wind, a wave rolls in through the cavity, mounts the escarpment, and leaps high above the opening with a roar like the booming of heavy ordnance. These natural curiosities are not unfrequent along the

CAVE OF THE SEA, SCHOONER HEAD.

coast. There is one of considerable power at Cape Arundel, Maine, that I have heard when two miles from the spot. Unfortunately for the tourist, these grand displays are usually in storms, when few care to be abroad; undoubtedly, the outward man may be protected and the inward exalted at such times. Some of the more adventurous go through the Horn: I went around it.

I saw here a few ruminant sheep gazing off upon the sea. What should a sheep see in the ocean?

On the farther side of the cove is a sea-cavern that has the reputation of being the finest on the island. Within its gloomy recesses are rock pools of rare interest to the naturalist. In proper season they will be found inhabited by the sea-anemone and other and more debatable forms of animal life. Some of these aquaria I have seen are of marvelous beauty, recalling the lines,

"Full many a gem of purest ray serene
 The dark unfathomed caves of ocean bear."

Lined with mother-of-pearl and scarlet mussels, resting on beds of soft sponge or purple moss-tufts, these fairy grottoes are the favorite retreat of King Crab and his myrmidons, of the star-fish and sea-urchin. Twice in every twenty-four hours the basins are refilled with pure sea-water, than which nothing can be more transparent. Strange that these rugged crags, where the grasp of man would be loosened by the first wave, should be instinct with life! It required some force to detach a mussel from its bed,

CLIFFS AT SCHOONER HEAD.

and you must have recourse to your knife to remove the barnacles with

DEVIL'S DEN AND SCHOONER HEAD.

which the smoother rocks are incrusted. John Adams, when he first saw the sea-anemone, compared it, in figure and feeling, to a young girl's breast.

Mount Desert has been familiar to two of the greatest of American naturalists. When Audubon was preparing his magnificent "Birds of America," he visited the island, and I have no doubt the report of his rifle was often heard echoing among the mountains or along the shores. Agassiz was also here, interrogating the rocks, rapping their stony knuckles with his hammer, or pressing their gaunt ribs with playful familiarity. Audubon died in 1851. Agassiz is more freshly remembered by the present generation, to whom he made the pathway of Natural Science bright by his genius, and pleasant, by his genuine, whole-hearted *bonhomie*.

In 1858 the French Government devoted itself, with extreme solicitude, to the reorganization of the administration of the Museum of Natural History of the *Jardin des Plantes* at Paris. It appears that, in spite of a first refusal, several times repeated, Agassiz at length consented to accept the direction of the museum. The Emperor, who had formed a personal acquaintance with the celebrated naturalist during his sojourn in Switzerland, pursued with customary pertinacity his favorite idea of alluring M. Agassiz to Paris. He was offered a salary of twenty-five thousand francs; and it was understood he was promised, besides, elevation to the dignity of senator, of which the appointments were worth twenty-five thousand francs more.

I have thought it fitting to give Agassiz's own report of his first introduction to an American public:

"When I came to Boston," said he, "the first course which I gave had five thousand auditors, and I was obliged to divide them into two sections of twenty-five hundred each, and to repeat each lesson. This course was given in the large hall of the Tremont Temple."

"Do you think," he was asked, "that in such a crowd it was the fashion or the desire for instruction which dominated?"

"No doubt," he replied, "it was a serious desire for instruction. I have plenty of proofs of it coming from persons belonging to the lower classes. For instance, it is usual here to accord to persons who go out to service full liberty after a certain hour in the evening, solely to go to the course of lectures; that is made a part of the agreement. A lady who had a very strong desire to hear me, told me that it was impossible for her to do so. Her cook was the first informed of my announcement, took the initiative, and obtained her promise of liberty for the hour of the evening when I taught, and left her mistress to take care of the house alone. On her return she explained very clearly what I had said."

The slow sale of Agassiz's works in Europe decided him to pass fifteen months in the United States; and the revolution of 1848 changed this intention into a purpose of permanent residence. Agassiz was tall, corpulent, bent, rather by continual study than with age. His forehead was broad, high, and a little retreating; his countenance conspicuously Swiss, by the largeness of his features, the gravity and benevolence of his expression. His hair was gray, and little abundant. He spoke German and English with facility, but had to some extent unlearned his French. Although his conversation was without volubility, when he grew animated in talking upon great questions his expression became noble and majestic. "There was in him a remarkable force of thought and will. He appeared like a man who makes haste slowly; but notwithstanding the adage, no one can withhold an involuntary astonishment at the great works he has been able to achieve." Agassiz belonged to the *noblesse* of science and of literature. When such men die they can not be said to leave legitimate successors.

Mount Desert has itself produced a man of marked usefulness in David Wasgatt Clark, D.D., a Wesleyan divine, who was elected bishop in 1864. He accomplished extensive literary labors, was intrusted with high and responsible positions, and although a puny boy, the jest of his companions of a more robust mould, completed nearly threescore years of a laborious and eventful life.

From Schooner Head I pursued my way by the road to Great Head. And while *en route* I should not forget the Lynam Homestead, to which Cole, Church, Gifford, Hart, Parsons, Warren, Bierstadt, and others renowned in American art have from time to time resorted to enrich their studios from the abounding wealth of the neighborhood.

One of the first artists to come to the island was Fisher. Church, whose name is associated with its rediscovery, did not always come for work. On one occasion, as leader of a merry party, he was lost on Beech Mountain, and passed the night there. With rare prevision he had provided an axe, with plenty of robes and wraps. At the foot of the mountain the carriage was sent back to the village. Church was too good a woodman not to use his axe to make a shanty of boughs, while the robes, when spread upon fragrant heaps of spruce, made excellent couches for the laughing girls that were under his protection. Meanwhile consternation reigned at Somesville. Messengers were sent hither and thither in haste; but no tidings arrived of the absent ones until the next morning, when they entered the village as if nothing unusual had happened.

Great Head is easily found. The road we have been pursuing comes to an abrupt ending at a house within a short half-mile of it. Follow the shore backward toward Schooner Head, and you will stand in presence of the boldest headland in all New England. I saw that no foot-print but my own had lately passed that way. There was something in thus having it all to one's self.

To appreciate Great Head one must stand underneath it; but the descent, always difficult, was rendered perilous by the newly-formed ice. By dint of perseverance I at last stood upon the ledge beneath, that extends out like a platform for some distance toward deep water. It was the right stage of the tide. I looked up at the face of the cliff. It was bearded with icicles, like the Genius of Winter. Along the upper edge appeared the interlacing roots of old trees grasping the scanty soil like monster talons. Stunted birches, bent by storms, skirted its brow, and at sea add to its height. From top to bottom the face of the cliff is a mass of hard granite, overhanging its foundations in impending ruin, shivered and splintered as if torn by some tremendous explosion. I could only think of the last sketch of Delaroche.

The sea rolls in great waves that overwhelm every thing within their reach. More than once I started back at the approach of one of them. Just outside the first line of breakers rode a flock of wild fowl, and occasionally the mournful cry of a loon, or shriller scream of a sea-gull, mingled with the roar of the surf. Farther out, at the distance of a mile, a wicked-looking rock and ledge was flinging off the seas, flecking its tawny flanks with foam, like a war-horse impatiently champing at his bit.

Looking off from Great Head to the eastward, the main-land is perceived trending away until it loses itself in the ocean. At the extremity of this land is Schoodic Point and Mountain, with Mosquito Harbor indenting it The water between is not the true "Baye Françoise" of Champlain, Lescarbot, and others. The appellation belongs of right to the Bay of Fundy, perpetuating as it does the misadventure of Nicolas Aubri, one of the company of De Monts, who was lost in the woods there. As this is not the only historic an-

GREAT HEAD.

achronism by many that may be met with on our coasts, I do not propose to quarrel with it, the less that a Frenchman was the first white here. The name has been current for about a century, though on old French maps it is found to lie farther east.

The north wind was beating down yesterday's sea, sweeping over the billows, and whirling their crests far away to leeward. Along the rocks the foam lay like wool-fleeces, or was whisked about, dabbling the grim face of the cliff with creamy spots. Other headlands were mailed in ice.

Mount Desert Rock is about twenty miles south-south-east of the island, and from fourteen to eighteen from the nearest land. It has a light-house, built upon naked, shapeless ledges. There is another on Baker's Island, off the entrance to Somes's Sound.

Natural sea-marks, like Great Head Cliff, are preferred by mariners to artificial buoys or beacons. No one that has seen them will be likely to forget the Pan of Matanzas, or the Cabanas of Havana. Before the excellent system inaugurated by the United States Coast Survey, trees, standing singly or in groups, often gave direction how to steer on a dangerous coast. Sometimes they were lopped on one side, or made to take some peculiarity of shape that would distinguish them from all others. Thus some solitary old cedar becomes a guide-board known to all who travel on ocean highways.

The next point of interest will be found at Otter Creek, which may be reached in good weather by sailing, by the direct road from Bar Harbor, already mentioned, or by crossing the lower ridge of Newport Mountain from Great Head.

After a last look at the sea, which was of a dingy green, and broke angrily as far as the eye could reach in the offing, I entered the trail that was to bring me to Otter Creek.

Newport's southern peak was just overhead, its sharp protuberances made smooth by knobs of ice that resembled the bosses of a target. There reached me occasional rapid glimpses of the sea in ascending, but I walked chiefly in a dense growth that excluded all light, except when the glint of the sun through the tree-tops fell in golden bars across my way. Prostrate and uselessly rotting was wood enough to have kept a good-sized village through the winter. The air was light and elastic. I do not think a pleasanter ramble is to be had on the island than this forest-walk.

> "O'er windy hill, through clogged ravine,
> And woodland paths that wound between
> Low drooping pine-boughs winter-weighed."

At Otter Creek is a scattered settlement and an inlet of the sea, into which the creek empties. The island traditions say the place was once the favorite retreat of the otter. There are cliffs to admire or study on the seashore, and Thunder Cave is there to explore.

In this pocket-edition of Somes's Sound we find ourselves once more under the shadow of Green Mountain, and upon looking back up the valley a pass opens between it and Newport, through which the road finds its way to Bar Harbor.

The dwellings here, as elsewhere on the island, are humble, and bespeak, in many instances, a near approach to poverty. In the larger villages there are comfortable and even substantial residences, but the impression of unthrift is associated with the proper population. The reasons are obvious. The first inhabitants got their livelihood by fishing, and formerly many vessels were fitted out from the Sound. Perhaps not a few went for the Government bounty. With the failure of this industry little was left on which to depend. A scanty subsistence at most could be wrung from the soil, though Williamson, the historian of Maine, avers this was once strong and fertile in the valleys. The land, by the removal of crops without restoring the elements essential to it, has been growing poorer year by year. A little hay is cut on the uplands, and at Pretty Marsh are some hundreds of acres of salt meadow. The mountains have been stripped of their wood to the last merchantable tree. At this unpromising juncture the island became suddenly famous, and is now among the most frequented of American summer resorts. None could be more astonished at their own prosperity than these islanders, who, being, as a whole and in a marked degree, incapable of appreciating the grandeur of the scenes with which they have from infancy been familiar, look with scarce concealed disdain upon the admiration they inspire in others.

Some handsome cottages have already sprung out of the prevailing ugliness at Bar Harbor. At Great Head a tract of considerable extent has been inclosed. The star of Mount Desert is clearly in the ascendant, as, however prudent the city man may be at home, all purse-strings are loosened at the sea-side. The French proverb, "*Il faut faire ou se taire*," is usually construed into the modern barbaric "play or pay" at the shore. Not one of these worthy landlords was ever known to fall, like Vatel, on his own sword because there was not enough roast meat. Nevertheless, at the risk of forfeiting the reader's good opinion, I will say that there are landlords with consciences, and I have both seen and spoken with such on Mount Desert.

Another of my excursions, which afforded new entertainment with new scenes, was a pedestrian jaunt from Otter Creek to North-east Harbor. This route commands fine ocean views in the direction of the entrance to the Sound and of the outlying islands. You first open Seal Cove, and, crossing the shingle road at its head, in two miles and a half of farther progress skirting the eastern shore of the Sound, arrive at the head of North-east Harbor, an inconsiderable village, in which Williamson conjectures La Saussaye finally landed.

Seven miles more along the eastern base of Brown's Mountain, in the sombre shadows of which the road nestles, brings us back to the tavern door at Somesville. This road crosses a limb of Hadlock's Pond, and is skirted for some distance by a fine grove of beeches. In summer-time this part of the route is traversed under a canopy of overarching branches, whose dense foliage excludes all but a few straggling rays that let fall a shimmer of delicious sunlight, for the moment glorifying all that pass beneath.

It may chance that the visitor will first pass over the section already traversed in these pages; or it may so fall out that he will decide to undertake a run by the shore north of Bar Harbor in advance of other excursions. In this case Saulsbury's Cove and the "Ovens" become his objective.

I have already forewarned the reader that it is six or seven miles from any initial point to any other given point on Mount Desert Island. This equality of distance sometimes makes a choice embarrassing, since in selecting from two routes the preference is usually given to the shorter. But it will sometimes happen that he will find these longer than statute miles, or that when pursuing his way with all

THE OVENS, SAULSBURY'S COVE.

imaginable confidence, it is suddenly blocked by a mountain or a precipice. These contingencies make walking preferable. A horse is no doubt a very useful animal where there are roads.

It is practicable at low tide to reach the Ovens by the beach, but as this involves many difficulties, it is better to take the road beyond Hull's Cove, two miles from Bar Harbor. The cove is said to have been named for a brother of General William Hull. It was resorted to quite early in the settlement of the island. Here was the dwelling-place of the Gregoires, to whom Massachusetts ceded the whole island upon proof, exhibited in 1787, that Madame Gregoire was the lineal descendant of Cadillac, who claimed under his grant from Louis XIV. in 1688.[1] The meditative reader may ponder upon this resumption under a French title as an evidence that time at last makes all things even. It would not seem inappropriate, inasmuch as two women have had so prominent a share in the history of Mount Desert, to perpetuate the names of Guercheville and Gregoire. The graves of the Gregoires may be seen near the north-east corner of the burial-ground. Monsieur is asserted to have been a *bon-vivant*.

The Ovens are caverns hollowed out by the waves in the softer masses of the cliffs. When the tide is completely down a pebbly beach shelves away to low-water mark. The feldspar and porphyry of which the rocks are composed impart a cheerfulness to the walls of these grottoes more pleasing after descending into the gloomy recesses of the south shore. Near the Ovens is a passage driven through a projecting cliff, known as *Via Mala*.

In passing, the reader will give me leave to mention another woman whose influence was felt in the affairs of Acadia. It was Henrietta, Duchesse d'Orleans, and aunt of Louis XIV., who obtained the relinquishment of Acadia by her husband, Charles I. of unfortunate memory, under the peace of 1632. The fate of the widowed queen is involved in one of the most repulsive chapters of history. According to contemporary accounts, she fell a victim to the reign of the poisoners in the time of Louis. By the testimony of the Marquis Dangeau and other annalists of the times, the poison had been sent by the Chevalier De Lorraine, her lover, then in England.

The reader may now complete the circuit of the island at leisure. In taking leave of these hills, I would observe that although not every one is possessed of a knowledge of woodcraft, or of the muscles of a mountaineer, it is far better to depart the beaten paths and to seek out new conquests. For my own part, I may safely guarantee that in finding himself for the first time on Mount Desert, the visitor will be as thoroughly surprised as impressed in the presence of natural scenes so pronounced in character, and so unique in their relation to and environment by the sea.

---

[1] See Williamson, vol. i., p. 79; "Resolves of Massachusetts," July and November, 1787; "New York Colonial Documents," vol. ix., p. 594. Mr. De Costa has given a summary of these in his pleasant little book.

In my way to and from this remote corner of New England, it was my fortune to encounter a single instance of that inquisitorial propensity known the world over as Yankee curiosity. On arriving at a late hour at Ellsworth, the landlord, a great burly fellow, drew a chair close to mine, pushed his hat back from his brows—every body here wears his hat in the house—spat in the grate, smote his knees with his big palms, and said,

"Look a here, mister! I know 'tan't none o' my business; but what might you be agoin' to Mount Desart arter?" And in the same breath, "I'm from Mount Desart."

"Certes," thought I, "if it's none of your business, why do you ask?"

The same publican afterward let a fellow-wayfarer and myself a sick horse that proved unfit to travel when we were well upon our journey. I forgave him all but the making me the unwilling instrument of his cruelty to a dumb beast.

CASTINE, APPROACHING FROM ISLESBORO.

CHAPTER IV.

CASTINE.

"A wind came up out of the sea,
And said, 'O mists, make room for me.'"
LONGFELLOW.

WHOEVER has turned over the pages of early New England history can not fail to have had his curiosity piqued by the relations of old French writers respecting this extreme outpost of French empire in America. The traditions of the existence of an ancient and populous city, going far beyond any English attempt in this corner of the continent, are of themselves sufficient to excite the ardent pursuit of an antiquary, and to set all the busy hives of historical searchers in a buzz of excitement.

That scoffer, Lescarbot, would dispose of the ancient city of Norumbega as Voltaire would have disposed of the Christian religion—with a sarcasm; but, if there be truth in the apothegm that "seeing is believing," the forerunners of Champlain came, saw, and made a note of it. "Now," says the advocate, "if that beautiful city was ever in nature, I should like to know who demolished it; for there are only a few cabins here and there, made of poles and covered with the bark of trees or skins; and both habitation and river are called Pemptegoet, and not Agguncia."[1]

I approached the famed river in a dense fog, in which the steamer cautiously threaded her way. Earth, sky, and water were equally indistinguishable. A volume of pent steam gushing from the pipes hoarsely trumpeted our approach, and then streamed in a snow-white plume over the taffrail, and was lost in the surrounding obscurity. The decks were wet with the damps of

---

[1] Lescarbot, vol. ii., p. 471.

the morning; the few passengers stirring seemed lifeless and unsocial. Here and there, as we floated in the midst of this cloud, the paddles impatiently beating the water, were visible the topmasts of vessels at anchor, though in the dimness they seemed wonderfully like the protruding spars of so many sunken craft. Hails or voices from them sounded preternaturally loud and distinct, as also did the noise of oars in fog-bewildered boats. The blast of a fog-horn near or far occasionally sounded a hoarse refrain to the warning that issued from the brazen throat of the Titan chained in our galley.

At this instant the sun emerging from his dip into the sea, glowing with power, put the mists to flight. First they parted on each side of a broad pathway in which sky and water re-appeared. Then, before brighter gleams, they overthrew and trampled upon each other in disorderly rout. A few scattered remnants drifted into upper air and vanished; other masses clung to the shores as if inclined still to dispute the field. Owl's Head light-house came out at the call of the enchanter, blinking its drowsy eyes; then sunlit steeples and lofty spars glanced up and out of the fog-cloud that enveloped the city of Rockland.

The vicinity of a town had been announced by cock-crowing, the rattling of wheels, or occasional sound of a bell from some church-tower; but all these sounds seemed to heighten the illusions produced by the fog, and to endow its impalpable mass with ghostly life. Vessels under sail appeared weird and spectral—phantom ships, that came into view for a moment and dissolved an instant after—masts, shrouds, and canvas melting away—

"As clouds with clouds embrace."

Rockland is a busy and enterprising place in the inchoate condition of comparative newness, and of the hurry that postpones all improvements not of immediate utility. Until 1848 it had no place on the map. Back of the settled portion of Rockland is a range of dark green hills, with the easy slopes and smooth contours of a limestone region. I know not if Rockland will ever be finished, for it is continually disemboweling itself, coining its rock foundations, until perchance it may some day be left without a leg to stand on.

Penobscot Bay is magnificent in a clear day. The fastidious De Monts surveyed and passed it by. Singularly enough, the French, who searched the New England coast from time to time in quest of a milder climate and more fertile soil than that of Canada, were at last compelled to abide by their first discoveries, and inhabit a region sterile and inhospitable by comparison. Had it fallen out otherwise, Quebecs and Louisburgs might have bristled along her sea-coast, if not have changed her political destiny.

Maine has her forests, her townships of lime, her granite islands, her seas of ice—all, beyond dispute, raw products. Fleets detach themselves from the banks of the Penobscot and float every year away.

> "One goes abroad for merchandise and trading,
> Another stays to keep his country from invading,
> A third is coming home with rich and wealthy lading.
> Halloo! my fancie, whither wilt thou go?"

The sumptuous structures we erect of her granite are only so many monuments to Maine. I have seen, on the other side of the continent, a town wholly built of Maine lumber. While Boston was yet smoking, her neighbor was getting ready the lumber and granite to rebuild her better than ever. So these great rivers become as mere mill-streams in the broader sense, and, at need, a telegraphic order for a town or a fleet would be promptly filled.

There is no corner, however remote, into which Maine enterprise does not penetrate. The spirit of adventure and speculation has pushed its commerce everywhere. With a deck-load of lumber, some shingles, or barrels of lime, schooners of a few tons burden, and manned with three or four hands, may be met with hundreds of miles at sea, steering boldly on in search of a buyer. An English writer narrates his surprise at seeing in the latitude of Hatteras, at the very height of a terrific storm, when the sea, wreathed with foam, was rolling before the gale, one of these buoyant little vessels scudding like a spirit through the mingling tempest, with steady sail and dry decks, toward the distant Bahamas.

Rockland was formerly a part of Thomaston,[1] and is upon ground anciently covered by the Muscongus, or Waldo patent, which passed through the ownership of some personages celebrated in their day. A very brief *resumé* of this truly seignorial possession will assist the reader in forming some idea of the state of the old colonial magnates. It will also account to him for the names of the counties of Knox and Lincoln.

Prior to the French Revolution there were distinctions in society afterward unknown, the vestiges of colonial relations. Men in office, the wealthy, and above all, those who laid claim to good descent, were the gentry in the country. Habits of life and personal adornment were outward indications of superiority. The Revolution drove the larger number of this class into exile, but there still continued to be, on the patriots' side, well-defined ranks of society. There was also a class who held large landed estates, in imitation of the great proprietors of England. These persons formed a country gentry, and were the great men of their respective counties. They held civil and military offices, and were members of the Great and General Court.

The Muscongus patent was granted by the Council of Plymouth, in 1630, to John Beauchamp of London, and John Leverett of Boston, England. It embraced a tract thirty miles square, extending between the Muscongus and Penobscot, being limited on the west and north by the Kennebec patent,

---

[1] Named for General John Thomas, of the Revolution.

mentioned hereafter as granted to our colony of Plymouth. Besides Rockland and Thomaston, the towns of Belfast, Camden, Warren, and Waldoboro are within its former bounds. In 1719 the Muscongus grant was divided for the purpose of settlement into ten shares, the ten proprietors assigning two-thirds of it to twenty associates. I have examined the stiff black-letter parchment of 1719, and glanced at its pompous formalities. At this time there was not a house between Georgetown and Annapolis, except on Damariscove Island.[1]

The Waldo family became in time the largest owners of the patent. Samuel Waldo, the brigadier, was the intimate friend of Sir William Pepperell, with whom he had served at Louisburg. They were born in the same year, and died at nearly the same time. Their friendship was to have perpetuated itself by a match between Hannah, the brigadier's daughter, and Andrew, the son of Sir William.

GENERAL HENRY KNOX.

After a deal of courtly correspondence that plainly enough foreshadows the bitter disappointment of the old friends, Hannah refused to marry Andrew, the scape-grace. In six weeks she gave her hand, a pretty one, 'tis said, to Thomas Flucker, and with it went a nice large slice of the patent. Flucker became the last secretary, under crown rule, of Massachusetts. He decamped with his friends the royalists, in 1776, but his daughter, Lucy, remained behind, for she had given her heart to Henry Knox, the handsome young book-seller of colonial Boston, the trusted friend whom Washington caressed with tears when parting from his comrades of the deathless little army of '76.

The old brigadier fell dead of apoplexy at the feet of Governor Pownall, while in the act of pointing out to him the boundary of his lands. Mrs. Knox, the artillerist's wife, inherited a portion of the Waldo patent, and her

---

[1] Williamson's "History of Maine."

husband, after the Revolution, acquired the residue by purchase. Here his troubles began; but I can not enter upon them. He built an elegant mansion at Thomaston, which he called Montpelier.¹ The house has been demolished by the demands of the railway, for which one of its outbuildings now serves as a station.

General Knox involved in his personal difficulties his old comrade, General Lincoln, though not quite so badly as Mr. Jefferson would make it appear in his letter to Mr. Madison, in which he says, "He took in General Lincoln for one hundred and fifty thousand dollars, which breaks him." The same writer has also recorded his opinion that Knox was a fool; but the resentments of Mr. Jefferson are known to have outrun his understanding. Through the embarrassments incurred by his friendship, General Lincoln became interested in the Waldo patent.

GENERAL BENJAMIN LINCOLN.

Lincoln was about five feet nine, so extremely corpulent as to seem much shorter than he really was. He wore his hair unpowdered, combed back from his forehead, and gathered in a long cue. He had a full, round face, light complexion, and blue eyes. His dress was usually a blue coat, and buff small-clothes. An enormous cocked hat, as indispensable to an old officer of the Revolution as to the Little Corporal, or as the capital to the Corinthian column, completed his attire. He had been wounded in the leg in the battles with Burgoyne, and always wore boots to conceal the deformity, as Knox concealed his mutilated hand in a handkerchief.

This old soldier, Lincoln, who had passed very creditably through the Revolution, was, like the fat boy in "Pickwick," afflicted with somnolency. In the old Hingham church, in conversation at table, and it is affirmed also while driving himself in a chaise, he would fall sound asleep. During his campaign against Shays and the Massachusetts insurgents of 1786, he snored and dictated between sentences. He considered this an infirmity, and his friends never ventured to speak to him of it.

Another charming picture is the approach to the Camden Hills. I saw their summits peering above fog-drifts, flung like scarfs of gossamer across their breasts. Heavier masses sailed along the valleys, presenting a series of ever-shifting, ever-dissolving views, dim and mysterious, with transient

---

¹ Jefferson had his Monticello, Washington his Mount Vernon.

glimpses of church-spires and white cottages, or of the tops of trees curiously skirting a fog-bank. Sometimes you caught the warm color of the new-mown hill-sides, or the outlines of nearer and greener swells. These hills are a noted landmark for seamen, and the last object visible at sea in leaving the Penobscot. The highest of the Megunticook peaks rises more than fourteen thousand feet, commanding an unsurpassed view of the bay.

After touching at Camden, the steamer continued her voyage. The genial warmth of the sun, with the beauty of the panorama unrolled before them, had brought the passengers to the deck to gaze and admire. I chanced on one family group making a lunch off a dry-salted fish and crackers, the females eating with good appetites. Near by was a German, breakfasting on a hard-boiled egg and a thick slice of black bread. My own compatriots preferred the most indigestible of pies and tarts, with pea-nuts à *discretion*. Relics of these repasts were scattered about the decks. The good-humor and jollity that had returned with a few rays of sunshine led me to think on the depression caused by the long nights of an Arctic winter, as related by Franklin, Parry, Kane, and Hays. A greeting to the sun! May he never cease to shine where I walk or lie!

Driving her sharp prow onward, the boat soon entered Belfast Bay. Many vessels, some of them fully rigged for sea, were on the stocks in the ship-yards of Belfast. The Duke of Rochefoucauld Liancourt, during his visit in 1797, noticed that some houses were painted. The town

FORT POINT.

then contained the only church in the Waldo patent. As might be inferred, the name is from Belfast, Ireland![1]

The bay begins to contract above Camden, bringing its shores within the meaning of a noble river. Indeed, as far as I ascended it, the Penobscot will not lose by comparison with the Hudson. The river is considered to begin at Fort Point, the site of Governor Pownall's fort. Above the flow of tidewater its volume decreases, for the Penobscot does not drain an extensive region like the St. Lawrence, nor has it such a reservoir at its source as the Kennebec. At Orphan Island the river divides into two channels, making

---

[1] Its Indian name was Passageewakeag—"the place of sights, or ghosts." It contained originally one thousand acres, which the settlers bought of the heirs of Brigadier Waldo at two shillings the acre. Belfast was the first incorporated town on the Penobscot. It suffered severely in the Revolution from the British garrison of Castine.

a narrow pass of extreme beauty and picturesqueness between the island and the western shore. Nowhere else, except in the Vineyard Sound, have I seen such a movement of shipping as here. A fleet of coasters were standing wing and wing through the Narrows. Tow-boats, dragging as many as a dozen heavy-laden lumbermen outward-bound, came puffing down the stream. As they entered the broad reach near Fort Point, one vessel after another hoisted sail and dashed down the bay. The Narrows are commanded by Fort Knox, opposite Bucksport.[1]

In coming out of Belfast we approached Brigadier's Island, from which the forest had wholly disappeared. General Knox, whose patent covered all islands within three miles of the shore, offered three thousand dollars to the seven farmers who then occupied it, in land and ready money, to relinquish their possession. Vessels were formerly built on the island, and it was famous for its plentiful supplies of salmon. In old times a family usually took from ten to sixty barrels in a season, which brought in market eight dollars the barrel. The fish were speared or taken in nets. Owners of jutting points made great captures.

The shores of the river are seen fringed with weirs. Salmon, shad, alewives, and smelts are taken in proper season, the crops of the sea succeeding each other with the same certainty as those of the land. Before the beginning of the century salmon had ceased to be numerous. Their scarcity was imputed to the Penobscot Indians, who destroyed them by fishing every day in the year, including Sundays. This king among fishes formerly frequented the Kennebec, the Merrimac, and were even taken in Ipswich River, and the small streams flowing into Massachusetts Bay.

From Belfast I crossed the bay by Islesboro to Castine. I confess I looked upon this famous peninsula, crowned with a fortress, furrowed with the intrenchments of forgotten wars, deserted by a commerce once considerable, little frequented by the present generation, with an interest hardly inferior to that stimulated by the associations of any spot of ground in New England.

The peninsula of Castine presents to view two eminences with regular outlines, of which the westernmost is the most commanding. Both are smoothly rounded, and have steep though not difficult ascents. The present town is built along the base and climbs the declivity of the eastern hill, its principal street conducting from the water straight up to its crest, surmounted by the still solid ramparts of Fort George. The long occupation of the peninsula has nearly denuded it of trees. Its external aspects belong rather to the milder types of inland scenery than to the rugged grandeur of the near sea-coast.

Passing by a bold promontory, on which the light-tower stands, the tide

---

[1] In 1797 there were twenty vessels owned in Penobscot River, two of which were in European trade.

carries you swiftly through the Narrows to the anchorage before the town. Ships of any class may be carried into Castine, while its adjacent waters would furnish snug harbors for fleets. You have seen, as you glided by the shores, traces, more or less distinct, of the sovereignty of Louis XIV., of George III., and of the republic of the United States. Puritans and Jesuits, Huguenots and Papists, kings and commons, have all schemed and striven for the possession of this little corner of land. Richelieu, Mazarin, and Colbert have plotted for it; Thurloe, Clarendon, and Bolingbroke have counter-plotted. It has been fought over no end of times, conquered and reconquered, and is now of no more political consequence than the distant peak of Katahdin.

There is very little appearance of business about Castine. It is delightfully lethargic. Few old houses of earlier date than the Revolution remain to give the place a character of antiquity conformable with its history. Nevertheless, there are pleasant mansions, and cool, well-shaded by-ways, quiet and still, in which the echo of your own footfall is the only audible sound. The peninsula, which the inhabitants call the "Neck," in distinction from the larger fraction of the town, is of small extent. You may ramble all over it in an afternoon.[1]

If it is a good maxim to sleep on a weighty matter, so it is well to dine before forming a judgment of a place you are visiting for the first time. Having broken bread and tasted salt, you believe yourself to have acquired some of the rights of citizenship; and if you have dined well, are not indisposed to regard all you may see with a genial and not too critical an eye. Upon this conviction I acted.

At the tavern, the speech of the girl who waited on the table was impeded by the gum she was chewing. While she was repeating the *carte*, the only words I was able to distinguish were, "Raw fish and clams." As I am not partial to either, I admit I was a little disconcerted, until a young man at my elbow interpreted, *sotto voce*, the jargon into "Corned fish and roast lamb." At intervals in the repast, the waiting-girl would run into the parlor and beat the keys of the piano, until recalled by energetic pounding upon the table with the haft of a knife. Below stairs I was present at a friendly altercation between the landlord and maid of all work, as to whether the towel for common use had been hanging a week or only six days. But "travelers," says Touchstone, "must be content;" and he was no fool though he wore motley.

I ascended the hill above the town on which the Normal School is situated, and in a few moments stood on the parapet of Fort George. And perhaps in no part of New England can a more beautiful and extensive view be had with so little trouble. It was simply enchanting. Such a combination

---

[1] The upper and larger part is called North Castine.

of land and water is seldom embraced within a single *coup d'œil*. The vision is bounded by those portals of the bay, the Camden range on the southwest, and the heights of Mount Desert in the east. A little north of east is the solitary Blue Hill, with the windings and broad reaches of water by which Castine proper is nearly isolated from the main-land. Turning still northward, and now with your back to the town, you perceive Old Fort Point, where, in 1759, Governor Pownall built a work to command the entrance to the river. Farther to the westward is Brigadier's Island, and the bay expanding three leagues over to Belfast.

VIEW FROM FORT GEORGE.

Fort George, a square, bastioned work, is the best preserved earth-work of its years in New England. A few hours would put it in a very tolerable condition of defense. The moat, excavated down to the solid rock, is intact; the esplanade hardly broken in outline. The position of the barracks, magazine, and guard-house may be easily traced on the parade, though no buildings now remain inside the fortress. The approach on three sides is by a steep ascent; especially is this the case on the side of the town. Each bastion was pierced with four embrasures. The position was of great strength, and would have been an ugly place to carry by escalade. A matter of a few hours once determined the ownership of Castine for England or the Colonies in arms.

Now let us take a walk over to the more elevated summit west of Fort George. Here are also evidences of military occupation in fast-perishing embankments and heaps of beach pebbles. What are left of the lines look over toward the English fort and the cove between it and the main-land. A broad, level plateau of greensward extends between the two summits, over which neither you nor I would have liked to walk in the teeth of rattling volleys of musketry. Yet such things have been on this very hill-top.

The story of these fortifications is drawn from one of the most disgraceful chapters of the Revolutionary war. It is of a well-conceived enterprise brought to a disastrous issue through incapacity, discord, and blundering. There are no longer susceptibilities to be wounded by the relation, though for many years after the event it was seldom spoken of save with mingled shame and indignation. Little enough is said of it in the newspapers of the time, for it was a terrible blow to Massachusetts pride, and struck home.

In June, 1779, Colonel Francis M'Lean was sent from Halifax with nine hundred men to seize and fortify the peninsula, then generally known as Penobscot.[1] He landed on the 12th of June, and with the energy and decision of a good soldier began the work of establishing himself firmly in his position.

In the British ranks was one notable combatant, Captain John Moore, of the Fifty-first foot, who fell under the walls of Corunna while commanding the British army in Spain. As his military career began in America, I may narrate an incident illustrating his remarkable popularity with his soldiers. In 1799, at Egmont-op-zee, the Ninety-second fiercely charged a French brigade.

SIR JOHN MOORE.

A terrific *mêlée* ensued, in which the French were forced to retreat. In the midst of the combat two soldiers of the Ninety-second discovered General Moore lying on his face, apparently dead; for he was wounded and unconscious. "Here is the general; let us take him away," said one of them, and, suiting the action to the word, they bore him to the rear. The general offered a reward of twenty pounds; but could never discover either of the soldiers who had aided him. Moore's death inspired Wolfe's admired lines, pronounced by Lord Byron "the most perfect ode in the language:"

> "Not a drum was heard, not a funeral note,
> As his corpse to the rampart we hurried;
> Not a soldier discharged his farewell shot
> O'er the grave where our hero we buried."

"Moore," said Napoleon, "was a brave soldier, an excellent officer, and a man of talent. He made a few mistakes, inseparable, perhaps, from the difficulties with which he was surrounded." Being reminded that Moore was al-

---

[1] Castine was not incorporated under its present name until 1796. The Indian name of the peninsula was Bagaduce, or Biguyduce.

ways in the front of battle, and generally unfortunate enough to be wounded, he added, "Ah! it is necessary sometimes. He died gloriously; he died like a soldier."

Great alarm was produced by M'Lean's bold dash. Immediate application was made to Massachusetts, of which Maine still formed a part, for aid to expel the invader. Hancock was then governor. General Gates commanded the Eastern Department, with head-quarters at Providence. The Massachusetts rulers put their heads together, and, thinking on the brilliant achievement of their fathers at Louisburg in 1745, resolved to emulate it. They raised a large land and naval force with the utmost expedition, laying an embargo for forty days in order to man their fleet with sailors. General Gates was neither consulted nor applied to for the Continental troops under his orders.[1]

FORT GRIFFITH.

The Massachusetts armament appeared off Penobscot on the 25th of July. The army was commanded by Solomon Lovell, the fleet by Captain Saltonstall, of the *Warren*, a fine new Continental frigate of thirty-two guns. Peleg Wadsworth was second in command to Lovell; Paul Revere, whom Longfellow has immortalized, had charge of the artillery. The land forces did not number more than twelve hundred men, but might be augmented to fifteen hundred or more with marines from the fleet. These troops were militia, and had only once paraded together under arms. The flotilla was formidable in appearance and in the number of guns it carried, but lacked unity and discipline quite as much as the army. Plenty of courage and plenty of means do not make soldiers or win battles.

M'Lean had received intelligence of the sailing of the Massachusetts armada. His fort was not yet capable of defense. Two bastions were not begun; the two remaining, with the curtains, had not been raised more than four or five feet, and he had not a single gun mounted. Captain Mowatt of detestable memory,[2] with three British vessels of small force, was in the harbor. He took a position to prevent a landing on the south side of the peninsula. A deep trench was cut across the isthmus connecting with the mainland, securing that passage. No landing could be effected except beneath the precipice, two hundred feet high, on the west. M'Lean dispatched a messenger to Halifax, and redoubled his efforts to strengthen his fort.

---

[1] Gordon, vol. iii., p. 304.   [2] The man who destroyed Falmouth, now Portland.

CASTINE.

On the third day after their arrival the Americans succeeded in landing, and, after a gallant fight, gained the heights. This action—an augury, it would seem, of good success to the assailants, for the enemy had every advantage of position and knowledge of the ground—is the single crumb of comfort to be drawn from the annals of the expedition. Captain Moore was in this affair.

Instead of pursuing his advantage, General Lovell took a position within seven hundred and fifty yards of the enemy's works, and began to intrench. There was fatal disagreement between the general and Saltonstall. The sum of the matter was that Lovell, fearing to attack with his present force, sent to Boston for re-enforcements. Then General Gates was applied to for help. Two weeks passed in regular approaches on Lovell's part, and in exertions by M'Lean to render his fort impregnable.

FORT GEORGE.

At the end of this time, Sir George Collier arrived from New York with a fleet, and raised the siege. General Lovell says the army under his orders had very short notice of the arrival of this force, by reason of a fog that prevented its being seen until its near approach. The land forces succeeded in gaining the western shore of the river at various points, but had then to make their way through a wilderness to the settlements on the Kennebec. The fleet of Saltonstall was either destroyed or captured.

It was not long after the complete dispersion of the ill-starred Penobscot expedition that General Peleg Wadsworth succeeded in entering the British fort on the hill at Bagaduce. He had more difficulty in leaving it.

After the disbanding of his militia, the general made his quarters at Thomaston, where he lived with his wife in apparent security. A young lady named Fenno and a guard of six militia-men completed his garrison. General Campbell, commanding at Bagaduce, was well informed of Wadsworth's defenseless condition, and resolved to send him an invitation to come and reside in the fortress. A lieutenant and twenty-five men arrived at dead of night with the message at Wadsworth's house. The sentinel challenged and fled. General Wadsworth defended himself with Spartan bravery. Armed with a brace of pistols, a fusee, and a blunderbuss, he fought his assailants away from his windows and the door, through which they had followed the retreating sentinel. In his shirt, with his bayonet only, he disdained to yield for some time longer, until a shot disabled his left arm. Then, with five or six men lying wounded around him, the windows shattered, and the house on fire, Peleg Wadsworth was able to say, "I surrender." They took him, exhausted with his exertions and benumbed with cold, to the fort, where he was kept close prisoner. Some time after, Major Burton, who had served with the general, was also made prisoner, and lodged in the same room with him. Wadsworth applied for a parole. It was refused. Governor Hancock sent a cartel with an offer of exchange. It was denied. One day he was visited by Miss Fenno, who in five words gave him to know he was to be detained till the end of the war. Peleg Wadsworth then resolved to escape.

The prisoners were confined in a room of the officers' quarters, the window grated, the door provided with a sash, through which the sentinel, constantly on duty in the passage, could look into the room as he paced on his round. At either end of this passage was a door, opening upon the parade of the fort, at which other sentinels were posted. At sunset the gates were closed, and the number of sentinels on the parapet increased. A picket was also stationed at the narrow isthmus connecting with the main-land.

These were not all the difficulties in their way. Supposing them able to pass the sentinels in the passage and at the outer door of their quarters, they must then cross the open space and ascend the wall under the eye of the guards posted on the parapet. Admitting the summit of the rampart gained, the exterior wall was defended with strong pickets driven obliquely into the earthen wall of the fort. From this point was a sheer descent of twenty feet to the bottom of the ditch. Arrived here, the fugitives must ascend the counterscarp, and cross the *chevaux-de-frise* with which it was furnished. They were then without the fortress, with no possible means of gaining their freedom except by water. To elude the picket at the Neck was not to be thought of.

The prisoners' room was ceiled with pine boards. Upon some pretext they procured a gimlet of a servant, with which they perforated a board so as to make an aperture sufficiently large to admit the body of a man. The interstices were cut through with a penknife, leaving the corners intact until the moment for action should arrive. They then filled the holes with bread, and carefully removed the dust from the floor. This work had to be executed while the sentinel traversed a distance equal to twice the depth of their own room. The prisoners paced their floor, keeping step with the sentry; and as soon as he had passed by, Burton, who was the taller, and could reach the ceiling, commenced work, while Wadsworth walked on. On the approach of the soldier Burton quickly rejoined his companion. Three weeks were required to execute this task. Each was provided with a blanket and a strong staff, sharpened at the end. For food they kept their crusts and dried bits of their meat. They waited until one night when a violent thunder-storm swept over the peninsula. It became intensely dark. The rain fell in torrents upon the roof of the barracks. The moment for action had come.

The prisoners undressed themselves as usual, and went to bed, observed by the sentinel. They then extinguished their candle, and quickly arose. Their plan was to gain the vacant space above their room, creeping along the joists until they reached the passage next beyond, which they knew to be unguarded. Thence they were to make their way to the north bastion, acting as circumstances might determine.

Burton was the first to pass through the opening. He had advanced but a little way before he encountered a flock of fowls, whose roost he had invaded. Wadsworth listened with breathless anxiety to the cackling that apprised him for the first time of this new danger. At length it ceased without having attracted the attention of the guards, and the general with difficulty ascended in his turn. He passed over the distance to the gallery unnoticed, and gained the outside by the door that Burton had left open. Feeling his way along the wall of the barracks to the western side, he made a bold push for the embankment, gaining the rampart by an oblique path. At this moment the door of the guard-house was flung open, and a voice exclaimed, "Relief, turn out!" Fortunately the guard passed without seeing the fugitive. He reached the bastion agreed upon as a rendezvous, but Burton was not there. No time was to be lost. Securing his blanket to a picket, he lowered himself as far as it would permit, and dropped without accident into the ditch. From here he passed softly out by the water-course, and stood in the open air without the fort. It being low tide, the general waded the cove to the main-land, and made the best of his way up the river. In the morning he was rejoined by his companion, and both, after exertions that exacted all their fortitude, gained the opposite shore of the Penobscot in safety. Their evasion is like a romance of the Bastile in the day of Richelieu.

The gallant old general removed to Falmouth, now Portland. One of his sons, an intrepid spirit, was killed by the explosion of a fire-ship before Tripoli, in which he was a volunteer. A daughter married Hon. Stephen Longfellow, of Portland, father of the poet.

When the *corps d'armée* of Rochambeau was at Newport, the French general conceived the idea of sending an expedition to recapture Penobscot, and solicited the consent of Washington to do so. The French officers much preferred acting on an independent line, but the proposal was wisely negatived by the commander in chief. The man to whom Rochambeau expected to intrust the naval operations was La Peyrouse, the distinguished but ill-fated navigator.

Other earth-works besides those already mentioned may be traced. Two small batteries that guarded the approaches on the side of the cove are distinct. Some of these works were renovated during the reoccupation of Castine by the British in 1812. Others seen on the shores of the harbor are of more recent date.

A speaking reminder of by-gone strife is an old cannon, lying on the greensward under the walls of Fort George, of whose grim muzzle school-girls were wont to make a post-office. There was poetry in the conceit. Never before had it been so delicately charged, though I have known a perfumed billet-doux do more damage than this fellow, double-shotted and at point-blank, might effect.

RUINS OF FORT PENTAGOËT, CASTINE.

CHAPTER V.

CASTINE—*continued*.

"Baron Castine of St. Castine
Has left his château in the Pyrenees,
And sailed across the western seas."
LONGFELLOW.

I CONFESS I would rather stand in presence of the Pyramids, or walk in the streets of buried Pompeii, than assist at the unwrapping of many fleshless bodies. No other medium than the material eye can grasp a fact with the same distinctness. It becomes rooted, and you may hang your legends or traditions on its branches. It is true there is a class who journey from Dan to Beersheba, finding all barren; but the average American, though far from unappreciative, too often makes a business of his recreation, and devours in an hour what might be viewed with advantage in a week or a month.

After this frank declaration, the reader will not expect me to hurry him through a place that contains so much of the crust of antiquity as Castine, and is linked in with the Old-world chronicles of a period of surpassing interest, both in history and romance.

Very little of the fort of the Baron Castin and his predecessors, yet enough to reward the research of the stranger, is to be seen on the margin of the shore of the harbor, less than half a mile from the central portion of the town. The grass-grown ramparts have sunk too low to be distinguished from the water in passing, but are evident to a person standing on the ground itself. Not many years will elapse before these indistinct traces are wholly obliterated.[1]

The bank here is not much elevated above high-water mark, while at the wharves it rises to a higher level, and is ascended by stairs. The old fort was

---

[1] In 1759 Governor Pownall took possession of the peninsula of Castine, and hoisted the English flag on the fort. He found the settlement deserted and in ruins.—*Gov.* POWNALL'S *Journal.*

placed near the narrowest part of the harbor, with a firm pebbly beach before it. Small boats may land directly under the walls of the work at high tide, or lie protected by the curvature of the shore from the heavy seas rolling in from the outer harbor. The high hills over which we were rambling in the preceding chapter ward off the northern winds.

A portion of the ground covered by old Fort Pentagoët is now occupied by buildings, a barn standing within the circumvallation, and the dwelling of Mr. Webb between the shore and the road. A little stream of sweet water trickles along the south-west face of the work, and then loses itself among the pebbles of the beach.

Fort Pentagoët, at its rendition by Sir Thomas Temple, in 1670, after the treaty of Breda, was a rectangular work with four bastions. The height of the curtains within was eight feet. On entering the fort a *corps de garde*, twelve paces long and six broad, stood at the left, with a *logis*, or quarter, on the opposite side of the entrance. On the left side were also two store-houses, each thirty-six paces long by twelve in breadth, covered with shingles. Underneath the store-houses was a cellar of about half their extent, in which a well had been sunk. Above the entrance was a turret, built of timber, plastered with clay, and furnished with a bell. At the right hand was a barrack of the same length and breadth as the store-houses, and built of stone. Sixty paces from the fort was a cabin of planks, in which the cattle were housed; and at some distance farther was a garden in good condition, having fruit-trees. There were mounted on the ramparts six six-pounder and two four-pounder iron cannon, with two culverins. Six other pieces were lying, useless and dismounted, on the parapet. Overlooking the sea and detached from the fort was a platform, with two iron eight-pounders in position.

The occupant of the nearest house told me an oven constructed of flat slate-stones was discovered in an angle of the work; also that shot had been picked up on the beach, and a tomahawk and stone pipe taken from the well. The whole ground has been explored with the divining-rod, as well within as without the fort, for treasure-trove; though little or nothing rewarded the search, except the discovery of a subterranean passage opening at the shore.

These examinations were no doubt whetted by an extraordinary piece of good luck that befell farmer Stephen Grindle, while hauling wood from a rocky hill-side on the point at the second narrows of Bagaduce River, about six miles from Castine peninsula. In 1840 this worthy husbandman saw a shining object lying in the track of his oxen. He stooped and picked up a silver coin, as bright as if struck within a twelvemonth. On looking at the date, he found it to be two hundred years old. Farther search was rewarded by the discovery of several other pieces. A fall of snow interrupted the farmer's investigations until the next spring, when, in or near an old trail leading across the point, frequented by the Indians from immemorial time, some seven hundred coins of the nominal value of four hundred dollars were unearthed near the surface. All the pieces were of silver.

The honest farmer kept his own counsel, using his treasure from time to time to pay his store bills in the town, dollar for dollar, accounting one of Master Hull's pine-tree shillings at a shilling. The storekeepers readily accepted the exchange at the farmer's valuation; but the possession of such a priceless collection was soon betrayed by its circulation abroad.

PINE-TREE SHILLING.

Dr. Joseph L. Stevens, the esteemed antiquary of Castine, of whom I had these particulars, exhibited to me a number of the coins. They would have made a numismatist's mouth water. French écus, Portuguese and Spanish pieces-of-eight, Bremen dollars, piasters, and cob-money,[1] clipped and battered, with illegible dates, but melodious ring, chinked in better fellowship than the sovereigns whose effigies they bore had lived in. A single gold coin, the only one found in the neighborhood of Castine, was picked up on the beach opposite the fort.[2]

The theory of the presence of so large a sum on the spot where it was found is that when Castin was driven from the fort by Colonel Church, in 1704, these coins were left by some of his party in their retreat, where they remained undiscovered for more than a century and a quarter. Or it may have been the hoard of one of the two countrymen of Castin, who, he says, were living two miles from him in 1687.

The detail of old Fort Pentagoët just given is believed to describe the place as it had existed since 1654, when captured by the colony forces of Massachusetts. General Sedgwick then spoke of it as "a small fort, yet very strong, and a very well composed peese, with eight peese of ordnance, one

---

[1] "The clumsy, shapeless coinage, both of gold and silver, called in Mexico *máquina de papa, lote y cruz* ("windmill and cross-money"), and in this country by the briefer appellation of "cobs." These were of the lawful standards, or nearly so, but scarcely deserved the name of coin, being rather lumps of bullion flattened and impressed by a hammer, the edge presenting every variety of form except that of a circle, and affording ample scope for the practice of clipping: notwithstanding they are generally found, even to this day, within a few grains of lawful weight. They are generally about a century old, but some are dated as late as 1770. They are distinguished by a large cross, of which the four arms are equal in length, and loaded at the ends. The date generally omits the *thousandth* place; so that 736, for example, is to be read 1736. The letters PLVS VLTRA (*plus ultra*) are crowded in without attention to order. These coins were formerly brought here in large quantities for recoinage, but have now become scarce."—WILLIAM E. DUBOIS, *United States Mint.*

I think the name of "cob" was applied to money earlier than the date given by Mr. Dubois. Its derivation is uncertain, but was probably either "lump," or from the Welsh, for "thump," *i. e.*, struck money.

[2] On an old map of unknown date Castin's houses are located here.

brass, three murtherers, about eighteen barrels of powder, and eighteen men in garrison."[1]

It would require a volume to set forth *in extenso* the annals of these mounds, scarce lifted above the surface of the surrounding plateau. But to arouse the reader's curiosity without an endeavor to gratify it were indeed churlish. I submit, therefore, with the brevity, and I hope also the simplicity, that should characterize the historic style, the essence of the matter as it has dropped from my alembic.

The reader is referred to what is already narrated of Norumbega for the earliest knowledge of the Penobscot by white men. The first vessel that ascended the river was probably the bark of Du Guast, Sieur de Monts, in the year 1604. De Poutrincourt was there in the year 1606.[2]

No establishment appears to have been begun on the Bagaduce peninsula until our colonists of New Plymouth fixed upon it for the site of a trading-post, about 1629.[3] Here they erected a house, defended, probably, after the fashion of the time, with palisades, loop-holed for musketry. They were a long way from home, and had need to keep a wary eye abroad. Governor Bradford mentions that the house was robbed by some "Isle of Rhé gentlemen" in 1632.

The Plymouth people kept possession until 1635, when they were dispossessed by an expedition sent from La Have, in Acadia, commanded by the Chevalier Charles de Menou, or, as he is usually styled, D'Aulnay Charnisay. The chevalier's orders from Razilly, who had then the general command in Canada, were to expel all the English as far as Pemaquid.

Plymouth Colony endeavored to retake the place by force. A large ship for that day, the *Hope*, of Ipswich, England, Girling commander, was fitted out, and attacked the post in such a disorderly, unskillful manner that Girling expended his ammunition before having made the least impression. Standish, the redoubtable, was there in a small bark, fuming at the incompetency of the commander of the *Hope*, who had been hired to do the job for so much beaver if he succeeded, nothing if he failed. Standish, with the beaver, returned to Plymouth, after sending Girling a new supply of powder from Pemaquid; but no further effort is known to have been made to reduce the place.

The Pilgrims then turned to their natural allies, the Puritans of the Bay; but, as Rochefoucauld cunningly says, there is something in the misfortunes

---

[1] Sedgwick's Letter, *Historical Magazine*, July, 1873, p. 38.

[2] Williamson thinks the name of Cape Rosier a distinct reminder of Weymouth's voyage.

[3] Though Hutchinson says "about 1627," I think it an error, as Allerton, the promoter of the project, was in England in that year, as well as in 1626 and 1628, as agent of the colony. Nor was the proposal brought forward until Sherley and Hatherly, two of the adventurers, wrote to Governor Bradford, in 1629, that they had determined upon it in connection with Allerton, and invited Plymouth to join with them.

of our friends that does not displease us. They got smooth speeches in plenty, but no help. It is curious to observe that at this time the two colonies combined were too weak to raise and equip a hundred soldiers on a sudden call. So the French remained in possession until 1654.

An attempt was made by Plymouth Colony to liberate their men captured at Penobscot. Isaac Allerton was sent to demand them of La Tour, who in haughty terms refused to deliver them up, saying all the country from Cape Sable to Cape Cod belonged to the king, his master, and if the English persisted in trading east of Pemaquid he would capture them.

"Will monseigneur deign to show me his commission?"

The chevalier laid his hand significantly on his sword-hilt. "This," said he, "is my commission."

I have mentioned three Frenchmen: Sir Isaac de Razilly, a soldier of the monastic order of Malta; La Tour, a heretic; and D'Aulnay, a zealous papist.

Razilly's commission is dated at St. Germain en Laye, May 10th, 1632. He was to take possession of Port Royal, so named by De Monts, from its glorious harbor, and ceded to France under the treaty of 1629. This was the year after the taking of La Rochelle; so that we are now in the times of the great cardinal and his puissant adversary, Buckingham. The knight of Malta was so well pleased with Acadia that he craved permission of the grand master to remain in the country. He was recalled, with a reminder of the subjection exacted by that semi-military, semi-ecclesiastical body of its members. Hutchinson says he died soon after 1635. There is evidence he was alive in 1636.

In 1638 Louis XIII. addressed the following letter to D'Aulnay: "You are my lieutenant-general in the country of the Etchemins, from the middle of the main-land of Frenchman's Bay to the district of Canceaux. Thus you may not change any regulation in the establishment on the River St. John made by the said Sieur De la Tour, etc."[1] Three years afterward the king sent his commands to La Tour to return to France immediately; if he refused, D'Aulnay was ordered to seize his person.

Whether the death of Louis, and also of his Eminence, at this time diverted the danger with which La Tour was threatened, is a matter of conjecture. D'Aulnay, however, had possessed himself, in 1643, of La Tour's fort, and the latter was a suppliant to the English at Boston for aid to displace his adversary. He obtained it, and recovered his own again, but was unable to eject D'Aulnay from Penobscot. A second attempt, also unsuccessful, was made the following year. The treaty between Governor Endicott and La Tour in this year was afterward ratified by the United Colonies.

In 1645 D'Aulnay was in France, receiving the thanks of the king and queen-mother for his zeal in preserving Acadia from the treasonable designs

---

[1] "Archives of Massachusetts."

of La Tour. The next year a treaty of peace was concluded at Boston between the English and D'Aulnay; and in 1647, the king granted him letters patent of lieutenant-general from the St. Lawrence to Acadia. He died May 24th, 1650, from freezing, while out in the bay with his valet in a canoe. La Tour finished by marrying the widow of D'Aulnay, thus composing, and forever, his feud with the husband.[1]

For some years quiet reigned in the peninsula, or until 1654, when an expedition was fitted out by Massachusetts against Stuyvesant and the Dutch at Manhattan. Peace having been concluded before it was in readiness, the Puritans, with true thrift, launched their armament against the unsuspecting Mounseers of Penobscot. Although peace also existed between Cromwell and Louis, the expenditure of much money without some gain was not to be thought of in the Bay. For a pretext, they had always the old grudge of prior right, going back to Elizabeth's patent of 1578 to Sir Humphrey Gilbert.

Robert Sedgwick and John Leverett were two as marked men as could be found in New England. They sailed from Nantasket on the 4th of July, 1654, with three ships, a ketch, and two hundred soldiers of Old and New England. Port Royal, the fort on St. John's River, and Penobscot, were all captured. Afterward they served the Protector in England. Sedgwick was chosen by Cromwell to command his insubordinate and starving army at Jamaica, and died, it is said, of a broken heart, from the weight of responsibility imposed on him.

Although the King of France testified great displeasure because the forts in Acadia were not restored to him, Cromwell continued to hold them fast, nor were they given up until after the treaty of Breda, when Pentagoët, in 1669–'70, was delivered by Sir Thomas Temple to M. De Grand Fontaine, who, in 1673, turned over the command to M. De Chambly.

On the 10th of August, 1674, M. De Chambly was assaulted by a buccaneer that had touched at Boston, where an English pilot, as M. De Frontenac says, was taken on board. An Englishman, who had been four days in the place in disguise, gave the pirates every assistance.[2] They landed one hundred and ten men, and fell with fury on the little garrison of thirty badly armed and disaffected Frenchmen. After sustaining the onset for an hour, M. De Chambly fell, shot through the body. His ensign was also struck down, when the fort surrendered at discretion. The sea-robbers pillaged the fort, carried off the cannon, and conducted the Sieur De Chambly to Boston, along with M. De Marson, whom they took in the River St. John. Chambly was put to ransom of a thousand beaver-skins. Colbert, then minister, expressed

---

[1] Aglate la Tour, granddaughter of the chevalier, sold the seigniory of Acadia to the crown for two thousand guineas.—DOUGLASS.

[2] Mr. Shea (Charlevoix) says this was John Rhoade, and the vessel the *Flying Horse*, Captain Jurriaen Aernouts, with a commission from the Prince of Orange.

his surprise to Frontenac that the forts of Pentagoët and Gemisée had been taken and pillaged by a freebooter. No rupture then existed between the crowns of England and France.

Another subject of Louis le Grand now raps with his sword-hilt for admission to our gallant company of noble French gentlemen who have followed the lead of De Monts into the wilds of Acadia. Baron La Hontan, writing in 1683, says, "The Baron St. Castin, a gentleman of Oleron, in Bearne, having lived among the Abenaquis after the savage way for above twenty years, is so much respected by the savages that they look upon him as their tutelar god."

COLBERT.

Vincent, Baron St. Castin, came to America with his regiment about 1665. He was ensign in the regiment Carignan, of which Henry de Chapelas was colonel. Chambly and Sorel, who were his comrades, have also left their names impressed on the map of New France. The regiment was disbanded, the governor-general allowing each officer three or four leagues' extent of good land, with as much depth as they pleased. The officers, in turn, gave their soldiers as much ground as they wished upon payment of a crown per *arpent* by way of fief.[1] Chambly we have seen in command at Pentagoët in 1673. Castin appears to have plunged into the wilderness, making his abode with the fierce Abenaquis.

The young Bearnese soon acquired a wonderful ascendency among them. He mastered their language, and received, after the savage's romantic fashion, the hand of a princess of the nation, the daughter of Madocawando, the implacable foe of the English. They made him their great chief, or leader,

---

[1] Estates are still conveyed in St. Louis by the *arpent*.

and at his summons all the warriors of the Abenaquis gathered around him. Exercising a regal power in his forest dominions, he no doubt felt every inch a chieftain. The French governors courted him; the English feared and hated him. In 1696, with Iberville, he overran their stronghold at Pemaquid. He fought at Port Royal in 1706, and again in 1707, receiving a wound there. He was, says M. Denonville, of a daring and enterprising character, thirsting for distinction. In 1702 he proposed a descent on Boston, to be made in winter by a competent land and naval force. Magazines were to be formed at Piscataqua and Marblehead.

It is known that some earlier passages of Castin's life in Acadia were not free from reproach. Denonville,[1] in recommending him to Louvois as the proper person to succeed M. Perrot at Port Royal ("si M. Perrot degoutait de son gouvernment"), admits he had been addicted in the past to riot and debauchery; "but," continues the viceroy, "I am assured that he is now quite reformed, and has very proper sentiments on the subject." Perrot, jealous of Castin, put him in arrest for six weeks for some foolish affair among the *filles* of Port Royal.

> "For man is fire and woman is tow,
> And the Somebody comes and begins to blow."

In 1686 Castin was at Pentagoët. The place must have fallen into sad neglect, for the Governor of Canada made its fortification and advantages the subject of a memoir to his Government. It became the rendezvous for projects against New England. Quebec was not difficult of access by river and land to Castin's fleet Abenaquis. Port Royal was within supporting distance. The Indians interposed a barrier between English aggression and the French settlements. They were the weapon freely used by all the French rulers until, from long service, it became blunted and unserviceable. They were then left to shift for themselves.

Here Castin continued with his dusky wife and brethren, although he had inherited an income of five million livres while in Acadia. By degrees he had likewise amassed a fortune of two or three hundred thousand crowns "in good dry gold;" but the only use he made of it was to buy presents for his fellow-savages, who, upon their return from the hunt, repaid him with usury in beaver-skins and peltries.[2] In 1688 his trading-house was plundered by the English. It is said he died in America, but of this I have not the evidence.

Vincent de Castin never changed his wife, as the Indian customs permitted, wishing, it is supposed, by his example to impress upon them the sanctity

---

[1] Denonville, who succeeded M. De la Barre as governor-general, was *maitre de camp* to the queen's dragoons. He was succeeded by Frontenac.

[2] Denonville's and La Hontan's letters.

of marriage as a part of the Christian religion. He had several daughters, all of whom were well married to Frenchmen, and had good dowries; one was captured by Colonel Church in 1704. He had also a son.

In 1721, during what was known as Lovewell's war, in which Mather intimates, with many nods and winks set down in print, the English were the aggressors, Castin the younger was kidnaped, and carried to Boston a prisoner. His offense was in attending a council of the Abenaquis in his capacity of chief. He was brought before the council and interrogated. His mien was frank and fearless. In his uniform of a French officer, he stood with true Indian *sang froid* in the presence of men who he knew were able to deal heavy blows.

"I am," said he, "an Abenaquis by my mother. All my life has been passed among the nation that has made me chief and commander over it. I could not be absent from a council where the interests of my brethren were to be discussed. The Governor of Canada sent me no orders. The dress I now wear is not a uniform, but one becoming my rank and birth as an officer in the troops of the most Christian king, my master."

The young baron was placed in the custody of the sheriff of Middlesex. He was kept seven months a prisoner, and then released before his friends, the Abenaquis, could strike a blow for his deliverance. This once formidable tribe was such no longer. In 1689 it scarcely numbered a hundred warriors. English policy had set a price upon the head of every hostile Indian. Castin, soon after his release, returned to the old family chateau among the Pyrenees.

"The choir is singing the matin song;
   The doors of the church are opened wide;
   The people crowd, and press, and throng
      To see the bridegroom and the bride.
   They enter and pass along the nave;
   They stand upon the farthest grave;
   The bells are ringing soft and slow;
   The living above and the dead below
   Give their blessing on one and twain;
   The warm wind blows from the hills of Spain,
   The birds are building, the leaves are green,
   The Baron Castine of St. Castine
   Hath come at last to his own again."

According to the French historian, Charlevoix, the Capuchins had a hospice here in 1646, when visited by Père Dreuillettes. I may not neglect these worthy fathers, whose disputes about sleeves and cowls, Voltaire says, were more than any among the philosophers. The shrewdness of these old monks in the choice of a location has been justified by the cities and towns sprung from the sites of their primitive missions. Here, as elsewhere,

"—These black crows
Had pitched by instinct on the fattest fallows."

"I," said Napoleon, at St. Helena, "rendered all the burying-places independent of the priests. I hated friars" (*frati*), "and was the annihilator of them and of their receptacles of crime, the monasteries, where every vice was practiced with impunity. A set of miscreants" (*scelerati*) "who in general are a dishonor to the human race. Of priests I would have always allowed a sufficient number, but no *frati*." A Capuchin, says an old dictionary of 1676, is a friar of St. Francis's order, wearing a cowl, or capouch, but no shirt nor breeches.[1]

Opening our history at the epoch of the settlement of New France, and turning over page by page the period we have been reviewing, there is no more hideous chapter than the infernal cruelties of the Society of Jesus. Their agency in the terrible persecutions of the Huguenots is too well known to need repetition. St. Bartholomew, the broken pledge of the Edict of Nantes, the massacres of Vivarais, of Rouergue, and of Languedoc are among their monuments.

The rigor with which infractions of the discipline of the order were punished would be difficult to believe, if unsupported by trustworthy testimony. Francis Seldon, a young pupil of the Jesuit College at Paris, was imprisoned thirty-one years, seventeen of which were passed at St. Marguerite, and fourteen in the Bastile. His crime was a lampoon of two lines affixed to the college door. A *lettre de cachet* from Louis XIV. consigned this poor lad of only sixteen to the Bastile in 1674, from which he only emerged in 1705, by the assignment of a rich inheritance to the Society, impiously called, of Jesus.

The siege of La Rochelle, and slaughter of the Huguenots, is believed to have been nothing more than a duel between Richelieu and Buckingham, for the favor of Anne of Austria. It was, however, in the name of religion that the population of France was decimated. Colbert, in endeavoring to stem the tide of persecution, fell in disgrace. Louvois seconded with devilish zeal the projects of the Jesuits, which had no other end than the total destruction of the reformed faith. In 1675 Père Lachaise entered on his functions of father-confessor to the king. He was powerfully seconded by his society; but they, fearing his Majesty might regard it as a pendant of St. Bartholomew, hesitated to press a decisive *coup d'état* against the Protestants.

There was at the court of Louis the widow Scarron, become De Maintenon, declared mistress of the king, who modestly aspired to replace Marie Therese of Austria upon the throne of France. To her the Jesuits addressed themselves. It is believed the compact between the worthy contracting parties exacted no less of each than the advancement of their mutual projects through the seductions of the courtesan, and the fears for his salvation the Jesuits were to inspire in the mind of the king. Louis believed in the arguments of Madame De Maintenon, and signed the Edict of Nantes; he

---

[1] Capuchin, a cowl or hood.

ceded to the threats or counsels of his confessor, and secretly espoused Madame De Maintenon. The 25th October, 1685, the royal seal was, it is not doubted by her inspiration, appended to the barbarous edict, drawn up by the Père Le Tellier, under the auspices of the Society of Jesus.[1]

France had already lost a hundred thousand of her bravest and most skillful children. She was now to lose many more. Among the fugitives driven from the fatherland were many who fled, as the Pilgrims had done into Holland. Some sought the New World, and their descendants were such men as John Jay, Elias Boudinot, James Bowdoin, and Peter Faneuil.

Before the famous edict of 1685, the Huguenots had been forbidden to establish themselves either in Canada or Acadia. They were permitted to visit the ports for trade, but not to exercise their religion. The Jesuits took care that the edict was enforced in the French possessions. I have thought the oft-cited intolerance of the Puritans might be effectively contrasted with the diabolical zeal with which Catholic Christendom pursued the annihilation of the reformed religion.

The Jesuits obtained at an early day a preponderating influence in Canada and in Acadia. It is believed the governor-generals had not such real power as the bishops of Quebec. At a later day, they were able well-nigh to paralyze Montcalm's defense of Quebec. The fathers of the order, with the crucifix held aloft, preached crusades against the English to the savages they were sent to convert. One of the fiercest Canabas chiefs related to an English divine that the friars told his people the blessed Virgin was a French lady, and that her son, Jesus Christ, had been killed by the English.[2] One might say the gray hairs of old men and the blood-dabbled ringlets of innocent children were laid on the altars of their chapels.

We can afford to smile at the forecast of Louis, when he says to M. De la Barre in 1683, "I am persuaded, like you, that the discoveries of Sieur La Salle are altogether useless, and it is necessary, hereafter, to put a stop to such enterprises, which can have no other effect than to scatter the inhabitants by the hope of gain, and to diminish the supply of beaver." We still preserve in Louisiana the shadow of the sceptre of this monarch, whose needy successor at Versailles sold us, for fifteen millions, a territory that could pay the German subsidy with a year's harvest.

Doubtless the little bell in the hospice turret, tolling for matins or vespers, was often heard by the fisher in the bay, as he rested on his oars and repeated an *ave*, or chanted the parting hymn of the Provençal:

> "O, vierge! O, Marie!
> Pour moi priez Dieu;
> Adieu, adieu, patrie,
> Provençe, adieu."

---

[1] Count Frontenac was a relative of De Maintenon.   [2] Cotton Mather.

There is a pleasant ramble over the hill by the cemetery, with the same accompaniments of green turf, limpid bay, and cool breezes everywhere. Intermitting puffs, ruffling the water here and there, fill the sails of coasting craft, while others lie becalmed within a few cable-lengths of them. Near the north-west corner of the ground I discovered vestiges of another small battery.

Castine having assumed the functions of a town within a period comparatively recent, her cemetery shows few interesting stones. The ancients of the little Acadian hamlet lie in forgotten graves; no moss-covered tablets for the antiquary to kneel beside, and trace the time-worn course of the chisel, are there. Numbers of graves are indicated only by the significant heaving of the turf. In one part of the field is a large and rudely fashioned slate-stone standing at the head of a tumulus. A tablet with these lines is affixed:

IN MEMORY OF
CHARLES STEWART,
The earliest occupant of this Mansion of the Dead,
A Native of Scotland,
And 1st Lieut. Comm. of his B. M. 74th Regt. of foot, or Argyle Highlanders,
Who died in this Town, while it was in possession of the Enemy,
March, A.D. 1783,
And was interred beneath this stone,
Æt. about 40 yrs.

This Tablet was inserted
A.D. 1849.

The tablet has a tale to tell. It runs that Stewart quarreled with a brother officer at the mess-table, and challenged him. Hearing of the intended duel, the commanding officer reprimanded the hot-blooded Scotsman in such terms that, stung to the quick, he fell, Roman-like, on his own sword.

Elsewhere I read the name of Captain Isaiah Skinner, who, as master of a packet plying to the opposite shore, "thirty thousand times braved the perils of our bay."

While I was in Castine I paid a visit to the factory in which lobsters are canned for market. A literally "smashing" business was carrying on, but with an uncleanness that for many months impaired my predilection for this delicate crustacean. The lobsters are brought in small vessels from the lower bay. They are then tossed, while living, into vats containing salt water boiling hot, where they receive a thorough steaming. They are next transferred to long tables, and, after cooling, are opened. Only the flesh of the larger claws and tail is used, the remainder being cast aside. The reserved portions are put into tin cans that, after being tightly soldered, are subjected to a new steaming of five and a half hours to keep them fresh.[1]

In order to arrest the wholesale slaughter of the lobster, stringent laws

---

[1] Isle au Haut is particularly renowned for the size and quality of these fish.

have been made in Maine and Massachusetts. The fishery is prohibited during certain months, and a fine is imposed for every fish exposed for sale of less than a certain growth. Of a heap containing some eight hundred lobsters brought to the factory, not fifty were of this size; a large proportion were not eight inches long. Frequent boiling in the same water, with the slovenly appearance of the operatives, male and female, would suggest a doubt whether plain Penobscot lobster is as toothsome as is supposed. The whole process was in marked contrast with the scrupulous neatness with which similar operations are elsewhere conducted; nor was there particular scrutiny as to whether the lobsters were already dead when received from the vessels.

Wood, in the "New England Prospect," mentions that lobsters were so

LOBSTER POT.

plenty and little esteemed they were seldom eaten. They were frequently, he says, of twenty pounds' weight. The Indians used lobsters to bait their hooks, and ate them when they could not get bass. I have seen an account of a lobster that weighed thirty-five pounds. Josselyn mentions that he saw one weighing twenty pounds, and that the Indians dried them for food as they did lampreys and oysters.

The first-comers into New England waters were not more puzzled to find the ancient city of Norumbega than I to reach the fabulous Down East of the moderns. In San Francisco the name is vaguely applied to the territory east of the Mississippi, though more frequently the rest of the republic is alluded to as "The States." South of the obliterated Mason and Dixon's line, the region east of the Alleghanies and north of the Potomac is Down East, and no mistake about it. In New York you are as far as ever from this *terra incognita*. In Connecticut they shrug their shoulders and point you about north-north-east. Down East, say Massachusetts people, is just across our eastern border. Arrived on the Penobscot, I fancied myself there at last.

"Whither bound?" I asked of a fisherman, getting up his foresail before loosing from the wharf.

"Sir, to you. Down East."

The evident determination to shift the responsibility forbade further pursuit of this fictitious land. Besides, Maine people are indisposed to accept without challenge the name so universally applied to them of Down Easters. We do not say down to the North Pole, and we do say down South. The higher latitude we make northwardly the farther down we get. Nevertheless, disposed as I avow myself to present the case fairly, the people of Maine uniformly say "up to the westward," when speaking of Massachusetts. Of one thing I am persuaded—Down East is nowhere in New England.

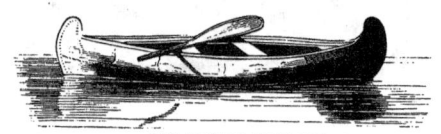

OLD FORT FREDERICK, PEMAQUID POINT.

CHAPTER VI.

PEMAQUID POINT.

"Love thou thy land, with love far-brought
From out the storied Past, and used
Within the Present, but transfused
Thro' future time by power of thought."
                                          TENNYSON.

A VERY small fraction of the people of New England, I venture to say, know more of Pemaquid than that such a place once existed somewhere within her limits; yet it is scarcely possible to take up a book on New England in which the name does not occur with a frequency that is of itself a spur to inquiry. If a few volumes be consulted, the materials for history become abundant. After accumulating for two hundred years, or more, what belongs to the imperishable things of earth, this old outpost of English power has returned into second childhood, and become what it originally was, namely, a fishing-village.

But those who delight in ferreting through the chinks and crannies of an out-of-the-way locality, will be repaid by starting from Damariscotta on a coastwise voyage of discovery. In traveling by railway from Portland, with your face to the rising sun, you catch occasional glimpses of the ocean, and you receive imperfect impressions of the estuaries that indent her "hundred-harbored" shores; but from the window of a stage-coach journeying at six miles an hour the material and mental eye may receive and fix ideas more distinct and enduring.

I reached the little village of New Harbor, at Pemaquid Point, in time to see the sun crimson in setting, a cloudless sky, and an unruffled sea. Monhegan Island grew of a deep purple in the twilight shadows. The tower lamps were alight, and from neighboring islands other beacons twinkled pleasantly on the waters. Coasting vessels trimmed their sails to catch the land-breeze of evening. Then the moon arose.

The little harbor beneath me contained a few small fishing-vessels at anchor.

"THE LAND-BREEZE OF EVENING."

One or two others were slowly working their way in. The cottages straggling by the shore were not numerous or noticeable. It was still some three miles to the light-house at the extremity of the point.

At Bristol Mills I had exchanged the stage for a beach-wagon. The driver was evidently a person of consequence here, as he usually becomes in such isolated neighborhoods out of the beaten paths of travel. His loquacity was marvelous. He had either a message or a missive for every one he met; and at the noise of our wheels house doors opened, and the noses and lips of youngsters were flattened in a whimsical manner against the window-panes. I observed that he invariably saluted the girls by their Christian names as they stood shyly peeping through half-opened doors; adding the middle name to the baptismal whenever one might be claimed, as Olive Ann, Matilda Jane, or Hannah Ann. I should have called some of them plain Olive, or Matilda, or Hannah. The men answered to such names as Dominicus, Jott, and 'Life (Eliphalet). Thus this brisk little fellow's passing was the great event over four miles of road.

I should have gone directly to the old settlement on the other side of the Neck, now known as "The Factory;" but here, for a wonder, were no hotels, and travelers are dependent upon private hospitality. "Do you think they will take me in over there?" I queried, pointing to the old mansion on the site of Fort Frederick. The driver shook his head.

"Are they quite full?"

"Solid," was his reply, given with an emphasis that conveyed the impression of sardines in a box. So I was fain to rest with a fisherman turned storekeeper.

The little rock-environed harbor on the side of Muscongus Bay is a mere roadstead, unfit for shipping in heavy easterly weather. This place, like many neighboring sea-coast hamlets, was busily engaged in the mackerel and menhaden fishery. The latter fish, usually called "porgee," is in demand at the factories along shore for its oil, and among Bank fishermen as bait. Some old cellars on the north side of New Harbor indicated the *locale* of a former generation of fishermen. On this side, too, there existed, not many years ago, remains of a fortification of ancient date.[1] Shot, household utensils, etc., have been excavated there. There is also by the shore what was either the lair of wild beasts, or a place of concealment frequented by savages. Mr. M'Farland, one of the oldest residents, mentioned that he had found an arrow-head in the den. Various coins and Indian implements, some of which I saw, have been turned up with the soil on this neck of land.

The visitor will not leave New Harbor without hearing of sharp work done there in the war of 1812. The enemy's cruisers kept the coast in perpetual alarm by their marauding excursions in defenseless harbors. One day a British frigate hove to in the Bay, and in a short time a number of barges were seen to push off, fully manned, for the shore. The small militia guard then stationed in Old Fort Frederick was notified, and the residents of New Harbor prepared for action. As the leading British barge entered the harbor, it was hailed by an aged fisherman, who warned the officer in charge not to attempt to land. "If a single gun is fired," replied the Briton, "the town shall be destroyed."

Not a single gun, but a deadly volley, answered the threat. The rocks were bristling with old queen's arms and ducking-guns, in the grasp of a score of resolute fellows. Every shot was well aimed. The barge drifted helplessly out with the tide, and the captain of the frigate had a sorry dispatch for the admiral at Halifax.

Leaving New Harbor, I crossed a by-path that conducted to the factory road. Here and elsewhere I had listened to the story of the destruction of the menhaden, from the fishermen's point of view. They apprehend nothing less than the total disappearance of this fish at no distant day. "What are we poor fellows going to do when they catch up all the porgees?" asked one. The fishery, as conducted by the factories, is regarded by the fishermen proper as the introduction of improved machinery that dispenses with labor is looked upon by the operative. Although the oil factories purchase the catch that is brought in, the owners are considered intruders, and experience many petty vexations. As men of capital, possessed of all needful appliances for their business, they are really independent of the resident population, to whom, on the other hand, they disburse money and give employment. The question with which the political economist will have to deal is the expected extinction of the menhaden.

I went through the factory at Pemaquid Point, and was persuaded the fish could not long support the drain upon them. The porgee begins to fre-

---

[1] This work is on an old map of the Kennebec patent. It was about twenty rods square, with a bastion. A house now stands in the space it formerly occupied.

quent these waters in June. The first-comers are lean, and will make only a gallon of oil to the barrel; those of September yield four gallons. A fleet of propellers, as well as sailing-craft of forty to fifty tons burden, are kept constantly employed.

At Pemaquid harbor, the fish cargoes are transferred from the steamer to an elevated tank of the capacity of four thousand barrels. Underneath the tank a tram-way, conducting by an inclined plane to the second story of the factory, is laid upon the wharf. In the bottom of the tank is a trap-door that, upon being opened, quickly fills a car placed below. The fish are then taken into the factory and dumped into other tanks, containing each three car-loads, or about sixty barrels. Here steam is introduced, rapidly converting the fish into unsavory chowder, or "mash." As many as a dozen of these vats were in constant use. The oil and water being drawn off into other vats, the product is obtained through the simplest of machinery, and the well-known principle that in an admixture with water oil will rise to the surface. The residuum from the first process is shoveled into perforated iron cylinders, by men standing up to their knees in the steaming mass. It is then subjected to hydraulic pressure, and, after the extraction of every drop of oil, is carefully housed, to be converted into phosphates. The water is passed from tank to tank until completely free of oil. Nothing is lost.

This factory had a capacity of three thousand barrels per day, though not of the largest class. Others were working day and night through the season, which continues for about three months.

I walked afterward by the side of a seine two hundred fathoms in length, spread upon the grass in order to contract the meshes. One of them frequently costs above a thousand dollars, and is sometimes destroyed at the first casting by being caught on the ledges in shallow water.

An old hand can easily tell the difference between a school of mackerel and one of menhaden. The former rush in a body on the top of the water, while the shoal of porgees merely ripples the surface, as is sometimes seen when a moving body of water impinges against a counter-current. The mackerel takes the hook, while the porgee and herring never do.

The talk was more fishy here than in any place I have visited. Here they call a school, or shoal, "a pod of fish;" "we sot round a pod" being a common expression. The small vessels are called seiners. When they approach a school, the seine is carried out in boats, one end being attached to the vessel, except when a bad sea is running. I have seen the men standing up to the middle among the fish they were hauling in; and they are sometimes obliged to abandon half their draught.

The whole process of rendering menhaden into oil is less offensive to the olfactories than might be supposed. The works at Pemaquid Point are owned by Judson, Tarr, and Co., of Rockport, Massachusetts. As against the generally received opinion that they were destroying fish faster than the losses could be repaired, the unusual abundance of mackerel the last year was cited. Mackerel, however, are not ground up at the rate of many thousand barrels per day. It is easy to conjecture that present profit is more looked to than future scarcity. The product of menhaden is chiefly used in the adulteration of linseed-oil. This fish is probably the same called by the French "*gasparot*," and found by them in great abundance on the coasts of Acadia.

Some account of the habits of the mackerel, as given by veteran fishermen, is of interest to such as esteem this valuable fish—and the number is legion—if not in explanation of the seemingly purposeless drifting of the mackerel fleet along shore, which is, nevertheless, guided by calculation.

In early spring the old breeding fish come into the bays and rivers to spawn. They then return northward. These mackerel are not apt to take the hook, but are caught in weirs and seines, a practice tending to inevitable scarcity in the future. The parent fish come back, in September, to the localities where they have spawned, and, taking their young in charge, proceed to the warmer waters west and south. Few if any mackerel spawn south of Cape Cod.

By the time this migration occurs, the young fish have grown to six or seven inches in length, and are called "tinkers." They frequently take the bait with avidity, but are too small for market. When this school comes along, the fishermen prepare to follow, saying, "The mackerel are bound west, and we must work west with them." These first-comers are usually followed by a second school of better size and quality. I have often seen numbers of young mackerel, of three to four inches in length, left in shallow pools upon the flats by the tide in midsummer.

In the midst of a "biting school" no sport could be more exciting or satisfying. At such times the mackerel resemble famished wolves, snapping and crowding for the bait, rather than harmless fishes. This unexampled voracity makes them an easy prey, and they are taken as fast as the line can be thrown over. It not unfrequently happens that the school will either sink or suddenly refuse the bait, even while swarming about the sides of the vessels. This is vexatious, but there is no help for it. The fleet must lie idle until the capricious or overfed fish is hungry.

Mackerel swim in deep water, and are brought to the surface by casting over quantities of ground bait. If they happen to be on the surface in a storm, at the first peal of thunder they will sink to the bottom. The movements of the fish in the water are like a gleam of light, and it dies hard when out of it. The mackerel was in great abundance when New England was first visited.

In the confusion naturally incident to accounts of early discoveries on our coast of New England, it is pleasant to find one vantage-ground from which you can not be dislodged. In this respect Pemaquid stands almost alone. It has never been called by any other name. Possibly it may have embraced either more or less of the surrounding territory or adjacent waters than at present; still there is eminent satisfaction in standing at Pemaquid on impregnable ground.

In the minds of some old writers Pemaquid was unquestionably confounded with the Penobscot. There is a description of Pemaquid River from the Hakluyt papers,[1] which makes it the easternmost river, one excepted, of Mavoshen, manifestly a name erroneously applied, as the description is as far from coinciding with the true Pemaquid as is its location by Hakluyt. In this account the Sagadahoc and town of Kennebec are also mentioned. Like many others, it is more curious than instructive.

It also appears, to the student's dismay, that in some instances the discoverers were apprehensive of drawing attention to any new-found port or harbor, as it would render their monopoly of less value. The account of Weymouth's voyage by James Rosier omitted the latitude, doubtless with this object. His narrative, if not written to mislead, was confessedly not intended to instruct. How is the historian to follow such a clue? Fortunately, after many puzzling and unsatisfactory conjectures, the account of William Strachey makes all clear, so far as Pemaquid is in question. Weymouth's first landfall was in 42°, and he coasted northward to 44°. Strachey speaks of "the isles and rivers, together with that little one of Pemaquid."

Sir F. Gorges, in his "Brief Narration," mentions that "it pleased God" to bring Captain Weymouth, on his return in 1605, into the harbor of Plymouth, where he, Sir Ferdinando, then commanded.[2] Captain Weymouth, he continues, had been dispatched by the Lord Arundel of Wardour in search of the North-west Passage, but falling short of his course, had happened into a river on the coast of America called Pemaquid. In the reprint of Sir F. Gorges's invaluable narrative[3] the word Penobscot is placed after Pemaquid in brackets. It does not appear in the original.

Pemaquid, then, becomes one of the pivotal points of New England discovery, as it subsequently was of her history. As the French had directed their early efforts toward the Penobscot, so the English had imbibed strong predilections for the Sagadahoc, or Kennebec. Weymouth and Pring had paved the way; the Indians transported to England had been able to give an intelligible account of the country, the configuration of the coasts, the magnitude of the rivers, and power of the nations peopling the banks.

The Kennebec was known to the French earlier than to the English, and by its proper name. Champlain's voyage in the autumn of 1604 extended, it is believed, as far as Monhegan, as he names an isle ten leagues from "*Quinebequi*," and says he went three or four leagues beyond it. Moreover,

---

[1] "Purchas," vol. iv., 1874.
[2] In 1603 Gorges was deprived of the command, but had it restored to him the same year.
[3] "Collections of the Massachusetts Historical Society," vol. vi., 3d series.

he had coasted both shores of the Penobscot bay, penetrating at least as far as the Narrows, below Bucksport. He calls the Camden hills Bedabedec, and says the Kennebec and Penobscot Indians were at enmity. De Monts followed Champlain in June, 1605, having sailed from St. Croix two days after Weymouth's departure from the coast for England. He was more than two months in exploring a hundred and twenty leagues of sea-coast, visiting and observing the Kennebec, of which a straightforward story is told. Even then the river was known as a thoroughfare to Canada.[1]

The mouth of the Kennebec is interesting as the scene of the third attempt to obtain a foothold on New England's soil. This was the colony of Chief-justice Popham, which arrived off Monhegan in August, 1607.[2] This undertaking was intended to be permanent. There were two well-provided ships, and a hundred and twenty colonists.[3] The leader of the enterprise, George Popham, was accompanied by Captain Raleigh Gilbert, nephew and namesake of Sir Walter Raleigh.

A settlement was effected on Hunnewell's Point, at the mouth of the Kennebec. The winter was one of unexampled severity, and the new-comers had been late in preparing for it. Encountering privations similar to those afterward endured by the Plymouth settlers, they lost courage, and when news of the death of their patron, the chief-justice, reached them, were ready to abandon the project. Popham, having died in February, was succeeded by Gilbert, whose affairs recalling him to England, the whole colony deserted their settlement at Fort St. George in the spring of 1608. Popham was the first English magistrate in New England.

Mather attributes the failure of attempts to colonize the parts of New England north of Plymouth to their being founded upon the advancement of worldly interests. "A constant series of disasters has confounded them," avers the witch-hating old divine. One minister, he says, was exhorting the eastern settlers to be more religious, putting the case to them much in this way, when a voice from the congregation cried out, "Sir, you are mistaken; you think you are preaching to the people of the Bay. Our main end was to catch fish."

"Did you ever see Cotton Mather's 'History of New England?'—one of the oddest books I ever perused, but deeply interesting." The question is put by Southey, and I repeat it, as, if you have not read Mather's "Magnalia Christi Americana," you have not seen the corner-stone of New England historical and ecclesiastical literature.

Apropos of the immigration into New England, it was openly bruited in England that King Charles I. would have been glad if the thousands who went over were drowned in the sea. Between the years 1628 and 1635 the

---

[1] See Lescarbot, p. 497.   [2] Strachey. Gorges says August 8th; Smith, August 11th.
[3] A fly-boat, the *Gift of God*, George Popham; *Mary and John*, of London, Raleigh Gilbert.

exodus was very great, and gave the king much displeasure. No one was permitted to remove without the royal permission. Even young Harry Vane had to solicit the good offices of his father, Sir Harry, to obtain a pass. He

COTTON MATHER.

was then out of favor at court and at home, through his Geneva notions about kneeling to receive the Sacrament, and other Puritan ideas. "Let him go," growls an old writer; "has not Sir Harry other sons but him?"

The colony of Popham began better than it ended. A fort, doubtless no more than a palisade with platforms for guns, was marked out. A trench was dug about it, and twelve pieces of ordnance were mounted. Within its protection fifty houses, besides a church and storehouse, were built. The carpenters framed a "prytty pynnace" of thirty tons, which they christened the *Virginia*. There is no earlier record of ship-building in Maine.

The tenacity of the English character has become proverbial. Nevertheless, the opinion is hazarded that no nation so ill accommodates itself to a new country. The English colonies of Virginia, New England, and Jamaica are striking examples of barrenness of resource when confronted with unforeseen privations. The Frenchman, on the contrary, possesses in an eminent degree the capacity to adapt himself to strange scenes and unaccustomed modes of life. Every thing is made to contribute to his wants. Let the reader consult, if he will, the campaign of the Crimea, where thousands of English soldiers gave way to hardships unknown in the French camps. The elastic gayety of the one is in contrast with the gloomy despondency of the other. The Popham colony abandoned a well-matured, ably-seconded design through dread of a New England winter and through homesickness. Clearly it was not of the stuff to found a State.

The previous winter was passed by the French at their new settlement of

Port Royal, commenced within two years. The seasons of 1605 and of 1606 were extremely rigorous. The colony of De Monts went through the first in rude cabins, hastily constructed, on the island of St. Croix. The next autumn the settlement was transferred to Port Royal. Winter found them domiciled in their new quarters under no better roofs than they had quitted. Though their leader, Du Guast, had left them, they were animated by an irrepressible spirit of fun, altogether French. They made roads through the forest, or joined with the Indians in hunting-parties, managing these native Americans with an address that won their confidence and good help.

ANCIENT PEMAQUID.

Finally, at the suggestion of Champlain, in order to keep up an unflagging good-fellowship, and to render themselves free of all anxiety on the subject of provisions, the ever-famous "L'Ordre de Bon Temps" was inaugurated. It is deserving of remembrance along with the coterie of the Knights of the Round Table.

Once in fifteen days each member of the order officiated as *maitre d'hotel* of De Poutrincourt's table. It was his care on that day that his comrades should be well and honorably entertained; and although, as the old chronicler quaintly says, "our gourmands often reminded us that we were not in the *Rue aux Ours* at Paris, yet so well was the rule observed that we ordinarily made as good cheer as we should have known how to do in the *Rue aux Ours*, and at less cost."

There was not a fellow of the order who, two days before his turn came, did not absent himself until he could return with some delicacy to add to their ordinary fare. They had always fish or flesh at breakfast, and were never without one or both at the repasts of noon and evening. It became their great festival.

The steward, or *maitre d'hotel*, having caused all things to be made ready, marched with his napkin on his shoulder, his staff of office in his hand, and the collar of the order, that we are told was worth more than four French crowns, about his neck. Behind him walked the brothers of the order, each one bearing his plate. In the evening, after giving thanks to God, the host of the day resigned the collar to his successor, each pledging the other in a glass of wine.

On such occasions they had always twenty or thirty savages—men, women, and children—looking on. To these they gave bread from the table; but when, as was often the case, the sagamores—those fierce, intractable barbarians—presented themselves, they were, says Lescarbot, "at table eating and drinking like us, and we right glad to see them, as, on the contrary, their absence would have made us sorry."

At Pemaquid we enter the domain of Samoset, that chivalric New Englander whom historians delight to honor. He was a sagamore without guile. Chronologically speaking, he should first appear at Plymouth, in the act of offering to those doubting Pilgrims the right hand of fellowship. He told them he was sagamore of Morattigon, distant from Plymouth " a daye's sayle with a great wind, and five dayes by land." In 1623 he extended a kindly reception to Christopher Levett, to whom he proffered a friendship, to continue until the Great Spirit carried them to his wigwam. All the old writers speak well of Samoset, whom we call a savage.[1]

CHARLEVOIX.

I next visited the little point of land on which are the ruins of old Fort Frederick. Little difficulty is experienced in retracing the exterior and interior lines of a fortress designed as the strongest bulwark of English power in New England. It was built upon a green slope, above a rocky shore, commanding the approach from the sea; but was itself dominated by the heights of the western shore of John's River, a circumstance that did not escape the notice of D'Iberville in 1696. At the south-east angle of the work is a high rock,

---

[1] Samoset, in 1625, sold Pemaquid to John Brown. His sign-manual was a bended bow, with an arrow fitted to the string. The deed to Brown also fixes the residence, at Pemaquid, of Abraham Shurt, agent of Elbridge and Aldworth, in the year 1626.

overgrown with a tangle of climbing vines and shrubs. This rock formed a gart of the old magazine, and is now the conspicuous feature of the ruined fortress. A projecting spur of the opposite shore was called "the Barbican." The importance of Pemaquid as a check to French aggression was very great. It covered the approaches to the Kennebec, the Sheepscot, Damariscotta, and Pemaquid rivers. It was also, being at their doors, a standing menace against the Indian allies of the French, with a garrison ready to launch upon their villages, or intercept the advance of war parties toward the New England settlements. Its presence exasperated the Abenaquis, on whose territory it was, beyond measure: the French found them ever ready to second projects for its destruction.

On the other hand, the remoteness of Pemaquid rendered it impracticable to relieve it when once invested by an enemy. Only a few feeble settlements skirted the sea-coast between it and Casco Bay, so the same causes combined to render it both weak and formidable. Old Pentagoët, which the reader knows for Castine, and Pemaquid, were the mailed hands of each nationality, always clenched ready to strike.

The fort erected at Pemaquid in 1677, by Governor Andros, was a wooden redoubt mounting two guns, with an outwork having two bastions, in each of which were two great guns, and another at the gate.[1] This work was named Fort Charles. It was captured and destroyed by the Indians in 1689.

Sir William Phips, under instructions from Whitehall, built a new fort at Pemaquid in 1692, which he called William Henry. Captains Wing and Bancroft were the engineers, the work being completed by Captain March.[2] The English believed it impregnable. Mather, who says it was the finest that had been seen in those parts of America, has a significant allusion to the architect of a fortress in Poland whose eyes were put out lest he should build another such. From this vantage-ground the English, for the fifth time, obtained possession of Acadia.

In the same year D'Iberville made a demonstration against it with two French frigates, but finding an English vessel anchored under the walls, abandoned his design, to the chagrin of a large band of auxiliary warriors who had assembled under Villebon, and who now vented their displeasure by stamping upon the ground.

The reduction of Fort William Henry was part of a general scheme to

---

[1] "New York Colonial Documents," vol. iii., p. 256. Some primitive defensive works had existed as early as 1630, rifled in 1632 by the freebooter, Dixy Bull.

[2] It was of stone; a quadrangle seven hundred and thirty-seven feet in compass without the outer walls, one hundred and eight feet square within the inner ones; pierced with embrasures for twenty-eight cannons, and mounting fourteen, six being eighteen-pounders. The south wall fronting the sea was twenty-two feet high, and six feet thick at the ports. The great flanker, or round tower, at the west end of the line was twenty-nine feet high. It stood about a score of rods from high-water mark.—MATHER, vol. ii., p. 537.

FRENCH FRIGATE, SEVENTEENTH CENTURY.

overrun and destroy the English settlements as far as the Piscataqua. The English were forewarned. John Nelson, of Boston, whose biography is worth the writing, was then a prisoner at Quebec. Madocawando was also there, in consultation with Count Frontenac. The Abenaqui chief, dissatisfied with his presents, gave open expression of his disgust at the niggardliness of his white ally. Nelson was well acquainted with the Indian tongue. He cajoled the chief into talking of his projects, and as soon as they were in his possession acted like a man of decision. He bribed two Frenchmen — Arnaud du Vignon and Francis Albert — to carry the intelligence to Boston. On their return to Canada both were shot, and Nelson was sent to France, where he became for five years an inmate of the Bastile.

The life of John Nelson contains all the requisites of romance. Although an Episcopalian, he put himself at the head of the revolution against the tyranny of Andros. As a prisoner, he risked his own life to acquaint his countrymen with the dangers that menaced them; and it is said he was even carried to the place of execution along with his detected messengers. The French called him "le plus audacieux et le plus acharné," in the design of conquering Canada. Released from the Bastile on his parole, after visiting England he returned to France to fulfill its conditions, although forbidden to do so by King William. A man of address, courage, and high sense of honor was this John Nelson.

In 1696, a second and more successful expedition was conducted against Pemaquid. In August, D'Iberville[1] and Bonaventure sailed with the royal order to attack and reduce it. They called at Pentagoët, receiving there a re-enforcement of two hundred Indians, who embarked in their canoes, led by St. Castin. On the 13th the expedition appeared before the place, and the next day it was invested.

---

[1] " D'Iberville, monseigneur, est un tres sage garçon, entreprenant et qui scait ce qu'il fait."— M. DENONVILLE.

Fort William Henry was then commanded by Captain Pascho Chubb, with a garrison of about a hundred men. Fifteen pieces of artillery were in position. The French expected an obstinate resistance, as the place was well able to withstand a siege.

Chubb, on being summoned, returned a defiant answer. D'Iberville then began to erect his batteries. The account of Charlevoix states that the French got possession of ten or twelve stone houses, forming a street leading from the village square to the fort. They then intrenched themselves, partly at the cellar-door of the house next the fort, and partly behind a rock on the sea-shore. A second demand made by St. Castin, accompanied by the threat that if the place were assaulted the garrison might expect no quarter, decided the valiant Chubb, after a feeble and inglorious defense, to surrender. The gates were opened to the besiegers.

HUTCHINSON.

On finding an Indian in irons in the fortress, Castin's warriors began a massacre of the prisoners, which was arrested by their removal, at command of D'Iberville, to an island, where they were protected by a strong guard from further violence. The name of William Henry has been synonymous with disaster to colonial strongholds. The massacre of 1757 at Lake George, forever infamous, obscures with blood the fair fame of Montcalm. The novelist Cooper, in making it the groundwork of his "Mohicans," has not overstated the horrors of the tragedy enacted by the placid St. Sacrament.

Two days were occupied by the French in the destruction of Pemaquid fort. They then set sail for St. John's River, narrowly escaping capture by a fleet sent from Boston in pursuit. The French, who had before claimed to the Kennebec, subsequently established their boundary of Acadia at St. George's River.

On the beach, below where the martello tower had stood, I discovered many fragments of bricks among the rock débris. Some of these were as large as were commonly used in the hearths of our most ancient houses. The arch by which the tower was perhaps supported remained nearly intact, though completely concealed by a thicket formed of interweaving shrubs. Some have conjectured it to have been a hiding-place of smugglers. Fragments of shot and shell have likewise been picked up among the rubbish of the old fortress. Not far from the spot is a grave-yard, in which time and neglect have done their work.

It has been attempted to show that a large and populous settlement existed from a very early time at Pemaquid, with paved streets and some of the belongings of a permanent population. Within a few years excavations have been made, exhibiting the remains of pavement of beach-pebble at some distance below the surface of the ground.

It is not doubted that a small plantation was maintained here antecedent to the settlement in Massachusetts Bay, but it as certainly lacks confirmation that it had assumed either the proportions or outward appearance of a well and regularly built town at any time during the seventeenth century. If it were true, as Sullivan states, that in 1630 there were, exclusive of fishermen, eighty-four families about Sheepscot, Pemaquid, and St. George's, it also becomes important to know by what means these settlements were depopulated previous to the Indian wars.

The commissioners of Charles II., sent over in 1665, reported that upon the rivers Kennebec, Sheepscot, and Pemaquid were three plantations, the largest containing not more than thirty houses, inhabited, say they, "by the worst of men." The commissioners gave impartial testimony here, for they were trying to dispossess Massachusetts of the government she had assumed over Maine since 1652. They wrote further, that neither Kittery, York, Wells, Scarborough, nor Falmouth had more than thirty houses, and those mean ones. This was the entirety of the grand old Pine-tree State two centuries ago.

Colonel Romer had recommended, about 1699, the fortifying anew of Pemaquid, and the building of supporting works at the next point of land, and on John's Island. Nothing, however, appears to have been done until the arrival of Colonel David Dunbar, in 1730, to resume possession of the Sagadahoc territory in the name of the crown.

Dunbar repaired the old works, giving them the name of Fort Frederick. At Pemaquid Point he laid out the plan of a city which he divided into lots, inviting settlers to repopulate the country. Old grants and titles were considered extinct. His possession at Pemaquid conflicting with the Muscongus patent was revoked through the efforts of Samuel Waldo. The garrison was replaced by Massachusetts troops, and the so-called Sagadahoc territory annexed to the County of York.[1]

When in the neighborhood, the visitor will feel a desire to inspect the extensive shell heaps of the Damariscotta, about a mile above the town of Newcastle. They occur on a jutting point of land, in such masses as to resemble low chalk cliffs of guano deposits. The shells are of the oyster, now no longer native in New England waters, but once abundant, as these and other remains testify. The highest point of the bank is twenty-five feet above the river. The deposits are rather more than a hundred rods in length, with a

---

[1] As it is inconsistent with the purpose and limits of these chapters to give the detail of charters, patents, and titles by which Pemaquid has acquired much historical prominence, the reader may, in addition to authorities named in the text, consult Thornton's "Ancient Pemaquid," vol. v. "Maine Historical Collections;" Johnston's "Bristol, Bremen, and Pemaquid;" Hough's "Pemaquid Papers," etc.

variable width of from eighty to a hundred rods. The shells lie in regular layers, bleached by sun and weather. Among the many naturalists who have visited them may be named Dr. Charles T. Jackson,[1] and Professor Chadbourne, of Bowdoin College. Some animal remains found among the shells were submitted to Agassiz, who concurred in the received opinion that the shells were heaped up by men.

From point to point excavations have been made with the expectation of finding the Indian implements which have occasionally rewarded such investigations. Williamson mentions a tradition that human skeletons had been discovered in these beds. The bones of animals and of birds have been found in them. Situated in the immediate vicinity of the shell deposits is a kiln for converting the shells into lime, which is produced of as good quality as that obtained from limestone rock.

In walking along the beach at low tide, I had an excellent opportunity of surveying these remains. A considerable growth of trees had sprung from the soil collected above them, the roots of some having penetrated completely through the superincumbent shells to the earth beneath. From an observation of several cavities near the surface and in the sides of the oyster banks, the shells, in some instances, appear to have been subjected to fire. The entire stratum was in a state of decomposition that sufficiently attests the work of years. Even those shells lying nearest the surface in most cases crumbled in the hands, while at a greater depth the closely-packed valves were little else than a heap of lime.

The shell heaps are of common occurrence all along the coast. The reader knows them for the feeding-places of the hordes preceding European civilization. Here they regaled themselves on a delicacy that disappeared when they vanished from the land. The Indians not only satisfied present hunger, but dried the oyster for winter consumption. Their summer camps were pitched in the neighborhood of well-known oyster deposits, the squaws being occupied in gathering shell-fish, while the men were engaged in fishing or in hunting.

Josselyn mentions the long-shelled oysters peculiar to these deposits. He notes them of nine inches in length from the "joint to the toe, that were to be cut in three pieces before they could be eaten." Wood professes to have seen them of a foot in length. I found many of the shells here of six inches in length. Winthrop alludes to the oyster banks of Mystic River, Massachusetts, that impeded its navigation. During recent dredgings here oyster-shells of six to eight inches in length were frequently brought to the surface. The problem of the oyster's disappearance is yet to be solved.[2]

---

[1] While making his geological survey of Maine.

[2] Williamson mentions the heaps on the eastern bank, not so high as on the western, extending back twenty rods from the river, and rendering the land useless. The shell heaps of Georgia and Florida are more extensive than any in New England.

MONHEGAN ISLAND.

CHAPTER VII.

MONHEGAN ISLAND.

" From gray sea-fog, from icy drift,
From peril and from pain,
The home-bound fisher greets thy lights,
Oh hundred-harbored Maine!"
WHITTIER.

THE most famous island you can find on the New England map is Monhegan Island. To it the voyages of Weymouth, of Popham, and of Smith converge. The latter has put it down as one of the landmarks of our coast. Rosier calls it an excellent landfall. It is undoubtedly Monhegan that is seen on the oldest charts of New England. Champlain, with the same aptness and originality recognized in Mount Desert and Isle au Haut, names it La Tortue. Take from the shelf Bradford, Winthrop, Prince, or Hubbard, and you will find this island to figure conspicuously in their pages. Bradford says starving Plymouth was succored from Monhegan as early as 1622. The Boston colonists of 1630 were boarded when entering Salem by a Plymouth man, going about his business at Pemaquid. English fishing ships hovered about the island for a dozen years before the *Mayflower* swung to her anchorage in the "ice-rimmed" bay. The embers of some camp-fire were always smouldering there.

Sailing once from Boston on a Penobscot steamboat, a few hours brought us up with Cape Ann. I asked the pilot for what land he now steered.

"M'nhiggin."

In returning, the boat came down through the Mussel Ridge Channel like a race-horse over a well-beaten course. We rounded Monhegan again, and then steered by the compass. Monhegan is still a landmark.

A wintry passage is not always to be commended, especially when the

Atlantic gets unruly. Leaving the wharf on one well-remembered occasion, we steamed down the bay in smooth water at fourteen miles an hour. All on board were in possession of their customary equipoise. Soon the gong sounded a noisy summons to supper. We descended. The cabin tables were quickly occupied by a merry company of both sexes. There was a clatter of plates and sharp clicking of knives and forks; waiters ran hither and thither; the buzz of conversation and ripple of suppressed laughter began to diffuse themselves with the good cheer, when, suddenly, the boat, mounting a sea, fell off into the trough with a measured movement that thrilled every victim of old Neptune to the marrow.

THATCHER'S ISLAND LIGHT AND FOG SIGNALS, CAPE ANN.

It would be difficult to conceive a more instantaneous metamorphosis than that which now took place. Maidens who had been chatting or wickedly flirting, laid down their knives and forks and turned pale as their napkins. Youths that were all smiles and attention to some adorable companion suddenly behaved as if oblivious of her presence. Another plunge of the boat! My *vis-à-vis*, an old gourmand, had intrenched himself behind a rampart of delicacies. He stops short in the act of carving a fowl, and reels to the cabin stairs. Soon he has many followers. Wives are separated from husbands, the lover deserts his mistress. A heavier sea lifts the bow, and goes rolling with gathered volume astern, accompanied by the crash of crockery and trembling of the chandeliers. That did the business. The commercial traveler who told me he was never sea-sick laid down the morsel he was in the act of conveying to his mouth. He tried to look unconcerned as he staggered from the table, but it was a wretched failure. Two waiters, each bearing a well-laden tray, were sent sliding down the incline to the leeward side of the cabin, where, coming in crashing collision, they finally deposited their burdens in a berth in which some unfortunate was already reposing. All except a handful of well-seasoned voyagers sought the upper cabins, where they remained pale as statues, and as silent. The rows of deserted seats, unused plates, the joints sent away untouched, presented a melancholy evidence of the triumph of matter over mind.

Early in the morning we made out Monhegan, as I have no doubt it was descried from the mast-head of the *Archangel*, Weymouth's ship, two hundred and seventy years ago. The sea was shrouded in vapor, so that we saw the island long before the main-land was visible. Sea-faring people call it high land for this part of the world.

Near the westward shore of the southern half of this remarkable island is a little islet, called Mananas, which forms the only harbor it can boast. Captain Smith says, "Between Monahiggon and Monanis is a small harbour, where we rid." The entrance is considered practicable only from the south, though the captain of a coasting vessel pointed out where he had run his vessel through the ragged reefs that shelter the northern end, and saved it. It was a desperate strait, he said, and the by-standers shook their heads, in thinking on the peril of the attempt.[1]

The inhabitants are hospitable, and many even well to do. Their harbor is providentially situated for vessels that are forced on the coast in heavy gales, and are able to reach its shelter. At such times exhausted mariners are sure of a kind reception, every house opening its doors to relieve their distresses. Having all the requirements of snug harboring, excellent rock fishing, with room enough for extended rambling up and down, the island must one day become a resort as famous as the Isles of Shoals. At present there is a peculiar flavor of originality and freshness about the people, who are as yet free from the money-getting aptitudes of the recognized watering-place.

George Weymouth made his anchorage under Monhegan on the 18th of May, 1805. "It appeared," says Rosier, "a mean high land, as we afterward found it, being an island of some six miles in compass, but, I hope, the most fortunate ever yet discovered. About twelve o'clock that day, we came to

---

[1] Monhegan lies nine miles south of the George's group, twelve south-east from Pemaquid, and nine west of Metinic. It contains upward of one thousand acres of land. According to Williamson, it had, in 1832, about one hundred inhabitants, twelve or fourteen dwellings, and a school-house. The able-bodied men were engaged in the Bank fishery; the elders and boys in tending the flocks and tilling the soil. At that time there was not an officer of any kind upon the island; not even a justice of the peace. The people governed themselves according to local usage, and were strangers to taxation. A light-house was built on the island in 1824.

an anchor on the north side of this island, about a league from the shore. About two o'clock our captain with twelve men rowed in his ship-boat to the shore, where we made no long stay, but laded our boat with dry wood of old trees upon the shore side, and returned to our ship, where we rode that night." * * *

"This island is woody, grown with fir, birch, oak, and beech, as far as we saw along the shore; and so likely to be within. On the verge grow gooseberries, strawberries, wild pease, and wild rose-bushes. The water issued forth down the cliffs in many places; and much fowl of divers kinds breeds upon the shore and rocks."

The main-land possessed greater attraction for Weymouth. Thinking his anchorage insecure, he brought his vessel the next day to the islands "more adjoining to the main, and in the road directly with the mountains, about three leagues from the island where he had first anchored."

I read this description while standing on the deck of the *Katahdin*, and found it to answer admirably the conditions under which I then surveyed the land. We were near enough to make out the varied features of a long line of sea-coast stretching northward for many a mile. There were St. George's Islands, three leagues distant, and more adjoining to the main. And there were the Camden Mountains in the distance.[1]

Weymouth landed at Pemaquid, and traded with the Indians there. In order to impress them with the belief that he and his comrades were supernatural beings, he caused his own and Rosier's swords to be touched with the loadstone, and then with the blades took up knives and needles, much mystifying the simple savages with his jugglery. It took, however, six whites to capture two of the natives, unarmed and thrown off their guard by feigned friendship.

But one compensation can be found for Weymouth's treachery in kidnaping five Indians here, and that is in the assertion of Sir F. Gorges that this circumstance first directed his attention to New England colonization. At least two of the captive Indians found their way back again. One returned the next year; another—Skitwarres—came over with Popham. A strange tale these savages must have told of their adventures beyond seas.[2]

Some credence has been given to the report of the existence of a rock inscription on Monhegan Island, supposed by some to be a reminiscence

---

[1] A good many arguments may be found in the "Collections of the Maine Historical Society" as to whether Weymouth ascended the Penobscot or the Kennebec. All assume Monhegan to have been the first island seen. This being conceded, the landmarks given in the text follow, without reasonable ground for controversy.

[2] In 1607 Weymouth was granted a pension of three shillings and fourpence per diem. Smith was at Monhegan in 1614, Captain Dermer in 1619, and some mutineers from Rocroft's ship had passed the winter of 1618-'19 there. The existence of a small plantation is ascertained in 1622. In 1626 the island was sold to Giles Elbridge and Robert Aldworth for fifty pounds.

of the Northmen. The Society of Northern Antiquaries of Copenhagen has reproduced it in their printed proceedings. The best informed American antiquaries do not believe it to possess any archæological significance. I also heard of another of the "devil's foot-prints" on Mananas, but did not see it.

Between Monhegan and Pemaquid Point was the scene of the sea-fight between the *Enterprise* and *Boxer*. Some of the particulars I shall relate I had of eye-witnesses of the battle.

In September, 1814, the American brig *Enterprise* quitted Portsmouth roads. She had seen service in the wars with the French Directory and with Algiers. She had been rebuilt in 1811, and had already gained the name of a lucky vessel. Her cruising-ground was along the Maine coast, where a sharp lookout was to be kept for privateers coming out of the enemy's ports. In times past her commanders were such men as Sterrett, Hull, Decatur, and Blakely, in whom was no more flinching than in the mainmast.

Lieutenant Burrows, who now took her to sea, had been first officer of a merchant ship and a prisoner to the enemy. As soon as exchanged he was given the command of the *Enterprise*. He was a good seaman, bound up in his profession, and the darling of the common sailors. Taciturn and misanthropic among equals, he liked to disguise himself in a pea-jacket and visit the low haunts of his shipmates. It was believed he would be killed sooner than surrender.

The *Boxer* had been fitted out at St. Johns with a view of meeting and fighting the *Enterprise*. Every care that experience and seamanship could suggest had been bestowed upon her equipment. She was, moreover, a new and strong vessel. In armament and crews the two vessels were about equal, the inferiority, if any, being on the side of the American. The two brigs were, in fact, as equally matched as could well be. They were prepared, rubbed down, and polished off, like pugilists by their respective trainers. They were in quest of each other. The conquered, however, attributed their defeat to every cause but the true one, namely, that of being beaten in a fair fight on their favorite element.

The *Boxer*, after worrying the fishermen, and keeping the sea-coast villages in continual alarm, dropped anchor in Pemaquid Bay on Saturday, September 4th, 1814. There was then a small militia guard in old Fort Frederick. The inhabitants of Pemaquid Point, fearing an attack, withdrew into the woods, where they heard at evening the music played on board the enemy's cruiser.

The next morning, a peaceful Sabbath, the lookout of the *Boxer* made out the *Enterprise* coming down from the westward with a fair wind. In an instant the Briton's decks were alive with men. Sails were let fall and sheeted home with marvelous quickness, and the *Boxer*, with every rag of canvas spread, stood out of the bay. From her anchorage to the westward of John's

Island, the *Boxer*, as she got under way, threw several shot over the island into the fort by way of farewell. Both vessels bore off the land about three miles, when they stripped to fighting canvas. The American, being to windward, had the weather-gage, and, after taking a good look at her antagonist, brought her to action at twenty minutes past three o'clock in the afternoon. Anxious spectators crowded the shores; but after the first broadsides, for the forty minutes the action continued, nothing could be seen except the flashes of the guns; both vessels were enveloped in a cloud. At length the firing slackened, and it was seen the *Boxer's* maintop-mast had been shot away. The battle was decided.

This combat, which proved fatal to both commanders, was, for the time it lasted, desperately contested. The *Enterprise* returned to Portland, with the *Boxer* in company, on the 7th. The bodies of Captain Samuel Blythe, late commander of the English brig, and of Lieutenant William Burrows, of the *Enterprise*, were brought on shore draped with the flags each had so bravely defended. The same honors were paid the remains of each, and they were interred side by side in the cemetery at Portland. Blythe had been one of poor Lawrence's pall-bearers.

GRAVES OF BURROWS AND BLYTHE, PORTLAND.

This was the first success that had befallen the American navy since the loss of the *Chesapeake*. It revived, in a measure, the confidence that disaster had shaken. The *Boxer* went into action with her colors nailed to the mast— a useless bravado that no doubt cost many lives. Her ensign is now among the trophies of the Naval Academy at Annapolis, while that of the *Enterprise* has but lately been reclaimed from among the forgotten things of the past, to array its tattered folds beside the flags of the *Bonhomme Richard* and of Fort M'Henry.[1]

Among the recollections of his " Lost Youth," the author of " Evangeline," a native of Portland, tells us:

> "I remember the sea-fight far away,
> How it thundered o'er the tide!
> And the dead captains, as they lay
> In their graves o'erlooking the tranquil bay,
> Where they in battle died."

---

[1] This flag inspired the national lyric, "The Star-spangled Banner."

BURROWS'S MEDAL.

GORGE, BALD HEAD CLIFF.

CHAPTER VIII.

FROM WELLS TO OLD YORK.

> "A shipman was there, wonned far by west;
> For aught I wot, he was of Dartëmouth."
> CHAUCER.

ONE hot, slumberous morning in August I found myself in the town of Wells. I was traveling, as New England ought to be traversed by every young man of average health and active habits, on foot, and at leisure, along the beautiful road to Old York. Now Wells, as Victor Hugo says of a village in Brittany, is not a town, but a street, stretching for five or six miles along the shore, and everywhere commanding an extensive and unbroken ocean view.

THE NEW ENGLAND COAST.

The place itself, though bristling with history, has been stripped of its antiques, and is in appearance the counterpart of a score of neat, thrifty villages of my acquaintance. I paused for a moment at the site of the Storer garrison, in which Captain Converse made so manful a defense when Frontenac, in 1692, let slip his French and Indians on our border settlements.[1] Some fragments of the timbers of the garrison are preserved in the vicinity, one of which I saw among the collections of a village antiquary. In the annals of Wells the names of John Wheelwright and of George Burroughs occur, the former celebrated as the founder of Exeter, the latter a victim of the witchcraft horror of '92.

John Wheelwright, the classmate and friend of Cromwell, fills a large space in the early history of the Bay Colony. A fugitive, like John Cotton, from the persecutions of Laud, he came to Boston in 1636, and became the pastor of a church at Braintree, then forming part of Boston. He was the brother-in-law of the famous Ann Hutchinson, who was near creating a revolution in Winthrop's government,[2] and shared her Antinomian opinions. For this he was banished, and became the founder of Exeter in 1638. In 1643, Massachusetts having claimed jurisdiction over that town, Wheelwright removed to Wells, where he remained two years. Becoming reconciled to the Massachusetts government, he removed to Hampton, was in England in 1657, returning to New England in 1660. He became pastor of the church in Salisbury, and died there in 1679; but the place of his burial, Allen says, is not known. He was the oldest minister in the colony at the time of his death, and a man of pronounced character. The settlement of the island of Rhode Island occurred through the removal of William Coddington and others at the same time, and for the same reasons that caused the expulsion of Wheelwright from Boston, as Roger Williams had been expelled from Salem seven years before.

"Wheelwright's Deed" has been the subject of a long and animated controversy among antiquaries; some, like Mr. Savage, pronouncing it a forgery because it is dated in 1629, the year before the settlement of Boston. This deed was a conveyance from the Indian sagamores to Wheelwright of the land on which stands the flourishing town of Exeter; and although copies of it have been recorded in several places, the original long ago disappeared. Cotton Mather, who saw it, testifies to its appearance of antiquity, and the advocates of its validity do not appear as yet to have the worst of the argument.[3]

---

[1] Colonel Storer kept up the stockades and one or more of the flankarts until after the year 1760, as a memorial rather than a defense.

[2] This relationship is disputed by Mr. Joseph L. Chester, the eminent antiquary. Winthrop, it would seem, ought to have known; Eliot and Allen repeat the authority, the latter giving the full name of Mary Hutchinson.

[3] Both sides have been ably presented by Dr. N. Bouton and Hon. Charles H. Bell.

George Burroughs, who fell fighting against terrorism on Gallows Hill—a single spot may claim in New England the terrible distinction of this name—was, if tradition says truly, apprehended by officers of the Bloody Council at the church door, as he was leaving it after divine service. A little dark man, and an athlete, whose muscular strength was turned against him to fatal account. An Indian, at Falmouth, had held out a heavy fowling-piece at arms-length by simply thrusting his finger in at the muzzle. Poor Burroughs, who would not stand by and see an Englishman outdone by a redskin, repeated the feat on the spot, and this was the most ruinous piece of evidence brought forth at his trial. A man could not be strong then, or the devil was in it.

The road was good, and the way plain. As the shores are for some miles intersected by creeks intrenched behind sandy downs, the route follows a level shelf along the high land. There are pleasant strips of beach, where the sea breaks noiselessly when the wind is off shore, but where it comes thundering in when driven before a north-east gale. Now and then a vessel is embayed here in thick weather, or, failing to make due allowance for the strong drift to the westward, is set bodily on these sands, as the fishermen say, "all standing." While I was in the neighborhood no less than three came ashore within a few hours of each other. The first, a timber vessel, missing her course a little, went on the beach; but at the next tide, by carrying an anchor into deep water and kedging, she was floated again. Another luckless craft struck on the rocks within half a mile of the first, and became a wreck, the crew owing their lives to a smooth sea. The third, a Bank fisherman, was left by the ebb high up on a dangerous reef, with a hole in her bottom. She was abandoned to the underwriters, and sold for a few dollars. To the surprise even of the knowing ones, the shrewd Yankee who bought her succeeded at low tide in getting some empty casks into her hold, and brought her into port.

Notwithstanding these sands are hard and firm as a granite floor, they are subject to shiftings which at first appear almost unaccountable. Many years ago, while sauntering along the beach, I came across the timbers of a stranded vessel. So deeply were they imbedded in the sand, that they had the appearance rather of formidable rows of teeth belonging to some antique sea-monster than of the work of human hands. How long the wreck had lain there no one could say; but at intervals it disappeared beneath the sands, to come to the surface again. I have often walked over the spot where it lay buried out of sight; and yet, after the lapse of years, there it was again, like a grave that would not remain closed.

A few years ago, an English vessel, the *Clotilde*, went ashore on Wells Beach, and remained there high and dry for nearly a year. She was deeply laden with railway iron, and, after being relieved of her cargo, was successfully launched. During the time the ship lay on the beach, she became so

OLD WRECKS ON THE BEACH.

deeply buried in the sand that a person might walk on board without difficulty. Ways were built underneath her, and, after a terrible wrenching, she was got afloat. Heavy objects, such as kegs of lead paint, and even pigs of iron, have been exposed by the action of the waves, after having, in some instances, been twenty years under the surface. I have picked up whole bricks, lost overboard from some coaster, that have come ashore with their edges smoothly rounded by the abrasion of the sand and sea. There is an authentic account of the re-appearance of a wrecked ship's caboose more than a hundred and seventy years after her loss on Cape Cod. After a heavy easterly gale, the beach is always sprinkled with a fine, dark gravel, which disappears again with a few days of ordinary weather.

Besides being the inexhaustible resource of summer idlers, the beach has its practical aspects. The sand, fine, white, and "sharp," is not only used by builders—and there is no fear of exhausting the supply—but is hauled away by farmers along shore, and housed in their barns as bedding for cattle, or to mix with heavy soils. The sea-weed and kelp that comes ashore in such vast quantities after a heavy blow is carefully harvested, and goes to enrich the lands with its lime and salt. It formerly supplied the commercial demand for soda, and was gathered on the coasts of Ireland, Scotland, France, and Spain for the purpose. It is the *varec* of Brittany and Normandy, the *blanquette* of Frontignan and Aigues-mortes, and the *salicor* of Narbonne. After being dried, it was reduced to ashes in rude furnaces. Iodine is also the product of sea-weed. You may sometimes see at high-water mark winrows of Irish moss (*carrageen*) bleaching in the sun, though for my blanc-mange I give the preference to that cast up on the shingle, as more free from sand. This plant grows only on the farthest ledges. The pebble usually heaped above the line of sand, or in little coves among the ledges, is used for ballast, and for mending roads and garden-walks. Turning to the sandy waste that skirts the beach, I seldom fail of finding the beach-pea, with its beautiful blossoms of blue and purple. In spring the vine is edible, and has been long used for food by the poorer people.

The beach is much frequented after a storm by crows in quest of a dinner *al fresco*. They haunt it as persistently as do the wreckers, and seldom fail of finding a stranded fish, a crab, or a mussel. They are the self-appointed scavengers of the strand, removing much of the offal cast up by the sea. The crow is a crafty fellow, and knows a thing or two, as I have had reason to observe. The large sea-mussel is much affected by him, and when found is at once pounced upon. Taking it in his talons, the crow flies to the nearest ledge of rocks, and, calculating his distance with mathematical eye, lets his prize fall. Of course the mussel is dashed in pieces, and the crow proceeds to make a frugal meal. I have seen this operation frequently repeated, and have as often scared the bird from his repast to convince myself of his success.

His method of taking the clam is equally ingenious. He walks upon the clam-bank at low tide, and seizes upon the first unlucky head he finds protruding from the shell. Then ensues a series of laughable efforts on the crow's part to rise with his prey, while the clam tries in vain to draw in its head. The crow, after many sharp tugs and much flapping of his wings, finally secures the clam, and disposes of him as he would of a mussel. The Indians, whose chief dependence in summer was upon shell-fish, complained that the English swine watched the receding tide as their women were accustomed to do, feeding on the clams they turned up with their snouts.

In the olden time the beach was the high-road over which the settlers traveled when, as was long the case, it was their only way of safety. It was often beset with danger; so much so that tradition says the mail from Portsmouth to Wells was for seven years brought by a dog, the pouch being attached to his collar. This faithful messenger was at last killed by the savages. For miles around this bay the long-abandoned King's Highway may be traced where it hugged the verge of the shore, climbing the roughest ledges, or crossing from one beach to another by a strip of shingle. Here and there an old cellar remains to identify its course and tell of the stern lives those pioneers led.

When the tide is out, I also keep at low-water mark, scrambling over ledges, or delving among the crannies for specimens. It does not take long to fill your pockets with many-hued pebbles of quartz, jasper, or porphyry that, in going a few rods farther, you are sure to reject for others more brilliant. At full sea I walk along the shore, where, from between those envious little stone walls, I can still survey the Unchanged.

After all that has been printed since the "Tractatus Petri Hispani," it is a question whether there are not as many popular superstitions to-day among plain New England country-folk as at any time since the settlement of the country. The belief in the virtue of a horseshoe is unabated. At York I saw one nailed to the end of a coaster's bowsprit. To spill salt, break a looking-glass, or dream of a white horse, are still regarded as of sinister augury. A tooth-pick made from a splinter of a tree that has been struck by lightning is a sure preventive of the toothache. Exceeding all these, however, is the generally accepted superstition that has led to the practice of bathing on Saco Beach on the 26th of June in each year. On this day, it is religiously believed that the waters, like Siloam of old, have miraculous power of healing all diseases with which humanity is afflicted. The people flock to the beach from all the country round, in every description of vehicle, to dip in the enchanted tide. A similar belief existed with regard to a medicinal spring on the River Dee, in Scotland, called Januarich Wells, one author gravely asserting that so great was the faith in its efficacy that those afflicted with broken legs have gone there for restoration of the limb.

I have found it always impracticable to argue with the pilgrims as to the grounds of their belief. They are ready to recount any number of wonderful cures at too great a distance for my investigation to reach, and may not, therefore, be gainsaid. It is a custom.

All this time I was nearing Ogunquit, a little fishing village spliced to the outskirts of Wells, being itself within the limits of York. At my right I caught a glimpse of the green bulk of Mount Agamenticus, and on the other hand, almost at my elbow, was the sea. So we marched on, as it were, arm in arm; for I was beginning to feel pretty well acquainted with a companion that kept thus constantly at my side. This morning it was Prussian blue, which it presently put off for a warmer hue. There it lay, sunning itself, cool, silent, impenetrable, like a great blue turquoise on the bare bosom of Mother Earth, nor looking as if a little ruffling of its surface could put it in such a towering passion.

My sachel always contains a luncheon, a book, and a telescopic drinking-cup. At noon, having left eight miles of road behind me, I sought the shelter of a tree by the roadside, and found my appetite by no means impaired by the jaunt. At such a time I read, like Rousseau, while eating, in default of a tête-à-tête. I alternately devour a page and a piece. While under my tree, a cow came to partake of the shade, of which there was enough for both of us. She gazed at me with a calm, but, as I conceived also, a puzzled look, ruminating meanwhile, or stretching out her head and snuffing the air within a foot of my hand. Perhaps she was wondering whether I had two stomachs, and a tail to brush off the flies.

From the village of Ogunquit there are two roads. I chose the one which kept the shore, in order to take in my way Bald Head Cliff, a natural curiosity well worth going some distance to see. The road so winds across the rocky waste on which the village is in part built that in some places you almost double on your own footsteps. Occasionally a narrow lane issues from among the ledges, tumbling rather than descending to some little cove, where you catch a glimpse of brown-roofed cottages and a fishing-boat or two, snugly moored. The inhabitants say there is not enough soil in Ogunquit with which to repair the roads, a statement no one who tries it with a vehicle will be inclined to dispute. Literally the houses are built upon rocks, incrusted with yellow lichens in room of grass. Wherever a dip occurs through which a little patch of blue sea peeps out, a house is posted, and I saw a few carefully-tended garden spots among hollows of the rock in which a handful of mould had accumulated. The wintry aspect is little short of desolation: in storms, from its elevation and exposure, the place receives the full shock of the tempest, as you may see by the weather-stained appearance of the houses.

A native directed me by a short cut "how to take another ox-bow out of the road," and in a few minutes I stood on the brow of the cliff. What a sight! The eye spans twenty miles of sea horizon. Wells, with its white meeting-houses and shore hotels, was behind me. Far up in the bight of the bay Great Hill headland, Hart's and Gooch's beaches—the latter mere ribbons of white sand—gleamed in the sunlight. Kennebunkport and its shipyards lay beneath yonder smoky cloud, with Cape Porpoise Light beyond. There, below me, looking as if it had floated off from the main, was the barren rock called the Nubble, the farthest land in this direction, with Cape Neddock harbor in full view. All the rest was ocean. The mackerel fleet that I had seen all day—fifty sail, sixty, yes, and more—was off Boon Island, with their jibs down, the solitary gray shaft of the light-house standing grimly up among the white sails, a mile-stone of the sea.

There are very few who would be able to approach the farthest edge of the precipice called the Pulpit, and bend over its sheer face without a quickening of the pulse. As in all these grand displays in which Nature puts forth her powers, you shrink in proportion as she exalts herself. For the time being, at least, the conceit is taken out of you, and you are thoroughly put down. Here is a perpendicular wall of rock ninety feet in height (as well as I could estimate it), and about a hundred and fifty in length, with a greater than Niagara raging at its foot—a rock buttress, with its foundations deeply rooted in the earth, breasting off the Atlantic; and the massy fragments lying splintered at its base, or heaved loosely about the summit, told of many a desperate wrestling-match, with a constant gain for the old athlete. The sea is gnawing its way into the coast slowly, but as surely as the cataract is approaching the lake; and the cliff, though it may for a thousand years oppose this terrible battering, will at last, like some sea fortress, crumble before it.

Underneath the cliff is one of those curious basins hollowed out almost with the regularity of art, in which a vessel of large tonnage might be floated. On the farther side of this basin, the ledges, though jagged and wave-worn, descend with regular incline, making a sort of platform. On the top of the cliff the rock débris and line of soil show unmistakably that in severe gales the sea leaps to this great height, drenching the summit with salt spray. At such a time the sea must be superb, though awful; for I doubt if a human being could stand erect before such a storm.

The exposed side of Bald Head Cliff faces south of east, and is the result of ages of wear and tear. The sea undermines it, assails it in front and from all sides. Here are dikes, as at Star Island, in which the trap-rock has given way to the continual pounding, thus affording a vantage-ground for the great lifting power of the waves. The strata of rock lie in perpendicular masses, welded together as if by fire, and injected with crystal quartz seams, knotted like veins in a Titan's forehead. Blocks of granite weighing many tons, honey-combed by the action of the water, are loosely piled where the cliff overhangs the waves; and you may descend by regular steps to the verge of the abyss. The time to inspect this curiosity is at low tide, when, if there be sea enough, the waves come grandly in, whelming the shaggy rocks, down whose sides a hundred miniature cascades pour as the waters recede.

Beneath the cliff the incoming tides have worn the trap-rock to glassy smoothness, rendering it difficult to walk about when they are wetted by the spray. From this stand-point it is apparent the wall that rises before you is the remaining side of one of those chasms which the sea has driven right into the heart of the crag. The other face is what lies scattered about on all sides in picturesque ruin. If the view from the summit was invigorating, the situation below was far from inspiring. It needed all the cheerful light and warmth the afternoon sun could give to brighten up that bleak and rugged shore. The spot had for me a certain sombre fascination; for it was here, more than thirty years ago, the *Isidore*, a brand-new vessel, and only a few hours from port, was lost with every soul on board. Often have I heard the tale of that winter's night from relatives of the ill-fated ship's crew; and as I stood here within their tomb, realizing the hopelessness of human effort when opposed to those merciless crags, I thought of Schiller's lines:

> "Oh many a bark to that breast grappled fast
> Has gone down to the fearful and fathomless grave;
> Again, crashed together the keel and the mast,
> To be seen tossed aloft in the glee of the wave!
> Like the growth of a storm, ever louder and clearer,
> Grows the roar of the gulf rising nearer and nearer."

Over there, where the smoke lies above the tree-tops, is Kennebunkport,[1] where they build as staunch vessels as float on any sea. The village and its ship-yards lie along the banks of a little river, or, more properly speaking, an arm of the sea. It is a queer old place, or rather was, before it became trans-

---

[1] Once, and much better, Arundel, from the Earl of Arundel.

lated into a summer resort; but now silk jostles homespun, and for three months in the year it is invaded by an army of pleasure-seekers, who ransack its secret places, and after taking their fill of sea and shore, flee before the first frosts of autumn. The town then hibernates.

The *Isidore* was built a few miles up river, where the stream is so narrow and crooked that you can scarce conceive how ships of any size could be successfully launched. At a point below the "Landing" the banks are so near together as to admit of a lock to retain the full tide when a launch took place. A big ship usually brings up in the soft ooze of the opposite bank, but is got off at the next flood by the help of a few yoke of oxen and a strong hawser. Besides its ship-building, Kennebunkport once boasted a considerable commerce with the West Indies, and the foundations of many snug fortunes have been laid in rum and sugar. The decaying wharves and empty warehouses now tell their own story.

I was one afternoon at the humble cottage of a less ancient, though more coherent, mariner than Coleridge's, who, after forty years battling with storms, was now laid up like an old hulk that will never more be fit for sea. Together we rehearsed the first and last voyage of the *Isidore*.

"Thirty years ago come Thanksgiving," said Ben, in a voice pitched below his usual key, "the *Isidore* lay at the wharf with her topsails loose, waiting for a slant of wind to put to sea. She was named for the builder's daughter, a mighty pretty gal, sir; but the boys didn't like the name because it sounded outlandish-like, and would have rather had an out-an'-out Yankee one any day of the week."

"There is, then," I suggested, "something in a name at sea as well as ashore?"

"Lor' bless your dear soul, I've seen them barkeys as could almost ship a crew for nothing, they had such spanking, saucy names. Captain R—— was as good a sailor as ever stepped, but dretful profane. He was as brave as a lion, and had rescued the crew of an Englishman from certain death while drifting a helpless wreck before a gale. No boat could live in the sea that was running; but Captain R—— bore down for the sinking ship, and passed it so close that the crew saved themselves by jumping aboard of him. Seven or eight times he stood for that wreck, until all but one man were saved. He had the ill-luck afterward to get a cotton ship ashore at Three Acres, near where the *Isidore* was lost, and said, as I've heard, 'he hoped the next vessel that went ashore he should be under her keel.' He had his wish, most likely.

"The *Isidore* was light, just on top of water, and never ought to have gone to sea in that plight; but she had been a good while wind-bound, and all hands began to be impatient to be off. Her crew, fifteen as likely lads as ever reefed a topsail, all belonged in the neighborhood. One of 'em didn't feel noways right about the v'y'ge, and couldn't make up his mind to go until the ship was over the bar, when he had to be set aboard in a wherry. Another dreamed three nights running the same dream, and every blessed time he saw the *Isidore* strike on a lee shore with the sea a-flying as high as the maintop. Every time he woke up in a cold sweat, with the cries of his shipmates ringing in his ears as plain as we hear the rote on Gooch's Beach this minute. So, when the *Isidore* set her colors and dropped down the river, Joe, though he had signed the articles and got the advance, took to the woods. Most every body thought it scandalous for the ship to unmoor, but Captain R—— said he would go to sea if he went to h—l the next minute. Dretful profane man, sir—dretful.

"The weather warn't exactly foul weather, and the sea was smooth enough, but all the air there was was dead ahead, and it looked dirty to wind'ard. The ship slipped out through the piers, and stood off to the east-'ard on the port tack. I recollect she was so nigh the shore that I could see who was at the wheel. She didn't work handy, for all the ropes were new and full of turns, and I knew they were having it lively aboard of her. Early in the afternoon it began to snow, first lightly, then thick and fast, and the wind began to freshen up considerable. The ship made one or two tacks to work out of the bay, but about four o'clock it closed in thick, and we lost her.

"I saw the Nubble all night long, for the snow come in gusts; but it blowed fresh from the no'th-east; *fresh*," he repeated, raising his eyes to mine and shaking his gray head by way of emphasis. "I was afeard the ship was in the bay, and couldn't sleep, but went to the door and looked out between whiles."

It was, indeed, as I have heard, a dreadful night, and many a vigil was kept by wife, mother, and sweetheart. At day-break the snow lay heaped in drifts in the village streets and garden areas. It was not long before a messenger came riding in at full speed with the news that the shores of Ogunquit were fringed with the wreck of a large vessel, and that not one of her crew was left to tell the tale. The word passed from house to house. Silence and gloom reigned within the snow-beleaguered village.

It was supposed the ship struck about midnight, as the Ogunquit fishermen heard in their cabins cries and groans at this hour above the noise of the tempest. They were powerless to aid; no boat could have been launched in that sea. If any lights were shown on board the ship, they were not seen; neither were any guns heard. The ropes, stiffened with ice, would not run through the sheaves, which rendered the working of the ship difficult, if not impossible. No doubt the doomed vessel drove helplessly to her destruction, the frozen sails hanging idly to the yards, while her exhausted crew miserably perished with the lights of their homes before their eyes.

All the morning after the wreck the people along shore were searching amidst the tangled masses of drift and sea-wrack the storm had cast up for the remains of the crew. They were too much mangled for recognition, except in a single instance. Captain G——, a passenger, had by accident put on his red-flannel drawers the wrong side out the morning the *Isidore* sailed, observing to his wife that, as it was good luck, he would not change them. One leg was found encased in the drawers. The mutilated fragments were brought to the village, and buried in a common grave.

THE MORNING ROUND.

Some of the old people at the Port declare to this day that on the night of the wreck they heard shrieks as plainly as ever issued from human throats; and you could not argue it out of them, though the spot where the *Isidore's* anchors were found is ten miles away. As for Joe B——, the runaway, he can not refrain from shedding tears when the *Isidore* is mentioned.

"But, Ben, do you believe in dreams?" I asked, with my hand on the latch.

"B'leeve in dreams!" he repeated; "why, Joe's a living man; but where's his mates?"

Perhaps they

> "Died as men should die, clinging round their lonely wreck,
> Their winding-sheet the sky, and their sepulchre the deck;
> And the steersman held the helm till his breath
> Grew faint and fainter still;
> There was one short fatal thrill,
> Then he sank into the chill
> Arms of Death."

I turned away from the spot with the old sailor's words in mind: "A wicked place where she struck; and the sea drove right on. A ragged place, sir—ragged."

Leaving the cliff, I struck across the pastures to the road, making no farther halt except to gather a few huckleberries that grew on high bushes by the roadside. The fruit is large, either black or blue, with an agreeable though different flavor from any of the low-bushed varieties. The local name for the shrub is "bilberry." It frequently grows higher than a man's head, and a single one will often yield nearly a quart.

It was a year of plenty, and I had seen the pickers busy in the berry pastures as I passed by. The fruit, being for the time a sort of currency—not quite so hard, by-the-bye, as the musket-bullets of the colonists—is received in barter at the stores. Whole families engage in the harvest, making fair wages, the annual yield exceeding in value that of the corn crop of the State. Maine grows her corn on the Western prairies, and pays for it with canned fish and berries.

At the village store I saw a woman drive up with a bushel of huckleberries, with which she bought enough calico for a gown, half a pound of tobacco, and some knickknacks for the children at home. Affixed in a conspicuous place to the wall was the motto, "Quick sales and small profits." Half an hour was spent in beating the shop-keeper down a cent in the yard, and another quarter of an hour to induce him to "heave in," as she said, a spool of cotton. The man, after stoutly contesting the claim, finally yielded both points. "The woman," thought I, "evidently only half believes in your seductive motto."

All along the road I had met women and children, going or returning, with pails or baskets. One man, evidently a fast picker, had filled the sleeves of his jacket with berries, after having first tied them at the wrists. Another, who vaulted over the stone wall at my side, when asked if he was going to try the huckleberries, replied,

"Wa'al, yes; think I'll try and *accumulate* a few."

Descending the last hill before reaching Cape Neddock Harbor, I had a good view of the Nubble, which several writers have believed was the Savage Rock of Gosnold, and the first land in New England to receive an English name. The reliable accounts of the early voyagers to our coasts are much too vague to enable later historians to fix the points where they made the land with the confidence with which many undertake to fix them. A careful examination of these accounts justifies the opinion that Gosnold made his land-fall off Agamenticus, and first dropped anchor, since leaving Falmouth, at Cape Ann. The latitude, if accurately taken, would of itself put the question beyond controversy; but as the methods of observing the exact position of a ship were greatly inferior to what they became later in the seventeenth century, I at first doubted, and was then constrained to admit, that the reckoning of Gosnold, Pring, and Champlain ought to be accepted as trustworthy. Gabriel Archer, who was with Gosnold, says, "They held themselves by computation well neere the latitude of 43 degrees," or a little northward of the Isles of Shoals. John Brereton, also of Gosnold's company, says they fell in with the coast in thick weather, and first made land with the lead. By all accounts the *Concord*, Gosnold's ship, was to the northward of Cape Ann. Land was sighted at six in the morning of the 14th of May, 1602, and Gosnold stood "fair along by the shore" until noon, which would have carried him across Ipswich Bay, even if the *Concord* were a dull sailer. In 1603 Martin Pring sailed over nearly the same track as Gosnold. It is by comparing these two voyages that Savage Rock appears to be located at Cape Ann.

Pring, says Gorges, observing his instructions (to keep to the northward as high as Cape Breton), arrived safely out and back, bringing with him "the most exact discovery of that coast that ever came to my hands since; and indeed he was the best able to perform it of any I met withal to this present." Pring's relation wrought such an impression on Sir F. Gorges and Lord Chief-justice Popham that, notwithstanding their first disasters, they resolved on another effort. He had no doubt seen and talked with Gosnold after his return; perhaps had obtained from him his courses after he fell in with the coast.

The *Speedwell*, Pring's vessel, also made land in forty-three degrees. It proved to be a multitude of small islands. Pring, after anchoring under the lee of the largest, coasted the main-land with his boats. The narrative continues to relate that they "came to the mayne in 43½, and ranged to southwest, in which course we found several inlets, the more easterly of which was barred at the mouth. Having passed over the bar, we ran up into it five miles. Coming out and sailing south-west, we lighted upon two other inlets; the fourth and most westerly was best, which we rowed up ten or twelve miles." Between forty-three and forty-three and a half degrees are the Saco, then barred at the mouth,¹ the Mousam, York, and the Piscataqua, the "most westerly and best."

"We (meeting with no sassafras)"—to follow the narrative—"left these places and *shaped our course for Savage's Rocks*, discovered the year before by Captain Gosnold." Savage Rock, then, was by both these accounts (Archer and Pring) to the southward of forty-three degrees, while the Nubble, or rather Agamenticus, is in forty-three degrees sixteen minutes.

"Departing hence, we bare into that great gulf which Captain Gosnold overshot the year before." This could be no other than Massachusetts Bay, for Gosnold, according to Brereton, after leaving Savage Rock, shaped his course southward ("standing off southerly into the sea") the rest of that day and night (May 15th), and on the following morning found himself "embayed with a mighty headland," which was Cape Cod. Pring, on the contrary, steered into the bay, "coasting, and finding people on the north side thereof." If my conjecture be correct, he was the first English mariner in Boston Bay.

It is hardly possible that a navigator falling in with the New England coast in forty-three or forty-three and a half degrees, and steering south-west, should not recognize in Cape Ann one of its remarkable features, or pass it by unperceived in the night. He would have been likely to find Savage Rock and end his voyage at the same moment. Champlain and Smith are both in

---

¹ An old sea-chart says, "Saco River bear place at low water."

evidence. The former, who examined the coast minutely two years after Pring (June, 1605), has delineated "Cap des Isles" on his map of 1612, which accompanied the first edition of his voyages. The account he gives of its position is as clear as that of Archer is obscure. Says the Frenchman, in his own way:

"Mettant le cap au su pour nous esloigner afin de mouiller l'ancre, ayant fait environ deux lieux nous apperçumes un cap a la grande terre au su quart de suest de nous ou il pouvoit avoit six lieues; a l'est deux lieues apperçumes trois ou quatre isles assez hautes et a l'ouest un grand cu de sac."

Here are the bearings of Cape Ann, the Isles of Shoals, and of Ipswich Bay defined with precision. Champlain also puts the latitude of Kennebunk River at forty-three degrees twenty-five minutes, which shows Pring could hardly have explored to the eastward of Cape Elizabeth. Smith, in 1614, described Cape Ann and Cape Cod as the two great headlands of New England, giving to the former the name of Tragabigzanda; but Champlain had preceded him, as Gosnold had preceded Champlain. On the whole, Gosnold, Pring, and Champlain agree remarkably in their latitude and in their itinerary.

At Cape Neddock I "put up," or rather was put up—an expression applied alike to man and beast in every public-house in New England—at the old Freeman Tavern, a famous stopping-place in by-gone years, when the mail-coach between Boston and Portland passed this way. Since I knew it the house had been brushed up with a coat of paint on the outside, the tall sign-post was gone, and nothing looked quite natural except the capacious red barn belonging to the hostel. The bar-room, however, was unchanged, and the aroma of old Santa Cruz still lingered there, though the pretty hostess assured me, on the word of a landlady, there was nothing in the house stronger than small beer. It was not so of yore, when all comers appeared to have taken the famous Highgate oath: "Never to drink small beer when you could get ale, unless you liked small beer best."

The evening tempted me to a stroll down to the harbor, to see the wood-coasters go out with the flood. Afterward I walked on the beach. The full moon shone out clear in the heavens, lighting up a radiant aisle incrusted with silver pavement on the still waters, broad at the shore, receding until lost in the deepening mystery of the farther sea. The ground-swell rose and fell with regular heaving, as of Old Ocean asleep. As a breaker wavered and toppled over, a bright gleam ran along its broken arch like the swift flashing of a train. Occasionally some craft crossed the moon's track, where it stood out for a moment with surprising distinctness, to be swallowed up an instant later in the surrounding blackness. Boon Island had unclosed its brilliant eye—its light in the window for the mariner. It had been a perfect day, but the night was enchanting.

WHAT THE SEA CAN DO.

CHAPTER IX.

AGAMENTICUS, THE ANCIENT CITY.

"Land of the forest and the rock,
 Of dark-blue lake and mighty river,
Of mountains reared aloft to mock
 The storm's career, the lightning's shock—
My own green land forever."
WHITTIER.

HO for Agamenticus! It is an old saying, attributed to the Iron Duke, that when a man wants to turn over it is time for him to turn out. As there are six good miles to get over to the mountain, and as many to return, I was early astir. The road is chiefly used by wood teams, and was well beaten to within half a mile of the hills. From thence it dwindled into a green lane, which in turn becomes a footpath bordered by dense undergrowth. Agamenticus is not a high mountain, although so noted a landmark. There are in reality three summits of nearly equal altitude, ranging north-east and south-west, the westernmost being the highest. At the mountain's foot is a scattered hamlet of a few unthrifty-looking cabins, tenanted by wood-cutters, for, notwithstanding the axe has played sad havoc in the neighboring forests, there are still some clumps of tall pines there fit for the king's ships. You obtain your first glimpse of the hills when still two miles distant, the road then crossing the country for the rest of the way, with the mountain looming up before you.

Along shore, and in the country-side, the people call the mount indifferently "Eddymenticus" and "Head o' Menticus." Some, who had lived within a few miles of it since childhood, told me they had never had the curiosity to try the ascent. One man, who lived within half a mile of the base of the western hill, had never been on any of the others. The name is unmistakably of Indian origin. General Gookin, in his "Historical Collections of the Indians in New England," written in 1674, has the following in relation to the tribes inhabiting this region: "The Pawtuckett is the fifth and last great sachemship of Indians. Their country lieth north and north-east from the Massachusetts, whose dominion reacheth so far as the English jurisdiction, or colony of the Massachusetts, now doth extend, and had under them several other small sagamores, as the Pennacooks, Agawomes, Naamkeeks, Pascatawayes, Accomintas, and others."[1]

The climb is only fatiguing; it is not at all difficult. The native forest has disappeared, but a new growth of deciduous trees, with a fair sprinkling of evergreens, is fast replacing it. In some places the slender stems of the birch or pine shoot up, as it were, out of the solid rock. Following the dry bed of a mountain torrent, and turning at every step to wonder and admire, in half an hour I stood on the top. The summit contains an acre or more of bare granite ledge, with tufts of wiry grass and clumps of tangled vines growing among the crevices. Some scattered blocks had been collected at the highest point, and a cairn built. I seated myself on the topmost stone of the monument.

A solitary mountain lifting itself above the surrounding country is always impressive. Agamenticus seems an outpost of the White Hills, left stranded here by the glacier, or upheaved by some tremendous throe. The day was not of the clearest, or, rather, the morning mists still hung in heavy folds about the ocean, making it look from my airy perch as if sky and sea had changed places. Capes and headlands were revealed in a striking and mystical way, as objects dimly seen through a veil. Large ships resembled toys, except that the blue space grasped by the eye was too vast for playthings. Cape Elizabeth northward and Cape Ann in the southern board stretched far out into the sea, as if seeking to draw tribute of all passing ships into the ports between. Here were the Isles of Shoals, lying in a heap together. That luminous, misty belt was Rye Beach. And here was the Piscataqua, and here Portsmouth, Kittery, and Old York, with all the sea-shore villages I had so lately traversed. As the sun rose higher, the murky curtain was rolled away, and the ocean appeared in its brightest azure.

The sea is what you seldom tire of, especially where its nearness to the chief New England marts shows it crowded with sails bearing up for port. Craft of every build, flags of every nation, pass Agamenticus and its three peaks in endless procession—stately ships

"'That court'sy to them, do them reverence
As they fly by on their woven wings.'"

---

[1] "Massachusetts Historical Collections," 1792, vol. i.

Old Ocean parts before the eager prow. You fancy you see the foam roll away and go glancing astern. Here is a bark with the bottom of the Tagus, and another with the sands of the Golden Horn, sticking to the anchor-fluke; and here a smoke on the horizon's rim heralds a swifter messenger from the Old World—some steamship climbing the earth's rotundity; and yet water, they say, will not run up hill! When I looked forth upon this moving scene my lungs began to "crow like chanticleer." I waved my hat, and shouted "a good voyage" to sailors that could not hear me. I had no fear of listeners, for the Old Man of the Mountain tells no tales. To stand on a mountain-top is better, to my mind, than to be up any distance in a balloon. You have, at least, something under you, and can come down when you like. What a fulcrum Agamenticus would have made for the lever of Archimedes!

Landward, the horizon is bounded by the White Hills — the "Crystal Mountains, daunting terrible," of the first explorer.[1] They look shadowy enough at this distance—seventy miles as the crow flies—Mount Washington, grand and grim, its head muffled in a mantle of clouds, overtopping all. The lofty ranges issuing from these resemble a broken wall as they stretch away to the Connecticut, with Moosehillock towering above.

> "To me they seemed the barriers of a world,
> Saying, 'Thus far, no farther!'"

The busy towns of Dover and Great Falls, with the nearer villages of Eliot and Berwick, are grouped about in picturesque confusion, a spire peeping out of a seeming forest, a broad river dwindling to a rivulet.

After feasting for an hour upon this sight, I became more than ever persuaded that, except in that rare condition of the atmosphere when the White Hills are visible far out to sea, Agamenticus must be the first land made out in approaching the coast anywhere within half a degree of the forty-third parallel. Juan Verazzani, perchance, certainly Masters Gosnold and Pring, saw it as plainly as I now saw the ships below me, where they had sailed.

I thought it fitting here, on the top of Agamenticus, with as good a map of the coast spread before me as I ever expect to see, to hold a little chat with the discoverers. If Hendrik Hudson haunts the fastnesses of the Catskills—and a veracious historian asserts that he has been both seen and spoken with—why may not the shade of Captain John Smith be lurking about this headland, where of yore he trafficked, and, for aught I know, clambered as I have done?

Right over against me, though I could not see them, were the Basque provinces, whose people the Romans could not subdue, and whose language, says the old French proverb, the devil himself could not learn. Cape Finisterre was there, with its shoals of sardines and its impotent conclusion of a

---

[1] An Irishman, Darby Field by name.

name, as if it had been the end of the world indeed! Archer says, in his relation of Gosnold's voyage,[1] that the day before they made the land they had sweet smelling of the shore as from the southern cape and Andalusia, in Spain. It was, says Brereton, "a Basque shallop, with mast and sail, an iron grapple and a kettle of copper, came boldly aboard of us." In 1578 there were a hundred sail of Spanish fishermen on the Banks of Newfoundland to fifty English. Spanish Biscay sent twenty or thirty vessels there to kill whales; France sent a hundred and fifty; and Portugal fifty craft of small tonnage to fish for cod. The Indians who boarded Gosnold could name Placentia and Newfoundland, and might have come from thence in their shallop, since they so well knew how to use it. But if Brereton's surmise was right, then some of those daring fellows from the Basse Pyrenees were first at Savage Rock. He says, "It seemed, by some words and signs they made, that some Basques, or of St. John de Luz, have fished or traded in this place, being in the latitude of 43 degrees."

Because there was no sassafras, it is not much we know about Savage Rock. The root of this aromatic tree was worth in England three shillings the pound, or three hundred and thirty-six pounds the ton, when Gosnold found store of it on the Elizabeth Islands; but as he was informed, "before his going forth that a ton of it would cloy England," few of his crew, "and those but easy laborers," were employed in gathering it. "The powder of sassafras," says Archer, "in twelve hours cured one of our company that had taken a great surfeit by eating the bellies of dog-fish, a very delicious meat."

That the medicinal qualities of sassafras were highly esteemed may be inferred from what is said of it in "An English Exposition," printed at Cambridge (England), in 1676, by John Hayes, printer to the University.

"*Sassafras.*—A tree of great vertue, which groweth in Florida, in the West Indies; the rinde herof hath a sweete smell like cinnamon. It comforteth the liver and stomach, and openeth obstructions of the inward parts, being hot and dry in the second degree. The best of the tree is the root, next the boughs, then the body, but the principal goodnesse of all resteth in the rinde."

One Master Robert Meriton, of Gosnold's company, was "the finder of the sassafras in these parts," from which it would appear that the shrub in its wild state was little known to these voyagers.

Coming down from my high antiquarian steed, and from Agamenticus at the same time, I walked back to the tavern by dinner-time, having fully settled in my own mind the oft-repeated question, the touch-stone by which even one's pleasures must be regulated, "Will it pay?" And I say it will pay in solid nuggets of healthful enjoyment, even if no higher aspirations are de-

---

[1] Purchas, vol. iv., 1647.

veloped, in standing where at every instant man and his works diminish, while those of the Creator expand before you.

Douglass remarks that "Aquamenticus Hills were known among our sailors as a noted and useful land-making for vessels that fall in northward of Boston or Massachusetts Bay."

Leaving my comfortable quarters at Cape Neddock, I pursued my walk to Old York the same afternoon, taking the Long Sands in my way. It was farther by the beach than by the road, but as I was in no haste I chose the shore. I noticed that the little harbor I had quitted was so shallow as to be left almost dry by the receding tide, the channel being no more than a rivulet, easily forded within a few rods of the sea. Between this harbor and Wells Bay I had passed several coves where, in a smooth sea and during a westerly wind, small vessels were formerly hauled ashore, and loaded with wood at one tide with ease and safety. York Beach is about a mile across. I did not find it a long one.

It being low tide and a fine afternoon, the beach was for the time being turned into a highway, broader and smoother than any race-course could be, over which all manner of vehicles were being driven, from the old-fashioned gig of the village doctor to the aristocratic landau, fresh from town. The sands are hard and gently shelving, with here and there a fresh-water brooklet trickling through the bulk-head of ballast heaped up at the top by the sea. These little streams, after channeling the beach a certain distance, disappeared in the sand, just as the Platte and Arkansas sink out of sight into the plain.

There was a fresh breeze outside, so that the coasters bowled merrily along with bellying sails before it, or else bent until gunwale under as they hugged it close. The color of the sea had deepened to a steely blue. White caps were flying, and the clouds betokened more wind as they rose and unrolled like cannon-smoke above the horizon, producing effects such as Stanfield liked to transfer to his canvas. Mackerel gulls were wheeling and circling above the breakers with shrill screams. Down at low-water mark the seas came bounding in, driven by the gale, leaping over each other, and beating upon the strand with ceaseless roar.

The beach, I saw, had been badly gullied by the late storm, but the sea, like some shrewish housewife, after exhausting its rage, had set about putting things to rights again. I found shells of the deep-sea mussel, of quahaug and giant sea clam, bleaching there, but did not see the small razor-clam I have picked up on Nahant and other more southerly beaches.

The sea-mussel, as I have read, was in the olden time considered a cure for piles and hemorrhoids, being dried and pulverized for the purpose. William Wood speaks of a scarlet mussel found at Piscataqua, that, on being pricked with a pin, gave out a purple juice, dying linen so that no washing would wear it out. "We mark our handkerchiefs and shirts with it," says this writer.[1] The large mussel is very toothsome. Like the oyster and clam, it was dried for winter use by the Indians.

The giant or hen clam-shell, found in every buttery within fifty miles of the coast, was the Indian's garden hoe. After a storm many clams would be cast up on the beaches, which the natives, taking out of the shells, carried home in baskets. A large shell will hold a plentiful draught of water, and is unequaled for a milk-skimmer. Only a part of the fish is used for food, as there is a general belief that a portion is poisonous, like the head of a lobster. Mourt's relation of the landing of the pilgrims at Cape Cod says they found "great mussels, and very fat and full of sea-pearle, but we could not eat them, for they made us all sicke that did eat, as well saylers as passengers." As they are only found on the beach after an easterly storm, they become well filled with sand, and require thorough cleansing before cooking, while those taken from the water near the shore are better, because free from sand. The common clam is not eaten along shore during the summer, except at the hotels and boarding-houses, not being considered wholesome by the resident population in any month that has not the letter R. The same idea is current with respect to the oyster. In either case the summer is inferior to the winter fish, and as Charles XII. once said of the army bread, "It is not good, but may be eaten."

There was but little sea-weed or kelp thrown up, though above high-water mark I noticed large stacks of it ready to be hauled away, containing as many varieties as commonly grow among the rocks hereaway. But there were innumerable cockles and periwinkles lately come ashore, and emitting no pleasant odor. The natives used both these shells to manufacture their wampum, or wampumpeag, the delicate inner wreath of the periwinkle being preferred. Now and then I picked up a sea-chestnut, or "whore's egg," as they are called by the fishermen. But the sand roller, or circle, is the curiosity of the beach as a specimen of ocean handicraft. I passed many of them scattered about, though a perfect one is rarely found, except on shallow bars beyond low-water mark. Looking down over the side of a boat, I have seen more than I was able to count readily, but they are too fragile to bear the buffeting of the surf. In appearance they are like a section taken off the top of a jug where the cork is put in, and as neatly rounded as if turned off a potter's lathe. Naturalists call them the nest of the cockle.

Going down the sands as far as the sea would allow, I remarked that the nearest breakers were discolored with the rubbish of shredded sea-weed, and

---

[1] In England there is a cockle called the purple, from the coloring matter it contains, believed to be one of the sources from which the celebrated Tyrian dye was obtained. The discovery is attributed in mythical story to a dog. The Tyrian Hercules was one day walking with his sweetheart by the shore, followed by her lap-dog, when the animal seized a shell just cast upon the beach. Its lips were stained with the beautiful purple flowing from the shell, and its mistress, charmed with the color, demanded a dress dyed with it of her lover.

by the particles of sand they held in solution. As I walked on, countless sand-fleas skipped out of my path, as I have seen grasshoppers in a stubble-field out West. The sandpipers ran eagerly about in pursuit, giving little plaintive squeaks, and leaving their tiny tracks impressed upon the wet sand. Little sprites they seemed as they chased the refluent wave for their food, sometimes overtaken and borne off their feet by the glancing surf. I remember having seen a flock of hens scratching among the sea-moss for these very beach-fleas in one of the coves I passed.

Old Neptune's garden contains as wonderful plants as any above high-water mark, though the latter do well with less watering. I have thought the botany of the sea worth studying, and, as it is sometimes inconvenient to pluck a plant or a flower when you want it, the beach is the place for specimens. Some years ago delicate sea-mosses were in request. They were kept in albums, pressed like autumn leaves, or displayed in frames on the walls at home. It was a pretty conceit, and employed many leisure fingers at the sea-side, but appears to have been discarded of late.

One day, during a storm, I went down to the beach, to find it encumbered with "devils' apron" and kelp, whitening where it lay. I picked up a plant having a long stalk, slender and hollow, of more than ten feet in length, resembling a gutta-percha tube. The root was firmly clasped around five deep-sea mussels, while the other end terminated in broad, plaited leaves. It had been torn from its bed in some sea-cranny, to be combined with terrestrial vegetation; but to the mussels it was equal whether they died of thirst or of the grip of the talon-like root of the kelp. There were tons upon tons of weed and moss, which the farmers were pitching with forks higher up the beach, out of reach of the sea, the kelp, as it was being tossed about, quivering as if there were life in it. I found the largest mass of sponge I have ever seen on shore—as big as a man's head—and was at a loss how to describe it, until I thought of the mops used on shipboard, and made of rope-yarns; for this body of sponge was composed of slender branches of six to twelve inches in length, each branching again, coral-like, into three or four offshoots. The pores were alive with sand-fleas, who showed great partiality for it.

What at first seems paradoxical is, that with the wind blowing directly on shore, the kelp will not land, but is kept just beyond the surf by the under-tow; it requires an inshore wind to bring it in. One who has walked on the beach weaves of its sea-weed a garland:

> " From Bermuda's reefs, from edges
>   Of sunken ledges,
> On some far-off, bright Azore;
> From Bahama and the dashing,
>   Silver-flashing
> Surges of San Salvador:
>   *   *   *   *   *

> Ever drifting, drifting, drifting
> On the shifting
> Currents of the restless main."

I had before walked round the cape one way, and now, passing it from a contrary direction, had fairly doubled it. After leaving York Beach I pushed on for Old York, finding little to arrest my steps, until at night-fall I arrived at the harbor, after a twenty-mile tramp, with an appetite that augured ill for mine host.

It was not my first visit to Old York, but I found the place strangely altered from its usual quiet and dullness. The summer, as Charles Lamb says, had set in with its usual severity, and I saw fishers in varnished boots, boatmen in tight-fitting trowsers, and enough young Americans in navy blue to man a fleet by-and-by. Parasols fluttered about the fields, and silks swept the wet floor of the beach. I had examined with a critical eye as I walked the impressions of dainty boots in the sand, keeping step with others of more masculine shape, and marked where the pace had slackened or quickened, and where the larger pair had diverged for a moment to pick up a stone or a pebble, or perchance in hurried self-communing for a question of mighty import. Sometimes the foot-prints diverged not to meet again, and I saw the gentleman had walked off with rapid strides in the opposite direction. For hours on the beach I had watched these human tracks, almost as devious as the bird's, until I fancied I should know their makers. Not unfrequently I espied a monogram, traced with a stick or the point of a parasol, the lesser initials lovingly twined about the greater. Faith! I came to regard the beach itself as a larger sort of tablet graven with hieroglyphics, easy to decipher if you have the key.

The hotel[1] appeared deserted, but it was only a seclusion of calculation. After supper the guests set about what I may call their usual avocations. Not a few "paired off," as they say at Washington, for a walk on the beach, springing down the path with elastic step and voices full of joyous mirth. One or two maidens I had seen rowing on the river showed blistered hands to condoling cavaliers. Young matrons, carefully shawled by their husbands, sauntered off for a quiet evening ramble, or mingled in the frolic of the juveniles going on in the parlor. The dowagers all sought a particular side of the house, where, out of ear-shot of the piano, they solaced themselves with the evening newspapers, damp from presses sixty miles away. A few choice spirits gathered in the smoking-room, where they maintained a frigid reserve toward all new-comers, their conversation coming out between puffs, as void of warmth as the vapor that rises from ice. On the beach, and alone with inanimate objects, I had company enough and to spare; here, with a hundred

---

[1] Situated on Stage Neck, a rocky peninsula connected with the main shore by a narrow isthmus, on which is a beach. There was formerly a fort on the north-east point of the Neck.

of my own species, it was positively dreary. I took a turn on the piazza, and soon retired to my cell; for in these large caravansaries man loses his individuality and becomes a number.

Old York, be it remembered, is one of those places toward which the history of a country or a section converges. Thus, when you are in Maine all roads, historically speaking, lead to York. Long before there was any settlement it had become well known from its mountain and its position near the mouth of the Piscataqua. Its first name was Agamenticus. Says Smith, "Accominticus and Pascataquack are two convenient harbors for small barks, and a good country within their craggy cliffs:" this in 1614. He could not have sounded, perhaps not even ascended, the Piscataqua.

Christopher Levett, in his voyage, begun in 1623 and ended in 1624, says of this situation: "About two leagues farther to the east (of Piscataqua) is another great river, called Aquamenticus. There, I think, a good plantation may be settled; for there is a good harbor for ships, good ground, and much already cleared, fit for planting of corn and other fruits, having heretofore been planted by the savages, who are all dead. There is good timber, and likely to be good fishing; but as yet there hath been no trial made that I can hear of." Levett was one of the Council of New England, joined with Robert Gorges, Francis West, and Governor Bradford. From his account, Agamenticus appears to have been a permanent habitation of the Indians, who had been stricken by the same plague that desolated what was afterward New Plymouth.

The first English settlement was begun probably in 1624, but not earlier than 1623, on both sides of York River, by Francis Norton, who had raised himself at home from the rank of a common soldier to be a lieutenant-colonel in the army. This was Norton's project, and he had the address to persuade Sir Ferdinando Gorges to unite in the undertaking. Artificers to build mills, cattle, and other necessaries for establishing the plantation, were sent over. A patent passed to Ferdinando Gorges, Norton, and others, of twelve thousand acres on the east to Norton, and twelve thousand on the west of Agamenticus River to Gorges. Captain William Gorges was sent out by his uncle to represent that interest.[1]

The plantation at Agamenticus was incorporated into a borough in 1641, and subsequently, in 1642, into a city, under the name of Gorgeana. Thomas Gorges, cousin of Sir F. Gorges, and father of Ferdinando, was the first mayor. It was also made a free port. Though Gorgeana was probably the first incorporated city in America, it was in reality no more than an inconsiderable sea-coast village, with a few houses in some of the best places for fishing and navigation. Its territory was, however, ample, embracing twenty-one square miles. There was little order or morality among the people, and in one ac-

---

[1] Sir F. Gorges's own relation.

count it is said "they had as many shares in a woman as a fishing boat.[1] All the earlier authorities I have seen agree in giving Gorgeana an indifferent character, and I was not surprised to find a couplet still extant, expressive of the local estimate in which its villages were once held.

"Cape Neddock and the Nubble,
Old York and the d—l."

Governor Winthrop, of Massachusetts, made, in 1643, the following entry in his "Journal:" "Those of Sir Ferdinando Gorge his province beyond Piscat were not admitted to the confederation,[2] because they ran a different course from us, both in their ministry and civil administration; for they had lately made Accomenticus (a poor village) a corporation, and had made a taylor their mayor, and had entertained one Mr. Hull, an excommunicated person, and very contentious, for their minister." A Boston man, and a magistrate, stood thus early on his dignity.

Sir F. Gorges makes his appearance in that brilliant and eventful period when Elizabeth ruled in England, Henry IV. in France, and Philip II. in Spain. He is said to have revealed the conspiracy of Devereux, earl of Essex, to Sir Walter Raleigh, after having himself been privy to it.[3] This act, a bar-sinister in the biography of Gorges, sullies his escutcheon at the outset. History must nevertheless award that he was the most zealous, the most indefatigable, and the most influential of those who freely gave their talents and their wealth to the cause of American colonization. Gorges deserves to be called the father of New England. For more than forty years—extending through the reigns of James I. and of Charles I., the Commonwealth, and the Restoration—he pursued his favorite idea with a constancy that seems almost marvelous when the troublous times in which he lived are passed in review. In a letter to Buckingham on the affairs of Spain, Gorges says he was sometimes thought worthy to be consulted by Elizabeth.

Sir Ferdinando commanded at Plymouth, England, with his nephew William for his lieutenant, when Captain Weymouth returned to that port from New England. On board Weymouth's ship were five natives, of whom three were seized by Gorges. They were detained by him until they were able to give an account of the topography, resources, and peoples of their far-off country. From this circumstance dates Gorges's active participation in New England affairs.

He was interested in Lord John Popham's ineffectual attempt. Finding

---

[1] About 1647 the settlements at Agamenticus were made a town by the name of York, probably from English York.

[2] Confederation of the colonies for mutual protection.

[3] Elizabeth died while Martin Pring was preparing to sail for America; and Essex and Raleigh both went to the block.

the disasters of that expedition, at home and abroad, had so disheartened his associates that he could no longer reckon on their assistance, he dispatched Richard Vines and others at his own charge, about 1617, to the same coast the Popham colonists had branded, on their return, as too cold to be inhabited by Englishmen. Vines established himself at or near the mouth of the Saco. Between the years 1617 and 1620, Gorges sent Captains Hobson, Rocroft, and Dermer to New England, but their voyages were barren of results. In 1620 Gorges and others obtained from the king a separate patent, with similar privileges, exemption from custom, subsidies, etc., such as had formerly been granted the Virginia Company.

By this patent the adventurers to what had heretofore been known as the "Northern Colony in Virginia," and "The Second Colony in Virginia," obtained an enlargement of territory, so as to include all between the fortieth and forty-eighth parallels, and extending westward to the South Sea or Pacific Ocean. This was the Great Charter of New England, out of which were made the subsequent grants within its territory. The incorporators were styled "The Council of Plymouth."[1]

The Virginia Company, whose rights were invaded, attempted to annul the Plymouth Company's patent. Defeated before the Lords, they brought the subject the next year, 1621, before Parliament, as a monopoly and a grievance of the Commonwealth. Gorges was cited to appear at the bar of the House, and made his defense, Sir Edward Coke[2] being then Speaker. After hearing the arguments of Gorges and his lawyers on three several occasions, the House, in presenting the grievances of the kingdom to the throne, placed "Sir Ferd. Gorges's patent for sole fishing in New England" at the head of the catalogue; but Parliament, having made itself obnoxious to James, was dissolved, and some of its members committed to the Tower. The patent was saved for a time.

Before this affair of the Parliament the Pilgrims had made their ever-famous landing in New England. Finding themselves, contrary to their first intention, located within the New England patent, they applied through their solicitor in England to Gorges for a grant, and in 1623 they obtained it. This was the first patent of Plymouth Colony; in 1629 they had another, made to William Bradford and his associates.

In 1623 the frequent complaints to the Council of Plymouth of the abuses and disorders committed by fishermen and other intruders within their patent, determined them to send out an officer to represent their authority on the spot. Robert Gorges, son of Sir Ferdinando, was fixed upon, and became for a short time invested with the powers of a civil magistrate. According to Belknap, he was styled "Lieutenant-general of New England." George Popham was the first to exercise a local authority within her limits.

---

[1] The insertion of the lengthy title in full appears unnecessary. [2] The celebrated commentator.

The Great Charter of New England was surrendered to the crown in April, 1635, and the territory embraced within it was parceled out among the patentees, Gorges receiving for his share a tract of sixty miles in extent, from the Merrimac to the Kennebec, reaching into the country one hundred and twenty miles. This tract was called the province of Maine. It was divided by Gorges into eight bailiwicks or counties, and these again into sixteen hundreds, after the manner of the Chiltern Hundreds, a fief of the English crown. The Hundreds were subdivided into parishes and tithings.

It would fatigue the reader to enter into the details of the government established by Gorges within what he calls "my province of Maine." It was exceedingly cumbrous, and the few inhabitants were in as great danger of being governed too much as later communities have often been. An annual rental was laid on the lands, and no sale or transfer could be made without consent of the Council. This distinction, as against the neighboring colony of Massachusetts, where all were freeholders, was fatal. The crown, in confirming the grant to Gorges, vested him with privileges and powers similar to those of the lords palatine of the ancient city of Durham. Under this authority the plantation at Agamenticus was raised to the dignity of a city, and a *quasi* ecclesiastical government founded in New England.

Belknap says further that there was no provision for public institutions. Schools were unknown, and they had no minister till, in pity of their deplorable state, two went thither from Boston on a voluntary mission.

There are yet some interesting objects to be seen in York, though few of the old houses are remaining at the harbor. These few will, however, repay a visit. Prominent among her antiquities is the meeting-house of the first parish. An inscription in the foundation records as follows:

YORK MEETING-HOUSE.

"Founded A. D. 1747.
The Revd. Mr. Moody, Pas."

The church is placed on a grassy knoll, with the parsonage behind it. Its exterior is plain. If such a distinction may be made, it belongs to the third order of New England churches, succeeding to the square tunnel-roofed edifice, as that had succeeded the original barn-like house of worship. Entering the porch, I saw two biers leaning against the staircase of the bell-tower, and noticed that the bell-ringer or his assistants had indulged a passion for scribbling on the walls, though not, as might be inferred, from Scripture texts. The interior is as severe as the exterior. Besides its rows of straight-backed pews, it was furnished at one end with a mahogany pulpit, communion-table, and sofa covered with black hair-cloth. Hanging in a frame against the pulpit are fac-similes of letters from the church at York to that of Rowley, bearing the date of 1673. The tower is an ingenious piece of joinery that reminded me of Hingham church.

Shubael Dummer, the first minister of this parish, was killed in 1692, at the sacking of the place by the Indians. He was shot down in the act of mounting his horse at his own door, a short distance toward the harbor. Mather, in his "Magnalia," indulges in a strain of eulogy toward this gentleman that we should now call *hifalutin*. Dummer's successor was Samuel Moody, an eccentric but useful minister, still spoken of as "Parson Moody." He was Sir William Pepperell's chaplain in the Louisburg expedition, and noted for the length and fervor of his prayers.

After the capitulation Sir William gave a dinner to the superior officers of the army and fleet. Knowing the prolixity of his chaplain, he was embarrassed by the thought that the parson's long-winded grace might weary the admiral and others of his guests. In this dilemma, he was astonished to see the parson advance and address the throne of grace in these words: "O Lord, we have so many things to thank thee for, that time will be infinitely too short for it; we must therefore leave it for the work of eternity."

A second parish was formed in York about 1730. Rev. Joseph Moody, the son of Samuel, was ordained its first pastor, in 1732. At the death of his wife he fell into a settled melancholy, and constantly appeared with his face covered with a handkerchief. From this circumstance he was called "Handkerchief Moody." He was possessed of wit, and some dreary anecdotes are related of him. Mr. Hawthorne has made the incident of the handkerchief the frame-work of one of his gloomiest tales. I know of no authority other than tradition to support the statement made in a note accompanying the tale, that "in early life he (Moody) had accidentally killed a beloved friend."[1]

It is only a short distance from the church to the old burying-ground, and I was soon busy among the inscriptions, though I did not find them as interesting as I had anticipated. The place seemed wholly uncared for. The grass grew rank and tangled, making the examination difficult, and at every step I sank to the knee in some hollow. The yard is ridged with graves, and must have received the dust of many generations, going back even to those who acknowledged the first James for their dread lord and sovereign.

---

[1] We are warranted in the belief that the first services held in this plantation were those of the Church of England. The first, or borough, charter mentions the church chapel. Robert Gorges, in 1623, brought over an Episcopal chaplain, William Morrell, and with him also came, as is supposed, Rev. William Blackstone, the first inhabitant of Boston.

As usual, the older stones, when I had found them, were too much defaced to be deciphered, and I remarked that the slate grave-stone of Parson Moody preserved but few of its original lines. Beside him lay the remains of his wife. The following is his own epitaph:

> "Here lies the body of the
> REV'D SAMUEL MOODY, A.M.
> The zealous, faithful, and successful pastor of the
> First Church of Christ in York.
> Was born in Newbury, January 4th, 1675.
> Graduated 1697. Came hither May 16th,
> Died here November 13th, 1747.
> For his farther character read the 2d Corinthians,
> 3d chapter and first six verses."

In the corner of the ground next the main street is the monumental tablet of Hon. David Sewall. A plain slab of slate at his side marks the resting-place of his wife. On this are enumerated some of the public offices held by her husband, and the two monuments might furnish the reader with materials for a biography.

Mr. Adams, in his "Diary," notes meeting his "old friend and classmate" at York, when he was going the circuit in 1770. Sewall had just returned from a party of pleasure at Agamenticus, and the talk was of erecting a beacon upon it. At this time he was looked upon as a Tory, but became a zealous Whig before hostilities with the mother country began.

JAIL AT OLD YORK.

In 1640, says Lechford, nothing was read nor any funeral sermon made at a burial, but at the tolling of the bell all the neighborhood came together, and after bearing the dead solemnly to the grave, stood by until it was closed. The ministers were commonly, but not always, present. In these few and simple rites our fathers testified

> "The emptiness of human pride,
> The nothingness of man."

On a rising ground opposite the town-house is the old jail of York. I have deemed it worthy a passing notice. It is a quaint old structure, and has held many culprits in former times, when York was the seat of justice for the county, though it would not keep your modern burglar an hour. It is perched, like a bird of ill omen, on a rocky ledge, where all might see it in passing over the high-road. Thus, in the early day, the traveler on entering the county town encountered, first, the stocks and whipping-post; continuing his route, he in due time came to the gallows, at the town's end. The exterior of the jail is not especially repulsive, now that it is no longer a prison; but the inside is a relic of barbarism —just such a place as I have often imagined the miserable witchcraft prisoners might have been confined in. The back wall is of stone. The doors are six inches of solid oak, studded with heavy nails; the gratings secured with the blades of mill saws, having the jagged teeth upward; the sills, locks, and bolts are ponderous, and unlike any thing the present century has produced.

PILLORY.

The dungeons, of which there are two, admitted no ray of light except when the doors were opened; and these doors were of two thicknesses of oaken planks banded between with plates of iron, and on the outside with rusty blades of mill saws, as were also the crevices through which the jailer passed bread and water to the wretched criminals. The gloom and squalor of these *cachots* oppressed the spirits of even the casual visitor, free to come and go at pleasure; what must it, then, have been to the wretches condemned to inhabit them? Above these dungeons were two or three cells, secured by precautions similar to those below; while other apartments were reserved for the jailer's use. The house was inhabited, and children were playing about the floor. I fancied their merry laughter issuing from solitary dungeons where nothing but groans and imprecations had once been heard. Perchance there have been Hester Prynnes and Cassandra Southwicks immured within these walls.

STOCKS.

As I never feel quite at home within a prison, I made haste to get into the open air again. I noticed, what is common in the country, that an underpinning of boards had been placed around the foundation at the distance of a foot, the space within being filled with earth. "That," said a whimsical fellow, "is to keep the coarsest of the cold out."

They have a jail at Alfred hardly more secure than the old. I was told of a prisoner who coolly informed the jailer one morning that if he did not supply him with better victuals he would not stay another day. He was as good as his word, making his escape soon after. Wagner, the Isles of Shoals murderer, also broke jail at Alfred, but was recaptured.

I should have liked to devote a few moments to the old court-house, its eminent and distinguished judges and barristers of the provincial courts, not forgetting its crier and constables. I should, I repeat, like to open the court, and marshal the jurors, witnesses, and even the idlers to their places in the king's name. I should like to hear some of those now antiquated, but then oft-quoted, scraps of law from the statutes of Richard II. or Sixth Edward. But it is all past. Bag-wigs, black gowns, and silver buckles are no more seen, except in family portraits of the time, and the learned counsel of to-day no more address each other as "Brother A———" or "B———." There do remain, however, in front of the old court-house four beautifully spreading elms, planted by David Sewall in 1773. To look at them now, it is not easy to fancy they could be grasped with the hand when the battle of Lexington was fought.

I passed on by the old tavern-stand where Woodbridge, in 1770, swung his sign of "Billy Pitt," and underneath, the words "Entertainment for the Sons of Liberty"—a hint to Tories to take their custom elsewhere. I should have enjoyed a pipe with that landlord, as John Adams says he did.

In Old York they have a precinct known as Scotland, said to have been first settled by some of the prisoners of Cromwell's victory at Dunbar, and shipped over seas to be sold as apprentices for a term of years. I was bound thither to see the garrison houses that had withstood the onset of the Indians in King William's war.

It is four miles from the village to Scotland parish, the road passing through broad acres of cleared land or ancient orchards, with now and then a by-way of green turf leading to a farm-house on the river, or a gleam of the stream itself winding through the meadows as you mount the rocky hills in your route.

Cider Hill is a classic locality, which the traveler must pass through. It is well named, I should say, the trees, though old, being laden with apples, fit only for the cider-press. I was struck with the age of the orchards, and indeed with the evidences on all sides of the long occupancy of the land. In going up and down the traveled roads of York the impression is everywhere gained of an old settled country.

By the side of the road is the withered trunk of an ancient tree, said to have been brought from England in a tub more than two hundred years ago. Nothing remains but the hollow shell, which still puts forth a few green shoots. Next to the rocks, it is the oldest object on the road. At a little distance it has sent up an offshoot, now a tree bearing fruit, and has thus risen again, as it were, from its own ashes. This tree deserves to be remembered along with the Stuyvesant and Endicott pear-trees. There is, or was, another apple-tree of equal age with this in Bristol.

"You have a good many apples this year," I said to a farmer.

"Oh, a marster sight on 'em, sir, marster sight; but they don't fetch nothing."

"Is the cool summer injuring your corn?" I pursued.

"Snouted it, sir; snouted it."

OLD GARRISON-HOUSE.

The Junkins's garrison is the first reached. It is on the brow of a high hill overlooking the river meadows, where, if good watch were kept, a foe could hardly have approached unseen. It can not survive much longer. It is dilapidated inside and out to a degree that every blast searches it through and through. The doors stood ajar; the floors were littered with corn-fodder, and a hen was brooding in a corner of the best room. Having served as dwelling and castle, it embodies the economy of the one with the security of the other. The chimney is of itself a tower; the floor timbers of the upper story project on all sides, so as to allow it to overhang the lower. This was a type of building imported from England by the early settlers, common enough in their day, and of which specimens are still extant in such of our older towns as Boston, Salem, and Marblehead. Its form admitted, however, of a good defense. The walls are of hewn timber about six inches thick, and bullet-proof. On the north-east, and where the timbers were ten inches thick, they have rotted away under their long exposure to the weather. I observed a loop-hole or two that had not been closed up, and that the roof frame was of oak, with the bark adhering to it.[1]

In one room was an old hand-loom; in another a spinning-wheel lay overturned; and in the fire-place the iron crane, blackened with soot, was still fixed as it might have been when the garrison was beset in '92. Between

---

[1] Hutchinson says: "In every frontier settlement there were more or less garrison houses, some with a flankart at two opposite angles, others at each corner of the house; some houses surrounded with palisadoes; others, which were smaller, built with square timber, one piece laid horizontally upon another, and loop-holes at every side of the house; and besides these, generally in any more considerable plantation there was one garrison house capable of containing soldiers sent for the defense of the plantation, and the families near, whose houses were not so fortified. It was thought justifiable and necessary, whatever the general rule of law might be, to erect such forts, castles, or bulwarks as these upon a man's own ground, without commission or special license therefor."—"History of Massachusetts," vol. ii., p. 67.

the house and the road is the Junkins's family burying-ground. The house attracts many curious visitors, though it lacks its ancient warlike accessories, its lookouts, palisades, and flankarts.

A few rods farther on, in descending the hill, is the M'Intire garrison. It is on the opposite side of the Berwick road from the house through which I have just hurried the reader; and, except that a newer addition has been joined to the garrison part, does not materially differ from it. Mr. M'Intire, now the owner of both houses, showed me an opening in the floor of the projection through which, according to the family tradition, boiling water was poured upon the heads of any who might try to force an entrance.

It has been supposed that these two garrisons were erected as early as 1640 or 1650. As no motive existed for building such houses at that time, the tradition is not entitled to credit. Few of the Indians were possessed of fire-arms, as the sale to them was strictly prohibited in the English colonies. The digging up of the hatchet by the eastern Indians, in 1676, during Philip's war, probably first led to the building of fortified houses in all the sea-coast towns. During the attack of 1692, the four garrisons in York saved the lives of those they sheltered, while fifty of the defenseless inhabitants were killed outright, and one hundred and fifty were led prisoners to Canada.

It is not my purpose to pursue farther the history of ancient Agamenticus. The state of the settlement five years after its destruction by the Indians appears in a memorial to the French minister, prepared in order to show the feasibility of a thorough wiping out of the English settlements from Boston to Pemaquid:

"From Wells Bay to York is a distance of five leagues. There is a fort within a river. All the houses having been destroyed five years ago by the Indians, the English have re-assembled at this place, in order to cultivate their lands. The fort is worthless, and may have a garrison of forty men."

As a memorial of the dark days when settler fought with savage, the Junkins's garrison-house appeals for protection in its decrepit old age. Its frame is still strong. A few boards and a kindly hand should not be wanting to stay its ruin. I left it as for nearly two hundred years it has stood,

"On its windy site uplifting gabled roof and palisade,
And rough walls of unhewn timber with the moonlight overlaid."

PORTSMOUTH, NEW HAMPSHIRE, FROM KITTERY BRIDGE.

CHAPTER X.

AT KITTERY POINT, MAINE.

"We have no title-deeds to house or lands;
Owners and occupants of earlier dates
From graves forgotten stretch their dusty hands,
And hold in mortmain still their old estates."

LONGFELLOW.

LOUIS XV. said to Bouret, the financier, "You are indeed a singular person not to have seen Marly! Call upon me there, and I will show it to you."

Our way lies from Old York to Kittery Point.[1] To get from the one to the other you must pass the bridge over York River, built in 1761. It inaugurated in New England the then novel method of laying the bridge superstructure on a frame-work formed of wooden piles driven into the bed of the river. The inventor was Major Samuel Sewall, of York, whose bridge was the model of those subsequently built over the Charles, Mystic, and Merrimac.

Kittery Point is separated from Kittery Foreside by Spruce Creek. It is also divided from Gerrish's Island, the outermost land of the eastern shore

---

[1] The name of Kittery Point is from a little hamlet in England. It is the first and oldest town in the State, having been settled in 1623. Gorgeana, settled 1624, was a city corporate, and not a town. Kittery first included North and South Berwick and Eliot.

of the Piscataqua, by Chauncy's Creek. It is important at Kittery Point to get used to the names of Cutts, Gerrish, Sparhawk, Pepperell, Waldron, Chauncy, and Champernowne. They recur with remarkable frequency.

If coming from Portsmouth, the visitor will first traverse the village, with its quaint little church, built in 1714, its secluded cemetery, and fine old elms. They say the frame of the meeting-house was hewn somewhere about Dover, and floated down the stream. There are few older churches in New England, or that embody more of its ancient homeliness, material and spiritual. Since I was there it has been removed about sixty feet northward, and now fronts the south, entirely changing the appearance of that locality.

NAVY-YARD, KITTERY, MAINE.

Formerly, in leaving the church door, you were confronted by a sombre old mansion, having, in despite of some relics of a former splendor, an unmistakable air of neglect and decay. The massive entrance door hung by a single fastening, the fluted pilasters on either side were rotting away, window panes were shattered, chimney tops in ruins, the fences prostrate. It was nothing but a wreck ashore. This was the house built by Lady Pepperell, after the death of Sir William. Report said it was haunted; indeed I found it so, and by a living phantom.

Repeated and long-continued knocking was at length answered by a tremulous effort from within to open the door, which required the help of my companion and myself to effect. I shall never forget the figure that appeared to us:

"We stood and gazed;
Gazed on her sunburned face with silent awe,
Her tattered mantle and her hood of straw."

Poor Sally Cutts, a harmless maniac, was the sole inhabitant of the old house; she and it were fallen into hopeless ruin together. Her appearance was weird and witch-like, and betokened squalid poverty. An old calash almost concealed her features from observation, except when she raised her head and glanced at us in a scared, furtive sort of way. Yet beneath this wreck, and what touched us keenly to see, was the instinct of a lady of gentle breeding that seemed the last and only link between her and the world. With the air and manner of the drawing-room of fifty years ago she led the way from room to room.

We tracked with our feet the snow that had drifted in underneath the hall door. The floors were bare, and echoed to our tread. Fragments of the original paper, representing ancient ruins, had peeled off the walls, and vandal hands had wrenched away the pictured tiles from the fire-places. The upper rooms were but a repetition of the disorder and misery below stairs.

Our hostess, after conducting us to her own apartment, relapsed into imbecility, and seemed little conscious of our presence. Some antiquated furniture, doubtless family heir-looms, a small stove, and a bed, constituted all her worldly goods. As she crooned over a scanty fire of two or three wet sticks, muttering to herself, and striving to warm her withered hands, I thought I beheld in her the impersonation of Want and Despair.

Her family was one of the most distinguished of New England, but a strain of insanity developed itself in her branch of the genealogical tree. Of three brothers—John, Richard, and Robert Cutt—who, in 1641, emigrated from Wales, the first became president of the Province of New Hampshire, the second settled on the Isles of Shoals, and the third at Kittery, where he became noted as a builder of ships.

This house had come into the possession of Captain Joseph Cutts[1] about the beginning of the century. He was a large ship-owner, and a successful and wealthy merchant. Ruined by Mr. Jefferson's embargo and by the war of 1812, he lost his reason, and now lies in the village church-yard. Two of his sons inherited their father's blighting misfortune: one fell by his own hand in Lady Pepperell's bed-chamber. Sally, the last survivor, has joined them within a twelvemonth.

---

[1] Captain Joseph Cutts was born in 1764, and died on his birthday anniversary, aged ninety-seven. He married a granddaughter of President Chauncy, of Harvard College. Sarah Chauncy, known to us as "Sally Cutts," was removed during her last illness to the house of her cousin, where she was kindly cared for. When near her end she became more rational, and was sensible of the attentions of her friends. She died June 30th, 1874. Her brother Charles was hopelessly insane forty-four years, and often so violent as to make it necessary to chain him. Joseph, the other brother, entered the navy: overtaken by his malady, he was sent home. Under these repeated misfortunes, added to the care of her father and brothers, Sally's reason also gave way. The town allowed a small sum for the board of her father and brothers, and her friends provided wood and clothing. Her house even was sold to satisfy a Government claim for duties, owed by her father. It has now been renovated, and is occupied by Oliver Cutts, Esquire.

Poor Sally Cutts! She rose to take leave of us with the same ceremonious politeness which had marked her reception. Her slight and shrunken figure was long in my memory, her crazy buffet, and broken, antiquated chairs, to which she clung as the most precious of earthly possessions. It was one of her hallucinations to be always expecting the arrival of a messenger from Washington with full reparation of the broken fortunes of her family. Some charitable souls cared for her necessities, but such was the poor creature's pride that artifice was necessary to effect their purpose. Flitting through the deserted halls of the gloomy old mansion—dreading the stranger's approach, the gossip of the neighborhood, the jibes of village urchins—Sally remained its mistress until summoned to a better and kindlier mansion. I said the house was haunted, and I believe it.

A short walk beyond the cemetery brings you up with Fort M'Clary,[1] its block-house, loop-holed for musketry, its derricks, and general disarray. Not

BLOCK-HOUSE AND FORT, KITTERY POINT.

many would have remembered the gallantry of Major Andrew M'Clary at Bunker Hill, but for this monument to his memory. The site has been fortified from an early day by garrison-house, stockade, or earth-work. It should have retained its earliest name of Fort Pepperell. John Stark's giant comrade might have been elsewhere commemorated.

It is said no village is so humble but that a great man may be born in it. Sir William Pepperell was the great man of Kittery Point. He was what is now called a self-made man, raising himself from the ranks through native genius backed by strength of will. Smollett calls him a Piscataquay trader,

---

[1] My appearance within Fort M'Clary caused a panic in the garrison. A few unimportant questions concerning the old works were answered only after a hurried consultation between the sergeant in charge and the head workman. The Government was then meditating war with Spain, and I had reason to believe I was looked upon as a Spanish emissary.

with little or no education, and utterly unacquainted with military operations. Though contemptuous, the description is literally true.

Sir William's father is first noticed in the annals of the Isles of Shoals. The mansion now seen near the Pepperell Hotel was built partly by him and in part by his more eminent son. The building was once much more extensive than it now appears, having been, about twenty years ago, shortened ten feet at either end. Until the death of the elder Pepperell, in 1734, the house was occupied by his own and his son's families. The lawn in front reached to the sea, and an avenue, a quarter of a mile in length, bordered by fine old trees, led to the house of Colonel Sparhawk, east of the village church. With its homely exterior the mansion of the Pepperells represents one of the greatest fortunes of colonial New England. It used to be said Sir William might ride to the Saco without going off his own possessions.[1]

SIR WILLIAM PEPPERELL'S HOUSE, KITTERY POINT.

There is hanging in the large hall of the Essex Institute, at Salem, a two-thirds length of Sir William Pepperell, painted in 1751 by Smibert, when the baronet was in London. It represents him in scarlet coat, waistcoat, and breeches, a smooth-shaven face and powdered periwig: the waistcoat, richly

---

[1] The house was also occupied at one time as a tenement by fishermen. It exhibits no marks, either inside or out, of the wealth and social consequence of its old proprietor.

gold-embroidered, as was then the fashion, was worn long, descending almost to the knee, and formed the most conspicuous article of dress. In one hand Sir William grasps a truncheon, and in the background the painter has depicted the siege of Louisburg.[1]

Smollett accredits Auchmuty, judge-advocate of the Court of Admiralty of New England, with the plan of the conquest of Louisburg, which he pronounces the most important achievement of the war. Mr. Hartwell said in the House of Commons that the colonists took Louisburg from the French single-handed, without any European assistance—"as mettled an enterprise as any in our history," he calls it. The honor of the Louisburg expedition has also been claimed for James Gibson, of Boston, and Colonel William Vaughan, of Damariscotta. But the central figures appear to have been Governor William Shirley and Sir William Pepperell.[2]

SIR WILLIAM PEPPERELL.

The year of Louisburg was an eventful one, for all Europe was in arms. The petty German princes were striving for the imperial crown vacant by the death of the emperor, Charles VII. France supports the pretensions of the Grand Duke of Tuscany with a powerful army under her illustrious profligate, Maurice de Saxe; Austria invades Bohemia; the old Brummbär swoops down upon Saxony, and his cannon growl under the walls of Dresden; the Rhenish frontiers, Silesia, Hungary, and Italy, are all ablaze.

England must have a hand in the fighting. Lord Chesterfield's mission to the Hague, the Quadruple Alliance at Warsaw, are succeeded by the stunning blow of Fontenoy. The allied army recoiled, and drew itself together under the walls of Brussels. The Duke of Cumberland was defeated by a sick man.[3]

It was at this moment of defeat that the news of the fall of Louisburg reached the allies. The Dunkirk of America had capitulated to a "trader of

---

[1] Mr. Longfellow has, at Cambridge, a painting by Copley, representing two children in a park. These children are William Pepperell and his sister, Elizabeth Royall Pepperell, children of the last baronet.

[2] Both were made colonels in the regular British establishment; their regiments, numbered the Fiftieth and Fifty-first respectively, were afterward disbanded.

[3] Marshal Saxe, unable to mount his horse, was carried along his lines in a litter.

Piscataquay." It put new life into the beaten army, and was celebrated with great rejoicings in its camps.[1]

Among those who served with distinction under Pepperell were Richard Gridley, who afterward placed the redoubt on Bunker Hill; Wooster, who fell at Norwalk; Thornton, a signer of our Magna Charta; and Nixon and Whiting, of the Continental army. It was sought to give the expedition something of the character of a crusade. George Whitefield furnished for its banner the motto,

"*Nil Desperandum, Christo Duce.*"

A little more family history is necessary to give the reader the *entrée* of the four old houses at Kittery Point.

The elder Sir William, by his will, made the son of his daughter Elizabeth and Colonel Sparhawk his residuary legatee, requiring him, at the same time, to relinquish the name of Sparhawk for that of Pepperell. The baronetcy, extinct with the death of Sir William, was revived by the king for the benefit of his grandson, a royalist of 1775, who went to England at the outbreak of hostilities. The large family estates were confiscated by the patriots.

The tomb of the Pepperells, built in 1734, is seen between the road and the Pepperell Hotel.[2] When it was repaired some years ago, at the instance of Harriet Hirst Sparhawk, the remains were found lying in a promiscuous heap at the bottom, the wooden shelves at the sides having given way, precipitating the coffins upon the floor of the vault. The planks first used to close the entrance had yielded to the pressure of the feet of cattle grazing in the common field, filling the tomb with rubbish. About thirty skulls were found in various stages of decomposition. A crypt was built in a corner, and the scattered relics carefully placed within.[3]

Dr. Eliot, the pioneer among American biographers, says Dr. Belknap often mentioned to him that his desire to preserve the letters of Sir William Pepperell led to the founding of the Massachusetts Historical Society. This object does not seem to have been wholly accomplished, as it is well known the baronet's papers have become widely scattered.[4]

Not far from the mansion of the Pepperells is the very ancient dwelling of Bray, whose daughter, Margery, became Lady Pepperell. It was long be-

---

[1] The year 1745 was also signalized by the death of Pope in June, and of the old Duchess of Marlborough in October, who died at eighty-five, immensely rich, and "very little regretted either by her own family or the world in general."—SMOLLETT.

[2] Mr. E. F. Safford, the proprietor, exercises watch and ward over this and other relics of the Pepperells with a care worthy of imitation all along the coast.

[3] Mr. Sabine notes in his "Loyalists" that the tomb, when entered some years ago, contained little else than bones strewed in confusion about its muddy bottom; among them, of course, the remains of the victor of Louisburg, deposited in it at his decease in 1759.

[4] The best biography of Sir William Pepperell is that by Dr. Usher Parsons.

fore the old shipwright made up his mind to consent to match his daughter so unequally. This house is considered to be two hundred and twenty-five years old, and is still habitable. Down at the water-side are seen the rotting timbers of the wharf where the Pepperells, father and son, conducted an extensive trade.

A little east of the hotel and the pleasant manse below the river makes a noble sweep, inclosing a favorite anchorage for storm or wind bound craft.

KITTERY POINT, MAINE.

Not unfrequently a hundred may be seen quietly riding out a north-easter at snug moorings. At such times this harbor and Gloucester are havens of refuge for all coasters caught along shore. The sight of the fleet getting under way with the return of fine weather is worth going to see.

When at Kittery Point the visitor may indulge in a variety of agreeable excursions by land or water; the means are always at hand for boating and driving, and there is no lack of pleasant rambles. I first went to Gerrish's

Island on a wild November day, and in a north-east snow-storm. I never enjoyed myself better.

In the first place, this island is one of the headlands of history as well as of the Piscataqua. It was conveyed as early as 1636, by Sir F. Gorges, to Arthur Champernowne, a gentleman of Devon.[1] The island was to take the name of Dartington, from the manor of the Champernownes.[2] In this indenture Brave Boat Harbor is mentioned. The Province of Maine was then sometimes called New Somersetshire.

There is something in this endeavor of all the promoters of New England to graft upon her soil the time-honored names of the Old, to plant with her civilization something to keep her in loving remembrance, that appeals to our protection. These names are historical and significant. They link us to the high renown of our mother isle. No political separation can disinherit us. I think the tie is like the mystery of the electric wave that passes under the sea, unseen yet acknowledged of all, active though invisible.

The island, with many contiguous acres, became the property of Francis, son of Arthur Champernowne, and nephew of Sir F. Gorges, who is buried there, his grave distinguished by a heap of stones. Tradition said he forbade in his last testament any stone to be raised to his memory.[3] In the hands of subsequent proprietors the island was called Cutts's, Fryer's, and Gerrish's Island. It is usually spoken of as two islands, being nearly though not quite subdivided by Chauncy's Creek. The venerable Cutts's farm-house on the shore of the island is two hundred and thirty years old by family account.

All the islands lying northward of the ship channel belong to Kittery.[4] Many of them have interesting associations. Trefethren's, the largest, projects far out into the river, and is garnished with the earth-works of old Fort Sullivan, from which shot might be pitched with ease on the decks of invading ships. Fernald's, now Navy Yard Island, became in 1806 the property of the United States, by purchase of Captain William Dennett, for the sum of five thousand five hundred dollars.

Badger's, anciently Langdon's Island, is a reminiscence of one of the no-

---

[1] The relation in Purchas, vol. iv., p. 1935, of the voyage of Robert, earl of Essex, to the Azores in 1597, has a supplementary or larger relation, written by Sir Arthur Gorges, knight, a captain in the earl's fleet of the ship *Wast-Spite*. There is mention of a Captain Arthur Champernowne, who appears to have sailed with the admiral in this expedition.

[2] The father of James Anthony Froude, the historian, was rector of Dartington; the historian was born there.

[3] He is fully recognized as a personage of distinction in the beginnings of Kittery. Charles W. Tuttle gives him a touch of royal blood. I failed to find such a provision in his own draft of his will.

[4] They are, in descending the river, Badger's, Navy Yard, Trefethren's, or Seavey's, Clark's, and Gerrish's Island.

GOVERNOR LANGDON'S MANSION, PORTSMOUTH.

blest of the old Romans of the revolutionary time. His still elegant mansion adorns one of the handsomest streets in Portsmouth.[1] Washington, when there, considered it the finest private house in the town.

Langdon was six feet tall, with a very noble presence. Duke Rochefoucauld Liancourt mentions that he had followed the sea first as mate, then as master of a ship. He ultimately became an eminent merchant and ship-builder. A devoted patriot, he was one of the leaders in the first act of aggression committed by the Portsmouth Whigs against the crown. As the words of a man of action and a model legislator in time of invasion by a foreign enemy, his well-known speech to the New Hampshire Assembly is worth the quoting. This is his manner of cutting short useless debate: "Gentlemen, you may talk as much as you please; but I know the enemy is upon our frontiers, and I am going to take my pistols and mount my horse, and go and fight in the ranks of my fellow-citizens." And he did it.

Yet a little more about Langdon. Chastellux relates that when on his way to Gates's camp he was followed by a favorite slave. The negro, who beheld the energy with which his master pressed on, without other repose than could be snatched in the woods, said to him, at last, "Master, you undergo great hardships, but you go to fight for liberty. I also should suffer patiently if I had the same liberty to defend." "Then you shall have it," said John Langdon; "from this moment I give you your freedom."

Continental Agent Langdon became the superintendent of war ships ordered here by Congress. He presided at the building of the *Ranger*, the *Alliance*, and the *America*, the last a seventy-four gun ship, generously given to Louis XVI. for one of his lost on our coast. Paul Jones was much here; a brave braggart, quarreling with Langdon and Congress, writing quires of

---

[1] In Pleasant, near Court Street.

memorials, little esteemed among his peers, though a lion on his own quarter-deck.

Though Langdon was a member elect of the Old Congress, as his State stipulated that only two of the delegates were to go to Philadelphia, his does not appear among the names signed to the Declaration. Matthew Thornton, elected after Langdon, was allowed to sign when he took his seat in November. Langdon became an opponent of the measures and administration of Washington, joining with Jefferson, Pierce Butler, and a few others in organizing the Republican party of that day. They had five votes in the Senate. In the House was Andrew Jackson, a member from Tennessee, who attracted little attention, though he voted with the small coterie of the Upper House, including Langdon, Butler, and Colonel Burr.

Jacob Sheaffe, who in his day carried on a more extensive business than any other merchant in Portsmouth, became the successor of Langdon as Government agent. It is said he purchased the island where the Navy Yard now is. One of the six frigates ordered under Washington's administration was begun here. We had voted to build these vessels to punish the Algerine corsairs; we then countermanded them; afterward a treaty was made with these pirates by which they were to have a new frigate of thirty-two guns, which was laid down at Portsmouth.

The family name of Sheaffe was once much more familiar in New England than now. It was of Peggy Sheaffe, a celebrated Boston beauty, that Baron Steuben perpetrated the following *mot:* When introduced to her at the house of Mrs. Livingstone, mother of the chancellor, the baron exclaimed, in his broken English, "I have been cautioned from my youth against *Mischief*, but had no idea her charms were so irresistible."

Kittery is mentioned by Josselyn as the most populous of all the plantations in the Province of Maine. It engrosses the left bank of the Piscataqua from the great bridge at Portsmouth to the sea. The booming of guns at the Navy Yard often announces the presence of some dignitary, yet none, I fancy, more distinguished than Washington have set foot in Kittery. I regret he has not much to say of it, but more of the fishing-party of which he was, at the moment, a member.

"Having lines," he says, "we proceeded to the fishing banks without the harbor, and fished for cod, but it not being a proper time of tide, we caught but two." The impregnable character of the President for truthfulness forbids the presumption that want of skill had aught to do with his ill-luck.

It would be matter for general regret if the selectmen of Kittery should again, as long ago happened, be presented by a grand jury for not taking care that their children were taught their catechism, and educated according to law. The number of steeples and school-houses seen by the way indicates, in this respect, a healthy public opinion. Kittery church-yard contains many mute appeals to linger and glean its dead secrets. Mrs. Thaxter sweetly sings as she felt the story of one of these mildewed stones :

> "Crushing the scarlet strawberries in the grass,
> I kneel to read the slanting stone. Alas!
> How sharp a sorrow speaks! A hundred years
> And more have vanished, with their smiles and tears,
> Since here was laid, upon an April day,
> Sweet Mary Chauncey in the grave away,
> A hundred years since here her lover stood
> Beside her grave."   *   *   *

I found both banks of the Piscataqua charming. The hotels at Newcastle, Kittery, Old York, etc., are of the smaller class, adapted to the comfortable entertainment of families; and as they are removed from the intrusion of that disagreeable constituent of city life known over-seas as the "swell mob," real comfort is attainable. They are not faultless, but one may always confidently reckon on a good bed, a polite, accommodating host, and well-provided table.

WHALE'S-BACK LIGHT.

CHAPTER XI.

THE ISLES OF SHOALS.

"O warning lights, burn bright and clear,
 Hither the storm comes! Leagues away
It moans and thunders low and drear—
 Burn 'til the break of day!"
                                    CELIA THAXTER.

ON the 15th of July, 1605, as the sun was declining in the west, a little bark of fifteen tons, manned by Frenchmen, was standing along the coast of New England, in quest of a situation to begin a settlement. The principal personage on board was Pierre du Guast, Sieur de Monts, a noble gentleman, and an officer of the household of Henry IV. His commission of lieutenant-general bore date at Fontainebleau in the year 1603. He was em-

THE NEW ENGLAND COAST.

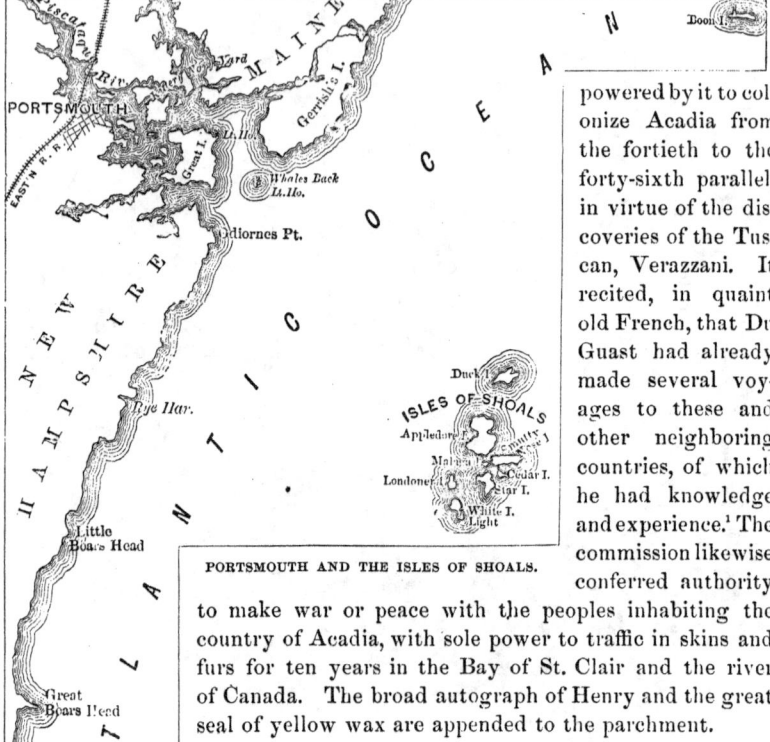

PORTSMOUTH AND THE ISLES OF SHOALS.

powered by it to colonize Acadia from the fortieth to the forty-sixth parallel, in virtue of the discoveries of the Tuscan, Verazzani. It recited, in quaint old French, that Du Guast had already made several voyages to these and other neighboring countries, of which he had knowledge and experience.[1] The commission likewise conferred authority to make war or peace with the peoples inhabiting the country of Acadia, with sole power to traffic in skins and furs for ten years in the Bay of St. Clair and the river of Canada. The broad autograph of Henry and the great seal of yellow wax are appended to the parchment.

On board the bark, besides the leader of the expedition, were a few gentlemen adventurers and twenty sailors. The name of De Monts's pilot was Champdoré.[2] The geographer of the expedition was Samuel Champlain. Accompanying De Monts, as guides and interpreters, were two natives, Panounias and his wife.

Since the 15th of June De Monts had been minutely examining the New England coast from St. Croix, where he had wintered, to near the forty-third parallel, in the hope of finding "a place more suitable for habitation and of a milder temperature" than the inhospitable region he had first pitched upon. The greater part of De Monts's colony remained at the Isle of St. Croix.

After leaving the mouth of the Saco, and looking in at the entrance of

---

[1] "Et en la connoissance et experience que vous avez de la qualité, condition et situation dudit païs de la Cadie, pour les diverses navigations, voyages, et frequentations que vous avez faits en ces terres et autres proches et circonvoisines."

[2] Williamson erroneously calls Champlain the pilot.

Kennebunk River, De Monts, still keeping as close in as was prudent with the land, which Champlain describes as flat and sandy (*platte et sabloneuse*), found himself on that July afternoon in presence of three striking landmarks.[1] Cape Ann bore south, a quarter east, six leagues distant. To the west was a deep bay into which, the savages afterward told him, a river emptied; and in the offing they perceived three or four islands of fair elevation. These last, historians agree, were the Isles of Shoals.

Notwithstanding the isles are not identified on either of Champlain's maps (1612 and 1632), it is no longer doubtful that De Monts made them out nine years before Smith saw them, though the latter has first given them on a map a locality and a name. But I take Pring to have been the first to mention them, when, two years before De Monts, he sighted a multitude of small islands in about forty-three degrees, and anchored under the shelter of the greatest.[2] Gosnold must have seen the isles, but thought them hardly worth entering in his log. Prince Charles, afterward Charles I., graciously confirmed the name Smith had, in 1614, given the isles. Yet he has little or no title to be considered their discoverer, and has left no evidence that he ever landed upon them. The French, Smith relates, had two ships forty leagues to the westward (of Monhegan) that had made great trade while he was on the coast. Beyond all these, the Basque shallop seen in these waters by Gosnold remains a nut for historians to crack.

De Poutrincourt's expedition of 1606 into Massachusetts Bay was the sequel to that of 1605. De Monts, a heretic, through the jealousy of rivals and Jesuit intrigue, was soon deprived of the privileges with which he had been endowed by his fickle monarch. In this his experience was not unlike that of Gorges and the Council of Plymouth. De Monts was really the head of a commercial company, organized by Chauvin, governor of Dieppe.[3] The detail of his voyage along the New England coast in 1605 is the first intelligible record to be found. Shall we not, at last, have to do the tardy justice of acknowledging him the chief and guiding spirit of the expedition, now universally referred to as Champlain's? The latter has become the prominent figure, while Du Guast is not even mentioned in some of our so-called school histories.

Christopher Levett is the first Englishman to give an account of the isles worthy of the name. Its brevity may be advantageously contrasted with later descriptions, though the natural features remain, in many respects, the same. He says, writing seven years after Captain Smith:

---

[1] A little book I have seen translates rather freely in making Champlain say "and on the west Ipswitch Bay." See p. 122 for Champlain's exact language.

[2] Pring came to the main-land in forty-three and a half degrees—his farthest point westward on this voyage—and worked along the coast to the south-west. I know of no other islands between Cape Ann and his land-fall answering his description.

[3] De Monts sailed from Havre de Grace March 7th, 1604.

"The first place I set my foot upon in New England was the Isle of Shoals, being islands in the sea about two leagues from the main.

"Upon these islands I neither could see one good timber-tree nor so much good ground as to make a garden.

"The place is found to be a good fishing-place for six ships, but more can not well be there, for want of convenient stage room, as this year's experience hath proved."

The year 1623 is the earliest date I have seen of the islands being occupied as a fishing station. Monhegan was earlier known, and more frequented by English vessels for this purpose. A word or two about the fishery of those days.

Cabot notices the cod under the name of "bacalo;" Jean Alfonse speaks of the "bacaillos;" Captain Uring calls it "baccalew;" the Indian name was "tamwock." Smith says the fish on our coast were much better than those taken at Newfoundland, which he styles "poor John," a nickname ever since current up the Mediterranean. One of his ships, in 1614, loaded with dry fish for Spain, where the cargo brought "forty ryalls," or five dollars, the quintal. Fifteen or eighteen men, by his relation, took with the hook alone sixty thousand fish in a month.

Charlevoix believed this fish could turn itself inside out, like a pocket. He says they found bits of iron and glass, and even pieces of broken pots, in the stomachs of fish caught on the Banks of Newfoundland; and adds that some people believed they could digest them. Josselyn says the fishermen used to tan their sails and nets with hemlock-bark to preserve them.

Allusion has been made to the number of fishermen frequenting the Grand Banks in 1578. Without the evidence few would be willing to believe the fishery had attained such proportions at that early day, on a coast we have been accustomed to regard as almost unknown. It certainly goes very far toward dispelling illusions respecting the knowledge that was had of our own shores by those adventurous "toilers of the sea."

In Captain Richard Whitbourne's relation of his voyages and observations in Newfoundland (Purchas, vol. iv., p. 1882), he says:

"More than four hundred sail of fishing ships were annually sent to the Grand Banks by the French and Portuguese, making two voyages a year, fishing winter and summer.

"In the year 1615, when I was at Newfoundland," he adds, "there were then on that coast of your Majestie's subjects two hundred and fiftie saile of ships, great and small. The burthens and tonnage of them all, one with another, so neere as I could take notice, allowing every ship to be at least three-score tun (for as some of them contained lesse, so many of them held more), amounting to more than 15,000 tunnes. Now, for every three-score tun burthen, according to the usual manning of ships in those voyages, agreeing with the note I then tooke, there are to be set doune twentie men and boyes; by which computation in these two hundred and fiftie saile there were no lesse than five thousand persons."

De Poutrincourt, writing to Paris in 1618 from Port Royal, estimates the fishery to be then worth a "*million d'or*" annually to France. He declares he would not exchange Canada for Peru if it were once seriously settled; and foreshadows the designs of the English on New France as soon as they should have made themselves strong in Virginia. By a royal edict of 1669 the French fishermen of New France were allowed to land their fish in all the ports of the mother country, except Havre, free of duty.

The advantages possessed by the Isles of Shoals were deep water, with a reasonably secure haven for ships, free from molestation by the savages, while the crews were engaged in taking and curing their fish. To this ought to be added their nearness to the best fishing grounds. All along shore the islands were, as a rule, earlier frequented than the main-land. Levett says (and he thought it a fatal objection) the ships that fished at Cape Ann in 1623 had to send their boats *twenty miles* to take their fish, and the masters were in great fear of not making their voyages. "I fear there hath been too fair a gloss set upon Cape Ann," writes Levett.

La Hontan, writing from Quebec in 1683, says of the cod-fishery on the Banks of Newfoundland: "You can scarce imagine what quantities of cod-fish were catch'd there by our seamen in the space of a quarter of an hour; for though we had thirty-two fathom water, yet the hook was no sooner at the bottom than the fish was catch'd; so that they had nothing to do but to throw in and take up without interruption. But, after all, such is the misfortune of this fishery that it does not succeed but upon certain banks, which are commonly past over without stopping. However, as we were plentifully entertain'd at the cost of these fishes, so such of 'em as continued in the sea made sufficient reprisals on the corpse of a captain and of several soldiers who died of the scurvy, and were thrown overboard three or four days after."

It is worthy of note that the *Trial*, the first vessel built in Boston, took a lading of fish to Bilboa, in 1643, that were sold to good profit. From thence she took freight for Malaga, and brought home wine, oil, fruit, iron, etc. She was then sent to trade with La Tour and Acadia. The *Trial* was of about a hundred and sixty tons burden.[1] In the year 1700 there were two hundred New England vessels loaded in Acadia with fish. The cargoes were taken to Boston, and there distributed to different parts of the world.

After the isles became permanently inhabited the fishery continued prosperous, and by 1730 three or four vessels were annually loaded for Bilboa. Before the Revolution seven or eight schooners hailed from the islands, but from this period the fishery dates its decay. In 1800 only shore-fishing was

---

[1] Winthrop's "Journal."

pursued, which employed thirteen whale-boats similar to those now in use, and the best of all boats in a sea.

Besides the fish itself, the liver of the cod, as is well known, is saved for the oil it contains. Hake sounds are of greater value than the fish, being extensively used in the manufacture of isinglass. The efficacy of the cod's liver was early known. "Their livers and sounds eaten," says an old writer, "is a good medicine for to restore them that have melted their grease."

The interest with which the obscure lives of these islanders and the cluster of inhospitable rocks on which they dwell are invested is remarkable enough. It may be in a measure owing to the irregular intercourse formerly held with the main-land, and to the consequently limited knowledge of them. And it is heightened in no small degree by the mystery of a residence in the midst of the sea, where all ties with the adjacent continent would seem to be dissevered. But if the open Polar Sea be a fact and not a myth, the continents are themselves but larger islands with more expanded horizons.

I happened one day to be in Portsmouth. *Entre nous*, if you want to be esteemed there you must say "Porchmouth," as even the lettered of that ilk do. The morning air had been freshened and sweetened by copious showers; little pools stood in the streets, and every

SHAG AND MINGO ROCKS, DUCK ISLAND.

blade of grass was tipped with a crystal rain-drop. Old Probabilities had foretold clearing weather. Every thing seemed propitious, except that it continued to rain "pitchforks," with the tines downward, and that the wind was steadily working round to the eastward. As the struggle between foul and fair seemed at length to incline to the latter, I went down to the wharf to find the packet for the Shoals had already unmoored, and was standing across the river. Unloosing a dory that was lying conveniently near, I boarded the *Marie* as she came about, thus putting myself *en rapport* with the Shoals by means of this little floating bridge, or island, as you may please to have it.

It being the first day of summer, the passengers were so few as to be easily taken in at a glance. They were chiefly workmen employed on the great hotel at Star Island, or, as they chose to style themselves, convicts going into servitude on a desert rock: so cheaply did they hold the attractions of the isles. Perhaps one or two of the passengers had no more business at the islands than myself.

It is not easy to have a more delightful sail than down the Piscataqua, or to find a more beautiful stream when its banks are clothed in green. It has often been described, and may again be, without fear of exhausting its capabilities. The movement of shipping to and fro; the shifting of objects as you glide by them, together with the historic renown with which its shores are incrusted, fill the eye while exciting the imagination. A few miles above Portsmouth the river expands into a broad basin, which receives the volume of tide, and then pours it into the sea between narrow banks.

We gained the narrows of the river with Pierce's Island on the right and Seavey's on the left, each crowned with grass-grown batteries thrown up in the Revolution to defend the pass. Here the stream is not a good rifle-shot in breadth, and moves with increased velocity within the contracted space, the swirl and eddying of the current resembling the boiling of a huge caldron. Its surface is ringed with miniature whirlpools, and at flood-tide the mid-channel seems lifted above the level of the river, as I have seen the mighty volume of the Missouri during its annual rise. It is not strange the place should have received the anathemas of mariners from immemorial time, or boast a name so unconventional withal as Pull-and-be-d—d Point.

Clearing the narrows, we left behind us the city steeples, the big ship-houses, lazy war ships, and tall chimneys on Kittery side. The wind being light, the skipper got up a stay-sail from the fore-hatch. As it was bent to the halyards, a bottle labeled "ginger ale," but smelling uncommonly like schnapps, rolled out of its folds. We were now slowly forging past Newcastle, or Great Island. The sun came out gloriously, lighting up the spire of the little church at Kittery Point and the masts of vessels lying at anchor in the roads.

Glancing astern, I remarked four wherries coming down at a great pace with the ebb. They kept directly abreast of each other, as if moved by a single oarsman, while the rowers talked and laughed as they might have done on the pavement ashore. I could see by the crates piled in the stern of each boat that they were lobstermen, going outside to look after their traps. As they went by they seemed so many huge water-spiders skimming the surface of the river.

Fort Constitution, with its dismantled walls and frowning port-holes, is now passed, and Whale's Back, with twin light-houses, shows its ledges above water. We open the mouth of the river with Odiorne's Point on the starboard and Gerrish's Island on the port bow, the swell of ocean lifting our little bark, and making her courtesy to the great deep.

The islands had appeared in view when we were off Newcastle, the hotel on Star Island, where it loomed like some gray sea-fortress, being the most conspicuous object. As we ran off the shore, the "cape of the main-land" and the "*cul-de-sac*" of Champlain came out, and fixed themselves where he had seen them. One by one the islands emerged from the dark mass that involved the whole, and became individuals. The wind dying away off Duck Island, I was fain to take an oar in the whale-boat towing astern. We rowed along under Appledore into the little haven between that island and Star, with no sound but the dip of our oars to break the stillness, and beached our boat as the evening shadows were deepening over a stormy sea.

There had been a striking sunset. Great banks of clouds were massed above the western horizon, showing rifts of molten gold where the sun burst through, which the sea, in its turn, reflected. As I looked over toward White Island, the lamps were lighted in the tower, turning their rays hither and thither over a blackness that recalled Poe's sensuous imagery of lamp-light gloating over purple velvet. The weather-wise predicted a north-easter, and I went to bed with the old sea "moaning all round about the island."

I passed my first night, and a rude one it was, on Star Island. When I arose in the morning and looked out I fancied myself at sea, as indeed I was. The ocean was on every side, the plash of the waters being the last sound heard at night and the first on waking. I saw the sun rise over Smutty Nose through the same storm-clouds in which it had set at evening. I am an early riser, but even before I was astir a wherry crossed the little harbor my window overlooked.

The islands lie in two States, and are seven in number. Duck Island, the most dangerous of the group; Appledore, sometimes called Hog Island; Smutty Nose, or Haley's, and Cedar, belong to Maine; Star, White, and Londoner's, or Lounging Island, are in New Hampshire. Appledore is the largest, and Cedar the smallest. In one instance I have known Star called Staten Island, though it was formerly better known as Gosport, the name of its fishing village, whose records go back to 1731. Counting Malaga, a little islet attached to Smutty Nose by a breakwater, and there are eight islands in the cluster. They are nine miles south-east of the entrance of the Piscataqua and twenty-one north-east from Newburyport Light. The harbor, originally formed by Appledore, Star, and Haley's Islands, was made more secure by a sea-wall, now much out of repair, from Smutty Nose to Cedar Island. The roadstead is open to the south-west, and is indifferently sheltered at best. Between Cedar and Star is a narrow passage used by small craft, through which the tide runs as in a sluice-way. The group is environed with several dangerous sunken rocks. Square Rock is to the westward of Londoner's; White Island Ledge south-west of that isle; Anderson's Ledge is south-east of Star Island; and Cedar Island Ledge south of Smutty Nose.[1]

---

[1] Star Island is three-fourths of a mile long and half a mile wide; White Island is also three-fourths of a mile in length. It is a mile and three quarters from Star Island. Londoner's is five-eighths of a mile in length, and one-eighth of a mile from Star Island. Duck Island is seven-

The name of the Isles of Shoals is first mentioned by Christopher Levett, in his narrative of 1623. The mariners of his day must have known of the description and the map of Smith, but they seem to have little affected the name he gave the islands. It would not be unreasonable to infer that the group was known by its present name even before it was seen by Smith, and that his claims were of little weight with those matter-of-fact fishermen. Some writers have made a difficulty of the meaning of the name, attributing it to the shoals, or schools, of fish seen there as everywhere along the coast at certain seasons of the year. East of the islands, toward the open sea, there is laid down on old charts of the Province an extensive shoal called Jeffrey's Ledge, named perhaps for one of the first inhabitants of the isles, and extending in the direction of the coast from the latitude of Cape Porpoise to the southward of the Shoals. On either side of this shallow, which is not of great breadth, are soundings in seventy fathoms, while on the ledge the lead brings up coarse sand in thirty, thirty-five, and forty-five fathoms. The presence of this reef tends to strengthen the theory that these islands, as well as the remarkable system of Casco Bay, once formed part of the main-land. The earlier navigators who approached the coast, cautiously feeling their way with the lead, soon after passing over this shoal came in sight of the islands, which, it is believed, served to mark its presence. Jeffrey's Ledge has been a fishing-ground of much resort for the islanders since its first discovery.[1]

To whatever cause science may attribute the origin of the isles, I was struck, at first sight, with their resemblance to the bald peaks of a submerged volcano thrust upward out of the waters, the little harbor being its crater. The remarkable fissures traversing the crust of the several members of the group, in some cases nearly parallel with the shores, strengthens the impression. In winter, or during violent storms, the savagery of these rocks, exposed to the full fury of the Atlantic, and surrounded by an almost perpetual surf, is overwhelming. You can with difficulty believe the island on which you stand is not reeling beneath your feet.

After exploring the shore and seeing with his own eyes the deep gashes in its mailed garment, the basins hollowed out of granite and flint, and the utter wantonness in which the sea has pitched about the fragments it has wrested from the solid rock, the futility of words in which to express this confusion comes home to the spectator. Mr. Hawthorne's idea greatly re-

---

eighths of a mile in length, and three miles from Star Island meeting-house. Appledore is seven-eighths of a mile from Star, and a mile in length. Haley's, or Smutty Nose, is a mile in length, and five-eighths of a mile from Star Island meeting-house. Cedar Island is one-third of a mile long, and three-eighths of a mile distant from the meeting-house. The whole group contains something in excess of six hundred acres.

[1] The term "Shoals of Isles" seems rather far-fetched, and scarcely significant to English sailors familiar with the hundred and sixty islands of the Hebrides. I can find no instance of these isles having been so called.

sembles the Indian legend of the origin of Nantucket. "As much as any thing else," he says, "it seems as if some of the massive materials of the world remained superfluous after the Creator had finished, and were carelessly thrown down here, where the millionth part of them emerge from the sea, and in the course of thousands of years have become partially bestrewn with a little soil."

The old navigators stigmatized Labrador as the place to which Cain was banished, no vegetation being produced among the rocks but thorns and moss. What a subject White Island would make for a painting of the Deluge!

A Finlander with whom I parleyed told me his country could show ruder places than these isles, and that the winters there were longer and colder. Parson Tucke used to say the winters at the Shoals were "a thin under-waistcoat, warmer" than on the opposite main-land. Doubtless the Orkneys or Hebrides equal these islands in desolateness and wildness of aspect, but they could scarce surpass them.

The islands are so alike in their natural features that a general description of one will apply to the rest of the cluster; and hence the first explored, so far as its crags, sea-caverns, and galleries are in question, is apt to make the strongest impression. But after closer acquaintance each of the seven is found to possess attractions, peculiarities even, of its own. They grow upon you and charm away your better judgment, until you find sermons, or what is better, in stones, and good health everywhere. The change comes over you imperceptibly, and you are metamorphosed for the time into a full-fledged "Shoaler," ready to climb a precipice or handle an oar with any native—I was about to say of the soil—but that would be quite too strong a figure for the Shoals.

The little church on Star Island is usually first visited. When I was before here, it was a strikingly picturesque object, surmounting the islands, and visible in clear weather twenty miles at sea. It is now dwarfed by the hotel, and is perhaps even no longer a sea-mark for the fishermen. Such quaint little turrets have I seen in old Dutch prints. The massive walls are of rough granite from the abundance of the isle. Its roof and tower are of wood, and, being here, what else could it have but a fish for its weather-vane? The bell was used, while I was there, to call the workmen to their daily labor; but its tones were always mournful, and vibrated with strange dissonance across the sea.

The whitewash the interior walls had received was plentifully bespattered upon the wooden benches. In a deeply recessed window one of the tiny sea-birds that frequent the islands was beating the panes with its wings. I gave the little fellow his liberty, but he did not stay for thanks. The church is not more than ten paces in length by six in breadth, yet was sufficient, no doubt, for all the church-goers of the seven islands. Its foundations are upon a rock, and it is altogether a queer thing in an odd place.

After the desertion of Appledore, a meeting-house was erected on Star Island, twenty-eight by forty-eight feet, with a bell. Mr. Moody, of Salisbury, Massachusetts, was, in 1706, called to be the first minister there. In 1730 he was succeeded by Rev. John Tucke.

Mather relates many anecdotes of Rev. John Brock, one of the early ministers at the islands, in illustration of the efficacy of prayer. The child of one Arnold, he says, lay sick, so nearly dead that those present believed it had really expired; "but Mr. Brock, perceiving some life in it, goes to prayer, and in his prayer uses this expression, 'Lord, wilt thou not grant some sign before we leave prayer that thou wilt spare and heal this child? We can not leave thee 'til we have it.' The child sneez'd immediately."

MEETING-HOUSE, STAR ISLAND.[1]

Going round the corner of the church, I came upon a coast pilot, peering through his glass for the smoke of a steamer, cable-freighted, that had been momentarily expected from Halifax for a week. His trim little boat lay in the harbor below us at her moorings. It was, he said, a favorite station from which to intercept inward-bound vessels. The pilot told me, with a quiet chuckle, of a coaster, manned by raw Irish hands, that had attempted in broad day to run into the harbor over the breakwater from Haley's to Cedar island. They did not get in, he said; but it being a full tide and smooth sea, the mole only knocked off the cut-water of their craft.

Behind the meeting-house is the little school-house, in as dire confusion

---

[1] Built in 1800, through the efforts of Dudley A. Tyng, of Newburyport, Massachusetts. Dedicated in November by Rev. Jedediah Morse, father of S. F. B. Morse. A school was for a time kept in it.

when I saw it as any bad boy could have wished. The windows were shattered, chairs and benches overturned, and a section of rusty stove-pipe hung from the ceiling, while the fragment of a wall map, pressed into service as a window-curtain, was being scanned through the dingy glass by an urchin with a turn for geography.

East of the church is a row of cottages, the remnant of the fishing village, serving to show what it was like before modern innovations had swept the moiety of ancient Gosport from the face of the island. Each had a bird-house on the peak of its gable. There was the semblance of regularity in the arrangement of these cottages, the school-house leading the van; but they were nearly or quite all unpainted, these homely abodes of a rude people.

On looking around, you perceived walled inclosures, some of them containing a little earth patched with green grass, but all thickly studded with boulders. Is it possible, you ask, that such a waste should ever be the cause of heart-burnings, or know the name of bond, mortgage, or warranty? Little did these impoverished islanders dream the day would come when their sterile rocks would be eagerly sought after by the fortunate possessors of abundance.

Star Island formerly afforded pasturage for a few sheep and cows. There is a record of a woman who died at Gosport in 1795, aged ninety. She kept two cows, fed in winter on hay cut by her in summer with a knife among the rocks. The cows were taken from her by the British in 1775, and killed, to the great grief of old Mrs. Pusley. Formerly there was more vegetation here, but at odd times the poor people have gathered and burned for fuel fully half the turf on the island. It is written in the book of records that the soil of the islands is gradually decreasing, and that a time would come when the dead must be buried in the sea or on the main-land.

From the year 1775 until 1820, the few inhabitants who remained on the islands lived in a deplorable condition of ignorance and vice. Some of them had lost their ages for want of a record. Each family was a law to itself. The town organization was abandoned. Even the marriage relation was forgotten, and the restraints and usages of civilized life set at naught. Some of the more debased, about 1790, pulled down and burned the old meeting-house, which had been a prominent landmark for seamen; but, says the record, "the special judgments of Heaven seem to have followed this piece of wickedness to those immediately concerned in it." The parsonage-house might have fared as ill, had it not been floated away to Old York by Mr. Tucke's son-in-law.

Rev. Jedediah Morse has entered in the record two marriages solemnized by him during the time he was on the islands, with the following remarks: "The two couples above mentioned had been published eight or ten years ago (but not married), and cohabited together since, and had each a number of children. —— had been formerly married to another woman; she had left him, and cohabited with her uncle, by whom she has a number of children. No regular divorce had been obtained. Considering the peculiar deranged state of the people on these islands, and the ignorance of the parties, it was thought expedient, in order as far as possible to prevent future sin, to marry them."[1]

THE GRAVES, WITH CAPTAIN JOHN SMITH'S MONUMENT, STAR ISLAND.

It is perhaps as well the visitor should be his own guide about the islands, leaving it to chance to direct his footsteps. After an inspection of the more prominent objects, such as may be taken in at a glance from the little church, I wandered at will, encountering at every few steps some new surprise. Some one says, if we seek for pleasure it is pretty sure to elude our pursuit, coming oftener to us unawares, and the more unexpected the higher the gratification. It was in some such mood I stumbled, to speak literally, on the old burial-place of the islands. I am aware that one does not, as a rule, seek enjoyment in a grave-yard; but I have ever found an unflagging interest in deciphering the tablets of a buried city or hamlet. These stones may be sententious or loquacious, pompous or humble, and sometimes grimly merry.

---

[1] For more than a century previous to the Revolution the islands were prosperous, containing from three to six hundred souls. In 1800 there were three families and twenty persons on Smutty Nose; fifteen families and ninety-two persons on Star Island, alias Gosport; eleven dwellings and ten fish-houses on the latter, and three decent dwellings on the former. At this time there was not an inhabitant on Appledore, alias Hog Island.

Our German friends call the church-yard "God's Field." Here are no inscriptions, except on the horizontal slabs of Tucke and Stephens. There is no difference between the rough stones protruding from the ground and the fragments strewn broadcast about the little house-lots. So far as this inclosure is concerned, the annals of the hamlet are as a closed book. The instinct which bids you forbear treading on a grave is at fault here. It requires sharp eyes and a close scrutiny to discover that some effort has been made to distinguish this handful of graves by head and foot stones; that some are of greater and some of lesser length; or that the little hollows and hillocks have their secret meaning.

The two shepherds lie at the head of their little fold, in vaults composed of the rude masses found ready at hand. For fear their inscriptions might one day be effaced, I transcribed them:

In Memory of
THE REV. JOSIAH STEPHENS,
A faithful Instructor of Youth, and pious
Minister of Jesus Christ.
Supported on this Island by the
Society for Propagating the Gospel,
who died July 2, 1804.
Aged 64 years.

Likewise of
MRS. SUSANNAH STEPHENS,
his beloved Wife,
who died Dec. 7, 1810.
Aged 54 years.

Underneath
are the Remains of
THE REV. JOHN TUCKE, A.M.
He graduated at Harvard College, A.D. 1723,
Was ordained here July 26, 1732,
And died Aug. 12, 1773.
Æt. 72.

He was affable and polite in his manner,
Amiable in his disposition,
Of great piety and integrity, given to hospitality,
Diligent and faithful in his pastoral office.
Well learned in History and Geography, as well as
General Science,
And a careful Physician both to the bodies
and the souls of his People.
Erected 1800.   In Memory of the Just.

For two-score years this pious man labored in his stony vineyard. His parishioners agreed to give him a quintal per man of winter fish—their best. They covenanted to carry his wood from the landing home for him. With this he was content. He was their minister, teacher, physician, and even kept the accounts of a little store in a scrupulously exact way. I have been poring over his old-time chirography, clear-cut and beautiful as copper-plate. There are the good old English names of Ruth, Nabby, and Judy, of Betty, Patsey, and Love. We get a glimpse of their household economy in the porringers, pewter lamps, and pint-pots; the horn combs, thread, tape, and endless rows of pins for women-folk; the knitting-needles that clicked by the fireside in long winter nights, while the lads were away on Jeffrey's Ledge.

From here I wended my way to Smith's monument, erected in 1864, a triangular shaft of marble, rising eight or ten feet above a craggy rock. It is placed on a pedestal of rough stone, and protected by a railing from vandal hands. Its situation on one of the highest eminences of Star Island has exposed the inscription to the weather, until it is become difficult to decipher. The three sides of the pillar are occupied by a lengthy eulogium on this hero of many adventures,

>Of moving accidents by flood and field;
>Of hair-breadth scapes i' the imminent deadly breach."

Like Temple Bar of old, the monument is crowned with heads—those of the three Moslems slain by Smith, and seen on his scutcheon, as given by Stow, where they are also quartered. I know of no other instance of decapitated heads being set up in New England since King Philip's was struck off and stuck on a pike at Plymouth, in 1676. Two of the heads had fallen down, and the third seemed inclined to follow. Then the monument will be as headless as the doughty captain's tombstone in the pavement of St. Sepulchre's, worn smooth by many feet. In brief, the three Turks' heads stick no better than the name given by Smith to the islands off Cape Ann—after they had been named by De Monts.

Smith says he had six or seven charts or maps of the coast so unlike each other as to do him no more good than waste paper. He gives credit to Gosnold and Weymouth for their relations.

A few rods south-east of the old burying-ground is a sheltered nook, in which are three little graves, wholly concealed by dwarf willows and wild rose-bushes. They are tenanted by three children—"Jessie," two years; "Millie," four years; and "Mittie," seven years old—the daughters of Rev. George Beebe, some time missionary to these isles. Under the name of the little one last named are these touching, tearful words: "I don't want to die, but I'll do just as Jesus wants me to." A gentle hand has formed this retreat, and protected it with a wooden fence. While I stood there a songbird perched above the entrance and poured forth his matin lay. There is a third burial-place on the harbor side, but it lacks interest.

Another historic spot is the ruined fort, on the west point of the island, overlooking the entrance to the roadstead. Its contour may be traced, and a little of the embankment of one face remains. The well was filled to the curb with water. It once mounted nine four-pounder cannon, but at the beginning of the Revolution was dismantled, and the guns taken to Newburyport. I suppose the inhabitants for a long time to have neglected precautions for defense, as Colonel Romer, in his report to the Lords of Trade, about 1699, makes no mention of any fortification here. One of its terrible four-pounders would not now make a mouthful for our sea-coast ordnance.

Continuing my walk by the shore, I came to the cavern popularly known as Betty Moody's Hole. It is formed by the lodgment of masses of rock, so as to cover one of the gulches common to the isle. Here, says tradition, Betty concealed herself, with her two children, while the Indians were ravaging the isles and carrying many females into captivity. The story goes that the children, becoming frightened in the cavern, began to cry, whereat their inhuman mother, in an excess of fear, strangled them both; others say she was drowned here. The affair is said to have happened during Philip's War. I do not find it mentioned by either Mather or Hubbard.[1] At times during the fishing season there was hardly a man left upon the islands, a circumstance well known to the Indians.

A memoir extracted from the French archives gives a picture of the Isles in 1702, when an attack appears to have been meditated. "The Isles de Chòòles are about three leagues from Peskatoué to the south-south-east from the embouchure of the river, where a great quantity of fish are taken. These are three isles in the form of a tripod, and at about a musket-shot one from the other." * * * "There are at these three islands about sixty fishing shallops, manned each by four men. Besides these are the masters of the fishing stages, and, as they are assisted by the women in taking care of the fish, there may be in all about two hundred and eighty men; but it is necessary to observe that from Monday to Saturday there are hardly any left on shore, all being at sea on the fishing-grounds."

Taking note of the ragged fissures, which tradition ascribes to the day

---

[1] 1691. A considerable body of Eastern Indians came down from the interior, with the intention of sacking the Isles of Shoals, but on August 4th came upon some English forces at Maquoit, under Captain March, and had a fight with them. This prevented their proceeding, and saved the Shoals.—"Magnalia," vol. xi., p. 611.

1692. Governor Fletcher examined three deserters, or renegadoes, as he calls them, from Quebec, who came before him September 23d. They said two men-of-war had arrived at Quebec, and were fitting out for an expedition along the coast, "with a design to fall on Wells, Isle of Shoals, Piscataqua, etc."—"New York Colonial Documents," vol. iii., p. 855.

1724. After the Indians had cut off Captain Winslow and thirteen of his men in the River St. George, encouraged by this success, the enemy made a still greater attempt by water, and seized two shallops at the Isles of Shoals.—HUTCHINSON'S "Massachusetts," vol. ii., p. 307.

of the Crucifixion, I clambered down one of the rocky gorges from which the softer formation has been eaten out by the consuming appetite of the waves. Sometimes the descent was made easy by irregular steps of trap-rock, and again a flying leap was necessary from stone to stone. The perpendicular walls of the gorge rose near fifty feet at its outlet, at the shore. It was a

GORGE, STAR ISLAND.

relief to emerge from the dripping sides and pent-up space into the open air. The Flume, on Star Island, is a fine specimen of the intrusion of igneous rock among the harder formation.

If you would know what the sea can do, go down one of these gulches to the water's edge and be satisfied. I could not find a round pebble among the débris of shattered rock that lay tumbled about; only fractured pieces of irregular shapes. Those rocks submerged by the tide were blackened as if by fire, and shagged with weed. Overhead the precipitous cliffs caught the sun's rays on countless glittering points, the mica with which they are so plentifully bespangled dazzling the eye with its brilliancy. Elsewhere they were flint, of which there was more than enough to have furnished all Europe in the Thirty Years' War, or else granite. Looking up from among the *abattis* which girds the isle about, you are confronted by masses of overhanging rocks that threaten to detach themselves from the cliff and bury you in their ruins.

It is not for the timid to attempt a ramble among the rocks on the Atlantic side at low tide. He should be sure-footed and supple-jointed who undertakes it, with an eye to estimate the exact distance where the incoming surf-wave is to break. The illusions produced in the mind by the great waves that roll past are not the least striking sensations experienced. The speed with which they press in, and the noise accompanying their passage through the gullies and rents of the shore, contribute to make them seem much larger than they really are. It was only by continually watching the waves and measuring their farthest reach that I was able to await one of these curling monsters with composure; and even then I could not avoid looking suddenly round on hearing the rush of a breaker behind me; and ever and anon one of greater volume destroyed all confidence by bursting far above the boundaries the mind had assigned for its utmost limits.

Nothing struck me more than the idea of such mighty forces going to pure waste. A lifting power the Syracusan never dreamed of literally throwing itself away! An engine sufficient to turn all the machinery in Christendom lying idle at our very doors. What might not be accomplished if Old Neptune would put his shoulder to the wheel, instead of making all this magnificent but useless pother!

I noticed that the waves, after churning themselves into foam, assumed emerald tints, and caught a momentary gleam of sapphire, melting into amethyst, during the rapid changes from the bluish-green of solid water to its greatest state of disintegration. The same change of color has been observed in the Hebrides, and elsewhere.

The place that held for me more of fascination and sublimity than others was the bluff that looks out upon the vast ocean. I was often there. The swell of the Atlantic is not like the long regular roll of the Pacific, but it beats with steady rhythm. The grandest effects are produced after a heavy north-east blow, when the waves assume the larger and more flattened form known as the ground-swell. I was fortunate enough to stand on the cliff after three or four days of "easterly weather" had produced this effect. Such billows as poured with solid impact on the rocks, leaping twenty feet in the air, or heaped themselves in fountains of boiling foam around its base, give a competent idea of resistless power! The shock and recoil seemed to shake the foundations of the island.

Upon a shelf or platform of this cliff a young lady-teacher lost her life in September, 1848. Since then the rock on which she was seated has been called "Miss Underhill's Chair." Other accidents have occurred on the same spot, insufficient, it would seem, to prevent the foolhardy from risking their lives for a seat in this fatal chair.

There are circumstances that cast a melancholy interest around the fate of Miss Underhill. In early life she had been betrothed, and the banns, as was then the custom, had been published in the village church. Her father, a stern old Quaker, opposed the match, threatening to tear down the marriage intention rather than see his daughter wed with one of another sect. Whether from this or other cause, the suitor ceased his attentions, and not long after took another wife in the same village.

The disappointment was believed to have made a deep impression on a girl of Miss Underhill's strength of character. She was a Methodist, deeply imbued with the religious zeal of that denomination. Hearing from one who had been at the Isles of Shoals that the people were in as great need of a missionary as those of Burmah or of the Gold Coast, it became an affair of conscience with her to go there and teach.

She came to the islands, and applied herself with ardor to the work before her, a labor from which any but an enthusiast would have recoiled. It is asserted that no spot of American soil contained so debased a community as this.

It was her habit every pleasant day, at the close of school, to repair to the high cliff on the eastern shore of Star Island, where a rock conveniently placed by nature became her favorite seat. Here, with her Bible or other book, she was accustomed to pass the time in reading and contemplation. She was accompanied on her last visit by a gentleman, erroneously thought to have been her lover, who ventured on the rock with her. A tidal wave of unusual magnitude swept them from their feet. The gentleman succeeded in regaining his foothold, but the lady was no more seen.

Search was made for the body without success. A week after the occurrence it was found on York Beach, where the tide had left it. There was not the least disorder in the ill-fated lady's dress; the bonnet still covered her head, the ear-rings were in her ears, and her shawl was pinned across her breast. In a word, all was just as when she had set out for her walk. The kind-hearted man who found the poor waif took it home, and cared for it as if it had been his own dead. An advertisement caught the eye of Miss Underhill's brother. She was carried to Chester, New Hampshire, her native place, and there buried.

Notwithstanding the humble surroundings of her home, Miss Underhill was a person of superior and striking appearance. Her face was winning and her self-possessed manner is still the talk of her old-time associates. I have heard, as a sequel to the school-teacher's story, that some years after the fatal accident her old suitor came to the Isles, and, while bathing there, was drowned. The recovery of the body of the lady uninjured seems little short of miraculous, and confirms the presence of a strong under-tow, as I had suspected on seeing the floats of the lobster-men moored within a few feet of the rocks.

Schiller may have stood, in imagination, on some such crag as this when his wicked king flung his golden goblet into the mad sea, and with it the life of the hapless stripling who plunged, at his challenge, down into

> "The endless and measureless world of the deep."

In a neighboring ravine I found a spring of fresh water, though rather brackish to the taste; and in the more sheltered places were heaps of mussel-shells, the outer surface of a beautiful purple. They look better where they are than in my cabinet, though the lining of those I secured have an enamel of mother-of-pearl. Another remarkable feature I observed were the deposits of gravel among the crevices; but I saw no flint among the water-worn boulders wedged, as if by a heavy pressure, in fissures of the rocks. I remarked also the presence of a poor schistus intersecting the strata here and there. Some of it I could break off with my hands.

Another delightful ramble is on the harbor side, from the old fort round to Caswell's Peak or beyond. Passing by the little hand-breadth of sandy beach where the dories may land, once paved, the chronicles tell us, many feet deep with fish-bones, I observed with pleasure the green oasis spread out between the hotel and the shore. The proprietor seemed resolved that the very rocks should blossom, and already "a garden smiled" above the flint.

There is a sight worth seeing from the cupola of the hotel; of the White Hills, and Agamenticus, with the sands of Rye, Hampton, and Squam stretching along shore. I could see the steeples of Portsmouth and of Newburyport, the bluff at Boar's Head, and the smoke of a score of inland villages. Following with the eye the south coast where it sweeps round Ipswich Bay one sees Cape Ann and Thatcher's Island outlying; the gate-way of the busy bay beyond, into which all manner of craft were pressing sail. Northward were Newcastle, Kittery, and York, and farther eastward the lonely rock of Boon Island. Shoreward is Appledore, with the turret of its hotel visible above; and right below us the little harbor so often a welcome haven to the storm-tossed mariner.[1]

Most visitors to the islands are familiar with the terrible story of the wreck of the *Nottingham* galley, of London, in the year 1710. She was bound into Boston, and having made the land to the eastward of the Piscataqua, shaped her course southward, driven before a north-east gale, accompanied with rain, hail, and snow. For ten or twelve days succeeding they had no observation. On the night of the 11th of December, while under easy sail, the vessel struck on Boon Island.

With great difficulty the crew gained the rocks. The ship having immediately broken up, they were able to recover nothing eatable, except three small cheeses found entangled among the rock-weed. Some pieces of the spars and sails that came ashore gave them a temporary shelter, but every

---

[1] *Mountains seen off the coast:* Agamenticus, twelve miles north of the entrance of the Piscataqua; three inferior summits, known as Frost's Hills, at a less distance on the north-west. In New Hampshire the first ridge is twenty or thirty miles from sea, in the towns of Barrington, Nottingham, and Rochester—the summits known as Teneriffe, Saddleback, Tuckaway, etc. Their general name is the Blue Hills. Beyond these are several detached summits — Mount Major, Moose Mountain, etc.; also a third range farther inland, with Chocorua, Ossipee, and Kearsarge. In the lofty ridge separating the waters of the Merrimac and the Connecticut is Grand Monadnock, twenty-two miles east of the Connecticut River; thirty miles north of this is Sunapee, and forty-eight farther, Moosehillock. The ranges then trend away north-east, and are massed in the White Hills.

thing else had been carried away from the island by the strong drift. In a day or two the cook died. Day by day their sufferings from cold and hunger increased. The main-land being in full view before them, they built a boat and got it into the water. It was overset, and dashed in pieces against the rocks. One day they descried three boats in the offing, but no signals they were able to make could attract notice. Then, when reduced to a miserable band of emaciated, hopeless wretches, they undertook and with great labor constructed a raft, upon which two men ventured to attempt to reach the shore. Two days afterward it was found on the beach, with one of its crew lying dead at some distance. After this they were obliged to resort to cannibalism in order to sustain life, subsisting on the body of the carpenter, sparingly doled out to them by the captain's hand. To make an end of this chapter of horrors, the survivors were rescued after having been twenty-four days on the island. The raft was, after all, for them a messenger of preservation, for it induced a search for the builders.

No one can read this narrative without feeling his sympathy strongly excited for the brave John Deane, master of the wrecked vessel. He seemed possessed of more than human fortitude, and has told with a sailor's simple directness of his heroic struggle for life. His account was first published in 1711, appended to a sermon by Cotton Mather. Deane afterward commanded a ship of war in the service of the Czar, Peter the Great.[1]

Few who have seen the light-house tower on this lonely rock, distant not more than a dozen miles from the coast, receiving daily and nightly obeisance of hundreds of passing sails, can realize that the story of the *Nottingham* could be true. It is a terrible injunction to keep the lamps trimmed and brightly burning.[2]

Proceeding onward in this direction, I came to the fish-houses that remain on the isle. Tubs of trawls, a barrel or two of fish-oil, a pile of split fish, and the half of a hogshead, in which a " kentle" or so of " merchantable fish" had just been salted down, were here and there; a hand-barrow on which to carry the fish from the boat, a lobster-pot, and a pair of rusty scales, ought to be added to the inventory. Sou'-westers and suits of oil-skin clothing hung against the walls; and in the loft overhead were a spare block or two and a parcel of oars, evidently picked up adrift, there being no two of the same length. In some of the houses were whale-boats, that had been hauled up to be calked and painted, that the men were preparing to launch. They were all schooner-rigged, and some were decked over so as to furnish a little cuddy for bad weather. No more sea-worthy craft can be found, and under guidance of a practiced hand one will sail, as sea-folk say, "like a witch." They

---

[1] John Ward Dean, of Boston, the accomplished antiquary, has elicited this and other facts relative to his namesake.

[2] On Boone Island it is said there is no soil except what has been carried there.

usually contained a coil of half-inch line for the road, a "killick," and a brace of powder-kegs for the trawls.

The process of curing, or, as it is called by the islanders, "saving," fish is familiar to all who live near the sea-shore, and has not changed in two hundred years. It is described as practiced here in 1800, by Dr. Morse:

"The fish, in the first place, are thrown from the boat in piles on the shore. The cutter then takes them and cuts their throat, and rips open their bellies. In this state he hands them to the header, who takes out the entrails (detaching the livers, which are preserved for the sake of the oil they contain), and breaks off their heads. The splitter then takes out the backbone, and splits them completely open, and hands them to the salter, who salts and piles them in bulk, where they lie from ten to twenty hours, as is most convenient. The shoremen and the women then wash and spread them on the flakes. Here they remain three or four weeks, according to the weather, during which time they are often turned, piled in fagots, and then spread again, until they are completely cured for market."

The "dun," or winter fish, formerly cured here, were larger and thicker than the summer fish. Great pains were taken in drying them, the fish-women often covering the "fagots" with bed-quilts to keep them clean. Being cured in cold weather, they required but little salt, and were almost transparent when held up to the light. These fish sometimes weighed a hundred pounds or more. The dun fish were of great esteem in Spain and in the Mediterranean ports, bringing the highest price during Lent. They found their way to Madrid, where many a platter, smoking hot, has doubtless graced the table of the Escurial. In 1745 a quintal would sell for a guinea.

In 1775 the revolting colonies, unable to protect the islands, ordered their abandonment. A few of the inhabitants remained, but the larger number removed to the near main-land, and were scattered among the neighboring towns. The Shoals became through the war a rendezvous for British ships. The last official act of the last royal governor of New Hampshire was performed here in 1775, when Sir John Wentworth prorogued the Assembly of his majesty's lost province.

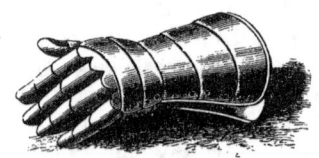

CLIFFS, WHITE ISLAND.

CHAPTER XII.

THE ISLES OF SHOALS—*continued*.

"—There be land-rats and water-rats, water thieves and land thieves; I mean pirates."—*Merchant of Venice.*

MY next excursion was to Smutty Nose, or Haley's. Seen from Star Island it shows two eminences, with a little hamlet of four houses, all having their gable-ends toward the harbor, on the nearest rising ground. Round the south-west point of Smutty Nose is the little haven already alluded to in the previous chapter, made by building a causeway of stone over to Malaga, where formerly the sea ran through. This Mr. Samuel Haley did at his own cost, expending part of a handsome fortune on the work. Into this little haven, we are told, many distressed vessels have put in and found safe anchorage. The chronicles, speaking by the pen of a fair islander, say old Mr. Haley, in building a wall, turned over a large flat stone, beneath which lay four bars of solid silver; with which, adds tradition, he began his sea mole. I should have thought, had this precious discovery gained currency, no stone would have been left unturned by the islanders, and that Haley's wall might have risen with magical celerity.

It is certain these islands were in former times the resort of freebooters, with such names as Dixy Bull, Low, and Argall (a licensed and titled buccaneer), who left the traces of their own lawlessness in the manner of life of the islanders. It was a convenient place in which to refit or obtain fresh provisions without the asking of troublesome questions.[1] The pirates could expect little booty from the fishermen, but they often picked them up at sea to replenish their crews.

In the year 1689 two noted buccaneers, Thomas Hawkins and Thomas Pound, cruised on the coast of New England, committing many depredations. The Bay colony determined on their capture, and dispatched an armed sloop called the *Mary*, Samuel Pease commander, which put to sea in October of that year. Hearing the pirates had been cruising at the mouth of Buzzard's Bay, Captain Pease made all sail in that direction. The *Mary* overhauled the outlaw off Wood's Hole. Pease ran down to her, hailed, and ordered her to heave to. The freebooter ran up a blood-red flag in defiance, when the *Mary* fired a shot athwart her forefoot, and again hailed, with a demand to strike her colors. Pound, who stood upon his quarter-deck, answered the hail with, "Come on, you dogs, and I will strike you." Waving his sword, his men poured a volley into the *Mary*, and the action for some time raged fiercely, no quarter being expected. Captain Pease at length carried his adversary by boarding, receiving wounds in the hand-to-hand conflict of which he died.

In 1723 the sloop *Dolphin*, of Cape Ann, was taken on the Banks by Phillips, a noted pirate. The able-bodied of the *Dolphin* were forced to join the pirate crew. Among the luckless fishermen was John Fillmore, of Ipswich. Phillips, to quiet their scruples, promised *on his honor* to set them at liberty at the end of three months. Finding no other hope of escape, for of course the liar and pirate never meant to keep his word, Fillmore, with the help of Edward Cheesman and an Indian, seizing his opportunity, killed three of the chief pirates, including Phillips, on the spot. The rest of the crew,

---

[1] 1670. The General Court being informed that there is a ship riding in the road at the Isle of Shoales suspected to be a pirat, and hath pirattically seized the sayd ship and goods from some of the French nation in amity with the English, and doeth not come under comand, this Court doeth declare and order that neither the sayd ship or goods or any of the company shall come into our jurisdiction, or be brought into any of our ports, upon penalty of being seized upon and secured to answer what shall be objected against them.—"Massachusetts Colonial Records," vol. iv., part ii., p. 449.

made up in part of pressed men, submitted, and the captured vessel was brought into Boston by the conquerors on the 3d of May, 1724. John Fillmore, the quasi pirate, was the great-grandfather of Millard Fillmore, thirteenth President of the United States.

It is affirmed on the authority of Charles Chauncy that Low once captured some fishermen from the "Shoals." Disappointed, perhaps, in his expectation of booty, he first caused the captives to be barbarously flogged, and afterward required each of them three times to curse Parson Mather or be hanged. The prisoners did not reject the alternative.

No doubt these pirates had heard of the sermons Cotton Mather was in the habit of preaching before the execution of many of their confederates. In his time it was the custom to march condemned prisoners under a strong guard to some church on the Sabbath preceding the day on which they were to suffer. There, marshaled in the broad aisle, they listened to a discourse on the enormity of their crimes and the torments that awaited them in the other world, this being the manner in which the old divines administered the consolations of religion to such desperate malefactors.

New England could contribute a thick volume to the annals of piracy in the New World from the records of a hundred years subsequent to her settlement. The name of Kidd was long a bugbear with which to terrify wayward children into obedience, and the search for his treasure continues, as we have seen, to this day. Bradish, Bellamy, and Quelch sailed these seas like true followers of those dreaded rovers who swept the English coasts, and sent their defiance to the king himself:

"Go tell the King of England, go tell him thus from me,
Though he reigns king o'er all the land, I will reign king at sea."

They have still the ghost of a pirate on Appledore, one of Kidd's men. There has consequently been much seeking after treasure. The face of the spectre is "pale, and very dreadful" to behold; and its neck, it is averred, shows the livid mark of the hangman's noose. It answers to the name of "Old Bab." Once no islander could be found hardy enough to venture on Appledore after night-fall. I shrewdly suspect "Old Bab" to be in the pay of the Laightons.

In 1700, Rear-admiral Benbow was lying at Piscataqua, with nine of Kidd's pirates on board for transportation to England. Robert Bradenham, Kidd's surgeon, says the Earl of Bellomont, was the "obstinatest and most hardened of 'em all." In the year 1726 the pirates William Fly, Samuel Cole, and Henry Greenville were taken and put to death at Boston, after having been well preached to in Old Brattle Street by Dr. Colman. Fly, the captain, like a truculent knave, refused to come into church, and on the way to execution bore himself with great bravado. He jumped briskly into the cart with a nosegay in his hand, smiling and bowing to the spectators, as he passed along, with real or affected unconcern. At the gallows he showed the same obstinacy until his face was covered.[1]

The various legends relative to the corsairs, and the secreting of their ill-gotten gains among these rocks, would of themselves occupy a lengthy chapter; and the recital of the fearful sights and sounds which have confronted such as were hardy enough to seek for treasure would satisfy the most inveterate marvel-monger in the land.

Among others to whom it is said these islands were known was the celebrated Captain Teach, or Blackbeard, as he was often called. He is supposed to have buried immense treasure here, some of which, like Haley's ingots, has been dug up and appropriated by the islanders. On one of his cruises, while lying off the Scottish coast waiting for a rich trader, he was boarded by a stranger, who came off in a small boat from the shore. The new-comer demanded to be led before the pirate chief, in whose cabin he remained some time shut up. At length Teach appeared on deck with the stranger, whom he introduced to the crew as a comrade. The vessel they were expecting soon came in sight, and after a bloody conflict became the prize of Blackbeard. It was determined by the corsair to man and arm the captured vessel. The unknown had fought with undaunted bravery and address during the battle. He was given the command of the prize.

BLACKBEARD, THE PIRATE.

The stranger Scot was not long in gaining the bad eminence of being as good a pirate as his renowned commander. His crew thought him invincible, and followed where he led. At last, after his appetite for wealth had been satisfied by the rich booty of the Southern seas, he arrived on the coast of his native land. His boat was manned, and landed him on the beach near an humble dwelling, whence he soon returned, bearing in his arms the lifeless form of a woman.

The pirate ship immediately set sail for America, and in due time dropped her anchor in the road of the Isles of Shoals. Here the crew passed their

---

[1] After execution the bodies of the pirates were taken to the little island in Boston harbor known as Nix's Mate, on which there is a monument. Fly was hung in chains, and the other two buried on the beach. The total disappearance of this island before the encroachments of the sea is the foundation of a legend. Bird Island, in the same harbor, on which pirates have been executed, has also disappeared. It formerly contained a considerable area.

time in secreting their riches and in carousal. The commander's portion was buried on an island apart from the rest. He roamed over the isles with his beautiful companion, forgetful, it would seem, of his fearful trade, until one morning a sail was seen standing in for the islands. All was now activity on board the pirate; but before getting under way the outlaw carried the maiden to the island where he had buried his treasure, and made her take a fearful oath to guard the spot from mortals until his return, were it not 'til doomsday. He then put to sea.

The strange sail proved to be a warlike vessel in search of the freebooter. A long and desperate battle ensued, in which the cruiser at last silenced her adversary's guns. The vessels were grappled for a last struggle, when a terrific explosion strewed the sea with the fragments of both. Stung to madness by defeat, knowing that if taken alive the gibbet awaited him, the rover had fired the magazine, involving friend and foe in a common fate.

A few mangled wretches succeeded in reaching the islands, only to perish miserably, one by one, from cold and hunger. The pirate's mistress remained true to her oath to the last, or until she also succumbed to want and exposure. By report, she has been seen more than once on White Island—a tall, shapely figure, wrapped in a long sea-cloak, her head and neck uncovered, except by a profusion of golden hair. Her face is described as exquisitely rounded, but pale and still as marble. She takes her stand on the verge of a low, projecting point, gazing fixedly out upon the ocean in an attitude of intense expectation. A former race of fishermen avouched that her ghost was doomed to haunt those rocks until the last trump shall sound, and that the ancient graves to be found on the islands were tenanted by Blackbeard's men.[1]

These islands were also the favorite haunt of smugglers.[2] Many a runlet of Canary has been "passed" here that never paid duty to king or Congress. It must have been a very paradise of free-traders, who, doubtless, had the sympathies of the inhabitants in their illicit traffic. "What a smuggler's isle!" was my mental ejaculation when I first set foot on Star Island; what a retreat for some Dirck Hatteraick or outlawed Jean Lafitte!

I rowed over to Smutty Nose in a wherry. The name has a rough sig-

---

[1] A somewhat more authentic naval conflict occurred during the war of 1812 with Great Britain, when the American privateer, *Governor Plummer*, was captured on Jeffrey's Ledge by a British cruiser, the *Sir John Sherbroke*. The American had previously made many captures. Off Newfoundland she sustained a hard fight with a vessel of twelve guns, sent out to take her. She also beat off six barges sent on the same errand.

[2] 1686. Ordered that no shipps do unliver any part of their lading at the Isles of Shoals before they have first entered with the Collector of H. M. Customs, and also with the officer receiving his maj^s imposts and revenues arising upon wine, sperm, &c., imported either in Boston, Salem, or Piscataqua; and that all shipps and vessells trading to the eastward of Cape Porpus shall enter at some of the aforesaid Ports, or at the town of Falmouth in the Prov. of Maine.—"Massachusetts Council Records," vol. i., p. 43.

nificance. Looking at the islands at low tide, they present well-defined belts of color. First is the dark line of submerged rock-weed, which led some acute fisherman to hit off with effect the more popular name of Haley's Island; next comes a strip almost as green as the grass in the rocky pastures; above these again, shaded into browns or dingy yellows, the rocks appear of a tawny hue, and then blanched to a ghastly whiteness, a little relieved by dusky patches of green.

I remarked that the schooners of twenty or thirty tons' burden lying in the harbor were all at moorings, ready to run after a school of fish or away from a storm. It is only a few years since three of these vessels were blown from their moorings and stranded on the rocks of Smutty Nose and Appledore.

In 1635 the ship *James*, Captain Taylor, of Bristol, England, had a narrow escape from being wrecked here. After losing three anchors, she was with difficulty guided past the great rocks into the open sea. The curious reader will find the details quaintly set forth in the journal of Rev. Richard Mather, the ancestor of a celebrated family of New England divines.[1] She had on board a hundred passengers for the Massachusetts Colony.

While lying on our oars in this basin, where so many antique craft have been berthed, it is perhaps not amiss to allude to Thomas Morton, of Mount Wollaston,[2] alias Merry Mount. To do so it will not only be necessary to clamber up the crumbling side of the ship in which he was being sent a prisoner to England, but to surmount prejudices equally decrepit, that, like the spectre of "Old Bab," continue to appear long after they have been decently gibbeted. The incident derives a certain interest from the fact that Morton's was the first instance of banishment in the New England colonies. The only consequence of Thomas Morton, of Clifford's Inn, gent., is due to the effort to cast obloquy upon the Pilgrims.

In the year 1628 the ship *Whale* was riding at the Isles of Shoals, Morton having been seized by order of Plymouth Colony, and put on board for transportation to England. What manner of ship the *Whale* was may be gathered from Morton's own account of her. The master he calls "Mr. Weathercock," and the ship "a pitiful, weather-beaten craft," in which he was "in more danger than Jonah in the whale's belly."

The cause of Morton's banishment is often asserted to have been simply his licentious conduct, and what some have been pleased to call indulgence in such "hearty old English pastimes" as dancing about a May-pole, singing songs of no doubtful import, holding high wassail the while, like the mad, roystering rogues his followers were. The Pilgrim Fathers are indicted by a class of historians desirous of displaying to the world the intolerance of the "Plymouth Separatists," as distinguished from the liberality which marked

---

[1] Boston, 1850: original in possession of Dorchester Antiquarian Society.
[2] Mount Wollaston, Quincy, Massachusetts; present residence of John Quincy Adams, Esq.

the religious views of the settlers east of the Merrimac. Our forefathers, say they, did not come to the New World for religious liberty, but to fish and trade.

Morton's offense is stated by Governor Bradford, in his letters to the Council for New England and to Sir F. Gorges, to have been the selling of arms and ammunition to the Indians in such quantities as to endanger the safety of the infant plantations. He was arrested, and his association of Merry Mount broken up, after repeated and friendly efforts to dissuade him from this course had been met with insolence and bravado. It stands thus in Governor Bradford's letter-book:

"*To the Honourable his Majesty's Council for New England, these, Right Honourable and our very good Lords:*

"Necessity hath forced us, his Majesty's subjects of New England in general (after long patience), to take this course with this troublesome planter, Mr. Thomas Morton, whom we have sent unto your honours that you may be pleased to take that course with him which to your honourable wisdom shall seem fit; who hath been often admonished not to trade or truck with the Indians either pieces, powder, or shot, which yet he hath done, and duly makes provision to do, and could not be restrained, taking it in high scorn (as he speaks) that any here should controul therein. Now the general weakness of us his Majesty's subjects, the strength of the Indians, and at this time their great preparations to do some affront upon us, and the evil example which it gives unto others, and having no subordinate general government under your honours in this land to restrain such misdemeanours, causeth us to be troublesome to your Lordships to send this party unto you for remedy and redress hereof."

The letter to Sir F. Gorges[1] is in greater detail, but its length prevents its insertion with the foregoing extract. The Governor of New Plymouth makes a similar allegation with regard to the fishing ships. It is noticeable that all the plantations took part in this affair, Piscataqua, the Isles of Shoals, Edward Hilton, and others paying their proportion of the expense of sending Morton out of the country.

Morton's offense, therefore, was political and not religious, and his extradition a measure of self-preservation, an inexorable law in 1628 to that handful of settlers. If, at the end of nearly two centuries and a half, the Government those Pilgrims contributed to found deemed it necessary to the public safety to banish individuals from its borders, how, then, may we challenge this act of a few men who dwelt in a wilderness, and worshiped their God with the Bible in one hand and a musket in the other?

---

[1] See "Massachusetts Historical Collections," vol. iii., p. 63.

Morton defied the proclamation of the king promulgated in 1622, saying there was no penalty attached to it. Its terms forbade " any to trade to the portion of America called New England, being the whole breadth of the land between forty and forty-eight degrees of north latitude, excepting those of the Virginia Company, the plantation having been much injured by interlopers, who have injured the woods, damaged the harbors, trafficked with the savages, and even sold them weapons, and taught them the use thereof."[1]

Of the May-pole, which the Pilgrims regarded with grim discontent, Stubbes gives the manner in England of bringing it home from the woods.

" But," he says, " their cheefest jewell they bring home with greate veneration, as thus: they have twentie or fourtie yoke of oxen, every oxe havyng a sweete nosegaie of flowers tyed on the tippe of his hornes, and these oxen drawe home this Maie-poole, which is covered all over with flowers and hearbes, bounde rounde aboute with stringes from the top to the bottome, and sometyme painted with variable colours, with two or three hundred men, women, and children followyng it with great devotion. And thus beying reared up with handkercheifes and flagges streamyng on the toppe, they strawe the grounde aboute, binde green boughes about it, sett up Sommer haules, Bowers, and Arbours hard by. And then fall they to banquet and feast, to leape and dance aboute it, as the Heathen people did at the dedication of their idolles, whereof this is a perfect patterne, or rather the thynge itself."

SMUTTY NOSE.

Smutty Nose, the most verdant of the islands, was one of the earliest settled. The stranger for the first time feels something like soil beneath his feet. There is a wharf and a little landing-place, where a boat may be

---

[1] British State Papers, Calendars.

beached. When within Haley's little cove, I looked down into the water, and saw the perch (cunners) swimming lazily about. This was the only place where the old-time industry of the isles showed even a flake, so to speak, of its former greatness. There were a few men engaged in drying their fish near the landing. Clear weather with westerly winds is best for this purpose; dull or foggy weather spoils the fish.

HALEY DOCK AND HOMESTEAD.
(In the third House from the left the Wagner Murder was committed.)

At a little distance, shorn of some of its former adornments, is the homestead of Samuel Haley, who with his two sons and their families occupied the island many years ago. Not far off is the little family grave-yard of the Haleys, with the palings falling in decay, and the mounds overgrown with a tangle of rank grass. At one time, by his energy, Mr. Haley had made of his island a self-sustaining possession. Before the Revolution he had built a windmill, salt-works, and rope-walk; a bakehouse, brewery, distillery, blacksmith's and cooper's shops succeeded in the first year of peace—all going to decay within his lifetime. By all report of him, he was a good and humane man, and I hereby set up his prostrate grave-stone on my page:

"IN MEMORY OF MR. SAMUEL HALEY
Who died in the year 1811
Aged 84
He was a man of great Ingenuity
Industry Honor and Honesty, true to his
Country & A man who did A great
Public good in Building A
Dock & Receiving into his
Enclosure many a poor
Distressed Seaman & Fisherman
In distress of Weather."

A few steps farther on are the graves of fourteen shipwrecked mariners, marked by rude boulders. It is entered in the Gosport records: "1813, *Jan. 14th*, ship *Sagunto* stranded on Smutty Nose Isle; *Jan.* 15*th*, one man found; 16*th*, six men found; 21*st*, seven men found." The record sums up the number as twelve bodies found, whereas the total appears to be fourteen.

Although the ship *Sagunto* was not stranded on Smutty Nose Isle, the wreck of a ship, either Spanish or Portuguese, with all on board, remains a terrible fact but too well attested by these graves.[1] The horror of the event is deepened and strengthened by the simple word "Unknown." When this ship crashed and filled and went down, the *Sagunto* was lying, after a terrible buffeting, within a safe harbor.

It was in a blinding snow-storm, and a gale that strewed the shore from the Penobscot to Hatteras with wrecks, that a ship built of cedar and mahogany was thrown on these rocks. Not a living soul was left to tell the tale of that bitter January night. The ill-fated vessel was richly laden, no doubt, for boxes of raisins and almonds from Malaga drifted on shore the next morning. On a piece of the wreck that came in a silver watch of English make was found, with the letters "P. S." graven on the seals; and among the débris was a Spanish and part of an American ensign, for it was war-time then between England and the American States. The watch had stopped at exactly four o'clock, or when time ceased for those hapless Spaniards. There were also found some twenty letters, addressed south of New York. Conjecture said it was a Spanish ship from Cadiz, bound for Philadelphia.

This is the story of this little clump of graves, and of the wreck, to this day unknown. It has been told many times in prose and poetry, but not often truly. Samuel Haley had been quietly lying in his grave two years. The reader may or may not believe he found the frozen bodies of some of the crew next morning reclining on his wall. Here is a wild flower of island growth, of a handful cast upon these fading mounds:

> "O sailors, did sweet eyes look after you
> The day you sailed away from sunny Spain?
> Bright eyes that followed fading ship and crew,
> Melting in tender rain?"

I wondered that these fourteen the old sea had strangled and flung up here could rest so peacefully in ground unblessed by Holy Church. Perchance the spot has witnessed midnight mass, with incense and with missal: no doubt beads have been told, and a *pater* and *ave* said by pious pilgrims.

---

[1] Spanish ship *Sagunto*, Carrera, seventy-three days from Cadiz for New York, arrived at Newport on Monday, January 11th, out of provisions and water, and the crew frost-bitten. Cargo, wine, raisins, and salt. Saw no English cruisers, and spoke only one vessel, a Baltimore privateer.—*Columbian Centinel*, January 16th, 1813.

It is not pleasant to think that the island has become more widely known through the medium of an atrocious murder committed here in March, 1873. Formerly the islanders dated from some well-remembered wreck; now it is before or since the murder on Smutty Nose they reckon.

On the morning of March 6th the Norwegian who lives opposite Star Island, on Appledore, heard a cry for help. Going to the shore, he saw a woman standing on the rocks of Malaga in her night-dress. He crossed over and brought the poor creature to his cottage, when it appeared that her feet were frozen. She was half dead with fright and exposure, but told her tale as soon as she was able.

John Hontvet, a fisherman, occupied one of the three houses on Smutty Nose; the third counting from the little cove, as you look at it from Star Island. On the night of the 5th of March he was at Portsmouth, leaving three women—Mary, his wife; Annethe and Karen Christensen—at home. They went to bed as usual, Annethe with Mrs. Hontvet in the bedroom; Karen on a couch in the kitchen. It was a fine moonlight night, though cold, and there was snow on the ground.

Some time during the night a man entered the house, it is supposed for the purpose of robbery. He fastened the door between the kitchen, which he first entered, and the bedroom, thus isolating the sleeping women. Karen, having awoke, cried out, when she was attacked by the intruder with a chair. The noise having aroused the two women in the bedroom, Mary Hontvet jumped out of bed, forced open the door leading into the kitchen, and succeeded in getting hold of the wounded girl, Karen, whom she drew within her own chamber. All this took place in the dark. Mary then bade Annethe, her brother's wife, to jump out of the window, and she did so, but was too much terrified to go beyond the corner of the house. Mary, meanwhile, was holding the door of the kitchen against the attempts of their assailant to force it open. Foiled here, the villain left the house, and meeting the young wife, Annethe, was seen by Mary, in the clear moonlight, to deal her three terrible blows with an axe. But before she was struck down the girl had recognized her murderer, and shrieked out, "Louis, Louis!"

After this accursed deed the man went back to the house, and Mary also made her escape by the window. Karen was too badly hurt to follow. The clear-grit Norwegian woman ran first to the dock, but finding no boat there, hid herself among the rocks. She durst not shout, for fear the sound of her voice would bring the murderer to the spot. There she remained, like another Betty Moody, until sunrise, when she took courage and went across the sea-wall to Malaga and was rescued. I was told that when she fled, with rare presence of mind, she took her little dog under her arm, for fear it might prove her destruction.

It resulted that Louis Wagner, a Prussian, was arrested, tried for the murder, and condemned as guilty. The fatal recognition by Annethe, the figure seen with uplifted axe through the window by Mary, and the prisoner's absence from his lodgings on the night of the murder, pointed infallibly to him as the chief actor in this night of horrors. To have committed this crime he must have rowed from Portsmouth to the Islands and back again on the night in question; no great feat for one of those hardy islanders, and Wagner was noted for muscular strength. It is said he was of a churlish disposition, and would seldom speak unless addressed, when he would answer shortly. He was not considered a bad fellow, but a poor companion.

I went to the house. Relic-hunters had left it in a sorry plight; taking away even the sashes of the windows, shelves, and every thing movable. Even the paper had been torn from the walls, and carried off for its blood-stains. Hontvet described, with the phlegm of his race, the appearance of the house on the morning of the tragedy: "Karen lay dere; Annethe lay here," he said. I saw they were preparing to make it habitable again: better burn it, say I.

We had a sun-dog at evening and a rainbow in the morning, full-arched, and rising out of the sea, a sure forerunner, say veteran observers, of foul weather. Says the quatrain of the forecastle:

> Rainbow in the morning,
> Sailors take warning;
> Rainbow at night,
> Is the sailor's delight."

LEDGE OF ROCKS, SMUTTY NOSE.

I spent a quiet, breezy afternoon in exploring Appledore. The landing from the harbor side has to be made in some cleft of the rock, and is not practicable when there is a sea running. Passing by the cottage at the shore, I first went up the rocky declivity to the site of the abandoned settlement of so long ago. It may still be recognized by the cellars, rough stone walls, and fragments of bricks lying scattered about. Thistles, raspberry-bushes, and dwarf cherry-trees in fragrant bloom, were growing in the depressions which marked these broken hearth-stones of a forgotten people. The poisonous ivy, sometimes called mercury, so often found clinging to old walls, was here. Some country-folk pretend its potency is such that they who look on it are inoculated with the poison; a scratch, as I know to my cost, will suffice.

Here was a strip of green grass running along the harbor side, and, for the first time, the semblance of a road; I followed it until it lost itself among the rocks. A horse and a yoke of oxen were browsing by the way, and on a distant shelf of rock I saw a cow, much exaggerated in size, contentedly ruminative. Clumps of huckleberry and fragrant bayberry were frequent, with blackberry and other vines clustering above the surface rocks.

I am inclined to doubt whether, after all, the habitation of Appledore[1] was abandoned on account of the Indians, for Star Island, as has been remarked, could give no better security. Probably the landing had much to do with it. Without some moving cause the inhabitants would hardly have left Appledore and its verdure for the bald crags of

SOUTH-EAST END OF APPLEDORE, LOOKING SOUTH.

---

[1] Appledore, a small sea-port of England, County of Devon, parish of Northampton, on the Torridge, at its mouth in Barnstable Bay, two and a quarter miles north of Bideford. It is resorted to in summer as a bathing-place, and has a harbor subordinate to the port of Barnstable.— "Gazetteer."

Star Island. The choice of Appledore by the first settlers was probably due to its spring of pure water, the only one on the islands.

The year 1628 is the first in which we can locate actual settlers at the Shoals. Mr. Jeffrey and Mr. Burslem, then assessed two pounds for the expenses of Morton's affair, are supposed to have been living there. By 1640 the Rev. Mr. Hull, of Agamenticus, paid parochial visits to the Isles, and some time before 1661, says Dr. Morse, they had a meeting-house on Hog Island, though the service of the Church of England was the first performed there. The three brothers Cutt, of Wales, settled there about 1645, removing soon to the main-land, where they became distinguished. Antipas Maverick is mentioned as resident in 1647. Another settler whom the chronicles do not omit was William Pepperell, of Cornwall, England, father of the man of Louisburg, who was here about 1676. The removal of the brothers Cutt within two years, and of Pepperell and Gibbons after a brief residence, does not confirm the view that the islands at that early day possessed attractions to men of the better class sometimes claimed for them. Pepperell and Gibbons left the choice of a future residence to chance, with an indifference worthy a Bedouin of the Great Desert. Holding their staves between thumb and finger until perpendicularly poised, they let them fall, departing, the tradition avers, in the direction in which each pointed—Pepperell to Kittery, Gibbons to Muscongus.

The first woman mentioned who came to reside at Hog Island was Mrs. John Reynolds, and she came in defiance of an act of court prohibiting women from living on the islands. One of the Cutts, Richard by name, petitioned for her removal, together with the hogs and swine running at large on the island belonging to John Reynolds. The court, however, permitted her to remain during good behavior. This occurred in 1647. It gives a glimpse

DUCK ISLAND, FROM APPLEDORE.

of what society must hitherto have been on the islands to call for such enactments. No wonder men of substance left the worse than barren rocks, and that right speedily.

I walked around the shores of Appledore, stopping to explore the chasms in my way. One of them I could liken to nothing but a coffin, it seemed so exactly fashioned to receive the hull of some unlucky ship. On some of the rocks I remarked impressions, as if made with the heel of a human foot. In the offing Duck Island showed its jagged teeth, around which the tide swelled and broke until it seemed frothing at the mouth.

Another Smith's monument is on the highest part of the island, all the others being within view from it. It is a rude cairn of rough stone, thrown together with little effort at regularity. The surface stones are overgrown with lichens, which add to its appearance of antiquity. It is known to have stood here rather more than a century, and is said to have been built by Captain John Smith himself. Howsoever the tradition may have originated, it is all we have, and are so fain to be content; but I marvel that so modest a man as Captain John should have said nothing about it in the book writ with his own hand. By some the monument has been believed to be a beacon built to mark the fishing-grounds.

Smith arrived at Monhegan in April, 1614, and was back again at Plymouth, England, on the 5th of August. He was one of those who came to "fish and trade," seeking out the habitations of the Indians for his purpose. There were no savages at the Isles.[1] Of his map Smith writes: "Although there be many things to be observed which the haste of other affairs did cause me to omit, for being sent more to get present commodities than knowledge by discoveries for any future good, I had not power to search as I would," etc. I should add, in passing, that Smith, who admits having seen the relation of Gosnold, does not allow him the credit of the name he gave to Martha's Vineyard, but speaks of it as Capawock.

One of the remarkable features of Appledore is the valley issuing from the cove, dividing the island in two. This ravine is a real curiosity, the great depression occurring where the hotel buildings are situated affording a snug cove on the west of the island. Just behind the house enough soil had accumulated to furnish a thriving and well-kept vegetable garden, evidently an object of solicitude to the proprietors. From the veranda of the hotel you may see the ocean on the east and the bay on the west. In Mr. Hawthorne's account of his visit here in 1852, he relates that in the same storm that overthrew Minot's Light, a great wave passed entirely through this valley; "and," he continues, "Laighton describes it when it came in from the sea as toppling over to the height of the cupola of his hotel. It roared and whitened through, from sea to sea, twenty feet abreast, rolling along huge

---

[1] Levett says, "Upon these islands are no salvages at all."

LAIGHTON'S GRAVE.

rocks in its passage. It passed beneath his veranda, which stands on posts, and probably filled the valley completely. Would I had been here to see!"

When I came back to the harbor side, both wind and tide had risen. I was ferried across by a lad of not more than ten years. At times the swift current got the better and swept the boat to leeward, but he stoutly refused to give me the oars, the pride of an islander being involved in the matter. The little fellow flung his woolen cap to the bottom of the dory, his hair flying loosely in the wind as he bent to his task. After taking in more water than was for our comfort, he was at last obliged to accept my aid. These islanders are amphibious, brought up with "one foot on sea, one foot on shore." I doubt if half their lives are passed on *terra firma*.

Duck Island is for the sportsman. He will find there in proper season the canvas-back, mallard, teal, white-winged coot, sheldrake, etc. Few land, except gunners in pursuit of sea-fowl. I contented myself with sailing along its shores, watching the play of the surf and the gambols of a colony of small sea-gulls that seemed in peaceable possession. Duck Island proper has a cluster of wicked-looking ledges encircling it from south-west to south-east. The mariner should give it a wide berth. Its ill-shapen rocks project on all sides, and a reef makes out half a mile into the sea from the north-west. Shag and Mingo are two of its satellites. This island was resorted to by the Indians for the seals frequenting it.

I had observed lying above the landing on Star Island a queer-looking craft, which might with great propriety be called a shell. It consisted of a frame of slats neatly fitted together, over which a covering of tarred canvas had been stretched. I at first thought some Kanaka's canoe had found its way through the North-west Passage, and drifted in here; but Mr. Poor assured me it belonged on the islands, and was owned and sailed by Tom Leha, whose dwelling on Londoner's he pointed out. As Tom Leha was the Celtic skipper of the *Creed*, I had some speech of him. His boat, he said, was such as is used in the Shannon, where it is called the "saint's canoe," because first used by one of the Irish saints. It was a good surf-boat, light as a cork, and as buoyant.

One night Leha, with his wife and three children, arrived at the Shoals in his canoe, which a strong man might easily carry. No one knew whence they came. Their speech was unintelligible. There they were, and there they seemed inclined to remain. Your *bona fide* Shoaler likes not intruders. The islanders gave Leha and his a cold welcome, but this did not discompose him. He was faithful and industrious, and in time saved money enough to buy Londoner's. He waved his hand toward his island home, as if to say,

"An ill-favored thing, sir, but mine own."

As seen from Star Island, Londoner's shows two rugged knobs connected by a narrower strip of shingle. It has its cove, and a reasonably good land-

LONDONER'S, FROM STAR ISLAND.

ing. Half-way between it and Star are hidden rocks over which the sea breaks. It was not occupied by its owner when I was there.

It was a lovely morning when I rowed over to White Island. Once clear of the harbor, I found outside what sailors call "an old sea," the relics of the late north-easter. But these wherries will live in any sea that runs on the New England coast. I have heard of the Bank fishermen being out in them for days together when their vessel could not lie at anchor in the tremendous swell.

White Island is now the most picturesque of the group, a distinction once conceded to Star. It owes this preference to its light-house, standing on a cliff at the east head of the isle, that rises full fifty feet out of water; at least it seemed so high to me as I lay underneath it in my little boat at low tide. Against this cliff the waves continually swelled, rushing into crannies, where

I could hear them gurgling and soughing as if some monster were choking to death in their depths.

This is not so forbidding as Boon Island, but it is enough. The light-house was of brick, as I could see where the weather had worn off last year's coat of whitewash. It was not yet time for the tender to come and brighten it up again. The long gallery conducting from the keeper's cottage up to the tower was once torn away from its fastenings, and hurled into the deep gorge of the rocks which it spans. I saw nothing to hinder if the Atlantic had a mind again to play at bowls with it.

The island owes its name to the blanched appearance of its crags, little different in this respect from its fellows. At high tides the westward end is isolated from the rest, making two islands of it in appearance, but inseparable as the Siamese twins. The light-house is much visited in summer, especially by those of a romantic turn, and by those to whom its winding stairs, huge tanks of oil, and powerful Fresnel, possess the charm of novelty. By its side is the section of an earlier building, a reminiscence of the former state of the Isles. For many years the keeper of the light was Thomas B. Laighton, afterward proprietor of Appledore. On account of some political disappointment, he removed from Portsmouth to the Isles, making, it is said, a vow never again to set foot on the main-land. Fortune followed the would-be recluse against his will. As keeper of a boarding-house on Appledore, he is reported to have expressed little pleasure at the coming of visitors, even while receiving them with due hospitality. He was glad of congenial spirits, but loved not overmuch the stranger within his gates. His sons succeeded to their father at the Appledore. His daughter[1] has told with charming *naiveté* the story of the light-house, whose lamps she often trimmed and lighted with her own hands.

"I lit the lamps in the light-house tower,
For the sun dropped down and the day was dead;
They shone like a glorious clustered flower,
Two golden and five red."

In 1793 there were only eight light-houses within the jurisdiction of Massachusetts. Of these one was at the entrance of Nantucket, and another of Boston harbor. There were twin lights on the north point of Plymouth harbor, on Thatcher's Island, off Cape Ann, and at the northerly end of Plum Island, at the mouth of the Merrimac. The latter were not erected until 1787. They were of wood, so contrived as to be removed at pleasure, in order to conform to the shifting of the sand-bar on which they stood. The lights on Baker's Island, at the entrance of the port of Salem, were not built until 1798.

But neither compass, sextant, fixed and revolving lights, storm signals, careful soundings, buoys, nor beacons, with all the improvements in modern

---

[1] Mrs. Celia Laighton Thaxter.

COVERED WAY AND LIGHT-HOUSE, WHITE ISLAND.

ship-building, have yet reduced traveling over the sea to the same certainty as traveling over the land. We commit ourselves to the mercy of Father Neptune just as fearfully as ever, and annually pay a costly tribute of lives for the privilege of traversing his dominions.

During the winter of 18—, so runs the story, the keeper of this light was a young islander, with a single assistant. For nearly a week north-easterly winds had prevailed, bringing in from the sea a cold, impenetrable haze, that enveloped the islands, and rendered it impossible to discern objects within a cable's length of the light-house. At the turn of the tide on the sixth day, the expected storm burst upon them with inconceivable fury. The sea grew blacker beneath the dead white of the falling snow. The waves, urged on by the gale, made a fair breach over the light-house rock, driving the keeper from his little dwelling to the tower for shelter.

The violence of the gale increased until midnight, when it began to lull.

The spirits of the oppressed watchers rose as the storm abated. One made ready a smoking platter of fish and potatoes, while the other prepared to snatch a few moments' sleep. While thus occupied, a loud knock was heard at the door. It was repeated. The two men stood rooted to the spot. They knew no living thing except themselves was on the island; they knew nothing of mortal shape might approach it in such a fearful tempest. At a third knock the assistant, who was preparing their frugal meal, fell upon his knees, making the sign of the cross, and calling upon all the saints in the calendar for protection, like the good Catholic he was.

The keeper, who had time to recollect himself, advanced to the door and threw it open. On the outside stood a gigantic negro, of muscular frame, clothed in a few rags, the blood streaming from twenty gashes in his body and limbs. A brig had been cast away on the rocks a few rods distant from the light, and the intrepid black had ventured to attempt to gain the lighthouse.

The keeper ran to the spot. Peering into the darkness, he could discover the position of the vessel only by the flapping of her torn sails in the wind. The roar of the sea drowned every other sound. If the shipwrecked crew had cried for help, they could not have been heard. Availing himself of his knowledge of every inch of the shore, the keeper succeeded in gaining a projecting ledge, from which he attracted the attention of those on board the brig, and after many fruitless efforts a line was got to land. The wreck, as the keeper could now see, was driven in a little under the shelter of a projecting point. Moments were precious. He sought in vain for some projection on which he might fasten his rope. He did not hesitate, but wound it about his body, and fixed himself as firmly as he could in a crevice of the rock. Here, with his feet planted on the slippery ledge, where every sea that came in drenched him to the skin, the brave fellow stood fast until every man of the crew had been saved.

WHITE ISLAND LIGHT.

There is nothing that moves the imagination like a light-house. John Quincy Adams said when he saw one in the evening he was reminded of the light Columbus saw the night he discovered the New World. I have been moved to call them telegraph posts, standing along the coast, each flashing its spark from cape to headland, the almost commingling rays being golden threads of happy intelligence to all mariners. What a glorious vision it would be to see the kindling of each tower from Florida to Prima Vista, as the broad streets of the city are lighted, lamp by lamp!

Here ended my wanderings among these islands, seated like immortals in the midst of eternity. The strong south-westerly current bore me swiftly from the light-house rock. We hoisted sail, and laid the prow of our little bark for the river's mouth; but I leaned over the taffrail and looked back at the beacon-tower 'til it faded and was lost.

"Even at this distance I can see the tides,
　Upheaving, break unheard along its base;
　A speechless wrath that rises and subsides
　In the white lip and tremor of the face.

"'Sail on!' it says, 'Sail on, ye stately ships!
　And with your floating bridge the ocean span;
　Be mine to guard this light from all eclipse,
　Be yours to bring man nearer unto man.'"

WENTWORTH HOUSE, LITTLE HARBOR.

CHAPTER XIII.

NEWCASTLE AND NEIGHBORHOOD.

"Yes—from the sepulchre we'll gather flowers,
Then feast like spirits in their promised bowers,
Then plunge and revel in the rolling surf,
Then lay our limbs along the tender turf."—BYRON.

ANOTHER delightfully ruinous old corner is Newcastle, which occupies the island opposite Kittery Point, usually called Great Island. Between Newcastle and Kittery is the main ship-channel, with deep water and plenty of sea-room. On the south of Great Island is another entrance called Little Harbor, with shallow water and sandy bottom; its communication with the main river is now valueless, and little used except by fishing-craft of small tonnage.

In going from Portsmouth there are three bridges to be crossed to reach the town of Newcastle, situated on the northern shore of the island; or, if your aim be the southern shore, it is equally a pleasant drive or walk to the ancient seat of the Wentworths, at Little Harbor, from which you may, if a ferry-man be not at hand, hail the first passing boat to take you to the island. I went there by the former route, so as to pass an hour among the tombstones in the old Point of Graves burial-ground, and returned by the latter in order to visit the Wentworth mansion.

The three bridges before mentioned connect as many islands with Portsmouth. They were built, it is said, at the suggestion of President Monroe, when he found Great Island somewhat difficult of access.

There appeared some symptoms of activity in the island fishery. As I passed down, I noticed two Bankers lying in the diminutive harbor, and an acre or so of ground spread with flakes, on which codfish were being cured.

The little cove which makes the harbor of Newcastle has several wharves, some of them in ruins, and all left "high and dry" at low tide. The rotting timbers, sticking in crevices of the rocks, hung with sea-weed and studded with barnacles, told very plainly that the trade of the island was numbered among the things of the past.

POINT OF GRAVES.

Between the upper end of Great Island and the town of Portsmouth is a broad, deep, still basin, called in former times, and yet, as I suspect, by some of the oldsters, the Pool. This was the anchorage of the mast ships, which made annual voyages between England and the Piscataqua, convoyed in wartime by a vessel of force. The arrival, lading, and departure of the mast ships were the three events of the year in this old sea-place. Sometimes as many as seven were loading here at once, even as early as 1665. In the Pool, the *Astrea*, a twenty-gun ship, was destroyed by fire one cold morning in January, 1744.

The Earl of Bellomont, an Irish peer, writes to the Lords of Trade, in 1699, of the Piscataqua: "It is a most noble harbour," says his lordship; "the biggest ships the king hath can lie against the bank at Portsmouth." He then advises the building of war vessels there for the king's service; and mentions that Charles II. had complimented the French king with the draughts of the best ships in the British navy, and had thereby "given vent to that precious secret."

In the day when all of old Portsmouth was crowded between what is now Pleasant Street and the river, it is easy to imagine the water-side streets and alleys frequented by sailors in pigtails and petticoats; the mighty carousals and roaring choruses; the dingy, well-smoked dram-shops; the stews and slums of back streets, and the jolly larks and affrays with the night-watch. Rear-admiral "the brave Benbow, sirs," has landed at these old quays from his barge, followed as closely as a rolling gait would permit by some old sea-dog of a valet, with cutlass stuck in a broad, leathern belt, exactly at the middle of his back. The admiral was doubtless on his way to some convivial rencounter, where the punch was strong, and where the night not infrequently terminated little to the advantage of the quarter-deck over the forecastle.

The ships of that day were wonderfully made. Their bows crouched low in the water, their curiously carved and ornamented sterns rose high above it. The bowsprit was crossed by a heavy spar, on which a square-sail was hoisted. Chain cables had not been invented, and hempen ones, as thick as the mainmast, held the ship at her anchors. Colored battle lanterns were fixed above the taffrail; watches and broadsides were regulated by the hour-glass. The sterns and bulging quarter-galleries of Spanish, French, and Portuguese war ships were so incrusted with gilding it seemed a pity to batter them with shot. Think of Nelson knocking the *Holy Trinity* into a cocked hat, or the *Twelve Apostles* into the middle of next week!

There are many old houses on Great Island. The quaintness of one that stands within twenty yards of the river is always remarked in sailing by. I could not learn its age, but hazard the conjecture it was there before James II. abdicated.

OLD HOUSE, GREAT ISLAND.

The visitor, as in duty bound, should go to the chamber of the selectmen, where the town charter given by William and Mary, in 1693, is displayed on the wall, engrossed in almost unintelligible black-letter.[1] The records of Newcastle have had a curious history. After a disappearance of nearly fifty years, they were recovered within a year or

---

[1] The Act of Corporation, though well preserved, appeared little valued; it hung by a corner and in a light that was every day dimming the ink with which it had been engrossed.

two in England. The first volume is bound in vellum, and, though somewhat dog-eared, is perfect. The entries are in a fair round-hand, beginning in 1693, when Lieutenant-governor Usher signed the grant for the township of Newcastle.

Among the earliest records, I noticed one of five shillings paid for a pair of stocks; and of a gallery put up, in 1694, in the meeting-house, for the women to sit in. Any townsman entertaining a stranger above fourteen days, without acquainting the selectmen, was to be fined. What would now be thought of domiciliary visits like the following? "One householder or more to walk every day in sermon-time with the constable to every publick-house in ye town, to suppress ill orders, and, if they think convenient, to private houses also."

I found the town quiet enough, but the youngsters noisy and ill-bred. There seemed also to be an unusual number of loiterers about the village stores; I sometimes passed a row of them, squatted, like greyhounds, on their heels, in the sun. Those I noticed whittled, tossed coppers, or laughed and talked loudly. Many of the men were employed at Kittery Navy Yard.

From observation and inquiry I am well assured our Government dock-yards are, as a rule, of little benefit to the neighboring population. The Government pays a higher price for less labor than private persons find it for their interest to do. The work is intermittent; and it happens quite too frequently that the dock-yard employé is always expecting to be taken on, and will not go to work outside of the yard; he is especially unwilling at wages less than the Government ordinarily pays, upon which labor in the vicinity of the yard is usually gauged.

A charming ramble of an afternoon is to Fort Constitution, built on a protruding point of rocks washed by the tide. When I saw it the old fortress was casting its shell, lobster-like, for a stronger. The odd old foot-paths among the ledges zigzag now to the right or left, as they are thrust aside by intruding ledges. Much history is contained within the four walls of the work.[1] Adjoining is a light-house, originally erected in 1771.

OLD TOWER, NEWCASTLE.

---

[1] The reader will do well to consult Belknap's admirable "History of New Hampshire," vol. ii.; Adams's "Annals," or Brewster's "Rambles about Portsmouth." Some sort of defense was begun here very early. In 1665 the commissioners of Charles II. attempted to fortify, but were met by a prohibition from Massachusetts. In 1700 there existed on Great Island a fort mounting thirty guns, pronounced by Earl Bellomont incapable of defending the river. Colonel Romer made the plan of a new work, and recommended a strong tower on the point of Fryer's (Gerrish's) Island,

While engaged in sketching the gate-way and portcullis of old Fort Constitution, I was accosted by a person, with a strong German accent, who repeated, word for word, as I should judge, a mandate of the War Office against the taking of any of its old ruins by wandering *artists*. He then walked away, leaving me to finish my sketch without further interruption.

On a rocky eminence overlooking the fortress is a martello tower, built during the war of 1812, to guarantee the main work against a landing on the beach at the south side. It has three embrasures, and was begun on a Sunday, while two English frigates were lying off the Isles of Shoals. Sally-port and casemates are choked with débris, the parapet grass-grown, and the whole in picturesque ruin. Many of these towers were erected on the south coast of England during the Napoleonic wars to repel the expected invasion.

GATEWAY, OLD FORT CONSTITUTION.

Another pleasant walk is to Little Harbor, taking by the way a look at the old house near Jaffrey's Point, that is verging on two hundred years, yet seems staunch and strong. The owner believes it to be the same in which Governor Cranfield[1] held colonial courts. This was one of the attractive sites of the island, until Government began the construction of formidable earth-works at a short distance from the farmstead. The Isles of Shoals are plainly distinguished, and with a field-glass the little church on Star Island may be made out in clear weather. I enjoyed a walk on the rampart at evening, when the lights on Whale's Back, Boon Island, White Island, and Squam were seen flashing their take-heed through the darkness.

Little Harbor, where there is a summer hotel, was the site of the first settlement on the island. At Odiorne's Point, on the opposite shore, was commenced, in 1623, the settlement of New Hampshire. It is now proposed to commemorate the event itself, and the spot on which the first house was built, by a monument.[2]

---

with batteries on Wood and Clark's islands. In December, 1774, John Langdon and John Sullivan committed open rebellion by leading a party to seize the powder here. The fort was then called William and Mary. Old Fort Constitution has the date of 1808 on the key-stone of the arch of the gate-way. Its walls were carried to a certain height with rough stone topped with brick. It was a parallelogram, and mounted barbette guns only. The present work is of granite, inclosing the old walls. The new earth-works on Jaffrey's Point and Gerrish's Island render it of little importance.

[1] Governor of New Hampshire from 1682 to 1685. The house is the residence of Mr. Alber.

[2] Odiorne's Point is in Rye, New Hampshire. The settlement began under the auspices of a

Captain John Mason is known as the founder of New Hampshire. His biography is interwoven with the times of the giant Richelieu and the pigmy Buckingham. He was treasurer and pay-master of the king's armies during the war with Spain. He was governor of Portsmouth Castle when Felton struck his knife into the duke's left side; it is said, in Mason's own house. The name of Portsmouth in New Hampshire was given by him to this outgrowth of Portsmouth in old Hampshire. At a time when all England was fermenting, it seems passing strange Gorges and Mason should have persisted in their scheme to gain a lodgment in New England.

In Sir Walter Scott's "Ivanhoe" the following passage occurs: "The ancient forest of Sherwood lay between Sheffield and Doncaster. The remains of this extensive wood are still to be seen at the noble seat of Wentworth. * * * Here hunted of yore the fabulous Dragon of Wantley, and here were fought many of the most desperate battles during the Civil Wars of the Roses; and here also flourished in ancient times those bands of gallant outlaws whose deeds have been rendered so popular in English story."

Reginald Wentworth, lord of the manor of Wentworth, in Berks, A.D. 1066, is considered the common ancestor of the Wentworths of England and America. The unfortunate Earl of Strafford was a Wentworth. On the dissolution of the monasteries,

SIR THOMAS WENTWORTH, WENTWORTH HOUSE, LITTLE HARBOR.

---

company, in which Gorges and Mason were leading spirits. Their grant covered the territory between the Merrimac and Sagadahoc rivers. Under its authority, David Thompson and others settled at Little Harbor, and built what was subsequently known as Mason's Hall. Disliking his situation, Thompson removed the next spring to the island now bearing his name in Boston Bay. From this nucleus sprang the settlements at Great Island and Portsmouth. The settlement at Hilton's Point was nearly coincident.

Newstead Abbey was conferred on Sir John Byron by Henry VIII. Its site was in the midst of the fertile and interesting region once known as Sherwood Forest. Here was passed the early youth of the brilliant and gifted George, Lord Byron, and in the little church of Newstead his remains were laid. The name and title of Baroness Wentworth were in 1856 assumed by Lady Byron, whose grandfather was Sir Edward Noel, Lord Wentworth.

Another of the distinguished of this illustrious family was the Marquis of Rockingham, who voted for the repeal of the Stamp Act, and acted with Chatham against Lord North.[1] It was at him, while minister, the pasquinade was leveled,

MARQUIS OF ROCKINGHAM.

"You had better declare, which you may without shocking 'em,
The nation's asleep and the minister Rock-ing'em."

The seat of the Wentworths at Little Harbor is at the mouth of Sagamore Creek, not more than two miles from town. Among a group of aged houses in the older quarter of Portsmouth, that of Samuel Wentworth is still pointed out.[2] His monument may also be seen in the ancient burial-place of Point of Graves. The family seem to have been statesmen by inheritance. There were three chief-magistrates of New Hampshire of the name, viz.: John, the son of Samuel; Benning, the son of John; and John, the nephew of Benning.

The exterior of the mansion does not of itself keep touch and time with the preconceived idea of colonial magnificence. Its architectural deformity would have put Ruskin beside himself. A rambling collection of buildings, seemingly the outgrowth of different periods and conditions, are incorporated into an inharmonious whole. The result is an oddity in wood. Doubtless the builder was content with it. If so, I have little disposition to be critical.

---

[1] Peace with the thirteen colonies was proposed under the administration of Rockingham, about the last official act of his life. His name is often met with in Portsmouth.

[2] The house stands at the north end of Manning, formerly Wentworth Street, and is thought from its size to have been a public-house. The same house was also occupied by Lieutenant-Governor John, son of Samuel Wentworth. Samuel was the son of William, the first settler of the name. He had been an innkeeper, and had swung his sign of the "Dolphin" on Great Island. Hon. John Wentworth, of Chicago, is the biographer of his family.

Beyond this, the visitor may not refuse his unqualified approval of the site, which is charming, of the surroundings—the mansion was embowered in blooming lilacs when I saw it—and of the general air of snugness and of comfort, rather than elegance, which seems the proper atmosphere of the Wentworth House.

Built in 1750, it commands a view up and down Little Harbor, though concealed by an eminence from the road. I had a brief glimpse of it while going on Great Island *via* the bridges. It is said it originally contained as many as fifty-two rooms, though by the removal of a good-sized tenement to the opposite island the number has been diminished to forty-five. There is, therefore, plenty of elbow-room. The cellar was sometimes used as a stable: it was large enough to have accommodated a troop, or, at a pinch, a squadron.

IN THE WENTWORTH HOUSE, LITTLE HARBOR.

Prepared for an interior as little attractive as the outside, the conjecture of the visitor is again at fault, for this queer old bundle of joiners' patchwork contains apartments which indicate that the old beau, Benning Wentworth, cared less for the rind than the fruit.

> "Within unwonted splendors met the eye,
>   Panels and floors of oak and tapestry;
>   Carved chimney-pieces where on brazen dogs
>   Reveled and roared the Christmas fires of logs;
>   Doors opening into darkness unawares,
>   Mysterious passages and flights of stairs;
>   And on the walls in heavy gilded frames,
>   The ancestral Wentworths with old Scripture names."

The council chamber contains a gem of a mantel, enriched with elaborate carving of busts of Indian princesses, chaplets, and garlands—a year's labor, it is said, of the workman. The wainscot is waist-high, and heavy beams divide the ceiling. As we entered we noticed the rack in which the muskets of the Governor's guard were deposited.

But what catches the eye of the visitor soonest and retains it longest, is the portraits on the walls. First is a canvas representing the Earl of Strafford[1] dictating to his secretary, in the Tower, on the day before his execution. At his trial, says an eye-witness, "he was always in the same suit of black, as in doole" (mourning). When the lieutenant of the Tower offered him a coach, lest he should be torn in pieces by the mob in going to execution, he replied, "I die to please the people, and I will die in their own way."

LADY HANCOCK'S PORTRAIT (BY COPLEY) IN THE WENTWORTH HOUSE.

Here is a portrait from the brush of Copley, who reveled in rich draperies and in the accessories of his portraits quite as much as in painting rounded arms, beautiful hands, and shapely figures. This one in pink satin, with over-dress of white lace, short sleeves

---

[1] His second wife was Henrietta du Roy, daughter of Frederick Charles du Roy, generalissimo to the King of Denmark.

with deep ruffles, and coquettish lace cap, is Dorothy Quincy, the greatest belle and breaker of hearts of her day. It was not, it is said, her fault that she became Mrs. Governor Hancock, instead of Mrs. Aaron Burr. When in later years, as Madam Scott, she retained all the vivacity of eighteen, she was fond of relating how the hand now seen touching rather than supporting her cheek, had been kissed by marquises, dukes, and counts, who had experienced the hospitality of the Hancock mansion; and how D'Estaing, put to bed after too much wine, had torn her best damask coverlet with the spurs he had forgotten to remove.

Other portraits are—Of Queen Christina of Sweden, who looks down with the same pitiless eyes that exulted in the murder of her equerry, Monaldeschi; one said to be Secretary Waldron, a right noble countenance and martial figure; and of Mr. and Mrs. Jacob Sheaffe.

I could be loquacious on the subject of these portraits, the fading impressions of histories varied or startling, of experiences more curious than profitable to narrate. In their presence we take a step backward into the past, that past whose lessons we will not heed. Hawthorne, standing before a wall covered with such old counterfeits, was moved to say: "Nothing gives a stronger idea of old worm-eaten aristocracy, of a family being crazy with age, and of its being time that it was extinct, than these black, dusty, faded, antique-dressed portraits."

The old furniture standing about was richly carved, and covered with faded green damask. In the billiard-room was an ancient spinet, quite as much out of tune as out of date. Doubtless, the flashing of white hands across those same yellow keys has often struck an answering chord in the breasts of colonial youth. Here are more portraits; and a buffet, a sideboard, and a sedan-chair. Punch has flowed, and laughter echoed here.

The reader knows the pretty story, so gracefully told by Mr. Longfellow, of Martha Hilton, who became the second wife of Governor Benning,[1] and thus Lady Wentworth of the Hall.

We can see her as she goes along the street, swinging the pail, a trifle heavy for her, and splashing with the water her naked feet. We hear her ringing laughter, and the saucy answer to Mistress Stavers in her furbelows, as that buxom landlady flings at her, in passing, the sharp reproof:

"O Martha Hilton! Fie! how dare you go
About the town half-dressed and looking so?"

The poet's tale is at once a history and a picture, full of pretty conceits and picturesque situations. Fancy the battered effigy of the Earl of Halifax on the innkeeper's sign falling at the feet of Mrs. Stavers to declare his passion.

---

[1] Bennington, Vermont, is named from Governor Wentworth.

But Benning Wentworth, governor though he was, was none too good for Martha Hilton.[1] It was the pride of the Hiltons made her say, "I yet shall ride in my own chariot." The widowed governor was gouty, passionate, and had imbibed with his long residence in Spain the hauteur of the Spaniard. He left office in 1776 in disgrace.

The last of the colonial Wentworths was Sir John, in whose favor his uncle had been allowed to screen himself by a resignation. There are some odd coincidences in the family records of both uncle and nephew. The former's widow made a second marriage to a Wentworth; the latter married his widowed cousin, Frances Wentworth.[2]

GOVERNOR BENNING WENTWORTH.

The mansion of Sir John may be seen in Pleasant Street, Portsmouth. He was the last royal governor of New Hampshire. John Adams mentions

---

[1] Her grandfather, Hon. Richard Hilton, of Newmarket, was grandson of Edward, the original settler of Dover, New Hampshire, and had been a justice of the Superior Court of the Province.— JOHN WENTWORTH.

[2] Frances Deering Wentworth married John just two weeks after the decease of her first husband, Theodore Atkinson, also her cousin, and in the same church from which he had been buried —matter for such condolence and reproof as Talleyrand's celebrated "Ah, madame," and "Oh, madame." Benning Wentworth's widow married Colonel Michael Wentworth, said to have been a retired British officer. He was a great horseman and a free liver. Once he rode from Boston to Portsmouth between sunrise and sunset. Having run through a handsome estate, he died under suspicion of suicide, leaving his own epitaph, "I have eaten my cake." Colonel Michael was the host, at the Hall, of Washington. In 1817, the house at Little Harbor was purchased by Charles Cushing, whose widow was a daughter of Jacob Sheaffe.

that as he was leaving his box at the theatre one night in Paris, a gentleman seized him by the hand: "'Governor Wentworth, sir,' said the gentleman. At first I was embarrassed, and knew not how to behave toward him. As my classmate and friend at college, and ever since, I could have pressed him to my bosom with most cordial affection. But we now belonged to two different nations, at war with each other, and consequently were enemies."

The king afterward gave Sir John the government of Nova Scotia. The poet Moore mentions the baronet's kind treatment of him in 1805, during his American tour. He is said to have kept sixteen horses in his stable at Portsmouth, and to have been a free-liver. A man of unquestioned ability to govern, who went down under the great revolutionary wave of 1775, but rose again to the surface and struck boldly out.

There is now in the possession of James Lenox, of New York, a portrait of the baronet's wife, by Copley, painted in his best manner. The lady was a celebrated beauty. The face has caught an expression, indescribably arch, as if its owner repressed an invincible desire to torment the artist. In it are set a pair of eyes, black and dangerous, with high-arched brows, a tempting yet mocking mouth, and nose a little *retroussé*. Her natural hair is decorated with pearls; a string of them encircles her throat. The corsage is very low, displaying a pair of white shoulders such as the poet imagined:

"She has a bosom as white as snow,
    Take care!
She knows how much it is best to show,
    Beware! beware!"

BARON STEUBEN.

In 1777 Baron Steuben arrived in Portsmouth, in the *Flamand*. Franklin had snubbed him, St. Germain urged him, but Beaumarchais offered him a thousand louis-d'or.' On the day the baron joined the army at Valley Forge his name was the watch-word in all the camps.

---

[1] "Paul Jones shall equip his *Bonne Homme Richard;* weapons, military stores can be smuggled over (if the English do not seize them); wherein, once more Beaumarchais, dimly as the Giant Smuggler, becomes visible—filling his own lank pocket withal."—CARLYLE, "French Revolution," vol. i., p. 43.

WITCH HILL, SALEM.

CHAPTER XIV.

SALEM VILLAGE, AND '92.

Banquo. "Were such things here as we do speak about?
Or have we eaten of the insane root,
That takes the reason prisoner?"—*Macbeth.*

SALEM VILLAGE has a sorrowful celebrity. It would seem as if an adverse spell still hung over it, for in the changes brought by time to its neighbors it has no part, remaining, as it is likely to remain, Salem Village—that is to say, distinctively antiquated, sombre, and lifeless.

A collection of houses scattered along the old high-road from Salem to Andover, decent-looking, brown-roofed, though humble dwellings, a somewhat pretending village church, and pleasant, home-like, parsonage; old trees, partly verdant, partly withered, stretching naked boughs above the gables of houses even older than themselves, embody something of the impressions of oft-repeated walks in what is known as the "Witch Neighborhood."

The village contains one central point of paramount interest. It is an inclosed space of grass ground, a short distance from the principal and only street, reached by a well-trodden by-path. Within this now naked field once stood a house, with a garden and orchard surrounding. Of the house nothing remains except a slight depression in the soil; of the orchard and garden there is no trace; yet hard by I chanced on a bank of aromatic thyme once held of singular potency in witchcraft—as in the "Faërie Queen," the tree laments to the knight:

"I chanced to see her in her proper hue,
Bathing herself in origan and thyme."

In this quiet, out-of-the-way little nook, Salem witchcraft had its beginning. The sunken cavity is what remains of the Ministry House, so called, pulled down in 1785 (not a day too soon); the den of error in which the plague-spot first appeared. No one would have thought, standing here, that he surveyed the focus of malevolence so deadly as the wretched delirium of '92.

The well-informed reader is everywhere familiar with the origin and development of Salem witchcraft.[1] It has employed the best pens as it has puzzled the best brains among us; until to-day the whole affair remains enveloped in a mystery which the theories of nearly two hundred years have failed wholly to penetrate.

The writer has had frequent occasion to know how wide-spread is the belief that witchcraft began in New England, and particularly in Salem. This is to be classed among popular errors upon which repeated denials have little effect. Nevertheless, witchcraft did not originate in New England; no, nor in old England either, for that matter. The belief in it was earlier than the *Mayflower*, older than the Norman Conquest, and antedated the Roman Empire. The first written account of it is contained in Scripture.[2]

Saul incurred the anger of God by consulting the Witch of Endor. Joan of Arc was burned as a witch in 1431. About fifty years later the Church of Rome fulminated a bull against witchcraft. The number of suspected persons already burned at the stake or subjected to the most cruel torments is estimated at many thousands.

In taking leave of the Dark Ages we do not take our leave of witchcraft. More than a hundred thousand victims had perished in Germany and France alone before the *Mayflower* sailed from Delft. The Pilgrims, I engage, believed in it to a man.

Old England! Why, the statute against witchcraft was not repealed until 1736, in the second George's time, though it had lain dormant some years. The last recorded execution in the British Islands occurred in Scotland, as late as 1722. The sixth chapter of Lord Coke's "Third Institutes" is devoted to a panegyric on the statutes for punishing "conjuration, sorcery, witchcraft, or enchantment." The laws of England were the fundamental law of New England; witchcraft was in the list of recognized crimes throughout Christendom.

France, under Louis le Grand, whose style history will change, notwithstanding his famous "*L' état c'est moi*," to Louis the Little, was immeshed in the net of superstition. The highest personages of the court resorted to the astrologers for horoscopes, charms, or philters. We might see later the magic

---

[1] Mather and Hutchinson deal largely with it. Upham and Drake have compiled, arranged, and analyzed it.

[2] Exod. xxii., 18 (1491 B.C.): "Thou shalt not suffer a witch to live."

and sorcery of the sixteenth century and of the seventeenth transformed into studies in chemistry under the Regency, and become experiments in magnetism in the eighteenth century.

The settlers in New England, who brought all their Old-World superstitions with them, were not surprised to find the Indians fully impregnated with a belief in magic equal to their own. The wonderful cures of the Indian magicians or medicine-men were thoroughly believed in, and are vouched for by white evidence. One of their favorite methods of revenging private injury was by enchanting a hair, which entered the bodies of their enemies and killed them while sleeping. It is noted that Tituba, an Indian, had much to do with the outbreak in Salem village.

Sir William Phips, an illiterate but not incapable man, had been appointed Governor of Massachusetts Bay, under the new charter of William and Mary. The charter conferred the power of civil government, and separated the legislative from the judicial authority. Sir William constituted a commission of seven to try the witchcraft cases at Salem. As he had no power to create such a court under the charter, one of the saddest reflections that arise from these bloody proceedings is that twenty persons suffered death for an imaginary crime, inflicted by an illegal tribunal. The province law of 1692 decreed death for "enchantment, sorcery, charm, or conjuration, or invocation, or to feed any wicked spirit."

The first authenticated case of witchcraft in New England, and also the first execution, took place at Boston, as early as 1648. The culprit, Margaret Jones, of Charlestown, was suspected of having and using the "malignant touch." She professed some knowledge of medicine, and probably availed herself of the awe in which she was held by the superstitious to ply her trade. Many other cases are mentioned in the other colonies, Connecticut bearing her full share, before the climax of 1692 is reached. Then, as afterward, the accusations fell chiefly upon women; the old, friendless, or half-witted bearing the burden of every accident in their neighborhood.

An English writer gravely says in 1690: "Several old women suspected for witches in and about Lancashire have been often noted to have beards of considerable growth, tho' that's no general rule, some of the reverend and virtuous being often liable to the same." Everywhere witchcraft was received as a stubborn fact. The criminal codes of nearly if not quite all the colonies recognized it. In Pennsylvania, if tradition may be believed, the fact was met by no less stubborn common sense. It is said, when Philadelphia was three years old, a woman was brought before Governor Penn, charged with witchcraft and riding through the air on a broomstick. Although the woman confessed her guilt, she was dismissed by the Quaker magistrate with the assurance that, as there was no law against it, she might ride a broomstick as often as she pleased.

Could a full and candid confession be obtained of the present generation

CUSTOM-HOUSE, SALEM, MASSACHUSETTS.

there would appear more superstition than we wot of, such as would show us legitimate descendants of credulous colonists. It is not long since a staid old town in Massachusetts was in consternation at the report of a ghost in a school-room. Signs and portents have been handed down and are religiously believed in by other than the ignorant and credulous, as has been already stated in a former chapter. A very small proportion of the skeptical could be induced to enter a church-yard at night. There is some subtle principle of our nature that gives ready adhesion to the mystical or the marvelous; and it is believed they were not differently constituted in 1692.

REBECCA NURSE'S HOUSE.

Leaving the Witch Ground, the visitor, in retracing his steps, will pass near the old Nurse House, a memorial of one of the most damning of the innocent sacrifices to superstition. It is not easy to sit down and write of it with the indifference of the professional historian.

Rebecca Nurse, aged and infirm, universally beloved by her neighbors, was accused. The jury, moved by her innocence, having brought in a verdict of "not guilty," the court sent them out again with instructions to find her guilty. She was executed. The tradition is that her sons disinterred her body by stealth from the foot of the gallows, where it had been thrown, and brought it to the old homestead, laying it reverently and with many tears in the little burying-ground which the family always kept, and which is still seen near by.

But briefly to our history. We there discover that twenty persons lost their lives through the denunciation of eight simple country girls, the youngest being eleven, and the oldest not more than twenty years of age.[1] These maidens met at the house of Samuel Parris, the then minister of the village, and on the spot where the earth is now trying to heal the scar left by the old cellar. They formed what was then and is still known as a "circle" in New England, devoted in these more modern days to clothing the heathen and bewitching the youth who enter their influence.

---

[1] Abigail Williams, eleven; Mary Walcut, seventeen; Ann Putnam, twelve; Mercy Lewis, seventeen; Mary Warren, twenty; Elizabeth Booth, eighteen; Sarah Churchill, twenty; Susannah Sheldon, age not known.

The most plausible, and therefore the commonly received opinion is, that these girls, having at first practiced some of the well-known methods of performing magic, were led into a series of false accusations which, from being conceived in a spirit of mischief, grew into crimes of the first magnitude as they found themselves carried away by a frenzy they had not moral courage to stay. Another presumption supposes the girls believers in their own powers. This view is sustained by the universal belief in witchcraft, the ready adhesion given to their charges, the support they received from the judges, and the terrible power with which they found themselves possessed. Another solution is found in the occult influences of second-sight so widely credited in Scotland in years by-gone, the psychology and clairvoyance of the present day. Dr. Samuel Johnson said he would rather believe in second-sight than in the poetry of Ossian.

PROCTER HOUSE.

If the soundest thinkers of the nineteenth century are staggered to account for the phenomena of spirit-rappings, it is wise to defer a hasty condemnation of the "possessed damosels" of Salem village. Instead of plying its needles, the circle was engaged in attempts to discover the future. Rev. John Hale, in his "Modest Inquiry into the Nature of Witchcraft," has this to say:

"I fear some young persons, through a vain curiosity to know their future condition, have tampered with devil's tools, so far that thereby one door was opened to Satan to play those pranks—*Anno* 1692. I knew one of the Afflicted persons, who (as I was credibly informed), did try with an egg and a glass to find her future husband's calling; till there came up a coffin, that is, a spectre in likeness of a coffin. And she was afterward followed with diabolical molestation to her death; and so dyed a single person. A just warning to others, to take heed of handling the devil's weapons lest they get a wound thereby." This John Hale, teacher of the people, was at first a zealous believer. Perhaps the denunciation of his own wife had something to do with his backsliding into common sense.

The accusing girls were believed infallible witch-finders. Their services were consequently in demand as their fame spread abroad. Some of them were taken to Andover, leaving distrust, dismay, and death in the quiet old

West Parish. "In a short time," says the annalist, "it was commonly reported forty men of Andover could raise the devil as well as any astrologer."

A "Boston Man" having taken his sick child to Salem in order to consult the afflicted ones, obtained the names of two of his own towns-people as the authors of its distemper; but the Boston justices refused warrants to apprehend them, and Increase Mather asked the father if there was not a God in Boston that he must go to the devil in Salem. These two persons are said to have been Mrs. Thatcher, mother-in-law of Curwin, one of the judges,[1] and the wife of Sir William Phips.

As soon as the prosecutions stopped, it was remarked that the apparitions ceased. Once or twice the accuser recoiled before a sharp and swift reproof, as at Lieutenant Ingersoll's, when one of them cried out, "There's Goody Procter!" Raymond and Goody Ingersoll told her flatly she lied; there was nothing. The girl was cowed, and "said she did it for sport."

Even the witchcraft horrors have a humorous side—grimly humorous, it is true, like the jokes cracked in a dissecting-room. The thought of pots and kettles jumping on the crane, of anchors leaping overboard of themselves, and of hay-cocks found hanging to trees is rather mirth-provoking. Mirrors were daily consulted by maids and widows looking for a husband. A matter of life and death could not prevent George Jacobs, the old grandfather, from laughing heartily at the spasmodic antics of Abigail Williams.

It seems a pity that New England in her greatest need should have found no champion, like St. Dunstan, to argue with and finally compel the devil to own himself confuted, as, according to vulgar belief, he did, by taking the fiend by the nose with a pair of red-hot tongs; or as Ignatius Loyola, who, when disturbed at his devotions by the devil, seized his cudgel and drubbed him away.[2] Montmorency, a peer and marshal of France, son of the famous Bouteville, whom Richelieu had caused to be decapitated for fighting a duel at midday in the Place Royal, was weak enough to visit La Voisin, the renowned conjuror and fabricator of poisons in the reign of Louis XIV. La Voisin had promised to show him the devil, and the duke was curious. When the maréchal whipped out his rapier and thrust vigorously at the spectre, it fell on its knees, and begged its life. The devil proved to be a confederate of La Voisin. Archibald, duke of Argyle, was haunted by blue phantoms—the origin of our epithet for melancholy, "blue devils."

In the village tavern there was a battle with spectres that Abigail Williams and Mary Walcut declared were present. Benjamin Hutchinson and Eleazer Williams pulled out their swords and cut and stabbed the air until, as the two girls averred, the floor was deep in ghostly blood!

A ride through the woods then was little coveted by the stoutest hearts. A spark of fear is soon blown into uncontrollable panic. Bushes grew spec-

---

[1] Account of Thomas Brattle. [2] See his life, page 80.

tres and trees outstretched goblin arms. Elizabeth Hubbard was riding home from meeting on the crupper, behind old Clement Coldum. The rustling leaves were witches' whisperings, the white birches seemed ghosts in their winding-sheets. The woman, faint-hearted and overmastered by a nameless dread, cried out to the goodman to ride for life—the woods were full of devils. Though he could see none, the valiant rider spurred his horse like mad, and rode as Tam O'Shanter rode his fearful race when pursued by the witches of Kirk Alloway.

The trysting-place of the witches was in Parris's pasture. It was here Abigail Hobbs, who had sold herself to the "Old Boy," attending, saw the sacrament of the "red bread and the red wine" administered to the devil's elect. Poor George Burroughs, whom we met for a moment in our walk through Wells, was denounced for summoning with a trumpet the attending witches. Obedient to the sound, from far and near, the withered beldams, toothless hags in short petticoats, white linen hoods, and conical high crowned hats, come flocking on flying broomsticks. Satan is there in person, not playing the bagpipe, as in Tam O'Shanter's fearful conclave, but with the conventional book written in letters of blood.

Certes, these were but rude ghosts. Nowadays the devil is raised as easily, but conducts himself with greater propriety, as becomes the devil of the nineteenth century. The damp grass of the church-yard and the witches' den are bugbears no longer. We sit in a comfortable apartment around a mahogany table. Our ghost no more appears in mouldy shroud, but, like a well-bred spectre, knocks for admittance. Soon his card will be handed in on a salver, and we may perhaps in time expect daily weather reports from the nether world.

Before leaving the village, I turned into one of those old abandoned roads in which I like so well to walk. Left on one side by a shorter cut, saving some rods to this hurrying age, the deserted by-way conducts you into solitudes proper for communion with the past. Grass has sprung up so thickly as almost to conceal traces of the once well-worn ruts, now only two indistinct lines of lighter green. Young pines, a foot high, are rooted in the cartway; stone walls, moss-grown and tumbling down. Here and there are the ghastly remains of some old orchard, the ground strewed with withered branches. A half-obliterated cellar denotes a former habitation; even the land betrays evidences of having been turned by the plows of two centuries ago. Who have passed this way? Perhaps the laying-out of this very road begot disputes transmitted from father to son.

A mile beyond the Witch Neighborhood the Andover road crosses the Newburyport turnpike. At the junction of the two roads stands the old farm-house in which Israel Putnam, the "Old Put" of the Revolutionary army, was born.

The house, or rather houses, for two structures compose it, is still occupied by Putnams. The newer building, already old by comparison with some of its neighbors, was built in 1744; the original in 1650, or thereabouts, according to family tradition. One object, to which the attention of every visitor is directed, is the old pollard of enormous girth standing near the house. House and tree seem types of the sturdy, indomitable old man, who at nearly three-score was full of the rage of battle.

By the courtesy of the family, ever ready to indulge a proper curiosity, I looked over the old house from garret to cellar. The little room in which the general was born remains just as when its rough-hewn posts and thick beams were revealed to his astonished gaze. There are few relics of the general remaining.

BIRTHPLACE OF PUTNAM.

While in the Wadsworth Museum at Hartford, I lately saw the damaged sign displayed by Putnam when he kept an inn at Brooklyn, Connecticut, about 1768. Another famous soldier, Murat, was the son of an *aubergiste*, and Napoleon was not too willing on this account to give him the hand of his sister.

The Putnams settled early in Salem. John, the first emigrant, came from Buckinghamshire, in 1634, with three sons, Thomas, Nathaniel, and John. Some of the name exercised a fatal influence during the reign of witchcraft. Israel was already an old man when he left his plow in the furrow to gallop to Cambridge, having been born in 1718. At twenty-one he removed to

PUTNAM IN BRITISH UNIFORM.

Pomfret, Connecticut. Putnam was prompt, resolute, and incapable of fear—full of fight, and always ready. Washington, who did not judge badly, thought him the only fit man to make an assault on Boston. Though uneducated, Putnam wrote pithily, as to Governor Tryon:

"Sir,—Nathan Palmer, a lieutenant in your king's service, was taken in my camp as a spy; he was condemned as a spy; and he shall be hanged as a spy.

"P. S.—*Afternoon.* He is hanged."

Danvers, in whose territory we have been rambling, is an aggregate of several widely scattered villages taken from Salem in the last century. Some of its villages have grown into good-sized, prosperous towns, and one has taken the name of her eminent banker-philanthropist, George Peabody. When at Salem, the visitor may easily reach Peabody, Danvers, and the Witch Neighborhood by rail, having in the latter instance a walk of a mile before him on leaving the little station near the Putnam House. In a circuit of several miles, embracing what is to be seen of interest on this side, it is, perhaps, better to leave Salem by the old Boston road and return to it by the Andover highway. Following this route, we successively pass by Governor Endicott's farm, on which is still seen the aged pear-

ENDICOTT PEAR-TREE.

tree, sole relic of the ancient orchard,¹ the house which became the headquarters in 1774 of General Gage, and the Witch Neighborhood. But before hurrying away from Peabody, it will be well to read the inscription on the monument which one sees in the main street,² examine the memorials of royal munificence in the library of the Institute,³ and, if the stranger be of my mind, to halt for a moment before the humble dwelling in which Bowditch was born. As there is no place in New England which so highly prizes its antique memorials and traditions as Salem, the first person you meet will be able to direct you to the one or relate to you the other.

---

¹ Endicott had a grant of three hundred acres on the tongue of land between Cow-house and Duck rivers. The site does justice to his discernment.

² Raised in 1837 to the memory of soldiers of Danvers killed in the battle of Lexington.

³ The Queen's portrait by Tilt, the gold box and medal presented by the city of London and by Congress to Mr. Peabody.

PUTNAM'S TAVERN SIGN.

WASHINGTON STREET, SALEM.

CHAPTER XV.

A WALK TO WITCH HILL.

> "Do not the hist'ries of all ages
> Relate miraculous presages,
> Of strange turns in the world's affairs,
> Foreseen by astrologers, soothsayers,
> Chaldeans, learned genethliacs,
> And some that have writ almanacs?"
> *Hudibras.*

IN 1692 Salem may have contained four hundred houses. A few specimens of this time now remain in odd corners—Rip Van Winkles or Wandering Jews of old houses, that have outlived their day of usefulness, and would now be at rest. Objects of scorn to the present generation, they have silently endured the contemptuous flings of the passer-by, as well, perchance, as the frowns and haughty stare of rows of plate-glass windows along the street. As well put new wine in old bottles, as an old house in a new dress; it is always an old house, despite the thin veneer of miscalled improvements. The architect can do nothing with it to the purpose; the carpenter can make nothing of it. There they are, with occupants equally old-fashioned—of, yet not belonging to the present. Some have stood so long in particular neighborhoods, have outlived so many modern structures, as to become points of direction, like London Stone or Charing-cross. The stranger's puzzled questioning is often met with, "You know that old house in such a street?" And so the old

BIRTHPLACE OF HAWTHORNE.

house helps us to find our way not alone to the past, but in the present.

Undoubted among such specimens as will be met with in the neighborhood of the wharves, or between Essex Street and the water-side, is the old gambrel-roofed, portly-chimneyed house in which our "Wizard of the North" first drew breath. It stands in Union Street, at the left as you pass down. Many pilgrims loiter and ponder there over these words:

"SALEM, October 4th, Union Street [Family Mansion].

"Here I sit in my old accustomed chamber, where I used to sit in days gone by. Here I have written many tales—many that have been burned to ashes, many that doubtless deserved the same fate. This claims to be called a haunted chamber, for thousands upon thousands of visions have appeared to me in it; and some few of them have become visible to the world. If ever I should have a biographer, he ought to make great mention of this chamber in my memoirs, because so much of my lonely youth was wasted here, and here my mind and character were formed; and here I have been glad and hopeful, and here

SHATTUCK HOUSE.

ROOM IN WHICH HAWTHORNE WAS BORN.

I have been despondent. And here I sat a long, long time, waiting patiently for the world to know me, and sometimes wondering why it did not know me sooner, or whether it would ever know me at all — at least, till I were in my grave."

It is not my purpose to attempt a description of Salem, or of what is to be seen there. Her merchants are princes. No doubt they were in Josselyn's mind when he said some of the New Englanders were "damnable rich." French writers of that day speak of her "*bourgeois entièrement riches.*" Those substantial mansions of red brick, tree-shaded and ivy-trellised, represent what Carlyle named the "noblesse of commerce," with money in its pocket.

Writing in 1685 upon the English invasions of Acadia, Sieur Bergier thus characterizes Salem and Boston:

"The English who inhabit these two straggling boroughs (*bourgades*) are for the greater part fugitives out of England, guilty of the death of the late king (Charles Stuart), and accused of conspiring against the reigning sovereign. The rest are corsairs and sea-robbers, who have united themselves with the former in a sort of independent republic." This is rather earlier than the date usually fixed for the planting of democracy in America, but perhaps none too early. Endicott had then cut the cross from the standard of England with his poniard; and Charles II. had been humbled in the persons of his commissioners.

Let us walk on through Essex Street, unheeding the throng, unmindful of the statelier buildings, until we approach an ancient landmark at the corner of North Street. Its claims on our attention are twofold. It is said to have been the dwelling of Roger Williams, for whom Southey, when reminded that Wales had been more famous for mutton than great men, avowed he had a sincere respect, yet it is even more celebrated as the scene of examinations during the Reign of Terror in 1692.[1]

---

[1] Considerable changes were necessary so long ago as 1674–'75, when it became the property of Jonathan Corwin, of witchcraft notoriety. In 1745, and again about 1772, it underwent other repairs, leaving it as now seen.

In appearance the original house might have been transplanted out of old London. Its peaked gables, with pine-apples carved in wood surmounting, its latticed windows, and colossal chimney, put it unmistakably in the age of ruffs, Spanish cloaks, and long rapiers. It has long been divested of its antique English character, now appearing no more than a reminiscence of its former self. However, from a recessed area at the back its narrow casements and excrescent stairways are yet to be seen. A massive frame, filled between with brick, plastered with clay, with the help of its tower-like chimney, has stood immovable against the assaults of time. Such houses, and their num-

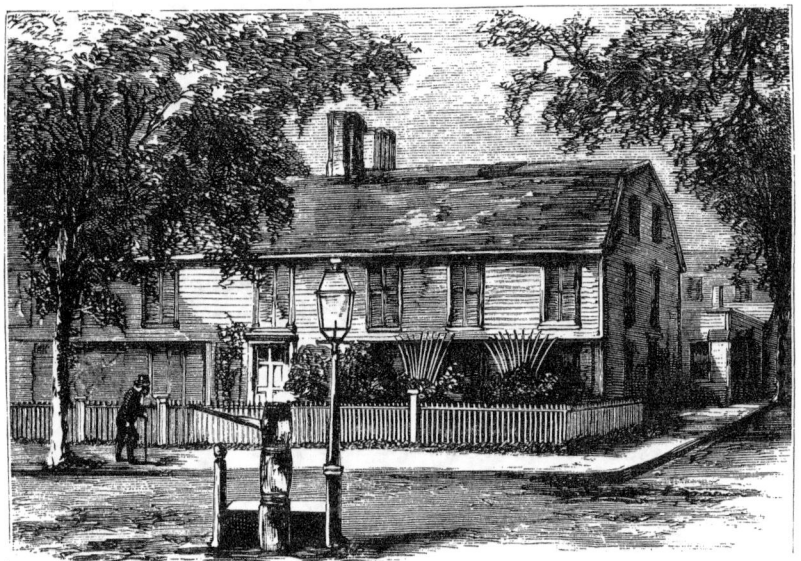

THE OLD WITCH HOUSE.

ber is not large, represent the original forest that stood on the site of ancient Salem.

Jonathan Corwin, or Curwin, made a councilor under the new charter granted by King William, was one of the judges before whom the preliminary examinations were held, both here and at the Village. Governor Corwin, of Ohio, is accounted a descendant, as was the author of "The Scarlet Letter" of another witch-judge, John Hathorne. The reader may imagine the novelist on his knees before the grave-stone of his ancestor, striving to scrape the moss from its half-obliterated characters.[1] Other examinations took place in Thomas Beadle's tavern.

---

[1] A scene from life in the old Copp's Hill burial-ground at Boston.

> The Examination of Rebekah Nurse at Salem Village 24. Mar. 1691/2
>
> Mr. Hathorn — What do you say (speaking to one afflicted) have you seen this woman hurt you?
> Yes, she beat me this morning
> Abigail Have you been hurt by this Woman?
> Yes
> Ann Putnam in a grievous fit cryed out that she hurt her.
> Goody Nurse, here are two An: Putnam the child & Abigail Williams complains of your hurting them what do you say to it
> N. I can say before my Eternal father I am innocent, & God will clear my innocency
>
> - - - - - - - - -
>
> you do know whither you are guilty. & have familiarity with the Devil, & now when you are here present to see such a thing as these testify a black man whispering in your ear, & birds about you what do you say to it
> It is all false I am clear
>
> Is it not an unaccountable case that when you are examined these persons are afflicted & I have got no body to look to but God
>
> John Hathorne
> Jonathan Corwin } Assistants

FRAGMENT OF EXAMINATION OF REBECCA NURSE,
In Handwriting of Rev. Samuel Parris.[1]

Knowing the world believed in witchcraft, our horror at the atrocities of '92 is moderated by the probability that nothing less than the shedding of innocent blood could have annihilated the delusion. The king believed in it,

---

[1] In the library of Harvard College is a book having the name of Parris on the fly-leaf.

the governor and judges believed in it, and the most sensible and learned gave ample credence to it. Queen Anne wrote a letter to Phips that shows she admitted it as a thing unquestioned.[1] The clergy, with singular unanimity, recognized it.

THOMAS BEADLE'S TAVERN, 1692.

The revulsion that followed equaled the precipitation that had marked the proceedings. One of the judges made public confession of his error.[2] Officers of the court were persecuted until the day of their death.

There is one hard, inflexible character, that was never known to have relented. William Stoughton, lieutenant-governor, presided at these trials. It is related that once, on hearing of a reprieve granted some of the condemned, he left the bench, exclaiming, "We were in a way to have cleared the land of these. Who is it obstructs the course of justice I know not. The Lord be merciful to the country."

This pudding-faced, sanctimonious, yet merciless judge had listened to the heart-broken appeals of the victims, raising their manacled hands to heaven for that justice denied them upon earth. "I have got nobody to look to but God." "There is another judgment, dear child." "The Lord will not suffer it." Others as passionately reproached their accusers, but all were confounded, because all were believers in the fact of witchcraft.[3]

Whether Witch Hill be the first or last place visited, it is there Salem witchcraft culminates. There is seen, in approaching by the railway from Boston, a bleak and rocky eminence bestrown with a little soil. Houses of the poorer sort straggle up its eastern acclivity, while the south and west faces remain as formed by nature, abrupt and precipitous. The hill is one of a range stretching away northward in a broken line toward the Merrimac. On the summit is a tolerably level area of several acres. Not a tree was growing on it when I was there. The bleak winds sweep over it without hinderance.

---

[1] She approved Governor Phips's conduct, but advised the utmost moderation and circumspection in all proceedings for witchcraft.—" Manuscript Files."

[2] Samuel Sewall, afterward chief-justice of the Supreme Court of the province.

[3] Some of the pins said to have been thrust by witches into the bodies of their victims are still preserved in Salem.

On the 19th of July, 1692, an unusual stir might have been observed in Salem. We may suppose the town excited beyond any thing that had been known in its history. The condemned witches, Sarah Good, Sarah Wildes, Elizabeth Howe, Susannah Martin, and Rebecca Nurse, are to be hanged on Gallows Hill.

The narrow lane in which the common jail is situated is thronged with knots of men and women, wearing gloomy, awe-struck faces, conversing in under-tones. Before the jail door are musketeers of the train-band, armed and watchful. The crowd gives way on the approach of a cart that stops in front of the prison door, which is now wide opened. On one side stands the jailer, with ponderous keys hanging at his girdle; on the other is the sheriff, grasping his staff of office. The guard clears a passage, and then the sheriff's voice is heard calling upon the condemned to come forth.

There are five of them, all women. They look pale, haggard, despairing. At sight of them a murmur ripples through the crowd, succeeded by solemn stillness. As they mount the cart with weak and tottering steps—for some are old and feeble and gray-haired—audible sobs are heard among the by-standers. Men's lips are compressed and teeth clenched as they look on with white faces. All is ready. The guard surrounds the cart, as if a rescue were feared. It takes a score of strong men, armed to the teeth, to conduct five helpless women to death!

I suppose there were outcries, hootings, and imprecations, as is the rabble's wont. If so, I believe they were borne with the resignation and heroism that make woman the superior of man in supreme moments. At last the cavalcade is grouped around the place of execution. The gallows and the fatal ladder are there, grotesque yet horrible. To each of those five women they meant martyrdom, and nothing less.

The provost-marshal commands silence while he reads the warrant. This formality ended, he replaces it in his belt. Expectation is intense as the condemned are seen to take leave of each other, like people who have done with this world. Then a shiver, like an electric spark, runs through the multitude as the hangman seizes them, pinions and blindfolds them, and, in the name of King William and Queen Mary, hangs them by the neck until dead.

Being leagued with Satan, they were denied the consolations of religion vouchsafed to pirates, murderers, and like malefactors. Poor old Rebecca Nurse had been led, heavily ironed, up the broad aisle of Salem Church to be thrust out of its communion. At the scaffold Rev. Mr. Noyes, of Salem, insulted the last moments of Sarah Good. "You are a witch, and you know it," said this servant of Christ. She turned upon him fiercely, "You lie, and if you take away my life God will give you blood to drink."[1] That few of

---

[1] This incident appears in Hawthorne's "Seven Gables." The tradition is that Noyes was choked with blood—dying by a hemorrhage.

INTERIOR OF FIRST CHURCH.[1]

the martyrs chose to buy their lives with a lie has ennobled their memories for all time. It is written: "If I would but go to hell for an eternal moment or so, I might be knighted."

Other executions took place in August and September, swelling the number of victims hanged to nineteen. Giles Corey was, by the old English law, pressed to death for standing mute when told to plead.

John Adams mentions a visit to this hill in 1766, then called Witchcraft Hill. Somebody, he says, within a few years had planted a number of locust-trees over the graves. In 1793 Dr. Morse notes that the graves might still be traced. I felt no regret at their total disappearance. Would that the bloody chapter might as easily disappear from history!

---

[1] The frame of the old First Church of Salem has been preserved. It is now standing in the rear of Plummer Hall, a depository of olden relics.

IRESON'S HOUSE, OAKUM BAY, MARBLEHEAD.

CHAPTER XVI.

MARBLEHEAD.

"*Launcelot.* Turn up on your right hand at the next turning, but at the next turning of all on your left; marry, at the very next turning, turn of no hand, but turn down indirectly to the Jew's house."—*Merchant of Venice.*

MARBLEHEAD is a backbone of granite, a vertebra of syenite and porphyry thrust out into Massachusetts Bay in the direction of Cape Ann, and hedged about with rocky islets. It is somewhat sheltered from the weight of north-east storms by the sweep of the cape, which launches itself right out to sea, and gallantly receives the first buffetings of the Atlantic. The promontory of Marblehead may once have been a prolongation of Cape Ann, the whole coast hereabouts looking as if the ocean had licked out the softer parts, leaving nothing that was digestible behind. This rock, on which a settlement was begun two hundred and forty odd years ago, performs its part by making Salem Harbor on one hand, and another for its own shipping on the east, where an appendage known as Marblehead Neck[1] is joined to it by a ligature of sand and shingle. The port is open to the north-east, and vessels are sometimes blown from their anchorage upon the sand-banks at

---

[1] Captain Goelet calls it an island.

GREAT HEAD.

the head of the harbor, though the water is generally deep and the shores bold. At the entrance a light-house is built on the extreme point of the Neck; and on a tongue of land of the opposite shore is Fort Sewall—a beckoning finger and a clenched fist.

The harbor, as the "Gazetteer" would say, has a general direction from north-east to south-west. It is a mile and a half long by half a mile wide, with generally good holding ground, though in places the bottom is rocky. La Touche Treville lost the *Hermione's* anchor here in 1780, when he brought over M. De Lafayette, sent by the king to announce the speedy arrival of Rochambeau's army.[1] Probably the good news was first proclaimed in the narrow streets of Marblehead, though it has hitherto escaped a spirited lyric from some disciple of Mr. Browning.

The geologist will find Marblehead and the adjacent islands an interesting ground, with some tolerably hard nuts for his hammer. The westerly shore of the harbor is indented with little coves niched in the rock, and having each a number, though the Marbleheaders have other names

---

[1] Treville was the man thought most worthy by Napoleon to lead his fleet in the long-meditated descent on England.

for them. One or two wharves are fitted in these coves, but I did not see a vessel unlading or a bale of merchandise there. The flow of the tide as it sucked around the wooden piles was the only evidence of life about them.

The varying formations of these shores go very far to redeem the haggard landscape. Even the coves differ in the materials with which their walls are built, feldspar, porphyry, and jasper variegating their rugged features with pleasing effect. The floor of one of these coves is littered with fractured rock of a reddish brown, from which it is locally known as Red Stone Cove. Captain Smith says this coast resembled Devonshire with its "tinctured veines of divers colors." The Rev. Mr. Higginson, of Salem, in 1629, speaks of the stone found here as "marble stone, that we have great rocks of it, and a harbor hard by. Our plantation is from thence called Marble Harbor." His marble was perhaps the porphyritic rock which it resembles when wetted by sea moisture.

"THE CHURN."

The beach is the mall of Marblehead. It opens upon Nahant Bay, and is much exposed to the force of south-east gales. Over this beach a causeway is built, which from time to time has required extensive repairs. Under the province, and as late even as 1812, the favorite method of raising moneys for such purposes was by lottery, duly authorized. In this way a work of public necessity was relegated to the public cupidity.

A run over the Neck revealed many points of interest. There are rock cavities of glassy smoothness, worn by the action of pebbles, chasms that receive the coming wave and derisively toss it high in air; and there are precipitous cliffs which the old stone-cutter and lapidary can never blunt, though he may fret and fume forever at their base. Looking off to sea, the eye is everywhere intercepted by islands or sunken ledges belted with surf. They have such names as Satan, Roaring Bull, Great and Little Misery, Great and Little Haste, Cut-throat Ledge, the Brimbles, Cat Island, and the like. Each would have a story, if it were challenged, how it came by its name. The number of these islands is something surprising. In fact they appear like a system, connecting the craggy promontory of Marblehead with the cape side. At some time the sea must have burst through this rocky barrier, carrying all before its resistless onset. The channels are intricate among these islands, and must be hit with the nicest precision, or a strong vessel would go to pieces at the first blow on the sharp rocks.

The Neck is the peculiar domain of a transient population of care-worn fugitives from the city. The red-roofed cottages were picturesque objects among the rocks, but bore marks of the disorder in which the winter had left them. They seemed shivering up there on the ledges, though it was the seventh day of May, for there had been a light fall of snow, followed by a searching north-west wind. Not even a curl of smoke issued from the chimneys to take off the prevailing chilliness. Down at the harbor side there was an old farmstead with some noble trees I liked better. On the beach I had trod in Hawthorne's " Footprints." I might here rekindle Longfellow's " Fire of Drift-wood :"

"We sat within the farm-house old,
 Whose windows, looking o'er the bay,
 Gave to the sea-breeze, damp and cold,
 An easy entrance night and day.

"Not far away we saw the port,
 The strange old-fashioned silent town,
 The light-house, the dismantled fort,
 The wooden houses quaint and brown."

The light-keeper, whom I found at home, indulged me in a few moments' chat. He could not account, he said, for the extraordinary predilection of the Light-house Board for whitewash. Dwelling, covered way, and tower were each and all besmeared; and the keeper seemed not overconfident that he might not soon receive an order to put on a coat of it himself. He did not object to the summer, but in winter his berth was not so pleasant. I already felt convinced of this. To a question he replied that Government estimated his services at five hundred dollars per annum; and he pointedly asked me how he was to support a family on the stipend? Yet he must keep his light trimmed and burning; for if that goes out, so does he.

All the light-houses are supplied with lard-oil, which burns without incrusting the wick of the lamp; but the keeper objected that it was always chilled in cold weather, and that he usually had to take it into the dwelling and heat it on the stove before it could be used. A good deal of moisture collects on the plate-glass windows of the lantern when the wind is off shore, but if it be off the land the glass is dry. In very cold weather, when it becomes coated with frost, the light is visible but a short distance at sea. To remedy this evil, spirits of wine are furnished to keepers, but does not wholly remove the difficulty.

DRYING FISH, LITTLE HARBOR.

Afterward we spoke of the commerce of Marblehead. The only craft now in port were five or six ballast-lighters that had wintered in the upper harbor; with this exception it was deserted. The keeper had been master of a fishing vessel. I could not help remarking to him on this ominous state of things.

"I have seen as many as a hundred and twenty vessels lying below us here, getting ready for a cruise on the Banks," he said.

"And now?"

"Now there are not more than fifteen sail that hail out of here."

"So that fishing, as a business—"

"Is knocked higher than a kite."

Will it ever come down again?

MARBLEHEAD.

We commiserate the situation of an individual out of business; what shall we, then, say of a town thrown out of employment? Before the Revolution, Marblehead was our principal fishing port. When the war came this industry was broken up for the seven years of the contest. Most of the men went into the army, one entire regiment being raised here. Many entered on board privateers or the public armed vessels of the revolted colonies. At the close of the war, great destitution prevailed by reason of the losses in men the town had sustained; and as usual a lottery was resorted to for the benefit of the survivors. The War of 1812 again drove the Marblehead fishermen from their peaceful calling to man our little navy. At its close five hundred of her sons were in British prisons.

Fisheries have often been called the agriculture of the seas. Sir Walter Raleigh attributed the wealth and power of Holland, not to its commerce or carrying trade, but to its fisheries. Captain John Smith was of this opinion; so were Mirabeau and De Witt. Franklin seemed to prefer the fisheries of America to agriculture; and Edmund Burke paid our fishermen the noblest panegyric of them all:

"No sea but is vexed by their fisheries. No climate that is not witness to their toils. Neither the perseverance of Holland, nor the activity of France, nor the dexterous and firm sagacity of English enterprise ever carried this most perilous mode of hardy industry to the extent to which it has been pushed by this recent people—a people who are still, as it were, but in the gristle, and not yet hardened into the bone of manhood."[1]

Add to this Napoleon's opinion that the American was the superior of the English seaman, and national self-complacency may safely rest on two such eminent authorities.

The light-keeper, who had been on the Banks, informed me that it was still the custom, when lying to in a heavy blow, to pour oil on the waves alongside the vessel; and that it was effectual in smoothing the sea—not a wave breaking within its influence. Dr. Franklin's experiments are the first I remember to have read of. A single tea-spoonful, he says, quieted the ruffled surface of near half an acre of water in a windy day, and rendered it as smooth as a looking-glass.[2] This man would have triumphed over nature herself.

Without doubt Marblehead owes a large share of her naval renown to her fishery; to those men who entered the sea-service at the bowsprit, like the great navigator, Cook, and not at the cabin windows. They gave a distinctively American character to our little navies of 1776 and 1812. Southey, while writing his "Life of Nelson," flings down his pen in despair to say: "What a miserable thing is this loss of a second frigate to the Americans. It is a cruel stroke; and, though their frigates are larger ships than ours, must be felt as a disgrace, and in fact is disgrace. It looks as if there was a

---

[1] "Address to the Electors of Bristol."   [2] "Philosophical Transactions," vol. lxiv., part ii.

dry-rot in our wooden walls. Is it that this captain also is a youngster hoisted up by interest, or that the Americans were manned by Englishmen, or that our men do not fight heartily, or that their men are better than ours?"

One writer calls the fishery "a great nursery of the marine, from whence a constant supply of men, inured to the perils of the sea, are constantly ready for the service of their country." Supposing this doctrine correct, it becomes an interesting question where the sailors of future navies are to come from? The whale-fishery has been fairly beaten out of the field by oil-spouting rocks. Why should we brave the perils of the Arctic circle when by sinking a tube in Pennsylvania we may strike a fellow of a thousand barrels, and wax rich while asleep? New London, Nantucket, New Bedford, and Edgartown have answered. The cod and mackerel fisheries have dwindled into like insignificance, say Marblehead, Gloucester, and all fishing ports along shore. When these towns, once so exclusively maritime, found the fishery slipping through their fingers, they took up shoe-making, and at present you will see plenty of Crispins, but not many blue-jackets, in Marblehead. Cobbling is now carried on in the barn-lofts, fish-houses, and cottages. Yet this change of condition is not met, as in the failing whale-fishery, by a supply from a different source; fish continues to be as highly esteemed and in greater request than ever; it is the supply, not the demand, that is diminishing.

There are some of those larger shoe-factories in the town where hides are received at the front door, and are delivered at the back, in an incredibly short time, ready for wear. The young men I saw in long aprons at the benches had none of the rugged look of their fathers. Their white arms showed little of the brawn that comes from constant handling of the oar. The air of the workshop was stifling, and I gladly left it, thinking these were hardly the fellows to stand by the guns or reef-tackles. One old man with whom I conversed bitterly deplored that shoe-making had killed fishing, and had made the young men, as he phrased it, "nash," which is what they say of fish that the sun has spoiled. At the time I was there shoe-making itself was suffering from a depression of trade, and many of the inhabitants appeared to be in a state of uncertainty as to their future that, I imagine, may become chronic. One individual, while lamenting the decline of business, brightened up as he said, "But I understand they an't much better off at Beverly."

The decline of the cod-fishery is attributed to the use of trawls, and to the greed that kills the goose that has laid the golden egg. Formerly fish were taken with hand-lines only, over the side of the vessel. Then they began to carry dories, in which the crew sought out the best places. The men lost in fogs or bad weather while looking for or visiting their trawls swell the list of casualties year by year. Fitting out fishing-vessels, instead of being the simple matter it once was, has become an affair of capital, the trawls for a vessel sometimes costing fifteen hundred dollars.

MARBLEHEAD.

Douglass gives some particulars of the fishery, as practiced in his own and at an earlier day. He says the North Sea cod, and those taken on the Irish coast were considered better than the American fish, but were inadequate to the supply. No fish were considered merchantable in England or Ireland less than eighteen inches long from the first fin to the beginning of the tail. In Newfoundland they worked their fish "belly down;" in New England they were worked with their backs downward, to receive more salt, and add to their weight. The stock-fish of Norway and Iceland were cured without salt, by hanging them in winter upon sticks called by the Dutch "stocks"—this may have been the origin of our dunfish. The fish made in Marblehead for

UNLOADING FISH.

Spain were known as "Bilboa drithe," and could be held out horizontally by the tail. Those cured for the western market were called "Albany drithe," from the fact that Albany was the head-quarters of that trade.

To quote from Douglass, he says: "In 1746 Marblehead ships off more dried cod than all the rest of New England besides. Anno 1732 a good fish year, and in profound peace, Marblehead had about one hundred and twenty schooners of about fifty tons burden, seven men aboard, and one man ashore to make the fish, or about one thousand men employed, besides the seamen who carry the fish to market. Two hundred quintals considered a fare. In 1747 they have not exceeding seventy schooners, and make five fares yearly to I. Sables, St. George's Banks, etc."

M. Rochefoucauld Liancourt, who visited New England in 1799, making a tour of the coast as far as the Penobscot, says at that time the vessels were usually of seventy tons, and had a master, seven seamen, and a boy. The owner had a quarter, the dryer on the coast an eighth, and the rest was shared by the master and seamen, in proportion to the fish they had taken. Every man took care of his own fish.

As early as 1631 Governor Matthew Cradock established a fishing station at Marblehead, in charge of Isaac Allerton, whose name appears fifth on the celebrated compact of the Pilgrims, signed at Cape Cod, November 11th, 1620.[1] Winthrop mentions in his journal that as the *Arabella* was standing in for Naumkeag, on the 12th of June, 1630, Mr. Allerton boarded her in a shallop as he was sailing to Pemaquid. Moses Maverick lived at Marblehead with Allerton, and married his daughter Sarah. In 1635 Allerton conveyed to his son-in-law all the houses, buildings, and stages he had at Marblehead. In 1638 Moses was licensed to sell a tun of wine a year.

In Winthrop's "Journal," under the date of 1633, is the following with reference to this plantation:[2]

"*February* 1.—Mr. Cradock's house at Marblehead was burnt down about midnight before, there being then in it Mr. Allerton, and many fishermen whom he employed that season, who all were preserved by a special providence of God, with most of his goods therein, by a tailor, who sat up that night at work in the house, and, hearing a noise, looked out and saw the house on fire above the oven in the thatch."[3]

While retracing my steps back to town, I pictured the harbor in its day of prosperity. A hundred sail would have given it a degree of animation quite marvelous to see. Six hours a hundred sharp prows point up the harbor, and six they look out to sea. Above the tapering forest of equal growth are thrust the crossed spars of ships from Cadiz, in Spain. Innumerable wherries dart about, rowed by two men each; they are strongly built, for baiting trawls on the banks and in a sea is no child's play. The cheery cries, rattling of blocks, and universal bustle aboard the fleet announce the preparations for sailing. At the top of the flood up go a score of sails, and round go as many

---

[1] A headland of Boston Harbor is named for him, Point Allerton.

[2] "Moses Maverick testifieth that in the yeare 1640 or 41 the toune of Salem granted unto the inhabitants of Marblehead the land we now injoy, with one of Salem, to act with us, w^h acordingly was acordingly attended unto the yeare 1648, in which yeare Marblehead was confirmed a toune, and to that time y^t never knew or understood he desented from what was acted in layeing out land or stinting the Comons, and have beene accounted a Toune, and payd dutyes accordingly as it hath been required. Taken vpon oath; 19: 1mo $\frac{78}{4}$.   WM. HATHORNE, *Afft.*
"(Original Document.)   Vera Copia, taken the 25 of May, 1674, by me, Robert Ford, Cleric."

[3] Relics of Indian occupation have been found in Marblehead at various times. There is a shell heap on the Wyman Farm, on the line of the Eastern Railway, quite near the farm-house.

windlasses to a rattling chorus. Anchors are hove short in a trice. The vessels first under way draw out from among the fleet, clear the mouth of the harbor, and in a few minutes more are flinging the seas from their bows with Marblehead Light well under their lee.

I do not know who first discovered Marblehead. The vague idea associates it with a heap of sterile rocks, inhabited by fishermen speaking an unintelligible jargon. Though not twenty miles from the New England metropolis, and notwithstanding its past is interwoven with every page of our historic times, less is known of it than would seem credible to the intelligent reader. A faithful chronicle of its fortunes would, no doubt, be sufficiently

A GROUP OF ANTIQUES.

curious, though many would, I fear, prefer the stories of Tyre and Carthage. But Marblehead is unique; there is nothing like it on this side of the water.

I was struck, on entering the place, with Whitefield's observation when he asked where the dead were buried; for the great want appears to be earth. But a further acquaintance revealed more pleasant inclosures of turf, orchards, and garden-spots than its gaunt crags seemed capable of sustaining. The town may be said to embrace two very dissimilar portions, of which the larger appears paralyzed with age, and the other the outgrowth of a newer and more thriving generation. It is with the old town I have to do.

I preferred to commit myself to the guidance of the narrow streets, and drift about wherever they listed. The stranger need not try to settle his topography beforehand. He would lose his labor. It was only after a third visit that I began to have some notions of the maze of rocky lanes, alleys, and courts. Caprice seemed to have governed the location of a majority of the houses by the water-side, and the streets to have adjusted themselves to the wooden anarchy; or else the idea forced itself upon you that the houses must have been stranded here by the flood, remaining where the subsiding waters left them; for they stand anywhere and nowhere, in a ravine or atop a cliff, crowding upon and elbowing each other until no man, it would seem, might know his own. How one of those ancient mariners rolling heavily homeward after a night's carouse could have found his own dwelling, is a mystery I do not undertake to solve.

M. De Chastellux, who had a compliment ready-made for every thing American, was accosted when in Boston with the remark,

"Marquis, you find a crooked city in Boston?"

"Ah, ver good, ver good," said the chevalier; "it show de *liberté.*"

I found Washington Street a good base of operations. A modern dwelling is rarely met with between this thoroughfare and the water. On State (formerly King) Street there is but one house less than a century old, and the frame of that one was being raised the day Washington came to town. Even he was struck by the antiquated look of the buildings. The long exemption from fire is little less than miraculous, for a building of brick or stone is an exception. Old houses, gambrel-roofed, hip-roofed, and pitch-roofed, with an occasional reminiscence of London in Milton's day, are ranged on all sides; little altered in a hundred years, though I should have liked better to have chanced this way when the porches of some were projecting ten feet into the street. I enjoyed losing myself among them; for, certes, there is more of the crust of antiquity about Marblehead than any place of its years in America.

An air of snug and substantial comfort hung about many of the older houses, and some localities betokened there was an upper as well as a nether stratum of society in Marblehead. Fine old trees flourished in secluded neighborhoods, where the brass door-knockers shone with unwonted lustre. I think my fingers itched to grasp them, so suggestive were they of feudal times when stranger knight summoned castle-warden by striking with his sword-hilt on the oaken door. Fancy goes in unbidden at their portals, and roves among their cramped corridors and best rooms, peering into closets where choice china is kept, or rummaging among the curious lumber of the garrets, the accumulations of many generations. On the whole, the dwellings represent so far as they may a singular equality of condition. It is only by turning into some court or by-way that you come unexpectedly upon a mansion having about it some relics of a former splendor. Though Marblehead has its Billingsgate, I saw nothing of the squalor of our larger cities; and though it may have its Rotten Row, I remarked neither lackeys nor showy equipages.

There are few sidewalks in the older quarter. The streets are too narrow to afford such a luxury, averaging, I should say, not more than a rod in width in the older ones, with barely room for a single vehicle. The passer-by may, if he pleases, look into the first-floor sitting-rooms, and see the family gathered at its usual occupations. Whether it be a greater indiscretion to look in at the windows than to look out of them, as the matrons and maidens are in the habit of doing when a stranger is in the neighborhood, is a question I willingly remand to the decision of my readers; yet I confess I found the temptation too strong to be resisted. In order to protect those houses at the street corners, a massive stone post is often seen imbedded in the ground; but to give them a wide berth is impossible, and I looked for business to be brisk at the wheelwright's shop.

Again, as the street encounters a ledge in its way, one side of it mounts the acclivity, ten, twenty

LEE STREET.

feet above your head, while the other keeps the level as before. Such accidental looking-down upon their neighbors does not, perhaps, argue moral or material pre-eminence; but, for all that, there may be a shilling side. One thing about these old houses impressed me pleasantly; though many of them were guiltless of paint, and on some roofs mosses had begun to creep, and a yellow rust to cover the clapboards, there were few windows that did not boast a goodly show of scarlet geraniums, fuchsias, or mignonnette, with ivy clustering lovingly about the frames, making the dark old casements blossom again, and glow with a wealth of warm color.

I was too well acquainted with maritime towns to be surprised at finding fishing-boats, even of a few tons burden, a quarter of a mile from the water. They might even be said to crop out with remarkable frequency. Some were covered with boughs, their winter protection; others were being patched, painted, or calked, preparatory for launching, with an assiduity and solicitude that can only be appreciated by the owners of such craft. On the street that skirts the harbor I saw a fisherman just landed enter his cottage, "paying out," as he went, from a coil of rope, one end being, I ascertained, fastened to his wherry. I remember to have seen in Mexico the *vaqueros*, on alighting from their mules, take from the pommel of their saddles some fathoms of braided hair-rope, called a lariat, and, on entering a shop or dwelling, uncoil it as they went. The custom of these Marblehead fishermen seemed no less ingenious.

In a sea-port my instinct is for the water. I have a predilection for the wharves, and, though I could well enough dispense with their smells, for their sights and sounds. The cross-ways in Marblehead seem in search of the harbor as they go wriggling about the ledges. I should say they had been formed on the ancient footpaths leading down to the fishing stages. At the head of one pier, half imbedded in the earth, was an old honey-combed cannon that looked as if it might have spoken a word in the dispute with the mother country, but now played the part of a capstan, and truant boys were casting dirt between its blistered lips. In Red Stone Cove there lay, stranded and broken in two, a long-boat, brought years ago from China, perhaps, on the deck of some Indiaman. Its build was outlandish; so unlike the wherries that were by, yet so like the craft that swim in the turbid Yang Tse. I took a seat in it, and was carried to the land of pagodas, opium, and mandarins. Its sheathing of camphor-wood still exhaled the pungent odor of the aromatic tree. On either quarter was painted an enormous eye that seemed to follow you about the strand. In all these voyages some part of the Old World seems to have drifted westward, and attached itself to the shores of the New. Here it was a Portuguese from the Tagus, or a Spaniard of Alicante; elsewhere a Norwegian, Swede, or Finn, grafted on a strange clime and way of life.

The men I saw about the wharves, in woolen "jumpers" and heavy fishing boots, had the true "guinea-stamp" of the old Ironsides of the sea. To see those lumbering fishermen in the streets you would not think they could be so handy, or tread so lightly in a dory. I saw there an old foreign-looking seaman, one of those fellows with short, bowed legs, drooping shoulders, contracted eyelids, and hands dug in their pockets, who may be met with at all hours of the day and night hulking about the quays of a shipping town. This man eyed the preparations of amateur boatmen with the contemptuous curiosity often vouchsafed by such personages in the small affair of getting a pleasure-boat under way. One poor fellow, who kept a little shop where he could hear the wash of the tide on the loose pebbles of the cove, told me he

TUCKER'S WHARF—THE STEPS.

had lost his leg by the cable getting a turn round it. Though they have a rough outside, these men have hearts. His skipper, he said, had put about, though it was a dead loss to him, and sailed a hundred miles to land his mutilated shipmate.

How did Marblehead look in the olden time? Its early history is allied with that of Salem, of which it formed a part until 1648. Francis Higginson, who came over in 1629, says, in that year, "There are in all of us, both old and new planters, about three hundred, whereof two hundred of them are settled at Nehumkek, now called Salem; and the rest have planted themselves at Masathulets Bay, beginning to build a town there which wee do call

Cherton or Charles Town." His New England's "Plantation" is curious reading. I have observed in my researches that these old divines are often fond of drawing the long bow, a failing of which Higginson, one of the earliest, seems conscious when he asks in his exordium, "Shall such a man as I lye? No, verily!"

William Wood, describing the place in 1633, says of it: "Marvil Head is a place which lyeth 4 miles full south from Salem, and is a very convenient place for a plantation, especially for such as will set upon the trade of fishing. There was made here a ship's loading of fish the last year, where still stand the stages and drying scaffolds." In 1635, the court order that "there shalbe a Plantacion at Marblehead."

John Josselyn looked in here in 1663. "Marvil, or Marblehead," he says,

GREGORY STREET.

is "a small harbour, the shore rockie, on which the town is built, consisting of a few scattered houses; here they have stages for fishermen, orchards, and gardens half a mile within land, good pastures, and arable land."

It had now begun to emerge from the insignificance of a fishing village, and to assume a place among the number of maritime towns. In 1696 a French spy makes report: "Marvalet est composé de 100 ou 120 maisons pescheurs où il peut entrer de gros vaisseaux."

In 1707-'8 Marblehead was represented to the Lords of Trade as a smuggling port for Boston, for which it also furnished pilots. A few years earlier (1704) Quelch, the pirate, had been apprehended there, after having scattered his gold right and left. But it was not until an order had come from the Governor and Council at Boston that he was arrested, nor had there been a province law against piracy until within a few years.[1] Seven of Quelch's gang were taken by Major Stephen Sewall; and the inhabitants of Marblehead were required to bring in the gold coin, melted down, and silver plate they had not been unwilling to receive.

It was, no doubt, owing to the lawless habits introduced that the character of the sea-faring population partook of a certain wildness—such as good Parson Barnard inveighs against — manifesting itself in every-day transactions, and infusing into the men an adventurous and reckless spirit which fitted them in a measure for deeds of daring, and gave to the old sea-port no small portion of the notoriety it enjoys.

Mr. Barnard speaks of the earlier class of fishermen as a rude, swearing, fighting, and drunken crew. The Rev. Mr. Whitwell, in his discourse on the disasters of 1770, does not give them a better character. "No wonder," he says, "the children of such parents imitate their vices, and, when they return from their voyages, have learned to curse and damn their younger brothers." He continues to pour balm into their wounds in this wise: "We hope we shall hear no more cursing or profaneness from your mouths..... Instead of spending your time in those unmanly games which disgrace our children in the streets, we trust you will be seriously concerned for the salvation of your souls."

Austin, in his "Life of Elbridge Gerry," speaks of the fishermen as a sober and industrious class; but the testimony of local historians is wholly opposed to his assertion.[2] They passed their winters in a round of reckless dissipation, or until the arrival of the fishing season set half the town afloat again. It was then left in the hands of the women, the elders, and a few merchants. There is much in the annals of such a community to furnish materials for history, or, on a lesser scale, hints for romance. Captain Goelet, who was here in 1750, estimated the town to contain about four hundred and fifty houses.

"They were," he said, "all wood and clapboarded, the generality miserable buildings, mostly close in with the rocks, with rocky foundations very Cragy and Crasey. The whole towne is built upon a rock, which is heigh and steep to the water. The harbour is sheltered by an island, which runs along parallel to it and brakes off the sea. Vessels may ride here very safe; there is a path or way downe to the warf, which is but small, and on which is a large Ware House where they land their fish, etc. From this heigh Cliffty shore it took its name. I saw ab^t 5 topsail vessels and ab^t 10 schooners or sloops in the harbour; they had then ab^t 70 sail schooners a-fishing, with about 600 men and Boys imployd in the fishery: they take vast quantitys Cod, which they cure heere. Saw several thousand flakes then cureing. The place is noted for Children, and Nouriches the most of any place for its bigness in North America; it's said the chief cause is attributed to their feeding on Cod's heads, etc., which is their Principall Dish. The greatest distaste a person has to this place is the stench of the fish, the whole air seems tainted with it. It may in short be said it's a Dirty Erregular, Stincking place.'"[3]

---

[1] A bill against piracy was ordered to be brought in March 1st, 1686; March 4th the bill passed.

[2] The first mention of Marblehead in the colony records I have seen is of two men fined there for being drunk, in the year 1633.

[3] "New England Historical and Genealogical Register," 1870, p. 57.

The fortunes of the place were now greatly altered. The obscure fishing village had become a bustling port, with rich cargoes from Spain and the Antilles lying within its rock-bound shores. Ships were being built in the coves, and substantial mansions were going up in the streets—in whose cellars, as I have heard, were kegs of hard dollars, salted down, as one might say, like the staple of Marblehead.

John Adams, then a young lawyer on the circuit, enters in his diary, under date of 1766, the brief impression of a first visit to Marblehead:

"14, *Thursday*.—In the morning rode a single horse, in company with Mrs. Cranch and Mrs. Adams, in a chaise to Marblehead. The road from Salem to Marblehead, four miles, is pleasant indeed (so I found it). The grass plats and fields are delightful, but Marblehead differs from Salem. The streets are narrow and rugged and dirty, but there are some very grand buildings."

As John Adams saw it so does the stranger of to-day, ignoring such modern improvements as railway, gas-works, telegraph, and factories, and sticking closely to the skirts of the old town.

I should say Marblehead might still assert its title to the number of children it "nourishes." Certainly they seemed out of all proportion to the adult population. Instinct guides them to the water from their birth, and they may be seen paddling about the harbor in stray wherries or clambering up the rigging of some collier, in emulation of their elders. Even their talk has a salty flavor. I recollect an instance, which must lose by the relation. A young scape-grace having incurred the maternal displeasure, and then taken to his heels to escape chastisement, the good-wife gave chase, brandishing a broomstick aloft, and breathing vengeance on her unnatural offspring. Having the wind fair and a heavy spread of petticoat, she was rapidly gaining on the youngster, when a comrade, who was watching the progress of the race with a critical eye, bawled out, "Try her on the wind, Bill; try her *on the wind.*"

A sailor on shore is not unlike Napoleon's dismounted dragoon: he is emphatically a fish out of water. One talked of "making his horse fast;" another complained that his neckerchief was "tew taut;" and a third could not understand which way to move a boat until his companion called out, "Haul to the west'ard, can't ye?"

If not insular, your genuine Marbleheader is the next thing to it. The rest of the world is merged with him into a place to sell his fish and buy his salt. Even Salem, Beverly, and the parts adjacent draw but little on his sympathy or his fellowship: in short, they are not Marblehead. During the Native American excitement of 18—, the Marbleheaders entered into the movement with enthusiasm. A caucus being assembled to nominate town officers, one old fisherman came into the town hall in his baize apron, just as he had got out of his dory. He glanced over the list of officers with an approving grunt at each name until he came to that of Squire Fabens. Now Squire Fabens, though a Salem man born, had lived a score of years in Marblehead, had married, and held office there. Turning wrathfully to the person who had given him the ticket, the fisherman tore it in pieces, exclaiming as he did so, "D'ye call that a Native American ticket? Why, there's Squire Fabens on it; he an't a Marbleheader!"

Though it is true there are few instances of the fatal straight line in Marblehead, those who are native there are far from appreciating the impression its narrow and crooked ways make on the stranger. They, at any rate, appeared to find their way without the difficulty I at first experienced. I asked one I met if I was in the right route to the dépôt. "Go straight ahead," was his injunction, a direction nothing but a round-shot from Fort Sewall could have followed. But I should add that Marblehead is not a labyrinth, any more than it is a field for missionary work: it has churches, banks, schools, a newspaper, and even a debating society; and it has thoroughfares that may be traversed without a guide.

LEE HOUSE.

The great man of Marblehead in the colonial day was Colonel Jeremiah Lee, whose still elegant mansion is to be seen there. Unlike many of the gentry of his time, Colonel Lee was a thorough-going patriot. He was, with Orne and Gerry, a delegate to the first and second Provincial Congresses of 1774. When the famous Revolutionary Committee of Safety and Supplies was formed, he became and continued a member until his death in May, 1775. Colonel Lee was with the committee on the day before the battle of Lexington, and with Gerry and Orne remained to pass the night at the Black Horse tavern in Menotomy, now Arlington. When the British advance reached this house it was surrounded, the half-dressed patriots having barely time to escape to a neighboring corn-field, where they threw themselves upon the ground until the search was over. From the exposure incident to this adventure Lee got his death. His townsmen treasure his memory as one of the men who formed the Revolution, braved its dangers, and accepted its responsibilities. Colonel Lee was a stanch churchman, which makes his adhesion to the patriot side the more remarkable.

There is nothing about the exterior of the Lee mansion to attract the stranger's attention, though it cost the colonel, when furnished, ten thousand pounds sterling. As was customary, its offices were on one side and its stables on the other, with a court-yard paved with beach-pebble, in which the date of the house, 1768,[1] may be traced. Entrance was gained on front and side over massive freestone steps, that show the print of time to have pressed more heavily than human feet. The house, long since deserted by the family, is now occupied as a bank.

On entering the mansion of the Lees the visitor is struck with the expansive area of the hall, which is six paces broad, and of corresponding depth. Age has imparted a rich coloring to the mahogany wainscot and casing of the staircase. The balusters are curiously carved in many different patterns; the walls are still hung with their original paper, in panels representing Roman or Grecian ruins, with trophies of arms, or implements of agriculture or of the chase between. One panel represented a sea-fight of Blake and Van Tromp's day. Some of them have been permanently disfigured by the use of the hall, at one time, as a fish-market. In a corner, a trap-door led to the old merchant's wine-cellar, which he thus kept under his own eye. It was after a visit to some such mansion that Daniel Webster asked, "Did those old fellows go to bed in a coach-and-four?"

The rooms opening at the right and left of the hall are worthy of it, especially the first named, which is wainscoted from floor to ceiling, and enriched with elaborate carving. Over the fire-place of this room was formerly a portrait of Esther before Ahasuerus, beautifully painted on a panel. There is an upper hall of ample size, from which open sleeping apartments with pictured tiles, recessed windows, and panes that were the wonder of the town, in which none so large had been seen.

Would I had been here when the old colonel's slaves kept the antique brasses brightly polished, and stout logs crackled and snapped in the fire-places, in the day of coffin-clocks, French mirrors, and massive old plate, when the bowl of arrack-punch stood on the sideboard, and Copley's portraits of master and mistress graced the walls.[2] The painter has introduced the colonel in a brown velvet coat laced with gold, and full-bottomed wig. He was short in stature and rather portly, with an open face, thin nostril, and fine, intelligent eye. The head is slightly thrown back, a device of the artist to add height to the figure. Madam Lee is in a satin overdress, with a pelisse of ermine negligently cast about her bare shoulders. She looks a stately dame, with her black eyes and self-possessed air, or as if she might have kept the colonel's house, slaves included, in perfect order.[3]

When General Washington was making his triumphal tour of the Eastern States, in 1789, he came to Marblehead. It was, he says, "four miles out

---

[1] I have seen the date of 1766 assigned for its building.

[2] Think of Copley painting these two canvases, eight feet long by five wide, and in his best manner, for £25!

[3] These portraits are now in possession of Colonel William Raymond Lee, of Boston.

of the way; but I wanted to see it." And so he turned aside to ride through its rocky lanes, and look into the faces of the men who had followed him from Cambridge to Trenton, and from Trenton to Yorktown. How the sight of their chief must have warmed the hearts of those veterans! He jotted down in his diary very briefly what he saw and heard in Marblehead: "About 5000 souls are said to be in this place, which has the appearance of antiquity; the houses are old; the streets dirty; and the common people not very clean. Before we entered the town we were

TOWN HOUSE AND SQUARE.

met and attended by a com'e, till we were handed over to the Selectmen, who conducted us, saluted by artillery, into the town to the house of a Mrs. Lee, where there was a cold collation prepared; after partaking of which, we visited the harbor, etc." Lafayette, Monroe, and Jackson have been entertained in the same house.

When the Revolutionary junto wished to organize its artillery, William Raymond Lee was summoned to Cambridge to command one of the companies. He was nephew to the old colonel, valiantly taking up the cause where his uncle had laid it down. Afterward he served in Glover's regiment, passing through all the grades from captain to colonel. Another nephew was that John Lee who, while in command of a privateer belonging to the Tracys, with a battery, part of iron and partly of wooden guns, captured a rich vessel of superior force in the bay. Both the colonel's fighting nephews were of Manchester, on Cape Ann.

Threading my way onward, I came upon the old Town-house, the Faneuil Hall of Marblehead, in which much treason was hatched when George III. was king. The Whigs of Old Essex have often been heard there when grave questions were to be discussed, and the jarring atoms of society have oft been summoned greeting,

"To grand parading of town-meeting."

In the old Town-house Judge Story went to school and was fitted for college; the substantial dwelling in which he was born being nearly opposite, with its best parlor become an apothecary's, under the sign of Goodwin. This house was the dwelling of Dr. Elisha Story, of Revolutionary memory, and the birthplace of his son, the eminent jurist. The physicians of Dr. Story's time usually furnished their own medicines. In cocked hat and suit of rusty black, with saddle-bags and countenance severe, they were marked men in town or village. Since my visit to Marblehead the last of Dr. Story's eighteen children, Miss Caroline Story, died at the age of eighty-five. The chief-justice, her brother, was one of the most lovable of men, and was never, I believe, ashamed of the slight savor of the dialect that betrayed him native and to the manner born.

The Episcopal church in Marblehead is one of its old landmarks, concurring fully, so far as outward appearance goes, in the prevailing mouldiness. It is not remarkable in any way except as an oddity in wood, with a square

ST. MICHAEL'S, MARBLEHEAD.

tower of very modest height surmounting a broad and sloping roof. At a distance it is scarcely to be distinguished in the wooden chaos rising on all sides; and not long ago its front was masked by buildings, so that the entrance-door could only be reached by a winding path. The parish has at length cleared its ancient glebe of intruders, and the old church is no longer jostled by its dissenting neighbors. Immediately adjoining is a little church-yard, in which repose the ashes of former worshipers who loved these old walls, and would lie in their shadow.

St. Michael's, as originally built, must have been an antique gem. According to the account given me by the rector, it had seven gables, topped by a tower, from which sprung a shapely spire, with another on the north and one on the south side. The form of the building was a square, with entrances on the south and west. The aisles crossed each other at right angles; the ceiling, supported by oaken columns, was in the form of a St. Andrew's cross. The present barren area of pine shingles was built above the old roof, which it extinguished effectually. Cotton Mather—he did not allude to the Church of England—styled the New England churches golden candlesticks, set up to illuminate the country; but what would he have said had he lived to see the Puritan Thanksgiving and Fast gradually superseded by Christmas and by Easter?

The interior of the old church well repays a visit. Its antiquities are guarded as scrupulously as the old faith has been. Suspended from the ceiling is a chandelier, a wonderful affair in brass, the gift of a merchant of Bristol, England. The little pulpit, successor to an earlier one of wine-glass pattern, belongs to an era before the introduction of costly woods. Above the altar is the Decalogue, in the ancient lettering, done in England in 1714. Manifestly St. Michael's clings to its relics with greater affection than did that parish in the Old Country, which offered its second-hand Ten Commandments for sale, as it was going to buy new ones. In the organ-loft is a diminutive instrument, going as far back as the day of Snetzler. Notwithstanding the disappearance of the cross from its pinnacle, and of the royal emblems from their place (save the mark!) above the Decalogue, St. Michael's remains to-day an interesting memorial of Anglican worship in the colonies. It was the third church in Massachusetts, and the fourth in all New England, those of Boston, Newbury, and Newport alone having preceded it.

ELBRIDGE GERRY.

The names of famous people are perpetuated in the place of their birth in many ways. I noticed in Marblehead the streets bore the names of Selman, Tucker, Glover, etc. Academies, public halls, and engine-houses keep their memory green, or will do so until the era of snobbery ingulfs the place, and pulls the old signs down. Its future, I apprehend, is to become a summer resort. When that period of intermittent prosperity shall have set in in full tide, it will be difficult, if not impossible, to preserve the peculiar quaintness which now makes Marblehead the embodiment of the old New England life.

Elbridge Gerry was born in Marblehead. He was of middle stature, thin, of courteous, old-school manners, and gentlemanly address. He has the name

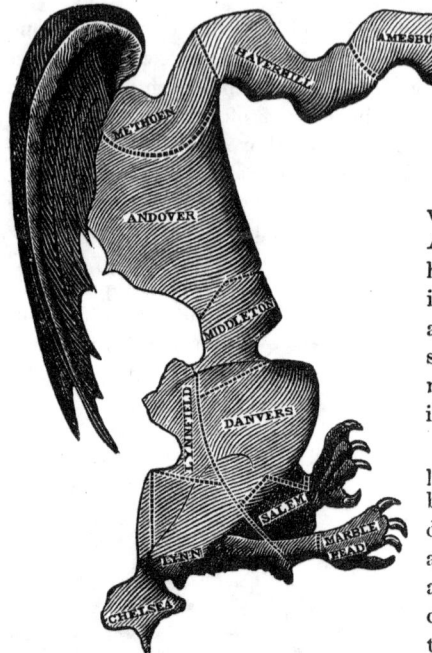

THE GERRYMANDER.

of a strong partisan, and of standing godfather to the geographical monstrosity called the Gerrymander, which has added a word to our political vocabulary.[1] A more effective party caricature has never appeared in America. It is admitted it has given its author a notoriety that has somewhat obscured eminent public service, and made his name a by-word for political chicanery.

Those who believe the worst phases of political controversy have been reserved to our own time would do well to read the history of the administrations of Washington, Adams, and Jefferson, whom we are accustomed to name with reverence as the fathers of the republic, yet who, while in office, were the objects of as much personal malignity and abuse as their successors have received. Mr. Gerry was invited to take a seat in the Massachusetts Convention when the constitution of 1787 was under consideration, in order that that body might have the benefit of his conceded sagacity and knowledge of affairs. He opposed the adoption of the constitution before the Convention. At heart Mr. Gerry was an undoubted patriot. Once, when he believed himself dying, he remarked that if he had but one day to live it should be devoted to his country.

Elbridge Gerry was destined for the practice of medicine, but engaged in mercantile pursuits instead; having acquired a competency at the time of the beginning of the Revolution, he was free to take part in the struggle. He held many important offices, and his public career, full of the incidents of stirring times, was marked also by some eccentricities. Mr. Gerry, as early as November, 1775, introduced a bill into the Provincial Congress for the fitting-out of armed vessels by Massachusetts. In the direction of inaugurating warfare with England at sea, he was, without doubt, the pioneer.

---

[1] It is not settled who is entitled to the authorship of the word "Gerrymander," for which a number of claimants have appeared. The map of Essex, which gave rise to the caricature, was drawn by Nathan Hale, who edited the *Boston Weekly Messenger*, in which the political deformity first appeared.

The number of naval heroes whom Marblehead may claim as her own is something surprising. There were John Selman and Nicholas Broughton, who sailed in two armed schooners from Beverly, as early as October, 1775, with instructions from Washington to intercept, if possible, some of the enemy's vessels in the Gulf of St. Lawrence. Failing in this object, they landed at St. John's, now Prince Edward Island, captured the fort, and brought off a number of provincial dignitaries of rank. Washington, who wanted powder, and not prisoners, was not well pleased with the result of this expedition, as he held it impolitic then to embroil the revolted colonies with Canada. Much was expected of the hereditary antipathy of the French Canadians for their English rulers, but in this respect the general's policy was founded in a mistaken judgment of those people.

"OLD NORTH" CONGREGATIONAL CHURCH.

Commodore Manly, to whom John Adams says the first British flag was struck, was either native born, or came in very early life to Marblehead. He was placed in command of the first cruiser that sailed with a regular commission from Washington, in 1775, signalizing his advent in the bay in the *Lee*—a schooner mounting only four guns—by the capture of a British vessel laden with military stores, of the utmost value to the Americans besieging Boston. When this windfall was reported to Congress, the members believed Divine Providence had interposed in their favor. Our officers declared their wants could not have been better supplied if they had themselves sent a schedule of military stores to Woolwich Arsenal. So apprehensive was the general that his prize might slip through his fingers, that all the carts to be obtained in the vicinity of Cape Ann were impressed, in order to bring the cargo to camp. Manly died in Boston, in 1793, in circumstances nearly allied to destitution. He was, says one who knew him well, "a handy, hearty, honest, benevolent, blunt man, with more courage than good conduct."

Another of these old sea-dogs was Commodore Samuel Tucker, the son of a ship-master. The old house in which he was born was standing on Rowland Hill. (I do not know that he of Surrey Chapel had any thing to do with the name in Marblehead.) It was before the door of this house that Tucker, in his shirt-sleeves, was chopping wood one evening, just at dusk, when a finely mounted officer clattered down the street. Seeing Tucker, the officer asked if he could inform him where the Honorable Samuel Tucker resided. Tucker, astonished at the question, answered in the negative, saying, "There is no such man lives here; there is no other Sam Tucker in this town but myself." At this reply, the officer raised his beaver, and, bowing low, presented him a commission in the navy.

SAMUEL TUCKER.

Tucker, in 1778, was taking John Adams to France in the old frigate *Boston*,[1] when he fell in with an enemy. While clearing his decks for action he espied Mr. Adams, musket in hand, among the marines. Laying a hand on the commissioner's shoulder, Tucker said to him, "I am commanded by the Continental Congress to carry you safely to Europe, and I will do it," at the same time conducting him below.

The brave Captain Mugford, whose exploit in capturing a vessel laden with

---

[1] The old frigate *Boston* was captured at Charleston in 1780 by the British. In 1804 Tom Moore went over to England in her, she being then commanded by Captain J. E. Douglas.

powder in Boston Harbor, in May, 1776, proved of inestimable value, was also an inhabitant of Marblehead. Like Selman and Broughton, he had been a captain in the famous Marblehead regiment, and his crew were volunteers from it. The year previous, Mugford, with others, had been impressed on board a British vessel, the *Lively*, then stationed at Marblehead. Mugford's wife, on hearing what had befallen her husband, went off to the frigate and interceded with the captain for his release, alleging that they were just married, and that he was her sole dependence for support. The Englishman, very generously, restored Mugford his liberty.

The Trevetts, father and son, were little less distinguished than any already named, adding to the high renown of Marblehead, both in the Old War and in the later contest with England.

Glover and his regiment conferred lasting honor on this old town by the sea. As soon as it had been determined to fit out armed vessels, Washington intrusted the details to Glover, and ordered the regiment to Beverly, where these amphibians first equipped and then manned the privateers. The regiment signalized itself at Long Island and at Trenton, and ought to have a monument on the highest point of land in Marblehead, with the names of its heroes inscribed in bronze. General Glover was long an invalid from the effects of disease contracted in the army, dying in 1797.[1] He had been a shoe-maker, and is, I imagine, the person referred to in the following extract from the memoirs of Madame Riedesel:

GENERAL GLOVER.

"Some of the generals who accompanied us were shoe-makers; and upon their halting days they made boots for our officers, and also mended nicely the shoes of our soldiers. One of our officers had worn his boots entirely into shreds. He saw that an American general had on a good pair, and said to him, jestingly, 'I will gladly give you a guinea for them.' Immediately the general alighted from his horse, took the guinea, gave up his boots, and put on the badly-worn ones of the officer, and again mounted his horse." General Glover's house is still standing on Glover Square. I made, as every body must make, in Marblehead, a pilgrimage to Oakum Bay, a classic precinct, and to the humble abode of Benjamin Ireson, whom Whittier has made

---

[1] William P. Upham, of Salem, has written a memoir of Glover.

immortal. Questionless the poet has done more to make Marblehead known than all the historians and magazine-writers put together, though the notoriety is little relished there. The facts were sufficiently dramatic as they existed; but Mr. Whittier has taken a poet's license, and arranged them to his fancy. Old Flood Ireson suffered in the flesh, and his memory has been pilloried in verse for a crime he did not commit. Nevertheless, I doubt that the people of Marblehead forget that Pegasus has wings, and can no more amble at the historian's slow place than he can thrive on bran and water.

It is not many years since Ireson was alive, broken in spirit under the obloquy of his hideous ride. Later in life he followed shore-fishing, and was once blown off to sea, where he was providentially picked up by a coaster bound to some Eastern port. I do not think he could have declared his right name, for sailors are superstitious folk, and he would have been accounted a Jonah in any ship that sailed these seas. His wherry having been cut adrift, was found, and Old Flood Ireson was believed to have gone to the bottom of the bay, when, to the genuine astonishment of his townsmen, he appeared one day plodding wearily along the streets. Some charitable souls gave him another wherry, but the boys followed the old man about as he cried his fish with their cruel shouts of,

> "I, Flood Ireson, for leaving a wrack,
> Was blowed out to sea, and couldn't get back."

There is book authority for the terrible aspect of the vengeance of the fish-wives of Marblehead, so picturesquely portrayed in the poet's lines. Increase Mather, in a letter to Mr. Cotton, 23d of Fifth month, 1677, mentions an instance of rage against two Eastern Indians, then prisoners at Marblehead: "Sabbath-day was sennight, the women at Marblehead, *as they came out of the meeting-house,* fell upon two Indians that were brought in as captives, and, in a tumultuous way, very barbarously murdered them. Doubtless, if the Indians hear of it, the captives among them will be served accordingly." This episode recalls the rage of the fish-women of Paris during the Reign of Terror, those unsexed and pitiless viragos of La Halle.

I could discover little of the old Marblehead dialect, once so distinctive that even the better class were not free from it. It is true a few old people still retain in their conversation the savor of it; but it is dying out. Your true Marbleheader would say, "barn in a burn" for "born in a barn." His speech was thick and guttural; only an occasional word falling familiarly on the unaccustomed ear. All the world over he was known so soon as he opened his mouth. The idiom may have been the outgrowth of the place, or perchance a reminiscence of the speech of old-time fishermen, grounded, as I apprehend, more in the long custom of an illiterate people than any supposed relationship with our English mother-tongue. Whittier was acquainted with the jargon, and the question is open to the philologist.

There is a legend about the cove near Ireson's of a "screeching woman" done to death by pirates a century and a half or more past—a shadowy memorial of the fact of their presence here so long ago. They brought her on shore from their ship, and murdered her. On each anniversary of her death, says the legend, the town was thrilled to its marrow by the unearthly outcries of the pirates' victim. Many believed the story, while not a few had heard the screams. Chief-justice Story was among those who asserted that they had listened to those midnight cries of fear.

Passing over the causeway and under the gate-way of Fort Sewall, said to have been named from Chief-justice Stephen Sewall,[1] who once taught school in Marblehead, I entered the spacious parade, on which a full regiment might easily be formed. The fort was built about 1742, and until what was so long known as "the late war" with England, remained substantially in its original picturesque condition. A very old man, whom I

FORT SEWALL.

encountered on my way hither, bemoaned the demolition of the old work, which had been pulled to pieces and made more destructive during the Great Civil War. The walls were originally of rough stone, little capable of withstanding the projectiles of modern artillery. There is another fort on the summit of a rocky eminence that overlooks the approach to the Neck, built also during the Rebellion. When I visited it, the earthen walls of one face had fallen in the ditch, where the remainder of the work bid fair, at no distant day, to follow. There is still remaining in the town the quaint little powder-house built in 1755, with a roof like the cup of an acorn.

Seated under the muzzle of one of the big guns of Fort Sewall that pointed seaward, I could descry Baker's Isle with its brace of lights, and the narrow strait through which the *Abigail* sailed in 1628, with Endicott and the founders of Salem on board. Two years later the *Arabella* "came to an anchor a little within the island." Winthrop tells us how the storm-tossed voyagers went upon the land at Cape Ann, and regaled themselves with store of

---

[1] Son of Major Stephen, of Newbury.

strawberries. Boston was settled. The little colony gave its left hand to Salem, and its right to Plymouth. It waxed strong, and no power has prevailed against it.

Little Harbor, north-west of the fort, is the reputed site of the first settlement at Marblehead. On Gerry's Island, which lies close under the shore, was the house of the first regularly ordained minister; the cellar and pebble-paved yard were, not long ago, identified. Near by, on the main-land, is the supposed site of the "Fountain Inn," which, like the "Earl of Halifax," has its romance of a noble gentleman taken in the toils of a pretty wench.¹ Sir Charles Frankland, collector of his Majesty's customs, visits Marblehead, and becomes enamored of the handmaid of the inn, Agnes Surriage. He makes her his mistress, but at length, having saved his life during the great earthquake at Lisbon, she receives the reward of love and heroism at the altar as the baronet's wedded wife. Arthur Sandeyn, who was the first publican in Marblehead, was allowed to keep an ordinary there in 1640. The port was fortified after some fashion as early as 1643–'44.

POWDER-HOUSE, 1755.

I had pointed out to me the spot where the *Constitution* dropped anchor when chased in here by two British frigates in April, 1814. They threatened for a time to fetch her out again; but as Stewart laid the old invincible with her grim broadside to the entrance of the port, and the fort prepared to receive them in a becoming manner, they prudently hauled off. The battle between the *Chesapeake* and *Shannon* was also visible from the high shores here, an eye-witness, then in a fishing-boat off in the bay, relating that nothing was to be seen except the two ships enveloped in a thick smoke, and nothing to be heard but the roar of the guns. When the smoke drifted to leeward, and the cannonade was over, the British ensign was seen waving above the Stars and Stripes.

Poor, chivalric, ill-starred Lawrence! He had given a challenge to the commander of the *Bonne Citoyen*, and durst not decline one.² At the *Shan-*

---

¹ See "Old Landmarks of Boston," pp. 162, 163.
² It has been erroneously stated that Bainbridge accompanied Lawrence to the pier and tried to dissuade him from engaging the *Shannon*. They had not met for several days.

non's invitation, he put to sea with an unlucky ship, and a mutinous crew fresh from the grog-shops and brothels of Ann Street. He besought them in burning words to show themselves worthy the name of American sailors. They replied with sullen murmurs. One wretch, a Portuguese named Joseph Antonio, came forward as their spokesman. His appearance was singularly fantastic. He wore a checked shirt, a laced jacket, rings in his ears, and a bandana handkerchief about his head. Laying his hand on his breast, he made a profound inclination to his captain as he said:

"Pardon me, sir, but fair play be one jewel all over the world, and we no touchee the specie for our last cruise with Capitaine Evans. The Congress is ver' munificent; they keep our piasters in treasury, and pay us grape and canister. Good fashion in Portuguee ship, when take rich prize is not pay *poco a poco*, but break bulk and share out dollar on drum-head of capstan."[1]

Already wounded in the leg, Lawrence was struck by a grape-shot on the medal he wore in honor of his former victory. His words, as he was borne from the deck, have become a watchword in our navy.[2] Samuel Livermore, of Boston, who accompanied Lawrence on this cruise out of personal regard, attempted to avenge him. His shot missed Captain Broke. Lawrence hearing from below the firing cease, sent his surgeon to tell his officers to fight on. "The colors shall wave while I live!" he constantly repeated. He was only thirty-four; sixteen years of his life had been passed in his country's service. His figure was tall and commanding, and in battle he was the incarnation of a warrior.

When Mr. Croker read the statement of the action in the House of Commons, the members from all parts interrupted him with loud and continued cheering. Perhaps a greater compliment to American valor could not have been paid than this. The capture of a single ship of any nation had never before called forth such a triumphant outburst.

JAMES LAWRENCE.

The oldest burial-ground in Marblehead is on the summit and slopes of the highest of its rocky eminences. Here, also, the settlers raised the frame of their primitive church; some part

---

[1] This fact was established by Geoffrey Crayon (Washington Irving) in one of his philippics against Great Britain, of which he so slyly concealed the authorship in the preface to his "Sketch Book."   [2] "Don't give up the ship."

of which, I was told, has since been translated into a more secular edifice. At the head of a little pond, where a clump of dwarfish willows has become rooted, is a sheltered nook, in which are the oldest stones now to be seen. This was probably the choice spot of the whole field, but it now wears the same air of neglect common to all these old cemeteries. A stone of 1690 with the name of "Mr. Christopher Latimore, about 70 years," was the oldest I discovered.

As I picked my way among the thick-set head-stones, for there was no path, and I always avoid treading on a grave, I came upon a grave-digger busily employed, with whom I held a few moments' parley. The man, already up to his waistband in the pit, seemed chiefly concerned lest he should not be able to go much farther before coming to the ledge, which, even in the hollow places, you are sure of finding at no great depth. On one side of the grave was a heap of yellow mould, smelling of the earth earthy, and on the other side a lesser one of human bones, that the spade had once more brought above ground.

GLIMPSE OF THE SEAMEN'S MONUMENT AND OLD BURIAL-GROUND.

After observing that he should be lucky to get down six feet, the workman told me the grave was destined to receive the remains of an old lady of ninety-four, recently deceased, who, as if fearful her rest might be less quiet in the midst of a generation to which she did not belong, had begged she might be buried here among her old friends and neighbors. Although interments had long been interdicted in the overcrowded ground, her prayer was granted. An examination of the inscriptions confirmed what I had heard relative to the longevity of the inhabitants of Marblehead, of which the grave-digger also recounted more instances than I am able to remember.

I asked him what was done with the bones I saw lying there, adding to the heap a fragment or two that had fallen unnoticed from his spade.

"Why, you see, I bury them underneath the grave I am digging, before the folks get here. We often find such bones on the surface, where they have been left after filling up a grave," was his reply. This did not appear surprising, for those I saw were nearly the color of the earth itself. Seeing my look directed with a sort of fascination toward these relics of frail mortality, the man, evidently misconstruing my thought, took up an arm-bone with playful familiarity, and observed, "You should have seen the thigh-bone I found under the old Episcopal Church! I could have knocked a man down with it easy. These," he said, throwing the bone upon the heap, with a gesture of contempt, "are mere rotten things." Who would be put to bed with that man's shovel!

On a grassy knoll, on the brow of the hill, is a marble monument erected by the Marblehead Charitable Seamen's Society, in memory of its members deceased on shore and at sea. On one face are the names of those who have died on shore, and on the east those lost at sea, from the society's institution in 1831 to the year 1848. On the north are the names of sixty-five men and boys lost in the memorable gale of September 19th, 1846. This number comprised forty-three heads of families; as many widows, and one hundred and fifty-five fatherless children, were left to mourn the fatality.

The grave-digger told me that brave Captain Mugford had been buried on this hill, but the spot was now unknown. I could well believe it, for never had I seen so many graves with nothing more than a shapeless boulder at the head and foot to mark them. Many stones were broken and defaced, and I saw the fragments of one unearthed while standing by. There is no material so durable as the old blue slate, whereon you may often read an inscription cut two hundred years ago, while those on freestone and marble need renewing every fifty years. General Glover's tomb here is inscribed:

> Erected with filial respect
> to
> The Memory of
> The Hon. JOHN GLOVER, Esquire,
> Brigadier General in the late Continental Army.
> Died January 30th, 1797,
> Aged 64.

Many of the old graves were covered with freshly springing "life-everlasting," beautifully symbolizing the rest of such as sleep in the faith. From the Seamen's Monument, at the foot of which some wooden benches are placed, is seen a broad horizon, dotted with white sails. I never knew a sailor who did not wish to be buried as near as possible to the sea, though never in it. "Don't throw me overboard, Hardy," was Nelson's dying request. There are clumps of lone graves on the verge of some headland all over New England, and one old grave-yard on Stage Island, in Maine, has been wholly washed away.

In allusion to the loss of life caused by disasters to the fishing fleets from time to time, an old man with whom I talked thought it was not greater than would occur through the ordinary chances of a life on shore. It is wonderful how a sea-faring population come to associate the idea of safety with the sea. Earthquakes, conflagrations, falling buildings, and like accidents are more dreaded than hurricanes, squalls, or a lee-shore.

LONE GRAVES.

By an estimate taken from the *Essex Gazette*, of January 2d, 1770, it appears that in the two preceding years Marblehead lost twenty-three sail of vessels, with their crews, numbering one hundred and sixty-two souls, without taking into account those who were lost from vessels on their return. There were few families that did not mourn a relative, and some of the older inhabitants remember to have heard their elders speak of it with a shudder.

These are the annals that doubtless suggested Miss Larcom's "Hannah Bind-

"SITTING, STITCHING IN A MOURNFUL MUSE."

ing Shoes," and the long, lingering, yet fruitless watching for those who never come back. The last shake of the hand, the last kiss, and the last flashing of the white sail are much like the farewell on the day of battle.

THE HOE, ENGLISH PLYMOUTH.

CHAPTER XVII.

PLYMOUTH.

"What constitutes a state?
Not high raised battlements or labored mound,
Thick walls or moated gate."

PLYMOUTH is the American Mecca. It does not contain the tomb of the Prophet, but the Rock of the Forefathers, their traditions, and their graves. The first impressions of a stranger are disappointing, for the oldest town in New England looks as fresh as if built within the century. There is not much that is suggestive of the old life to be seen there. Except the hills, the haven, and the sea, there is nothing antique; save a few carefully cherished relics, nothing that has survived the day of the Pilgrims.

Somehow monuments—and Plymouth is to be well furnished in the future —do not compensate for the absence of living facts. The house of William Bradford would have been worth more to me than any of them. Even the rusty iron pot and sword of Standish are more satisfying to the common run of us than the shaft they are building on Captain's Hill to his memory. They, at least, link us to the personality of the man. And with a sigh that it was so—for I had hoped otherwise—I was obliged to admit that Old Plymouth had been rubbed out, and that I was too late by a century at least to realize my ideal.

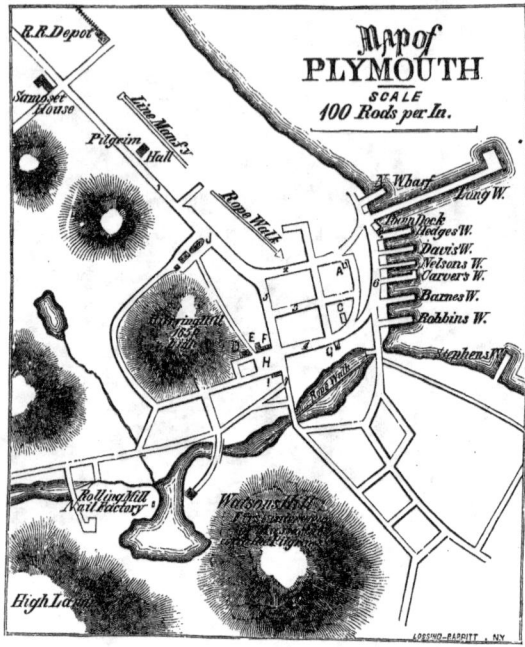

A, Joanna Davis House—Cole's Hill; B, Plymouth Rock and Wells's Store; C, Universalist Church; D, First Church; E, Church of the Pilgrimage; F, Post-office—Site of Governor Bradford's House; G, Samuel D. Holmes's House—Site of Common House; H, Town Square; I, Town-house; J, Court-house Square.
1, Court Street; 2, North Street; 3, Middle Street; 4, Leyden Street; 5, Main Street; 6, Water Street; 7, Market Street.

The most impressive thing about Plymouth is its quiet; though I would not have the reader think it deserted. There are workshops and factories, but I did not suspect their vicinity. Even the railway train slips furtively in and out, as if its rumbling might awaken the slumbering old seaport. Although the foundation of a commonwealth, the town, as we see, has not become one of the centres of traffic. It has shared the fate of Salem, in having its commercial marrow sucked out by a metropolis "opulent, enlarged, and still increasing," leaving the first-born of New England nothing but her glorious past, and the old fires still burning on her altars.

Court Street is a pleasant and well-built thoroughfare. It runs along the base of three of the hills on whose slopes the town lies, taking at length the name of Main, which it exchanges again beyond the town square for Market Street. If you follow Court Street northwardly, you will find it merging in a country road that will conduct you to Kingston; if you pursue it with your face to the south, you will in due time arrive at Sandwich. Trees, of which there is a variety, are the glory of Court Street. I saw in some streets magnificent lindens, horse-chestnuts, and elms branching quite across them; and in the areas such early flowering shrubs as forsythia, spiræa, pyrus japonica, and lilac.

Many houses are old, but there are none left of the originals; nor any so peculiar as to demand description. On some of the most venerable the chimneys are masterpieces of masonry, showing curious designs, or, in some instances, a stack of angular projections. The chimney of Governor Bradford's house is said to have been furnished with a sun-dial.

PILGRIM HALL.

Pursuing your way along Court Street, you will first reach Pilgrim Hall, a structure of rough granite, in the style of a Greek temple, the prevailing taste in New England fifty years ago for all public and even for private buildings. Within are collected many souvenirs of the Pilgrims, and of the tribes inhabiting the Old Colony. Lying in the grass-plot before the hall is a fragment of Forefathers' Rock, surrounded by a circular iron fence, and labeled in figures occupying the larger part of its surface, with the date of 1620. In this place it became nothing but a vulgar stone. I did not feel my pulses at all quickened on beholding it.

BREWSTER'S CHEST, AND STANDISH'S POT.

One end of the hall is occupied by the well-known painting of the "Landing of the Pilgrims," by Sargent. To heighten the effect, the artist has introduced an Indian in the foreground, an historic anachronism. A tall, soldierly figure is designated as Miles Standish, who is reported as being short, and scarce manly in appearance. The canvas is of large size, and the grouping does not lack merit, but its interest is made to depend on the figures of Governor Carver and of Samoset, in the foreground —both larger than life. We do not recognize, in the crouching attitude of the Indian, the erect and dauntless Samoset portrayed by Mourt, Bradford, and Winslow. This painting, which must have cost the artist great labor, was generously presented to the Pilgrim Society. I have seen a painting of the "Landing" in which a boat is represented approaching the shore, filled with soldiers in red coats.[1] The late Professor Morse also made it the subject of his pencil.

LANDING OF THE PILGRIMS, FROM SARGENT'S PAINTING.

There are on the walls portraits of Governor Edward Winslow, Governor Josiah Winslow and wife, and of General John Winslow, all copies of originals in the gallery of the Massachusetts Historical Society. The original of Edward Winslow is believed to be a Vandyke. There is also a portrait of Hon. John Trumbull, presented by Colonel John, the painter.[2]

---

[1] In possession of New England Historic Genealogical Society, Boston. It is by Corné, a marine painter of some repute in his day.

[2] Other portraits are of Dr. James Thacher, by Frothingham, and of John Alden, great-grandson of John, of the *Mayflower*, who died at the great age of one hundred and two years. He was of Middleborough. Dr. Thacher, a surgeon of the old Continental army, deserves more space than I am able to give him. He has embodied a great deal of Revolutionary history, in a very interesting way, in his "Military Journal," having been present at the principal battles.

The cabinets contain many interesting memorials of the first settlers, their arms, implements, household furniture, and apparel. I refer the reader to the

CARVER'S CHAIR.

BREWSTER'S CHAIR.

guide-books for an enumeration of them. The chairs of Governor Carver and of Elder Brewster are good specimens of the uncomfortable yet quaint furnishing of their time; as the capacious iron pots, pewter platters, and wooden trenchers are suggestive of a primitive people, whose town was a camp. I fancy there were few breakages among the dishes of these Pilgrims, for they were as hard as their owners; nor were there serious deductions to be made from the maids' wages on the day of reckoning. I confess I should have liked to see here, instead of the somewhat confusing jumble of articles pertaining to Pilgrim or

MINCING-KNIFE.

PEREGRINE WHITE'S CABINET.

Indian, an apartment exclusively devoted to the household economy of the first-comers, with furniture suitably arranged, and the evidences of their frugal housewifery garnishing the walls.

Many of the articles said to have been brought over in the *Mayflower* are doubtless authentic, but the number of objects still existing and claiming some part of the immortality of that little bark would freight an Indiaman of good tonnage. There is a still pretty sampler, embroidered by the spider fingers of a Puritan maiden, with a sentiment worth the copying by any fair damsel in the land:

> "Lorea Standish is my name.
> Lord, guide my hart that I may doe thy will;
> Also fill my hands with such convenient skill
> As may conduce to virtue void of shame;
> And I will give the glory to thy name."

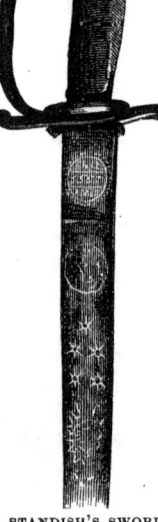

STANDISH'S SWORD.

And here is the carnal weapon of Miles Standish, the living sword-blade of the colony. It lacks not much of an English ell from hilt to point, and looks still able to push its way in the world if well grasped. The weapon has a brass cross and guard, and resembles those trenchant Florentine blades of the sixteenth century, with its channels, curved point, and fine temper. The sword figures in Mr. Longfellow's "Courtship of Miles Standish," where we may hear it clank at the captain's heels as he goes from his wrathful interview with John Alden, slamming the door after him, no doubt, like the tempestuous little tea-pot he was. The inscription on the blade has baffled the *savans*. For such a hot-tempered captain it should have been that engraved on the Earl of Shrewsbury's sword,

> "I am Talbot's, for to slay his foes."

It could hardly have been this legend, with a point inscribed on a broadsword of the seventeenth century:

> "*Qui gladio ferit*
> *Gladio perit.*"

Speaking of swords, I am reminded that the first duel in New England was at Plymouth, in the year 1621. It was between Edward Doty or Doten, and Edward Leister, servants of Steven Hopkins. They fought with sword and dagger, like their betters, and were both wounded. Having no statute against the offense, the Pilgrims met in council to determine on the punishment. It was exemplary. The parties were ordered to be tied together, hand and foot, and to remain twenty-four hours without food or drink. The intercession of their master and their own entreaties procured their release before the sentence was carried out.

In the front of the court-house is a mural tablet, with the seal of the Old Colony sculptured in relief. The quarterings of the shield represent four kneeling figures, having each a flaming heart in its hands. On one side of the figures is a small tree, indicative, I suppose, of the infant growth of the plantation. The attitude and semi-nude appearance indicate an Indian, the subsequent device of Massachusetts, and are at once significant of his subjection, hearty welcome, and ultimate loyalty. The colony seal is said to have been abstracted from the archives in Andros's time, and never recovered.[1] Its legend was "Plimovth Nov-Anglia, Sigillvm Societatis," with the date of 1620 above the shield. The union with Massachusetts, in 1692, dispensed with the necessity for a separate seal.

I saw, in the office of the Register, the records of the First Church of Plymouth, begun and continued by Nathaniel Morton to 1680. The court records, as well as the ancient charter, on which the ink is so faded as to be scarcely legible, are carefully kept.

But the compact, that august instrument, I did not see, nor is the fate of the original known. Its language bears an extraordinary similitude to the preamble of the Constitution of the United States, in its spirit and idea. The name of the king is there in good set phrase; but the soul of the thing is its assumption of sovereignty in the people. See now how King James figures at the head and the tail of it, and then look into the heart of the matter:

THE OLD COLONY SEAL.

"In yᵉ name of God, Amen. We whose names are underwritten, the loyall subjects of our dread soveraigne Lord, King James, by yᵉ grace of God, of Great Britaine, Franc, & Ireland, King, defender of yᵉ faith, &c., haveing undertaken, for yᵉ glorie of God and advancement of yᵉ Christian faith and honour of our king & countrie, a voyage to plant yᵉ first colonie in yᵉ Northerne parts of Virginia, doe by these presents solemnly & mutualy in yᵉ presence of God, and one of another, covenant and combine our selves togeather in a civill body politick, for our better ordering & preservation & furtherance of yᵉ ends aforesaid; and by vertue hearof to enacte, constitute, and frame such just & equall lawes, ordinances, acts, constitutions & offices, from time to time, as shall be thought most meete & convenient for yᵉ generall good of yᵉ Colonie, unto which we promise all due submission and obedience. In witnes wherof we have hereunder subscribed our names at Cap-Codd yᵉ 11 of November, in yᵉ year of yᵉ raigne of our soveraigne lord, King James of England, Franc, & Ireland yᵉ eighteenth & of Scotland yᵉ fiftie fourth, Anᵒ: Dom. 1620."

Bradford says the bond was partly due to the mutinous spirit of some of the strangers on board the *Mayflower*, and partly to the belief that such an act might be as firm as any patent, and in some respects more sure. It is impossible not to be interested in the lives of such men; they were deeply in earnest.

In 1630 the first public execution took place in Plymouth. The culprit was John Billington, who, as Bradford wrote home to England, was a knave, and so would live and die. Billington had waylaid and shot one of the town,[2] and was adjudged guilty of murder. The colony patent could not confer a power it did not itself possess to inflict the death penalty, so they took coun-

---

[1] "Pilgrim Memorial."   [2] John Newcomen.

sel of their friends just come into Massachusetts Bay, and were advised to "purge the land of blood."

In 1658, the crime of adultery appears to be first noticed in the laws. The punishment of this offense was two whippings, the persons convicted to wear two capital letters "A. D." cut in cloth and sewed on their uppermost garment, on their arm or back; if they removed the letters, they were again to be publicly whipped. Another law, that would bear rather hardly on the present generation, was as follows:'Any persons "who behaved themselves profanely by being without doors at the meeting-houses on the Lord's day, in time of exercise, and there misdemeaning themselves by jestings, sleepings, or the like," were first to be admonished, and if they did not refrain, set in the stocks; and if still unreclaimed, cited before the court.

Josselyn, writing of the old "Body of Laws of 1646," says, "Scolds they gag and set them at their doors for certain hours, for all comers and goers by to gaze at." And here is material for the "Scarlet Letter:" "An English woman suffering an Indian to have carnal knowledge of her was obliged to wear an Indian cut out of red cloth sewed upon her right arm, and worn twelve months." Swearing was punished by boring through the tongue with a hot iron; adultery with death.

The chronicles of the Pilgrims have undergone many strange vicissitudes, but are fortunately quite full and complete. It would be pleasant to know more of their lives during their first year at Plymouth than is given by Bradford or Morton. Governor Bradford's manuscript history of Plymouth plantation was probably purloined form the New England Library deposited in the Old South Church of Boston, during the siege of 1775. It found its way to the Fulham Library in England, was discovered, and a copy made which has since been printed, after remaining in manuscript more than two hundred years. The letter-book of Governor Bradford has a similar history. It was rescued from a grocer's shop in Halifax, after the destruction of half its invaluable contents.

The next best thing to be done is probably to go at once to the top of Burial Hill, which is here what the Hoe is to English Plymouth. Here, at least, are plenty of memorials of the Pilgrims, and here town and harbor are outspread for perusal. Seen at full tide, the harbor appears a goodly port enough, but it is left as bare by the ebb as if the sea had been commanded to remove and become dry land. Nothing except a broad expanse of sand-bars and mussel shoals, with luxuriant growth of eel-grass, meets the eye. Through these a narrow and devious channel makes its way. The bay, however, could not be called tame with two such landmarks as Captain's Hill on Duxbury side, and the promontory of Manomet on the shoulder of the Cape.

Plymouth Bay is formed by the jutting-out of Manomet on the south, and by the long-attenuated strip of sand known as Duxbury Beach, on the north.

This beach terminates in a smaller pattern of the celebrated Italian boot that looks equally ready to play at foot-ball with Sicily or to kick intruders out of the Mediterranean. The heel of the boot is toward the sea, and called The Gurnet; the toe points landward, and is called Saquish Head. Just within the toe of the boot is Clark's Island, named from the master's mate of the *Mayflower;* then comes Captain's Hill, making, with the beach, Duxbury Harbor; and in the farthest reach of the bay to the westward is Kingston, where a little water-course, called after the master of the *Mayflower*,[1] makes up into the land. In the southern board Cape Cod is seen on a clear day far out at sea; a mere shining streak of white sand it appears at this distance.

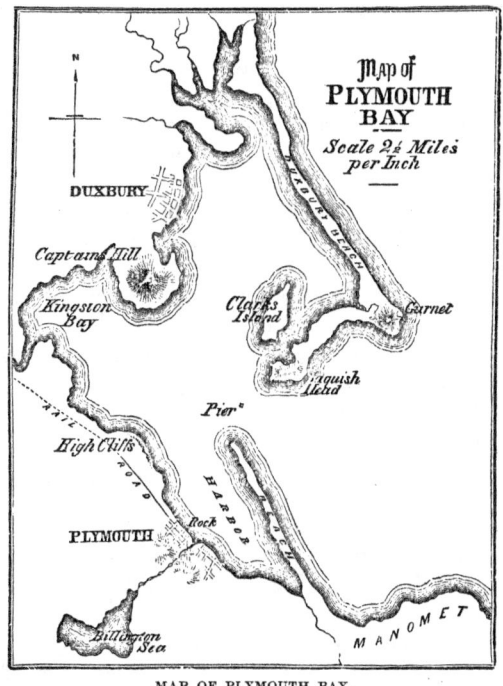

MAP OF PLYMOUTH BAY.

Plymouth harbor proper is formed by a long sand-spit parallel with the shore, that serves as a breakwater for the shallow roadstead. It is anchored where it is, for the winds would blow it away else, by wooden cribs on which the drifting sands are mounded; and it is also tethered by beach-grass rooted in the hillocks or downs that fringe the harbor-side. Now and then extensive repairs are necessary to make good the ravages of a winter's sea-lashings, as many as six hundred tons of stone having been added to the breakwater at the Point at one time. Brush is placed in the jetties, and thousands of roots of beach-grass are planted to catch and stay the shifting sands. The harbor is lighted at evening by twin lights on the Gurnet, and by a single one off Plymouth Beach. The latter is a caisson of iron rooted to the rock by a filling of concrete, and is washed on all sides by the waters of the harbor.

Sand is everywhere; the "stern and rock-bound coast" of Mrs. Hemans nowhere. Except one little cluster by the northern shore of the harbor, the Forefathers' is the only rock on which those pious men could have landed

---

[1] Jones's River.

with dry feet. A few boulders, noticeably infrequent, are scattered along the beach as you approach from Kingston. The hills on which the town is built appear lean and emaciated, as if the light yellow earth with which they are furnished were a compromise between sand and soil. The gardens and house-plots, nevertheless, thrive if they have moisture enough. Few vessels were lying in the harbor, for Plymouth has at present little or no commerce; yet of these, two small colliers were larger than the little *Mayflower* that carried a greater than Cæsar and his fortunes.[1]

The Pilgrims brought the name of their settlement along with them, though Captain John Smith gives it first the Indian name of Accomack, changed by Prince Charles to Plimouth, as it appears on the map accompanying "Advertisements for the Unexperienced." The port was, however, earlier known to both French and English. Samoset told the Pilgrims, at his first interview with them, the Indian name was Patuxet.[2] Prince, indeed, assigns a date (December 31st) for the formal assumption of the English name.[3]

Plymouth, England, from which the Pilgrims finally set sail on the 6th of September, 1619, is situated at the extreme north-west corner of Devonshire, and is divided from Cornwall only by the river Tamar. The name has no other significance than the mouth of the river *Plym*. Exmouth and Dartmouth have the like derivation. Plymouth was long the residence of Sir Francis Drake, and was the birthplace of Sir John Hawkins; also of the painters Northcote, Prout, and B. Haydon. Captain John Davis, the intrepid navigator, and Sir Humphrey Gilbert, who, Queen Elizabeth said, was a " man of noe good happ by sea," were also of Devonshire. It is of the two rivers upon which the "Three Towns" stand that old Michael Drayton writes:

"Plym that claims by right
The christening of that Bay, which bears her noble name."

In spite of historic antecedents, English Plymouth was distasteful to Lord Nelson, who says, in one of his letters to Lady Hamilton, " I hate Plymouth." American Plymouth should owe no grudge to his memory, for he did a very noble act to one of her townsmen. While cruising on our coast in the *Albemarle*, in 1782, Nelson captured a fishing schooner belonging to Plymouth. The cargo of the vessel constituted nearly the whole property of Captain Carver, the master, who had a large family at home anxiously awaiting his return. There being no officer on board the *Albemarle* acquainted with Boston Bay, Nelson ordered the master of the prize to act as pilot. He performed the service to the satisfaction of his captor, who requited him by giving him his vessel and cargo back again, with a certificate to prevent recapture by

---

[1] The *Mayflower* was only one hundred and eighty tons burden. [2] Mourt.
[3] I do not find any exact authority for this.

other British cruisers. Sir N. Harris Nicolas relates that Nelson accompanied this generous act with words equally generous: "You have rendered me, sir, a very essential service, and it is not the custom of English seamen to be ungrateful. In the name, therefore, and with the approbation of the officers of this ship, I return your schooner, and with it this certificate of your good conduct.[1] Farewell! and may God bless you."

The choice of the site of Plymouth by the Pilgrims was due rather to the pressing necessities of their situation than to a well-considered determination. Arriving on our coast in the beginning of winter, after nearly six weeks passed in explorations that enfeebled the hardiest among them, they found their provisions failing, while the increasing rigor of the season called for a speedy decision. As it was not their destination, so it may readily be conceived they were not prepared beforehand with such knowledge of the coast as might now be most serviceable to them. Cheated by their captain, they had thrown away the valuable time spent in searching the barren cape for a harbor fit for settlement. Smith, in his egotism, administers a rebuke to them in this wise:

"Yet at the first landing at *Cape Cod*, being an hundred passengers, besides twenty they had left behind at *Plimouth* for want of good take heed, thinking to find all things better than I advised them, spent six or seven weeks in wandering up and downe in frost and snow, wind and raine, among the woods, cricks, and swamps, forty of them died, and three-score were left in a most miserable estate at New Plimouth, where their ship left them, and but nine leagues by sea from where they landed, whose misery and variable opinions, for want of experience, occasioned much faction, till necessity agreed them."

It is not easily understood why they should have remained in so unpromising a location after a better knowledge of the country had been obtained. To the north was Massachusetts, called by Smith "the paradise of those parts." South-west of them was the fertile Narraganset country, with fair Aquidneck within their patent. In thirteen or fourteen years the whole of Plymouth colony would not have made one populous town. But there are indications that a removal was kept in view. Their brethren in Leyden, who saw the hand of God in their first choice, advised them not to abandon it. In 1633 they established a trading-house on the Connecticut, and when afterward dispossessed by Massachusetts, alleged as a reason for holding a post there that "they lived upon a barren place, where they were by necessity cast, and neither they nor theirs could long continue upon the same, and why should they be deprived of that which they had provided and intended

---

[1] "This is to certify that I took the schooner *Harmony*, Nathaniel Carver, master, belonging to Plymouth, but, on account of his good services, have given him up his vessel again.
"HORATIO NELSON.
"Dated on board H. M. ship *Albemarle*, 17th August, 1782."

to remove to as soon as they were able?"[1] Yet, like fatalists they continued on the very shores to which Providence had directed them.

When the Pilgrims explored the bay, they were at first undetermined whether to make choice of Clark's Island, the shores of the little river at Kingston, or the spot on the main-land which became their ultimate abode. The high ground of Plymouth shore, the "sweete brooke" under the hill-side, and the large tract of land ready cleared for their use, settled the question; the high hill from which they might see Cape Cod, and withal very fit for a citadel, clenched their decision.

It did not seem to occur to the Pilgrims that to pitch their residence in a place desolated by the visitation of God was at all ill-omened. In their circuit of the bay they did not see an Indian or an Indian wigwam, though they met with traces of a former habitation. Added to the sadness and gloom of the landscape, the frozen earth, the bare and leafless trees, was a silence not alone of nature, but of death. The plague had cleared the way for them; they built upon graves.

This terrible forerunner of the English is alluded to by several of the old writers. It swept the coast from the Fresh Water River to the Penobscot, with a destructiveness like to that witnessed in London a few years later. Sir F. Gorges tells us that the Indians inhabiting the region round about the embouchure of the Saco were sorely afflicted with it, "so that the country was in a manner left void of inhabitants." Vines, Sir Ferdinando's agent, with his companions, slept in the cabins with those that died; but, to their good fortune, as the narrative quaintly sets forth, "not one of them ever felt their heads to ache while they stayed there." This was in the year 1616–'17. Levett says the Indians at "Aquamenticus" were all dead when he was there. Samoset explains, in his broken English, to the Pilgrims that the lawful occupants of Patuxet had, four years before, been swept away by an extraordinary plague. The Indians had never seen or heard of the disease before. Villages withered away when the blight fell upon them; tribes were obliterated, and nations were reduced to tribes. Doubtless, this disaster had much to do with the peaceable settlement of Plymouth, Salem, and Boston. Had the Pilgrims been everywhere resisted, as at Nauset, they could hardly have planted their colony in Plymouth Bay.

There was another cause to which the English owed their safety, as related to them by many aged Indians. A French ship had been cast away on Cape Cod. The crew succeeded in landing, but the Indians, less merciful than the sea, butchered all but three of them. Two were ransomed by Dermer, one of Sir F. Gorges's captains. The other remained with the savages, acquired their language, and died among them. Before his death he foretold that God was angry, and would destroy them, and give their heritage to a strange peo-

---

[1] Governor Bradford's "History of Plymouth."

ple. They derided him, and answered boastfully, they were so strong and numerous that the Manitou could not kill them all. Soon after the pestilence depopulated the country. Then came the Englishmen in their ships. The savages assembled in a dark swamp, where their conjurors, with incantations lasting several days, solemnly cursed the pale-faces, devoting them to destruction. Thus the English found safety in the superstitious awe of the natives. The story of the terrible plague is as yet unwritten. Governor Bradford says that when Winslow went to confer with Massasoit, he passed by numbers of unburied skulls and bones of those who had died.

Captain Levett is corroborative of the Pilgrims' settled intention to depart from their original place of settlement. He observes in his "Voyage into New England:" "Neither was I at New Plymouth, but I fear that place is not so good as many others; for if it were, in my conceit, they would content themselves with it, and not seek for any other, having ten times so much ground as would serve ten times so many people as they have now among them. But it seems they have no fish to make benefit of; for this year they had one ship fish at Pemaquid, and another at Cape Ann, where they have begun a new plantation, but how long it will continue I know not."

It is evident from the testimony that the settlement at Plymouth was illconsidered, and that the Pilgrims were themselves far from satisfied with it. In this, too, we have the solution of the rapid overshadowing of the Old Colony by its neighbors, and the fading away of its political and commercial importance.

There is no manner of doubt that Plymouth had been visited by whites long before the advent of the *Mayflower's* band. Hutchinson erroneously says De Monts "did not go into the Massachusetts bay, but struck over from some part of the eastern shore to Cape Ann, and so to Cape Cod, and sailed farther southward." Definite is this!

It was the object of De Monts to examine the coast, and his pilot seems to have kept in with it as closely as possible, making a harbor every night where one was to be found. The Indian pilot proved to have little knowledge of the shores or of the language of the tribes to the westward of the Saco; for on being confronted with the natives of the Massachusetts country, he was not able to understand them. Gorges recounts that his natives from Pemaquid and from Martha's Vineyard at first hardly comprehended each other.

Hutchinson, it is probable, saw the edition of "Champlain's Voyages" of 1632, contenting himself with a cursory examination of it. An attentive reading of the text of the edition of 1613 would have undeceived him as to the movements of De Monts. Although the reprint of 1632 gives the substance of the voyage, it is so mutilated in its details as to afford scanty satisfaction to the student.

After leaving Cape Ann, De Monts entered Boston Bay and saw Charles

River, named by his company "Rivière du Gas," in compliment to their chief. From thence they continued their route to a place that has for the moment a greater interest. Given the latitude, the physical features, and the distance from Cape Ann, we are at no loss to put the finger on Plymouth Bay, of which the geographer of the expedition is the first to give us a description.

The wind coming contrary, they dropped anchor in a little roadstead.[1] While lying there they were boarded by canoes that had been out fishing for cod. These, going to shore, notified their companions, who assembled on the sands, dancing and gesticulating in token of amity and welcome. A canoe from the bark landed with a few trifles with which the simple natives were well pleased, and begged their strange visitors to come and visit them within their river. The man-stealers had not yet been among them. They offered a simple but sincere hospitality.

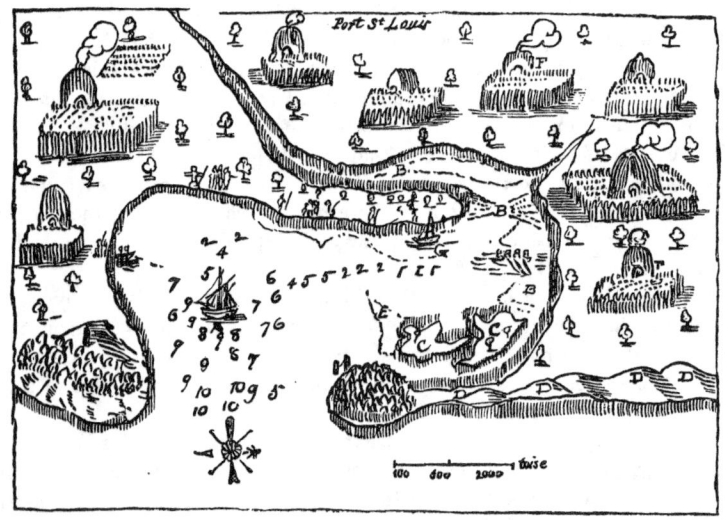

CHAMPLAIN'S MAP.—PORT CAPE ST. LOUIS.

Let us have recourse to the musty pages and antiquated French of Champlain, following in the wake of the bark as it weathers the Gurnet, and doubles Saquish, with the cheery cry of the leadsman, and the eyes of De Monts, Champlain, and Champdoré fixed on the shores of coming renown:

"Nous levames l'ancre pour ce faire, mais nous n'y peusmes entrer à cause du peu d'eau que nous y trouvames estans de basse mer et fumes contrainctes de mouiller l'ancre à l'entrée d'icelle. Je decendis à terre où j'eu vis quantité d'autres qui nous reçeurent fort gratieusement : et fus recognoistre la rivière, où n'y a vey autre chose qu'un bras d'eau qui s'estant quelque peu

---

[1] Green's Harbor, perhaps.

dans les terres qui font en partie desertées : dedans lequel il n'y a qu'un ruisseau qui ne peut porter basteaux sinon de pleine mer. Ce lieu peut avoir une lieue de circuit. En l'une des entrées duquel y a une manière d'icelle couverte de bois et principalement de pins qui tient d'un coste à des dunes de sable, qui font assez longues : l'autre coste est une terre assez haute. Il y a deux islets dans lad. Baye, qu'on ne voit point si l'on n'est dedans, où autour at la mer asséche presque toute de basse mer. Ce lieu est fort remarquable de la mer ; d'autant que la coste est fort basse, hormis le cap de l'entrée de la Baye qu'avons nommé le port du cap St. Louys distant dud. cap deux lieues et dix du Cap aux Isles. Il est environ par le hauteur du Cap St. Louys."

TRANSLATION.[1]

We raised the anchor to do this, but we could not enter therein by reason of the little water which we found there, being low sea, and were constrained to let go the anchor at the entrance of it. I went ashore, where I saw numbers of natives who received us very graciously, and surveyed the river, which is nothing more than an arm of water that makes a little way in the lands which are in part deserted, within which it is only a rivulet that can not float vessels except at full sea. This place may be a league in circuit. At one of the entrances is a sort of island, which is covered with wood, principally pines, which holds to a coast of sandy downs of some length ; the other shore is pretty high land. There are two isles in the said Bay which are not perceived until you are within, which the sea leaves almost entirely at low tide. This place is very remarkable from the sea, inasmuch as the coast is very low, except the cape at the entrance of the Bay, which we have named Port Cape St. Louis, distant from the said Cape two leagues, and ten from the Cape of Islands. It is about the latitude of Cape St. Louis.[2]

In this description the Gurnet and Manomet stand out for easy recognition. The sandy downs of Duxbury Beach, the shallow harbor, the river, even the soundings establish the identity of Port St. Louis with Plymouth; and the two islands become further evidence, if more were needed.

To account for the hostility of the Indians inhabiting the Cape when the Pilgrims were reconnoitring there, it is only necessary to cite a few facts. Cabot stole three savages and carried them to England, where, says Stow, in ludicrous astonishment, after two years' residence they could not be told from Englishmen. In 1508, it is said, Thomas Aubert, a pilot of Dieppe, excited great curiosity by bringing over several natives to France. Cartier took two back with him to France, but with their own consent; and they were eventually, I believe, restored to their native country. Weymouth, in 1605, seized five at Pemaquid; Harlow, in 1611, five more; and Hunt, the greatest thief of them all, kidnaped in this very harbor of Plymouth, in the year 1614, twenty-four of those silly savages, and sold them in Spain for reals of eight. After such treachery it is not strange the red men looked on these new-comers as their natural enemies. It is more extraordinary that Samoset, on entering their weak village some months after their landing, should have greeted them with the memorable " Welcome, Englishmen !"

The Pilgrims saw in the evidences of prior intercourse with Europeans, that they were not the pioneers in this wilderness of New England. They found

---

[1] Followed as literally as possible, to preserve the style.
[2] Named by De Monts, and supposed to be Brant Point.

implements and utensils of civilized manufacture, though no fire-arms. These articles were probably obtained by barter with the fishing or trading ships.

On William Wood's map of 1634,[1] Old Plymouth is laid down on the eastern shore of Narraganset Bay, while New Plymouth has its proper position. "New Plimouth" is placed on Blauw's map at the head of a small bay, into which a large river flows. One of the headlands of the bay is named C. Blanco Gallis, and the bay itself Crane Bay. Josselyn has also this reference to Old Plymouth:

"At the farther end of the bay, by the mouth of Narraganset River, on the south side thereof was Old Plymouth plantation, *Anno* 1602." He may have borrowed his itinerary in part from Wood, who, as I take it, referred to Gosnold's attempt at the mouth of Buzzard's Bay. In his summary, under date of 1607, Josselyn notes, "Plimouth plantation in New England attempted."

I spent some hours among the grave-stones on Burial Hill. Here, as in the streets of the living inhabitants, the old familiar names of the *Mayflower's* passengers are to be met with. And in every burial-place in the land, I make no doubt, are to be found Howlands and Winslows, Bradfords and Brewsters, side by side. I have felt myself much moved in thinking on the story of those stern men and self-contained, trustful women. Their whole lives might justly be called a pilgrimage. Consider their gathering in the Old England they loved so well; then their dispersion, suffering, and hurried flight into Holland; afterward the staking their all on the issue of their venture in the New World, and the painful, anxious lives they led; despoiling the young of their youth, and the elders of a peaceful old age.

This spot, as is well known, was not the Pilgrims' original place of interment. They who first died were buried on Cole's Hill, nearer the shore, and to the strait limits of their little hamlet. They lost one half their number during the first dismal winter, and there was room enough without going far to make their graves. Tradition says that, fearing their wretchedness might inspire the Indians with the hope of exterminating them, those early graves were first leveled and then planted upon in order to conceal their losses. It is said that sixty years elapsed before a grave-stone with an inscription was set up in Plymouth; certain it is that none older has been found than that of Edward Gray, merchant, who died in 1681.

The obliterated grave-yard on Cole's Hill, which was nothing more than a sea-bluff overhanging the shore, was flooded by a freshet about 1735, laying bare many of the graves, and carrying along with it to the sea many of the remains. It is the supposed resting-place of Carver, the first governor of Plymouth, and of his wife, who did not long survive him. It contained the ashes of fifty of the one hundred and two that had landed in December. In

---

[1] "The south part of New England, as it is planted this yeare, 1634."

the time of the first winter's sickness, says Hutchinson, there were not above seven men capable of bearing arms. And yet, when they were almost too few to bury their own dead, they talked of war with Canonicus as if it were mere bagatelle, answering defiance with defiance. I fancy those Pilgrims were of the right stuff!

On Burial Hill is a monument to the memory of Governor Bradford, who succeeded Carver, and was annually chosen from 1621 until his death, in 1657 —except during the years 1633, 1636, 1638, and 1644, when Edward Winslow, and in 1634, when Thomas Prence, administered the colony affairs. In seventy years there were only six different persons governors of Plymouth. Roger White, the friend of Bradford, writes him a letter from Leyden, December, 1625, counseling rotation in office, more than hinting that the constant re-election of himself to the chief office in the colony tended to an oligarchy.[1] Bradford was among the earliest to go into Holland for conscience' sake. He was of good estate, and had learned the art of silk-dyeing in Amsterdam. His residence in the New World began in affliction, for, before a site for settlement had been fixed upon, his wife, Dorothy May, fell from the vessel into the sea and was drowned. His monument was erected, some years ago, by descendants.

In a conspicuous position is the monument raised, in 1858, by the descendants of Robert Cushman, and of Thomas Cushman, his son, for forty-three years ruling elder of the church of the Pilgrims. Of all the original memorial tablets in this old cemetery, those of Thomas Cushman, who came in 1621, in the *Fortune*, and of Thomas Clark, a passenger by the *Ann*, in 1623, alone were remaining. The grave of John Howland, an emigrant of the *Mayflower*, has been identified, and furnished with a handsome head-stone. In some instances boards bearing simply the name and age of the deceased have replaced the aged and no longer legible stones, as in the cases of Elder Thomas Faunce, William Crowe, and others. The stone of Thomas Clark was the most curious I saw, and in general the inscriptions do not possess other interest than the recollections they summon up. The grave of Dr. Adoniram Judson is also here.

Burial Hill is also memorable as the site of the second[2] regular church edifice in New England, built to serve the double purpose of church and citadel. From this cause the eminence was long called Fort Hill. By February, 1621, after the defiance of Canonicus, the town was inclosed within a palisade, taking in the top of the hill under which it was situated. In 1622 the colonists built their church-fortress; it should have been dedicated with Luther's anthem:

---

[1] "Collections of the Massachusetts Historical Society."

[2] See Popham's settlement on the Kennebec; the Episcopal service was doubtless the first religious exercise in New England.

> "God is a castle and defense,
> When troubles and distress invade,
> He'll help and free us from offense,
> And ever shield us with his aid."

Ever willing to turn an honest penny, the Dutch, in 1627, opened a correspondence between Fort Amsterdam and Plymouth, with offers of trade. They followed it with an embassy in the person of Isaac de Rasieres, who, says Bradford, was their chief merchant, and second to their governor. He came into Plymouth "honorably attended with a noise of trumpeters." It is in a letter of De Rasieres, found at The Hague by Mr. Brodhead, that we obtain a circumstantial account of town and fortress as they then existed.

"Upon the hill," he writes, "they have a large, square house, with a flat roof, made of thick sawn planks, stayed with oak beams, upon the top of which they have six cannons, which shoot iron balls of four and five pounds, and command the surrounding country. The lower part they use for their church, where they preach on Sundays and the usual holidays."[1]

A looker-on here in 1807 found in this burying-ground and on the summit of the hill the remains of the ditch that surrounded the ancient fortification erected in 1675, on the approach of Philip's war. This was a work of greater magnitude than that of the first adventurers, inclosing a space one hundred feet square, strongly palisaded with pickets ten and a half feet high. As late as 1844 the whole circuit of this work was distinctly visible.[2] The head of Wittuwamet, one of the chiefs killed by Standish's party at Weymouth in 1623, was set up on the battlements of the fort, as was afterward that of the renowned King Philip. The vaunting, the exasperating mockery of a savage, is in these lines:

> "'Who is there here to fight with the brave Wattawamat?'
> Then he unsheathed his knife, and, whetting the blade on his left hand,
> Held it aloft and displayed a woman's face on the handle,
> Saying, with bitter expression and look of sinister meaning,
> 'I have another at home, with the face of a man on the handle;
> By-and-by they shall marry; and there will be plenty of children.'"

According to Edward Winslow, the English stood to their guns when Indians came among them. To allay distrust in the minds of the savages, they were told it was an act of courtesy observed by the English, both on

---

[1] Captain John Smith, speaking of the town in 1624, says of this fortress, there was "within a high mount a fort, with a watch-tower, well built of stone, lome, and wood, their ordnance well mounted."

[2] During some excavations made on the hill, remains of the watch-tower of brick came to light, indicating its position to have been in the vicinity of the Judson monument. There also existed on the hill, until about 1860, a powder-house of antique fashion, built in 1770. It had an oval slab of slate imbedded in the wall, with a Latin inscription; and there were also engraved upon it a powder-horn, cartridge, and a cannon.—"Pilgrim Memorial."

land and sea. The sentinel who paced his lonely round here in 1622 should have had steady nerves. The nearest outpost was his fellow-watcher on the ramparts of Fort Amsterdam. He could hardly pass the word on "All's well!" to Jamestown or Saint Augustine, or hear the challenge from Port Royal, in Acadia. Behind him was the wilderness, out of which it was a wonder the Indians did not burst, it was so easy to overwhelm the devoted little band of Englishmen and brush them away into the sea. I make no account of the few scattered cabins along the northern coast, and the Pilgrims made no account of them. Thus they lived for ten years within the narrow limits of an intrenched camp, a picket lodged within an enemy's country, until the settlement in Massachusetts Bay enabled them to draw breath. Why might they not say to those after-comers,

"We are the Jasons; we have won the fleece?"

The procession of the Pilgrims to their church was a sight that must have exceedingly stirred the sluggish blood of the Dutch emissary. He found them attentive to proffers of trade; acute, as might be expected of the first Yankees, where profits were in question; but there was no doubt about the quality of their piety. At the hour of worship the silent village was assembled by drum-beat, as was befitting in the Church Militant. At this signal the house-doors open and give passage to each family. The men wear their sad-colored mantles, and are armed to the teeth, as if going to battle. Silently they take their places in front of the captain's door, three abreast, with match-locks shouldered. The tall, stern-visaged ones, we may suppose, lead the rest. In front is the sergeant. Behind the armed men comes Bradford, in a long robe. At his right hand is Elder Brewster, with his cloak on. At the governor's left marches Miles Standish, his rapier lifting up the corner of his mantle, and carrying a small cane in his hand. The women in sober gowns, kerchiefs, and hoods, their garments poor, but scrupulously neat, follow next; the lowlier yielding precedence to those of better condition. At command, they take their way up the hill in this order, and, entering within the rude temple they have raised, each man sets down his musket where he may lay hand upon it. "Thus," says De Rasieres, "they are on their guard night and day."

Thomas Lechford, "of Clement's Inn, Gent," in his "Plain Dealing," says he once looked in the church-door in Boston where the sacrament was being administered. He thus noted down what he saw: "They come together about nine o'clock by ringing of a bell. Pastor prayed for a quarter of an hour. The teacher then readeth and expoundeth a chapter; then a psalm is sung, which one of the ruling Elders dictates. Afterward the pastor preaches a sermon, or exhorts *ex tempore*."

This is the way in which they made contributions: "On Sundays, in the afternoon, when the sermon is ended, the people in the galleries come down and march two abreast up one aisle and down the other, until they come before the desk, for pulpit they have none. Before the desk is a long pue where the elders and deacons sit, one of them with a money-box in his hand, into which the people, as they pass, put their offering, some a shill, some 2s., some half a crown, five s., according to their ability. Then they conclude with a prayer."

Lechford adds that the congregation used to pass up by the deacon's seat, giving either money, or valuable articles, or paper promises to pay, and so to their seats again, the chief men or magistrates first. The same author describes the method of excommunication practiced in some of the New England churches. "At New Haven, *alias* Quinapeag," he says, " where Master Davenport is pastor, the excommunicate is held out of the meeting, at the doore, if he will heare, in frost, snow, and raine."

The Pilgrims are often called Puritans, a term of reproach first applied to the whole body of Dissenters, but in their day belonging strictly to those who renounced the forms and ceremonies while believing in the doctrines and sacraments of the Church of England. Boston was settled by Puritans, who, according to Governor Winthrop, adhered to the mother-church when they left Old England. It is curious to observe that the Boston Puritans became rigid Separatists, while the Plymouth Separatists became more and more moderate. The Pilgrims were originally of the sect called Brownists, from Robert Brown, a school-master in Southwark about 1580, and a relation of Cecil, Lord Burghley.[1] Cardinal Bentivoglio erroneously calls the Holland refugees a distinct sect by the name of Puritans. Hutchinson, usually well informed, observes, "If all in England who called themselves Brownists and Independents at that day had come over with them (the Pilgrims), they would scarcely have made one considerable town." Yet in 1592 there were said to be twenty thousand Independents in England.

The Church of the Pilgrims, formed, in 1602, of people living on the borders of Nottinghamshire, Lincolnshire, and Yorkshire, made their way, after innumerable difficulties, into Holland. Their pastor, John Robinson, is usually regarded as the author of Independency. A residence on the scene of the Reformation softened, in many respects, the inflexible religious character of the Brownists. They discarded the name rendered odious on many accounts. It is stated, on the authority of Edward Winslow, that Robinson and his Church did not require renunciation of the Church of England, acknowledging the other reformed churches, and allowing occasional communion with

---

[1] Robert Brown, the founder of the sect, after thirty-two imprisonments, eventually conformed. Henry Penay, Henry Barrow, and other Brownists, were cruelly executed for alleged sedition, May 29th, 1593. Elizabeth's celebrated Act of 1593 visited a refusal to make a declaration of conformity with the Church of England with banishment and forfeiture of citizenship; death if the offender returned into the realm.

them. It is also evident from what Bradford says that the Pilgrims chose the Huguenots as their models in Church affairs.[1]

Both in regard to civil and ecclesiastical affairs the Pilgrims were placed in a situation of serious difficulty. The King of England promised not to interfere with them in religious matters, but would not acknowledge them by any public act under his hand and seal. Some of the most influential of the company of English merchants, by whom they were transported to New England, did not sympathize with them in their religious views, and at length broke off from them, and left them to struggle on alone as best they might. This is apparent in the plan to prevent the remnant of the Church of Leyden from coming over. It is also clear that neither the motives nor the intentions of the Pilgrims were well understood by the adventurers at the outset, and that as soon as these were fully developed, the merchants, or a majority of them, preferred to augment their colony with a more pliant and less obnoxious class of emigrants than the first-comers had proved. In examining the charges and complaints of the one, and the explanations of the other, it is difficult to avoid the conclusion that a good deal of duplicity was used by the Pilgrims to keep the breath of life in their infant plantation.

It appears that the settlers in Massachusetts Bay were not acquainted with the form of worship practiced by the Pilgrims, as Endicott writes to Governor Bradford from "Naumkeak, May 11th, 1629 : I acknowledge myself much bound to you for your kind love and care in sending Mr. Fuller among us, and rejoice much that I am by him satisfied touching your judgments of the outward form of God's worship; it is (as far as I can yet gather) no other than is warranted by the evidence of truth, and the same which I have professed and maintained ever since the Lord in his mercy revealed himself unto me, being far differing from the common reports that hath been spread of you touching that particular."[2]

I have thought it worth mentioning that the church at Salem was the first completely organized Congregational church in America. It was gathered August 6th, 1619, when Rev. Mr. Higginson was ordained teacher, and Mr. Skelton pastor.[3] Governor Bradford and others deputed from the church at Plymouth, coming into the assembly in the hour of the solemnity, gave them the right hand of fellowship. Robinson never having come over, Plymouth was without a pastor for some years.

---

[1] Sir Matthew Hale used to say, "Those of the Separation were good men, but they had narrow souls, or they would not break the peace of the Church about such inconsiderable matters as the points of difference were." In this country the Independents took the name of Congregationalists. They held, among other things, that one church may advise or reprove another, but had no power to excommunicate. The churches outside of Plymouth did, however, practice excommunication.

[2] Governor Bradford's Letter-book.

[3] The teacher explained doctrines; the pastor enforced them by suitable exhortations.

Under Charles I. the Pilgrims fared little better than in the preceding reign; but they had seated themselves firmly by the period of the Civil War. On the day before his arrival at Shrewsbury, the king caused the military orders to be read at the head of each regiment. Then, mounting his horse, and placing himself in the midst, where all might hear, he made a speech to his soldiers, in which this passage occurs:

"Gentlemen, you have heard these orders read; it is your part, in your severall places, to observe them exactly. .... I can not suspect your Courage and Resolution; your Conscience and your Loyalty hath brought you hither to fight for your Religion, your King, and the Laws of the Land; you shall fight with no Enemies, but Traitours, most of them Brownists, Anabaptists, and Atheists, such who desire to destroy both Church and State, and who have already condemned you to ruin for being Loyall to vs."

Here, then, were a handful of men repudiated by their king, cast off by their commercial partners, a prey to the consequences of civil war at home, and living by sufferance in the midst of a fierce and warlike people, compelled at last to work out their own political destiny. What wonder that with them self-preservation stood first, last, and always! All other settlements in New England were made with the hope of gain alone, few, if any, colonists meaning to make a permanent home in its wilds. We may not withhold the respect due to these Pilgrims, who were essentially a unit, embodying the germ of civil, political, and religious liberty. They beheld from the beach the vanishing sail of the *Mayflower* as men who had accepted what fate may bring to them. They did not mean to go back.

THE PILGRIMS' FIRST ENCOUNTER.

CHAPTER XVIII.

PLYMOUTH, CLARK'S ISLAND, AND DUXBURY.

"Ay, call it holy ground,
 The soil where first they trod!
They have left unstain'd what there they found—
 Freedom to worship God!"—MRS. HEMANS.

LET us now take a walk in Leyden Street. Until 1802 the principal street of the Pilgrims was without a name; it was then proposed to give it the one it now so appropriately bears. In my descent of the hill into the town square, I passed under the shade of some magnificent elms just putting forth their spring buds. Some of those natural enemies of trees were talking of cutting down the noblest of them all, that has stood for nearly a hundred years, and long shaded Governor Bradford's house.[1]

Consulting again our old guide, De Rasieres, I find he tells us, "New Plymouth lies on the slope of a hill stretching east, toward the sea-coast,

---

[1] These trees are said to have been planted in 1783, by Thomas Davis.

with a broad street about a cannon-shot of eight hundred [yards] long leading down the hill; with a street crossing in the middle northward to the rivulet and southward to the land. The houses are constructed of hewn planks, with gardens, also inclosed behind and at the sides with hewn planks; so that their houses and court-yards are arranged in very good order, with a stockade against a sudden attack; and at the ends of the streets there are three wooden gates.

BUILDING ON THE SITE OF BRADFORD'S MANSION.

In the centre, on the cross-street, stands the governor's house, before which is a square inclosure, upon which four pateros [steenstucken] are mounted, so as to flank along the streets." We are standing, then, in the ancient place of arms of the Pilgrims.

Nearest to us, on the north side of the square, is the site of Governor Bradford's house, with the Church of the Pilgrimage just beyond. The dwelling of the governor was long ago removed to the north part of the town, and this, its successor, does not fulfill our want, as the veritable habitation of the much-honored magistrate would do. Nearly opposite is the old county courthouse, erected in 1749. Up at the head of this inclosed space, which long custom miscalls a square, is the First Church, its pinnacles appearing dimly through the interweaving branches of tall elms. There is a coolness as well as a repose about the spot that makes us loiter.

After the tragic death of his first wife, Bradford bethought him of Mrs. Southworth, whom he had known and wooed in old England as Alice Carpenter. She was now a widow. He renewed his suit, and she hearkened to him. But as the governor could not leave his magistracy, the lady, ceding her woman's rights, took ship, and came to Plymouth in August, 1623. In a fortnight they were married.

Bradford tells how the passengers of the ship *Ann*, of whom Mistress Southworth was one, were affected by what they saw when they first set foot in Plymouth. They were met by a band of haggard men and women, meanly appareled, and in some cases little better than half-naked. The best dish they could set before their friends was a lobster or piece of fish, without other drink than a cup of water. Some of the newly arrived fell weeping; others wished themselves in England again, while even the joy of meeting friends from whom they had long been separated could not dispel the sadness of others in beholding their miserable condition. The governor has not told us of the coming of Alice Southworth, but says simply there were " some very useful persons" on board the ship *Ann.*

Here the governor entertained Père Gabriel Dreuillettes, in 1650, with a fish dinner, because, says the good old Jesuit, it was a Friday. The governor was equal to the courtesy; yet, I fancy, fish dinners were often eaten in Plymouth.

Bradford's second wife survived him thirteen years. With her came his brother-in-law, George Morton, her sister, Bridget Fuller,[1] and two daughters of Elder Brewster. She lived thirty years with her second husband, and, from the tribute of Nathaniel Morton,[2] must have been a woman of an exemplary and beautiful character. Her sister, Mary Carpenter, lived to be ninety years old. She is referred to in the church records of Plymouth as " a godly old maid, never married."

Apropos of the governor's wedding, I extract this notice of the first marriage in the colony from his history: "May 12th, 1621, was ye first marriage in this place, which, according to ye laudable custome of ye Low Countries, was thought most requisite to be performed by the magistrate, as being a civill thing, upon which many questions aboute inheritance doe depende," etc.

When Edward Winslow was in England as agent of the colony, and was interrogated at the instance of Laud, Archbishop of Canterbury, before the Lords Commissioners of the Plantations, he was, among other things, questioned upon this practice of marriage by magistrates. He answered boldly that he found nothing in Scripture to restrict marriage to the clergy. He also alleged that the plantation had long been without a minister, and finished by citing, as a precedent, his own marriage by a magistrate at the *Staathaus* in Holland. Morton, who appeared as an accuser of Winslow, says, "The people of New England held the use of a ring in marriage to be a relique of popery, a diabolical circle for the Devell to daunce in."

As soon as they had definitely settled upon a location, the colonists went to work building their town. They began to prepare timber as early as the 23d of December, but the inclemency of the season and the distance every thing was to be transported—there were no trees standing within an eighth of a mile of the present Leyden Street—made the work painfully laborious and the progress slow. On the twenty-eighth day the company was consoli-

---

[1] Wife of Samuel Fuller. She gave the church the lot of ground on which the parsonage stood.—*Allen.*
[2] See Appendix to Bradford's History.

dated into nineteen families, the single men joining some household in order to lessen the number of houses to be built. They then staked out the ground, giving every person half a pole in breadth and three in length. Each head of a family chose his homestead by lot, and each man was required to build his own house. By Tuesday, the 9th of January, the Common House wanted nothing but the thatch to be complete; still, although it was only twenty feet square, the weather was so inclement that it took four days to cover it. They could seldom work half the week.

Captain Smith says, in 1624, the town consisted of two-and-thirty houses and about a hundred and eighty people. The Common House is believed to have stood on the south side of Leyden Street, where the abrupt descent of the hill begins. In digging a cellar on the spot, in 1801, sundry tools and a plate of iron were discovered, seven feet below the surface of the ground. This house is supposed to have served the colonists for every purpose of a public nature until the building of their fortress on Burial Hill. Mourt calls it their rendezvous, and relates that a few days after completion it took fire from a spark in the thatch. At the time of the accident Governor Carver and William Bradford were lying sick within, with their muskets charged, and the thatch blazing above them, to their very great danger. In this Common House the working parties slept until their dwellings were made ready.

SITE OF THE COMMON HOUSE.

It was worth living two hundred years ago to have witnessed one street scene that took place here. John Oldham, the contentious, the incorrigible, dared to return to Plymouth after banishment. He had, with Lyford, tried to breed a revolt among the disaffected of the colony. A rough and tough malignant was Oldham, fiercely denouncing the magistrates to their teeth when called to answer for his misdeeds. He defied them roundly in their grave assembly. Turning to the by-standers, he exclaimed:

"My maisters whar is your harts? now show your courage, you have oft complained to me so and so; now is ye tyme if you will doe any thing, I will stand by you."

He returned more choleric than before, calling those he met rebels and traitors, in his mad fury. They put him under guard until his wrath had time to cool, and set their invention to work. He was compelled to pass through a double file of musketeers, every one of whom "was ordered to give

PLYMOUTH, CLARK'S ISLAND, AND DUXBURY.

him a thump on ye brich, with ye but end of his musket," and was then conveyed to the water-side, where a boat was in readiness to carry him away. They then bid him go and mend his manners. The idea of the gantlet was, I suspect, borrowed from the Indians.

This little colony of pilgrims was at first a patriarchal community. Every thing was in common. Each year an acre of land was allotted to every inhabitant to cultivate. The complete failure of the experiment ought to stand for a precedent, though it seems somehow to have been forgotten. Men, they found, would not work for the common interest as for themselves, and so the idea of a community of dependents was abandoned for an association of independent factors. From this time they began to get on. The rent-day did not trouble them. "We are all freeholders," writes Edward Hilton home to England. In 1626 the planters bought themselves free of the undertakers, who oppressed them with ruinous charges for every thing furnished the colony. Allerton, who was sent over in 1625 to beg the loan of one hundred pounds sterling, was obliged to pay thirty pounds in the hundred interest for the two hundred pounds he had obtained. In the year 1627 they divided all their stock into shares, giving each person, or share, twenty acres of land, besides the single acre already allotted.

It is time to resume our walk down Leyden Street. On reaching the bluff before mentioned the street divides, one branch descending the declivity toward the water, while the other skirts the hill-side. The Universalist Church at the corner marks the site of the Allyne House, an ancient dwelling demolished about 1826. By the Plymouth records, it appears that, in 1699, Mr. Joseph Allyne married Mary Doten, daughter of Edward, and granddaughter of that Edward Doten who had come in the *Mayflower*. Among the children of Joseph Allyne born in the old

THE ALLYNE HOUSE.

homestead was Mary, who became the mother of that "flame of fire," James Otis. The house commanded a fine view of the bay, its foundations being higher than the chimneys in the streets below. It may not, perhaps, be generally known that James Otis, after completing his studies in the office of Jeremiah Gridley, then the most eminent lawyer in the province, came from Boston to Plymouth, where he took an office in the main street. He practiced there during the years 1748–'49, when his talents called him to a broader field.

Mercy, the sister of James Otis, married James Warren, a native of Plymouth. He succeeded General Joseph Warren as president of the Provincial Congress of Massachusetts, but is better known as the author of the celebrated "Committee of Correspondence," which he proposed to Samuel Adams while the latter was at his house. Mrs. Warren, at the age of seventy, was visited by the Duke De Liancourt. "She then retained," he says, "the activity of mind which distinguished her as a sister of James Otis; nor had she lost the graces of person or conversational powers, which made her still a charming companion." For reasons apparent to the reader, she resolved not to send her "History of the Revolution" to the press during her husband's lifetime.

THE JOANNA DAVIS HOUSE, COLE'S HILL.

Going beyond the church, we come upon the open space of greensward, intersected by footpaths, known as Cole's Hill. Some defensive works were erected on this bank in 1742, in the Revolution, and again in 1814. I have already traversed it in imagination, when standing on the summit of Burial Hill. It is no longer a place of graves, nor does it in the least suggest, by any monumental symbol, the tragedy of the Pilgrims' first winter here, when, as Bradford touchingly says, "Y^e well were not in any measure sufficient to tend ye sicke; nor the living scarce able to burie the dead." Their greatest strait was in May and June, when there were no wild fowl. Winslow says they were without good tackle or seines to take the fish that swam so abundantly in the harbor and creeks.

PLYMOUTH, CLARK'S ISLAND, AND DUXBURY.

We may not disguise the fact. The least attractive object is the Rock of the Forefathers. The stranger who comes prepared to do homage to the spot the Pilgrims' feet first pressed, finds his sensibility stricken in a vital place. The insignificant appearance of the rock itself, buried out of sight beneath a shrine made with hands, and the separation of the sacred ledge into two fragments, each of which claims a divided regard, give a death-blow to the emotions of awe and reverence with which he approaches this corner-stone of American history.

Plymouth Rock, or rather what is left of it in its original position, is reached by following Water Street, which, as its name indicates, skirts the shore, conducting you through a region once devoted to commerce, now apparently consigned to irretrievable decay. Near Hedge's Wharf, and in close vicinity to the old Town Dock, is the object of our present search. A canopy, designed by Billings, has been built above it. I entered. In the stone pavement is a cavity of perhaps two feet square, and underneath the uneven surface the rock appears. I had often wished to stand here, but now all enthusiasm was gone

PLYMOUTH ROCK IN 1850.

out of me. I had rather have contented myself with the small piece so long treasured, and with the loom of the rock as my imagination had beheld it, than to stand in the actual presence of it.

By the building of street and wharf on a higher level the rock is now at some little distance from high-water mark.[1] At one time the sea had heaped the sand upon it to the depth of twenty feet, but the tradition of the spot had been well kept, and at the dawn of the Revolution the sand was cleared away, and the rock again laid bare. This was in 1774. In the attempt to remove it from its bed it split asunder, the superstitious seeing in this accidental fracture a presage of the division of the British empire in America. The upper half, or shell, of Forefathers' Rock was removed to the middle of the village, and placed at the end of a wall, where, along with vulgar stones, it

---

[1] In 1741, when it was proposed to build a wharf near the rock, it was pointed out as the identical landing-place of the Pilgrims by Elder Thomas Faunce, who, having been born in 1646, had received the fact from the original settlers.

19

propped the embankment. In 1834 the fractured half was removed from the town square to its present position in front of Pilgrim Hall, where it is now lying.

The honor of having first set foot on this threshold of fame is claimed for John Alden and Mary Chilton. The question of precedence will probably never be settled. It is also claimed for the exploring party who landed from the shallop on Monday, the $\frac{11}{21}$st of December, commonly called Forefathers' Day.[1]

For more than two hundred years the 22d of December had been observed as the day of the landing; that is, in effect, to say, it had been so observed by the Pilgrims themselves, by their descendants around their firesides, and had received the sanction of formal commemoration, in 1769, by the Old Colony Club. Men were then living who were within two generations of the first comers, and retained all their traditions unimpaired. After this long period had elapsed, it was assumed that the Pilgrims had designed to signalize the landing of the exploring party of eighteen, rather than that from the *Mayflower*, and upon this theory, by adopting the new style, the landing was fixed for the 21st, a substitution which has been generally acquiesced in by recent writers. Unless it is believed that the landing of the party of discovery possessed greater significance to the Pilgrims, and to those who lived within hearing of the voices of the *Mayflower*, than the disembarkation of the whole body of colonists on the very strand they had finally adopted for their future home, the presumption of error in computing the difference between old and new style has little force.

For six weeks these explorations had continued all along the coast-line of Cape Cod, and nothing had been settled until the return of the last party to the ship. The *Mayflower* then sailed for Plymouth, and cast anchor in the harbor on the 16th; but the explorations continued, nor was there a decision until the 20th as to the best point for fixing the settlement. Moreover, there are no precise reasons for saying that the first exploring party landed anywhere within the limits of the present town of Plymouth, nor any tradition of its making the rock a stepping-stone.

We prefer to believe that the Pilgrims meant to illustrate the landing from the *Mayflower*—the event emphasized by poets, painters, and orators—as marking the true era of settlement; that the 22d of December was intelli-

---

[1] This party consisted of eighteen persons—viz., Miles Standish, John Carver, William Bradford, Edward Winslow, John Tilley, Edward Tilley, John Howland, Richard Warren, Steven Hopkins, and Edward Doten. Besides these were two seamen, John Alderton and Thomas English. Of the ship's company were Clark and Coppin, two of the master's mates, the master-gunner, and three sailors. This little band of discoverers left the ship at anchor at Cape Cod Harbor on the $\frac{8}{16}$th of December. Mourt calls Alderton and English "two of our seamen," in distinction from the ship's company proper, they having been sent over by the undertakers, in the service of the plantation.

gently adopted by those best able to judge of their intentions; and that an unbroken custom of more than two centuries should remain undisturbed, even if it had originated in a technical error, which we do not believe was the case. "This rock," says the gifted De Tocqueville, "has become an object of veneration in the United States. I have seen bits of it carefully preserved in several towns of the Union. Does not this sufficiently show that all human power and greatness is in the soul of man? Here is a stone which the feet of a few outcasts pressed for an instant, and the stone becomes famous; it is treasured by a great nation; its very dust is shared as a relic. And what has become of the gate-ways of a thousand palaces? Who cares for them?"

The skeleton of a body was here before them, but, as Carlyle says, the soul was wanting until these men and women came. Mr. Sherley, writing to Bradford, says, "You are the people that must make a plantation and erect a city in those remote places when all others fail and return."

I do not find such conspicuous examples of intolerance among the Pilgrims as afterward existed in the Bay Colony. Lyford said they were Jesuits in their ecclesiastical polity, but they permitted him to gather a separate church and perform the Episcopal service among them. Beyond question, they were not willing to see the hierarchy from which they had fled establish itself in their midst. The intrigues of such men as Lyford within the colony, and Weston in the company at home, kept back the remnant of their own chosen associates, and re-enforced them with churchmen, or else men of no particular religion or helpfulness.

In November, 1621, the planters received an accession of thirty-five persons by the *Fortune*.[1] It was the custom in the plantation for the governor to call all the able-bodied men together every day, and lead them to their work in the fields or elsewhere. On Christmas-day they were summoned as usual, but most of the new-comers excused themselves, saying it was against their consciences to work on that day. The governor told them if they made it a matter of conscience he would spare them until they were better informed. He then led away the rest. When those who had worked came home at noon they found the conscientious observers of the day in the street, at play; some pitching the bar, and some at stool-ball and like sports. The governor went to them, took away their implements, and told them it was against his conscience they should play while others worked. If they made keeping the day a matter of devotion, they must keep their houses, but there must be no gaming or reveling in the streets. Assuredly there was some fun in William Bradford, governor.

---

[1] On her return voyage the *Fortune* was seized by a French man-of-war, Captain Frontenan de Pennart, who took Thomas Barton, master, and the rest prisoners to the Isle of Rhe, plundering the vessel of beaver worth five hundred pounds, belonging to the Pilgrims. The vessel and crew were discharged after a brief detention.—"British Archives."

Hutchinson—after all the abuse of him, the fairest historian as to what transpired in advance of the Revolutionary period—gives the Plymouth colonists credit for moderation. When Mrs. Hutchinson was banished by Massachusetts, she and her adherents applied for and obtained leave to settle on Aquidneck, then acknowledged to be within the Plymouth patent. Before this, Roger Williams, who had been their minister, was, after his banishment from Salem, kindly used, though requested to remove beyond their limits, for fear of giving offense to the Massachusetts colony. Many Quakers probably saved their lives by fleeing to Plymouth, although the Pilgrims detested their worship and enacted laws against them. The town of Swanzey[1] was almost wholly settled by Baptists.

The relations of the Pilgrims with the Indians were founded in right and justice, and stood on broader grounds than mere policy. This is shown in the unswerving attachment of Massasoit, the fidelity of Samoset, and the friendship of Squanto. The appearance of Samoset in the Pilgrim village was of good augury to the colony, and is worthy of a more appreciative pencil than has yet essayed it.

About the middle of March, after many false alarms of the savages, an Indian stalked into the town. Passing silently by the houses, he made straight for the rendezvous. I think I see the matrons and maids peeping through their lattices at the dusky intruder. He was tall, straight of limb, and comely, with long black hair streaming down his bare back, for, except a narrow girdle about his loins, he was stark naked. When he would have gone into the rendezvous the guard intercepted him. He was armed with a bow, and in his quiver were only two arrows, one headed, the other unheaded, as indicating the pacific nature of his mission. His bearing was frank and fearless, as became a sagamore. "Welcome, Englishmen," he said to the by-standers, astounded, as well they might be, on hearing such familiar salutation from the lips of a savage.

The first thing this Indian asked for was beer. The Pilgrims themselves preferred it to water, but they had none left; so they feasted him on good English cheer, and gave him strong waters to wash it down. His naked body excited astonishment, and a compassionate Pilgrim cast a horseman's cloak about him. Of all the assembly that encircled him, Samoset alone seemed unconcerned. The settlers had seen skulking savages on the hills, but they knew not what to make of this fellow, who thus dropped in on them, as it were, for a morning call. Since their first encounter with the Nauset Indians, they expected enmity, and not friendship. A midnight assault in their unprepared state was the thing most dreaded. Peace or war seemed to reside in the person of this Indian. They watched him narrowly. At night-fall they hoped he would take his leave; but he showed neither disposition to depart,

---

[1] First spelled Swansea, and named from Swansea, in South Wales.

nor distrust at beholding himself the evident object of mingled fear and suspicion. They concluded to send him on board the *Mayflower* for safe-keeping, and Samoset went willingly to the shallop; but it was low tide, and they could not reach the vessel. So they lodged him in Steven Hopkins's house. The next day he left them to go to Massasoit, and they finished by recognizing him as a friend, sent them by Heaven. Samoset was the Pemaquid chief, of whom we should gladly know more than we do. His communications were of importance to the Pilgrims, for Bradford admits that the exact description he gave them of his own country and of its resources was very profitable to them. I suppose it led to their establishing the trading-houses at Penobscot and Kennebec, and to the addition of the strip of country on the latter river to their patent of 1629, afterward enlarged by other tracts purchased of the Indians. The Pilgrims preferred trading to fishing, and no subsequent colony had such an opportunity to enrich themselves; but it was the policy of the English adventurers to keep them poor, and it may be questioned whether they developed the shrewdness in traffic for which their descendants have become renowned.

Samoset's coming paved the way for that of Massasoit, who made his entry into Plymouth with Indian pomp, in March. He was preceded by Samoset and Squanto,[1] who informed the settlers that the king was close at hand. The Pilgrims were then assembled under arms on the top of Burial Hill, engaged in military exercise, and witnessed the approach of Massasoit with his savage retinue of sixty warriors. Here were two representative delegations of the Old World and the New; the English in steel caps and corslets, the Indians in wild beasts' skins, paint, and feathers. The bearing of the Christians was not more martial than that of the savages.

The Pilgrims stood on their dignity, and waited. At the king's request, Edward Winslow went out to hold parley with him. His shining armor delighted the Indian sachem, who would have bought it, together with his sword, on the spot, but Winslow was unwilling to part with either. After mutual salutations and some talk of King James, Massasoit, accompanied by twenty, proceeds to the town, leaving Winslow a hostage in the hands of Quadequina, his brother. At the town brook Massasoit is met by Standish with half a dozen musketeers. Here are more grave salutations, and then the king is conducted to an unfinished house, where the utmost state the Pilgrims could contrive was a green rug and three or four cushions placed on the floor. There is a roll of drum and blast of trumpet in the street, and Bradford, attended by musketeers, enters. He kisses the hand of the New England prince—"tho'," says Mourt, "the king looked greasily"—and the savage

---

[1] Squanto was one of the Indians kidnaped by Hunt, and the last surviving native inhabitant of Plymouth. He had lived in London with John Slany, merchant, treasurer of the Newfoundland Company.

kisses Bradford. Then they sit. The governor calls for a stoup of strong waters, which he quaffs to the king, after the manner of chivalry; the royal savage drinks, in return, a great draught, that makes him "sweate all the time after."

> "Give me the cups,
> And let the kettle to the trumpet speak,
> The trumpet to the cannoneer without,
> The cannons to the heavens, the heaven to earth.
> 'Now the king drinks to Hamlet.' Come, begin."

It may interest some readers to know what a real Indian king was like. "He was," says an eye-witness, "a very lustie man, in his best yeares, an able body, grave of countenance, and spare of speech; in his Attyre little or nothing differing from the rest of his followers, only in a great Chaine of white bone Beades about his necke; and at it behinde his necke hangs a little bagg of Tobacco, which he dranke and gave us to drinke; his face was painted with a sad red like murry, and oyled both head and face, that hee looked greasily. All his followers, likewise, were in their faces in whole or in part painted, some blacke, some red, some yellow, and some white, some with crosses, and other Antick workes, some had skins on them, and some naked, all strong, tall, all men in appearance.

"One thing I forgot; the king had in his bosome, hanging to a string, a great long knife. He marvelled much at our trumpet, and some of his men would sound it as well as they could." Mourt also states that the king trembled with fear while he sat by the governor, and that the savages showed such apprehension of the fire-arms that the governor caused them to be removed during the conference.

This was the first American Congress of which I have found mention. The Indians knew what a treaty of amity meant. They needed no instruction in international law. I believe they knew the Golden Rule, or had a strong inkling of it. That was a convention more famous than the Field of the Cloth of Gold, though there were but a green rug and a few cushions. "The peace," Bradford writes, "hath now (1645) continued this twenty-four years." "To which I may add," says Prince, "*yea*, 30 *years longer, viz., to* 1675."

The Indians, at the entertainment given them in Plymouth, partook heartily of the food set before them, but they could not be induced to taste spices or condiments. Salt was not used by them. Gosnold regaled them with a picnic at the Vineyard, of which John Brereton says, "the Indians misliked nothing but our mustard, whereat they made many a sowre face." I doubt not the English spread it thickly on the meat, even at the hazard of good understanding.

It took these simple natives a long time to comprehend the English method of correspondence. They could not penetrate the mystery of talking paper. There is a story of an Indian sent by Governor Dudley to a lady with some oranges, the present being accompanied with a letter in which the number was mentioned. When out of the town, the Indian put the letter under a stone, and going a short distance off, ate one of the oranges. His astonishment at finding the theft discovered was unbounded.

I did not omit a ramble among the wharves, but saw little that would interest the reader. When you are there, the proper thing to do is to take a boat and cross the bay to Clark's Island and Duxbury. We sailed over the submerged piles at the end of Long Wharf; for the pier, once the pride of Plymouth, was fast going to wreck. The tops of the piles, covered with sea-weed kept in motion by the waves, bore an unpleasant resemblance to drowned human heads bobbing up and down. As we passed close to the new light-house off Beach Point, the boatman remarked that when it was being placed in position the caisson slipped in the slings, and dropped to the bottom nearer the edge of the channel than was desirable.

Having wind enough, we were soon up with Saquish Head, and in a few minutes more were fast moored to the little jetty at Clark's Island. The presence at one time of two islands in Plymouth Bay is fully attested by competent witnesses. Many have supposed Brown's Island, a shoal seaward of Beach Point, to have been one of these, tradition affirming that the stumps of trees have been seen there. One author[1] believes Brown's Island to have been above water in the time of the Pilgrims. Champlain locates two islands on Duxbury side, with particulars that leave no doubt where they then were. Mourt twice mentions them, and they are on Blauw's map inside the Gurnet headland. In an account of Plymouth Harbor, printed near the close of the last century, two islands are mentioned: "Clark's, consisting of about one hundred acres of excellent land, and Saquish, which was joined to the Gurnet by a narrow piece of sand: for several years the water has made its way across and insulated it. The Gurnet is an eminence at the southern extremity of the beach, on which is a light-house, built by the State."[2]

Bradford mentions the narrow escape of their pinnace from shipwreck on her return from Narraganset in 1623, by "driving on y^e *flats* that lye without, caled Brown's Ilands." Winthrop relates that in 1635 "two shallops, going, laden with goods, to Connecticut, were taken in the night with an easterly storm and cast away upon Brown's Island, near the Gurnett's Nose, and the men all drowned." In 1806 it was, as now, a shoal. There can be little dispute as to Saquish having been permanently united to the main-land by those shifting movements common to a sea-coast of sand.[3]

---

[1] Winsor, "History of Duxbury," p. 26, note.
[2] See *ante*, also "Massachusetts Historical Collections," vol. ii., p. 5. First light-house erected 1763; burned 1801.
[3] Saquish is the Indian for clams. They are of extraordinary size in Plymouth and Duxbury.

THE GURNET.

It is rather remarkable that, with a sea-coast exceeding that of the other New England colonies, Plymouth had so few good harbors. The beach, the safeguard of Plymouth, was once covered on the inner side with plum and wild cherry trees, pitch-pines, and undergrowth similar to that existing on Cape Cod and the adjacent islands. The sea has, in great storms, made a clean breach through it, digging channels by which vessels passed. There was a shocking disaster within the harbor in December, 1778, when the privateer brig *General Arnold* broke from her anchorage in the Cow Yard,[1] and was driven by the violence of the gale upon the sand-flats. Twenty-four hours elapsed before assistance could be rendered, and when it arrived seventy-five of the crew had perished from freezing and exhaustion, and the remainder were more dead than alive.[2]

As we sailed I observed shoals of herring breaking water, or, as the fishermen word it, "scooting." Formerly they were taken in prodigious quantity, and used by the Pilgrims to enrich their land. Squanto gave them the hint of putting one in every hill of corn. His manner of fishing for eels, I may add, was new to me. He trod them out of the mud with his feet, and caught them in his hands. I was surprised at the number of seals continually rising

---

[1] An anchorage near Clark's Island, so called from a cow-whale having been taken there.

[2] The following account of what straits light-keepers have been subjected to in coast-harbors during the past winter will perhaps be read with some surprise by those acquainted with Plymouth only in its summer aspect: "On Tuesday evening, February 9th, 1875, the United States revenue steamer *Gallatin* put into Plymouth harbor for the night, to avoid a north-west gale blowing outside. On the morning of the 10th, at daylight, when getting under way, Captain Selden discovered a signal of distress flying on Duxbury Pier Light. The light-house was so surrounded by ice that he was utterly unable to reach the pier with a boat; the captain, therefore, steamed the vessel through the ice near enough to converse with the keeper, and found that he had had no communication with any one outside of the light since December 22d, 1874; that his fuel and water were out; and that they had been on an allowance of a pint of water a day since February 6th, 1875. The steamer forced her way to within some fifty or seventy-five yards of the pier, when Lieutenants Weston and Clayton, with the boats, succeeded, after two hours' hard work cutting through the ice, in reaching the pier, and furnished the keeper and his wife with plenty of wood and water."

within half a cable's length of the boat, at which they curiously gazed with their bright liquid eyes. We did them no harm as ever and anon one pushed his sleek round head and whiskered muzzle above water. Hundreds of them disport themselves here in summer, though in winter they usually migrate.

It is only a little way from the landing-place at Clark's Island to the venerable Watson mansion, seen embowered among trees as we approached.[1] The parent house was removed from its first situation, rather nearer the water than it now stands, and has incorporated with itself newer additions, till it is quite lost in the transformation it has undergone. The island is a charming spot, and the house a substantial, hospitable one. I did not like it the less because it was old, and seemed to carry me something nearer to the Pilgrims than any of the white band of houses I saw across the bay. Ducks, turkeys, geese, and fowls lived in good-fellowship together in the barn-yard, where were piled unseaworthy boats; and store of old lumber-drifts the sea had provided against the winter. The jaw-bone of a whale, that Mr. Watson said he had found stranded on the beach, and brought home on his back, lay bleaching in the front yard. I may have looked a trifle incredulous, for the hale old gentleman, turned, I should say, of three-score, drew himself up as if he would say, "Sir, I can do it again."

WATSON'S HOUSE, CLARK'S ISLAND.

After showing us his family portraits, ancient furniture, and other heirlooms, our host told us how Sir Edmund Andros had tried to dispossess his ancestors. My companion and myself then took the path leading to Election Rock, that owes its name, doubtless, to some local event. It is a large boulder, about twelve feet high, on the highest point of the island. Two of its

---

[1] There is tradition for it that Edward Dotey, the fighting serving-man, was the first who attempted to land on Clark's Island, but was checked for his presumption. Elkanah Watson was one of the three original grantees of the island, which has remained in the family since 1690. Previous to that time it belonged to the town. The other proprietors were Samuel Lucas and George Morton.

faces are precipitous, while the western side offers an easy ascent. At the instance of the Pilgrim Society, the following words, from "Mourt's Relation," have been graven on its face:

"On the Sabboth Day wee rested. 20 December, 1620."

ELECTION ROCK, CLARK'S ISLAND.

As is well known to all who have followed the fortunes of the little band of eighteen—and who has not followed them in their toilsome progress in search of a haven of rest?—their shallop, after narrowly escaping wreck among the shoals of Saquish, gained a safe anchorage under the shelter of one of the then existing islands. It is probable that when they rounded Saquish Head they found themselves in smoother water.

The gale had carried away their mast and sail. Their pilot proved not only ignorant of the place into which he was steering, but a coward when the pinch came. They were on the point of beaching the shallop in a cove full of breakers, when one of the sailors bid them about with her, if they were men, or else they would be all lost. So that the fortunes of the infant colony hung, at this critical moment, on the presence of mind of a nameless mariner.

Cold, hungry, and wet to the skin, they remained all night in a situation which none but the roughest campaigner would know how rightly to estimate. The Indians had met them, at Eastham, with such determined hostility that they expected no better reception here. Their arms were wet and unserviceable. As usual, present discomfort triumphed over their fears, for many were so much exhausted that they could no longer endure their misery on board the shallop. Some of them gained the shore, where with great difficulty they lighted a fire of the wet wood they were able to collect. The remainder of the party were glad to join them before midnight; for the wind shifted to north-west, and it began to freeze. They had little idea where they were, having come upon the land in the dark. It was not until daybreak that they knew it to be an island. Surely, these were times to try the souls of men, and to wring the selfishness out of them.

This night bivouac, this vigil of the Pilgrims around their blazing campfire, the flames painting their bronzed faces, and sending a grateful warmth into benumbed bodies, was a subject worthy the pencil of Rembrandt. I doubt that they dared lay their armor aside or shut their eyes the live-long night. I believe they were glad of the dawn of a bright and glorious December day.¹ They dried their buff coats, cleansed their arms of rust, and felt themselves once more men fit for action. Then they shouldered their muskets and reconnoitred the island. Probably the eighteen stood on the summit of this rock.

I found Clark's Island to possess a charm exceeding any so-called restoration or monumental inscription — the charm of an undisturbed state. No doubt much of the original forest has disappeared, and Boston has yet to return the cedar gate-posts so carefully noted by every succeeding chronicler of the Old Colony. A few scrubby originals of this variety yet, however, remain; and the eastern side of the island is not destitute of trees. The air was sweet and wholesome, the sea-breeze invigorating. In the quietude of the isle the student may open his history, and read on page and scene the story of a hundred English hearts sorely tried, but triumphing at last.

History has not told us how the eighteen adventurous Pilgrims passed their first Sabbath on Clark's Island. One writer says very simply "wee rested;" and his language re-appears on the tablet of imperishable rock. Bradford says, on the "last day of ye weeke they prepared ther to keepe ye Sabbath." If ever they had need of rest it was on this day; and if ever they had reason to give thanks for their "manifold deliverances," now was the occasion. They would hardly have stirred on any enterprise without their Bible; and probably one having the imprint of Geneva, with figured verses, was now produced. Bradford, yet ignorant of his wife's death, may have prayed, and Winslow exhorted, as both admit they often did in the church. Master Carver may have struck the key-note of the Hundredth Psalm, "the grand old Puritan anthem;" and even Miles Standish and the "saylers" three, may have joined in the forest hymnal.²

Hood, in his "History of Music in New England," speaking of the early part of the eighteenth century, says: "Singing psalms, at that day, had not become an amusement among the people. It was used, as it ever ought to be, only as a devotional act. So great was the reverence in which their psalm-tunes were held, that the people put off their hats, as they would in prayer, whenever they heard one sung, though not a word was uttered."

On leaving Clark's Island we steered for Captain's Hill. By this time the water had become much roughened, or, to borrow a word from the boatmen's vocabulary, "choppy;" I should have called it hilly. Our attempt to land at Duxbury was met with great kicking, bouncing, and squabbling on the part of the boat, which seemed to like the chafing of the wharf as little as we did the idea of a return to Plymouth against wind and tide. Quiet persever-

---

¹ Saturday, December 9th, Old Style.
² No reasonable doubt can be entertained that the Pilgrims' first religious services were held in Provincetown Harbor, either on board the *Mayflower* or on shore. They were not the men and women to permit several Sabbaths to pass by without devotional exercises.

ance, however, prevailed, and, after clambering up the piles, we stood upon the wharf. A short walk by the cart-way, built to fetch stone from the pier to the monument, brought us to the brow of the hill.

Captain's Hill, named from Captain Miles Standish, its early possessor, is on a peninsula jutting out between Duxbury and Plymouth bays. Its surface is smooth, with few trees, except those belonging to the farm-houses near its base. The soil, that is elsewhere in Duxbury sandy and unproductive, is here rather fertile, which accounts for its having become the seat of the puissant Captain Standish. The monument, already mentioned as in progress, had advanced as high as the foundations. As originally planned, it was to be built of stones contributed by each of the New England States, and by the several counties and military organizations of Massachusetts.

Standish, about 1632, settled upon this peninsula, building his house on a little rising ground south-east of the hill near the shore. All traces that are left of it will be found on the point of land opposite Mr. Stephen M. Allen's house. The cellar excavation was still visible when I visited it, with some of the foundation-stones lying loosely about. Except a clump of young trees that had become rooted in the hollows, the point is bare, and looks any thing but a desirable site for a homestead. Plymouth is in full view, as is also the harbor's open mouth. The space between the headland on which the house stood and Captain's Hill was at one time either an arm of the sea, or else in great gales the water broke over the level, forming a sort of lagoon. Mr. Winsor, in his "History of Duxbury," says the sea, according to the traditions of the place, once flowed between Standish's house and the hill. The ground about the house, he adds, has been turned up in years past, the search being rewarded by the recovery of several relics of the old inhabitant.[1] The house is said to have been burned, but so long ago that even the date has been quite forgotten. On this same neck Elder Brewster is believed to have lived, but the situation of his dwelling is at best doubtful.

The earliest reference I have seen to the tradition of John Alden "popping the question" to Priscilla Mullins for his friend, Miles Standish, is in "Alden's Epitaphs," printed in 1814. No mention is there of the snow-white bull,

> "Led by a cord that was tied to an iron ring in its nostrils,
> Covered with crimson cloth, and a cushion placed for a saddle."

John Alden's marriage took place, it is supposed, in 1621. The first cattle brought to Plymouth were a bull, a heifer, and "three or four jades," sent by Mr. Sherley, of the Merchant's Association, in 1624. They were consigned to

---

[1] The first substance discovered was a quantity of barley, charred and wrapped in a blanket. Ashes, as fresh as if the fire had just been extinguished, were found in the chimney-place, with pieces of an andiron, iron pot, and other articles. There were discovered, also, a gun-lock, sickle, hammer, whetstone, and fragments of stone and earthen ware. A sword-buckle, tomahawk, brass kettle, etc., with glass beads, showing the action of intense heat, likewise came to light.

Winslow and Allerton, to be sold. The tradition of the embassy of Alden, and of the incomparably arch rejoinder of Priscilla, "Prythee, John, why don't you speak for yourself?" was firmly believed in the family of Alden, where, along with that of the young cooper having first stepped on the ever-famous rock, it had passed from the mouth of one generation to another, without gainsaying.

I am not of those who experience a thrill of joy at destroying the illusions of long-hoarded family traditions. What of romance has been interwoven with the singularly austere lives of the Puritans, gracious reader, let us cherish and protect. The province of the Dryasdust of to-day is to bewilder, to deny the existence of facts that have passed without challenge for centuries. The farther he is from the event, the nearer he accounts himself to truth. Historic accuracy becomes another name for historic anarchy. Nothing is settled. The grand old characters he strips of their hard-earned fame can not confront him. Would they might! Columbus, Tell, Pocahontas, are impostors: Ireson's Ride and Standish's Courtship are rudely handled. His tactics would destroy the Christian religion. Without doubt mere historic truth is better written in prose, but by all means let us put a stop to the slaughter of all the first-born of New England poesy. Let us have Puritan lovers and sweethearts while we may. "What is your authority?" asked a visitor of the guide who was relating the story of a ruined castle. "We have tradition, and if you have any thing better we will be glad of it."

The position of Standish in the colony was in a degree anomalous, for he was neither a church member nor a devout man. But the Pilgrims, who knew on occasion how to smite with the sword, did not put too trifling an estimate upon the value of the little iron man. He seems to have deserved, as he certainly received, their confidence, as well in those affairs arising out of religious disorders among them as in those of a purely military character. When wanted, they knew where he was to be found.

After his fruitless embassy to England, Standish seems to have turned his sword into a pruning-hook, leading a life of rural simplicity, perhaps of comparative ease. He had, as the times went, a goodly estate. There is little doubt he was something "splenetic and rash," or that the elders feared he would bring them into trouble by his impetuous temper. He was of a race of soldiers.[1] Hubbard calls him a little chimney soon fired. Lyford speaks of him as looking like a silly boy, and in utter contempt. The Pilgrims managed his infirmities with address, and he served them faithfully as soldier and magistrate. It is passing strange a man of such consequence as he should sleep in an unknown grave.

Near the foot of Captain's Hill is an old gambrel-roofed house, with the

---

[1] I find that a Captain Standish, who is called a great commander, a captain of foot, was killed in an attack by Lord Strange on Manchester, England, during the Civil War, 1642.

date of 1666 on the chimney. At the entrance the stairs part on each side of an immense chimney-stack. The timbers, rough-hewn and exposed to view, are bolted with tree-nails. One fire-place would have contained a Yule-log from any tree in the primeval forest. The hearth was in breadth like a sidewalk. On the doors were wooden latches, or bobbins, with the latch-string out, as we read in nursery tales. The front of the house was covered with climbing vines, and, taken altogether, as it stood out against the dark background of the hill, was as picturesque an object as I have seen in many a day.[1]

I would like to walk with you two miles farther on, and visit the old Alden homestead, the third that has been inhabited by the family since pilgrim John built by the margin of Eagle Tree Pond. This old house, erected by Colonel Alden, grandson of the first-comer of the name, is still in the same family, and would well repay a visit; but time and tide wait for us.

Farther on I have rambled over ancient Careswell, the seat of the Winslows, a family with a continuous stream of history, from Edward, the governor, who became one of Cromwell's Americans, and died in his service (you may see his letters in the ponderous folios of Thurloe), down to the winner in the sea-fight between the *Kearsarge* and *Alabama*. Beyond is the mansion Daniel Webster inhabited in his lifetime, and the hill where, among the ancient graves, he lies entombed. Here, in Kingston, General John Thomas, of the Revolution, lived.

Another military chieftain, little less renowned than Standish, was Colonel Benjamin Church, the famous Indian fighter. He was Plymouth-born, but lived some time in Duxbury. In turning over the pages of Philip's and King William's wars, we meet him often enough, and always giving a good account of himself. One act of the Plymouth authorities during Philip's war deserves eternal infamy. It drew from Church the whole-hearted denunciation of a brave man.

During that war Dartmouth was destroyed. The Dartmouth Indians had not been concerned in this outrage, and after much persuasion were induced to surrender themselves to the Plymouth forces. They were conducted to Plymouth. The Government ordered all of them to be sold as slaves, and they were transported out of the country, to the number of one hundred and sixty.[2]

CHURCH'S SWORD.

I despaired of being able to match this act of treachery with any contemporaneous history. But here is a fragment that somewhat approaches it

---

[1] This house has been stated to have been built in part of materials from the house of Captain Miles Standish.

[2] Bayless's "New Plymouth."

in villainy. In 1684 the King of France wrote M. de la Barre, Governor of New France, to seize as many of the Iroquois as possible, and send them to France, where they were to serve in the galleys, in order to diminish the tribe, which was warlike, and waged war against the French. Many of them were actually in the galleys of Marseilles.[1]

The balance is still in our favor. In 1755 we expatriated the entire French population of Acadia. Mr. Longfellow tells the story graphically in "Evangeline." John Winslow, of Marshfield, was the instrument chosen by the home government for the work. It was conducted with savage barbarity. Families were separated, wives from husbands, children from parents. They were parceled out like cattle among the English settlements. Their aggregate number was nearly two thousand persons, thenceforth without home or country. One of these outcasts, describing his lot, said, "It was the hardest that had happened since our Saviour was upon earth." The story is true.

Our little boat worked her way gallantly back to Plymouth. Though thoroughly wet with the spray she had flung from her bows, I was not ill-pleased with the expedition. Figuratively speaking, my knapsack was packed, my staff and wallet waiting my grasp. With the iron horse that stood panting at the door I made in two hours the journey that Winthrop, Endicott, and Winslow took two days to accomplish. Certainly I found Plymouth much changed. The Pilgrims would hardly recognize it, though now, as in centuries before their coming,

"The waves that brought them o'er
Still roll in the bay, and throw their spray,
As they break along the shore."

---

[1] "Massachusetts Archives."

PROVINCETOWN FROM THE HILLS.

CHAPTER XIX.

PROVINCETOWN.

"A man may stand there and put all America behind him."—THOREAU.

AS it was already dark when I arrived in Provincetown, I saw only the glare from the lantern of Highland Light in passing through Truro, and the gleaming from those at Long Point and Wood End, before the train drew up at the station. It having been a rather busy day with me (I had embarked at Nantucket in the morning, idled away a few hours at Vineyard Haven, and rested as many at Cohasset Narrows), it will be easily understood why I left the investigation of my whereabouts to the morrow. My wants were at this moment reduced to a bed, a pair of clean sheets, and plenty of blankets; for though the almanac said it was July in Provincetown, the night breeze blowing freshly was strongly suggestive of November.

It was Swift, I think, who said he never knew a man reach eminence who was not an early riser. Doubtless the good doctor was right. But, then, if he had lodged as I lodged, and had risen as I did, two mortal hours before breakfast-time, he might have allowed his precept to have its exceptions. I devoted these hours to rambling about the town.

Though not more than half a hundred miles from Boston, as the crow flies, Cape Cod is regarded as a sort of *terra incognita* by fully half of New England. It has always been considered a good place to emigrate from, rather than as offering inducements for its young men and women to remain at home; though no class of New Englanders, I should add, are more warmly attached to the place of their nativity. The ride throughout the Cape affords the most impressive example of the tenacity with which a population clings to locality that has ever come under my observation. To one accustomed to the fertile shores of Narraganset Bay or the valley of the Connecticut, the region between Sandwich, where you enter upon the Cape, and Orleans, where you reach the bend of the fore-arm, is bad enough, though no desert. Beyond this is simply a wilderness of sand.

The surface of the country about Brewster and Orleans is rolling prairie, barren, yet thinly covered with an appearance of soil. Stone walls divide the fields, but from here down the Cape you will seldom see a stone of any size in going thirty miles. My faith in Pilgrim testimony began to diminish as I looked on all sides, and in vain, for a "spit's-depth of excellent black earth," such as they tell of. It has, perchance, been blown away, or buried out of sight in the shiftings constantly going on here. Eastham, Wellfleet, and

COHASSET NARROWS.

Truro grow more and more forbidding, as you approach the *Ultima Thule*, or land's end.[1]

Mr. Thoreau, who has embodied the results of several excursions to the Cape in some admirable sketches, calls it the bared and bended arm of Massachusetts. Mr. Everett had already used the same figure. To me it looks like a skinny, attenuated arm thrust within a stocking for mending—the bony elbow at Chatham, the wrist at Truro, and the half-closed fingers at Provincetown. It seems quite down at the heel about Orleans, and as if much darning would be needed to make it as good as new. It was something to conceive, and more to execute, such a tramp as Thoreau's, for no one ought to

---

[1] There is a well-defined line of demarkation between the almost uninterrupted rock wall of the north coast and the sand, which, beginning in the Old Colony, in Scituate, constitutes Cape Cod; and, if we consider Nantucket, Martha's Vineyard, and Long Island as having at some period formed the exterior shores, the almost unbroken belt of sand continues to Florida. This line is so little imaginary that it is plain to see where granite gives place to sand; and it is sufficiently curious to arrest the attention even of the unscientific explorer.

attempt it who can not rise superior to his surroundings, and shake off the gloom the weird and wide-spread desolateness of the landscape inspires. I would as lief have marched with Napoleon from Acre, by Mount Carmel, through the moving sands of Tentoura.

The resemblance of the Cape to a hook appears to have struck navigators quite early. On old Dutch maps it is delineated with tolerable accuracy, and named "Staaten Hoeck," and the bay inclosed within the bend of it "Staaten Bay." Massachusetts Bay is "Noord Zee," and Cape Malabar "Vlacke Hoeck." Milford Haven appears about where Eastham is now located. On the earliest map of Champlain the extremity of the Cape is called "C. Blanc," or the White Cape.[1] Mather says of Cape Cod, he supposes it will never lose the name "till swarms of codfish be seen swimming on the highest hills."

This hook, though a sandy one, caught many a school of migratory fish, and even whales found themselves often embayed in the bight of it, on their way south, until, from being so long hunted down, they learned to keep a good offing. It also caught all the southerly drift along shore, such as stray

HIGHLAND LIGHT, CAPE COD.

ships from France and England. Bartholomew Gosnold and John Brereton were the first white men to land on it. De Monts, Champlain, De Poutrincourt, Smith, and finally the Forefathers, were brought up and turned back by it.

Bradford, under date of 1620, writes thus in his journal: "A word or two by yᵉ way of this Cape: it was thus first named (Cape Cod) by Captain Gosnold and his company, An°: 1602, and after by Capten Smith was caled Cape James; but it retains yᵉ former name amongst sea-men. Also yᵗ pointe which

---

[1] "Lequel nous nommâmes C. Blanc pour ce que c'estoient sables et dunes qui paroissent ainsi."

first shewed those dangerous shoulds unto them, they called Point Care, and Tucker's Terrour;[1] but y° French and Dutch, to this day, call it Malabarr, by reason of those perilous shoulds, and y° losses they have suffered their."

Notwithstanding what Bradford says, the name of Mallebarre is affixed to the extreme point of Cape Cod on early French maps. In Smith's "New England" is the following description:

"Cape Cod is the next presents itselfe, which is onely a headland of high hills of sand, overgrowne with shrubbie pines, hurts, and such trash, but an excellent harbor for all weathers. The Cape is made by the maine sea on the one side and a great Bay on the other, in forme of a sickle; on it doth inhabit the people of Pawmet; and in the bottome of the Bay, the people of Chawum. Towards the south and south-west of this Cape is found a long and dangerous shoale of sands and rocks. But so farre as I encircled it, I found thirtie fadom water aboard the shore and a strong current, which makes mee thinke there is a channel about this Shoale, where is the best and greatest fish to be had, Winter and Summer, in all that Countrie. But the Salvages say there is no channel, but that the shoales beginne from the maine at Pawmet to the ile of Nausit, and so extends beyond their knowledge into the sea."

The historical outcome of the Cape is in the early navigations, and in the fact that Provincetown was the harbor entered by the Forefathers. The first land they saw, after Devon and Cornwall had sunk in the sea, was this sandbar, for it is nothing else. It appeared to their eager eyes, as it will probably never again be seen, wooded down to the shore. Whales, that they had not the means of taking, disported around them. They dropped anchor three-quarters of a mile from shore, and, in order to land, were forced to wade a "bow shoot," by which many coughs and colds were caught, and a foundation for the winter's sickness laid. The first landing was probably on Long Point. The men set about discovery; for the master had told them, with a sailor's bluntness, he would be rid of them as soon as possible. The women went also to shore to wash, thus initiating on Monday, November $\frac{13}{23}$d, the great New England washing-day.

Were there to be a day of general observance in New England commemorative of the landing of the Pilgrims, it should be that on which they first set foot on her soil at Cape Cod; the day, too, on which the compact was signed.[2] Whatever of sentiment attached to the event should, it would seem, be consecrated to the very spot their feet first pressed. There is yet time to rescue the day from unaccountable and unmerited neglect.

On the map of Cyprian Southack a thoroughfare is delineated from Massachusetts Bay to the ocean at Eastham, near Sandy Point. His words are:

---

[1] Named by Captain Gosnold, on account of the expressed fears of one of his company.

[2] Being the $\frac{11}{21}$st of November, it would fall quite near to the day usually set apart for Thanksgiving in New England, which is merely an arbitrary observance, commemorative of no particular occurrence.

"The place where I came through with a whale-boat, April 26th, 1717, to look after Bellame the pirate." I have never seen this map, which Douglass pronounces "a false and pernicious sea-chart."

From its barring their farther progress, Cape Cod was well known to the discoverers of the early part of the seventeenth century. According to Lescarbot, Poutrincourt spent fifteen days in a port on the south side. It had been formally taken possession of in the name of the French king. The first conflict between the whites and natives occurred there; and in its sands were interred the remains of the first Christian who died within the ancient limits of New England.[1]

The assault of the natives on De Poutrincourt is believed to have occurred at Chatham, ironically named by the French Port Fortuné, in remembrance of their mishaps there. It was the very first collision recorded between Europeans and savages in New England. Five of De Poutrincourt's men having slept on shore contrary to orders, and without keeping any watch, the Indians fell on them at day-break, October 15th, 1606, killing two outright. The rest, who were shot through and through with arrows, ran down to the shore, crying out, "Help! they are murdering us!" the savages pursuing with frightful whoopings.

Hearing these outcries and the appeal for help, the sentinel on board the bark gave the alarm: "*Aux armes!* they are killing our people!" Roused by the signal, those on board seized their arms, and ran on deck, without taking time to dress themselves. Fifteen or sixteen threw themselves into the shallop, without stopping to light their matches, and pushed for the shore. Finding they could not reach it on account of an intervening sand-bank, they leaped into the water and waded a musket-shot to land. De Poutrincourt, Champlain, Daniel Hay, Robert Gravé the younger, son of Du Pont Gravé, and the younger Poutrincourt, with their trumpeter and apothecary, were of the party that rushed pell-mell, almost stark naked, upon the savages.

The Indians, perceiving the rescuing band within a bow-shot of them, took to flight. It was idle to pursue those nimble-footed savages; so the Frenchmen brought their dead companions to the foot of the cross they had erected on the preceding day, and there buried them. While chanting the funeral prayers and orisons of the Church, the natives, from a safe distance, shouted derisively and danced to celebrate their treason. After their funeral rites were ended the French voyagers silently returned on board.

In a few hours, the tide being so low as to prevent the whites from landing, the natives again appeared on the shore. They threw down the cross, disinterred the bodies of the slain Frenchmen, and stripped them before the eyes of their exasperated comrades. Several shots were fired at them from

---

[1] One of De Monts's men ("*un charpentier Maloin*") was killed here in 1605 by the natives. In attempting to recover a kettle one of them had stolen, he was transfixed with arrows.

the bronze gun on board, the natives at every discharge throwing themselves flat on their faces. As soon as the French could land, they again set up the cross, and reinterred the dead. The natives, for the second time, fled to a distance.[1]

Provincetown was originally part of Truro. Its etymology explains that its territory belonged to the province of Massachusetts. The earliest inhabitants had no other title than possession, and their conveyance is by quitclaim. For many years the place experienced the alternations of thrift and decay, being at times well-nigh deserted. In 1749, says Douglass, in his "Summary," the town consisted of only two or three settled families, two or three cows, and six to ten sheep. The houses formerly stood in one range, without regularity, along the beach, with the drying-flakes around them.

WASHING FISH.

Fishing vessels were run upon the soft sand, and their cargoes thrown into the water, where, after being washed free from salt, the fish were taken up and carried to the flakes in hand-barrows. Cape Cod Harbor, by which name it is also familiar to the readers of Pilgrim chronicles, was the earliest name of Provincetown.

The place has now lost the peculiar character it owed to the windmills on

---

[1] Lescarbot adds that the natives, turning their backs to the vessel, threw the sand with both hands toward them from between their buttocks, in derision, yelling like wolves.

the sandy heights above the town and the salt-works on the beach before it. The streets, described by former writers as impassable, by reason of the deep sand, I found no difficulty in traversing. What with an admixture of clay, and a top-dressing of oyster-shells and pebble, brought from a distance, they have managed to make their principal thoroughfares solid enough. Step aside from these, if you would know what Provincetown was like in the past.

If the streets were better than I had thought, the houses were far better. The great number of them were of wood, looking as most New England houses look—ready for the torch. They usually had underpinnings of brick, instead of being, as formerly, built on posts, in order that the sand might blow underneath them. There were willows, poplars, locusts, and balm of Gilead, standing about in odd corners, and of good size. I saw a few sickly fruit-trees that appeared dying for lack of moisture; and some enterprising citizens were able to make a show of lilacs, syringas, pinks, and geraniums in their front yards. I talked with them, and saw that the unremitting struggle for life that attended the growth of these few simple flowers seemed to increase their love for them, and enlarge their feeling for what was beautiful. All the earth they have is imported. I called to mind those Spanish vineyards, where the peasant carries a hamper of soil up the sunny slopes of the mountain-sides, and in some crevice of the rocks plants his vine.

There are two principal streets in Provincetown. One of, I should imagine, more than a mile in length, runs along the harbor; the other follows an elevated ridge of the sand-hills, and is parallel with the first. A plank-walk is laid on one side of the avenue by the shore, the other side being occupied by stores, fish-houses, and wharves. No sinister meaning is attached to walking the plank in Provincetown; for what is the whole Cape if not a gangplank pushed out over the side of the continent?

Where the street on the ridge is carried across gaps among the hills, the retaining walls were of bog-peat, which was also laid on the sides of those hills exposed to the force of the wind. Whortleberry, bayberry, and wild rose were growing out of the interstices. They flourish as well as when the Pilgrims were here, though all the primitive forest disappeared long ago. I ascended the hill on which the town-hall building stands. You must go up the town road, or break the law, as I saw, by the straggling footpaths, the youngsters were in the habit of doing. Read sand for scoriæ, and the fate of Herculaneum seems impending over Provincetown. The safeguards taken to prevent the hills blowing down upon it impresses the stranger with a sense of insecurity, though the inhabitants do not seem much to mind it. I have heard that in exposed situations on the Cape window-glass becomes opaque by reason of the frequent sand-blasts rattling against the panes.

On the hill was formerly a windmill, having the flyers inside, so resembling, say the town annalists, a lofty tower. It was a famous landmark for

PROVINCETOWN.   311

vessels making the port. The chart-makers have now replaced it with the town hall, and every mariner steering for Provincetown has an eye to it.

The harbor is completely land-locked. There is good anchorage for vessels of the largest class. Ofttimes it is crowded with shipping seeking a haven of refuge. This morning there were perhaps fifty sail, of every kind of craft. An inward-bound vessel must steer around every point of the compass before the anchor is let go in safety. In the Revolution the port was made use of by the British squadrons, to refit, and procure water.[1] The tide flows on the bay side of the Cape about twenty feet, while at the back of it there is a flow of only five or six feet.

The town is of extreme length, compared with its breadth, being contracted between the range of high sand-hills behind it and the beach. It lies fronting the south-east, bordering the curve of the shore, which sweeps grandly around half the circumference of a circle on the bay side. In one direction extends the long line of shore. If Boston be your starting-point, you must travel a hundred and twenty miles to get fifty; and, by the time you arrive at the extremity of the Cape, should be able to box the compass. Looking south, Long Point terminates the land view. Following with the eye the outline of the hook, it rests an instant on the shaft of the light-house at Wood End, the extreme southerly point of the Cape. Thence the coast trends north-west as far as Race Point, which is shut out from view by intervening hills. Race Point is the outermost land of the Cape. All these names are well known to mariners, the world over.

The shores are bordered with dangerous bars and shallows. As shipping could not get up to the town, the town has gone off to it, in the shape of a wharf of great length. Our Pilgrim ancestors had to wade a " bow shoot " to get on dry land. A resident told me that with fishing-boots on I could cross to the head of Herring Cove at low tide. Assuredly, it is one of the most wonderful of havens, and little likely to be dispensed with, even if the vexed question of

> "A way for ships to shape,
> Instead of winding round the *Cape*
> A short-cut through the *collar*,"

be answered by a ship-canal from Barnstable to Buzzard's Bay.[2]

On the summit of Town Hill you are almost astride the Cape, having the Atlantic on one side, and Massachusetts Bay in full view on the other. The port is not what it was when some storm-tossed bark, in accepting its shelter, was the town talk for months. Ships come and go by scores and hun-

---

[1] Hubbard relates a terrific storm here. See "New England," p. 644. In 1813 there was a naval engagement at Provincetown.

[2] General Knox was interested in this project. Lemuel Cox, the celebrated bridge architect, was engaged in cutting it.

dreds, folding their wings and settling down on the water like weary sea-gulls.

With an outward appearance of prosperity, I found the people bemoaning the hard times. Taxes, they said, were twenty dollars in the thousand, and only ten at Wareham; fish were scarce, and prices low, too, though as to the last item consumers think otherwise. The fishermen I saw were burly, athletic fellows, apparently not more thrifty than their class everywhere. They are averse to doing any thing else than fish, and, if the times are bad, are content to potter about their boats and fishing-gear till better days, much as they would wait for wind and tide. If they can not go fishing they had as lief do nothing, though want threatens.

The boys take to the water by instinct. I saw one adrift in a boat without oars, making his way to land by tilting the side of the dory. They go to the fishing-banks with their fathers, and can hand, reef, and steer with an old salt. One traveler tells of a Provincetown cow-boy who captured and killed a blackfish he descried near the shore. As soon as they had strength to pull in a fish, they were put on board a boat.

I noticed the familiar names that have been transplanted and thriven everywhere. Those of Atwood, Nickerson, Newcomb, Rich, Ryder, Snow, and Doane have the Cape ring about them. In general they are "likely" men, as the phrase here is, getting on as might be expected of a people who literally cast their bread upon the waters, and live on a naked crust of earth that the sea is forever gnawing and growling at. The girls are pretty. I say it on the authority of an expert in such matters who accompanied me. Not all are sandy-haired.

There is a strong dash of humor about these people. They are piquant Capers, dry and sharp as the sand. One of them was relating that he had once watched for so long a time that he finally fell asleep while crossing the street to his boarding-house, and on going to bed had not waked for twenty-four hours. "Wa'al," said an old fellow, removing a short pipe from between his lips, "you was jest a-cannin' on it up, warn't ye?"

There is quite a colony of Portuguese in Provincetown. In my rambles I met with a band of them returning from the swamp region back of the town. They looked gypsy-like with their swarthy faces and gleaming eyes. The younger women had clear olive complexions, black eyes, and the elongated Madonna faces of their race; the older ones were grisly and witch-like, with shriveled bodies and wrinkled faces. All of them bore bundles of fagots on their heads that our tender women would have sunk under, yet they did not seem in the least to mind them. They chattered merrily as they passed by me, and I watched them until out of sight; for, picturesque objects anywhere, here they were doubly so. They had all gaudy handkerchiefs tied about their heads, and shawls worn sash-wise, and knotted at the hip, the bright bits of warm color contrasting kindly with the dead white of the sand.

There were shapely figures among them, but the men's boots they of necessity wore subtracted a little from the symmetry of outline and my admiration.

They number about fifty families—these Portuguese—and are increasing. One citizen expressed a vague apprehension lest they should exclude, eventually, the whites, as the whites had expelled the Indians. And why not? They believe in large families, while we believe in small ones or none at all. The Pilgrims were fewer than they when they came to Cape Cod, though they did believe in large families. Besides, Gaspard Cortereal, a "Portingale," fell in with the land hereabouts before any of our English. The Portuguese are reported to have stocked Sable Island with domestic animals thirty years before Gilbert's coming to Newfoundland.[1] Assuredly, Cortereal had as good a mortgage on the country as Cabot, who did not land, but only beheld it in sailing by. I had found the town effervescent. The killing of a Portuguese by his captain, in a quarrel on board a fishing vessel, had set the whole town talking. Coming from the city, where we average a murder a week, I was quite startled at the measure of horror and indignation the deed excited here. Sub-

MACKEREL.—A FAMILY GROUP.

sequently I learned that such crimes were rare, and that in this out-of-the-way corner of the land people had quite old-fashioned notions about the value of human life and limb.

The cod and mackerel fisheries have been the making of Provincetown, though they complained of dull times when I was there, the fleet not numbering more than fifty or sixty sail. Some schooners go whaling to the Gulf of Mexico, Western Islands, or far up the north coast; but the fares there are poor, they say, and growing poorer. The first mackerel exhibited in the spring in Boston market are taken in Provincetown Harbor.

---

[1] Champlain confirms this.

Former travelers have observed that the art as well as the name of hay-making was applied to the curing of the cod here, the fish, when made, being stacked in the same manner. Cattle are reported to have sometimes eaten them in lieu of salt hay. When the fishing season was at its height, it must have been something to have seen—the length and breadth of the town overspread with cod-fish, occupying the front yards and intervals between the houses. A goodwife then, instead of going to the garden for vegetables, would bring in a cod-fish from the flakes. Then the hook was well baited.

I suppose the phrase "cod-fish aristocracy" did not originate on the Cape, but may have a more ancient beginning than is generally believed, as the Dutch were, in the year 1347, engaged in a civil war which lasted many years, the rival parties being called "Hooks" and "Cod-fish," respectively. The former supported Margaret, Countess of Holland; the latter, William, her son.

Champlain relates that the Indians, in this bay, fished for cod with lines made of bark, to which a bone hook was attached, the bone being fashioned like a harpoon, and fastened to a piece of wood with what he believed to be hemp, such as they had in France. Bass, blue-fish, and sturgeon were taken by spearing.

A fish dinner is eaten at least once a week by every family in New England. In Catholic countries the supply of dried fish is usually exhausted by the end of Lent. We have seen that Bradford received a Jesuit at his own table, and regaled him with a fish dinner because it was Friday, a piece of old-time courtesy some would have us think the Pilgrims incapable of. Somewhat later they had a law in Massachusetts banishing Jesuits or other Roman Catholic ecclesiastics out of their jurisdiction on pain of death.

In effect, the cod-fish is to New England what roast beef is to old Albion. The likeness of one is hanging in the State-house at Boston, as the symbol of a leading Massachusetts industry. Down East the girls carry bits of it in their pockets, and it is set on the bar-room counters for luncheon. A Yankee can fatten on it where an Englishman would starve. The statement is fortified by what we call the truth of history.

In 1714 her Majesty of England concluded a peace with her restless neighbor across the Channel; or, as Pope rhymes it,

"At length great Anna said, 'Let discord cease;'
She said, the world obey'd, and all was peace."

This was the famous treaty that Matthew Prior, the negotiator-poet, calls "the d—d Peace of Utrecht." Prior went to Paris with Bolingbroke. Having arrived there during Lent, he was, by an edict, permitted to have roast beef as a mark of royal favor, and on, I presume, his own application. I rescue this *morceau* from the abyss of state archives:

"Nous Baron de Breteuil et de Preuilly, premier Baron de Touraine, Con^r

du Roy en ses Conseils, Introducteur des Ambassadeurs et Princes Etrangères pres de Sa Matie; Enjoignons au Boucher de l'Hôtel de Dieu de fournir pendant le Carême au *prix ordinaire*, suivant l'ordre du Roy, toute la viande de Boucherie, et Rotisserie qui sera necessaire pour la subsistance de la maison de plenipotentiaire de la Reyne de la Grande Bretagne, M. Prior."[1]

If the great staple of New England is so firmly associated with the Cape, its claims in another direction deserve also to be remembered. The whale-fishery of New England had its beginning here. The hook caught those leviathans as the Penobscot weirs catch salmon. It was long afterward that Nantucket bristled with harpoons. That sea-girt isle borrowed her art of the Cape, and induced a professor in whale-craft, Ichabod Paddock by name, to come over and teach it to her. The Pilgrims would have begun on the instant, but they had not the gear. The Indians followed it in their primitive way, and the exploring parties saw them stripping blubber from a stranded blackfish exactly as now practiced.

POND VILLAGE, CAPE COD.

During the years the whales swam along the shore by Cape Cod there was good fishing in boats. Watchmen stationed on the hills gave notice by signals when one was in sight. After some time they passed farther off on the banks, and sloops carrying whale-boats were used. Cotton Mather refers to the fishery here. Douglass notes a whale struck on the back of Cape Cod that yielded one hundred and thirty-four barrels of oil. In 1739 six small whales were taken in Provincetown Harbor. In 1746 not more than three or four whales were taken on the Cape.

The first whaling adventure to the Falkland Islands is referred to the

---

[1] Prior was personally acceptable to Louis XIV., who gave him a diamond box with his portrait. He was also well known to Boileau.

enterprise of two inhabitants of Truro, who received the hint from Admiral Montague, of the British navy, in 1774.[1]

This admiral, commonly called "Mad Montague," was a character. There is an anecdote of his causing his coxswain to put the hands of some drowned Dutch sailors in their pockets, and then betting fifty guineas to five they died thus. The only reminiscence of whaling that I saw in Provincetown was a gate-way formed of the ribs of a whale before the door of a cottage. Over the house-door was a gilded eagle, of wood, that had decorated some luckless craft. At the tavern the door was kept ajar by a curiously carved whale's tooth wedged underneath. My landlord, gray-haired, but still straight and sinewy, remarked, as he saw me examining it, " I struck that fellow."

But what I came to see here was the desert, and I had not yet seen it. Turning my back upon the town, I set out for Race Point, three miles distant. The last house I passed — and this was a slaughter-house — had the sign-board of a ship, the *Plymouth Rock*, nailed above the lintel. For a certain distance the path was easy to follow; it then became obscure, and I finally lost it altogether; but the sea on the Atlantic side was always roaring a hoarse halloo.

It was never before my fortune to thread so curious and at the same time so desolate a way as this. It filled up the pictures of my reading of the coasts of Barbary or of Lower Egypt. I first crossed a range of sand-hills thinly grown with beach-plum, whortleberry, brake, and sheep laurel, or wild rhododendron.[2] Now and then there was a grove of stunted pitch-pines on the hill-sides, and upon descending I found the hollows occupied by swamps more or less extensive, where the growth was denser and the stagnant water dotted with white blossoming lilies. There were also clumps of the fragrant white laurel in full bloom. In such places the bushes grew thickly, and I had to force my way through them.

The largest of these sunken ponds is named Shank Painter. Seeing what a share they have in preserving Provincetown, I shall always respect a bog or a morass. Over on the shore, between Race Point and Wood End, they have Shank Painter Bar. Here and there in the swamp were clearings of an acre or two planted with cranberry-vines, which yield a handsome return. It was blossoming-time, and the ground was starred with their delicate white flowers, having the corolla rolled back, as seen in the tiger-lily. I found ripe blueberries growing close to the sand, and wild strawberries, of excellent flavor, on the borders of cranberry meadows. An account says, cows might once be seen " wading, and even swimming, in these ponds, plunging their heads into the water up to their horns, picking up a scanty subsistence from the roots

---

[1] Captain David Smith and Captain Gamaliel Collins.
[2] In old times a decoction of checkerberry leaves was given to lambs poisoned by eating the young leaves of the laurel in spring.

PROVINCETOWN.

and herbs produced in the water." I saw birch, maple, and a few other forest trees of stinted growth in the swamp, and stumps of very large pines that had been, perhaps, many times covered and uncovered by sand.[1]

Cranberry culture, already briefly alluded to, has become an important industry on Cape Cod. It is pleasant to see the pickers busily gathering the fruit for market, a labor performed almost wholly by females. An instrument called a cranberry-rake was formerly used; but as it bruised the fruit, it has been discarded for hand-picking. Very little outlay is necessary in the preparation of a cranberry-bed, and much less labor than is usual with ordi-

PICKING AND SORTING CRANBERRIES—CAPE COD.

nary farm crops, while the return is much greater. Here the visitor is astonished at seeing the vine producing abundantly in what appears to be pure white sand. These cranberry plantations are very profitable. Captain Henry Hull, of Barnstable, was one of the earliest cultivators on the Cape.

Though it was raw and windy the marsh-flies bit shrewdly. After passing over the first hills beyond Shank Painter, a very different scene presented itself. Here was a stretch of lofty mounds of clean white sand, five miles in length and a mile and a half in breadth, bare of all vegetation, except scanty patches of beach grass. There was no longer a path, and though I

---

[1] There is an authentic account of ice being found here on the 4th of July, 1741.

saw occasional foot-prints, I did not meet any one. A carriage would be of no use where a horse would sink to his knees in the sand. It was Equality Lane, where pauper or millionaire must trudge for it. In some places the sand was soft and yielding, and again it was so hard beaten by the wind that the footfall would scarcely leave an impression. Scrambling to the summit of one of the highest hills, I found myself overlooking a remarkable hollow completely surrounded with sandy walls. A Bedouin might have been at home here, but shipwrecked sailors would wander aimlessly, until, caught in some such *cul-de-sac*, they gave up the ghost in despair. In wintry storms the route is impracticable. The tourist who has never been to Naples may here do Vesuvius *in poco*, taking care to empty his shoes after sliding from the top to the bottom of a sand-hill.

SAND-HILLS, PROVINCETOWN.

The beach grass, I noticed, resembled the buffalo grass of the plains. It grew at equal distances, even in spots where it had seeded itself. It is the sheet-anchor of the Cape; for, now that the woods are nearly gone, there is nothing else to prevent this avalanche of sand from advancing and overwhelming every thing in its way. Why may not the cotton-wood, which propagates itself in the sand on the borders of Western rivers, prove a valuable auxiliary here? I have known a newly formed sand-bar in the Missouri become a well-wooded island in ten years. There, the tree grows to a great size, and seems to care little for the kind of soil it gets. The poplar (of the same species) flourished well, I saw, in Provincetown and elsewhere on the Cape. The experiment is worth the trying.

In Dr. Belknap's account of Provincetown, printed in 1791, he says of this range of sand-hills: "This volume of sand is gradually rolling into the woods with the winds, and as it covers the trees to the tops, they die. The tops of the trees appear above the sand, but they are all dead. Where they have been lately covered the bark and twigs are still remaining; from others they have fallen off; some have been so long whipped and worn out with the sand and winds that there is nothing remaining but the hearts and knots of the trees; but over the greater part of this desert the trees have long since disappeared." The tops of the dead trees mentioned by Dr. Belknap, the remnant of the forest seen here by the Pilgrims, have been cut off for fuel, until few, if any, are to be seen.

After crossing the wilderness, I came to the shore. It was blowing half a gale, the sea being roughened by it, but not grand. There was but little drift, and that such "unconsidered trifles" of the sea as the vertebræ of fishes, jellyfish, a few tangled bunches of weed, and some pretty pebbles. Looking up and down the beach, I discovered one or two wreckers seeking out the night's harvest; and presently there came a cart in which were a man and woman, the man ever and anon jumping out to gather up a little bundle of drift-wood, with which he ran back to the cart, followed by a shaggy Newfoundland dog that barked and gamboled at his side. These wreckers claim what they have discovered by placing crossed sticks upon the heap, the mark being respected by all who come after.

I followed the bank by the verge of the beach, the tide having but just turned. Before me was the light-house, and the collection of huts at Race Point. A single vessel, bound for a Southern port, was in sight, that, after standing along, gunwale under, within half a mile of the shore, filled away on the other tack, rounding the point in good style. A hundred yards back of the usual high-water mark were well-defined lines of drift, indicating the limit where the sea in great storms had forced its way. I passed a group of huts, used perhaps at times by fishermen, and at others as a shelter for shipwrecked mariners. The doors were open, and, notwithstanding a palisade of barrel-staves, the sand had drifted to a considerable depth within. Here also were pieces of a vessel's bulwarks, the first vestiges of wreck I had seen.

In 1802 the Humane Society erected a hut of refuge at the head of Stout's Creek; but it being improperly built with a chimney, and placed on a spot where no beach grass grew, the strong winds blew the sand from its foundation, and the weight of the chimney brought it to the ground. A few weeks later the ship *Brutus* was cast away. Had the hut remained, it is probable the whole of the unfortunate crew might have been saved, as they gained the shore within a few rods of the spot where it had stood. Upon such trifles the lives of men sometimes depend.

The curvature of the shore south of Race Point, by which I was walking, is called Herring Cove. There is good anchorage here, and vessels may ride safely when the wind is from north-east to south-east. The shore between

Race Point and Stout's Creek, in Truro, was formerly considered the most dangerous on the Cape. Since the erection of Race Point Light, disasters have been less frequent. An attempt to penetrate through the hills to Provincetown by night would be attended with danger, especially in the winter season, but by day the steeple of the Methodist church is always in sight from the highest sand-hills.

Freeman, in his "History of Cape Cod," relates an occurrence that happened here in 1722. A sloop from Duxbury, in which the Rev. John Robinson and wife, and daughter Mary, had taken passage, was upset by a sudden tempest near Nantasket Beach, at the entrance of Boston Harbor. The body of Mrs. Robinson was found "in Herring Cove, a little within Race Point," by Indians, about six weeks after the event. It was identified by papers found in the stays, and by a gold necklace, that had been concealed from the natives by the swelling of the neck. A finger had been cut off, doubtless for the gold ring the unfortunate lady had worn.

The winter of 1874-'75 will be memorable in New England beyond the present generation, the extreme cold having fast locked up a greater number of her harbors than was ever before known. Provincetown, that is so providentially situated to receive the storm-tossed mariner, was hermetically sealed by a vast ice-field, which extended from Wood End to Manomet, a distance of twenty-two miles, grasping in its icy embrace all intermediate shores and havens. In the neighborhood of Provincetown a fleet of fishing vessels that was unable to reach the harbor became immovably imbedded in the floe, thus realizing at our very doors all the perils of Arctic navigation. A few were released by the aid of a steam-cutter, but by far the greater number remained helplessly imprisoned without other change than that caused by the occasional drift of the ice-floe in strong gales.

The sight was indeed a novel one. Where before was the expanse of blue-water, nothing could now be seen except the white slab, pure as marble, which entombed the harbors. All within the grasp of the eye was a Dead Sea. Flags of distress were displayed in every direction from the masts of crippled vessels that no help could reach. Their hulls, rigging, and tapering spars were so ice-crusted as to resemble strips of glass. As many as twenty signals of distress were counted at one time from the life-saving station at Provincetown. Some of these luckless craft were crushed and sunk to the bottom; others were abandoned by their crews, who had eaten their last crust and burned the bulwarks of their vessels for fuel. The remainder were at length released by the breaking-up of the ice-floe, which only relaxed its grip after having held them fast for a month.

It would not be extravagant to say that the beach on the ocean side, between Highland Light and Wood End, was strewed with wrecks. Vessel after vessel was dashed into pieces by waves that bore great blocks of drift-ice to aid in the work of destruction. One starless morning the *James Rommell* struck between Highland Light and Race Point. Instantly the ice-laden surges leaped upon her decks. Wood and iron were crushed like paper under the blows of sea and ice. The helpless vessel was forced sidewise toward the beach, where the waves began heaping up the loose sand on the leeward side, until it reached as high as her decks. When the vessel struck, the crew clambered up the rigging, and all were saved, in a perishing condition, with the help of rescuing hands from the life station. One poor fellow dropped dead on the shore he had periled life to gain, a frozen corpse. In twenty-four hours there was no more left of the *James Rommell* than could be carried away in the wreckers' carts.

But saddest of all was the loss of the Italian bark *Giovanni*. After eighty-one days of stormy voyage from Palermo, a terrible gale, which tore the frozen sails in shreds from her masts, drove her upon this dangerous coast. In the midst of a blinding snow-storm, the unmanageable vessel was borne steadily and mercilessly upon the shore. When she struck, the shock brought down portions of her rigging, leaving her a dismantled wreck. Her crew could see people moving about on the beach, but no human power could aid them. Soon the *Giovanni* began to sink into the sandy grave the waves were fast digging to receive her hull, and the seas sweeping her decks raged around the rigging, in which the sailors had taken refuge. One by one they were picked off by the waves. The wreckers' bombs failed to bring a line to them. A few of the ship's company

LIFE-BOAT STATION.—TRIAL OF THE BOMB AND LINE.

made a desperate push for the beach, which only one reached alive. All night long the wreckers kept their watch by the shore, hoping the gale might abate; but sea and wind beat and howled as wildly as before. When it was light enough to descry the *Giovanni*, six objects could be seen clinging in the rigging. The ship, it was perceived, was fast breaking up. God help them, for no other could! The spectators saw these poor fellows perish before their eyes. They saw the overstrained masts bend and shiver and break, crashing in ruin down upon the shattered hull. The next day only a piece of the bow remained, sticking up like a grave-stone on the reef.

Of the *Giovanni's* crew of fifteen only the one mentioned escaped. He could not speak a syllable of English, but was able, by signs, to identify the body of his captain, when it came ashore. The other bodies that came in were laid out in Provincetown church, three miles from the scene of the wreck. Stray portions of the ship's cargo of wine and fruit were washed up, and while any of the former was to be had the beach was not safe to be traversed. In the midst of this carnival of death, men drunk with wine wandered up and down in the bitter cold, intent upon robbery and violence. One or more of these beach pirates were found dead, the victims of their own debauch.

The configuration of the shores of the Cape on the Atlantic side is very different from what was observed by early voyagers. The Isle Nauset of Smith has, for more than a century, been "wiped out" by the sea.[1] Inlets to harbors have in some cases been closed and other passages opened, as at Eastham and Orleans. In 1863 remains of the hull of an ancient ship were uncovered at Nauset Beach in Orleans, imbedded in the mud of a meadow a quarter of a mile from any water that would have floated her. Curiosity was aroused by the situation as well as the singular build of the vessel, and what was left of her was released from the bed in which, it is believed, it had been inclosed for more than two centuries. A careful writer considers it to have been the wreck of the *Sparrow-hawk*, mentioned by Bradford as having been stranded here in 1626.[2]

There are generally two ranges of sand-bars on the ocean side of the Cape; the outward being about three-fourths of a mile from shore, and the inner range five hundred yards. As in the case of the ill-fated *Giovanni*, a vessel usually brings up on the outer bar, and pounds over it at the next tide, merely to encounter the inward shoal. Between these two ranges a tremendous cross-sea is always running in severe gales, and, if the wind has continued

---

[1] When the English first settled upon the Cape there was an island off Chatham, three leagues distant, called Webb's Island. It contained twenty acres, covered with red-cedar or savin. The Nantucket people resorted to it for fire-wood. In 1792, as Dr. Morse relates, it had ceased to exist for nearly a century. "A large rock," he says, "that was upon the island, and which settled as the earth washed away, now marks the place."

[2] Amos Otis, in the "New England Historical and Genealogical Register," 1865.

long from the same quarter, causing also a current that will float the *débris* of a wreck along the shore faster than a man can walk. With the wind at south-east the wreck stuff will not land, but is carried rapidly to the northwest. Shipwrecked mariners have to cross this hell gate to reach the beach. The mortars used at the life-stations will not carry a life-line to a vessel at five hundred yards from the shore in the teeth of a gale, and are therefore useless at that distance; but if the wreck is fortunate enough to be lifted over the inner bar by the sea, it will strike the beach at a distance where it is practicable to save life under ordinary contingencies. So great are the obstacles to be overcome on this shore, that there is no part of the New England coast, Nantucket perhaps excepted, where a sailor would not rather suffer shipwreck.

Standing here, I felt as if I had not lived in vain. I was as near Europe as my legs would carry me, at the extreme of this withered arm with a town in the hollow of its hand. You seem to have invaded the domain of old Neptune, and plucked him by the very beard. For centuries the storms have beaten upon this narrow strip of sand, behind which the commerce of a State lies intrenched. The assault is unflagging, the defense obstinate. Fresh columns are always forming outside for the attack, and the roll of ocean is forever beating the charge. Yet the Cape stands fast, and will not budge. It is as if it should say, "After me the Deluge."

A "SUNFISH."

NANTUCKET, FROM THE SEA.

CHAPTER XX.

NANTUCKET.

"God bless the sea-beat island!
And grant for evermore
That charity and freedom dwell,
As now, upon her shore."—WHITTIER.

THE sea-port of Nantucket, every body knows, rose, flourished, and fell with the whale-fishery. It lies snugly ensconced in the bottom of a bay on the north side of the island of the name, with a broad sound of water between it and the nearest main-land of Cape Cod. The first Englishman to leave a distinct record of it was Captain Dermer, who was here in 1620, though Weymouth probably became entangled among Nantucket Shoals in May, 1605. The relations of Archer and Brereton render it at least doubtful whether this island was not the first on which Gosnold landed, and to which he gave the name of Martha's Vineyard. The two accounts are too much at variance to enable the student to bring them into reciprocal agreement, yet that of Archer, being in the form of a diary, in which each day's transactions are noted, will be preferred to the narrative of Brereton, who wrote from recollection. To these the curious reader is referred.[1]

The name of "Nautican" is the first I have found applied to Nantucket

---

[1] Purchas, iv.; reprinted in "Massachusetts Historical Collections," iii., viii. I can not give space to those points that confirm my view, but they make a strong presumptive case. It has been alleged that De Poutrincourt landed here after his conflict with the Indians of Cape Cod. So far from landing on the island they saw, Champlain says they named it "*La Soupçonneuse*," from the doubts they had of it. Lescarbot adds that "they saw an island, six or seven leagues in length, which they were not able to reach, and so called '*Ile Douteuse*.'" The land, it is probable, was the Vineyard.

Island.[1] Whether the derivation is from the Latin *nauticus*, or a corruption of the Indian, is disputed, though the word has an unmistakably Indian sound and construction.[2] In the patents and other documents it is called Nantukes, Mantukes, or Nantucquet Isle, indifferently, showing, as may be suggested, as many efforts to construe good Indian into bad English. Previous to Gosnold's voyage the English had no knowledge of it, nor were the names he

MAP OF CAPE COD, NANTUCKET, AND MARTHA'S VINEYARD.

gave the isles discovered by him in general use until long afterward. One other derivation is too far-fetched for serious consideration, a mere *jeu de mot*, to which all readers of Gosnold's voyage are insensible. Historians and antiquaries having alike failed to solve these knotty questions, it is proposed

---

[1] By Sir F. Gorges.
[2] Nantasket, Namasket, Naushon, Sawtuckett, are Indian.

to refer them to a council of Spiritualists, with power to send for persons and papers.

Those who wish to enjoy a foretaste of crossing the British Channel may have it by going to Nantucket. The passage affords in a marked degree the peculiarities of a sea-voyage, and, in rough weather, is not exempt from its drawbacks. The land is nearly, if not quite, lost to view. You are on the real ocean, and the remainder of the voyage to Europe is merely a few more revolutions of the paddles. You have enjoyed the emotions incident to getting under way, of steering boldly out into the open sea, and of tossing for a few hours upon its billows: the rest is but a question of time and endurance.

Every one is prepossessed with Nantucket. Its isolation from the world surrounds it with a mysterious haze, that is the more fascinating because it exacts a certain faith in the invisible. Inviting the imagination to depict it for us, is far more interesting than if we could, by going down to the shore, see it any day. In order to get to it we must steer by the compass, and in thick weather look it up with the plummet. In brief, it answers many of the conditions of an undiscovered country. Although laid down on every good map of New England, and certified by the relations of many trustworthy writers, it is not enough; we do not know Nantucket.

APPROACH TO MARTHA'S VINEYARD.

No brighter or sunnier day could be wished for than the one on which the *Island Home* steamed out from Wood's Hole into the Vineyard Sound for the sea-girt isle. Besides the usual complement of health and pleasure seekers was a company of strolling players, from Boston, as they announced themselves — a very long way indeed, I venture to affirm. These abstracts and brief chronicles of the time" were soon "well bestowed" on the cabin sofas, the rising sea making it at least doubtful whether they would be able to perform before a Nantucket audience so soon as that night. From the old salt who rang the bell and urged immediate attendance at the captain's office, to the captain himself, with golden rings in his ears, and the Indian girl who officiated as stewardess, the belongings of the *Island Home* afloat were spiced with a novel yet agreeable foretaste of the island home fast anchored in the Atlantic.

The sail across the Vineyard Sound is more than beautiful; it is a poem. Trending away to the west, the Elizabeth Islands, like a gate ajar, half close the entrance into Buzzard's Bay. Among them nestles Cuttyhunk, where the very first English spade was driven into New England soil.[1] Straight over in front of the pathway the steamer is cleaving the Vineyard is looking its best and greenest, with oak-skirted highlands inclosing the sheltered harbor of Vineyard Haven,[2] famous on all this coast. Edgartown is seen at the bottom of a deep indentation, its roofs gleaming like scales on some huge reptile that has crawled out of the sea, and is basking on the warm yellow sands. Chappaquiddick Island, with its sandy tentacles, terminates in Cape Poge, on which is a light-house.

Between the shores, and as far as eye can discern, the fleet that passes almost without intermission is hurrying up and down the Sound. One column stretches away under bellying sails, like a fleet advancing in line of battle, but the van-guard is sinking beneath the distant waves. Still they come and go, speeding on to the appointed mart, threading their way securely among islands, capes, and shoals. Much they enliven the scene. A sea without a sail is a more impressive solitude than a deserted city.

We ran between the two sandy points, long and low, that inclose the harbor into smoother water. The captain went on the guard. "Heave your bow-line." "Ay, ay, sir." "Back her, sir" (to the pilot). "Hold on your spring." "Stop her." "Slack away the bow-line there." "Haul in." It is handsomely done, and this is Nantucket.

The wharf, I should infer, would be the best place in which to take the census of Nantucket. No small proportion of the inhabitants were assembled at the pier's head, waiting the arrival of the boat. You had first to make your way through a skirmishing line of hack-drivers and of boys eager to carry your luggage; then came the solid battalion of citizen idlers, and behind these was a reserve of carriages and carts. On the pier you gain the idea that Nantucket is populous; that what you see is merely the overflow; whereas it is the wharf that is populous, while the town is for the moment well-nigh deserted. There could be no better expression of the feeling of iso-. lation than the agitation produced by so simple an event as the arrival of the daily packet. Doors are slammed, shutters pulled to in a hurry, while a tide of curious humanity pours itself upon the landing-place. The coming steam-

---

[1] In 1602 by the colony of Bartholomew Gosnold, already so often mentioned in these pages.
[2] Better known as Holmes's Hole.

A BIT OF NANTUCKET—THE HOUSE-TOPS.

er is heralded by the town-crier's fish-horn, as soon as descried from the church-tower that is his observatory. In winter, when communication with the main-land is sometimes interrupted for several days together, the sense of separation from the world must be intensified.[1]

After running the gantlet of the crowd on the wharf, the stranger is at liberty to look about him.

The fire of 1846 having destroyed the business portion of the town, that part is not more interesting than the average New England towns of modern growth. Generally speaking, the houses are of wood, the idea of spaciousness seeming prominent with the builders. Plenty of house-room was no doubt synonymous with plenty of sea-room in the minds of retired shipmasters, whose battered hulks I saw safe moored in snug and quiet harbors. The streets are cleanly, and, having trees and flower-gardens, are often pretty and cheerful.

The roofs of many houses are surmounted by a railed platform, a reminder of the old whaling times. Here the dwellers might sit in the cool of the evening, and take note of the passing ships, or of some deep-laden whaleman with rusty sides and grimy spars wallowing toward the harbor. Here the merchant anxiously scanned the horizon for tidings of some loitering bark; and here superannuated skippers paced up and down, as they had done the quarter-deck. I question if the custom was not first brought here from the

---

[1] On the raising of the ice-blockade of the past winter seventeen mails were due, the greatest number since 1857, when twenty-five regular and two semi-monthly mails were landed at Quidnet.

tropics, for in Spanish-talking America the best room is not unfrequently the roof, to which the family resort on sweltering hot nights. Sometimes a storm arises, when the precipitancy with which the sleepers gather up their pallets and seek a shelter is the more amusing if witnessed near day-break. Formerly every other house in Nantucket had one of these lookouts, or a vane at the gable-end, to show if the wind was fair for vessels homeward-bound.

While other towns have increased, Nantucket for a length of time has stood still. I saw no evidences of squalid poverty or of actual want, though there was a striking absence of activity. The fire, of which they still talk, though it happened thirty years ago, can not be traced by such visible reminders as a mass of new buildings fitted into the burned space, or by a cordon of old houses drawn around its charred edges. The disaster caused the loss of many handsome buildings, among them Trinity Church, a beautiful little edifice, having latticed windows.

If there was no squalor obtruding itself upon the stranger, neither was there any display of ostentatious wealth. There were a few large square mansions of brick or wood, and even an aristocratic quarter, once known as India Row; but, on the whole, a remarkable equality existed in the houses of Nantucket. The old New England Greek temple greets you familiarly here and there. I read on the sign-boards the well-remembered names of Coffin, Folger, Bunker, Macy, Starbuck, etc., that could belong nowhere else than here. Whenever I have seen one of them in some distant corner of the continent, I have felt like raising the island slogan of other times, "There she blows!"

The Nantucket of colonial times was not more like the present than sailors in pigtails and high-crowned hats are like the close-cropped, wide-trowsered tars of to-day. Houses were scattered about without the semblance of order. The streets had never any names until the assessment of the direct tax in the administration of President Adams. Common convenience divided the town into neighborhoods, familiarly known as "Up-in-Town," "West Cove," or "North Shore." An old traveler says the stranger formerly received direction to Elisha Bunker's Street, or David Mitchell's Street, or Tristram Hussey's Street.

The average conversation is still interlarded with such sea phrases as "cruising about," "short allowance," "rigged out," etc. I heard one woman ask for the "bight" of a clothes-line. I had it from credible authority that a Cape Cod girl, when kissed, always presented the other cheek, saying, "You darsent do that again." A Nantucket lass would say, "Sheer off, or I'll split your mainsail with a typhoon."

There is a story of a "cute" Nantucket skipper, who boasted he could tell where his schooner might be in the thickest weather, simply by tasting what the sounding-lead brought up. His mates resolved to put him to the test.

The lead was well greased, and thrust into a box of earth, "a parsnip bed," that had been brought on board before sailing. It was then taken down to the skipper, and he was requested to tell the schooner's position. At the first taste

> "The skipper stormed, and tore his hair,
> Thrust on his boots, and roared to Marden,
> 'Nantucket's sunk, and here we are
> Right over old Marm Hackett's garden!'"

The streets avoid the fatal straight-line, though they are not remarkably crooked. In the business quarter they are paved with cobble-stones, showing ruts deeply worn by the commerce of other days. Grass was growing out of the interstices of the pavement, where once merchants most did congregate. One of the principal avenues is built along the brow of the sea-bluff, so that almost every house commands a broad sweep of ocean view. The sides of a great many houses were shingled, being warmer, as many will tell you, than if covered with clapboards. As in all maritime towns, the weather-vane is usually a fish, and that, of course, a whale. It is the first thing looked at in the morning by every male inhabitant of the island. Some of the lanes go reeling and twisting about in a remarkable manner.

Nantucket was larger than I had expected. The best view of it is obtained from the side of Coatue. A single old windmill on the summit of a hill behind the town adds to its picturesqueness, and somewhat relieves the too-familiar outlines of roof and steeple. But what, in a place of its size, is most remarkable, is the almost total absence of movement. It impressed me, the time I was there, as uninhabited. There were no troops of joyous children by day, nor throngs of promenaders by night; all was listless and still. Here, indeed, was the town, but where were the people? I was not at all surprised when accosted by one who, like me, wandered and wondered, with the question, "Does any body live in Nantucket?" In midwinter, said an old resident to me, you might have a hospital in the town market-place without danger of disturbing any body. The noise of wheels rattling over the stony street is not often heard.

Owing to the total loss of its great industry, the population of Nantucket is not greater than it was a hundred years ago, and not half what it was early in the century.[1] A large proportion of the houses, it would appear, were unoccupied; yet many that had long remained vacant were being thrown open to admit new guests, that are seeking

> "The breath of a new life—the healing of the seas!"

Old brasses were being furbished up, and cobwebs swept away by new and ruthless brooms. The town is being colonized from the main-land, and

---

[1] In 1837 its population was 9048; it is now a little more than 4000.

though the inhabitants welcome the change, the crust and flavor of originality can not survive it. Already the drift has set in: we may, perhaps, live to see a full-fledged lackey in Nantucket streets.

The wharves show the same decay as in Salem and Plymouth, except that here all are about equally dilapidated and grass-grown. Not a whaling vessel of any tonnage to be seen in Nantucket! The assertion seems incredible. In 1834 there were seventy-three ships and a fleet of smaller craft owned on the island. At this moment a brace of fishing schooners, called smacks, were the largest craft in the harbor. The dispersion of the shipping has been like to that of the inhabitants. I have seen those old whale-ships, with their bluff bows and flush decks, moored in a long line inside the Golden Gate. There they lay, rotting at their anchors, with topmasts struck, and great holes cut in their sides, big enough to drive a wagon right into their holds. To a landsman they looked not unlike a fleet in array of battle.

Others of these old hulks drifted into such ports as Acapulco and Panama, where they were used for coaling the steamships of that coast; and at Sacramento I saw they had converted one into a prison-ship. The last of them remaining in New England harbors were purchased by the Government, and sunk in rebel harbors, as unfit longer to swim the seas. It is not pleasant to think how the last vestiges of a commerce that carried the fame of the island to the remotest corners of the earth have been swept from the face of the ocean.

The whale-ship I was last on board of was the old *Peri*, of New London, that looked able to sail equally well bow or stern foremost. The brick try-house, thick with soot, remained on deck, the water-butt was still lashed to the mizzen-mast. How she smelled of oil! Her timbers were soaked with it, and, on looking down the hatchway, I could see it floating, in prismatic colors, on the surface of the bilge-water in her hold. Many a whale had been cut up alongside. Her decks were greasy as a butcher's block. Though her spars were aloft, she had a slipshod look that would have vexed a sailor beyond measure. The very manner in which the yards were crossed told as plainly of abandonment as unreeved blocks and slackened rigging betokened a careless indifference of her future.

In the days of whaling, a different scene presented itself from that now seen on Nantucket wharves. Ships were then constantly going and coming, discharging their cargoes, or getting ready for sea. The quays were encumbered with butts of oil and heaps of bone. The smith was busy at his forge, the cooper beside himself with work. Let us step into the warehouse. Oil is everywhere. The counting-house ceiling is smeared with it. The walls are hung with pictures of famous whalemen—in oil, of course—coming into port with flags aloft, and I know not how many barrels under their hatches. See the private signal at the mizzen, the foam falling from the bows, and bubbling astern! A brave sight; but become unfrequent of late.

LAST OF THE WHALE-SHIPS.

On the walls are also models of fortunate ships, neatly lettered with their names and voyages. I have seen the head and tusks of the walrus affixed to them, as the head and antlers of the stag might grace the halls of the huntsmen of the land. A strip of whalebone; maps or charts, smoke-blackened, and dotted with greasy finger-marks, indicating where ships had been spoken, or mayhap gone to Davy Jones's Locker; a South Sea javelin with barbed head, a war club and sheaf of envenomed arrows, or a paddle curiously carved, were the usual paraphernalia appropriate in such a place.

In the store-room are all the supplies necessary to a voyage. There are harpoons, lances, and cutting spades, with a rifle or two for the cabin. Coils of rigging, and lines for the boats, with a thousand other objects belonging to the ship's outfitting, are not wanting.

According to Langlet, the whale-fishery was first carried on by the Norwegians, in the ninth century. Up to the sixteenth century, Newfoundland and Iceland were the fishing-grounds. The use of bone was not known until 1578; consequently, says an old writer, "no stays were worn by the ladies." The English commenced whaling at Spitzbergen in 1598, but they had been preceded in those seas by the Dutch. As many as two thousand whales a year have been annually killed on the coast of Greenland.

Champlain says that in his time it was believed the whale was usually taken by balls fired from a cannon, and that several impudent liars had sustained this opinion to his face. The Basques, he continues, were the most skillful in this fishery. Leaving their vessels in some good harbor, they manned their shallops with good men, well provided with lines a hundred and fifty fathoms in length, of the best and strongest hemp. These were attached to the middle of the harpoons.[1] In each shallop was a harpooner, the most adroit and "*dispos*" among them, who had the largest share after the master, inasmuch as his was the most hazardous office. The boats were provided also with a number of partisans of the length of a half-pike, shod with an iron six inches broad and very trenchant.[2]

WHALING IN THE OLDEN TIME.

When at Provincetown, I referred to the beginning of the whale-fishery of Nantucket. Ichabod Paddock, in 1690, instructed the islanders how to kill whales from the shore in boats. The Indians of the island joined in the chase, and were as dexterous as any. Early in the eighteenth century small sloops and schooners of thirty or forty tons burden were fitted out, in which the blubber, after being first cut in large square pieces, was brought home, for trying out. In a few years vessels of sixty to eighty tons, fitted with tryworks, were employed.

Douglass gives some additional particulars. About 1746, he says, whaling

---

[1] The Dutch also whaled with long ropes, as is now our method.

[2] Weymouth also describes the Indian manner of taking whales: "One especial thing is their manner of killing the whale, which they call powdawe; and will describe his form; how he bloweth up the water; and that he is twelve fathoms long; and that they go in company of their King, with a multitude of their boats, and strike him with a bone made in the fashion of a harping-iron, fastened to a rope, which they make great and strong of the bark of trees, which they veer out after him; that all their boats come about him, and as he riseth above water, with their arrows they shoot him to death. When they have killed him and dragged him to shore, they call all their chief lords together, and sing a song of joy; and these chief lords, whom they call sagamores, divide the spoil, and give to every man a share, which pieces so distributed they hang up about their houses for provision; and when they boil them, they blow off the fat, and put to their pease, maize, and other pulse which they eat.—"Weymouth's Voyage."

was by sloops or schooners, each carrying two boats and thirteen men. In every boat were a harpooner, steersman, and four oarsmen, who used nooses for their oars, so that by letting them go they would trail alongside when they were fast to a whale. The "fast" was a rope of about twenty-five fathoms, attached to a drag made of plank, about two feet square, with a stick through its centre. To the end of this stick the tow-rope of fifteen fathoms was fastened.[1]

WHALE OF THE ANCIENTS.

It passes without challenge that the isle's men were the most skillful whalemen in the world. The boys, as soon as they could talk, made use of the Indian word "townor," meaning, "I have twice seen the whale;" and as soon as able they took to the oar, becoming expert oarsmen. Language would inadequately express the triumph of the youngster who landed in his native town after having struck his first whale. The Indian who proudly exhibits his first scalp could not rival him. Thus it happens that you suppose every man in Nantucket can handle the harpoon, and every woman the oar. Nor was it in whaling battles alone that the island prowess made itself famous. Reuben Chase, midshipman of the *Bonne Homme Richard* in the battle with the *Serapis*, became, under Mr. Cooper's hand, Long Tom Coffin of "The Pilot."

The Revolution was near giving the death-blow to Nantucket. In February, 1775, Lord North brought in his famous bill to restrain the trade and commerce of New England with Great Britain and her dependencies, and to prohibit their fishery on the Banks of Newfoundland.[2] It was represented to Parliament that of the population of the islands, amounting to some thousands, nine-tenths were Quakers; that the land was barren, but by astonishing industry one hundred and forty vessels were kept employed, of which all but eight were engaged in the whale-fishery.[3]

The inhabitants having been exempted from the restraining act of Parliament, the Continental Congress, in 1775, took steps to prevent the export of provisions to the island from the main-land, except what might be necessary for domestic use. The Provincial Congress of Massachusetts also prohibited the export of provisions until full satisfaction was given that they were not to be used for foreign consumption.[4] These precautions were necessary, because the enemy's ships made the island a rendezvous.

---

[1] Nantucket in 1744 had forty sloops and schooners in the whale-fishery. The catch was seven thousand to ten thousand barrels of oil per annum. There were nine hundred Indians on the island of great use in the fishery.—Douglass, vol. i., p. 405.

[2] State papers.   [3] Gordon, vol. i., p. 463.   [4] Records of Congress.

Some stigma has attached to the Nantucket Friends for their want of patriotism in the Revolution. They were perhaps in too great haste to apply for the protection of the crown to suit the temper of the day. Justice to their position requires the impartial historian to state that they were at the mercy of the enemy's fleets. They were virtually left to shift for themselves, and ought not to be censured for making the best terms possible. At the close of hostilities their commerce was, in fact, nearly destroyed. Starved by their friends, now become their enemies, and robbed by their enemies, of whom they had sought to make friends, they were in danger of being ground between the upper and nether millstones of a hard destiny.

I well enough remember the first sight I had of whale-ships on their cruising-grounds; of the watchmen in their tubs at the mast-head, where they looked like strange birds in strange nests; and of the great whales that rose to breathe, casting fountains of spray high in the air. They seemed not more animated than the black hull of a vessel drifting bottom-up, and rolling lazily from side to side, until, burying their huge heads deeper, a monster tail was lifted into view, remained an instant motionless, and then, following the rolling plunge of the unwieldy body, sunk majestically beneath the wave.

The curious interest with which, from the deck of a matter-of-fact steamship, I had watched the indolent gambols and puffings of the school, had caused me to lose sight of the whaleman, until an extraordinary commotion recalled her to my attention. Blocks were rattling, commands quick and sharp were ringing out, and I could plainly see the splash that followed the descent of the boats into the water. Away they went, the ashen blades bending like withes with the energy and vim of the stroke. Erect in the stern, his arms bared to the shoulder, his body inclined forward like a bended bow, was the boat-steerer. I fancied I could hear his voice and see his gestures as he shook his clenched fist in the faces of the boat's crew. This was the boat-steerer's speech:

"Now, boys, give it to her; lay back hard! Spring *hard*, I tell you! There she blows! Break your backs, you duff-eaters! Put me right on top of that whale, boys! There she is, boys — a beauty! One more lift, and hurra for Nantucket bar!"

After a weary and fruitless chase—for the whales had sounded—we were boarded by the mate's boat, and requested to report their vessel. I gazed with real curiosity at its crew. Every man had a bandana handkerchief bound tightly about his head. Faces, chests, and arms were the color of old mahogany well oiled. They were then two years out, they said, and inquired anxiously for news from the "States." They neither knew who was President, nor of the war raging between the great powers of Europe, and were thankful for the old newspapers that we tossed to them. At length they rowed off, cutting their way through the water with a powerful stroke, their boat mounting the seas like an egg-shell.

An ancient salt with whom I talked in Nantucket spoke of the disappearance of the whales, and of their turning up in new and unexpected waters. From the beginning of the century until the decline of the fishery, vessels usually made a straight course for Cape Horn; but of late years, whales, he said, had re-appeared in the Atlantic, making their way, it is believed, through the North-west Passage. Whales with harpoons sticking in them having the names of vessels that had entered the Arctic by way of Behring's Straits have been taken by other ships on the Atlantic side of the continent.

"When I first went whaling," quoth he, "you might wake up of a morning in the Sea of Japan with fifty sail of whalemen in sight. A fish darsent (durst not) show his head: some ship would take him."

"I have gone on deck off the Cape of Good Hope," he continued, "when we hadn't a bar'l of ile in the ship, an' the whales nearly blowin' on us out o' the water. We took in twelve hundred bar'ls afore we put out the fires."

Now, though they burn coal-oil in Nantucket, I believe they would prefer sperm. You could not convince an islander that the discovery of oil in the coal-fields was any thing to his advantage; nor would he waste words with you about the law of compensations. A few, I was told, still cling to the idea of a revival in the whale-fishery, but the greater number regard it as clean gone. I confess to a weakness for oil of sperm myself. There are the recollections of a shining row of brazen and pewter lamps on the mantel, the despair of house-maids. In coal-oil there is no poetry; Shakspeare and Milton did not study, nor Ben Jonson rhyme, by it. Napoleon dictated and Nelson died by the light of it. Nowadays there are no lanterns, no torches, worthy the name.

As there is not enough depth of water on Nantucket bar for large ships, Edgartown Harbor was formerly resorted to by the whalemen of this island, to obtain fresh water and fit their ships for sea. If they returned from a voyage in winter, they were obliged to discharge their cargoes into lighters at Edgartown before they could enter Nantucket Harbor. One of the Nantucket steeples was constructed with a lookout commanding the whole island, from which the watchman might, it is said, with a glass, distinguish vessels belonging here that occasionally came to anchor at Martha's Vineyard.

In time a huge floating dock that could be submerged, called a camel, was employed to bring vessels over the bar. After going on its knees and taking the ship on its back, the camel was pumped free of water, when both came into port. These machines are not of Yankee invention. They were originated by the celebrated De Witt, for the purpose of conveying large vessels from Amsterdam over the Pampus. They were also introduced into Russia by Peter the Great, who had obtained their model while working as a common shipwright in Holland. As invented, the camel was composed of two separate parts, each having a concave side to embrace the ship's hull, to which it was fastened with strong cables.

NANTUCKET.

The harbors of Edgartown, New London, and New Bedford, not being subject to the inconvenience of a bar before them, flourished to some extent at the expense of Nantucket; but all these ports have shared a common fate. The gold fever of 1849 broke out when whaling was at its ebb, and then scores of whale-ships for the last time doubled Cape Horn. Officers and men drifted into other employments, or continued to follow the sea in some less dangerous service. They were considered the best sailors in the world. I remember one athletic Islesman, a second-mate, who quelled a mutiny single-handed with sledge-hammer blows of his fist. When his captain appeared on deck with a brace of pistols, the affray was over. The ringleader bore the marks of a terrible punishment. "You've a heavy hand, Mr. Blank," said Captain G——. "I'm a Nantucket whaleman, and used to a long dart."

At the Nantucket Athenæum are exhibited some relics of whales and whaling, of which all true islanders love so well to talk. The jaw-bone of a sperm-whale may there be seen. It would have made Samson a better weapon than the one he used with such effect against the Philistines. This whale stores the spermaceti in his cheek. You can compress the oil from it with the hand, as from honey-comb. What is called the "case" is contained in the reservoir he carries in his head, from which barrels of it are sometimes dipped. What does he want with it? Or is it, mayhap, a softening of his great, sluggish brain?

The tremendous power the whale is able to put forth when enraged is illustrated by the tale of a collision with one that resulted in the loss of the ship *Essex*, of Nantucket. On the 13th of November, 1820, the ship was among whales, and three boats were lowered. A young whale was taken. Shortly after, another of great size, supposed to have been the dam of the one just killed, came against the ship with such violence as to tear away part of the false keel. It then remained some time alongside, endeavoring to grip the ship in its jaws; but, failing to make any impression, swam off about a quarter of a mile, when, suddenly turning about, it came with tremendous velocity toward the *Essex*. The concussion not only stopped the vessel's way, but actually forced her astern. Every man on deck was knocked down. The bows were completely stove. In a few minutes the vessel filled and went on her beam-ends.

Near one of the principal wharves is the Custom-house. It is situated at the bottom of the square already referred to, of which the Pacific Bank, established in 1805, occupies the upper end, the sides being bordered by shops. The first-floor of the Custom-house is used by a club of retired ship-masters, in which they meet to recount the perils and recall the spoils of whaling battles.

We are told by Macy, the historian of the island, that "the inhabitants live together like one great family. They not only know their nearest neighbors, but each one knows the rest. If you wish to see any man, you need but ask the first inhabitant you meet, and he will be able to conduct you to his residence, to tell you what occupation he is of, etc., etc." If one house entertained a stranger, the neighbors would send in whatever luxuries they might have. After a lapse of nearly forty years, I found Macy's account still true. All questionings were answered with civility and directness, and, as if that were not enough, persons volunteered to go out of their way to conduct me. In a whaling port there is no cod-fish aristocracy. Thackeray could not have found materials for his "Book of Snobs" in Nantucket, though, if rumor may be believed, a few of the genus are dropping in from the mainland.

I observed nothing peculiar about the principal centre of trade, except the manner of selling meat, vegetables, etc. When the butchers accumulate an overstock of any article they dispose of it by auction, the town-crier being dispatched to summon the inhabitants, greeting.

This functionary I met, swelling with importance, but a trifle blown from the frequent sounding of his clarion, to wit, a japanned fish-horn. Met him, did I say? I beg the indulgence of the reader. Wherever I wandered in my rambles, he was sure to turn the corner just ahead of me, or to spring from the covert of some blind alley. He was one of those who, Macy says, knew all the other inhabitants of the island; me he knew for a stranger. He stopped short. First he wound a terrific blast of his horn. Toot, toot, toot, it echoed down the street, like the discordant braying of a donkey. This he followed with lusty ringing of a large dinner-bell, peal on peal, until I was ready to exclaim with the Moor,

"Silence that dreadful bell! it frights the isle
From her propriety."

Then, placing the fish-horn under his arm, and taking the bell by the tongue, he delivered himself of his formula. I am not likely to forget it: "Two boats a day! Burgess's meat auction this evening! Corned beef! Boston Theatre, positively last night this evening!"

He was gone, and I heard bell and horn in the next street. He was the life of Nantucket while I was there; the only inhabitant I saw moving faster than a moderate walk. They said he had been a soldier, discharged, by his own account, for being "*non compos*," or something of the sort. I doubt there is any thing the matter with his lungs, or that his wits are, "like sweet bells jangled, out of tune and harsh;" yet of his fish-horn I would say,

"O would I might turn poet for an houre,
To satirize with a vindictive powere
Against the *blower!*"

The history of Nantucket is not involved in obscurity, though Dr. Morse, in his *Gazetteer*, printed in 1793, says no mention is made of the discovery and settlement of the island, under its present name, by any of our historians. Its settlement by English goes no further back than 1659, when Thomas Macy[1] removed from Salisbury, in Massachusetts, to the west end of the island, called by the Indians Maddequet, a name still retained by the harbor and fishing hamlet there. Edward Starbuck, James Coffin, and another of the name of Daget, or Daggett, came over from Martha's Vineyard, it is said, for the sake of the gunning, and lived with Macy. At that time there were nearly three thousand Indians on the island.

Nantucket annals show what kind of sailors may be made of Quakers. The illustration is not unique. In the same year that Macy came to the island a ship wholly manned by them went from Newfoundland to Lisbon with fish. Some of them much affronted the Portuguese whom they met in the streets by not taking off their hats to salute them. If the gravity of the matter had not been the subject of a state paper I should not have known it.[2]

Nantucket and Martha's Vineyard were not included in either of the four New England governments. All the islands between Cape Cod and Hudson River were claimed by the Earl of Sterling. In 1641 a deed was passed to Thomas Mayhew, of Martha's Vineyard, by James Forett, agent of the earl, and Richard Vines, the steward of Sir F. Gorges. The island, until the accession of William and Mary, was considered within the jurisdiction of New York, though we find the deed to Mayhew reciting that the government to be there established by him and his associates should be such as was then existing in Massachusetts, with the same privileges granted by the patent of that colony. In 1659 Mayhew conveyed to the associates mentioned in his deed, nine in number, equal portions of his grant, after reserving to himself Masquetuck Neck, or Quaise.[3] The consideration was thirty pounds of lawful money and two beaver hats, one for himself, and one for his wife. The first meeting of the proprietors was held at Salisbury, Massachusetts, in September

---

[1] Of Macy it is known that he fled from the rigorous persecution of the Quakers by the government of Massachusetts Bay. The penalties were ordinarily cropping the ears, branding with an iron, scourging, the pillory, or banishment. These cruelties, barbarous as they were, were merely borrowed from the England of that day, where the sect, saving capital punishment, was persecuted with as great rigor as it ever was in the colonies. The death-penalty inflicted in the Bay Colony brought the affairs of the Friends to the notice of the reigning king. Thereafter they were tolerated; but as persecution ceased the sect dwindled away, and in New England it is not numerous. The Friends' poet sings of Macy, the outcast:

"Far round the bleak and stormy Cape
The vent'rous Macy passed,
And on Nantucket's naked isle
Drew up his boat at last."

[2] Thurloe, vol. v., p. 422.

[3] The nine were Tristram Coffin, Thomas Macy, Christopher Hussey, Richard Swain, Thomas Barnard, Peter Coffin, Stephen Greenleaf, John Swain, and William Pile, who afterward sold his tenth to Richard Swain.

of the same year (1659), at which time ten other persons were admitted partners,[1] enlarging the whole number of proprietors to nineteen. After the removal to the island, the number was further increased to twenty-seven by the admission of Richard and Joseph Gardiner, Joseph Coleman, William Worth, Peter and Eleazer Folger, Samuel Stretor, and Nathaniel Wier.

The English settlers in 1660 obtained a confirmation of their title from the sachems Wanackmamack and Nickanoose, with certain reservations to the Indian inhabitants, driving, as usual, a hard, ungenerous bargain, as the Indians learned when too late. In 1700 their grievances were communicated by the Earl of Bellomont, then governor, to the crown. Their greatest complaint was, that the English had by calculation stripped them of the means of keeping cattle or live stock of any kind, even on their reserved lands, by means of concessions they did not comprehend. At that time the Indians had been decimated, numbering fewer than four hundred, while the whites had increased to eight hundred souls. The mortality of 1763 wasted the few remaining Indians to a handful.[2] In 1791 there were but four males and sixteen females. Abraham Quady, the last survivor, died within a few years.

The choice of the island by Macy is accounted for by the foregoing facts, doubtless within his knowledge, as many of the original proprietors were his townsmen.

Thomas Mayhew ought to be considered one of the fathers of English settlement in New England. He was of Watertown, in Massachusetts, and I presume the same person mentioned by Drake, in his "Founders," as desirous of passing, in 1637, into "fforaigne partes." He is styled Mr. Thomas Mayhew, Gent., a title raising him above the rank of tradesmen, artificers, and the like, who were not then considered gentlemen; nor is this distinction much weakened at the present day in England. Mayhew received his grant of Nantucket and two small islands adjoining in October, 1641, and on the 23d of the same month, of Martha's Vineyard and the Elizabeth Islands. The younger Mayhew, who, Mather says, settled at the Vineyard in 1642, seems to have devoted himself to the conversion of the Indians with the zeal of a missionary.[3] In 1657 he was drowned at sea, the ship in which he had sailed for England never having been heard from. He was taking with him one of the Vineyard Indians, with the hope of awakening an interest in their progress toward Christianity. Jonathan Mayhew, the celebrated divine, was of this stock.

The first settlement at Maddequet Harbor was abandoned after a more

---

[1] John Smith, Nathaniel Starbuck, Edward Starbuck, Thomas Look, Robert Barnard, James Coffin, Robert Pike, Tristram Coffin, Jun., Thomas Coleman, and John Bishop.

[2] Of three hundred and fifty-eight Indians alive in 1763, two hundred and twenty-two died by the distemper.

[3] Hutchinson.

thorough knowledge of the island and the accession of white inhabitants. The south side of the present harbor was first selected; but its inconvenience being soon felt, the town was located where it now is. By instruction of Governor Francis Lovelace it received, in 1673, the name of Sherburne, changed in 1795 to the more familiar one of Nantucket.

The town stands near the centre of the island, the place having formerly been known by the Indian name of "Wesko," signifying White Stone. This stone, which lay, like the rock of the Pilgrims, on the harbor shore, was in time covered by a wharf. The bluff at the west of the town still retains the name of Sherburne. I found the oldest houses at the extremities of the town.

E. JOHNSON'S STUDIO, NANTUCKET.

Another of the original proprietors is remembered with honor by the islanders. Peter Folger was looked up to as a superior sort of man. He was so well versed in the Indian tongue that his name is often found on the deeds from the natives. The mother of Benjamin Franklin was the daughter of Folger. They do not forget it. The name of Peter Folger is still continued, and family relics of interest are preserved by the descendants of the first Peter.

Any account of Nantucket must be incomplete that omits mention of Sir Isaac Coffin. Sir Isaac was a Bostonian. His family were out-and-out Tories in the Revolution, with more talent than in general falls to the share of one household. He was descended from an ancient family in the northern part of Devonshire, England. In 1773 Isaac Coffin was taken to sea by Lieutenant Hunter, of the *Gaspee*, at the recommendation of Admiral John Montague. His commanding officer said he never knew any young man acquire so much nautical knowledge in so short a time. After reaching the grade of post-captain, Coffin, for a breach of the regulations of the service, was deprived of his vessel, and Earl Howe struck his name from the list of post-captains. This act being illegal, he was reinstated in 1790. In 1804 he was made a baronet, and in 1814 became a full admiral in the British navy. One of his brothers was a British general.

On a visit to the United States, in 1826, Sir Isaac came to Nantucket. Finding that many of the inhabitants claimed descent from his own genealogical tree, he authorized the purchase of a building, and endowed it with a fund of twenty-five hundred pounds sterling, for the establishment of a school to which all descendants of Tristram Coffin, one of the first settlers, should be admitted. On one of his voyages to America the admiral suffered shipwreck.

During the war of 1812, it is related that the admiral made a visit to Dartmoor prison, for the purpose of releasing any American prisoners of his family name. Among others who presented themselves was a negro. "Ah," said the admiral, "you a Coffin too?" "Yes, massa." "How old are you?" "Me thirty years, massa." "Well, then, you are not one of the Coffins, for they never turn black until forty."

NANTUCKET.—OLD WINDMILL, LOOKING OCEANWARD.

CHAPTER XXI.

NANTUCKET—*continued.*

Muskeeget, Tuckanuck, Maddequet,
Sankoty, Coatue, Siasconset.

HISTORY is said to repeat itself, and why may not the whale-fishing? Now that the ships are all gone, a small whale is occasionally taken off the island, as in days of yore. While I was at Nantucket, a school of blackfish were good enough to come into the shallows not far from the harbor, and stupid enough to permit themselves to be taken. The manner of their capture was truly an example of the triumph of mind over matter.

When the school were discovered near the shore, the fishermen, getting outside of them in their dories, by hallooing, sounding of horns, and other noises, drove them, like frightened sheep, toward the beach. As soon as the hunters were in shoal water they left their boats, and jumped overboard, urging the silly fish on by outcries, splashing the water, and blows. Men, and even boys, waded boldly up to a fish, and led him ashore by a fin; or, if inclined to show fight, put their knives into him. They cuffed them, pricked them onward, filling the air with shouts, or with peals of laughter, as some pursuer, more eager than prudent, lost his footing, and became for the moment a fish. All this time the blackfish were nearing the shore, uttering sounds closely resembling groanings and lamentations. The calves kept close to the old ones, "squealing," as one of the captors told me, like young pigs. It was great sport, not wholly free from danger, for the fish can strike a powerful blow with its flukes; and the air was filled with jets of water where they had lashed it into foam. At length the whole school were landed, even to one poor calf that had wandered off, and now came back to seek its dam. The fishermen, after putting their marks upon them, went up to town to communicate their good luck. Sometimes a hundred or two are taken at once in this wise, here or on the Cape.

The oil of the blackfish is obtained in precisely the same manner as that of the whale, of which it is a pocket edition. The blubber, nearly resembling pork-fat, was stripped off and taken in dories to town. I saw the men tossing it with their pitchforks on the shore, whence it was loaded into carts, and carried to the try-house on one of the wharves. Here it was heaped in a palpitating and by no means savory mass. Men were busily engaged in trimming off the superfluous flesh, or in slicing it, with great knives resembling shingle-froes, into pieces suitable for the try-pot; and still others were tossing it into the smoking caldron.

But if whales are getting scarce round about Nantucket, the blue-fish is still plenty. This gamest and most delicious of salt-water fish is noted for its strength, voracity, and grit. He is a very pirate among fish, making prey of all alike. Cod, haddock, mackerel, or tautog, are glad to get out of his way; the smaller fry he chases among the surf-waves of the shore, much as the fishermen pursue the blackfish. Where the blue-fish abounds you need not try for other sort: he is lord high admiral of the finny tribes.

This fish has a curious history. Before the year 1763, in which the great pestilence occurred among the Indians of the island, and from the first coming of the Indians to Nantucket, a large, fat fish, called the blue-fish, thirty of which would fill a barrel, was caught in great plenty all around the island, from the 1st of July to the middle of October. It was remarked that in 1764, the year in which the sickness ended, they disappeared, and were not again seen until about fifty years ago.[1]

It was a delicious afternoon that I set sail for the "Opening," as it is called, between Nantucket and Tuckanuck,[2] an appanage of the former, and one of the five islands constituting the county of Nantucket. The tide runs with such swiftness that the boatmen do not venture through the Opening except with plenty of wind, and of the right sort. With a stiff breeze blowing, the breakers are superb, especially when wind and tide are battling with each other. With the wind blowing freshly over these shallow waters, it does not take long for the seas to assume proportions simply appalling to a lands-

---

[1] Zaccheus Macy, in his account of the island, written in 1792, says none had been taken up to that time—"a great loss to the islanders."

[2] The Indian name Tuckanuck signifies a loaf of bread.

CAPTURED PORPOISE AND BLACKFISH.

man. It was a magnificent sight! Great waves erected themselves into solid walls of green, advancing at first majestically, then rushing with increased momentum across our course to crash in clouds of foam upon the opposite shore. It needs a skillful boatman at the helm. What with the big seas, the seething tide-rips, and the scanty sea-room, the sail is of itself sufficiently exciting.

But the fishing, what of that? We cast our lines over the stern, and, as the boat was going at a great pace, they were straightened out in a trice. At the end of each was a wicked-looking hook of large size, having a leaden sinker run upon the shank of it. Over this hook, called by the fishermen hereabouts a "drail," an eel-skin was drawn, though I have known the blue-fish to bite well at a simple piece of canvas or leather. Away bounded the boat, while we stood braced in the standing-room to meet her plunging. Twenty fathoms with a pound of lead at the end seems fifty, at least, with your boat rushing headlong under all she can bear. Half an acre of smooth water wholly unruffled is just ahead. "I'm going to put you right into that slick," said our helmsman. "Now look out for a big one."

I felt a dead weight at my line. At the end of it a shining object leaped clear from the water and fell, with a loud plash, a yard in advance. Now, haul in steadily; don't be flurried; but, above all, mind your line does not slacken. I lost one splendid fellow by too great precipitation. The line is as rigid as steel wire, and, if your hands are tender, cuts deep into the flesh. Ah! he is now near enough to see the boat. How he plunges and tries to turn! He makes the water boil, and the line fairly sing. I had as lief try to hold an old hunter in a steeple-chase. Ha! here you are, my captive, under the counter; and now I lift you carefully over the gunwale. I enjoin on the inexperienced to be sure they land a fish in the boat, and not lose one, as I did, by throwing him on the gunwale.

The fish shows fight after he is in the tub, shutting his jaws with a vicious snap as he is being unhooked. Look out for him; he can bite, and sharply too. The blue-fish is not unlike the salmon in looks and in action. He is furnished with a backbone of steel, and is younger brother to the shark.

I looked over my shoulder. My companion, a cool hand ordinarily, was engaged in hauling in his line with affected nonchalance; but compressed lips, stern eye, and rigid figure said otherwise. There is a quick flash in the water, and in comes the fish. "Eight-pounder," says the boatman.

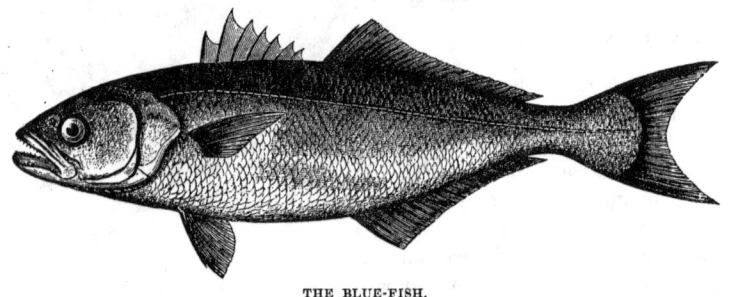

THE BLUE-FISH.

These "slicks" are not the least curious feature of blue-fishing. The fish seems to have the ability to exude an oil, by which he calms the water so that he may, in a way, look about him, showing himself in this an adept in applying a well-known principle in hydrostatics. A perceptible odor arises from the slicks, so that the boatmen will often say, "I smell blue-fish."

The boatman steered among the tide-rips, where each of us soon struck a fish, or, as the phrase here is, "got fast." The monster—I believe he was a ten-pounder at least—that took my hook threw himself bodily into the air, shaking his head as if he did not mean to come on board us. And he was as good as his threat: I saw the drail skipping on the top of the wave as my line came in empty.

In two hours we had filled a barrel with fish, and it was time to shape our course harborward. We saw the smoke of the *Island Home*, looking at first as if rising out of the Sound; then her funnel appeared, and at length her hull rose into view; but she was come within a mile of us before I could distinguish her walking-beam. Tuckanuck and Low Water Island were soon a-lee. Maddequet Harbor opened a moment for us, but we did not enter. We rounded Eel Point with a full sail, and shot past Whale Rock and the shoal of stranded blackfish I told you of. Ever and anon we had passed one adrift, stripped of his fatty epidermis, and now food for the sharks. They were grotesque objects, though now mere carrion, above which the fierce gulls

BLUE-FISHING.

screamed noisily. Here is Brant Point, and its light-house of red brick. We stand well over for Coatue, then about with her for the home stretch. "Fast bind fast find." Our bark is moored. With stiffened joints, but light hearts, we seek our lodgings. What do they say to us? I' faith I am not sorry I went blue-fishing. Reader, are you?

Many blue-fish are caught off the beach on the south shore of the island by casting a line among the breakers, and then hauling it quickly in. This method they call "heave and haul." It takes an expert to get the sleight of it. Gathering the line in a coil and swinging it a few times around his head, an old hand will cast it to an incredible distance. The fish is also frequently taken in seines in shallow creeks and inlets, but he as often escapes through the rents he has made in the net.

I had three excursions to make before I could say I had seen Nantucket. One was to the hills and sands toward Coatue, that curved like a sickle around the harbor; another was to Siasconset; and yet another to the south side. This being done, I had not left much of the island unexplored.

It was on a raw, blustering morning that I set out for a walk around the eastern shore of the harbor. I saw the steamboat go out over the bar, now settling down in the trough, and now shaking herself and staggering onward. Dismally it looked for a day in July, but I had not the mending of it. After getting well clear of the town I found the hills assuming some size and appearance of vegetation. They were overgrown with wild-cranberry vines bearing stunted fruit, each turning a little red cheek to be kissed by the morning sun. Some beautiful flowers sprung from among the neutral patches of heather. The Indian pea, unmatched in wild beauty, displayed its sumptuous plume among the gray moss or modest daisies.

The beach grass was rooted everywhere in the hillocks next the shore, and appeared to be gradually working its way inland. I attempted to pull some of it up, but only the stalks remained in my hand. Each leaf is like a sword-blade. Pass your hand across the under-surface, and it is prickly and rough. What there formerly was of soil has been growing thinner and thinner by being blown into the sea. Unlike the buffalo-grass of the plains, the beach grass possesses little nutriment, though cattle crop the tender shoots in spring. It was formerly much used for broom-stuff.

I picked up by the shore many scallop-shells, and on the hills saw many more lying where pleasure-seekers had held, as the saying is, their "*squantum*," or picnic. This is a historical shell. It surmounts the cap-stone of the monument built over the Rock of the Forefathers at Plymouth. In the Dark Ages, a scallop-shell fastened to the hat was the accepted sign that the wearer had made a pilgrimage to the Holy Land. We read in Parnell's "Hermit:"

> " He quits his cell, the pilgrim staff he bore,
> And fixed the scallop in his hat before."

Professor Gosse says there was a supposed mystical connection between the scallop-shell and St. James, the brother of the Lord, first bishop of Jerusalem. The scallop beds are usually in deep water, and the fish, therefore, can be obtained only by dredging. They are rather plentiful in Narraganset Bay. Some, of a poetic turn, have called them the "butterflies of the sea;" others a "frill," from their fancied resemblance to that once indispensable badge of gentility. As much as any thing they look like an open fan. Many other shells I found, particularly the valves of quahaugs, and a periwinkle six inches in length. Its shell is obtained by fastening a hook in the fish and suspending it by a string. In a few hours the inhabitant drops his integument. Amber is sometimes picked up on the shores, they say, but none came to my share.

Shells of the same kind as those now common to the shores of the island have been found at the depth of fifty feet, after penetrating several strata of earth and clay. In digging as deep as the sea-level, the same kind of sand is brought to the surface as now makes the beaches, and the same inclination has been observed that now exists on the shores. Mr. Adams, my landlord, told me he saw taken from a well, at the depth of sixty feet, a quantity of quahaug-shells of the size of a half-dollar. They usually have to go this depth in the sand, and then get poor, brackish water. There is an account of the finding of the bone of a whale thirty feet under-ground at Siasconset. I saw many covered wells in Nantucket streets that appeared to be the supply of their immediate neighborhoods.

The fogs that sometimes envelop Nantucket gave rise to a pleasant fiction, which smacks of the salt. A whaling ship, outward-bound, having been caught in one of unusual density in leaving the port, the captain made a peculiar mark in it with a harpoon, and on his return, after a three years' cruise, fell in with the harbor at the very same spot.

The Indian legend of the origin of Nantucket is that Mashope, the Indian giant, formed it by emptying the ashes of his pipe into the sea. This same Mashope, having in one of his excursions lighted his pipe on the island, and sat down for a comfortable smoke, caused the fogs that have since prevailed there. He probably waded across from the Vineyard, when he wanted a little distraction from domestic infelicities.

The residence of Mashope was in a cavern known as the Devil's Den, at Gay Head. Here he broiled the whale on a fire made of the largest trees, which he pulled up by the roots. After separating No Man's Land from Gay Head, metamorphosing his children into fishes, and throwing his wife on Seconnet Point, where she now lies, a misshapen rock, he broke up housekeeping and left for parts unknown.

Another Indian legend ascribed the discovery of Nantucket to the ravages made by an eagle among the children of the tribes on Cape Cod. The bird having seized a papoose, was followed by the parents in a canoe until they came to the island, where they found the bones of the child. The existence of the island was not before suspected.

Anciently, the dwellers were shepherds, living by their flocks as well as by fishing. Every inhabitant had the right to keep a certain number of sheep. One day in the year—formerly the only holiday kept on the island—every body repaired to the commons. The sheep were driven into pens and sheared. Sheep-shearing day continued the red-letter day on Nantucket well into the present century. I saw flocks browsing almost everywhere in my rambles, and thought them much more picturesque objects in the landscape than corn-fields or vegetable gardens. There is a freedom about a shepherd's life, a communion with and knowledge of nature in all her variable moods, that renders it more attractive than delving in the soil. No one is so weatherwise as a shepherd-boy. I liked to hear the tinkling of the bells, and watch the gambols of the lambs on the hill-sides.

In his day, Philip was lord and sagamore of the Nantucket Indians. He came once to the island, in pursuit of a subject who had violated savage laws by speaking the name of the dead. The culprit took refuge in the house of Thomas Macy, and Philip, by the payment of a considerable ransom, was induced to spare his life. This occurred in 1665.

The Indian prince was absolute lord on land and sea. Every thing stranded on his coasts—whales or other wreck of value found floating on the sea washing his shores—or brought and landed from any part of the sea, was no less his own. In the "Magnalia" is related an incident illustrating this absolutism of Indian sagamores. An Indian prince, with eighty well-armed attendants, came to Mr. Mayhew's house at Martha's Vineyard. Mayhew entered the room, but, being acquainted with their customs, took no notice of the visitors, it being with them a point of honor for an inferior to salute the superior. After a considerable time the chief broke silence, addressing Mr. Mayhew as sachem, a title importing only good or noble birth. The prince having preferred some request, Mayhew acceded to it, adding that he would confer with the whites to obtain their consent also. The Indian demanded why he recalled his promise, saying, "What I promise or speak is always true; but you, an English governor, can not be true, for you can not of yourself make true what you promise."

It has been observed that the island is gradually wasting away. On the east and south some hundreds of acres have been encroached upon by the sea, and, by the accounts of ancient inhabitants, as many more on the north. During some years the sea has contributed to extend the shores; in others the waste was arrested; but the result of a long series of observations shows a constant gain for the ocean. Smith's Point, now isolated from the mainland, once formed a part of it, the sea in 1786 making a clean breach through, and forming a strait half a mile wide.

I have no wish to depreciate the value of real estate upon Nantucket, but by the year 3000, according to our present calendar, I doubt if there will be more than a grease-spot remaining to mark the habitation of a race of vikings whose javelins were harpoons.

Siasconset is the paradise of the islander: not to see it would be in his eyes unpardonable. Therefore I went to Siasconset, or Sconset, as your true islander pronounces it, retaining all the kernel of the word. It is situated on the south-east shore of the island, seven miles from the town.

You may have, for your excursion, any sort of vehicle common to the main-land, but the islanders most affect a cart with high-boarded sides and a step behind, more resembling a city coal-cart than any thing else I can call to mind. Though not like an Irish jaunting-car, it is of quite as peculiar construction, and, when filled with its complement of gleeful excursionists, is no bad conveyance. For my own part, I would rather walk, but they will tell you every body rides to Sconset. Take any vehicle you will, you can have only a single horse, the road, or rather track, being so deeply rutted that, when once in it, the wheels run in grooves six to twelve inches in depth, while the horse jogs along in a sort of furrow.

I own to a rooted antipathy to carts, going much farther back than my visit to Nantucket. The one I rode in over a stony road in Maine, with a sack of hay for a cushion, put me out of conceit with carts. I would have admired the scenery, had not my time been occupied in holding on, and in catching my breath. I might have talked with the driver, had not the jolting put me under the necessity of swallowing my own words, and nobody, I fancy, quite likes to do that. What little was said came out by jerks, like the confession of a victim stretched on the rack. Henceforth I revolted against having my utterance broken on the wheel.

But when I came to be the involuntary witness of a family quarrel in a cart, I banished them altogether from the catalogue of vehicles. "You are kept so very close to it, in a cart, you see. There's thousands of couples among you getting on like sweet-ile on a whetstone, in houses five and six pairs of stairs high, that would go to the divorce court in a cart. Whether the jolting makes it worse, I don't undertake to decide, but in a cart it does come home to you, and stick to you. Violence in a cart is so violent, and aggrawation in a cart so aggrawating."

After leaving the town the way is skirted, for some distance, with scraggy, weird-looking pitch-pines, that are slowly replacing the native forest. At every mile is a stone—set at the roadside by the care of one native to this, and now an inhabitant of the most populous island in America.[1] They are painted white, and stand like sentinels by day, or ghosts by night, to point the way. In one place I noticed the bone of a shark stuck in the ground for a landmark. There are two roads to Siasconset, the old and the new. I chose the old.

A stretch of seven miles across a lonely prairie, with no other object for the eye to rest upon than a few bare hills or sunken ponds, brought us in sight of the village and of the sea.

The Siasconset of the past was neither more nor less than a collection of fishermen's huts, built of the simplest materials that would keep out wind and weather. In the beginnings of the English along our coast these little fishing-hamlets were called "stages." Other fishing-stages were at Weweeders, Peedee, Sesacacha, and Quidnet. Of these Siasconset alone has flourished. All early navigators and writers agree that the waters hereaway were abundantly stocked with the cod.

I found the village pleasantly seated along the margin of the bluff, that rises here well above the sea. Behind it the land swelled again so as to intercept the view of the town. Underneath the cliff is a terrace of sand, to which a flight of steps, eked out with a footpath, assists the descent. Here were lying a number of dories, and one or two singular-looking fish-carts, with a cask at one end for a wheel. A fish-house, with brush flakes about it, and a pile of wreck lumber, completed what man might have a title to. This terrace pitches abruptly into the sea, with a regularity of slope like the glacis of a fortress. It would never do to call the Atlantic a ditch, yet you seem

---

[1] Rev. F. C. Ewer, of New York.

HOMES OF THE FISHERMEN, SIASCONSET.

standing on a parapet of sand. The sand here appears composed of particles of granite; in other parts of the island it is like the drift at Cape Cod.

The village is an odd collection of one-story cottages, so alike that the first erected might have served as a pattern for all others. Iron cranes projected from angles of the houses, on which to hang lanterns at night-fall, in place of street-lamps. Fences, neatly whitewashed or painted, inclosed each householder's possession, and in many instances blooming flower-beds caused an involuntary glance at the window for their guardians. On many houses were the names of wrecks that had the seeming of grave-stones overlooking the sands that had entombed the ships that wore them. In one front yard was the carved figure of a woman that had been fillped by the foam of many a sea. Fresh from the loftier buildings and broader streets of the town, this seemed like one of those miniature villages that children delight in.

Looking off seaward, I could descry no sails. The last objects on the horizon line were white-crested breakers combing above the "gulf or ship-swallower" lying in wait beneath them. It is a dangerous sea, and Nantucket Shoals have obtained a terrible celebrity—unequaled, perhaps, even by the Goodwin Sands, that mariners shudder at the mention of. If a ship grounds on the Shoal she is speedily wrenched in pieces by the power of the surf. They will tell you of a brig (the *Poinsett*) that came ashore on the south side with her masts in her, apparently uninjured. Two days' pounding strewed the beach with her timbers. "A ship on the Shoals!" is a sound that will quicken the pulses of men familiar with danger. I suppose the calamitous boom of a minute-gun has often roused the little fishing-hamlet to exertions of which a few human lives were the guerdon. Heard amidst the accompaniments of tempest, gale, and the thunder of the breakers, it might well thrill the listener with fear; or, if unheard, the lightning flashes would tell the watchers that wood and iron still held together, and that hope was not yet extinct.

It may be that the great Nantucket South Shoal, forty-five miles in breadth by fifty in length, tends to the preservation of the island, for which it is a breakwater. The great extent of shallows on both sides of the island, with the known physical changes, would almost justify the belief that these sands and this island once formed part of the main-land of New England.

Much is claimed, doubtless with justice, for the salubrity of Siasconset air. Many resort thither during the heats of midsummer. I found denizens of Nantucket who, it would seem, had enough of sea and shore at home, domesticated in some wee cottage. The season over, houses are shut up, and the village goes into winter-quarters. The greensward, elevation above the sea, and pure air are its credentials. I saw it on a sunny day, looking its best.

The sand is coarse-grained and very soft. There is no beach on the island firm enough for driving, or even tolerable walking. The waves that came in here projected themselves fully forty feet up the escarpment of the bank that I

THE SEA-BLUFF, SIASCONSET.

have spoken of. I recollect that, having chosen what I believed a safe position, I was overtaken by a wave, and had to beat a hasty retreat. Bathing here is, on account of the under-tow and quicksands, attended with hazard, and ought not to be attempted except with the aid of ropes. Willis talks of the tenth wave. I know about the third of the swell, for I have often watched it. The first and second are only forerunners of the mighty one. The dories come in on it. A breaker fell here every five seconds, by the watch.

We returned by the foreland of Sankoty Head, on which a light-house stands. From an eminence here the sea is visible on both sides of the island. When built, this light was unsurpassed in brilliancy by any on the coast, and was considered equal to the magnificent beacon of the Morro. Fishermen called it the blazing star. Its flashes are very full, vivid, and striking, and its position is one of great importance, as warning the mariner to steer wide of the great Southern Shoal. Seven miles at sea the white flash takes a reddish hue.

HAULING A DORY OVER THE HILLS, NANTUCKET.

The following afternoon I walked across the island to the south shore at Surfside, a distance of perhaps three miles or more. A south-west gale that had prevailed for twenty-four hours led me to expect an angry and tumultuous sea; nor was I disappointed: the broad expanse between shore and horizon was a confused mass of foam and broken water. It was a mournful sea: not a sail nor a living soul was in sight. A few sand-birds and plover piped plaintively to the hoarse diapason of the billows.

Here I saw a sunset in a gale; the sun, as the sailors say, "setting up

NANTUCKET.

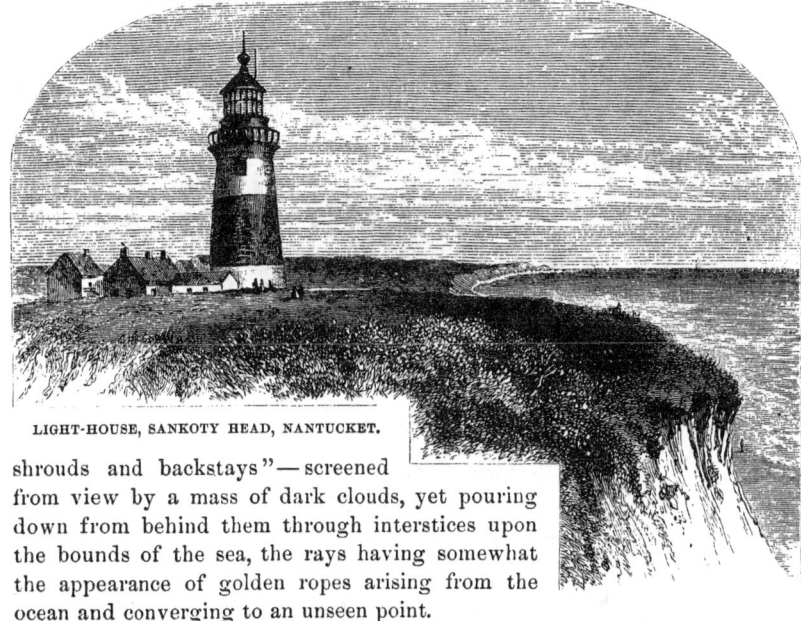

LIGHT-HOUSE, SANKOTY HEAD, NANTUCKET.

shrouds and backstays"— screened from view by a mass of dark clouds, yet pouring down from behind them through interstices upon the bounds of the sea, the rays having somewhat the appearance of golden ropes arising from the ocean and converging to an unseen point.

I seated myself in one of the dories on the beach and gazed my fill. Say what you will, there is a mighty fascination in the sea. Darkness surprised me before I had recrossed the lonely moor, and I held my way, guided by the deep cart-ruts, until the lights of the town twinkled their welcome before me. It was my last night on sea-girt Nantucket. I do not deny that I left it with reluctance.

NEWPORT, FROM FORT ADAMS.

CHAPTER XXII.

NEWPORT OF AQUIDNECK.

"This castle hath a pleasant seat: the air
Nimbly and sweetly recommends itself
Unto our gentle senses."—*Macbeth.*

NEWPORT is an equivoque. It is old, and yet not; grave, though gay; opulent and poor; splendid and mean; populous or deserted. As the only place in New England where those who flee from one city are content to inhabit another, it is anomalous.

In his "Trois Mousquetaires" Alexander Dumas makes his giant, Porthos, encounter a ludicrous adventure. The guardsman is the complacent possessor of a magnificent golden sword-belt, the envy of his comrades, until on one unlucky day it is discovered that the half concealed beneath his cloak is nothing but leather; whereupon some sword-thrusts occur. It was M. Besmeaux, afterward governor of the Bastile, who was the real hero of the sword-belt—half gold, half leather—that Dumas has hung on the shoulders of his gigantic guardsman.

Newport's ocean side is belted with modern villas, costly, showy, and ornate. They mask the town in splendid succession, as if each had been built to surpass its neighbor. This is the Newport of to-day. Behind it, old, gray, and commonplace by comparison, is the Newport of other days. The difference between the two is very marked. The old town is the effete body into which the new is infusing young blood, warming and invigorating it into new life. If the figure were permissible, we should say the Queen of Aquidneck had drunk of the elixir of life, so unexampled is the rapidity with which she transfigures herself.

I like Newport because it is old, quaint, and peculiar. Though far from insensible to its difficult feats in architecture, I did not come to see fine houses. To me they embody nothing besides the idea of wealth and luxurious ease. Many of them are as remarkable for elegance as are others for ugliness of design; yet I found it much the same as walking in Fifth Avenue or Beacon Street. They are at first bewildering, then monotonous; or, as Ruskin says of types of form, mere form, "You learn not to see them. You don't look at them."

I said Newport was commonplace, and I said it with mental reservation. It has a matchless site, glorious bay, and delicious climate, that many have been willing, perhaps a little too willing, to compare with Italy. If we have in New England any phase of climate we may safely match with that favored land,[1] I frankly concede Newport possesses it. The Gulf Stream approaches near enough to temper in summer the harshness of sea-breezes, and the rigor of cold northern winds in winter. The only faults I had to find with the summer and autumn aspects of Newport climate were the fogs and humidity of the nights. The pavements are frequently wet as if by light showers. This condition of the atmosphere is the plague of laundresses and hair-dressers at the great houses: the ringlets you see in Newport are natural.

When at the Isles of Shoals, we were a "thin under-waistcoat warmer" than on the main-land. Neal says it is a coat warmer in winter at Newport than at Boston. I remarked that evening promenaders in the streets there were more thinly clothed than would be considered prudent elsewhere. In Newport, according to Neal, it would lose much point to say a man was without a coat to his back. Mr. Cooper, in the "Red Rover," calls attention to the magnificent harbor of Newport in the language of the practiced seaman. It fully meets all the requisites of easy approach, safe anchorage, and quiet basin. Isles and promontories, frowning with batteries, shield it from danger or insult. The verdure of the shores is of the most brilliant green, and grows quite to the water's edge, or to the verge of the cliffs. In a calm day, when the water is ruffled only by light airs, the tints of sea and sky are scarcely different: then the bay really looks like

"Un pezzo di cielo caduto in terra."

In approaching Newport from sea, after weathering much-dreaded Point Judith,[2] we shall fall in with the light-vessel anchored off Brenton's Reef, the extreme south-west point of the island of Rhode Island. At the same time the light-house on Beaver Tail[3] flashes greeting, and we may now enter the

---

[1] At Naples the summer temperature is seldom above 73°; in winter it does not fall below 47°.

[2] Point Judith is named from Judith Quincy, the wife of John Hull, coiner of the rare old pine-tree shillings of 1652.

[3] Beaver Tail is a peninsula at the southern extremity of Canonicut Island, so named from its marked resemblance, on the map, to the appendage of the beaver.

port with confidence. Passing beside the "Dumplings" and the old round tower, perched on a projecting and almost insulated rock, we steer under the walls of Fort Adams.[1] Sleepy fishing-boats, coming in with the morning's flood, are sent, with rattling blocks, and sails idly flapping, reeling and rocking on big waves caused by the majestic onward march of our great steamer; the beat of the paddles comes audibly back from rocks washed for a moment by our attendant wave. As we round the fortress the bugles play. A ball goes quickly up to the very top of the flag-staff; there is a flash, and a roar of the morning gun; and when the smoke drifts slowly before the breeze, we see the dear old flag blowing out clear, with every stripe still there, and never a reproach in one of them. At our right, and close inshore, is Lime Rock Light, with its associations of female heroism.[2] At the left is Goat Island, long and low, with Fort Wolcott and pleasant cottages for the officers of the torpedo station.[3] Beyond, rising tier above tier, with the beautiful spire of Trinity Church in its midst, is Newport.

OLD FORT, DUMPLING ROCKS.

Newport has been compared to the Lothians and to the Isle of Wight, the British Eden. By all old travelers it was admitted to be the paradise of New England. Its beautiful and extensive bay reminds Scotsmen of the Clyde. In fact, every traveled person at once estimates it with what has hitherto impressed him most — an involuntary but sure recognition of its charms.

Previous to the Revolution, Newport was the fourth commercial town in the colonies, once having more than nine thousand inhabitants. It was at first tributary to Boston, sending its corn, pork, and tobacco to be exchanged

---

[1] Fort Adams is situated at the upper (northern) end of a point of land which helps to form the harbor of Newport; it also incloses a piece of water called Brenton's Cove.

[2] By our American Grace Darling, Miss Ida Lewis.

[3] Goat Island was the site of a colonial fortress. During the reign of King William, Colonel Romer advised the fortification of Rhode Island, which he says had never been done "by reason of the mean condition and refractoriness of the inhabitants." In 1744 the fort on Goat Island mounted twelve cannon. At the beginning of the Revolution General Lee, and afterward Colonel Knox, marked out defensive works; but they do not appear to have been executed when the British, on the same day that Washington crossed the Delaware, took possession of the island. The Whigs, in 1775, removed the cannon from the batteries in the harbor. Major L'Enfant, the engineer of West Point, was the author of Fort Wolcott.

for European goods. Its commercial recovery from the prostration in which the old war left it was again arrested by that of 1812; and this time it did not rise again. The whale-fishery was introduced and abandoned: writers of this period describe it as lifeless, with every mark of dilapidation and decay. The salubrity of the climate of Newport had long been acknowledged, and before 1820 it had become a place of resort for invalids from the Southern States and the West Indies. This one original gift has ever since been out at interest, until, where a few acres of grass once flourished, you might cover the ground with dollars before you became its owner.[1]

At Newport the visitor is challenged by past and present, each having large claims on his attention. I spent much of my time among old houses, monuments, and churches. Some of these are in public places and are easily found, while others are hidden away in forgotten corners, or screened from observation by the walls of intervening buildings. As is inevitable in such a place, the visitor will unwittingly pass by many objects that he will be curious to see, and in retracing his footsteps will have occasion to remark how much a scrap of history or tradition adds to the charm of an otherwise uninteresting structure.

The town along the water resembles Salem, except that it has neither its look of antiquity nor its dilapidation. Here the principal thoroughfare is Thames Street, long, narrow, and almost wholly built of wood. The narrowness of Thames Street has been referred to the encroachments of builders of a former time, the old houses standing at some distance back from the pavement being pointed to as evidence of the fact. I can only vouch for glimpses of some very habitable and inviting old residences in back courts and alleys opening upon the street. Here, too, old gambrel-roofed houses are plenty as blackberries in August. They have a portly, aldermanic look, with great breadth of beam, like ships of their day. When these houses that now stand end to the street had pleasant garden spots between, a walk here would have been worth the taking. When there were no sidewalks, it meant something to give the wall to your neighbor, and tact and breeding were requisite to know when to demand and when to decline it.

In Thames Street are several imperturbable notables in brick or wood. The City Hall—for as early as 1784 Newport had reached the dignity of a city—is usually first encountered. Notwithstanding they tell you it was one

---

[1] There should be added to the detail of maps given in the initial chapter that of Jerome Verrazani, in the College de Propaganda Fide, at Rome, of the supposed date of 1529. This map is described and discussed, together with the detail of Giovanni Verrazani's letter to Francis I., dated at Dieppe, July 8th, 1524, in "Verrazano, the Navigator," by J. C. Brevoort. A reduced copy of the map or "Planisphere" is there given. The author adopts the theory, not without plausibility, that Verrazani passed fifteen days at anchor in Narraganset Bay. As I have before said, there is something of fact in these early relations; but if tested by the only exact marks given (latitude, distances, and courses), they establish nothing.

of Peter Harrison's[1] buildings, it is very ordinary-looking, inside and out. It was built on arches, which indicates the lower floor to have been intended as a public promenade; and shows that the architect had the Old Royal Exchange in mind. For some time it was used as a market. This house came into the little world of Newport in 1763. A word of admiration from Allston has long been treasured.

In this building I saw hanging the escutcheon of William Coddington, who, as every body at all familiar with the history of Rhode Island knows, was one of the founders of Newport, and first governor of the little body politic organized upon the Isle of Aquidneck.

OLD-TIME HOUSES.

We have decided to cast a glance backward, and, to know our ground, must pay our duty to this old founder. William Coddington, Esquire, came to New England in 1630 with the Boston colonists, as one of the assistants named in their charter. He was several times rechosen to this important position, became a leading merchant in Boston, and is said to have built the first brick house there.[2] The house he afterward built and lived in at Newport, of the quaint old English pattern, was standing within the recollection of many older inhabitants.

Mr. Coddington became involved in the Anne Hutchinson controversy, as did Wheelwright, the founder of Exeter. Mrs. Hutchinson was banished, and took refuge with Coddington and others on Rhode Island. In the presence

---

[1] Harrison, the first architect of his day in New England, was the author of many of the older public buildings in Newport, Trinity Church and Redwood Library among others. He also designed King's Chapel, Boston, and did what he could to drag architecture out of the mire of Puritan ugliness and neglect.

[2] He owned, besides his house and garden in Boston, lands at Mount Wollaston, now Quincy, Massachusetts. Coddington is mentioned in Samuel Fuller's letter to Bradford, June, 1630. "Mrs. Cottington is dead," he also says.

of Governor Winthrop and of Dudley, his deputy; of the assistants, among whom were Endicott, Bradstreet, and Stoughton; confronted by the foremost and hardest-shelled ministers in the colony, such as Hugh Peters, Eliot, and Wilson, this woman defended herself, almost single-handed and with consummate address, against a court which had already prejudged her case, and which stubbornly refused, until the very last stage of the proceedings, to put the witnesses upon oath. As a specimen of the way in which justice was administered in the early day, and of judicial procedure, this trial is exceedingly curious.[1] Here is a specimen of brow-beating that recalls "Oliver Twist:"

RESIDENCE OF GOVERNOR CODDINGTON, NEWPORT, 1641.

Deputy-governor. "Let her witnesses be called."

Governor. "Who be they?"

Mrs. Hutchinson. "Mr. Leveret, and our teacher, and Mr. Coggeshall."

Governor. "Mr. Coggeshall was not present."

Mr. Coggeshall. "Yes, but I was, only I desired to be silent until I was called."

Governor. "Will you, Mr. Coggeshall, say that she did not say so?"

Mr. Coggeshall. "Yes, I dare say that she did not say all that which they lay against her."

Mr. Peters. "How dare you look into the court to say such a word?"

Mr. Coggeshall. "Mr. Peters takes upon him to forbid me. I shall be silent."

As the governor was about to pass sentence, Mr. Coddington arose and spoke some manly words:

---

[1] It may be found at length in Hutchinson, appendix, vol. ii. Governor Hutchinson was a relative of the schismatic Anne.

Mr. Coddington. "I do think that you are going to censure, therefore I desire to speak a word."

Governor. "I pray you speak."

Mr. Coddington. "There is one thing objected against the meetings. What if she designed to edify her own family in her own meetings, may none else be present?"

Governor. "If you have nothing else to say but that, it is a pity, Mr. Coddington, that you should interrupt us in proceeding to censure."

Despite this reproof, Mr. Coddington had his say, and one of the assistants (Stoughton) insisting, the ministers were compelled to repeat their testimony under oath; which they did after much parleying and with evident reluctance. It is curious to observe that in this trial the by-standers were several times appealed to for an expression of opinion on some knotty question.[1] Had it not involved the liberty and fortunes of many more than the Hutchinsons, its ludicrous side would scarcely have been surpassed by the celebrated cause of "Bardell *vs.* Pickwick."

There is something inexpressibly touching in the decay of an old and honorable name—in the struggle between grinding poverty and hereditary family pride. Instead of finding the Coddingtons, as might be expected, among the princes of Newport, a native of the place would only shake his head when questioned of them.

Touching the northern limits of Newport is a placid little basin called Coddington's Cove. It is a remembrancer of the old governor. The last Coddington inherited an ample estate, upon the principal of which, like Heine's monkey, who boiled and ate his own tail, he lived, until there was no more left. The Cossacks have a proverb: "He eats both ends of his candle at once." Having dissipated his ancestral patrimony to the last farthing, the thriftless and degenerate Coddington descended all the steps from shabby gentility to actual destitution; yet, through all these reverses, he maintained the bearing of a fine gentleman. One day he was offered a new suit of clothes —his own had the threadbare gloss of long application of the brush—for the Coddington escutcheon that had descended to him. Drawing himself up with the old look and air, he indignantly exclaimed, "What, sell the coat of arms of a Coddington!" Nevertheless, he at last became an inmate of the poorhouse at Coddington's Cove; and that is the way the family escutcheon came to be hanging in the City Hall. I tell you the story as it was told to me.

The Wanton House, still pointed out in Thames Street, may be known by its ornamented cornice and general air of superior condition. It stands within a stone's-throw of the City Hall. The Wantons, like the Malbones, Godfreys, Brentons, Wickhams, Cranstons, and other high-sounding Newport names,

---

[1] This was called an appeal to the country. A judge would hardly, at the present day, permit such an expression in court.

were merchants. Like the Wentworths of New Hampshire, this was a family, I might almost say a dynasty, of governors. When one Wanton went out, another came in. It was the house of Wanton, governing, with few intervals, from 1732, until swept from place by the Revolution.[1] As the king never dies, at the exit of a Wanton the sheriff should have announced, "The governor is dead. Long live the governor!"

Joseph Wanton, the last governor of Rhode Island under the crown, was the son of William. He was a Harvard man, amiable, wealthy, of elegant manners, and handsome person. In the description of his outward appearance we are told that he "wore a large white wig with three curls, one falling down his back, and one forward on each shoulder." I have nowhere met with an earlier claimant of the fashion so recently in vogue among young ladies who had hearts to lose.

Turning out of narrow and noisy Thames Street into the broader and quieter avenues ascending the hill, we find ourselves on the Parade before the State-house. Broad Street, which enters it on one side, was the old Boston high-road; Touro Street, debouching at the other, loses its identity ere long in Bellevue Avenue, and is, beyond comparison, the pleasantest walk in Newport.

NEWPORT STATE-HOUSE.

The Parade, also called Washington Square, is the delta into which the main avenues of Newport flow. It is, therefore, admirably calculated as a starting-point for those street rambles that every visitor has enjoyed in anticipation. On this ground I saw some companies of the Newport Artillery going through their evolutions with the steadiness of old soldiers. Their organization goes back to 1741, and is maintained with an *esprit de corps* that a people not long since engaged in war ought to know how to estimate at its true value. A custom of the corps, as I have heard, was to fire a *feu de joie* under the windows of a newly married comrade; if a commissioned officer, a field-piece.

At the right of the Parade, and a little above the hotel of his name, stands the house purchased by Commodore Perry after the battle of Lake Erie; in

---

[1] William Wanton, 1732 to 1734; John Wanton, 1734 to 1741; Gideon Wanton, 1745 to 1746, and from 1747 to 1748; Joseph Wanton, from 1769 to 1775. The last named left Newport with the British, in 1780, and died in New York. His son Joseph, junior, commanded the regiment of loyalists raised on the island.

Clarke Street, near-by, is the church in which Dr. Stiles, afterward president of Yale, preached, built in 1733; and next beyond is the gun-house of the Newport Artillery.

The State-house is a pleasing, though not imposing, building, known to all evening promenaders in Newport by the illuminated clock in the pediment of the façade. It is in the style of colonial architecture of the middle of the last century, having two stories, with a wooden balustrade surmounting the roof. The pediment of the front is topped by a cupola, and underneath is a balcony, from which proclamations, with "God save the king" at the end of them, have been read to assembled colonists; as in these latter days, on the last Tuesday of May, which is the annual election in Rhode Island, after a good deal of parading about the streets, the officials elect are here introduced by the high sheriff with a flourish of words: "Hear ye! Take notice that his Excellency, Governor ——, of Dashville, is elected governor, commander-in-chief, and captain-general of Rhode Island for the year ensuing. God save the State of Rhode Island, and Providence Plantations!" The candidate smiles, bows, and withdraws, and the populace, as in duty bound, cheers itself hoarse. It loves the old forms, though some of them seem cumbrous for "Little Rhody." Sometimes a sheriff has been known to get his formula "out of joint," and to tack the words "for the year ensuing" at the end of the invocation.

COMMODORE PERRY'S HOUSE.

During the Revolution the State-house was used as a hospital by British and French, and of course much abused. In the restoration some little savor of its ancient quaintness is missed. The interior has paneled wainscoting, carved balusters, and wood-work in the old style of elegance. The walls of the Senate chamber are sheathed quite up to the ceiling, in beautiful paneling, relieved by a massive cornice. Stuart's full-length portrait of Washington, in the well-known black velvet and ruffles, is here. I have somewhere seen that the French "desecrated," as some would say, the building by raising an altar on which to say mass for the sick and dying. In the garret I saw a section of the old pillory that formerly stood in the vacant space before the building. Many think the restoration of stocks, whipping-post, and pillory would do more to-day to suppress petty crimes than months of imprisonment. They still cling in Delaware to their whipping-post. There, they assert, the dread of public exposure tends to lessen crime.

The pillory, which a few living persons remember, was usually on a movable platform, which the sheriff could turn at pleasure, making the culprit front the different points of the compass it was the custom to insert in the sentence. Whipping at the cart's tail was also practiced.

One of the finest old characters Rhode Island has produced was Tristram Burgess, who administered to that dried-up bundle of malignity, John Randolph, a rebuke so scathing that the Virginian was for the time completely silenced. Having roused the Rhode Islander by his Satanic sneering at Northern character and thrift, his merciless criticism, and incomparably bitter sarcasm, Burgess dealt him this sentence on the floor of Congress: "Moral monsters can not propagate; we rejoice that the father of lies can never become the father of liars."

It was at first intended to place the State-house with its front toward what was then known as "the swamp," in the direction of Farewell Street. In 1743 it was completed. Rhode Island may with advantage follow the lead of Connecticut in abolishing one of its seats of government. At present its constitution provides that the Assembly shall meet and organize at Newport, and hold an adjourned session at Providence.[1]

JEWISH CEMETERY.

Walking onward and upward in Touro Street, the visitor sees at its junction with Kay Street what he might easily mistake for a pretty and and well-tended garden, but for the mortuary emblems sculptured on the gate-way. The chaste and beautiful design of this portal, even to the inverted flambeaux, is a counterpart of that of the Old Granary ground at Boston. This is the Jewish Cemetery.

> "How strange it seems! These Hebrews in their graves,
>   Close by the street of this fair sea-port town.
> Silent beside the never-silent waves,
>   At rest in all this moving up and down!
>
> "And these sepulchral stones, so old and brown,
>   That pave with level flags their burial-place,
> Seem like the tablets of the Law, thrown down
>   And broken by Moses at the mountain's base."

---

[1] One of the most curious chapters of Rhode Island's political history was the "Dorr Rebellion" of 1842, growing out of a partial and limited franchise under the old charter.

Close at hand is the synagogue, in which services are no longer held, though, like the cemetery, it is scrupulously cared for.[1] The silence and mystery which brood over each are deepened by this reverent guardianship of unseen hands. In 1762 the synagogue was dedicated with the solemnities of Jewish religious usage. It was then distinguished as the best building of its kind in the country. The interior was rich and elegant. Over the reading-desk hung a large brass chandelier; in the centre, and at proper distances around it, four others. On the front of the desk stood a pair of highly ornamented brass candlesticks, and at the entrance on the east side were four others of the same size and workmanship. As usual, there was for the women a gallery, screened with carved net-work, resting on columns. Over this gallery another rank of columns supported the roof. It was the commonly received opinion that the lamp hanging above the altar was never extinguished.

JEWS' SYNAGOGUE, NEWPORT.

The Hebrews began to settle on the island before 1677. The deed of their ancient burial-place is dated in this year. They first worshiped in a private house. Accessions came to them from Spain, from Portugal, and from Holland, with such names as Lopez, Riveriera, Seixas, and Touro, until the congregation numbered as many as three hundred families. The stranger becomes familiar with the name of Touro, which at first he would have Truro, from the street and park, no less than the respect with which it is pronounced by all old residents. The Hebrews of old Newport seem to have fulfilled the destiny of their race, becoming scattered, and finally extinct. Moses Lopez is said to have been the last resident Jew, though, unless I mistake, the Hebrew physiognomy met me more than once in Newport. This fraction formed one of the curious constituents of Newport society. Its history is ended, and "*Finis*" might be written above the entrances of synagogue and cemetery.

Lord Chesterfield once told Lady Shirley, in a serious conversation on the evidences of Christianity, that there was one which he thought to be invin-

---

[1] A fund bequeathed by Abraham Touro, who died in Boston in 1822, secures this object.

cible, namely, the present state of the Jews—a fact to be accounted for on no human principle. The Hebrew customs have remained inviolate amidst all the strange mutations which time has brought. The Sabbath by which Shylock registered his wicked oath is still the Christian's Saturday. In the Jewish burial rite the grave was filled in by the nearest of kin.

JUDAH TOURO.

In no other cemetery in New England have I been so impressed with the sanctity, the inviolability of the last resting-place of the dead, as here among the graves of a despised people. The idea of eternal rest seemed really present. Not long since I heard the people of a thriving suburb discussing the removal of their old burial-place, bodily—I mean no play upon the word —to the skirts of the town. Being done, it was thought the land would pay for the removal, and prove a profitable speculation. Since Abraham gave four hundred shekels of silver for the field of Ephron, the Israelites have reverenced the sepulchres wherein they bury their dead. Here is religion without ostentation. In our great mausoleums is plenty of ostentation, but little religion.

The visitor here may note another distinctive custom of this ancient people. The inscription above the gate reads, "Erected 5603, from a bequest made by Abraham Touro."[1] They compute the passage of time from the creation.

An hour, or many hours, may be well spent in the Redwood Library, founded by Abraham Redwood,[2] one of the Quaker magnates of old Newport.

---

[1] Judah Touro, the philanthropist, was born here in Newport, in 1775, the year of American revolt. His father, the old rabbi, Isaac, came from Holland, officiating as preacher in 1762 in Newport. When still a young man, Judah Touro removed to New Orleans, where he acquired a fortune. He was a volunteer in the battle of 1815, and was wounded by a cannon-ball in the hip. Though a Jew, Judah Touro was above sect, generously contributing to Christian church enterprises. Bunker Hill Monument, toward which he gave ten thousand dollars, is a memorial of his patriotic liberality.

[2] It was incorporated 1747: the same year Mr. Redwood gave five hundred pounds sterling, in books, or about thirteen hundred volumes. The lot was the gift of Henry Collins, in 1748; building erected 1748–'50; enlarged in 1758; and now (1875) a new building is erecting. Abraham

His fine and kindly face has been carefully reproduced in the engraving. The library building is in the pure yet severe style of a Greek temple. The painter Stuart considered it classical and refined. It has a cool and secluded look, standing back from the street and shaded by trees, that is inviting to the appreciative visitor. This is one of the institutions of Newport which all may praise without stint. It has grown with its growth; yet, after repeated enlargements, the increased collections in art and literature of this storehouse of thought have demanded greater space.

THE REDWOOD LIBRARY.

Another benefactor worthy to be ranked with Abraham Redwood was Charles Bird King, whose portrait is hanging in the hall. At his death he made a munificent bequest of real estate, yielding nine thousand dollars, his valuable library, engravings, and more than two hundred of the paintings which now adorn the walls.

Among other portraits here are those of Bishop Berkeley in canonicals, and of Governor Joseph Wanton, in scarlet coat and periwig, his face looking as if he and good living were no strangers to each other; of William Coddington, and of a long catalogue of soldiers and statesmen, many being copies by Mr. King. The library suffered from pilfering during the British occupation: it now numbers something in excess of twenty thousand volumes.[1]

I admit the first object in Newport I went to see was the Old Stone Mill. I went directly to it, and should not venture to conduct the reader by any route that did not lead to it. I returned often, and could only wonder at

---

Redwood was a native of Antigua. When the library sent its committee to Stuart, with a commission to paint a full-length portrait of Mr. Redwood, Stuart refused, for reasons of his own, to execute it.

[1] Dr. Ezra Stiles was librarian for twenty years.

the seeming indifference of people constantly passing, but never looking at it.

The Old Stone Mill stands within the pleasant inclosure of Touro Park, a place as fitting as any in Newport for the beginning of a sentimental journey. It is a pretty sight on a summer's evening, this green spot, dotted with moving figures sauntering up and down under the grim shadow of this picturesque ruin.[1] By moonlight it is superb.

No structure in America is probably so familiar to the great mass of the people as this ruined mill. The frequency of pictorial representation has fixed its general form and character until there is probably not a school-boy in his teens who would not be able to make a rude sketch of it on the blackboard. For years it has been the toughest historical *pièce de resistance* our antiquaries have had to deal with, and by many it was supposed to embody a secret as impenetrable as that of Stonehenge.

The Old Mill was dozing quietly away on this hill, when, in 1836, the Society of Northern Antiquaries, of Copenhagen, declared it to be evidence of the discovery and occupation of Newport by Northmen, in the eleventh century. An historical chain was immediately sought to be established between Dighton Rock, an exhumed skeleton at Fall River, and this tower, of which the inscription at Monhegan Island was believed to be another link.

Common opinion, prior to the declaration of the Danish antiquaries, was

ABRAHAM REDWOOD.

that the tower was the remains of a windmill, and nothing more. In a gazetteer of Rhode Island, printed in 1819, is the following paragraph: "In this town (Newport) there is now standing an ancient stone mill, the erection of which is beyond the date of its earliest records; but it is supposed to have been erected by the first settlers, about one hundred and eighty years ago. It is an interesting monument of antiquity."

---

[1] The discovery of any portion of the coast of New England by Northmen belongs to the realms of conjecture. It is not unreasonable to suppose that they may have fallen in with the continent; but what should have brought them so far south as Rhode Island, when Nova Scotia must have appeared to their eyes a paradise? The vine grows there. Champlain called Richmond's Island Isle de Bacchus, on account of its grapes.

About this time Timothy Dwight, formerly president of Yale, was in Newport. In his letters, published in 1822, he has something to say of the Old Stone Mill: "On a skirt of this town is the foundation of a windmill erected some time in the seventeenth century. The cement of this work, formed of shell-lime and beach gravel, has all the firmness of Roman mortar, and when broken off frequently brings with it part of the stone. Time has made no impression on it, except to increase its firmness. It would be an improvement in the art of building in this country, if mortar made in the same manner were to be generally employed."[1]

THE OLD STONE MILL.

All readers of early New England history know that nothing was too trivial, in the opinion of those old chroniclers, to be recorded. Winthrop mentions the digging-up of a French coin at Dorchester in 1643. It is pertinent to inquire why Roger Williams, Hubbard, Mather, the antiquary, and correspondent of the Royal Society, Prince, Hutchinson, and others, have wholly ignored the presence of an old ruin antedating the English occupation of Rhode Island? Would not Canonicus have led the white men to the spot, and there recounted the traditions of his people? No spot of ground in New England has had more learned and observing annalists. Where were Bishop

---

[1] "Travels in New England and New York:" New Haven, 1822, vol. iii., p. 56.

NEWPORT OF AQUIDNECK. 371

Berkeley, Rochambeau, Chastellux, Lauzun, Abbé Robin, Ségur, Dumas, and Deux-Ponts, that they make no mention, in their writings or memoirs, of the remarkable archæological remains at Newport? Yet, on the report of the Danish Society, nearly or quite all our American historians have admitted their theory of the origin of the Old Stone Mill to their pages. With this leading, and the ready credence the marvelous always obtains, the public rested satisfied.[1]

The windmill was an object of the first necessity to the settlers. More of them may be seen on Rhode Island to-day than in all the rest of New England. That this mill should have been built of stone is in no way surprising, considering that the surface of the ground must have been bestrewed with stones of proper size and shape ready to the builders' hands.[2] I saw these flat stones of which the tower is built turned up by the plowshare in the roads. Throughout the island the walls are composed of them.[3]

THE PERRY MONUMENT.

The cut on the preceding page represents the Old Stone Mill, with the moon's radiance illuminating its arches. It is a cylindrical tower, resting on eight rude columns, also circular. The arches have no proper key-stone,[4] and two of them appear broader than the others, as if designed for the entrance of some kind of vehicle. One column is so placed as to show an inner projection, an evident fault of workmanship. Two stages are also apparent, and

---

[1] Among the records of Newport was found one of 1740, in which Edward Pelham bequeathed to his daughter eight acres of land, "with an Old Stone Wind Mill thereon standing and being, and commonly called and known as the Mill Field." The lane now called Mill Street appears to have been so named from its conducting up the hill to the mill. The wife of Pelham was granddaughter of Governor Benedict Arnold. In the governor's will, dated in 1677, he gives direction for his burial in a piece of ground "being and lying in my land in or near yᵉ line or path from my dwelling-house, leading to my stone-built Wind Mill in yᵉ town of Newport above mentioned."

[2] I incline to the opinion that the Indians had here, as at Plymouth, cleared a considerable area. There the carpenters had to go an eighth of a mile for timber suitable for building.

[3] Within five miles of Boston is standing an ancient stone windmill, erected about 1710. It had been so long used as a powder-magazine that no tradition remained in the neighborhood that it had ever been a windmill. They still call it the Old Powder-house.

[4] The keys are compound, and, though rude, are tolerably defined. No two are alike; they are generally of a hard gray stone, instead of the slate used in the structure.

there are two windows and a fire-place. On the inside the haunches are cut to receive the timbers of the first-floor, just at the turn of the arch. Some cement is still seen adhering to the interior walls. The whole tower I estimated to be twenty-five feet high, with an inside diameter of twenty feet. This was probably nearly or quite its original height. For the rude materials, it is a remarkable specimen of masonry.[1]

I could see that even some of the best-informed Newporters with whom I talked were reluctant to let go the traditional antiquity of their Old Stone Mill. It is more interesting when tinged with the romance of Norse vikings than as the prosaic handiwork of English colonists, who had corn to grind, though American antiquaries have ceased to attribute to it any other origin. I confess to a feeling of remorse in aiding to destroy the illusion which has so long made the Old Mill a tower of strength to Newport. Its beauty, when seen draped in ivy and woodbine, clustering so thickly as to screen its gray walls from view, is at least not apocryphal.

---

[1] This building may have been mentioned by Church in his account of Philip's War, when, after some display of aversion on the part of a certain captain to a dangerous enterprise, he was advised by the Indian fighter to lead his men "to the windmill on Rhode Island, where they would be out of danger."

BOAT LANDING.

CHAPTER XXIII.

PICTURESQUE NEWPORT.

"Don't you see the silvery wave?
Don't you hear the voice of God?"
KIRKE WHITE.

THERE is a walk of singular beauty along the sea-bluffs that terminate the reverse of the hills on which Newport is built. It is known as the Cliff Walk. Every body walks there. A broken wall of rock overhanging or retreating from its base, but always rising high above the water, is bordered by a foot-path with pleasant windings and elastic turf. The face of the cliff is studded with stony pimples; its formation being the conglomerate, or pudding-stone, intermingled with schists. Color excepted, these rocks really look like the artificial cement used in laying the foundations of ponderous structures. They appear to resist the action of the sea with less power than the granite of the north coast. Masses of fallen rock are grouped along the beach underneath the cliff, around which the rising waves seethe and foam and hiss.

A persistent pedestrian, having reached the shore at Easton's Beach, may pass around the southern limb of the island to Fort Adams. He may then make his way back to town by the Fort Road, or take the little ferry-boat plying between Newport and Jamestown, on Canonicut. This ramble has been much, yet not undeservingly, praised.

My first walk here was on one of those rare October days that are to the New England climate what the bloom is to the peach. The air, after the sun had swept aside the vapors arising from the ocean, was intoxicating; it was so light and crystal, it seemed as if it might put new life into the most confirmed valetudinarian. On one side the sea glittered like silvery scales on fine armor. The intruding promontories of Sachuest and Seconnet bathed their feet in tranquil waves; and as the eye roved along the horizon it lodged an instant on the island known as Cormorant Rock, betrayed by the whitening foam around it. In the farthest sea-board a dark cloud of brooding vapor prolonged the land in seeming, and veiled the approach of ships.

THE BEACH.

Along the verge of the cliff where I walked the dash of the surf frequently tossed a shower of fine spray as high as the shelf itself, drenching the grass, and immeshing for an instant among its myriad drops the fleeting hues of the rainbow. The rocks had a prevailing purple mass of color, fringed at the edge with green grass, that sometimes crept down the face of the cliff and toyed with its wrinkles.

These rocks, constantly varnished by sea-spray, sparkle with glancing lights that relieve the hardness of their angular lineaments. As you walk on, they are always presenting new profiles of grotesque resemblances. Yet not a sphinx of them all would tell how long the sea had been battering at their rugged features, or of the fire that had baked their tooth-defying pudding—Old Ocean's daily repast. Now and then, when standing on the brink of some table-rock, the plunge of a billow underneath caused a sensible tremor. At various points the descent of the cliffs is facilitated by steps, and at proper stages of the tide the outlying rocks are the favorite resort of anglers for tautog, bass, and perch. The Forty Steps are of note as conducting to Conrad's Cave, a favorite haunt of lovers who have heart secrets they may no longer keep. The ways of such people are past finding out. At Niagara vows are whispered at the brink of the cataract. Perchance there is a savor of romance about these old sea caverns which plain matter-of-fact folk may not fathom.

Turning away from the sea, the rambler perceives the long line of cottages, villas, and country houses, Swiss, Italian, English, or nondescript, to which these territories pertain.[1] These houses represent the best and at the same time the most rational feature of a semi-residence at the sea-side. People are really at home, and may enjoy the natural beauties of their situation without the disadvantages inseparable from hotel life. To be sure, at Newport it is only Murray Hill or Beacon Hill transplanted. The social system revolves with much the same regularity as the planetary, and with no abatement of its exclusive privileges. But home life or cottage life at the sea-side is within the means of all those possessing moderate incomes, who are content to dispense with luxury or more house-room than they know what to do with; and it is remarkable how little may serve one's turn where outdoor life is the desideratum. Those who are content to leave all the surplusage at home, whether of frivolity or luggage, and honestly mean to enjoy the shore for itself, come where they may forget the world, the flesh, and money-getting. To this sort of life—a hint borrowed of English seaside customs—Newport has led the way. At Oak Bluffs a city has sprung into existence on this plan, and the shores of New England are dotted with little red-roofed cottages.

If he has come to the cliffs by the Bath road, the visitor sees, almost at the beginning of his ramble, the summer cottage of Charlotte Cushman, whose career has some resemblance to that of the gifted Mrs. Siddons. Both were poor

CLIFF WALK.

---

[1] Many of these so-called cottages cost from $50,000 to $200,000. For the season, $2000 is considered a moderate rental, and $5000 is frequently paid.

girls at the outset of their professional lives. The Englishwoman, even after she became famous, usually refused invitations to the houses of the great or opulent, excusing herself from accepting them on the ground that all her time was due to the public, whose continued favor she wished to merit by unremitting application to her studies.

Whatever money or taste or art has been able to do toward the embellishment of the grounds along the cliffs—and in this category are included Bellevue and other favored avenues—has not been omitted. A horticulturist would see something to notice everywhere. As the houses stand well back from the shore, the space between is laid out in bright-hued *parterres*, that look like Persian carpets spread on the well-kept lawns. The eye at times fairly revels in sumptuous masses of color. Yet Newport was now deserted by the fashionable world, in the month of months, when sea and shore are incomparably enticing and satisfying.

THE CLIFFS.

In the angle formed by the meeting of Ocean and Carroll avenues is Lily Pond, where knights of the rod love to loiter and cast a line. If still pursuing the cliffs, you pass by Gooseberry Island, whither the old-time magnates were wont to wend for fishing, bathing, and drinking-bouts. Spouting Rock, where, in gales, inrolling seas are forced high in air, lies this way. Bass Rock, of piscatory renown, and Brenton's Reef, the place of wrecks, show their jagged sides. Point Judith and Block Island are visible from Castle Hill, where in former times a watch-tower stood. No other day of the seven in Newport is quite equal to Fort Day. Then the very long line of equipages directs itself upon the point where Fort Adams is located. On this gala-day the commandant keeps open house, with colors flying, music playing, and gates opened wide. The procession winds around the parade, a very moving picture

A NEWPORT COTTAGE.

of peace in the lap of war. Gay scarfs instead of battle-flags wave, jewels instead of steel, and dog-carts instead of ammunition-carts flash and rumble. The crash, glitter, and animation are reminders of Hyde Park Corner or the Bois de Boulogne. The soldiers I saw were much improved in appearance since the war, and now seemed really proud of the dress they wore. They paced the jetty and rampart in jaunty shakos, white gloves, and well-fitting uniforms, as men not ashamed of themselves, and of whom Uncle Sam need not be ashamed.

CHARLOTTE CUSHMAN'S RESIDENCE.

Fort Adams was begun in the administration of the president whose name it bears. The father of the American navy intended Newport as a station for her squadrons of the future. To this end fortifications were begun, designed to guarantee the approaches to the harbor. At this time we were dreading our late ally, France, more than any other European power. Fortifying Newport against France now seems incredible, yet the Directory, with citizen Talleyrand at the helm, would either mould American politics to its will or trample the ancient amity in the dust. In 1798, a French cruiser, after the capture of several American vessels, had the impudence to bring her prize into one of our own ports to escape the more dreaded English.[1] Mr. Adams brought citizen Talleyrand and the Directoire Exécutif to their senses;[2] but Mr. Jefferson, who decidedly leaned to the French side of European politics, stopped the work begun by his predecessor.

SPOUTING ROCK.

In 1800, Mr. Humphreys, the naval constructer, was sent to examine the New England ports with regard to their eligibility as great national dock-yards. He reported that Newport possessed by far the most suitable harbor for such an establishment.

Fort Adams was chiefly constructed under the watchful supervision of the accomplished engineer, General J. G. Totten. It is said that during the progress of the work a full set of plans of the fortress mysteriously disappeared, and as mysteriously re-appeared after a long interval. It is believed in certain quarters that copies of these drawings might be found in the topographical bureau of the British War Office.

Before setting out for the campaign of 1812, the Emperor Napoleon, as Bourrienne relates, wished to have exact information respecting Ragusa and Illyria. He sent for Marmont, whose answers were not satisfactory. He then interrogated different generals to as little purpose. Dejean, inspector of engineers, was then summoned. "Have you," demanded the emperor, "among your officers any one who is acquainted with Ragusa?"

Dejean, after a moment's reflection, answered, "Sire, there is a chief of battalion who has been a long time forgotten, who is well acquainted with Ragusa."

"What do you call him?"

"Bernard."

"Ah, stop a little; Bernard—I recollect that name. Where is he?"

---

[1] "R. Goodloe Harper's Speeches, p. 275."
[2] By smashing their frigates, *L'Insurgente, La Vengeance, Berceau*, and making it generally unpleasant for them.

"Sire, he is at Antwerp, employed upon the fortifications."

"Send notice by the telegraph that he instantly mount his horse and repair to Paris."

The promptitude with which the emperor's orders were always executed is well known. A few days afterward Bernard was in Paris at the house of General Dejean, and shortly after in the cabinet of the emperor. He was graciously received, and Napoleon immediately said, "Tell me about Ragusa." When Bernard had done speaking, the emperor said, "*Colonel* Bernard, I now know Ragusa." He then conversed familiarly with him, and having a plan of the works at Antwerp before him, showed how he would successfully besiege the place. The newly made colonel explained so well how he would defend himself against the emperor's attacks that Napoleon was delighted, and immediately bestowed upon him a mark of distinction which, says Bourrienne, "he never, to my knowledge, granted but upon this one occasion." As he was going to preside at the council he desired Colonel Bernard to accompany him, and several times during the sitting requested his opinion upon the points under discussion. On the breaking-up of the council, Napoleon said to him, "You are my aid-de-camp."

Bourrienne continues: "At the end of the campaign he was made general of brigade; shortly after, general of division; and he is now known throughout Europe as the first officer of engineers in existence. A piece of folly of Clarke's[1] has deprived France of the services of this distinguished man, who, after refusing most brilliant offers made to him by different sovereigns of Europe, has retired to the United States of America, where he commands the engineers, and where he has constructed on the side of the Floridas fortifications which are by engineers declared to be masterpieces of military skill."[2]

Bernard came to the United States in 1816, and was associated with the late General Totten in carrying out the now discarded system of sea-coast fortifications. It is said that Colonel M'Cree, then chief of engineers, resigned rather than serve under him. Accord between the French engineer and Colonel Totten was only secured by a division of the works, and agreement to accept, on the part of each, the other's plans. Bernard wished to construct one great fortress, like Antwerp or the once famous strongholds of the Quadrilateral. Fortress Monroe is the result of this idea. He also planned the defenses of Mobile.[3]

From Fort Adams it is a short sail across to the Dumplings, and the circular tower of stone, built also in the administration of John Adams. This work, now in ruins, is second only in picturesqueness to the Old Stone Mill,

---

[1] Duke de Feltre, French minister of war.
[2] He afterward returned to France, and was made minister of war.
[3] Fort Morgan was constructed by him with twelve posterns, a statement significant to military engineers. General Totten closed six of them, and the Confederates, when besieged, all but two.

if indeed it should yield the first place to that singular structure. The parapet has crumbled, and the bomb-proofs are choked with rubbish. It is about

THE DUMPLINGS.

a hundred feet from the crown of the parapet to the water, and, though the elevation is inconsiderable, is one of the choice points of observation in Narraganset Bay. The neighboring rocks are of good report among fishermen, and the tower and its neighborhood are places much affected by picnic parties. Taken altogether, the old fort on Canonicut, with its swarthy rock foundations, is one of the last objects to fade from the recollection. Seen with the setting sun gilding the broken rampart or glancing from out its blackened embrasures, it embodies something of the idea of an antique castle by the sea.

Being here on the island of Canonicut, the visitor will find it pleasant sauntering along the shores, or across a broad, smooth road leading to the farther side of the island and the ferry to the opposite main-land. The water between is called the Western Passage. When I saw it, not fewer than a hundred vessels were lying wind-bound, their sails spread to catch the first puff of the land-breeze. Dutch Island, with its light-house, appears in full view, about midway of the passage. The rock formation of this side of Canonicut is largely slate, with abundant intrusion of white quartz. Along the beach the slate is so decomposed as to give way to the pressure of the foot.

Canonicut is a beautiful island, with graceful slopes and fertile soil. It is here, on the northern end, a cottage city is designed of summer houses, accessible to people who do not keep footmen or carriages, or give champagne breakfasts. Five hundred acres have been laid out in avenues, parks, and drives: the shores, by special reservation, are to remain forever open for the equal enjoyment of all who resort hither.[1]

At the coming of D'Estaing and the French fleet, Canonicut was garrisoned by Brown's provincial corps, and two regiments of Anspach, who were compelled to evacuate it. The French land troops then took possession of

---

[1] Canonicut is about seven miles long, its longest axis lying almost north and south. It includes a single township, incorporated 1678, by the name of Jamestown. The island was purchased from the Indians in 1657. Prudence Island, six miles long, is also attached to Jamestown.

the Dumpling and Beaver Tail batteries.[1] In the year 1749 a light-house was erected on Beaver Tail.

Newport has not treasured the memory of the Hessians. They were never in favor, being about equally feared and hated. At the battle of Long Island they pinned American soldiers to the trees with their bayonets. Loaded down with arms and accoutrements, they marched and fought with equal phlegm. As foragers they were even more to be dreaded than in battle, as they usually stripped a garden or a house of its last root or crust. Brutalized by the removal of the only incentive that is honorable in the soldier, they lived or died at so much per head.

Newport as a British garrison was the resort of numbers of courtesans, many of whom had followed the army from New York. Quarrels between Hessian and British officers, growing out of their amours, were frequent. A Hessian major and captain at last fought a duel about a woman of the town, in which glorious cause the major was run through the body and killed. General Prescott then ordered all the authors of these troubles to be confined in Newport jail.

HESSIAN GRENADIER.

Driving in Newport is one of the duties the fashionable world owes to itself and to society. On every fine day between four in the afternoon and dusk Bellevue Avenue is thronged with equipages, equestrians, and promenaders. Nowhere in America can so many elegant turnouts be seen as here: every species of vehicle known to the wheeled vocabulary is in requisition. The cortége is not, as might be supposed, a racing mob, but a decorous-paced, well-reined procession—a sort of reunion upon wheels of all that is brilliant and fascinating in Newport society. The quiet though elegant carriages with crests on them are Bostonian; the most "stylish" horse-furniture and mettled horses are at home in Central

---

[1] At this time four British frigates and several smaller craft were destroyed. The French forced the passage on the west of Canonicut, and raised the blockade of Providence.

COAST SCENE, NEWPORT.

Park; Philadelphia is self-contained, and of substantial elegance. Imagine this pageant of beautiful women and cultivated men passing and repassing, mingling and separating, smiling, saluting, admiring, and admired; the steady beat of hoofs on the hard gravel and continuous roll of wheels proceeding without intermission, until the whole becomes bewildering, confused, and indistinct, as if the whirl of wheels were indeed "in your brain."

When "The Drive" is spoken of, that through Bellevue and Ocean avenues —with, on Fort days (Wednesdays and Fridays), the *détour* to the fortress and so back to town—is meant. Another charming drive is by the Bath road, then skirting the beaches, to continue on through Middletown, where the hills are still blistered with the remains of Revolutionary intrenchments. Paradise and Purgatory are both reached by this road, and are within easy distance of any part of Newport.

On two occasions when I crossed the beaches the sea was running too heavily to make bathing practicable. The surf, too, was much discolored with sea-wrack and the nameless rubbish it is always turning over and over. Groups of bathing-houses were dispersed along the upper margin of the strand.

THE DRIVE.

They are not much larger than, and bear a strong resemblance to, sentry-boxes. When feasible, bathing is regulated by signals, flags of different colors being used to designate the hours assigned to males or females. The floor of the beach is hard and gently shelving. There being little tide, a plunge into the sea may be enjoyed without danger from quicksands or under-tow.

On the eastern side of Easton's Point, which divides what would otherwise be a continuous beach into two, is Purgatory Bluff, a mass of conglomerate split asunder by some unknown process of nature. The two faces of the fissure appear to correspond to each other, but no other force than that which smote may restore them. A place used to be shown on the irregular surface of the rocks above where the Evil Spirit of the red men once dragged a squaw, and, in spite of her frantic

PURGATORY BLUFF.

struggles, which might be traced, dispatched her, and flung the body into the chasm. Another and more recent legend is, that here a lover was dared by his mistress to leap across the chasm, some fourteen feet, her glove to be the guerdon of his success. The feat was performed, but the lover flung the glove into the face of his silly mistress. What seems curious in these fractures of pudding-stone, the pebbles break in the same direction as the mass of rock.[1]

---

[1] The chasm is one hundred and sixty feet in length, with an average depth of about sixty feet.

Hanging Rock, a favorite haunt of good Dean Berkeley, is a cavity or shelf where it would be practicable to sit, and, while looking off to sea, indulge in dreamy musings. Half a mile farther on is the house he built, and afterward, on his departure from the country, gave to Yale. It bears the pretending name of Whitehall, for, though comfortable-looking, it is little palatial.

The dean, it is said, told the painter, Smibert, who ventured to betray some distrust of his patron's sanguine belief in the future importance of Newport, "Truly, you have very little foresight, for in fifty years' time every foot of land in this place will be as valuable as in Cheapside." If he indeed made the remark attributed to him, he was only a century or so out of his reckoning.

WHITEHALL.

The name and fame of George, Bishop of Cloyne, the friend of Swift and of Steele, the professor of an ideal philosophy, and the projector of a Utopian scheme for evangelizing and educating the Indians, is dear to the people of Newport. He came to America in 1728 with the avowed purpose of establishing a college, "to be erected on the Summer Islands," the "still vext Bermoothes" of Shakspeare.

Berkeley is perhaps more familiar to American readers by four lines—of which the first is as often misquoted as any literary fragment I can call to mind—than by his philosophical treatises:

> "Westward the course of empire takes its way;
> The four first acts already past,
> A fifth shall close the drama with the day:
> Time's noblest offspring is the last."

The residence of the dean at Newport was a forced retirement, the sum of twenty thousand pounds promised by Sir Robert Walpole in aid of his college never having been paid. In this college, "he most exorbitantly proposed," as Swift humorously remarked, "a whole hundred pounds a year for himself, forty pounds for a fellow, and ten for a student." Seven years were passed in literary pursuits; "The Minute Philosopher," of which no one who comes to Newport may go ignorant away, being the offspring of his meditations. Along with the dean came John Smibert, of whose canvases a few remain scattered over New England, and whose chief excellence lay in infusing the love of his art into such men as Copley, Trumbull, and Allston.[1] Pope assigns to Berkeley "every virtue under heaven." There is no question but that he was as amiable and learned as he was thoroughly speculative and unpractical.

The return to town by Honyman's Hill, named from the first pastor of Trinity, is thoroughly enjoyable and interesting. The historical student may here see how near the Americans were advanced toward the capture of Newport. An old windmill or two or a farmhouse are picturesque objects by the way.

"I saw," says Miss Martineau, "the house which Berkeley built in Rhode Island — built in the particular spot where it is, that he might have to pass, in his rides, over the hill which lies between it and Newport, and feast himself with the tranquil beauty of the sea, the bay, and the downs as they appear from the ridge of the eminence. I saw the pile of rocks, with its ledges and recesses, where he is said to have meditated and composed his 'Minute Philosopher.' It was at first melancholy to visit these his retreats, and think how empty the land still is of the philosophy he loved."

WASHINGTON PARK, NEWPORT.

---

[1] Smibert planned the original Faneuil Hall, Boston. Trumbull painted in the studio left vacant by Smibert.

D'ESTAING.

CHAPTER XXIV.

THE FRENCH AT NEWPORT.

"Grenadiers, rendez-vous!"
"La Garde meurt et ne se rend pas."
"Braves Français, rendez-vous; vous serez traités comme les premiers soldats du monde."
"*La garde meurt et ne se rend pas.*"—OLD GUARD AT WATERLOO.

ANOTHER phase of Newport in by-gone days was the sojourn of our French allies in the Revolution. Then there were real counts, and dukes, and marquises in Newport. There had also been a British occupation; but the troops of his Britannic Majesty ruined the town, humiliated its pride, and crushed its prejudices under an armed heel. On the other hand, the French soldiers respected property, were considerate in their treatment of the inhabitants, and paid scrupulously for every thing they took. In time of war a garrisoned town is usually about equally abused by friend or enemy. Here the approach of the French was dreaded, and their departure regarded as a misfortune.

Apropos to the good behavior of our French friends is the testimony of an eye-witness, who says: " The different deputations of savages who came to view their camp exhibited no surprise at the sight of the cannon, the troops, or of their exercise; but they could not recover from their astonishment at seeing apple-trees loaded with fruit above the tents which the soldiers had been occupying for three months." The English, during their occupation, had burned almost the last forest-tree on the island.

The astonishing spectacle of monarchy aiding democracy against itself is one of the reflections suggested by the alliance. Besides Louis Seize, other crowned heads would willingly have helped America as against the old "Termagant of the Seas," had not the idea been too illogical. The Empress Catherine II. is reported as having hinted, in a private interview with Sir James Harris,[1] at the possibility of restoring European peace by renouncing the struggle England was making with her American colonies. "May I ask your Majesty," said the *ruse* old Briton, "if this would be your policy in case the colonies had belonged to you?"

"J'aimerais mieux perdre ma tête," replied the empress (I would sooner lose my head).

Kaiser Joseph repulsed the idea with equal candor and bluntness: "Madame, mon métier à moi c'est d'être royaliste." (Madam, my trade is to be a royalist).

This was not the first move France had made to detach the American colonies from the British crown. Far back in the day of the Puritans the thing had been attempted. Again, in 1767, M. de Choiseul dispatched Baron De Kalb on a secret mission. The baron came, saw, and made his report. He wrote from Boston in March, 1768, that he did not believe it possible to induce the Americans to accept foreign aid, on account of their fixed faith in their sovereign's justice.[2] We were still, while growling, licking the hand that smote us. And this little fragment shows that before the day of Caron Beaumarchais, of "Sleek Silas," of "Sleek Benjamin," the idea of assistance was already germinating. France was to heave away at the old British empire as soon as she had found a fulcrum on which to rest her lever.

D'Estaing came first to Newport; but his appearance, like that of a meteor, was very brilliant and very brief. Besides being vice-admiral, he was also lieutenant-general, and brought with him something in excess of fifteen hundred land soldiers, without counting the marines of his fleet. The chevalier advanced his squadron in two divisions, one ascending the Narraganset, the other the Seconnet passage. He cannonaded Sir Robert Pigot's batteries, de-

---

[1] British ambassador at St. Petersburg, afterward Lord Malmesbury.
[2] Massachusetts Files.

stroyed some British vessels, and caused some addition to the national debt of England. Then, when the pear was ready to fall, at sight of Earl Howe's fleet he put to sea, and was battered by his lordship and by storms until he brought his shattered vessels into Boston Harbor, where he should refit, and taste Governor Hancock's wine.

The Americans, who had advanced under Sullivan within two miles of Newport—old continentals, militia, and volunteer corps, full of fight and confident of success—were obliged to withdraw in good order but bad temper. Sullivan secured his retreat by a brilliant little action at the head of the island.

EARL HOWE.

The French at Boston found themselves very ill received. They were accused of having abandoned, betrayed Sullivan. French sailors and soldiers were beaten in the streets, and their officers seriously wounded in attempting to quell affrays with the populace. D'Estaing conducted himself with great circumspection. He refused to press the punishment of the leaders in these outrages; but, stung by the imputation of cowardice, offered to put himself, a vice-admiral of France, with seven hundred men, under the orders of Sullivan, who, says a French historian, "was lately nothing but a lawyer."

An extraordinary number of personages, distinguished in the Revolution, or under the empire, its successor, served France in America. The heads of many fell under the guillotine. In this way perished D'Estaing. He was in Paris during the Reign of Terror, and present at the trial of Marie Antoinette. One of those ladies who met him at Boston describes him as of dignified presence, affable, and gracious.

With D'Estaing came Jourdan, a shop-keeper, and the son of a doctor. At sixteen he was the comrade of Rochambeau, and in the same regiment Montcalm had commanded in 1743. The Limousin shows with pride to the stranger the old wooden house, with dark front, in which the conqueror of Fleurus was born. The marshal who had commanded the army of the *Sambre et Meuse* became the scape-goat of Vittoria.

After D'Estaing came Rochambeau, and with him a crowd of young officers of noble birth, fortune's favorites, who yet sought with the eagerness of knights-errant to enroll themselves in the ranks of the alliance. Gay, careless, chivalric, and debonair, carrying their high-bred courtesy even to the front of battle, they were worthy

ROCHAMBEAU.

sons of the men who at Fontenoy advanced, hat in hand, from the ranks, and saluted their English enemies: "Apres vous, messieurs les Anglais; nous ne tirons jamais les premiers" (After you, gentlemen; we never fire first).

Having in some respects remained much as when the French were here, there is no greater difficulty in beating our imaginary *rappel* than in supposing Newport peopled when walking at night through its deserted streets.

We suppose an intrenched camp drawn across the island from the sea to the harbor, having town, fleet, and transports under its wing, and batteries on all the points and islands. Twelve days sufficed to secure the position to the satisfaction of Rochambeau, who shrugged his shoulders, saying, as another and greater said after him, "I have them now, these English." Yet Washington, remembering Long Island and Fort Washington, wrote in July to General Heath, "I wish the Count de Rochambeau had taken a position on the main."[1]

ROCHAMBEAU'S HEAD-QUARTERS.

Under British rule, Newport wore a muzzle; under French, a collar bristling with steel. The white standard was unfolded to the breeze in all the camps and from the masts of shipping. Tents and marquees were pitched along the line and dotted the green of Canonicut, Rose Island, Coaster's and Goat islands. Bayonets brightly and cannon duskily flashed in the sun everywhere. Sentinels in white uniforms, black gaiters, and woolen epaulets tramped in little paths of their own making. Officers in white, splendidly gold-embroidered, with rich and elegant side-arms, put to the blush such of our poor fellows as chanced in their camps. In every shady spot groups of soldiers, gay and jovial, reclined on the grass, chattering all together, or laughing at the witticism of the company *gaillard*. The drum—the type military, which has scarcely changed its form

LOUIS XVI.

---

[1] Heath then commanded at Providence: he was ordered to meet Rochambeau on his arrival, and extend any assistance in his power.

in three hundred years — was improvised into the card-table. "*Ma fois*," "*paroles d'honneur*," "*sacrés*," and "*milles tonnerres*," flew thickly as bullets at Fontenoy.

A finer body of men had probably never taken the field. Many were seasoned in the Seven Years' War. Perfectly disciplined, commanded by generals of experience, they only asked to be led against the hereditary enemy of France. Officers who had mounted guard at the Tuileries, and had been intimate with crowned heads, embraced the campaign with the careless vivacity of school-boys.

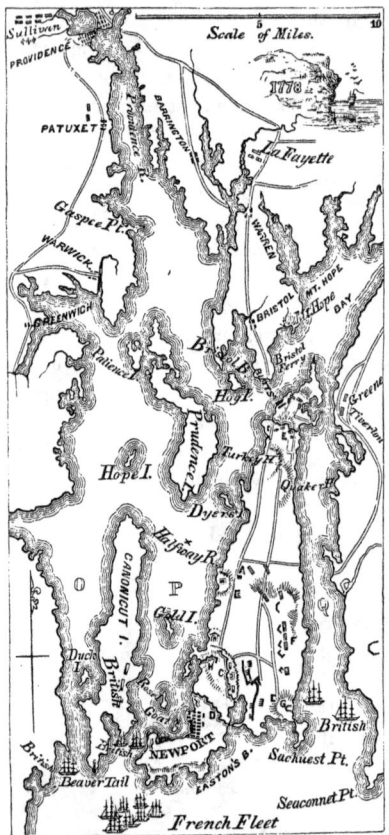

MILITARY MAP OF RHODE ISLAND, 1778.

In the present region of old houses is a mansion having a high air of respectability; it is situated at the corner of Clarke and Mary streets, and known as the Vernon House. This was the *Quartier Général* of the Count Rochambeau, one of the four supreme generals of France in those days. The count was a brave old soldier, rather short in stature, rather inclined to fat, with a humane soul and noble heart. He was hampered by his instructions, and his army lost time here, to the vexation of Washington, and chagrin, it is believed, of himself. Hear what he says when teased by a younger soldier to begin the fighting:

"I owe it to the most scrupulous examination of my conscience, that of about fifteeen thousand men killed or wounded under my orders in different grades and in the bloodiest actions, I have not to reproach myself with having caused the death of a single one to gratify my own ambition.

"LE VIEUX PÈRE ROCHAMBEAU."

It was to Lafayette, burning with the desire to see his countrymen signalize their coming otherwise than by balls, routs, and reviews, that the letter was addressed. Rochambeau was under the orders of Washington, yet many of his officers disliked being commanded by Lafayette, their junior in military service, or by lawyers, blacksmiths, and book-sellers.

THE FRENCH AT NEWPORT.

The career of M. de Ternay, admiral of the fleet, was soon ended. He died in Newport, and was buried in Trinity Church-yard. One of Rochambeau's staff-officers ascribes his death to chagrin in consequence of having permitted five English ships to escape him without a general engagement. These ships were then on their way to join Admiral Rodney. It is certain he was openly denounced by many officers of rank for too great caution. Rochambeau says:

LAFAYETTE.

"Newport, December 18th, 1780.

"I set out from here on the 12th to visit Boston and M. Hancock, leaving here M. de Ternay with a slight fever, which announced nothing serious. On the 16th, in the morning, I received a courier from Baron de Vioménil, announcing his death on the morning of the 15th. I returned at once, and reached here yesterday evening."

A mural tablet of black marble inscribed with golden letters was sent from France. The admiral's grave happening not to be contiguous to the church or church-yard wall, a wall was built to support the slab. Since then it has been removed to the vestibule of Trinity Church, and a granite stone, at the instance of the Marquis de Noailles, has replaced it above the grave. The first house, built in 1702, was succeeded in 1726 by the present edifice. An organ was presented by Bishop Berkeley, whose infant daughter lies in the church-yard.

In March, 1781, Washington, accompanied by Lafayette, came to Newport, and was received by Rochambeau in the Vernon House. The curious interest with which the American general was regarded by his allies is sufficiently evident in their accounts of him. He at once commanded all their admiration and respect, and was perhaps their only ideal not destroyed by actual contact. They still show the visitor the house in Church Street where Washington led the dance with "the beautiful Miss Champlin," and where the French officers, taking the instruments from the musicians' hands, played the minuet, "A successful Campaign."

BARON VIOMÉNIL.

Another of the *noblesse* of the army was the Viscount de Noailles, in whose regiment Napoleon was afterward a subaltern. Two grateful tasks fell to his share in the war. As ambassador to England, he delivered to Lord Weymouth intelligence of the alliance and acknowledgment of the independence of the thirteen States. His manner was said to have been very offensive, and considered tantamount to a challenge. An equally agreeable duty devolved upon him as one of the commissioners to arrange the capitulation of Yorktown.

The alliance was a bitter draught for England. She offered, in 1781, to cede Minorca to Russia if the empress would effect a peace between France, Spain, and herself; but stipulated that there should be an express condition that the French should immediately evacuate Rhode Island and every other part of his Majesty's colonies in America; "no stipulation or agreement whatever to be made with regard to H. M. rebellious subjects, who could never be suffered to treat through the medium of a foreign power."

TRINITY CHURCH.

The Dutch republic, influenced by John Adams, having declared for the alliance, England demanded satisfaction. Then Frederick the Great got his "dander" up. Said he, "Puisque les Anglais veulent la guerre avec tout le monde, ils l'auront" (Since the English wish war with all the world, they shall have it). So much for him who was then called in the court circles of Europe "Le Vieux de la Mon-

CHASTELLUX.

THE FRENCH AT NEWPORT.

tagne" (Old Man of the Mountain). Spain was arming. England continued to ply the empress through her favorite and debauchee, Potemkin. Russia, as head of the Northern League, now held the key of European politics. Potemkin was too adroit for British diplomacy. It is believed he had a secret understanding with the French ambassador, as the doctors whom Molière makes say to each other, "Passez-moi la rhubarbe et je vous passerai le séne."

In this same year, 1781, the mediating powers, Russia and Austria, proposed an armistice for a year, during which hostilities were to be suspended and peace negotiated. The American colonies were to be admitted to this arrangement, and no treaty signed in which they were not included. Lord Stormont, in notifying the refusal of England to this proposal, declining any intervention between herself and her colonies, pointed out that, in the then state of the struggle in America, a suspension of hostilities would be fatal to the success of his Majesty's arms.

England could not disentangle the knot of European politics, and Yorktown brought her to her knees. Many of the Continental powers openly rejoiced at her humiliation; Catharine could scarcely dissemble her joy. The news reached London on Sunday, November 25th. Lord Walsingham, who had been under-secretary of state, happened to be with Lord Germain when the messengers arrived. Without mentioning the disaster to any other persons, the two peers took a hackney-coach and drove to Lord Stormont's, in Portland Place. Imparting their intelligence, his lordship joined them, and they proceeded to the chancellor's, where, after a short consultation, it was determined they would communicate it in person to Lord North. The first minister's firmness, and even his presence of mind, gave way under this crushing blow. He is represented as having received it "as he would have taken a ball in his breast, for he opened his arms, exclaiming wildly, as he paced up and down the apartment, 'O God! it is all over!'"

LAUZUN.

The American is now living who will see justice done the memory of George III. He was neither a bad king nor a bad man. Like his antagonist, Louis Seize, he was possessed of strong good sense, which accounts, perhaps, says one, for the decapitation of Louis by the French. A well-informed authority attributes the insanity of George III. to the revolt of his American colonies. Just as he was taken ill, in 1788, he said, after the last levee he held, to Lord Thurlow, who was advising him to take care of himself, and return to Windsor, "You, then, too, my Lord Thurlow, forsake me and suppose me ill beyond recovery; but whatever you and Mr. Pitt may think or feel, I, that am born a gentleman, shall never lay my head on my last pillow in peace and quiet as long as I remember the loss of my American colonies."[1]

But to come back to our Frenchmen. Of others whose sabres and spurs have clanked or jingled on the well-worn door-stone of the Vernon House was Biron, better known as the *roué* Lauzun. There being no forage on the island, Lauzun's cavalry and the artillery horses were sent for the winter to Lebanon, Connecticut, a place the duke compares to Siberia. Lauzun had the talents that seduce men as well as women. Traveled, speaking English well, gay and audacious, he was among men the model of a finished gentleman, and among women the type of such dangerous raillery that many, in order to control him, gave the lie to the proverb, "We hate whom we fear."

MATHIEU DUMAS.

At Berlin Lauzun had been a prodigious favorite with Frederick. His connection with the Duke d'Orleans (Egalité) proved his ruin. At forty-six, having unsuccessfully commanded the republican armies in La Vendée, he was guillotined in 1793. Mademoiselle Laurent, his mistress, attended him to the last. He would not let his hands be tied. "We are both Frenchmen," said he to the executioner; "we shall do our duty." Thus *exit* Biron, capable of every thing, good for nothing.

The elegant and accomplished Marquis Chastellux, whose *petits soupers* at Newport were the talk of every one who had the good fortune to be invited, and whose "Travels in America," partly printed on board the French fleet, are so charmingly written; the brave Baron Vioménil, second in command, distinguished for gallantry

DEUX-PONTS.

at Yorktown; headlong Charles Lameth, who fought the young Duke de Castries in the Bois de Boulogne; Mathieu Dumas, aid to Rochambeau, and af-

---

[1] The manner and matter of his reception of Mr. Adams were equally those of gentleman and king. Contrast him with the Prince Regent, and his remark to the French ex-minister, Calonne, during his father's sudden illness, in 1801: "Savez-vous, Monsieur de Calonne, que mon père est aussi fou que jamais?" (Do you know, Monsieur de Calonne, that my father is as crazy as ever?) Thackeray could not do him justice.

terward fighting at Waterloo, were prominent figures in an army pre-eminent among armies for the distinction of its leaders.

La Peyrouse, in October, made his escape through the English blockade during a severe gale, in which his vessel was dismasted; though, fortunately, not until the enemy had given up the chase. He carried with him Rochambeau's son, charged with an account of the conference at Hartford and the necessities of the Americans.

Berthier, the military confidant of Napoleon, was of this army. He embarked for America, a captain of dragoons in the regiment of Lorraine, and here won the epaulets of a colonel. There were also two brothers serving under the name of Counts Deux-Ponts. One of them, Count Christian Deux-Ponts, was captured by Nelson, while on a boat excursion with several friends, off Porto Cavallo. Southey, in his "Life of Lord Nelson," says he was a prince of the German Empire, and brother to the heir of the Electorate of Bavaria. Nelson, then a young captain, after giving his prisoners a good dinner, released them.[1]

DE BARRAS.

It would require a broad muster-roll merely to enumerate the distinguished of Rochambeau's expeditionary army. I have not yet mentioned De Broglie, Vauban, Champcenetz, Chabannes, De Melfort, and Talleyrand; nor De Barras, La Touche, and La Clocheterie; nor Désoteux, leader of Chouans in the French Revolution. To have withstood the assaults of so much wit, gallantry, and condescension, Newport must have been a city of vestals; yet, according to the good Abbé Robin, his countrymen gave few examples of that gallantry for which their nation is famed. One remarkable instance of a wife reclaimed, when on the point of yielding to the seductions of an epauleted stranger, is related by him. The story has a fine moral for husbands as well as wives.

The expected arrival of this army spread terror in Newport. The French had been represented as man-eaters, whereas they were only frog-eaters. The country was deserted, and those whom curiosity had brought to Newport encountered nobody in the streets. Rochambeau landed in the evening. These fears were soon dissipated by the exact discipline enforced in the camps. They tell of pigs and fowls passing unmolested, and of fields of corn standing untouched in their midst.

Beautiful Miss Champlin, charming Redwood, the *distingué* Misses Hunter, and the Quaker vestal, Polly Lawton, are names escaped to us from the

---

[1] The fellow-prisoner of Count Christian Deux-Ponts was an Irishman, named Lynch, who belonged also to Rochambeau's army. Fearful that his nationality might be discovered, he begged the count to be on his guard. When at table, and heated with wine, the secret was divulged by the count; but Nelson, as Segur relates, pretended not to have heard it.

memoirs of Gallic admirers; yet there was only a single suicide in the French ranks justly chargeable to an American love account;[1] and this did not occur in Newport.

One of the French regiments at Yorktown was as famous in Old-World annals as any battalion that ever stood under arms. This was the regiment of Auvergne. Wherever men might march, Auvergne was seen or heard. Once, when in the advance of the army — it was always there — one of its captains, sent out to reconnoitre, was surrounded in the darkness by foes. A hundred bayonets were leveled at his breast. "Speak above a whisper and you die," said the German officer. Captain D'Assas saw himself in the midst of a multitude of enemies, who were stealthily approaching his weary and unsuspecting comrades. In an instant his resolution was taken. Raising himself to his full height, that he might give his voice greater effect, he cried out, "À moi, Auvergne! voilà les ennemis!"[2] and fell dead as the French drums beat "To arms!" The regiment was very proud of its motto, "*Sans tache*."

LATOUR D'AUVERGNE.

In this regiment was Philip d'Auvergne, "the first grenadier of France," of whose prowess stories little less than marvelous are told. When the corps came to America its name had been changed to Gatinais, whereat there was much grumbling among these aged mustaches. There were two redoubts at Yorktown to be taken. One was assigned to Lafayette and his Americans, the other to the French. The grenadiers of Gatinais were to lead this attack; and, as it was expected to be bloody, Rochambeau himself addressed them. "My friends," said he,

---

[1] That of Major Galvan, who pistoled himself on account of unrequited love.
[2] Rally, Auvergne! here is the enemy!

"if I should want you this night, I hope you have not forgotten that we have served together in that brave regiment of Auvergne, '*Sans Tache.*'" "Promise, general, to give us back our old name, and we will suffer ourselves to be killed, to the last man." The promise was given, the redoubt won, and King Louis confirmed the pledge. In token of its peerless valor Washington presented the regiment with one of the captured cannon.

The comfortable and contented lives of the French soldiers daily astonished our poor and tattered, but unconquerable ragamuffins. At parade they appeared so neat and gentleman-like as hardly to be distinguished from their officers. They were paid every week, and seemed to want for nothing. No sentinel was allowed to stand on his post without a warm watch-coat to cover him. The officers treated their soldiers with attention, humanity, and respect, neglecting no means of inculcating sentiments of honor. Stealing was held by them in abhorrence. As a consequence, punishments were extremely rare, desertions unfrequent, and the health of the troops excellent.

Speculations more or less unfavorable to French disinterestedness, more or less destructive of American enthusiasm for the alliance, must arise from a knowledge of the secret policy of France in coming to the aid of democracy. Possibly she hoped for the reconquest of Canada. Rochambeau would have first employed his forces against Castine, had he not been overruled. That would have been curious, indeed, to have seen France re-established at old Pentagoët, carrying war into Canada, as, more than a century previous and from the same vantage-ground, she had carried it into New England. Not much later she tried to wheedle and then to bully us into ceding to her the island of Rhode Island, in order, as urged by her, to prevent its being seized again at any future time by Great Britain. Her armed intervention was of little worth compared with the moral effect of the alliance.

Pierre du Guast had groped his way along the coast in 1605, seeking a habitation. He, and his lieutenant, Poutrincourt, had well-nigh reached their goal when compelled to turn back, baffled, for wintry Acadia. A French colony, in 1605, upon Aquidneck might have changed the order of history, and rendered impossible the events of which this chapter is the skeleton.

GRAVES ON THE BLUFF, FORT ROAD.

CHAPTER XXV.
NEWPORT CEMETERIES.

"Come, my spade. There is no ancient gentlemen but gardeners, ditchers, and grave-makers; they hold up Adam's profession."—SHAKSPEARE.

ASSUMING the looker-on to be free from all qualms on the subject of grave-yard associations, I invite him to loiter with me awhile among the tombstones of buried Newport. As we thread the streets of the town, sign-boards or door-plates inform us who are the occupants; and in pursuing the narrow paths of the burial-place, the tablets set up denote, not only the final residences, but symbolize the dread of the world's forgetfulness, of those who sleep there. The analogy might still be pursued, as it was an old custom to inscribe the occupation and birthplace upon a memorial stone. Here is one I found in the old ground adjoining Rhode Island Cemetery:

> Here lyeth the Body
> of Roger Baster
> Bachelor Block mackr
> Aged 66 yeres He Dyed
> 23 Day of Aprel 1687
>   He ⱻas one of the Fi
> rst Beginers of a Chv
> rch of Christ obsrving———
> Of the 7th Day Sab
> bath of ᚻE LORD ᛏN
> NE AD BEGAN 23D ᛁS 1671

The grave-yards are the first green spots. Dandelions, buttercups, and daisies blossom earliest there. The almost imperceptible shading-off of winter into spring is signaled by tufts of freshly springing grass on the sunny side of a grave-stone; the birds build betimes among the tree-branches of the cemetery. Your grave-maker is always a merry fellow, who cares no more for carved cross-bones than for the clay-pipes so artistically crossed in shop-windows.

I found many stones dating from 1726 to 1800, but even these had become much defaced by time. Where freestone slabs had been used, the inscriptions were either illegible or quite obliterated. Some of the older slate stones had been painted to protect them from the weather. The city takes commendable care of the grounds; yet I could not help thinking that a little money might be well spent in renewing the fading inscriptions. Throughout the inclosure the pious chisel of some "Old Mortality" is painfully in request.

In a retired part of the ground I found two horizontal slabs—one of white, the other red, freestone—lying side by side over man and wife. I transcribed the epitaph of the wife, as the more characteristic:

> HERE LYETH THE BODY OF HARTE
> GARDE THE WIFE OF IOHN GARDE
> MERCHANT WHO DEPARTED THIS
> THE 16 DAY OF SEPTEMBER AN
> DOM 1660
> AGED 55 YEARS.

Another slate stone contained the singular inscription given in the engraving; and still another was lettered:

> In Memory Of
> M$^{rs.}$ Elizabeth Lintu
> rn widow for many
> years a noted midwife
> She departed this life
> October 23^d 1758
> In the 63^d year of her age.

In the old Common Burying-ground is the following plaint:

> Here doth Simon Parrett lye
> Whose wrongs did for justice cry
> But none could haue
> And now the Graue
> Keeps him from Inivrie
> Who Departed this life
> ћe 23 Day of May 1718
> Aged 84 years.

Farewell Street, by which you approach the principal cemetery of Newport, is not ill-named. The ground, a generally level area, permits the eye to roam over the whole region of graves. Glimpses of the bay and of the islands dispersed so picturesquely about it harmonize with the calm of the place. Sails drift noiselessly by, and the fragrance of evergreens and of eglantine perfumes the air. There was breeze enough to bring the strains of martial music from the fort even here.

It is stated, I know not how authoritatively, that the Hessians, whose hospital was close at hand, defaced many stones here by altering the inscriptions. Here is buried William Ellery,[1] one of the signers of the Declaration. On the day of his death he rose as usual, dressed, and seated himself in the old flag-bottomed chair which he had sat in for more than half a century. Here he remained reading a volume of Cicero in Latin until his physician, who had dropped in, perceived that he could scarcely raise his eyelids to look at him. The doctor found his pulse gone. After giving him a little wine and water, Dr. W—— told him his pulse beat stronger. "Oh, yes, doctor, I have a charming pulse," expressing at the same time his conviction that his life was nearly ended, and his thankfulness that he was to pass away free from sickness or pain. He at last consented to be placed upright in bed, so that he might continue reading. He died thus without attracting the notice of his attendants, like a man who becomes drowsy and falls asleep, sitting in the same posture, with the book under his chin. Here is also the tomb of Governor Cranston, and the gray stone slab with typical skull and cross-bones, on which is graven the name of William Jefferay, said to have been one of Charles Stuart's judges. Among other specimens of grave-yard literature is the inscription to Christopher Ellery: "The Human Form respected for its honesty, and known for fifty-three years by the appellation of Christopher Ellery, began to dissolve in the month of February, 1789."

There is not so much quaintness in the epitaphs here as in the old Puritan grave-yards of Boston and Salem; less even of stateliness, of pomp, and of human pride than is usual. I missed the Latin, the blazonry, and the sounding detail of public service so often seen spread over every inch of crumbling old tombstones. The grotesque emblems of skull, cross-bones, and hour-glass —bugbears to frighten children—change in a generation or two to weeping-willows, urns, and winged cherubs. These are in turn discarded for sculptured types of angels, lambs, doves, and lilies; of broken columns and chaplets. This departure from the horrible for the beautiful is not matter for regret. In these symbols we get all the religion of the place, and Death is robbed of half his repulsiveness.

---

[1] William Ellery Channing, the pastor of "Old Federal Street," Boston, was one of the most gifted and eloquent men the American pulpit has produced. He married the old signer's daughter, and bore his name.

On a grassy knoll in Rhode Island Cemetery the visitor sees the granite obelisk, erected by the State to the memory of the victorious young captain who, at twenty-seven, gained imperishable renown. Ardent, chivalrous, and brave, Perry showed the true inspiration of battle in taking his flag to a ship still able to fight. His laconic dispatch, "We have met the enemy, and they are ours," is modestly exultant. The marble tablet of the monument's east face has the words,

OLIVER HAZARD PERRY.
At the Age of Twenty-seven Years,
He Achieved
The Victory of Lake Erie,
September 10, 1813.

PERRY'S MONUMENT.[1]

Within the neat iron fence that surrounds the monument are also the graves of Perry's widow, Elizabeth Champlin, and of his eldest son, Christopher Grant Perry, with the fresher one of Rev. Francis Vinton, whose wife was a daughter of the naval hero. From this spot the bay and all ancient Newport are visible. Another monument in the cemetery is in memory of General Isaac Ingalls Stevens, "dead on the field of honor."

OLIVER HAZARD PERRY.

A prevailing ingredient of Newport society in the olden days was, doubtless, the Quaker element. As the religious asylum of New England, it alike received Jew and Gentile, Quaker and Anabaptist, followers of the Church of England and of Rome. Its complexion at the beginning of the eighteenth century might be in harmony with religious freedom, though little homogeneous; and although there was plenty of toleration, its religious character has been vaunted overmuch. It commands a passing thought that

---

[1] The other faces of Commodore Perry's monument recite his age, birthplace, etc. He was born at South Kingston in 1785, and died at Port Spain, Trinidad, 1819. According to a resolve of Congress his remains were conveyed, in 1826, in an armed vessel to the United States.

all these human components intermingling and assimilating in the active duties of life, separate in death. Their burial must be distinct.

The Quaker-meeting has contributed to our vocabulary a synonym for dullness. Old England and New were in accord in persecuting the sect. It is related of a number under sentence of banishment to America, that soldiers from the Tower carried them on board the ships, the Friends refusing to walk and the sailors to hoist them on board. In the year 1662 Hannah Wright came from Long Island, several hundred miles to the "bloody town of Boston," into the court, and warned the magistrates to spill no more innocent blood. They were at first abashed by the solemn fervor of their accuser, until Rawson, the secretary, exclaimed, "What! Shall we be baffled by such a one as this? Come, let us drink a dram."

FRIENDS' MEETING-HOUSE.

The sufferings of the Friends in New England were heightened, no doubt, by the zeal of some to embrace martyrdom, who, in giving way to the promptings of religious fanaticism, outraged public decency, and shamed the name of modesty in woman. Deborah Wilson went through the streets of Salem naked as she came into the world, for which she was well whipped. Two other Quaker women, says Mather, were whipped in Boston, "who came as stark naked as ever they were born into our public assemblies." This exhibition was meant to be a sign of religious nakedness in others; but the Puritans preferred to consider it an offense against good morals, and not a Godiva-like penance for the general sinfulness.[1]

The Society of Friends is the youngest of the four surviving societies which date from the Reformation, and is, without doubt, the sternest protest against the ceremonial religion of Rome. George Fox, who preached at

---

[1] When appealed to by the United Colonies in 1657 to punish Quakers, Rhode Island objected that no law of that colony sanctioned it. The president, Benedict Arnold, however, replied that he (and the other magistrates) conceived the Quaker doctrines tended to "very absolute cutting down and overturning relations and civil government among men." He urged as a measure of public policy that the Quakers should not be molested, as they would not remain where the civil authority did not persecute them. This has, in fact, been the history of this sect in New England. —See Arnold's letter, Hutchinson, vol. i., appendix.

Newport,[1] was the son of a Leicestershire weaver, beginning his public assertion of religious sentiments at the age of twenty-two. The pillory sometimes served him for a pulpit. He once preached with such power to the populace that they rescued him "in a tumultuous manner," setting a clergyman who had been instrumental in his punishment upon the same pillory.

Pagan superstition having originated most of the names bestowed by custom on the days and months, the Friends ignore them, substituting in their place "first day" and "first month," "second day" and "second month" for those occurring at the beginning of our calendar. The Society does not sanction appeals by its members to courts of law, but refers disputes to arbitration, a practice well worthy imitation.

GEORGE FOX.

George Fox mentions in his "Journal" his interview in England with Simon Bradstreet and Rev. John Norton, the agents whom Massachusetts had sent over in answer to the command of Charles II. Says Fox, "We had several discourses with them concerning their murdering our friends, but they were ashamed to stand to their bloody actions. I asked Simon Bradstreet, one of the New England magistrates, whether he had not an hand in putting to death these four whom they hanged for being Quakers? He confessed he had. I then demanded of him and his associates then present if they acknowledged themselves subject to the laws of England? They said they did. I then said by what law do you put our friends to death? They answered, By the same law as the Jesuits were put to death in England. I then asked if those Friends were Jesuits? They said nay. Then, said I, ye have murdered them.'"[2]

---

[1] George Fox was in Rhode Island in 1672. On arriving at Newport, he went to the house of Nicholas Easton, who was then governor, and remained there during his sojourn. A yearly meeting of all the Friends in New England was held while he remained in Newport.—"George Fox his Journal," London, 1709.

[2] Josselyn mentions the sect: "Narraganset Bay, within which bay is Rhode Island, a harbor for the Shunamitish Brethren, as the saints errant, the Quakers, who are rather to be esteemed vagabonds than religious persons." He also attributes to them dealings in witchcraft. Whittier, the Quaker poet, has depicted in stirring verse the persecutions of this people. "Cassandra Southwick" is from real life.

The first Quakers came to Rhode Island in 1656. Roger Williams, in his "George Fox digged out of his Burrowes," shows that tolerance did not go so far with him as the Quaker fashion of wearing the hair long and flowing. Speaking of one he met who accosted him with the salutation, "Fear the Lord God," Williams says he retorted, "What God dost thou mean—a ruffian's God?" Through Fox's preaching some of Cromwell's soldiers became converted, and would not fight. He lies in the old London burying-ground of Bunhill Fields, among the Dissenters.

The objection of the sect to sepulchral stones leaves little to be remarked of the Quaker burying-ground in Newport.[1] Notwithstanding the non-resistant principles of the Friends, it stands in strong light that Nathaniel Greene, a Quaker, and Oliver Hazard Perry, the descendant of a Quaker, were conspicuous figures in two of our wars. Few innovations have appeared in the manners, customs, or dress of the followers of George Fox.[2] Their broad-brims, sober garb, and sedate carriage, their "thee" and "thou," may still occasionally be seen and heard in Newport streets.

Newport contains several widely scattered burial-places, some of them hardly more in appearance than family groups of graves. Not all exhibit the care bestowed upon such as are more prominently before the public eye. The little Clifton cemetery, at the head of Golden Hill Street, was in a wretched plight. A crazy wooden paling afforded little or no protection from intrusion. But there was no incentive to linger among its few corroded monuments and accumulated rubbish. Here are buried the Wantons, of whom Edward, the ancestor of the name in Newport, fled from Scituate, Massachusetts, during the Quaker persecutions.

CHARLES LEE.

When Washington was at Cambridge, besieging Boston, he sent Charles Lee to look after "those of Rhode Island" who were still for King George. Lee administered to the Tories who would take it an oath as whimsical as characteristic. He knew the fondness of these old royalists for old wine, good dinners, and fine raiment. They were required to

---

[1] Stones giving simply the name and date of decease are now allowed.
[2] In 1708 M. de Subercase solicited of his Government the means of attempting an enterprise against the island of Rhode Island. He says, "Cette isle est habitée par des Coakers qui sont tous gens riches."

swear fidelity to the Whig cause "by their hope of present ease and comfort, as well as the dread hereafter." Colonel Wanton refused the oath, and was, I presume, of those whom Lee had taken to Providence with the threat of forwarding them to the American camp.

Another isolated field of graves is that usually called the Coddington burial-ground, containing the remains of Governor Coddington and kindred. A stone erected on the second centennial anniversary of the settlement of Newport, compresses in a few lines the chief events of his history:

"To the memory of William Coddington, Esq., that illustrious man who first purchased this island from the Narraganset sachems, Canonicus and Miantonimo, for and on account of himself and seventeen others, his associates in the purchase and settlement. He presided many years as Chief Magistrate of the Island and Colony of Rhode Island, and died, much respected and lamented, November 1st, 1678, aged 78 years."[1]

Lechford, in his "Plain Dealing," relates a circumstance that has caused some inquiry into the ecclesiastical polity of Coddington and his associates. "There lately," he says, "they whipt one master Gorton, a grave man, for denying their power, and abusing some of their magistrates with uncivill tearmes; the governor, master Coddington, saying in court, 'You that are for the king, lay hold on Gorton;' and he again, on the other side, called forth, 'All you that are for the king, lay hold on Coddington.' Whereupon Gorton was banished the island." Gorton was the founder of Warwick, Rhode Island.

There is a little inclosure at the upper end of Thames Street in which is a granite obelisk to the memory of John Coggeshall, president of the plantations under their first patent. The name was originally Coxehall. It is the same John Coggeshall briefly met with in the trial scene, to whom a lineal descendant has raised this monument.

Other burial-places may be enumerated, but that lying in the shadow of Trinity Church is probably first to challenge the attention of such as seek to read the annals of the past on memorial stones. The church steeple, with gilded crown on the pinnacle—how these churchmen love the old emblems! —was in full view from my window, slender and graceful, the gilded vane flashing in the morning sun, itself a monument of its ancient flock below.

Here are the names of Hunter, of Kay, of Honyman, and of Malbone: all are to be met with in Newport streets or annals. The presence of foreign armies on the isle is emphasized by the burial of French and British officers in this church-yard. A few family escutcheons designate the ancient adherence to the dogma that all men were not created politically free and equal. One of the unaccustomed objects the stranger sees in peering through the

---

[1] Here also is the grave of Governor Henry Bull, who died in 1693, and whose ancient stone house is now standing in Thames, near Sherman street.

railings of these old church-yards is the blazonry of which the possessors were once so proud, and which is now carried with them to their graves. In cavities where leaden coats of arms have once been imbedded are little basins to catch the rain, where careless sparrows drink and take their morning baths, twittering and chirruping among the homesteads of the dead.

Stuart, who was fond of rambling through the old grave-yards, reading the inscriptions, went to Trinity. He mentions his pew, and the sweetness of the organ, the gift of Berkeley. The painter had a Scotsman's inordinate fondness for snuff, and would be most naturally drawn with palette in one hand and a huge pinch of snuff in the other. A resident of the same street once told me that when Stuart's table-cloth was shaken out at the window the whole street sneezed. He was a good talker and listener, though crabbed and eccentric to a degree.

I venture to contribute to the already portentous number the following anecdote of Stuart: Dining one day at the house of Josiah Quincy, his attention was attracted by an engraving of West's "Battle of the Boyne." "Ah!" said Stuart, "I was studying with West when he was at work on that picture, and had to lie for hours on the floor, dressed in armor, for him to paint me in the foreground as the Duke of Schomberg. At last West said, 'Are you dead, Stuart?' 'Only half, sir,' was my reply; and my answer was true; for the stiffness of the armor almost deprived me of sensation. Then I had to sit for hours on a horse belonging to King George, to represent King William. After the painting was finished, an Irishman who saw it observed to West, 'You have the battle-ground there correct enough, but where is the monument? I was in Ireland the other day and saw it.' He expected to see a memorial of the battle in a representation of its commencement."[1]

In the yard of the Congregational Church in Spring Street is a slate grave-stone to the memory of Dr. Samuel Hopkins, settled as pastor of the First Congregational Church of Newport, in 1770. At first his sentiments were so little pleasing to his people that it was voted by the church not to give him a call; but the doctor preached a farewell sermon of such beauty and impressiveness that the vote was recalled, and Hopkins consented to remain. The salient points of his character have furnished the hero for Mrs. Stowe's "Minister's Wooing." The First Congregational Church of Newport was established in 1720.

---

[1] Stuart was in Boston at the time of the battle of Lexington, and managed to escape a few days after Bunker Hill. His obituary in the Boston *Daily Advertiser*, a very noble tribute from one man of genius to another, was written by Allston.

MOUNT HOPE.

CHAPTER XXVI.

TO MOUNT HOPE, AND BEYOND.

"La mattina al monte, e la sera al fonte."—*Italian Proverb.*

MOHAMMED, it is said, on viewing the delicious and alluring situation of Damascus, would not enter that city, but turned away with the exclamation, "There is but one paradise for man, and I am determined to have mine in the other world."

I started on my morning walk up the island just as the clocks were striking eight. Spring comes in Newport very early and very verdant. The bloom of orchard and of lilac greeted me. At every step I crushed the perfume out of violets blossoming in the strip of greensward that bordered the broad band of road. I often looked back upon the fortunate city, mounting the green slopes and scattering itself among the quiet fields. The last point of land was visible even down to Point Judith. A faint roll of drums reached me from the fort. Good-bye to a pleasant place! I felt, in turning away, that if Damascus had been like Newport, I should have entered Damascus.

Distant about a mile from Newport is "Tonomy," or more properly Miantonimo Hill. It is the highest elevation in the southern part of the island, receiving its name as the seat of a sachem. Some remains of field-works are seen on its slopes.[1]

---

[1] It was the fortress of the British left wing. Two large and elegant country houses at its base, included within the lines, were occupied by the officers.

Near the southern foot of Miantonimo Hill is the old Malbone place, the site of a colonial mansion celebrated in its day as the finest in Newport. It was destroyed by fire rather more than a century ago. Tradition avers that Colonel Godfrey Malbone, seeing his house in flames, ordered the table removed to the lawn, and coolly finished his dinner there. It was a two-story stone-built house, which had cost the owner a hundred thousand dollars.

Many are the dark, vague, and mysterious hints let fall from time to time relative to the life of Malbone. As a merchant his ventures are said to have been lawless even for his lawless age. His corsairs preyed upon the commerce of Frenchman or Spaniard without regard for treaties. Rum and slaves were the commodities in which the Newport of his time trafficked largely. Smuggling was hardly deemed dishonorable in a merchant. As confirming this easy condition of commercial virtue, a writer mentions having seen in Malbone's garden the entrance of

THE GLEN.

one of those subterranean passages leading to the shore I have so often unearthed.

During the French war of George II., Newport, from its beginning to the year 1744, had armed and sent to sea more than a score of privateers. It was called the nursery of corsairs. It was also called rich; and the French, in planning its capture, facilitated by the information of a resident French merchant, a spy, calculated on levying a heavy contribution. "Perhaps we had better burn it, as a pernicious hole, from the number of privateers there fitted out, as dangerous in peace as in war; being a sort of freebooter, who confiscates *à tord et à travers*," say they. These harsh expressions sound strangely unfamiliar when contrasted with French panegyric of the next generation.

Edward G. Malbone, a natural son, belonged to a collateral branch of the family.[1] Newport was the birthplace of this exquisite miniature painter and most refined of men. This refinement appears in his works, which are full of artistic grace and dainty delicacy. Little of his life was passed here, though that little is much prized by all who know his worth as a man. Allston and Malbone are said to have worked together in Newport as pupils of Samuel King, beginning thus the friendship that so long subsisted between them.

About midway of the island, on the eastern shore, is The Glen, once more frequented than at present. A line carried across the island from this point would pass near the old farmstead, which was the quarters of the British general, Prescott. It is on the west road leading by the most direct route from Newport to Bristol Ferry.

A RHODE ISLAND WINDMILL.

Colonel Barton, whose station was at Tiverton, conceived the idea of releasing General Lee, then a prisoner, by securing General Prescott. Having matured his plans, he crossed over to Warwick Neck, where he was detained two days by a violent storm. With him were forty volunteers, who manned five whale-boats. The enemy were then in possession of both Canonicut and

---

[1] He was the son of John, the son of Godfrey Malbone.

Prudence islands, with some shipping lying under the little isle, called Hope, which is between Prudence and the western shore of the bay.

On the night of the 9th of July, 1777, every thing being favorable, Barton informed his men for the first time where they were going. His party embarked in their boats, rowing between Patience and Prudence in order to elude the enemy's guard-boats. Meeting with no obstacle, they coasted the west shore of Prudence, passed around the southern end, and landed on Rhode Island. They then pushed on for Overing's house, where they knew General Prescott was to be found.

WILLIAM BARTON.

The sentinel on duty was quickly seized and disarmed, and the house surrounded. On entering General Prescott's chamber, Barton saw him rising from his bed.

"Are you General Prescott?"

"Yes, sir."

"Then you are my prisoner."

The general was allowed to half dress himself, and was then conducted to the boats. His aid, Major Barrington, had also been taken. Arrived at the shore, General Prescott finished his toilet in the open air. Soon after leaving the island the alarm was given in the British camp. "Sir," said Prescott to Barton, as they stepped ashore at Warwick Neck, "you have made a d—d bold push to-night." The Americans had returned in just six and a half hours from the time they set out.

While on his way to the American head-quarters, Prescott was horse-whipped by an innkeeper whom he insulted. The situation of the house from which he was carried off is easily distinguished by the pond before it, whose overflow falls in a miniature cascade into the road. Very little, if any, of the original building is remaining.

Talbot's achievement the next year was in carrying off a British armed vessel, the *Pigot*, that guarded Seconnet Passage and the communication between the islands and

SILAS TALBOT.

the main-land. With a few troops from the camp at Providence he manned a small vessel and set sail. On coming near the *Pigot,* Talbot caused his vessel to drift down upon her, when he carried her by boarding. He took his prize successfully into Stonington.

The absence of forest-trees on the island gives it a general resemblance to the rolling prairie of the West. The slopes are gracefully rounded as the Vermont hills—ground-swells, over which the road rises or descends in regular irregularity. Over this road that discarded vehicle, the stage-coach, once rolled and lurched, and was more wondered at than the train that now rattles along under the hills by the shore.

PRESCOTT'S HEAD-QUARTERS.

It is said that Dexter Brown, "an enterprising man," set up a four-horse stage-coach between Boston and Providence as early as 1772. When "well regulated," it left Providence every Monday, and arrived in Boston on Tuesday night; returning, it left Boston on Thursday, reaching Providence on Friday night. The coach was chiefly patronized by people who visited Newport for their health. On a long route, the change from one coach into another, equally cramped, might not inaptly be said to resemble an exchange of prisoners.

All travelers here have remarked on the productiveness of Rhode Island. Its dairies and its poultry have always been celebrated. Orchards bursting with blossoms somewhat relieved the bare aspect of the hills. Fields of spinach and of clover varied the coloring of the pastures, which were shaded off on cool slopes into the dark green of Kentucky blue-grass. Groups of brown hay-ricks, left from the winter's store, stood impaled in barn-yards. Flocks of geese waddled by the roadside. Ox-teams, market-men, boys with droves of pigs, made the whole way a pastoral. On lifting the eye from the yellow band of road a windmill would be seen with its long arms beating the air. I liked to walk through the green lanes that led up to them, and hold brief chat with the boy or maid of the mill. I shall never look at one without thinking of Don Quixote and of Sancho Panza. The lack of streams and water-power is thus supplied by air-currents and wind-power. It is an ill wind indeed that blows nobody good on Rhode Island.

AGRICULTURAL PROSPERITY.

I have said nothing of the fish-market of the island, and that market is of course centred in Newport. Dr. Dwight enumerates twenty-six different species, to be found in their season. Sheep's-head, considered superior to turbot, were sometimes caught off Hanging Rocks. Blackfish (tautog) and scup, or scuppaug, are much esteemed. When I was last on the island, the fishermen were emptying their seines of the scup, which were so plenty as to be almost valueless, a string of fine fish, ready dressed, bringing only twelve cents. The flesh of a tautog is very firm, and he will live a long time out of water. The boats used here by fishermen have the mast well forward, in the manner known to experts along shore as the "Newport rig." Formerly they used "pinkeys," or Chebacco boats, so called from a famous fishing precinct of Essex County, Massachusetts.

The quartz imbedded in the stone makes the roadside walls appear as if splashed with whitewash. I saw few ledges from Newport to Lawton's Valley. The stones brought up by the plow were all small and flat, but at the upper end of the island I observed they were the round masses or pebbles met with on the opposite main-land. There is also on the western shore a coal vein of inferior quality. The dust from it mingles with that of the road before you arrive at Bristol ferry.

I made a brief halt at the old grass-grown earth-work on the crest of the hill overlooking Lawton's Valley. No wayfarer should lose the rare views to be had here. The fort forms a throne from which the Queen of Aquidneck, a voluptuous rather than virgin princess, a Cleopatra rather than an Elizabeth, might behold her empire. At the foot of the hill is the remarkable vale intersecting the island, sprinkled with cottages among orchards; on the left, part of Canonicut and all of Prudence lie outstretched along the sunny bay; farther north the steeples of Bristol distinctly, and of Providence dimly, are seen; to the right Mount Hope, Tiverton, and perhaps a faint spectral chimney or two at Fall River. The long dark line on the water from the island to Tiverton is the stone bridge.[1]

Turning to the southward is the battle-field of 1778, where Sullivan and Greene fought with Pigot and Prescott, and where Lafayette, though he had ridden from Boston in six hours, was not. This campaign, begun so auspiciously, terminated ingloriously. New England had been aroused to arms. Men of all ranks of society shouldered their firelocks and marched. Volunteers from Newburyport, a company of the first merchants of Salem, artillery and infantry corps from Boston, thronged the roads to Sullivan's camp. It was a good and salutary lesson to the Americans, not to put their faith in French appearances.[2]

FROM BUTTS'S HILL, LOOKING NORTH.

When Coddington and his associates determined to remove from Massachusetts, they meant to settle upon Long Island or in Delaware Bay. While their vessel was making the dangerous passage around Cape Cod without them, they came by land to Providence, where Mr. Williams courteously entertained and afterward influenced them to settle upon the Isle of Aquidneck. Plymouth having disclaimed jurisdiction over it, and promised to look upon and assist them as loving neighbors, in March, 1637-'38, the exiles organized their political community upon the northern end of the island. Sir H. Vane and Roger Williams were instrumental in procuring Rhode Island from the Narraganset chieftains, Miantonimo and Canonicus. By the next spring their

---

[1] The first bridge spanning what was known as Howland's Ferry was completed in 1795. It was of wood, destroyed and swept to sea by a storm; rebuilt, and again destroyed by worms. The present stone structure was built in 1809-'10, and, though injured by the gale of 1815, stands firm.

[2] The battle was fought in the valley below Quaker, sometimes called Meeting-house, Hill. Sullivan commanded in chief, though Greene is entitled to a large share of the credit of repulsing the British attack. It was a well-fought action. Pigot, by British accounts, had six thousand regular troops. Lafayette was mad as a March hare at their fighting without him.

QUAKER HILL FROM BUTTS'S HILL, LOOKING SOUTH.

numbers were so much augmented that some of the settlers removed to the southern or western shores. The island was divided into two townships——Portsmouth, which now engrosses its upper half, and Newport. In 1644 they named it the Isle of Rhodes, which was merely exchanging one pagan name for another.[1]

Mount Hope is scarcely more than two hundred feet high, though in its isolation it looks higher. It is commandingly situated on a point of land on the eastern shore of Bristol Neck, giving its name to a broad expanse of water that receives Taunton River in its course to the sea. On the eastern side the hill is precipitous, vastly more so than Horse Neck, down which the valiant Putnam urged his steed when pursued by British dragoons. Down this declivity Philip is said to have rolled like a cask when surprised by white enemies. Here, on the shores of Taunton River, is the scene of those hand-to-hand encounters between settler and savage in which the old historians are wont to mix up gunpowder with religion so perplexedly. In those days the fall of a red chieftain on the hunting-grounds of his fathers was hailed as a

BATTLE-GROUND OF AUGUST 29, 1778.

---

[1] Lechford, writing between 1637 and 1641, says: "At the island called Aquedney are about two hundred families. There was a church where one Master Clark was elder: the place where the church was is called Newport, but that church, I hear, is now dissolved. At the other end of the island there is another town called Portsmouth, but no church. Those of the island have a pretended civil government of their own erection without the king's patent."

special providence. Mount Hope was the sequel of Samoset's "Welcome, Englishmen."

By the river, in the forked branches of blasted sycamores, the fish-hawk builds and broods. Their nests are made of dried eel-grass from the shore interwoven with twigs. The shrill scream of the female at my coming was answered by the cry of the male, who left his fishing out on the river at the first signal of distress. An old traveler says this bird sometimes seems to lie expanded on the water, he hovers so close to it. Having by some attractive power drawn the fish within his reach, he darts suddenly upon them. The charm he makes use of is supposed to be an oil contained in a small bag in the body. In defense of his mate and her young the bird seems to forget fear.

After many agreeable surprises already encountered, I was unprepared for what I saw from the summit of Mount Hope. I felt it was good to be there. Every town in Rhode Island is said to be visible. All the islands dispersed about the bay are revealed at a glance. Glimmering in the distance was Providence. On the farther shore of Mount Hope Bay, Fall River appeared niched in the sheer side of a granite ledge. Here were Warren and Bristol, there Warwick; and, far down the greater bay, Newport was swathed in a hazy cloud. I had made a long walk, yet felt no fatigue, on the top of Mount Hope.

KING PHILIP, FROM AN OLD PRINT.

Near the brow of the hill Philip fixed his wigwam and held his dusky court. He has had Irving for his biographer, Southey for his bard, and Forrest for his ideal representative. In his own time he was the public enemy whom any should slay; in ours he is considered as a martyr to the idea of liberty—his idea of liberty not differing from that of Tell and Toussaint, whom we call heroes.

Philip did not comprehend the religion of the whites, but as he understood their policy he naturally distrusted their faith. When the prophet Eliot preached to him, he went up to that good man, and, pulling off a button from his doublet, said he valued his discourse as little as the piece of brass—"the monster!" exclaims pious Cotton Mather.

Such hills as Mount Hope were the settlers' sun-dials, when clocks and watches were luxuries known only to the wealthy few. The crest is a green nipple, having quartz cropping out everywhere; in fact, the basis of the hill is nearly a solid mass of quartz. Between the site of Philip's wigwam and the shore, where the escarpment is fifty feet, is a natural excavation, five or six feet from the ground, called "Philip's Throne." A small grass-plot is before it, and at its foot trickles a never-failing spring of water, known as "Philip's Spring."

The manner of Philip's death, as given in Church's history, is considered authentic. Church's party crossed the ferry, and reached Mount Hope about midnight. Detachments were placed in ambush at all the avenues of escape. Captain Golding, with a number of picked men and a guide, was ordered to assault the stronghold by break of day. One of Philip's Indians having showed himself, Golding fired a volley into the camp. The Indians then fled to the neighboring swamp, Philip the foremost. Having gained the shore, he ran directly upon Church's ambuscade. An Englishman snapped his gun at him without effect, when his companion, one of Church's Indian soldiers, sent a bullet through the heart of the chief. He fell on his face in the mud and water, with his gun under him. After the fight was over, Church ordered the body to be quartered and decapitated. The executioner was also an Indian, and before he struck the body made a short speech to it. Philip's head was taken to Plymouth in triumph, where, arriving on the very day the church was keeping a solemn thanksgiving, in the words of Mather, "God sent 'em in the head of a leviathan for a thanksgiving feast."

I made the ascent of Mount Hope from the south, where it is gradual; but on the west, where I descended, I found it abrupt, and covered with a grove of oak-trees sprinkled with stones among fern. With the exception of a few tumble-down stone walls that cross it, and now and then a cow quietly cropping the herbage, it is as wild as when it was the eyrie of the proud-spirited chieftain, "the Last of the Wampanoags."

At Bristol the railway will set you down opposite to Fall River, or by returning to Bristol ferry you may take, on the Rhode Island side, the rail for Dighton and its sculptured rock. This rock, which has puzzled so many learned brains both of the Old World and the New, lies near the eastern shore of Taunton River, opposite Dighton wharves.[1]

INSCRIPTION ON DIGHTON ROCK.

I wanted two things in Dighton —direction to the rock, and a skiff to cross the river to it. An ancient builder of boats, very tall and very lank,

---

[1] To be exact, the shores adjacent to the rock are in the town of Berkeley, formerly part of Dighton.

having his adze in his hand and his admeasurements chalked on the toes of his boots, supplied me with both.

"What on airth do you want to look at that rock for?" he expostulated rather than questioned. "I'd as lief look at the side of that house," pointing to his work-shop.

"You do not seem to value your archæological remains overmuch," I submitted.

"Bless you, I knew a gal born and brought up right in sight of that air rock, who got married and went to Baltimore to live, without ever having sot eyes on it. When she had staid there a spell she heard so much about Dighton Rock, she came all the way back a purpose to see it. *Fee*-male curiosity, you see, sir."

The river is half a mile broad at Dighton, with low, uninteresting shores. The "Writing Rock," a large boulder of fine-grained greenstone, is submerged either wholly or in part by the tidal flow, but when uncovered presents a smooth face, slightly inclined toward the open river. When so close as to lay hold of it, you are aware of faint impressions on its surface, yet these have become so nearly effaced by the action of the tides and the chafing of drift ice as to be fragmentary, and therefore disappointing. As is usual, the action of the salt air has turned this, as other rocks by the shores, to a dusky red color. Seventy years ago the characters or lines traced on the rock were by actual measurement an inch in breadth by half an inch in depth, and distinct enough to attract attention from the decks of passing vessels.

The rock is first mentioned, says Schoolcraft, in a sermon of Dr. Danforth, of 1680. The river had then been frequented by white men for sixty years. It is next alluded to in the dedication of a sermon to Sir H. Ashurst by Cotton Mather, in these words: "Among the other curiosities of New England one is that of a mighty rock, on a perpendicular side whereof, by a river which at high tide covers part of it, there are very deeply engraved, no man alive knows how or when, about half a score lines near ten foot long and a foot and a half broad, filled with strange characters, which would suggest as odd thoughts about them that were here before us as there are odd shapes in that elaborate monument, whereof you shall see the first line transcribed here."

In the "Philosophical Transactions" of the Royal Society of London, covering a period from 1700 to 1720, are several communications from Cotton Mather, one of which (part iv., p. 112) is as follows:

"At Taunton, by the side of a tiding river, part in, part out of the river, is a large Rock; on the perpendicular side of which, next to the Stream, are seven or eight lines, about seven or eight foot long, and about a foot wide, each of them ingraven with unaccountable characters, not like any known character."[1]

---

[1] A copy of the inscription, made by Professor Sewall, is deposited in the Museum at Cambridge.

Schoolcraft believed the work to have been performed by Indians. Washington, who had some knowledge of their hieroglyphics, was of this opinion. Dr. Belknap asserts that they were acquainted with sculpture, and also instances their descriptive drawings on the bark of trees. Sculptured rocks, of which the origin is unknown, have been found in other locations in the United States. Since the unsettling of Norse traditions, the characters on Dighton Rock are generally admitted to be of Indian creation; but if the work of white men, it would strengthen the theory of Verazzani's presence in these waters.

Another link of the supposed discovery by Northmen was the skeleton exhumed about 1834 at Fall River. It was found in a sitting posture, having a plate of brass upon its breast, with arrow-heads of the same metal lying near, thin, flat, and of triangular shape. The arrows had been contained within a quiver of bark, that fell in pieces when exposed to the air. The most remarkable thing about the remains was a belt encircling the body, composed of brass tubes four and a half inches in length, the width of the belt, and placed close together longitudinally. The breastplate, belt, and arrow-heads were considered so many evidences that the skeleton was that of some Scandinavian who had died and been buried here by the natives.

An antiquary would of course prize a dead Scandinavian more than many living ones. These mouldering bones and corroded trinkets were not, however, the key to Dighton Rock. The mode of sepulture was that practiced by the natives of this continent. In Archer's account of Gosnold's voyage he speaks of the Indians on the south of Cape Cod as follows:

"This day there came unto the ship's side divers canoes, the Indians appareled as aforesaid, with tobacco and pipes steeled with copper, skins, artificial strings, and other trifles, to barter; one had hanging about his neck a plate of rich copper, in length a foot, in breadth half a foot, for a breastplate."

John Brereton, of the same voyage, tells us more of the Indians of the Elizabeth Islands: "They have also great store of copper, some very red, and some of a paler color; none of them but have chains, ear-rings, or collars of this metal: they had some of their arrows herewith, much like our broad arrow-heads, very workmanly made. Their chains are many hollow pieces cemented together, each piece of the bigness of one of our reeds, a finger in length, ten or twelve of them together on a string, which they wear about their necks; their collars they wear about their bodies like bandeliers, a handful broad, all hollow pieces like the other, but somewhat shorter, four hundred pieces in a collar, very fine and evenly set together." Were this evi-

---

There is another copy, by James Winthrop; see plate in vol. iii., "Memoir American Academy," and description of method of taking it, vol. ii., part ii., p. 126. Many others have been taken, more or less imperfect; the best one recollected is in the hall of the Antiquarian Society, Worcester, Massachusetts.

dence less positive, we know from Champlain that the Indians would never have permitted the body of a stranger to remain buried longer than was necessary to disinter and despoil it. Verazzani's letter mentions the possession of copper trinkets by the Indians.

About two miles and a half from Taunton Green is the Leonard Forge, the oldest in America. The spot is exceedingly picturesque. The brook, overhung by trees, which of yore turned the mill-wheel, glides beneath a rustic bridge ere it tumbles over the dam and hurries on to meet the river. James and Henry Leonard built the forge in 1652.

Near the spot is the site of the dwelling they occupied, one of the distinctive old structures of its day. Philip lived in amity with the Leonards, who made for him spear and arrow heads when he came to hunt at the Fowling Pond, not far from the forge, where he had a hunting-lodge. When he had resolved to strike the English, it is said he gave strict

OLD LEONARD HOUSE, RAYNHAM.

orders not to hurt those Leonards, his good friends of the forge. Tradition has it that his head was afterward kept in the house some days.

My pilgrimage among the haunts of the Narragansets and Wampanoags of old fame extended no farther. Setting my face again toward the sea, when on board one of those floating hotels that ply between Fall River and New York, I thought of the prediction I had cut from the Boston *Daily Advertiser* of just half a century ago: "We believe the time will not be far distant when a steamboat will be provided to run regularly between New York and Taunton River, to come to Fall River and Dighton, and perhaps to the wharves in Taunton, a mile below the village. This route from New York to Boston would in some respects be preferable to that through Providence."

NEW LONDON IN 1813.

CHAPTER XXVII.

NEW LONDON AND NORWICH.

"It seems that you take pleasure in these walks, sir."—MASSINGER.

NEW LONDON is a city hiding within a river, three miles from its meeting with the waters of Long Island Sound. On the farthest seaward point of the western shore is a light-house. Before, and yet a little eastward of the river's mouth, is an island about nine miles long screening it from the full power of Atlantic storms, and forming, with Watch Hill,[1] the prolongation of the broken line of land stretching out into the Sound from the northern limb of the Long Island shore. Through this barrier, thrown across the entrance to the Sound, all vessels must pass. The island is Fisher's Island. It seems placed on purpose to turn into the Thames all commerce winging its way eastward. Across the western extremity of Fisher's Island, on a fair night, New London and Montauk lights exchange burning glances. From Watch Hill the low and distant shore of Long Island is easily distinguished by day, and by night its beacon-light flashes an answer to its twin-brother of Montauk. These two towers are the Pillars of Hercules of the Sound, on which are hung the long and radiant gleams that bridge its gate-way.

South-west of Fisher's Island are the two Gull Islets, on the smallest of

---

[1] Watch Hill, in the town of Westerly and near Stonington, is the south-western extremity of Rhode Island.

which is a light-house. The swift tide which washes them is called the Horse-race. Next comes Plum Island, separated from the Long Island shore by a narrow and swift channel known as Plum Gut, through which cunning yachtsmen sometimes steer. In 1667, Samuel Wyllys, of Hartford, bought Plum Island for a barrel of biscuit and a hundred awls and fish-hooks.

Any one who looks at the long ellipse of water embraced within Long Island and the Connecticut shore, and remarks the narrow and obstructed channel through which it communicates with the Hudson, the chain of islands at its meeting with the ocean on the east, must be impressed with the belief that he is beholding one of the greatest physical changes that have occurred on the New England coast. As it is, Long Island Sound lacks little of being an inland sea. The absence of any certain indications of the channels of the rivers emptying into the Sound west of the Connecticut favors the theory of the union, at some former time, of Long Island at its western end with the main-land.

To resume our survey of the coast, we see on the map, about midway between Point Judith and Montauk, the pear-shaped spot of land protruding

NEW LONDON HARBOR, NORTH VIEW.

above the ocean called Block Island.[1] It is about eight miles long, diversified with abrupt hills and narrow dales, but destitute of trees. A chain of ponds extending from the north and nearly to the centre, with several separate and smaller ones, constitutes about one-seventh of the island. There is no ship harbor, and in bad weather fishing-boats are obliged to be hauled on shore, though the sea-mole in process of construction by Government will afford both haven and safeguard against the surges of the Atlantic; for the island, having no rock foundation, is constantly wasting away. Cottages of wood, whitewashed every spring, are scattered promiscuously over the island, with wretched roads or lanes to accommodate every dwelling. The total disappearance of the island has often been predicted, and I recollect when the im-

---

[1] Named from Captain Adrian Blok, a Dutch navigator. Its Indian name was Manisses. There are about twelve hundred inhabitants on this island, all native-born, of whom two hundred and seventy-five are voters. There are also six schools, two Baptist churches, and two windmills, a hotel, and several summer boarding-houses. Two hundred fishing-boats are owned by the islanders. In 1636 John Oldham, mentioned in our ramble in Plymouth, was murdered here by the Pequots. Block Island in 1672 was made a township, by the name of New Shoreham.

pression prevailed to some extent on the main-land that the islanders had only an eye apiece.

Ascending now the river toward New London, wind, tide, or steam shall sweep us under the granite battlements of Fort Trumbull, on the one side, and the grassy mounds of Fort Griswold on the other.[1] Near the latter is standing a monument commemorating the infamy of Benedict Arnold and the heroism of a handful of brave men sacrificed to what is called the chances of war.

New London is seen straggling up the side of a steep and rocky hill, dominated by three pointed steeples. Descending from the crest, its principal street opens like the mouth of a tunnel at the water-side into a broad space, always its market-place and chief landing. Other avenues follow the natural shelf above the shore, or find their way deviously as streams might down the hill-side.

NEW LONDON LIGHT.

The glory of New London is in its trees, though in some streets they stand so thick as to exclude the sun-light, and oppress the wayfarer with the feeling of walking in a church-yard.

The destruction of New London by Arnold's command, in 1781, has left little that is suggestive of its beginning. Its English settlement goes no farther back than 1646. In that year and the next a band of pioneers from the Massachusetts colony, among whom was John Winthrop, Jun.,[2] built their cottages, and made these wilds echo with the sounds of their industry.

---

[1] The two forts, Trumbull and Griswold, are named from governors of Connecticut. They date from the Revolution. Fort Trumbull in its present form was completed in 1849, under the supervision of General G. W. Cullum, U. S. A. In passing through New London in April, 1776, General Knox, by Washington's direction, examined the harbor with the view of erecting fortifications, and reported, by letter, that it would, in connection with Newport, afford a safe retreat to the American navy or its prizes in any wind that blew.

[2] Son of Governor Winthrop, of Massachusetts. He passed his first winter on Fisher's Island, which remained in his family through six generations. The valuable manuscript collection known as the Winthrop papers was found some years ago on the island, which belongs to New York in consequence of the grants to the Earl of Stirling and the Duke of York. The origin of its present

NEW LONDON AND NORWICH.

Old London and Father Thames are repeated in New England, because, as these honest settlers avow, they loved the old names as much as they disliked the barbaric sounds of the aboriginal ones, though the latter were always typical of some salient characteristic. They settled upon the fair Mohegan, in the country of the Pequots, a race fierce and warlike, who in 1637 had made a death-grapple of it with the pale-faces, and had been blotted out from among the red nations. Pequot was the name of the harbor, changed in 1658 to New London.

OLD BLOCK HOUSE, FORT TRUMBULL.

I first visited New London in 1845. It was then a bustling place—a little too bustling, perhaps, when rival crews of whalemen in port joined battle in the market-place, unpaving the street of its oyster-shells, and shouting war-cries never before heard except at Otaheite or Juan Fernandez. A large fleet of vessels, engaged in whaling and sealing voyages, then sailed out of the Thames. The few old hulks laid up at the wharves, the rusty-looking oil-butts and discarded paraphernalia pertaining to the fishery, yet reminded me of the hunters who lassoed the wild coursers of sea-prairies.[1]

I have already confessed to a weakness for the wharves. There is one in New London, appropriated to the use of the Light-house Board, on which are piled hollow iron cylinders, spare anchors, chain cables, spars and spindles, buoys and beacons. A "relief" light-ship, and a tug-boat with steam up, lay beside it. The danger and privation of life in a light-house is not to be compared with that on board the light-ship, which is towed to its station on some dangerous shoal or near some reef, and there anchored. It not unfrequently happens in violent storms that the light-ship breaks from its moorings, and meets the fate it was intended to signal to other craft.[2] The sight of a

---

name is uncertain, though so called as early as 1636. Governor Winthrop relates to Cotton Mather a singular incident which happened on Fisher's Island the previous winter. During the severe snow-storms hundreds of sheep, besides cattle and horses, were buried in the snow. Even the wild beasts came into the settlements for shelter. Twenty-eight days after the storm alluded to, the tenants of Fisher's Island, in extricating the bodies of a hundred sheep from one bank of snow in the valley, found two alive in the drift, where they had subsisted by eating the fleeces of those lying dead near them.

[1] In 1834 New London employed thirty-six vessels in whaling and sealing. A few are still engaged in the latter fishery, in the extreme navigable waters of the Arctic and Antarctic seas.

[2] During the unexampled cold of the past winter (1874-'75), the light-boat off New London was, in fact, carried away from her moorings by an ice-field, and many others all along the coast were stranded.

raging sea as high as the decks of the vessel is one familiar to these hardy mariners. When I expressed surprise that men were willing to hazard their lives on these cockle-shells, a veteran sea-dog glanced at the scanty sail his vessel carried as he replied, "We can get somewhere."

On the light-ship the lanterns are protected by little houses, built around each mast, until lighted, when they are hoisted to the mast-head. A fog-bell is carried on the forecastle to be tolled in thick weather. A more funereal sound than its monotone, deep and heavy, vibrating across a sea shrouded in mist, can scarcely be imagined.

A LIGHT-SHIP ON HER STATION.

Old sailors are considered to make the best keepers of either floating or stationary beacons. Their long habit of keeping watches on shipboard renders them more reliable than landsmen to turn out in all kinds of weather, or on a sudden call. They are also far more observant of changes of the weather, of tides, or the position of passing vessels. I have found many persons in charge of our sea-coast lights who had been ship-masters, and were men of more than ordinary intelligence. When the Fresnel lenticular light was being considered, it was objected by those having our system in charge that it would be difficult to procure keepers of sufficient intelligence to manage the lens apparatus. M. Fresnel replied that this difficulty had been most singularly exaggerated, as in France the country keepers belonged almost always to the class of ordinary mechanics or laborers, who, with eight or ten days' instruction, were able to perform their duties satisfactorily.[1]

All visitors to New London find their way, sooner or later, to the Old Hempstead House, a venerable roof dotted with moss-tufts, situated on Jay Street, not far west of the court-house. It is one of the few antiques which time and the flames have spared. As one of the old garrison-houses standing in the midst of a populous city, it is an eloquent reminder of the race it has outlived. It was built and occupied by Sir Robert Hempstead, descending as entailed property to the seventh generation, who continued to inhabit it. The Hempstead House is near the cove around which the first settlement of the town appears to have clustered. The last remaining house built by the first settlers stood about half a mile west of the court-house, on what was called Cape Ann Street: it was taken down about 1824. Governor Winthrop lived at the head of the cove bearing his name at the north end of the city.

COURT-HOUSE, NEW LONDON.

The court-house standing at the head of State (formerly Court) Street has the date of 1784 on the pediment, having been rebuilt after the burning of the town by Arnold.[2] At the other end of the street was the jail. The court-house, which formerly had an exterior gallery, has a certain family resemblance to the State-house at Newport. It is built of wood, with some attempt at ornamentation. Freshened up with white paint and green blinds, it looked remarkably unlike a seat of justice, which is usually dirty enough in all its courts to be blind indeed.

In the chancel of St. James's repose the ashes of Samuel Seabury, the first Anglican bishop in the United States. He took orders in 1753 in London, and on returning to his native country entered upon the work of his ministry. In 1775, having subscribed to a royalist protest, declaring his "abhorrence of all unlawful congresses and committees," he was seized by the Whigs, and confined in New Haven jail. Later in the war, he became chaplain of Colonel

---

[1] At the light-houses I have visited in cold weather, the unvarying complaint is made of the poor quality of the oil furnished by the Light-house Board. One keeper told me he was obliged to shovel the congealed lard-oil out of the tank in the oil-room, and carry it into the dwelling, some rods distant, to heat it on his stove; sometimes repeating the operation frequently during the night, in order to keep his light burning.

[2] It is shown in the view of New London in 1813, at the head of this chapter.

Fanning's regiment of American loyalists. After the war, Mr. Seabury went to England in order to obtain consecration as bishop, but, meeting with obstacles there, he was consecrated in Scotland by three non-juring bishops. The monument reproduced is from the old burying-ground of New London.[1]

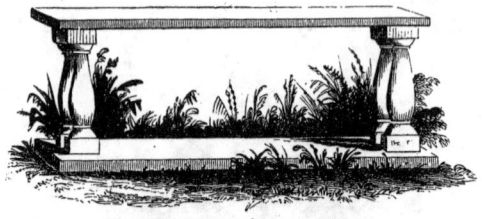

BISHOP SEABURY'S MONUMENT.

The ancient burial-place of New London is in the northern part of the city, on elevated ground, not far from the river. An old fractured slab of red sandstone once bore the now illegible inscription:

"An epitaph on Captaine Richard Lord, deceased May 17, 1662, Aetatis svæ 51.

"......Bright starre of ovr chivallrie lies here
To the state a covnsellorr fvll deare
And to ye trvth a friend of sweete content
To Hartford towne a silver ornament
Who can deny to poore he was releife
And in composing paroxyies he was cheife
To Marchantes as a patterne he might stand
Adventring dangers new by sea and land."

The harbor of New London being considered one of the best in New England, its claim to be a naval station has been urged from time to time upon the General Government. It is spacious, safe, and deep. During the past winter, which has so severely tested the capabilities of our coast harbors, closing many of them with an ice-blockade of long continuance, that of New London has remained open. In 1835, when the navigation of the harbor of New York was suspended, by being solidly frozen, New London harbor reremained unobstructed, vessels entering and departing as in summer.[2]

Among other observations made among the shipping, I may mention the operations of the destructive worm that perforates a ship's bottom or a thick

---

[1] Bishop Seabury was born in 1728, and died in 1796, aged 68. In person he was large, robust, and vigorous; dignified and commanding in appearance, and loved by his parishioners of low estate. After consecration he discharged the functions of bishop of the diocese of Connecticut and Rhode Island.

[2] The months of January and February, 1875, will be long remembered in New England for the intense and long-continued cold weather. Long Island Sound was a vast ice-field, which sealed up its harbors. For a time navigation was entirely suspended, the boats usually plying between Newport, Stonington, New London, and New York being obliged to discontinue their voyages. Gardiner's Bay was completely closed. The shore of Long Island, on its ocean side, was strewed with great blocks of ice. An unusual number of disasters signalized the ice embargo throughout the whole extent of the New England coast.

stick of timber with equal ease. I now had an opportunity of confirming what I had often been told, yet scarcely credited, that the worm could be distinctly heard while boring. The sound made by the borer exactly resembled that of an auger. It is not a little surprising to reflect that so insignificant a worm—not longer than a cambric needle when it first attacks the wood—is able to penetrate solid oak. I noticed evidences where these dreaded workmen were still busy, in little dust-heaps lying on the timber not yet removed from a vessel.

With the aid of a wheezy ferry-boat that landed me on Groton side, I still pursued my questionings or communings under the inspiration of a sunny afternoon, a transparent air, and a breeze brisk and bracing, bringing with it the full flavor of the sea.

GROTON MONUMENT.

A climb up the steep ascent leading to the old fort was rewarded by the most captivating views, and by gales that are above blowing in the superheated streets of a city.

The granite monument, which is our guide to the events these heights have witnessed, was built with the aid of a lottery. A marble tablet placed above its entrance is inscribed:

This Monument
was erected under the patronage of the State of Connecticut, A.D. 1830,
and in the 55th year of the Independence of the U. S. A.,
In Memory of the Brave Patriots
who fell in the massacre of Fort Griswold, near this spot,
on the 6th of September, A.D. 1781,
When the British, under the command of the Traitor,
BENEDICT ARNOLD,
burnt the towns of New London and Groton, and spread
desolation and woe throughout this region.

Westminster Abbey could not blot out that arraignment. Dr. Johnson did not know Benedict Arnold when he said, "Patriotism is the last refuge of a scoundrel." An American school-boy, if asked to name the greatest villain the world has produced, would unhesitatingly reply, "The traitor, Benedict Arnold." The sentence which history has passed upon him is eternal. Some voice is always repeating it.

Shortly after the peace of '83 Arnold was presented at court. While the king was conversing with him, Earl Balcarras, who had fought with Burgoyne in America, was announced. The king introduced them.

"What, sire," exclaimed the haughty old earl, refusing his hand, "the traitor Arnold!"

The consequence was a challenge from Arnold. The parties met, and it was arranged they should fire together. Arnold fired at the signal, but the earl, flinging down his pistol, turned on his heel, and was walking away, when his adversary called out,

"Why don't you fire, my lord?"

"Sir," said the earl, looking over his shoulder, "I leave you to the executioner."

The British attack on New London was not a blind stroke of premeditated cruelty, but a part of the only real grand strategy developed since the campaign of Trenton. Sir Henry Clinton had been completely deceived by Washington's movement upon Yorktown, and now launched his expedition upon Connecticut, with the hope of arresting his greater adversary's progress. Arnold was the suitable instrument for such work.

The expedition of 1781 landed on both sides of the harbor, one detachment under command of the traitor himself, near the light-house, the other at Groton Point. Fort Trumbull, being untenable, was evacuated, its little garrison crossing the river to Fort Griswold. Encountering nothing on his march except a desultory fire from scattered parties, Arnold entered New London, and proceeded to burn the shipping and warehouses near the river. In his official dispatch he disavows the general destruction of the town which ensued, but the testimony is conclusive that dwellings were fired and plundered in every direction by his troops, and under his eye.[1]

The force that landed upon Groton side was led by Lieutenant-colonel Eyre against Fort Griswold, which then contained one hundred and fifty men, under Lieutenant-colonel William Ledyard, cousin of the celebrated traveler. The surrender of the fort being demanded and refused, the British assaulted it on three sides. They were resisted with determined courage, but at length effected an entrance into the work. Eyre had been wounded, and his successor, Montgomery, killed in the assault. Finding himself overpowered, Ledyard advanced and offered his sword to Major Bromfield, now in command of the enemy, who asked, "Who commands this fort?"

"I did," courteously replied Ledyard; "but you do now."

Bromfield immediately stabbed Ledyard with his own sword, and the hero fell dead at the feet of the coward and assassin.[2] This revolting deed

---

[1] In all, the British destroyed one hundred and forty-three buildings, sixty-five of which were dwellings, and including the court-house, jail, and church.

[2] In the Wadsworth Museum, Hartford, the vest and shirt worn by Ledyard on the day of his death, are still shown to the visitor. Lafayette, when attacking the British redoubt at Yorktown, ordered his men, it is said with Washington's consent, to "remember New London." The continental soldiers could not or would not execute the command on prisoners who begged their lives on their knees.

was reserved for a Tory officer, of whom Arnold officially writes Sir H. Clinton, his "behavior on this occasion does him great honor." The survivors of the garrison were nearly all put to the sword, and even the wounded treated with incredible cruelty.[1]

Fort Griswold is a parallelogram, having a foundation of rough stone, on which very thick and solid embankments have been raised. It is the best preserved of any of the old earth-works I have seen since Fort George, at Castine. The position is naturally very strong, far stronger than Bunker Hill, which cost so many lives to carry. On all sides except the east the hill is precipitous; here the ascent is gradual, and having surmounted it, an attacking force would find itself on an almost level area of sufficient extent to form two thousand men. In consequence of the knowledge that this was their weak point of defense, the Americans constructed a small redoubt, the remains of which may still be seen about three hundred yards distant from the main work.

BENEDICT ARNOLD.

Groton was the seat of the Pequot power, the royal residence of Sassacus being situated on a commanding eminence called Fort Hill, four miles east of New London. This was his principal fortress, though there was another about eight miles distant from New London, near Mystic, which was the scene of the memorable encounter which all our historians from Cotton Mather to Dr. Palfrey have related with such minuteness. The conquest of the Pequots, with whom, man against man, no other of the red nations near their frontiers dared to contend, was heroic in the little band of Englishmen by whom it was effected. The reduction to a handful of outcasts of a nation that counted a thousand warriors was a stroke of fortune the English owed to the assistance of Uncas, a rebel against his lawful chieftain, Sassacus, and of Miantonimo, whose alliance had been secured by Roger Williams.[2]

Captain John Mason, who had served under Fairfax in the Netherlands, is

---

[1] Soon after the surrender a wagon loaded with wounded Americans was set in motion down the hill. In its descent it struck with great force against a tree, causing the instant death of several of its occupants.—"Gordon's Revolution," vol. iv., p. 179.

[2] Captain Mason, with the Connecticut and Massachusetts forces, numbering in all only ninety men, together with about four hundred Narragansets and Mohegans, attacked the Pequot fortress on the morning of May 26th, 1637. His Indian allies skulked in the rear. Mason's onset was a complete surprise; but he would not have succeeded had he not fired the fort, which created a panic among the enemy, and rendered them an easy prey to the English and friendly Indians surrounding it. Between six and seven hundred Pequots perished.

the ideal Puritan soldier. Before leading his men on to storm the Pequot stronghold, they knelt together in the moonlight, which shone brightly on that May morning, and commended themselves and their enterprise to God. Report says that the accompanying Narragansets and Mohegans were much astounded and troubled at the sight. Satisfied that he could not conquer the Pequots hand to hand with his little force, Mason himself applied a fire-brand to the wigwams. His own account of the Pequot war, reprinted by Prince in 1736, is the best and fullest narrative of its varying fortunes.

STORMING OF THE INDIAN FORTRESS.

Mason relates that he had but one pint of strong liquors in his army during its whole march. Like a prudent commander, he carried the bottle in his hand, and ingenuously says, when it was empty the very smelling of it would presently recover such as had fainted away from the extremity of the heat. Among the special providences of the day he mentions that Lieutenant Bull had an arrow shot into a hard piece of cheese he carried, that probably saved his life; "which may verify the old saying," adds the narrator, that "a little armor would serve, if a man knew where to place it."[1] Fuller, in one of his sermons, has another and a similar proverb: "It is better to fight naked than with bad armor, for the rags of a bad corselet make a deeper wound, and worse to be healed, than the bullet itself." Mason ultimately settled in Norwich, and died there.

---

[1] The English in these early wars fought in armor, that is to say, a steel cap and corselet, with a back and breast piece, over buff coats, the common equipment everywhere of that day for a horse or foot soldier.

Silas Deane was a native of Groton. Of the three men to whom Congress intrusted its secret negotiations with European powers, Franklin was the only one whose character did not permanently suffer, although he did not escape the malignity and envy of Arthur Lee. The Virginian's enmity and jealousy, aided by the influence of his brothers, were more successful in sullying the name and fame of Silas Deane. Yet Arthur Lee was a patriot and an honest man, whose public life was corroded by a morbid envy and distrust of his associates. A more disastrous appointment than his could hardly have been made, as his temperament especially unfitted him for a near approach to men who, with all the world's polish, were, in diplomatic phrase, able to cut an adversary's throat with a hair.

SILAS DEANE.

John Quincy Adams, who may perhaps have inherited his father's dislike of Deane, once said, in the course of a conversation with some friends:

"A son of Silas Deane was one of my school-fellows.[1] I never saw him again until last autumn, when I recognized him on board a steamboat, and introduced him to Lafayette, who said, 'Do you and Deane agree?' I said, 'Yes.' 'That's more than your fathers did before you,' replied the general.

"Silas Deane," continued Mr. Adams, "was a man of fine talents, but, like General Arnold, he was not true to his country. After he was dismissed from the service of the United States he went to England, lived for a long time on Lord Sheffield's patronage, and wrote a book which did more to widen the breach between England and America, and produce unpleasant feelings between the two countries, than any work that had been published. Finally he determined to return to America, but, in a fit of remorse and despair, committed suicide before the vessel left the Thames. His character and fate affected those of his son, who has lived in obscurity."[2]

It is possible that Silas Deane's patriotism was not proof against the ingratitude he had experienced, and that he became soured and disaffected; but it is scarcely just to his memory to call him traitor, or compare him with such an ignoble character as Arnold. Deane was the friend of Beaumarchais; he was also his confidant. He was the means of securing the services of Lafayette for America. There is little doubt that he exceeded his powers as commissioner, involving Congress in embarrassments, of which his recall was the solution. The malevolence of Lee and the crookedness of French diplomacy

---

[1] Mr. John Quincy Adams accompanied his father to France, and was placed at school near Paris.

[2] Miss E. S. Quincy's "Memoir."

did what was wanting to consign him to obscurity and poverty. The controversy over Deane's case produced a pamphlet from Thomas Paine, and caused John Jay to take the place resigned by Mr. Laurens as president of Congress. Deane and Beaumarchais were the scape-goats of the French alliance.[1]

John Ledyard was another monument of Groton. His first essay as a traveler exhibits his courage and resource. He entered Dartmouth as a divinity student; but poverty obliging him to withdraw from the college, and not having a shilling in his pocket, he made a canoe fifty feet long, with which he floated down the river one hundred and forty miles to Hartford. He then embarked for England as a common sailor, and while there, under the impulse of his passion for travel, enlisted with Captain Cook as a corporal of marines. He witnessed the tragical death of his captain. In 1771, after eight years' absence, Ledyard revisited his native country. His mother was then keeping a boarding-house at Southhold. Her son took lodgings with her without being recognized, as had once happened to Franklin in similar circumstances.

Ledyard's subsequent exploits in Europe, Asia, and Africa bear the impress of a daring and adventurous spirit. At last he offered himself for the more perilous enterprise of penetrating into the unknown regions of Central Africa. A letter from Sir Joseph Banks introduced him to the projectors of the expedition. "Before I had learned," says the gentleman to whom Sir Joseph's letter was addressed, " the name and business of my visitor, I was struck with the manliness of his person, the breadth of his chest, the openness of his countenance, and the inquietude of his eye. Spreading the map of Africa before him, and tracing a line from Cairo to Sennaar, and thence westward in the latitude and supposed direction of the Niger, I told him that was the route by which I was anxious that Africa might, if possible, be explored. He said he should consider himself singularly fortunate to be intrusted with the adventure. I asked him when he would set out. His answer was, 'To-morrow morning.' "[2]

New London's annals afford a passing glimpse of two men who, though enemies, were worthy of each other. During the war with England of 1812, Decatur, with the *United States*, *Macedonian*, and *Hornet*, was blockaded in New London by Sir T. M. Hardy with a squadron of superior force. The presence of the British fleet was a constant menace to the inhabitants, disquieted as they also were by the recollections of Arnold's descent. In vain Decatur tried to escape the iron grip of his adversary. Hardy's vigilance

---

[1] In 1835, when President Jackson demanded twenty-five millions of France on account of French spoliations, the claim of Beaumarchais was allowed, after deducting a million livres which had been advanced by Vergennes. Deane's heirs did not obtain an adjustment of his claims by Congress until 1842.

[2] Ledyard proceeded no farther than Cairo, where he died, in 1788, of a bilious fever.

never relaxed, and the American vessels remained as uselessly idle to the end of the war, as if laid up in ordinary. Once Decatur had prepared to slip away unperceived to sea, but signals made to the hostile fleet from the shore compelled him to abandon the attempt. He then proposed to Hardy a duel between his own and an equal force of British ships, which, though he did not absolutely decline the challenge,[1] it is pretty evident Sir Thomas never meant should happen.

Decatur was brave, fearless, and chivalric. He was the handsomest officer in the navy. Coleridge, who knew him well at Malta, always spoke of him in the highest terms. Our history does not afford a more impressive example of a useful life uselessly thrown away. Of his duel with Barron the following is probably a correct account of the closing scene: The combatants ap-

STEPHEN DECATUR.

proached within sixteen feet of each other, because one was near-sighted, and the rule was that both should take deliberate aim before the word was given. They both fired, and fell with their heads not ten feet apart. Each believed himself mortally hurt. Before their removal from the ground they were reconciled, and blessed each other, declaring there was nothing between them. All that was necessary to have prevented the meeting was a personal explanation.

Sir T. Hardy is well known as the captain of Nelson's famous flag-ship, the *Victory*, and as having received these last utterances of the dying hero: "Anchor, Hardy, anchor!" When the captain replied, "I suppose, my lord, Admiral Collingwood will now take upon himself the direction of affairs?" "Not while I live, I hope, Hardy!" cried the dying chief, endeavoring ineffectually to raise himself from the bed. "No," he added, "do *you* anchor, Hardy." "Shall *we* make the signal, sir?" "Yes," replied his lordship, "for if I live, I'll anchor. Take care of my dear Lady Hamilton, Hardy; take care of poor Lady Hamilton. Kiss me, Hardy."[2]

---

[1] Decatur offered to match the *United States* and *Macedonian* with the *Endymion* and *Statira*. Sir Thomas declined the proposal as made, but consented to a meeting between the *Statira* and *Macedonian* alone.

[2] Nelson commended almost with his latest breath Lady Hamilton and his daughter as a legacy to his country. Lady Hamilton, however, died in exile, sickness, and actual want at Calais, France, in 1815.

With whatever local preferences the traveler may have come, he will think the approach to Norwich charming. Through banks high and green, crested with groves, or decked with white villages, the river slips quietly away to mingle in the noisy world of waters beyond. In deeper shadows of the hills the pictures along the banks are reproduced with marvelous fidelity of form and coloring; and even the blue of the sky and white drifting clouds are mirrored there. All terrestrial things, however, appear, as in the camera, inverted— roofs or steeples pointing downward, men or animals walking with feet upward, along the banks, like flies on a ceiling. When autumn tints are on, the effects seen in the water are heightened by the confused masses of sumptuous foliage hung like garlands along the shores.

RUSTIC BRIDGE, NORWICH.

Norwich is ranged about a hill overlooking the Thames. It is on a point of rock-land infolded by two streams, the Yantic and Shetucket, that come tumbling and hurrying down from the higher northern ranges to meet and kiss each other in the Thames. Rising, terrace above terrace, the appearance of Norwich, as viewed from the river, is more striking in its *ensemble* than by reason of particular features. The water-side is the familiar dull red, above which glancing roofs and steeples among trees are seen retreating up the ascent. By night a ridged and chimneyed blackness bestrewed with lights rewards the curious gazer from the deck of a Sound steamboat. I admired in Norwich the broad avenues, the wealth of old trees, the luxurious spaciousness of the private grounds. Washington Street is one of the finest I have walked in. There is breathing-room everywhere, town and country seeming to meet and clasp hands, each giving to the other of the best it had to offer. I do not mean that Norwich is countrified; but its mid-city is so easily escaped as to do away with the feeling of imprisonment in a widerness of brick, stone, and plate-glass. The suburban homes of Norwich have an air of substantial comfort and delicious seclusion. In brief, wherever one has made up his mind to be buried, he would like to live in Norwich.

There are not a few picturesque objects about Norwich, especially by the shores of the Yantic, which, since being robbed of the falls, once its pride and glory, has become a prosaic mill-stream.[1] The water is of the blackness of Acheron, streaked with amber where it falls over rocks, and of a rusty brown in shallows, as if partaking of the color of bits of decayed wood or dead leaves which one sees at the bottom. The stream, after having been vexed by dams and tossed about by mill-wheels, bounds joyously, and with some touch of savage freedom, to strike hands with the Shetucket.

OLD MILL, NORWICH.

The practical reader should be told that the city of Norwich is the outgrowth and was of yore the landing of Norwich town, two miles above it. The city was then known as Chelsea and Norwich Landing. The Mohegans were lawful owners of the soil. Subsequent to the Pequot war hostilities broke out between Uncas, chief of the Mohegans, and Miantonimo, the Narraganset sachem. The Narragansets invaded the territory of the Mohegans, and a battle occurred on the Great Plains, near Greenville, a mile and a half below Norwich. The Narragansets suffered defeat, and their chief became a prisoner. He was delivered by Uncas to the English, who condemned him to death, and devolved upon Uncas the execution of the sentence. The captive chief was led to the spot where

---

[1] The falls were very beautiful, and have been celebrated by Trumbull's pencil and Mrs. Sigourney's verse. There still remain some curious cavities, worn in the rock by the prolonged rotary motion of loose stones. Lydia Huntley Sigourney, the most celebrated writer in prose or poetry of her day in New England, was a native of Norwich.

he had been made prisoner, and, while stalking with Indian stoicism in the midst of his enemies, was killed by one blow from a tomahawk at the signal of Uncas. Miantonimo was buried where he fell, and from him the spot takes its name of Sachem's Plain.[1]

War continued between the Narragansets and Mohegans, the former, led by a brother of Miantonimo, being again the assailants. Uncas was at length compelled to throw himself within his strong fortress, where he was closely besieged, and in danger of being overpowered. He found means to send intelligence to Saybrook, where Captain Mason commanded, that his supply of food was exhausted. Mason immediately sent Thomas Leffingwell with a boat-load of provision, which enabled Uncas to hold out until his enemy withdrew. For this act, which he performed single-handed, Leffingwell received from Uncas the greater part of Norwich; and in 1659, by a formal deed, signed by Uncas and his two sons, Owaneko and Attawanhood, he, with Mason, Rev. James Fitch, and others, became proprietors of the whole of Norwich.[2]

UNKOS, his mark
OWANEKO, his mark.
ATTAWAUHOOD, his mark.
SIGNATURES OF UNCAS AND HIS SONS.

I did not omit a visit to the ground where the "buried majesty" of Mohegan is lying. It is on the bank of the Yantic, in a secluded though populous neighborhood. A granite obelisk, with the name of Uncas in relief at its base, erected by citizens of Norwich, stands within the inclosure. The foundation was laid by President Jackson in 1833. Around are clustered a few mossy stones chiseled by English hands, with the brief record of the hereditary chieftains of a once powerful race.[3] In its native state the spot must have been singularly romantic and well chosen. A wooded height overhangs the river in full view of the falls, where their turbulence subsides into a placid onward flow, and where the chiefs, ere their de-

---

[1] Before the battle with the Narragansets, Uncas is said to have challenged Miantonimo to single combat, promising for himself and his nation to abide the result. Miantonimo refused. This chief, in his flight from the field, was overtaken by Mohegan warriors, who impeded him until Uncas could come up. When Uncas laid his hand on Miantonimo's shoulder, the latter sat down in token of submission, maintaining a sullen silence. Uncas is said to have eaten a piece of his flesh.

[2] The proprietors numbered thirty-five. Uncas received about seventy pounds for nine square miles. The settlement of Norwich is considered to have begun in 1660, when Rev. James Fitch removed from Saybrook to Norwich (town).

[3] The following inscriptions are from the royal burial-ground of the Mohegans:

"Here lies ye body of Pompi Uncas, son of Benjamin and Ann Uncas, and of ye royal blood, who died May ye first, 1740, in ye 21st year of his age."

"Here lies Sam Uncas, the 2d and beloved son of his father, John Uncas, who was the grandson of Uncas, grand sachem of Mohegan, the darling of his mother, being daughter of said Uncas, grand sachem. He died July 31st, 1741, in the 28th year of his age."

"In memory of Elizabeth Joquib, the daughter of Mahomet, great-grandchild to ye first Uncas, great sachem of Mohegan, who died July ye 5th, 1750, aged 33 years."

parture for the happy hunting-grounds, might look their last on the villages of their people. It was the Indian custom to bury by the margin of river, lake, or ocean. Here, doubtless, repose the bones of many grim warriors, seated in royal state, with their weapons and a pot of succotash beside them. The last interment here was of Ezekiel Mazeon, a descendant of Uncas, in 1826. The feeble remnant of the Mohegans followed him to the grave.[1]

UNCAS'S MONUMENT.

Mr. Sparks remarks that the history of the Indians, like that of the Carthaginians, has been written by their enemies. As the faithful, unwavering ally of the English, Uncas has received the encomiums of their historians. His statesmanship has been justified by time and history. By alliance with the English he preserved his people for many generations after the more numerous and powerful Pequots, Narragansets, and Wampanoags had ceased to exist. In 1638 he came with his present of wampum to Boston, and having convinced the English of his loyalty, thus addressed them: "This heart" (laying his hand upon his breast) "is not mine, but yours. Command me any difficult service, and I will do it. I have no men, but they are all yours. I will never believe any Indian against the English any more." It is this invincible fidelity, approved by important services, that should make his name and character respected by every descendant of the fathers of New England.

ARNOLD'S BIRTHPLACE.

About midway of the pleasant avenue that unites old Norwich with new is the birthplace of Benedict Arnold.[2]

---

[1] The hereditary chieftainship was extinct as long ago as the beginning of the century. The Mohegans occupied a strip of land containing two thousand seven hundred acres, lying on the Thames between Norwich and New London, above the mouth of Stony Brook, and between the river and Montville. In 1633 the Indian population of Connecticut was computed at eight persons to the square mile; the earliest enumeration of the Mohegans made their number one thousand six hundred and sixty-three souls; in 1797 only four hundred remained. By 1825 the nation was reduced to a score or two, a portion having emigrated to Stockbridge, Massachusetts. The Mohegan reserve was divided in 1790 among the remaining families of the nation. The Mohegans were probably a distinct nation, though Uncas was a vassal of the Pequots.

[2] On the Colchester road, or Town Street, near the junction of a street leading toward the Falls. The estate is now locally known as the Ripley Place.

Somewhat farther on, and when within half a mile of the town, you also see at the right the homely little building which was the apothecary's in which Arnold worked as a boy with pestle and mortar to the acceptance of his master, Dr. Lathrop, who lived in the adjoining mansion. One can better imagine Arnold dealing out musket-bullets than pills, and mixing brimstone with saltpetre rather than harmless drugs. As a boy he was bold, high-spirited, and cruel.

ELM-TREES BY THE WAYSIDE.

In this neighborhood I saw a group of elms unmatched for beauty in New England. One of them is a king among trees. They are on a grassy slope, before an inviting mansion, and are in the full glory of maturity. It was a feast to stand under their branching arms, and be fanned and soothed by the play of the breeze among their green tresses, that fell in fountains of rustling foliage from their crowned heads. A benison on those old trees! May they never fall into the clutches of that class who have a real and active hatred of every thing beautiful, or that appeals to more than their habitual perception is able to discover!

I made a brief visit at the mansion built by General Jedediah Huntington before he removed to New London after the Old War.[1]

In the dining-room was a full-length of General Eben Huntington, painted by Trumbull at the age of eighteen. On seeing it some years afterward, Trumbull took out his

GENERAL HUNTINGTON'S HOUSE.

---

[1] The general was appointed collector of New London by Washington. His first wife was a daughter of Governor Trumbull.

penknife and said to his host and friend, "Eb, let me put my knife through this." Another portrait by the same hand, representing the general at the siege of Yorktown, is in a far different manner. The three daughters of General Huntington, then living in the old family mansion, in referring to the warm friendship between their father and the painter, mentioned that the first and last portraits painted by Colonel Trumbull were of members of their family.

Near General Huntington's, where many of the choicest spirits of the Revolution have been entertained, is the handsome mansion of Governor Huntington, a remote connection of his military neighbor. Without the advantages of a liberal education, he became a member of the old Congress, and its president, chief-justice, and governor of Connecticut. President Dwight, who knew him well, extols his character and abilities warmly and highly.

MANSION OF GOVERNOR HUNTINGTON.

I had frequent opportunities of seeing, in my rambles about the environs of New London and Norwich, the beautiful dwarf flowering laurel (*Kalmia augustifolia*) that is almost unknown farther north. In the woods, where it was growing in wild luxuriance, it appeared like a gigantic azelia, ablaze with fragrant bloom of white and pink. It used to be said that honey collected by the bee from this flower was poisonous. The broad-leaved laurel, or calico-tree (*Kalmia latifolia*) was believed to be even more injurious, instances being mentioned where death had occurred from eating the flesh of pheasants that had fed on its leaves.

Norwich town represents the kernel from which the city has sprung, and retains also no little of the savor incident to a population that has held innovations at arms-length. It has quiet, freshness, and a certain rural comeliness. A broad green, or common, planted with trees, is skirted by houses, many of them a century or more old, among which I thought I now and then detected the no longer familiar well-sweep, with the "old oaken bucket" standing by the curb. On one side of the common the old court-house is still seen.

Take the path beside the meeting-house, ascending the overhanging rocks by some natural steps, and you will be richly repaid for the trifling exertion.

The view embraces a charming little valley watered by the Yantic, which here flows through rich meadow-lands and productive farms. Encompassing the settlement is another elevated range of the rocky hills common to this region, making a sort of amphitheatre in which the town is naturally placed.

CONGREGATIONAL CHURCH.

The old church of Norwich town formerly stood in the hollow between two high hills above its present site. The pound, now its next neighbor, is still a lawful inclosure in most of the New England States. Not many years ago, I knew of a town in Massachusetts that was presented by a grand jury for not having one. I visited the old grave-yard, remarkable for its near return to a state of nature. Many stones had fallen, and sometimes two were kept upright by leaning one against the other. Weeds, brambles, and vines impeded my footsteps or concealed the grave-stones. I must often repeat the story of the shameful neglect which involves most of our older cemeteries. One is not quite sure, in leaving them, that he does not carry away on his feet the dust of former generations. Some of the stones are the most curious in form and design I have met with. The family tombs of Governor and General Huntington are here.

PETER STUYVESANT.

CHAPTER XXVIII.

SAYBROOK.

" Says Tweed to Till,
  'What gars ye rin sae still?'
Says Till to Tweed,
  'Though ye rin wi' speed,
    An' I rin slaw,
  For ae man that ye droon,
    I droon twa.' "—*Old Song.*

RATHER more than a hundred miles from New York the railway crosses the Connecticut River, on one of those bridges that at a little distance resemble spiders' webs hung between the shores. From here one may look down quite to the river's mouth, where it enters the Sound; and if it be a warm summer's day, the bluish-gray streak of land across it may be seen. The Connecticut is the only river of importance emptying upon the New England coast that has not an island lodged in its throat.

It was on one of those parched days of midsummer, when the very air is quivering, and every green thing droops and shrivels under a vertical sun, that I first alighted at the station at Saybrook. The listless, fagged, and jaded air of city swells lounging about the platform, the flushed faces of blooming girls and watchful dowagers, betokened the general prostration of weary humanity, who yearned for the musical plash of sea-waves as the withering leaves and dusty grass longed for rain.

How feminine New England exaggerates, to be sure! A group of three young ladies exchange their views upon the sultriness of the day: one observes, "What a dreadful hot day!" a second declares it "horrid" (torrid, perhaps she meant to say); and the last pronounces it "perfectly frightful," emphasizing the opinion by opening her umbrella with a sharp snap. What they would have said to an earthquake, a conflagration, or a shipwreck, is left to bewildering conjecture.

In a certain unquiet portion of the American Union, the term Connecticut Yankee is expressive of concentrated dislike for shrewd bargaining, a nasal twang of speech, and a supposed desire to overreach one's neighbor. How often have I heard in the South the expression, "A mean Yankee;" as if, forsooth, meanness were sectional! Here in New England a Connecticut Yankee is spoken of as a cunning blade or sharp fellow; as an Englishman would say, "He's Yorkshire;" or an Italian, "È Spoletino."

The day of wooden nutmegs is past and gone, and Connecticut is more familiarly known as the "Land of Steady Habits." The whole State is a hive. Every smoky town you see is a busy work-shop. The problem of the Connecticut man is how to do the most work in the shortest time, whether by means of a sewing-machine, a Colt, or a *mitrailleuse*. If I should object to any thing in him, it would be the hurry and worry, the *drive*, which impels him through life—and in this I do not imagine he differs from the average American man of business—until, like one of his own engines that is always worked under a full pressure of steam, he stops running at last. That is why we see so many old men of thirty, and so many premature gray hairs in New England.

But what I chiefly lament is the disappearance of the Yankee—not the conventional Yankee of the theatre, for he had never an existence elsewhere; but the hearty yet suspicious, "cute" though green, drawling, whittling, unadulterated Yankee, with his broad humor, delicious *patois*, and large-hearted patriotism. His very mother-tongue is forgotten. Not once during these rambles have I heard his old familiar "I swaow," or "Git aout," or "Dew tell."[1] Railway and telegraph, factory and work-shop, penetrating into the

---

[1] The term "Brother Jonathan" originated with Washington, who applied it to Governor Jonathan Trumbull, of Connecticut. When any important matter was in agitation the general would say, "We must consult Brother Jonathan."

most secluded hamlets, have rubbed off all the crust of an originality so pronounced as to have become the type, and often the caricature too, of American nationality the world over.

One peculiarity I have noticed is that of calling spinsters, of whatever age, "girls." I knew two elderly maiden ladies, each verging on three-score, who were universally spoken of as the "Young girls," their names, I should perhaps explain, being Young. Once, when in quest of lodgings in a strange place, I was directed to apply to the two Brown girls, whose united ages, as I should judge, could not be less than a century and a quarter. But one is not to judge of New England girls by this sample.

Another practice which prevails in some villages is that of designating father and son, where both have a common Christian-name, as "Big Tom" and "Little Tom;" and brother and sister as "Bub" and "Sis." One can hardly maintain a serious countenance to hear a stalwart fellow of six feet alluded to as "Little" Tom, or Joe, or Bill, or a full-grown man or woman as "Bub" or "Sis." On the coast, nicknames are current principally among the sea-faring element; "Guinea Bill" or "Portugee Jack," presupposes the owner to have made a voyage to either of those distant lands.

The Italians count the whole twenty-four hours, beginning at half an hour after sunset. By this method of computation I reckoned on arriving at Saybrook Point at exactly twenty-two o'clock. I walked through the village leisurely observant of its outward aspect, which was that of undisturbed tranquillity. Modern life had been so long in reaching it, that it had been willing to accommodate itself to the old houses, and so far to the old life of the place. The toilets here, as elsewhere, encroached in many instances upon those of the last century, and were wonderfully like the portraits one sees of the time. Now, let us have the old manners back again.

One of the pleasantest old houses in Saybrook is the Hart mansion, which stands in the main street of the village, heavily draped by the foliage of three elm-trees of great size and beauty. It was a favorite retreat of that gallant sailor, Isaac Hull, who lost his heart there.[1] Like Nelson, he was the idol of his sailors, for he was as humane as he was brave. He seldom ordered one of his old sea-dogs to be flogged, but would call a culprit before him, and after scolding him soundly with affected roughness of tone and manner, would tell him to return to his duty. The *Old Ironsides* was loved with a love almost like that which man bears to woman. Ladies would have kissed the hem of her sails; men scraped the barnacles from her bottom, and carried them home in their pockets. I have seen no end of canes, picture-frames, and

---

[1] General William Hart, an old soldier of the Revolution, was a wealthy and highly esteemed citizen of Saybrook. In 1795, with Oliver Phelps and others, he purchased the tract in Ohio called the Western Reserve. The Commodores Hull, uncle and nephew, married sisters belonging to this family. Commodore Andrew Hull Foote was also a nephew of Commodore Isaac Hull, whose widow was still living when I visited Saybrook in 1874.

other souvenirs of this famous ship treasured by fortunate possessors; and one of the old merchants of Boston had his street door made of her oak.

ISAAC HULL.

Saybrook is languid. It is dispersed along one broad and handsome street, completely canopied by an arch of foliage. You seem, when at the entrance, to be looking through a green tunnel. In this street there is no noise and but little movement. The few shops were without custom. After the spasm of activity caused by the arrival of the train—when it seemed for the moment to rub its eyes and brisk up a little, carriages and pedestrians having mysteriously disappeared somewhere—the old town dozed again.

The Connecticut is here tame and uninteresting, with near shores of salt-marsh flatness. Yellow sand-bars, green hummocks, or jutting points skirted with pine-groves, inclose the stream, which is broad, placid, and shallow. There are no iron headlands, or dangerous reefs. Nature seems quite in harmony with the general quietude and restfulness.

A few years ago there existed at the Point the remains of a colonial fortress, with much history clustering around it. It was raised in the very infancy of English settlement at the mouth of the Connecticut; and when the Revolution came, the old dismounted cannon, that had perhaps done duty with Howard or Blake, were again placed on the ramparts. The railway people have reduced the hill on which it stood to a flat and dreary gravel waste.[1] This is walking into antiquity with a vengeance! It is perhaps fortunate that the Coliseum, Temple Bar, and St. Denis are not where they would be valued for the cubic yards of waste material they might afford.

The Dutch anticipated the English in the settlement on Connecticut River. The Hollanders at Fort Amsterdam, and the then rival colonies of Plymouth and Massachusetts Bay, were each desirous of obtaining a foothold which each felt too weak to undertake alone. The country had been subjugated by the Pequots, whose territory neither colony might invade without bringing the whole nation upon them.

---

[1] The eminence on which the fort stood, also called Tomb Hill, jutted into the river, being united to the shore by a beach, and bordered by salt-marshes. It was steep and unassailable from any near vantage-ground. In 1647 the first fort was accidentally destroyed by fire.

The Dutch were also first to visit the river, and to inform the Pilgrims of its beauty and advantages for traffic. In 1633, Massachusetts having rejected overtures for a joint occupation, Plymouth determined to establish a trading-post upon the river without her aid. Apprised of this intention, the Dutch dispatched an expedition, which disembarked where Hartford now is. A house was hastily erected, and ordnance mounted, with which the Hollanders gave notice that they meant to keep out intruders.

The Plymouth expedition, under command of William Holmes, ascended the river, and, notwithstanding an attempt to stop them, passed by the Dutch fort. They landed at Nattawanute, afterward Windsor, and, having made themselves secure, sent their vessel home. Word was sent to Fort Amsterdam of the invasion. A company of seventy dispatched to the scene advanced "brimful of wrath and cabbage," with drums beating and colors flying, against the English fort. Seeing the Pilgrims were in nowise disconcerted, the Dutch captain ordered a halt; a parley took place, and, having thus vindicated the national honor, Gualtier Twilley's men withdrew.[1]

The attempts of Plymouth to establish tributary plantations, with trading-posts, at the extreme eastern and western limits of New England, were equally disastrous. Massachusetts stood quietly by, and saw her rival dispossessed at Penobscot, but at Windsor the Plymouth people soon found themselves hemmed in between settlements made by emigrants from the bay. As a quarrel would perhaps have been alike fatal to both, Plymouth gave way to her more powerful neighbor.

The English settlement of Connecticut is usually assigned to the year 1635, the year of beginnings at Hartford, Wethersfield, and Saybrook. In the autumn the younger Winthrop sent a few men to take possession and fortify at the mouth of the Connecticut, as agent of Lords Say, Brook, and their associate owners of the patent.[2] This expedition forestalled by a few days only a new attempt to obtain possession by the Dutch, who, finding the English already landed and having cannon mounted, abandoned their design.

Through the agency of the celebrated Hugh Peters, the patentees engaged, and sent to New England, Lion Gardiner, a military engineer who had served in the Low Countries. He arrived at Boston in November, 1635, and proceeded to the fort at the mouth of the Connecticut. He was followed by George Fenwick, sent over by Lord Say to be resident agent of the English

---

[1] In the British State Paper Office is a translation of part of a letter, dated at Fort Amsterdam, in 1633, from Gualtier Twilley to the governor of Massachusetts Bay, concerning the right of the Dutch to the river. The governor says that he has taken possession of it in the name of the States General, and set up a house on the north side, with intent to plant. He desires Winthrop will defer his claims until their superior magistrates are agreed. The word "[Hudson?]" is placed after "river" in the calendars, but the date and other given facts are probably allusions to the Connecticut attempt.

[2] Lieutenant Gibbons, Sergeant Willard, and some carpenters. — "Lion Gardiner's Account."

proprietors. Fenwick, accompanied by Peters, reached the fort in the spring. The plantation was called Saybrook, as a compliment to the two principal personages interested in its founding.

Saybrook has perhaps acquired a certain importance in the eyes of historical writers to which no other spot of New England's soil can pretend. There is little room to doubt that Lord Say, and perhaps some of his associates, strongly entertained the idea of removing thither.[1] A more debatable assertion, which is, however, well fortified with authorities, represents Oliver Cromwell, John Hampden, Pym, and Sir Arthur Haselrig as having been prevented from embarking only by an express order from the king: some, indeed, assert that they actually embarked.[2]

In the old burial-place of Saybrook Point is the most curious sepulchral memorial in New England. I can compare it with nothing but a Druid monument, it is so massy, so roughly shaped, and so peculiar in form. Until a few years ago, it stood within a field south-west of the fort, over the dust of George Fenwick's wife, a woman of gentle blood. The "improvements" made by the railway in this vicinity caused the removal of the monument to its present position. When the remains of Lady Fenwick were disinterred, the skeleton was found to be nearly entire. Beneath the skull was lying a heavy braid of auburn hair, which was parceled out among the villagers. My informant offered to show me the tress that had fallen to his share.

A MOSS-GROWN MEMORIAL.

I acknowledge it, I am the fool of association; and when I see the spade thrust among graves, I wince a little. I would have Shakspeare's appeal and malediction inscribed over the entrance to every old grave-yard in New En-

---

[1] See the correspondence in Hutchinson's "History of Massachusetts," appendix, vol. i., between John Cotton and Lord Say.

[2] There is nothing improbable in the story, either from the rank or political importance of the personages mentioned; the civil commotions in England rather give it a groundwork of probability. The authorities in support of the emigration are Dr. George Bates, the physician of Cromwell, in his "*Elenchus Maluum Nuperorum in Anglia*," William Lilly's "Life and Times" (London, 1822), Sir William Dugdale's "Troubles in England," Mather's "Magnalia," Oldmixon's "British Empire in America," Neal's "History of New England," and Hutchinson's "History of Massachusetts." Hume, Chalmers, Grahame, Hallam, Russell, Macaulay, and others repeat the story with various modifications; Aiken, Forster, Bancroft, Young, and others deny or doubt it. The arguments *pro* and *con* may be consulted in the "New England Historical and Genealogical Register for 1866."

gland. But, after all, what is Shakspeare's malediction to these trouble-tombs who anticipate the Resurrection, and give the burial service the lie. Our bones ache at the thought of being tossed about on a laborer's shovel. Rather come cremation than mere tenure at will at the tender mercies of these levelers. When we have been "put to bed with a shovel," and have pulled our green coverlet over us, let us have the peace that passeth all understanding.

Not much is known of Lady Anne Boteler, or Butler, the wife of George Fenwick. It is surmised that she died in childbed. The inscription that her monument undoubtedly bore has been so long obliterated that no record remains of it. A newer one, with the simple name and date, "Lady Fenwick, died 1648," has been cut in the perishable sandstone. Some one has also caused the cross to be chiseled there.[1] Considering the peculiar aversion with which the Puritans regarded the cross, the appearance of one on the tombstone of Lady Fenwick is suggestive of the famous prohibition of the cemetery of Saint Médard:

"De par le roi, défense à Dieu
De faire miracle en ce lieu."

Dr. Dwight states, as of report, that Fenwick, before his return to England, made provision for having his wife's tomb kept in repair. The sale of the title of Lords Say and Brook by him, in 1644, to Connecticut, is considered evidence as well of the existence of the design of removal alluded to as of its abandonment. After the death of Lady Fenwick her husband returned to England, and is mentioned as one of the regicide-judges. He subsequently appears with the title of "colonel," and is believed to be the same person who besieged Hume Castle, in 1650, for Cromwell. On being summoned, the governor sent his defiance in verse:

"I, William of the Wastle,
Am now in my Castle:
And aw the dogs in the town
Shanna gar me gang down."[2]

The English at Saybrook Point protected the land approach with a pali-

---

[1] Lechford, in his "Plain Dealing," says, "There are five or six townes and Churches upon the River Connecticut where are worthy master Hooker, master Warham, master Hewet, and divers others, and master Fenwike, with the Lady Boteler, at the river's mouth in a faire house, and well fortified, and one master Higgison, a young man, their chaplain. These Plantations have a Patent; the Lady was lately admitted of Master Hooker's Church, and thereupon her child was baptized."

[2] Fenwick "played upon him" a little "with the great guns," which did gar him gang down more fool than he went up.—CARLYLE. Hutchinson places his death in 1657. There was a Lieutenant-colonel Fenwick killed in one of the battles between Condé and Turenne, in Flanders, in 1658. The action occurred before Dunkirk. Fenwick's last request of Lockhart, the English commander, was to be buried in Dunkirk.—THURLOE, vol. i., p.156.

sade drawn across the narrow isthmus, which very high tides overflowed and isolated from the main-land. Their corn-field was two miles distant from the fort, and skulking Pequots were always on the alert to waylay and murder them. Some of the Bay magistrates having spoken contemptuously of Indian arrows, Gardiner[1] sent them the rib of a man in which one, after passing through the body, had buried itself so that it could not be withdrawn.

Gardiner's manner of dealing with Indians was peculiar. When the expedition against the Pequots was at Saybrook Fort, distrusting Mohegan faith, he resolved to make a trial of it. He therefore called Uncas before him, and said, "You say you will help Major Mason, but I will first see it; therefore send you now twenty men to the Bass River, for there went yesternight six Indians in a canoe thither; fetch them now, dead or alive, and then you shall go with Major Mason, else not." So Uncas sent his men, who killed four and captured one, the sixth making his escape.

The old burial-ground of Saybrook is neat and well kept. Lady Fenwick's monument is just within the entrance, concealed by a clump of fir-trees. Not a quarter of the graves have stones, and that part of the ground occupied by the ancients of the village is so mounded and overcrowded that you may not avoid walking upon them. In another spot head-stones jutted above the turf at every variety of angle, and several monuments had cavities, showing where they had been robbed of leaden coats of arms—to run into bullets, perhaps. All are of ample dimensions, and on older ones creeping mosses conceal the inscriptions. The variety of color presented by slate, sandstone, or marble upon green is not unpleasing to the eye, yet those reckonings scored upon slate shall endure longest.

In the Hart inclosure repose the ashes of the once beautiful Jeannette M. M. Hart, whose slab bears the symbol of her faith. She, the fairest of all the sisters, renounced the world and, embracing the Roman faith, became a nun. Her remains were brought home from Rome, and laid to rest with the service of the Church of England. In a little separate inclosure, whispered to have been consecrated by the rite of Rome, another sister is lying. When Commodore Hull cruised in the old frigate *United States,* one of these beautiful girls was on board his ship. She was seen by Bolivar, who fell desperately in love with her at a ball, and became so attentive that the American officers believed they were betrothed.[2]

Saybrook was also the original site of Yale College, fifteen commence-

---

[1] Lion Gardiner became the owner of the fertile island bearing his name at the east end of Long Island. It is seven miles long and a mile broad, with excellent soil. Some time ago its peculiar beauty and salubrity caused it to be called the Isle of Wight. The island, I believe, still remains in the possession of the Gardiner family. For many years it descended regularly from father to son by entail. The Indian name was Munshongonuc, or "the place of Indian graves."

[2] One sister married Commodore Hull, as related; another married Hon. Heman Allen, minister to Chili; and a third, Rev. Dr. Jarvis, of St. Paul's, Boston.

SAYBROOK.

ments having occurred here. The building, which was of a single story, stood about midway between fort and palisade. Its removal, in 1718, to New Haven occasioned great excitement, and the library had to be carried away under the protection of a guard. The Saybrook Platform, so called, was adopted here after the commencement of 1708. Harvard and Yale were in infancy probably not different from those Scotch universities which Dr. Johnson said were like a besieged town, where every man had a mouthful, but no man a bellyful.

The shores about Saybrook offer little that is noteworthy. On the beach the tide softly laps the incline of sand, that looks like a slab of red freestone, fine-grained and hard. A dry spot flashing beneath your tread, or perhaps a sea-bird circling above your head, attends your loiterings.

Look now off upon the Sound, where the golden sunset is flowing over it, gilding the waves, the distant shores, and the sails of passing vessels with beams that in dying are transfused into celestial fires. Idle boats are rocked and caressed on this golden sea. Yonder distant gleam is a light-house, kindled with heavenly flame. The world is transfigured, that we may believe in Paradise. Soon yellow flushes into pale crimson, blending with a sapphire sky. Standing on the strand, we are transformed, and seem to quaff of the elixir of life. Now the violet twilight deepens into sombre shadows. A spark appears in the farther sea. Soon others shine out like glow-worms in your path; while twinkling stars, seen for a moment, disappear, as if they, too, revolved for some more distant shore. The Sound becomes a vague and heaving blackness. And now, with gentle murmurings, the rising tide effaces our wayward foot-prints.

INDEX.

A.

Acadia, New England, included in, 18; means taken to people, 25; expatriation of the French, 303.
Adams, John, resists the pretensions of the French Directory, 378, 392.
Agamenticus, called Snadoun Hill, 21; landfall of early navigators, 120; ascent of, 123; mountains seen from, 125.
Agassiz, Louis, at Mount Desert, 48; anecdotes of, and personal appearance, 49.
Alden, John, claimed to have first landed on Plymouth Rock, 290; tradition of his courtship, 300, 301.
Alexander, William (Earl of Sterling), islands in his patent, 339.
Alfonse, Jean, cited, 18; his manuscripts and account of him, 22.
Allerton, Isaac, at Marblehead, 236.
Appledore Island, 160, 187.
Argall, Sir Samuel, his descent at Mount Desert Island, 24, 36.
Arnold, Governor Benedict, extract from his will, 371, *note*.
Arnold, General Benedict, 427; anecdote of, 427, 428; attacks New London, 428, 429; birthplace, 437.
Aubert, Thomas, supposed discovery by, 21, 275.
Audubon, John James, at Mount Desert, 48.
Auvergne, Latour de, in America, 396.
Auvergne regiment, 396.

B.

Badger's Island, 149.
Bald Head Cliff (York, Maine), described, 115, 116; wreck at, 117.
Bar Harbor, visit to, 43.
Barton, Colonel William, carries off General Prescott, 409, 410.
Basques, on the New England coast, 125; at Newfoundland, 126.
Baye Françoise, the true Frenchman's Bay, 50.
Beauchamp, John, mentioned, 60.

Beaver Tail (Newport), 357, 381.
Beaver, the, former value of, 41, 42.
Beebe, Rev. George, at the Shoals, 167.
Belfast, Maine, name of, 63, *note*.
Belknap, Jeremy, his account of a sand-avalanche, 319.
Berkeley, George (Bishop), portrait of, 368; at Newport, 384.
Bernard, General Simon, Napoleon's estimate of, 378, 379; in the United States, 379; builds Fortress Monroe and Fort Morgan, 379, *note*.
Biard, Père, arrives at Port Royal, 35; at Mount Desert, 35.
Billington, John, executed at Plymouth, 267.
Biron, Duc de Lauzun, 394.
Blauw, or Blaeuv Guillaume, atlas cited, 21.
Block Island, 421. *See note.*
Blue-berries, their value in New England, 39; humors of the pickers, 120.
Blue-fish, singular disappearance of, 344.
Blythe, Captain Samuel, killed, 107.
Body of Laws, extracts from, 268.
Bon Temps, order of, 95, 96.
Boon Island, wreck of the *Nottingham*, 172, 173.
Boteler, Lady Anne. *See Fenwick.*
Bradford, William, his manuscript history of Plymouth, 277; monument at Plymouth, 277, 284, 285, 286, 290, *note*, 291; receives Massasoit, 293, 294; account of Cape Cod, 307.
Brevoort, J. Carson, 359, *note*.
Brigadier's Island, ownership and fishery at, 64.
Brock, Rev. John, anecdote of, 163.
Brodhead, John Romeyn, mentioned, 22, *note*, 278.
Bromfield, Major, kills Colonel Ledyard, 428.
Brother Jonathan, origin of the name, 442, *note*.
Broughton, Nicholas, 251.
Brown, Dexter, establishes first stage-coach between Boston and Providence, 411.
Brown, Robert, founder of Brownists, 280, *note*.
Brown's Island (Plymouth), disappearance of, 295.
Bull, Governor Henry, burial-place of, 405, *note*.
Burroughs, George, at Wells, 111.
Burrows, Lieutenant William, killed, 107.

C.

Cabot, Sebastian, voyage of, 20.
Camden Mountains, approach to, 62; Indian name of, 93.
Canonicut Island, visited, 380. *See note.*
Cape Ann, fishery at, 157.
Cape Arundel, spouting-horn at, 47.
Cape Breton, early knowledge of, 21.
Cape Cod, a *coup d'œil* of, 304–306; early accounts of, 307; Poutrincourt's fight at, 308; ship canal begun from Barnstable to Buzzard's Bay, 311, *note;* harbors frozen in 1875, 320; changes in its exterior shores, 322, 323.
Cape Cod Harbor (Provincetown).
Cape Neddock, 122.
Capuchins, at Pentagoët, 81; Napoleon's opinion of, 82.
Cartier, Jacques, sails for America, 20; manner of taking possession of Canada, 23.
Carver, John, supposed burial-place, 276.
Carver, Nathaniel, Lord Nelson's generous act to, 271.
Castin, the younger, kidnaped, 81; returns to France, 81.
Castin, Jean Vincent, Baron de, sketch of, 79, 80; in the attack on Pemaquid, 98.
Castine, approach to, 64, 65; views from Fort George, 65; seized and fortified by the British, 67; besieged, 68, 69; Indian name of, 67; Fort Pentagoët described, 74; singular discovery of coins at, 74, 75; its early history sketched, 76–82; old cemetery of, 84.
Cedar Island, 160.
Chambly, M. de, made prisoner at Pentagoët, 78.
Champernowne, Arthur, 149.
Champernowne, Francis, 149.
Champlain, Samuel, quoted, 18; title of his map, 22, *note;* names Mount Desert, 28; voyage of 1604, 92, 93; suggests "L'Ordre de Bon Temps," 95; descries Isles of Shoals, 122; description of Plymouth Bay, 274, 275; at Cape Cod, 308; account of Indian fishing, 314.
Channing, William Ellery, 400, *note.*
Charlevoix's account of siege of Fort William Henry, 99.
Chastellux, Marquis, 394.
Chilton, Mary, tradition about, 291.
Chouacouet. *See* Saco River.
Christmas, how observed in Plymouth, 292.
Chubb, Pascho, surrenders the fort at Pemaquid, 99.
Church, Colonel Benjamin, at Castine, 75, 302, 372.
Church, F. E., anecdote of, 50.
Clark, D. Wasgatt, a native of Mount Desert, 49.
Clark's Island (Plymouth), 269; sail to, 295;
Watson House, 297; Election Rock, 297, 298; landing of the exploring party, 298.
Clinton, Sir Henry, outgeneraled by Washington, 428.
Cob-money, specimens found at Castine, 75, *note.*
Cod-fish aristocracy, origin of the appellation, 314.
Cod-fishery in the sixteenth century, 156; in the seventeenth, 232–236; at Provincetown, 313, 314.
Coddington, William, sketch of, 360; at Anne Hutchinson's trial, 361; decay of his family, 362; burial-place of, 405.
Coffin, Sir Isaac, founds a school at Nantucket, 341, 342.
Coggeshall, John, at Anne Hutchinson's trial, 361; monument to, 405.
Colbert mentioned, 78, 82.
Collins, Captain Gamaliel, 316.
Colonial society described, 60.
Connecticut River, settlements on, 444, 445, 446.
Constitution, frigate, chased into Marblehead, 256.
Corey, Giles, pressed to death, 227.
Corwin, Jonathan, a witch-judge, 223.
Cousin, Captain, story of his discovery of America, 22.
Cradock, Governor Matthew, establishes fishing-station at Marblehead, 236.
Cranberry, the growth and culture of, 39, 317.
Cranberry Islands, 39.
Cromwell, Oliver, his proposed emigration to New England, 446.
Cushman, Charlotte, residence at Newport, 375.
Cushman, Robert, 277.
Cushman, Thomas, 277.
Cutts, Captain Joseph, 143.
Cutts, Sarah Chauncy, sad story of, 142, 143.
Cuttyhunk, first English colony at, 327. *See note.*

D.

Damariscotta, oyster-shell heaps at, visited and described, 100, 101.
Daniel, Father, his history mentioned, 23.
Dartmouth Indians sold as slaves, 302.
D'Aulnay Charnisay (Charles de Menou), at Pentagoët, 76; imbroglio with La Tour, 77; his death, 78.
Dean, John Ward, 173, *note.*
Deane, John, 173.
Deane, Silas, Mr. Adams's opinion of, 431.
Decatur, Stephen, blockaded at New London, 432; duel with Barron, 433. *See note.*
De Costa, B. F., mentioned, 22, *note.*
De Monts, efforts of to obtain colonists, 25; cedes his privileges in Acadia, 34, 35; his

INDEX. 453

commission and privileges, 153–155; descries the Isles of Shoals, 155; in Plymouth Bay, 273, 274, 275.
Dermer, Captain Thomas, at Nantucket, 324.
Deux-Ponts, Count Christian, anecdote of, 395. *See note.*
D'Iberville, makes a demonstration against Pemaquid, 97; captures Fort William Henry, 98. *See note.*
Dighton Rock, inscription attributed to Northmen, 369, 416, 417, 418.
Dorr Rebellion, 365, *note.*
Doty or Doten, Edward, fights a duel, 266, 297, *note.*
Douglass, William, quoted, 23, 24.
Down East, an undiscovered country, 85, 86.
Drake, Sir Bernard, manner of his death, 24.
Dreuillettes, Père Gabriel, at Plymouth, 285.
Duck Island, 160, 190.
Dummer, Shubael, minister of York, 135.
Dumplings, fort on, 358, 380, 381.
Dunbar, Colonel David, at Pemaquid, 100.
Dutch Island, 380.
Du Thet, Gilbert, killed at Mount Desert, 36.
Duxbury, sail to, from Plymouth, 299; Captain's Hill and monument, 300; historic personages of Duxbury, 300, *et seq.*
Dwight, Timothy, at Newport, 370.

E.

Ellery, William, his death, 400.
Endicott, Governor John, his farm, 218, 255.
Estaing, Count de, at Newport, 387; guillotined, 388.
Excommunication in New England churches, 280, 281, *note.*

F.

Faunce, Thomas, identifies Plymouth Rock, 289, *note.*
Fenwick, George, 445, 446, 447.
Fenwick, Lady, her remarkable monument, 446; her story, 447.
Fillmore, John, exploit of, 176.
Fisher's Island, 420, 422, *note.*
Flucker, Lucy, marries General Knox, 61.
Fly, William, the pirate, 177, 178.
Forefather's Day, its true date and significance, 290.
Fort Adams, 358; Fort Day, 377; history of the fortress, 377, 378.
Fort Constitution, Great Island, New Hampshire, 199, 200.
Fort Fenwick, Saybrook, 444, 445.
Fort Frederick, Pemaquid, described, 96.
Fort George, Castine, described, 66; siege of, 67, 68, 69; imprisonment and escape of General Wadsworth and Major Burton, 70, 71.
Fort Griswold, 422. *See note;* assault on, 428, 429. *See note.*
Fort M'Clary, 144.
Fortress Monroe, 379.
Fort Morgan, Mobile, 379, *note.*
Fort Pentagoët, Castine, described, 73, 74.
Fort Point, site of, 63, 66.
Fort Sewall, Marblehead, 255.
Fort Trumbull, 422. *See note,* 428.
Fort William Henry, Pemaquid, description and importance of, 97; captured by D'Iberville, 99.
Fort Wolcott, 358. *See note.*
Fox, George, at Newport, 403; denounces the New England magistrates, 403. *See note.*
Frankland, Sir Charles, romantic marriage of, 256.
Franklin, Benjamin, 341.
Fremont, General John C., mentioned, 43.
Friday not an unlucky day, 26.
Funeral customs, ancient, 136.

G.

Gardiner's Island, 448, *note.*
Gardiner, Lion, at Saybrook, 445, 448. *See note.*
Garrison-houses described, 139, 140.
Gay Head, Indian legend of, 349.
George III., cause of his insanity, 394.
Gerrish's Island, 149.
Gerry, Elbridge, 249, 250.
Gerrymander, the, origin of, 250, *note.*
Gibson, James, 146.
Gilbert, Raleigh, with Popham's colony, 93.
Gilbert, Sir H., method of taking possession of Newfoundland, 23.
Glover, General John, anecdote of, 253; tomb of, 259.
Goat Island, Newport, 358.
Gorgeana. *See* Old York.
Gorges, Sir F., notice of Weymouth's voyage, 92; plantation at Agamenticus, Old York, 131, *et seq.*
Gorges, Ferdinando, son of Thomas, 131.
Gorges, Robert, 133.
Gorges, Thomas, mayor of Gorgeana, 131.
Gorges, Captain William, 131.
Great Head Cliff, Mount Desert, 50.
Great Island. *See* Newcastle.
Gregoire, Madame, at Mount Desert, 56.
Gridley, Richard, at Louisburg, 147.
Groton, the battle monument, 427; British attack on, 426; the Pequots destroyed, 429, 430.
Guercheville, Madame de, attempts to colonize Mount Desert, 34, 35, 36.

H.

Hakluyt, Richard, quoted, 19.
Hale, Rev. John, on witchcraft, 214.
Haley's Island. *See* Smutty Nose.
Haley, Samuel, 175; his epitaph, 183.
Hamilton, Lady Emma, 433.
Hancock, Dorothy Quincy, 204, 205.
Hardy, Sir Thomas Masterman, off New London, 432; declines a duel of ships, 433; at Nelson's death-bed, 433.
Harrison, Peter, 360. *See note.*
Hart, General William, 433. *See note.*
Hawkins, Thomas, the pirate, 176.
Hawthorne, Nathaniel, birthplace of, 221.
Hebrews at Newport, 366, 367.
Hempstead, Sir Robert, 425.
Henrietta d'Orleans poisoned, 56.
Henry IV.'s projects in the New World, 20; assassinated, 35.
Herring Cove, 319, 320.
Hessians at Newport, 380, 381.
Higginson, Francis, account of Salem, etc., 241.
Hilton, Martha, romantic story of, 205, 206.
Hilton, Richard, 205. *See note.*
Hog Island. *See* Appledore.
Holmes's Hole, 327, *note.*
Hontvet, John, heroism of his wife, 185.
Hopkins, Dr. Samuel, 406.
Howe, Richard, Earl, naval action with D'Estaing, 388.
Howland's Ferry, 413, *note.*
Hull, Commodore Isaac, 443, 444.
Hull, General William, mentioned, 56.
Humphries, Joshua, report on establishing a dock-yard at Newport, 378.
Huntington, General Eben, 438, 439.
Huntington, General Jedidiah, 438.
Huntington, Governor Samuel, 439.
Hutchinson, Anne, her trial and banishment, 361, 362.

I.

Ireson, Benjamin (called Flood), of Marblehead, story of, 253, 254.
Isle au Haut, named, 29.
Isle Nauset, total disappearance of, 322.
Isle of Rhodes. *See* Rhode Island.
Isles of Shoals, De Monts sees them, 155; described by Smith and Levett, 155, 156; advantages for fishery, 157; sail from Portsmouth, 158; isles described, 160, *see note;* their name, 161; general aspect of, 162; Star Island rambles, 162, *et seq.;* semi-barbarous condition of ancient Gosport, 164, 165; burial-grounds, 166, 167; caverns and cliffs, 168, 169, 170; Miss Underhill's chair, 170, 171; mountains seen off the coast, 172, *note;* dun-fish, 174; Smutty Nose, 175; piracy in colonial time, 176–179; Blackbeard, 178; Thomas Morton, Gent., 180, 181; Samuel Haley, 183; the Spanish wreck, 184; Wagner, the murderer, 185, 186; Appledore, 186–190; Duck Island, 190; Londoner's, 191; White Island Light, 192.

J.

Jackson, Andrew, 151.
Jeffrey's Ledge, 161.
Jesuits, persecutions by, 82; intrigues of, 82, 83.
Jones, Margaret, executed as a witch, 210.
Jourdan, Jean Baptiste, Marshal of France, at Newport, 388.
Judson, Adoniram, 277.

K.

Kadesquit, probably Kenduskeag, 35.
Kalb, Baron de, in New England on a secret mission, 387.
Kennebec River, discovery and name, 92.
King, Charles Bird, 368.
Kittery Point, named, 141, *note;* the Cutts House, 142; Fort M'Clary, 144; the Pepperells, 144, *et seq.;* Pepperell tomb, 147; Gerrish's Island, 149; other islands, 149; John Langdon, 150, 151.
Knox, General Henry, connection with Waldo patent, 61; involves General Lincoln, 62.

L.

Lafayette, 390; at Newport, 391.
Laighton, Thomas B., 192.
Langdon, John, anecdotes of, 150, 151, 200, *note.*
La Peyrouse in America, 71.
La Tour, Aglate, sells the seigniory of Acadia, 78.
La Tour, Chevalier, mentioned, 76; troubles with D'Aulnay, 77, 78.
Lawrence, Captain James, death of, 257.
Lee, General Charles, at Newport, 356, *note,* 404.
Lee, Colonel Jeremiah, sketch of, 245.
Lee, John, 247.
Lee, William Raymond, 247.
Leffingwell, Thomas, relieves Uncas, 436.
Leonard Forge, Taunton, 419.
Lescarbot, Marc, his criticism of Alfonse, 18; quoted, 58.
Levett, Christopher, mentioned, 96; describes Agamenticus, 131; at Isles of Shoals, 155, 156, 161; notice of Plymouth, 273.
Leverett, John, a Muscongus patentee, 60; at Pentagoët, 78.

INDEX.   455

Lincoln, General Benjamin, sketch of, 61.
Livermore, Samuel, attempts to shoot Captain Broke, 257.
Lobsters, process of canning for market, 84; facts about, 85.
Longfellow, Hon. Stephen, 71.
Long Island Sound, 421.
Londoner's Island, 160, 191.
Louis XIV. marries De Maintenon, 82; opinion of La Salle's discoveries, 83.
Lovell, Solomon, commands in Penobscot expedition, 68; retreats, 69.

M.

Mackerel, habits of, 91.
Macy, Thomas, settles at Nantucket, 339.
"Magnalia," Mather's, Southey's opinion of, 93.
Maine, sea-coast of, 17, 18; embraces Norumbega, Mavoshen, 18; other names applied to her territory, 18; French occupation of, 18; her enterprise and products, 60; part of Massachusetts, 68.
Maintenon, Madame de, intrigue with the Jesuits, 82, 83.
Malaga Island, 160.
Malbone, Colonel Godfrey, 408, 409.
Malbone, Edward G., 409.
Mananas Island, 104.
Manly, John, 251, 252.
Mansell, Sir Robert, mentioned, 34.
Marblehead, its conformation and topography, 228, 229, 230, 231; Lafayette there, 229; islands off the port, 231; the Neck, 231; annals and decay of the cod-fishery, 232, 233, 234, 235; early settlement, 236, 241, 242; described, 238, 239, 240, 241; character of early fishermen, 243; Goelet's account, 243; Lee Mansion, 245, 246; St. Michael's, 248; the old sea-lions, 251, 252; the dialect, 254; Fort Sewall, 255; *Chesapeake* and *Shannon*, 256, 257; old burial-ground, 258; perils of the fishery, 259, 260.
Marriage, first, in New England, 285.
Mashope, legend of, 349.
Mason, Captain John, 201.
Mason, John, attacks the Pequot stronghold, 429, *note*, 430.
Massachusetts Bay, alleged discovery of, 18, 22.
Massachusetts Historical Society, motive of its founding, 147.
Massasoit, entry into Plymouth, 293, 294.
Masse, Enemond, at Mount Desert, 35.
Mavoshen, Maine, so styled, 18.
Mayhew, Thomas, purchases Nantucket, 339; owns Martha's Vineyard and Elizabeth Islands, 340.

May-pole, ancient custom of, 182.
M'Clary, Andrew, 144.
M'Lean, Colonel Francis, seizes and fortifies Castine, 67.
Mercator, atlas of, cited, 21.
Miantonimo makes war on Uncas, 435; is killed, 436.
Miantonimo Hill, 407, 408.
Mohegan Indians, 436, 437.
Monhegan Island, probably seen and named in 1604, 92, 102; early knowledge of, 102; described, 104; inscription at, 106; naval battle near, 106, 107, 324.
Moody, Joseph, Handkerchief, 135.
Moody, Rev. Samuel, anecdote of, 135; epitaph, 136.
Moore, Sir John, at Castine, 67; Napoleon's opinion of, 68.
Morse, Rev. Jedediah, at the Shoals, 164; describes curing fish, 174.
Morse, S. F. B., paints Landing of Pilgrims, 264.
Morton, Thomas, his banishment, 180, 181.
Mount Desert Island, discovered and named, 28; Champlain's description of, 29; mountain ranges, 29-32; approach from Ellsworth, 31; first settlers, 33; road to South-west Harbor, 33, 34; French colony on, 34, 35, 36; shell-heaps at, 37; neighborhood of South-west Harbor, 38, 39; islands off Somes's Sound, 39; Christmas on, 40, *et seq.*; route to Bar Harbor, 41, 42; island nomenclature, 42; islands off Bar Harbor, 43; shore rambles to Schooner Head and Great Head, 43-48; naturalists and artists who have visited, 48-50; excursion to Otter Creek and North-east Harbor, 53, 54; the Ovens, etc., 55, 56.
Mount Desert Rock, 53.
Mount Hope, 414, 415, 416.
Mugford, Captain James, 252, 253, 259.
Muscongus patent, history of, 60, 61.

N.

Nantucket, its early discovery, 324; name, 325, 341; voyage to, 326, 327; the town described, 328, 329, 330; whales, ships, and whaling, 331-334; Nantucket in the Revolution, 335; cruising for whales, 335; the camels, 336; whaling annals, 336, 337; white settlement of the island, 339, 340, 341; Coffin school and Admiral Sir Isaac Coffin, 342; black-fishing, 343, 344; blue-fishing at the Opening, 344, 345, 346; Coatue, 347; Indian legends, 349; Indian absolutism, 350; wasting of the shores, 350; Siasconset, 351, 352; the great South Shoal, 353; Sankoty Head, 354; Surfside, 354.

INDEX.

Narraganset Bay, Verrazani's supposed sojourn in, 359.
Nautican or Nauticon. See Nantucket.
Nelson, Horatio, Lord, chivalric conduct of, 395. See note; death-scene of, 433.
Nelson, John, important services of, 98.
Newcastle, 196, et seq.; the Pool, 197; old charter and records, 198, 199; Little Harbor, 200.
New England of ancient writers, 17-27; early names of, 18, 19; first called New England, 20; attempts to colonize, 24; quality of emigration to, 25; patents of, 133; supposed visit of Northmen, 369, note.
Newfoundland, English occupation of, 23; seizures of Portuguese at, 24; Basques at, 126; fisheries of, 156.
New France, New England included in, 20, 21.
New London, sail up the Thames, 422; the town and its beginnings, 422, 423; light-houses and light-ships, 423, 424; Hempstead House, 425; Court-house, 424; old burial-ground, 426; the harbor, 426; Arnold's descent, 428, 429.
Newport Artillery, 363, 364.
Newport, the old town, 356, et seq.; its climate, 357; approach from sea, 357, 358; its commerce, 359; street rambles, 359-372; City Hall, 360; Coddington's Cove, 362; the Wantons, 362, 363; State House, 363, 364; Jews' cemetery, 365, 366, 367; Redwood Library, 367, 368; Old Stone Mill, 369, 370, 371, 372; Cliff Walk, 373, et seq.; Forty Steps, 374; cottage life at the sea-side, 375; Lily Pond, Spouting Rock, and Brenton's Reef, 376; Fort Adams and Fort Day, 377, 378, 379; Napoleon's engineer, 378, 379; Dumplings, 380; Hessians, 381; the drives, 381, 382; the beaches and Purgatory, 382, 383; Hanging Rock and Whitehall, 384; the French occupation, 386, et seq.; French diplomacy, 387; attack of D'Estaing, 387, 388; celebrities of the French army and navy, 388-397; Rhode Island cemetery, 398, et seq.; Quaker annals, 401, et seq.; other burial-places, 405, 406.
Noailles, Viscount de, 391, 392.
Norembegue. See Norumbega.
North, Lord, how he received the news of Cornwallis's surrender, 393.
Northmen, supposed voyage to New England, 369, note.
Norton, Francis, settles at Agamenticus, 131.
Norumbega, river and country of, 18, 19, 21; explored by Champlain, 28.
Norwich, approach to, 434; the Mohegans, 435, 436, 437; the town, 439, 440, 441.
Nubble, The, not Savage Rock, 120.
Nurse, Rebecca, executed for witchcraft, 213, 224, 226.

O.

Oak Bluffs, cottage city at, 375.
Odiorne's Point, first settlement of New Hampshire at, 200.
Ogunquit described, 114, 115.
Old Colony, seal of, 267.
Oldham, John, his ingenious punishment at Plymouth, 286, 287; killed, 421.
Old South Church, Boston, New England, library in, plundered, 268.
Old Stone Mill, Newport, 369, 370, 371, 372.
Orleans, ancient wreck discovered at, 322.
Ortelius, map of, 19, 20.
Otis, James, at Plymouth, 288.

P.

Paddock, Ichabod, teaches Nantucket men how to take whales, 315.
Parris, Samuel, witch-finders at his house, 213; his minutes of examination, 224.
Peabody, George, 218.
Pease, Samuel, fight with pirates, 176.
Pemaquid Point, visit to, 87, et seq.; British descent at, repulsed, 89; porgee fishery at, 89, 90; early history, 92-101; Weymouth, at, 92; Fort Frederick, at, 96, 97; other fortifications, 97; Fort William Henry, at, captured, 99; ancient settlement at, 100; Indians kidnaped by Weymouth, 105.
Pemetiq. See Mount Desert.
Pentagoët, meaning of the name, 19, note; on Blauw's map, 21; how settled, 25. See Castine.
Penobscot Bay and River, Champlain's account of, 18, 19; called Pemetegoit, 19; meaning of name, 19, note; called Pembrock's Bay, 21; Smith's account of, 24; approach to in a fog, 58, 59; described, 63, 64.
Penobscot Expedition, history of, 68, 69.
Pepperell, Andrew, his affair with Hannah Waldo, 61.
Pepperell, Sir William, 61; sketch and residence of, 144-147; portrait of, 145, 146; his tomb, 147; Pepperell William, Sen., 188.
Perry, Oliver Hazard, 363; monument to, 401, 404.
Peters, Hugh, 445.
Philip, King, 349; seat at Mount Hope, 414; his capture, 416.
Phips, Sir William, builds Fort William Henry, 97; his connection with witchcraft, 210; accusation of his wife, 214.
Pigot, Sir Robert, defends Newport, 387.
Pilgrims, the, not strictly Puritans, 280; their church, 280, 281, 282; land at Cape Cod, 307.

INDEX. 457

Pillory, one described, 365.
Piscataqua, capture proposed, 80; sail down, 159; Earl Bellomont's opinion of, 197.
Plymouth Bay, 268, 274, 275.
Plymouth Beach, 269.
Plymouth, on Smith's map, 21; establishes a trading-house at Castine, 76; dispossessed, 76, 77; the colony patents, 133; Plymouth described, 262; Pilgrim memorials, 263-267; pictures of the "Landing," 264; first duel at Plymouth, 266; the colony seal, 267; the compact, 267; first execution, 267; Pilgrim laws and chronicles, 268; Burial Hill, 268, 276, 277, 278, 279; the harbor, 268, 269; names of the settlement, 270; why it was chosen, 271; desolated by a plague, 272, 273; French make the first landing, 274, 275; other settlements called Plymouth, 276; Pilgrims' first church, 278; church customs, 279, 280; Leyden Street, 283, *et seq.*; the town in 1627, 284; Governor Bradford's, 286; Allyne House, 287; Cole's Hill, 288; Plymouth Rock, 289; the Landing, 290, 291; Samoset, 292; entry of Massasoit, 293, 294; Clark's Island, 295, *et seq*. See article, Clark's Island, Plymouth Beach, 296.
Plymouth, England, 270.
Plum Island, 421.
Point Judith, 357. *See note.*
Point of Graves, 196, 202.
Poore, Ben Perley, mentioned, 22, *note*.
Popham, Chief-justice, efforts to colonize New England, 93, 94.
Popham, George, leader of the colony at the Kennebec, 93; death, 93.
Popular superstitions, some enumerated, 114.
Porcupine Islands, 43.
Port Royal settled, 95.
Port St. Louis. *See* Plymouth, 275.
Pound, Thomas, a pirate, 176.
Poutrincourt, Biencourt, arrives at Port Royal, 35.
Poutrincourt, Jean de, receives Port Royal from De Monts, 34; his fight with natives at Cape Cod, 308.
Pownall, Thomas, builds a fort on the Penobscot, 66.
Prior, Matthew, allowed roast beef in Lent, 314.
Provincetown, described, 309-312; Town Hill, 311; cape names, 312; Portuguese colony at, 312, 313; fishery of, 313, *et seq.*; whaling from, 315; the desert, 316; cranberry culture, 317; walk to Race Point, 316, *et seq.*; the sand-avalanche, 319; huts of refuge, Herring Cove, 319; the terrible winter of 1874-'75, 320; disasters on the ocean side, 321, 322.
Prudence Island, 380.
Purchas, Samuel, quoted, 24.

Purgatory Bluff, 383.
Puritans distinguished from Separatists, 280.
Putnam, General Israel, birthplace of, 217; laconic letter to Governor Tryon, 218.

Q.

Quakers as sailors, 339. *See note*, 401, *et seq.*; persecution in New England, 402, 403; burial customs, 404.
Quincy, Dorothy (Madam Hancock), 205.
Quincy, Josiah, 406.
Quincy, Judith, 357.

R.

Race Point, 311, 319.
Ramusio, Giambetta, map cited, 21.
Rasieres, Isaac de, at Plymouth, 278, 283.
Razilly, Isaac de, commands in Acadia, 77.
Redwood, Abraham, 367, 368. *See note.*
Redwood Library, Newport, 368. *See note.*
Revere, Paul, in Penobscot expedition, 68.
Rhode Island, island of, 407, *et seq.*; Tonomy Hill, 407; the Glen, 408; Prescott's capture, 409, 410; Talbot's feat, 410, 411; early stages, 411; Lawton's Valley, 412; early settlement of, 413, 414; Revolutionary earthworks and history, 413, 414.
Richmond's Island, 369, *note*.
Rochambeau, Count, proposes the capture of Penobscot, 71; at Newport, 388, 389, 390, 391.
Rockland, brief sketch of, 59, 60.

S.

Saco Beach, superstition relative to, 114.
Saco River, on Blauw's map, 21; Richard Vines at, 133; De Monts there, 154.
Salem in 1692, 220, 222; old witch house, 223; Witch Hill, 225; hanging the condemned witches at, 226; formation of church at, 281.
Salem Village, witchcraft at, 208, *et seq.*; Witch Ground, 213; names of the witch-finders, 213, *note;* their motives and power, 214; humors of witchcraft, 215, 216.
Salmon, disappearance of, 64.
Saltonstall, Captain, commands in Penobscot expedition, 68; disagreement with General Lovell, 69.
Samoset, sagamore of Pemaquid, 96, 264; at Plymouth, 292, 293.
Sandeyn, Arthur, 256.
Sankoty Head, 354.
Sargent, Henry, paints "Landing of Pilgrims," 264.
Sassafras, its medicinal virtues, 126.
Savage Rock, probably at Cape Ann, 120, 121.

INDEX.

Say, Lord, proposes to emigrate to New England, 446.
Saybrook, 441, *et seq.*; Hart mansion, 443; old fortress at the Point, 444; settled, 445; Cromwell's proposed emigration to, 446; old burial-place, 446, 447, 448.
Scallop-shell, its historical significance, 348.
Schooner Head, a visit to, 46.
Seabury, Samuel, Bishop, 425, 426. *See note.*
Sedgwick, Robert, at Pentagoët and Jamaica, 78.
Selman, John, 251.
Sewall, Samuel, recants his belief in witchcraft, 225.
Sewall, David, 136.
Sheaffe, Jacob, 151.
Sherburne. *See* Nantucket.
Shipwrecks: the *Isidore*, 117, *et seq.*; on Smutty Nose, 184; the *Nottingham*, 172, 173; at Cape Cod, 272; the *General Arnold*, 296; the *James Rommell*, 320, 321; the *Giovanni*, 321, 322; *Essex*, of Nantucket, 337.
Siasconset, Nantucket Island, visited, 350, 351, 352.
Siddons, Sarah, anecdote of, 376.
Smibert, John, at Newport, 384, 385. *See note.*
Smith, Captain David, 316, *note.*
Smith, John, names New England, 20; his map, 21; mentions Monhegan, 104; monument, Star Island, 167; Appledore, 189; account of Cape Cod, 307.
Smutty Nose Island, 160, 175, 182.
Somes's Sound, 31, *et passim.*
Somesville, Mount Desert, 30; first settlers of, 33.
Southack, Cyprian, his chart, 308.
Southworth, Alice (Carpenter), 284, 285.
Sparhawk, Harriet Hirst, 147.
Sparhawk, William (Pepperell), 147.
Standish, Miles, his sword, 266; residence, 300; sketch of, 301.
Star Island, 160, 162, *et seq.*
Stephens, Rev. Josiah, epitaph of, 166.
Steuben, Baron, arrival at Portsmouth, 207.
Stevens, General Isaac Ingalls, 401.
Stiles, Dr. Ezra, at Newport, 304, 368.
Story, Elisha, 248.
Story, Joseph, birthplace of, 248.
Stoughton, William, 225.
Strafford, Earl of, 204.
Stuart, Gilbert, anecdote of, 406.
Sullivan, John, 200, *note;* fights a battle on Rhode Island, 419. *See note.*
Surriage, Agnes, marries a baronet, 256.

T.

Talbot, Silas, brilliant achievement of, 410, 411.
Tarrantines, their country, 19, 24.
Taunton River, 414, 415, 416, 417.
Temple, Sir Thomas, renders Fort Pentagoët, 74, 78.
Ternay, M. de, Admiral, dies at Newport, 391.
Thatcher, James, 264, *note.*
Thaxter, Celia Laighton, 192.
Thevet, André, cited, 19, *note.*
Thomaston, Maine, named, 60, *note.*
Thompson, David, at Little Harbor, 201.
Totten, General Joseph Gilbert, builds Fort Adams, 378; relations with General Simon Bernard, 379.
Touro, Abraham, 366, *note*, 367.
Touro, Judah, 367, *note.*
Trevett, Samuel, 253.
Truro, Provincetown part of, 309.
Tucke, Rev. John, 163, 166, 167.
Tucker, Samuel, 252.
Tuckanuck Island, 344. *See note.*

U.

Uncas, fights and conquers Miantonimo, 435; slays him, 436; burial-place, 436; friendship for the English, 437. *See note.*
Underhill, Nancy J., death at Star Island, 170, 171.

V.

Vane, Henry, procures a pass for New England, 94, 413.
Vaughan, Colonel William, 146.
Verrazani, Juan, his voyage, 20; gives New England a Christian name, 20.
Vines, Richard, in New England, 133, 272.
Vinton, Rev. Francis, burial-place of, 401.

W.

Wadsworth, Peleg, in Penobscot expedition, 68; kidnaped, 69; escapes from Fort George, 70, 71.
Wagner, Louis, 138, 185, 186.
Waldo, Hannah, marries Thomas Flucker, 61.
Waldo patent. *See* Muscongus patent.
Waldo, Samuel, sketch of, 61.
Wanton, Joseph, his personal appearance, 363, *see note;* portrait of, 368; arrested, 405.
Warren, James, originates a Revolutionary junto, 288.
Warren, Mercy, her history of the Revolution, 288.
Washing-day in New England, inaugurated, 307.
Washington, George, at Kittery, 151; at Marblehead, 247; disapproves the occupation of Newport by Rochambeau, 389; at Newport, 391.

INDEX. 459

Watch Hill, Rhode Island, 420. *See note.*
Webster, Daniel, residence and burial-place, 302.
Wells, Maine, walks in, 110; beach rambles, 111, 112, 113.
Wentworth, Benning, his mansion, Little Harbor, 203, *et seq.*
Wentworth, Frances Deering, 206, 207.
Wentworth, Hon. John, 202.
Wentworth, John, 202.
Wentworth, Sir John, sketch of, 206, 207.
Wentworth, Colonel Michael, 206, *note.*
Wentworth, Samuel, 202.
Wentworth, Reginald, 201.
Weymouth, Captain George. *See note,* 76; accounts of his voyage, 92; at Monhegan Island, 104, 105.
Whale-fishery in New England, originates at Cape Cod, 315; of Nantucket, 331, *et seq.*
Wheelwright, John, sketch of him, 110.
White Island, 160, 192.

Whitefield, George, 147.
Williams, Roger, residence of, 222; on Quakers, 404, 413.
Winslow, General John, 303.
Winthrop, John, Jun., 422, 423, *note.*
Witchcraft. *See* Salem Village.
Wood End, 311.
Wyllys, Samuel, buys Plum Island, 421.

Y.

Yale College, founded at Saybrook, 448, 449.
Yankee, disappearance of the, 442.
York, called Boston, 21; Cape Neddock, 122; York Beach, 127; York Harbor, 130; historical résumé, 131; indifferent reputation of, 132; meeting-house, first parish, 134; old jail, 136; Woodbridge's tavern, 138; Cider Hill, 138; garrison-house, 139, 140; Sewall's bridge, 141.

THE END.

www.ingramcontent.com/pod-product-compliance
Lightning Source LLC
Chambersburg PA
CBHW071940220426
43662CB00009B/925